The MANIFESTO in Literature

VOLUME 2

The MANIFESTO *in Literature*

THE MODERNIST MOVEMENT: 1900-WWII

THOMAS RIGGS, *editor*

ST. JAMES PRESS

A part of Gale, Cengage Learning

Detroit • New York • San Francisco • New Haven, Conn • Waterville, Maine • London

The Manifesto in Literature

Thomas Riggs, Editor

Lisa Kumar, Project Editor

Artwork and photographs for *The Manifesto in Literature* covers were reproduced with the following kind permission.

Volume 1
For foreground painting "Writing the Declaration of Independence in 1776" by Jean Leon Gerome Ferris. © Virginia Historical Society, Richmond, VA/The Bridgeman Art Library.
For background image of the Declaration of Independence of the thirteen United States of America, 1776. © Private Collection/The Bridgeman Art Library.

Volume 2
For foreground portrait of Adolf Hitler. © INTERFOTO/awkz/Mary Evans.
For background image of the title page from the original publication of Mein Kampf, 1925-1926. © INTERFOTO/Alamy.

Volume 3
For foreground portrait of Albert Einstein. © Mary Evans/AISA Media.
For background image of the first page of the Russell-Einstein Manifesto. Courtesy Ava Helen and Linus Pauling Papers, Oregon State University Libraries.

LIBRARY OF CONGRESS CATALOGING-IN-PUBLICATION DATA

The Manifesto in Literature / Edited by Thomas Riggs.
  v. cm. — ()
  Includes bibliographical references and index.
  ISBN - 13: 978-1-55862-866-3 (set) -- ISBN - 13: 978-1-55862-867-0 (vol. 1) -- ISBN - 13: 978-1-55862-868-7 (vol. 2) -- ISBN - 13: 978-1-55862-869-4 (vol. 3)
  1. Revolutionary literature—History and criticism. 2. Literary manifestos.
3. Political manifestoes. 4. Politics and literature. 5. Authors—Political and social views.
I. Riggs, Thomas, 1963—editor of compilation.
  PN51.M26785 2013
  809.935—dc23

Gale
27500 Drake Rd.
Farmington Hills, MI, 48331-3535

978-1-55862-866-3 (set)   1-55862-866-5 (set)
978-1-55862-867-0 (vol. 1)   1-55862-867-3 (vol. 1)
978-1-55862-868-7 (vol. 2)   1-55862-868-1 (vol. 2)
978-1-55862-869-4 (vol. 3)   1-55862-869-X (vol. 3)

This title will also be available as an e-book.
ISBN-13: 978-1-55862-880-9 ISBN-10: 1-55862-880-0
Contact your Gale, a part of Cengage Learning, sales representative for ordering information.

Printed in the United States of America
1 2 3 4 5 6 7 17 16 15 14 13

ADVISORY BOARD

CHAIR

Martin Puchner
Byron and Anita Wien Professor of Drama and of English and Comparative Literature, Harvard University, Cambridge, Massachusetts. Author of *The Drama of Ideas: Platonic Provocations in Theater and Philosophy* (2010); *Poetry of the Revolution: Marx, Manifestos, and the Avant-Gardes* (2006); and *Stage Fright: Modernism, Anti-Theatricality, and Drama* (2002). Editor of *The Norton Anthology of World Literature*, 3rd edition (2012); and *The Communist Manifesto and Other Writings* (2005). Coeditor, with Alan Ackerman, of *Against Theatre: Creative Destructions on the Modernist Stage* (2006). Founding Director, Mellon Summer School of Theater and Performance Research.

ADVISORS

Rita Felski
William R. Kenan, Jr. Professor of English, University of Virginia, Charlottesville. Author of *Uses of Literature* (2008); *Literature after Feminism* (2003); *Doing Time: Feminist Theory and Postmodern Culture* (2000); *The Gender of Modernity* (1995); and *Beyond Feminist Aesthetics: Feminist Literature and Social Change* (1989). Editor of *Rethinking Tragedy* (2008). Coeditor of *Comparison: Theories, Approaches, Methods* (2013). Editor of *New Literary History*.

Janet Lyon
Associate Professor of English; Science, Technology and Society; and Women's Studies, Pennsylvania State University, University Park. Author of *Manifestoes: Provocations of the Modern* (1999). Contributor to *Gender in Modernism: New Geographies, Complex Intersections,* edited by Bonnie Kime Scott (2007); *The Cambridge Companion to American Modernism,* edited by Walter Kalaidjian (2005); and *Geomodernisms: Race, Modernism, Modernity,* edited by Laura Doyle and Laura Winkiel (2005).

Peter Nicholls
Professor of English, New York University, New York City. Author of *George Oppen and the Fate of Modernism* (2009); *Modernisms: A Literary Guide,* 2nd

edition (2009); and *Ezra Pound: Politics, Economics and Writing* (1984). Coeditor, with Sara Crangle, of *On Bathos: Literature, Art, Music* (2010); and, with Laura Marcus, of *The Cambridge History of Twentieth-Century English Literature* (2004). Contributor to *The Oxford Handbook of Modern and Contemporary American Poetry*, edited by Cary Nelson (2012); and *The Cambridge Companion to Modernist Poetry*, edited by Alex Davis and Lee M. Jenkins (2007).

Laura Winkiel
Associate Professor of English, University of Colorado Boulder. Author of *Modernism, Race and Manifestos* (2008). Coeditor, with Laura Doyle, of *Geomodernisms: Race, Modernism, Modernity* (2005). Contributor to *The Routledge Companion to Experimental Literature*, edited by Joe Bray, Alison Gibbons, and Brian McHale (2012); *The Invention of Politics in the European Avant-Garde* (1906-1940), edited by Sascha Bru and Gunther Martens (2006); and *Decentering the Avant-Garde: Towards a New Topography of the International Avant-Garde*, edited by Per Backstrom and Hubert van den Berg (forthcoming). Book project provisionally titled "Epic Proportions: Genre, Debt and Anticolonial Modernism." Senior editor of *English Language Notes*.

Sarah G. Wenzel
Librarian, English and Romance Literatures, University of Chicago, Illinois.

EDITORIAL AND PRODUCTION STAFF

ASSOCIATE PUBLISHER
Marc Cormier

PRODUCT MANAGER
Philip J. Virta

PROJECT EDITOR
Lisa Kumar

EDITORIAL ASSISTANCE
Andrea Henderson, Michelle Lee, and Rebecca Parks

ART DIRECTOR
Kristine Julien

COMPOSITION AND IMAGING
Evi Seoud, John Watkins

MANUFACTURING
Wendy Blurton

RIGHTS ACQUISITION AND MANAGEMENT
Kimberly Potvin, Robyn V. Young

TECHNICAL SUPPORT
Luann Brennan, Mike Weaver

TABLE OF CONTENTS

Introduction

Among the hundreds of manifestos that are represented in these three volumes, one stands out: *The Manifesto of the Communist Party* (1848). In a collaborative process that spanned several countries and included much trial and error, the two authors, Karl Marx and Friedrich Engels, did nothing less than invent the manifesto as we know it. To be sure, there were earlier texts that called themselves manifestos, but they existed side by side with declarations, proclamations, open letters, admonitions, refutations, theses, defenses, vindications, catechisms, and much more. "Manifesto" was just one more convenient name to give to a document intent on stating publicly—on making manifest—a set of rules or beliefs.

When they were charged with drawing up the beliefs of the newly established Communist League, Marx and Engels experimented with all of these rival forms. For example, they initially thought that the best way of expressing the principles of the new party would be in the form of a catechism, the question-and-answer testing of knowledge introduced by theologians of the Catholic Church. The finished text of the *Communist Manifesto* still bears traces of this early experiment. Gradually, however, the two authors realized that they were facing an unprecedented challenge—a challenge they needed to meet with an entirely new kind of text.

The problem they set themselves in 1847 was how to write a revolution. All across Europe monarchies and empires were entrenched, fortifying their positions of power. They watched jealously for any sign of new revolutionary groups threatening the status quo. The French revolution had long ago receded into history, but it had not been forgotten. Word was going around of a radical new movement sowing discontent abroad, but no one knew anything specific about it. Apparently, it was called communism.

There was something to the rumor. Carefully, Marx and Engels had begun to establish a network of the revolutionaries scattered across the continent. "There is a specter haunting Europe," the *Communist Manifesto* begins. With discontent in the air, the time had come for the secret society to become visible, public—manifest. To accomplish this purpose, the two authors recreated the manifesto as a new genre.

This manifesto did much more than make manifest the principles of communism. Marx, a trained philosopher, had developed a philosophy of history based on the struggle among different classes. This history culminated in the present moment, in the manifesto itself, which declared a kind of point zero: all subsequent history would be shaped by this crucial document. At the center of this turning point stood the proletariat, a newly defined class of workers utterly dependent on the owners of factories and capital. Everyone knew about disenfranchised workers, of course, but the *Communist Manifesto* took the unusual step of describing them as the future sovereigns of Europe and the world.

In addition to articles of belief, Marx and Engels's treatise includes this history of mankind, told at breathtaking speed, leading up to the present and into the future. In order to bring about this revolutionary future, the document introduced a new historical agent—the proletariat—and now had to call this agent into being. The burden of the *Communist Manifesto* was to forge out of the disenfranchised workers a coherent class. This class must be roused to action. If there was going to be a revolution, the manifesto itself must incite it. Ingeniously, Marx and Engels combined the crucial elements—declaration of principle; long view of history; creation of a turning point; introduction of a new agent—and couched them in a style singularly intent on transforming their ideas into action. Out of disparate ingredients the authors created a formula that was exemplified, for the first time, in the *Communist Manifesto*. Without this document, the three volumes presented here would not exist.

The *Communist Manifesto* is a lens through which we can look backward and forward, backward at the prehistory of the genre and forward to the many successors and imitators. A look back reveals a striking fact: many early manifestos were not revolutionary documents. They tended to be declarations by heads of states, emperors, or the Church, utterances by those with the power and authority to make laws and impose a vision of the world. Marx and Engels would cunningly change the genre, turning the manifesto into a tool not for those in power but for those seeking to usurp it.

Alongside these authoritative declarations, other, more subversive texts existed, although they didn't always designate themselves as manifestos. Martin Luther's *Ninety-Five Theses* (1517), nailed to the church door in Wittenberg, had the long-term, if perhaps unintended, consequence of revolutionizing the Church. Other, more explicitly insurrectional documents—for example those (such as the 1649 "Digger's Song") emanating from the so-called Diggers and Levellers in seventeenth-century England, who hoped to claim common property from landlords—explicitly sought to change the status quo. Like Luther, they made ample use of Christian texts to articulate their demands, quoting liberally from the Bible.

Religion was not the only language available to revolutionaries. In the eighteenth century, philosophers began to formulate, more and more cogently, a worldview premised on the human exercise of reason; their beliefs freed humanity from the humble subservience to God that had characterized many earlier revolutionary texts. The new philosophical attitude created a new age, the Enlightenment, and its principal philosopher, Immanuel Kant, authored the seminal text (which might have been called, retrospectively, the Enlightenment Manifesto) "What Is Enlightenment?" This undertaking was not just a matter of philosophy. It aided those hoping to reorganize the social order without recourse to older authorities—to place society on a new foundation.

The most famous experiment along these lines happened not in Europe but in the English colonies of North America, where revolutionaries declared their independence from England and from the monarchy. The Americans expressed the principles of their freedom in a text that soon became world famous and found many imitators of its own: the *Declaration of Independence* (1776). Like the *Communist Manifesto,* the *Declaration of Independence* did not just state new principles; together with the *Constitution* (1787), it called into being a new entity, the United States of America. More particularly, it created a new agent, the people of the United States of America, who would henceforth govern their own fate.

Although these documents and other, lesser-known manifestos tended to be phrased in the radical idiom of universality—as in the opening of the *Declaration of Independence,* which proclaimed, "All men are created equal"—their practice was often a good deal more restrictive, excluding slaves and women, among others. In response these discounted groups began to articulate their demands with recourse to the *Declaration,* holding the document, and those who endorsed it, to its original, radical vision. In 1848 a women's rights convention in Seneca Falls, New York, modeled its *Declaration of Sentiments* explicitly on the *Declaration of Independence,* demanding freedom and independence for the half of the nation that had been excluded in the original *Declaration.* Eighty years earlier, on the French colonial island of Saint-Dominique, a slave revolt inspired by the *Declaration of the Rights of Man and of the Citizen* (1789) had found expression in Jean-Jacques

Dessalines's "Liberty or Death" (1804), which charged Europeans with not living up to their own revolutionary ideas. Despite these forceful new manifestos, it would take centuries for their mandates to receive wider acceptance.

Protest literature, Enlightenment philosophy, a new type of Republican constitution—these were some of the strands that Marx and Engels knit into a new kind of text, the manifesto proper. Despite the later success of this document, which truly changed the world, its immediate effects were disappointing. The timing was right, or almost right—revolutions were erupting across Europe (although the *Communist Manifesto* was published in London, which was relatively isolated from those revolutions, and it was written in German). When the revolutionary energy of 1848 ebbed, however, enthusiasm for the document and its ilk ebbed as well, and it took decades and a concerted program of translation to catapult the *Communist Manifesto* to the forefront again. At the end of the nineteenth century, the treatise finally began its triumphant rise. Marx and Engels's new formula had taken a long time to become popular.

Two developments resulted from the increasingly visible success of the *Communist Manifesto*. The first was that the genre became the preferred form of political expression for the Left: Marx and Engels had inaugurated a long tradition of manifestos seeking to found communist or socialist parties or to update and revitalize the international communist movement. Several of these are collected in the second volume of this set, "The Modernist Movement." They include Emma Goldman's "Anarchism" (1910), in which the author explains the tenets of that movement; the "Zimmerwald Manifesto" (1915), a World War I socialist document condemning the fierce nationalism that held Europe's Left in its grip; and the *Spartacus Manifesto* (1918), a Marxist revolutionary treatise written by Rosa Luxemburg in postwar Germany. From time to time right-leaning groups tried to answer this leftist tradition with manifestos of their own but never with lasting success.

The second development, also represented in volume two, was more surprising. As the *Communist Manifesto* was gaining prominence, artists started to write texts specifically styled as manifestos. Most did not hope to create social revolutions; instead, they wanted to revolutionize the arts. Their treatises adopted many elements from political manifestos: the telling of a grand history (of art) that culminated in a complete rupture; the creation of a new entity or movement; an aggressive denunciation of predecessors or rivals; and lists of demands or actions to be taken. The trend began in the late nineteenth century, when a new group called the symbolists sought to articulate their break with the dominant artistic mode of the time, realism. The art manifesto movement really took off when the obscure Italian symbolist poet F. T. Marinetti recognized the form's potential in the artistic sphere and authored *Futurist Manifesto* (1909). The document created quite a stir, which encouraged Marinetti to write more manifestos until he was flooding the art market with his missives. No futurist artwork had been created yet; the new movement existed simply by virtue of having been founded, defended, and explained through manifestos. With the proclamation of futurism, the new artistic offshoot of the political manifesto had come into its own.

The artistic manifesto, too, had predecessors. Artists had always wanted to articulate their principles and views, sometimes quite succinctly or polemically; examples of these texts appear in the first volume of this series, "Origins of the Form." Percy Bysshe Shelley's *Defence of Poetry* for instance, written in 1821 and published in 1840, exalts Romantic poetry and poets in the face of detractors. Shelley's contemporary William Wordsworth had contented himself with writing the pointed "Preface" to the 1800 edition of *Lyrical Ballads* (poems by Wordsworth and Samuel Taylor Coleridge), which accomplished a similar purpose. Over the course of the nineteenth century, these declarations of aesthetic principles edged closer to the manifesto; Émile Zola's *Naturalism in the Theater* (1880) is a prominent example of this trend. Only after the turn of the century, with futurism, did the genre fully arrive in the world of art.

Once the manifesto gained entry into the artistic sphere, art was never the same again. Groups, splinter groups, and subformations sprang up everywhere, fiercely fighting over minor points of aesthetic doctrine, and most of the fighting was done through manifestos. The immediate effect was a new artistic landscape dominated by a proliferation of "isms." Many artists were no longer content simply to exercise their craft; they now felt the need to be part of a movement—futurism, Dadaism, surrealism, suprematism, and numerous others—until finally the war of the manifestos became more important than the artwork created under the auspices of any particular movement.

The competition even extended to the form of the manifesto itself. Marinetti had perfected a particularly aggressive style, intent on driving home its often extreme points with utmost force. The Dadaists responded with playful, whimsical manifestos that seemed not only to disagree with the content of futurist treatises but also with their bellicose tone. The surrealists differentiated themselves from both of these movements, not only by emphasizing the importance of dreams and of free association but also by writing meandering, essay-like manifestos that mirrored this new emphasis.

A term began to circulate throughout the new landscape: "avant-garde." Originally a military term designating the advanced guard of an army, it now described the ambition of artists to found the latest and most advanced ism through the latest and most advanced manifesto.

The two strands of the manifesto, the political and the artistic, existed side by side, sometimes merging, sometimes diverging. During World War II and its aftermath, however, the fortunes of the manifesto waned as fascism and fascist-leaning regimes took hold in Europe, quelling both leftist revolutionary energy and artistic revolutions. Even movements that had sided with fascism, such as Italian futurism, quieted, and once the war was over, these groups found themselves discredited. The time of the manifesto seemed to have ended.

Not for long. A second wave of both political and artistic manifestos swelled in the 1950s and gained momentum as the 1960s wore on. This next wave, represented in the third volume of this series, "Activism, Unrest, and the Neo-Avant-Garde," was different. The political manifestos, although still primarily leftist, were no longer used predominantly by communist parties but rather by disenfranchised groups seeking recognition and justice, including African Americans, feminists, immigrants, and gays.

Many of these groups could claim a substantial history of manifesto writing. Harlem Renaissance writers of the 1920s and 1930s, including Alain Locke and Richard Wright, outlined the aesthetic and political principles of their art in manifestos or manifesto-like statements, including Locke's "Legacy of Ancestral Arts" (1925) and Wright's "Blueprint for Negro Writing" (1937) (both represented in the second volume of the series). In 1966 the Black Panthers demanded rights for African Americans in a more political and forceful manifesto, the Black Panther Party Platform. They strategically ended their document with the first paragraph of the *Declaration of Independence,* recalling one of the most important documents in the prehistory of the manifesto. In her 1967 *SCUM* (Society for Cutting Up Men) *Manifesto,* Valerie Solanas notably used the standard "we" even though her movement consisted only of herself. She, too, could look back on a long history of feminist manifestos, including Mary Wollstonecraft's *A Vindication of the Rights of Woman* (1792), one of the most important early examples of the form.

Artistic and political manifestos had emerged outside Europe and the United States during the first part of the twentieth century, driven by the global rise of communism, an increasingly international modernism, and the avant-garde movements in the arts. In 1914 the Chilean poet Vicente Huidobro delivered the lecture "Non Serviam" (Latin for "I will not serve"), a manifesto declaring independence from authority in various forms; and in 1917 the future cofounder of the Chinese Communist Party Chen Duxiu wrote "On Literary Revolution," importing the form and its revolutionary zeal to China. By the 1960s the manifesto's international reach was no longer an exception but a commonplace occurrence. Frantz Fanon's *The Wretched of the Earth* (1961) became a manifesto for the independence movements of former colonies all over the world, and Nelson Mandela's 1961 "Manifesto of Umkhonto we Sizwe" played a role in the struggle against Apartheid in South Africa.

By the middle of the twentieth century, writing political manifestos was no longer an original act. On the contrary, it now meant joining a long tradition; it meant pledging allegiance to the institution of leftist thought even as the origin of the tradition, the *Communist Manifesto,* receded into history.

The artistic manifesto was going through a similar experience. Originally conceived as a means of declaring a new point of departure, a complete rupture with all preceding art, avant-garde manifestos now had to admit that they were part of a tradition—a tradition of manifesto writing. What to do? Some artists tried to surpass their early-twentieth-century predecessors by being even more radical and revolutionary; one group, the Situationists (whose founder Guy Debord produced "Situationist Theses on Traffic" in 1959), even declared that they were against the production of anything resembling art. Others found novelty in new technologies, from which they hoped a complete revolution would arise. Donna Haraway's "Manifesto for Cyborgs" (1985) envisioned a new form of existence in the symbiosis of humans and machines, while McKenzie Wark's *Hacker Manifesto* (2004) elevated hacking to the status of a new creative and radical activity.

The end of the twentieth century saw the demise of communism in politics and the emergence of the postmodernist movement in the arts—both seemed to spell, once again, the end of the manifesto. Without communism as a credible alternative to capitalism, how could political activists write in a genre inaugurated by the *Communist Manifesto?* And with the art world declaring that "anything goes," how could activist artists claim to do away with all preceding and rival art forms? If the late twentieth century did not experience the "end of history," as the political scientist Francis Fukuyama predicted in 1992 that it would, it certainly seemed to experience the end of the manifesto.

The manifesto has not disappeared entirely, however. An increasingly global capitalism still breeds resistance and resentment in those left behind; and 9/11 demonstrated that we still live in a world dominated by rival political systems and their sometimes violent clashes. At the same time, the ever-changing social media allow for new forms of revolutionary organizing, and new technological revolutions are changing the face of art even more rapidly now than during the early twentieth century.

The evidence of several hundred years of manifesto writing assembled in these volumes captures a breathtaking history of innovation, a history of men and women trying to make the world anew. The enduring impulse to declare a point zero and to envision a new departure, the audacity to break with tradition and to found new traditions, is nothing less than a history of modernity itself. Manifestos, the most characteristic form in which these ambitions have been expressed, can thus be regarded as the most representative and important documents of the modern world, a literature unto themselves.

Manifestos have routinely predicted the future even as they have tried to bring that future about. They may well continue to shape our world for the foreseeable future.

Martin Puchner,
Advisory Board Chair

EDITOR'S NOTE

The Manifesto in Literature, a three-volume reference guide, provides critical introductions to 300 manifestos throughout the world. As manifestos, all the works share a common trait. They challenge a traditional order, whether in politics, religion, social issues, art, literature, or technology, and propose a new vision of the future.

Among the earliest manifestos discussed in the guide are the *Ninety-Five Theses* (1517), a critique of the Roman Catholic Church by German priest and professor Martin Luther, and the *Politics of Obedience* (1552-53), in which French writer Étienne de la Boétie argues that people allow themselves to be ruled by tyrants out of habit and hope for personal gain. Of the twentieth-century art manifestos covered in the book, "Art, Revolution, and Decadence" (1926), by Peruvian marxist José Carlos Mariátegui, discusses the relationship between revolutionary art and politics, and "Gutai Manifesto" (1956), by Japanese artist Jiro Yoshihara, contends that representational art perpetuates a "fraud" by creating illusions. More recently, *Why Facebook Exists* (2012), by Mark Zuckerberg, the American founder of the social network, offers an idealistic vision for his company, arguing that its mission is not profit but increased interpersonal connectivity throughout the world and thus more democratic social, political, and economic institutions.

The structure and content of *The Manifesto in Literature* was planned with the help of the project's advisory board, chaired by Martin Puchner, Byron and Anita Wien Professor of Drama and of English and Comparative Literature at Harvard University. In his introduction to this guide, he discusses how *The Manifesto of the Communist Party,* written in 1848 by the German theorists Karl Marx and Frederick Engels, helped define the very idea of the manifesto.

ORGANIZATION

All entries share a common structure, providing consistent coverage of the works and a simple way of comparing basic elements of one text with another. Each entry has six parts: overview, historical and literary context, themes and style, critical discussion, sources, and further reading. Entries also have either an excerpt from the manifesto and/or a sidebar discussing a related topic, such as the life of the author.

The Manifesto in Literature is divided into three volumes, each with 100 entries. Volume 1, "Origins of the Form: Pre-1900," has six sections focusing on early concerns of manifesto writers—church and state, citizens and revolutionaries, proletarians, emancipation and independence, women, and artists and writers. "Church and State," for example, contains nineteen entries, such as the *People's Charter* by English activist William Lovett, who advocated electoral reforms aimed at helping British working classes. Volume 2, "The Modernist Movement: 1900-WWII," includes three sections—social and political upheavals, Harlem Renaissance, and avant gardes—the latter two including entries on art and literature manifestos. Volume 3, "Activism, Unrest, and the Neo-Avant-Garde," has eleven sections: art and architecture; film; feminisms; radical politics; queer politics; America left and right; global militants; philosophies; poetry and performance; students, activists, and situations; and technologies.

Among the criteria for selecting entry topics were the importance of the work in university curricula, the region and country of the author and text, and the time period. Entries can be looked up in the author and title indexes, as well as in the general subject index.

ACKNOWLEDGMENTS

Many people contributed time, effort, and ideas to *The Manifesto in Literature*. At Gale, Philip J. Virta, manager of new products, developed the original plan for the book, and Lisa Kumar, senior content project editor, served as the in-house manager for the project. *The Manifesto in Literature* owes its existence to their ideas and involvement.

We would like to express our appreciation to the advisors, who, in addition to creating the organization of *The Manifesto in Literature* and choosing the entry topics, identified other scholars to work on the project and answered many questions, both big and small. We would also like to thank the contributors for their accessible essays, often on difficult topics, as well as the scholars who reviewed the text for accuracy and coverage.

I am grateful to Erin Brown, senior project editor, especially for her work with the advisors and on the entry list; Greta Gard, project editor, who managed the writers; Mary Beth Curran, associate editor, who oversaw the editing process; David Hayes, associate editor, whose many contributions included organizing the workflow; and Hannah Soukup, assistant editor, who identified and corresponded with the academic reviewers. Other important assistance came from Mariko Fujinaka, managing editor; Anne Healey, senior editor; and Janet Moredock and Lee Esbenshade, associate editors. The line editors were Heather Campbell, Cheryl Collins, Tony Craine, Holli Fort, Laura Gabler, Harrabeth Haidusek, Ellen Henderson, Joan Hibler, Dehlia McCobb, Kathy Peacock, Donna Polydoros, Natalie Ruppert, Mary Russell, Lisa Trow, Will Wagner, and Whitney Ward.

Thomas Riggs

CONTRIBUTORS

DAVID AITCHISON

Aitchison is a PhD candidate in literary studies and a university instructor.

GREG BACH

Bach holds an MA in classics and is a freelance writer.

KIM BANION

Banion is a PhD student in English literature and a high school English instructor.

LISA BARCA

Barca holds a PhD in romance languages and literatures and is a university professor.

KATHERINE BARKER

Barker holds an MA in English literature.

CRAIG BARNES

Barnes holds an MFA in creative writing and has been a university instructor and a freelance writer.

MARIE BECKER

Becker holds an MA in humanities.

KAREN BENDER

Bender holds an MFA in creative writing and an MPhil in Anglo-Irish literature. She has taught high school English.

KATHERINE BISHOP

Bishop is a PhD student in English literature and has been a university instructor.

ALLISON BLECKER

Blecker is a PhD candidate in Near Eastern languages.

ELIZABETH BOEHEIM

Boeheim holds an MA in English literature and has been a university instructor.

MELANIE BREZNIAK

Brezniak is a PhD candidate in English literature and has been a university instructor.

WESLEY BORUCKI

Borucki holds a PhD in American history and is a university professor.

JOSEPH CAMPANA

Campana holds an MA in English literature and has been a university professor.

GERALD CARPENTER

Carpenter holds an MA in U.S. intellectual history and a PhD in early modern French history. He is a freelance writer.

CHRISTINA BROWN CELONA

Celona holds a PhD in English literature and creative writing and has been a university instructor and a freelance writer.

CURT CLONINGER

Cloninger holds an MFA in studio arts and is a university professor.

KEVIN COONEY

Cooney holds a PhD in English literature and is a university professor.

ALEX COVALCIUC

Covalciuc is a PhD candidate in English literature. He has been a university instructor and a freelance writer.

GIANO CROMLEY

Cromley holds an MFA in creative writing and is a university instructor.

MARIE DAVOL

Davol holds an MA in writing.

VICTORIA DeCUIR

DeCuir holds an MA in art history and is a university instructor.

ANNA DEEM

Deem holds an MA in education and is a freelance writer.

CAMERON DODWORTH

Dodworth holds a PhD in English literature and is a university instructor.

RICHARD ESBENSHADE

Esbenshade holds a PhD in history and has been a university professor and a freelance writer.

TAYLOR EVANS

Evans is a PhD student in English literature and has been a university instructor.

DENNIS FEHR

Fehr holds a PhD in art education and is a university professor.

ELEANOR FOGOLIN

Fogolin is pursuing an MA in English literature.

CAROL FRANCIS

Francis holds an MA in English literature and has been a university instructor.

DANIEL FRIED

Fried holds a PhD in East Asian studies and is a university professor.

DAISY GARD

Gard is a freelance writer with a background in English literature.

GRETA GARD

Gard is a PhD candidate in English literature and has been a university instructor and a freelance writer.

CLINT GARNER

Garner holds an MFA in creative writing and is a freelance writer.

KRISTEN GLEASON

Gleason holds an MFA in creative writing and has been a university instructor.

RODNEY HARRIS

Harris is pursuing a PhD in history and has been a university instructor.

JOSH HARTEIS

Harteis holds an MA in English literature and is a freelance writer.

MICHAEL HARTWELL

Hartwell holds an MFA in creative writing and has been a university instructor and a freelance writer.

RON HORTON

Horton holds an MFA in creative writing and has been a high school English instructor and a freelance writer.

ANNA IOANES

Ioanes is a PhD student in English language and literature and has been a university instructor.

MIRANDA JOHNSON

Johnson is a freelance writer with a background in art history.

EMILY JONES

Jones holds an MFA in creative writing and has been a university instructor.

REBECCA KASTLEMAN

Kastleman is a PhD candidate in English literature and a freelance writer.

KRISTIN KING-RIES

King-Ries holds an MFA in creative writing and has been a university instructor.

LISA KROGER

Kroger holds a PhD in English literature and has been a university instructor.

DAVID LOVE

Love is pursuing an MFA in creative writing and has been a freelance writer.

JENNY LUDWIG

Ludwig holds an MA in English literature and has been a university instructor and a freelance writer.

GREGORY LUTHER

Luther holds an MFA in creative writing and has been a university instructor and freelance writer.

KATIE MACNAMARA

Macnamara holds a PhD in English literature and has been a university instructor.

MAGGIE MAGNO

Magno has an MA in education. She has been a high school English teacher and a freelance writer.

ABIGAIL MANN

Mann holds a PhD in English literature and is a university professor.

THEODORE McDERMOTT

McDermott holds an MFA in creative writing and has been a university instructor and a freelance writer.

LISA MERTEL

Mertel holds an MA in library science and an MA in history.

STEPHEN MEYER

Meyer holds an MFA in creative writing and has been a university instructor and a freelance writer.

RACHEL MINDELL

Mindell holds an MFA in creative writing and has been a freelance writer.

JIM MLADENOVIC

Mladenovic holds an MS in clinical psychology and is pursuing an MA in library science.

CAITIE MOORE

Moore holds an MFA in creative writing and has been a university instructor.

ROBIN MORRIS

Morris holds a PhD in English literature and has been a university instructor.

JANET MULLANE

Mullane is a freelance writer and has been a high school English teacher.

ELLIOTT NIBLOCK

Niblock holds an MTS in the philosophy of religion.

ELIZABETH ORVIS

Orvis is a freelance writer with a background in English literature.

JAMES OVERHOLTZER

Overholtzer holds an MA in English literature and has been a university instructor.

JONATHAN REEVE

Reeve holds an MA in humanities and an MA in English literature and has been a university instructor.

EVELYN REYNOLDS

Reynolds is pursuing an MA in English literature and an MFA in creative writing and has been a freelance writer.

RICHARD ROTHROCK

Rothrock hold an MA in mass communication and has been a university instructor and a freelance writer.

REBECCA RUSTIN

Rustin holds an MA in English literature and is a freelance writer.

CARINA SAXON

Saxon is a PhD candidate in English literature and has been a university instructor and a freelance editor.

CATHERINE E. SAUNDERS

Saunders holds a PhD in English literature and is a university professor.

JACOB SCHMITT

Schmitt holds an MA in English literature and has been a freelance writer.

NANCY SIMPSON-YOUNGER

Simpson-Younger is a PhD candidate in literary studies and a university instructor.

NICHOLAS SNEAD

Snead is a PhD candidate in French language and literature and has been a university instructor.

HANNAH SOUKUP

Soukup holds an MFA in creative writing.

STEPHEN SQUIBB

Squibb is a PhD candidate in English literature and a freelance writer.

SARAH STOECKL

Stoeckl holds a PhD in English literature and is a university instructor and a freelance writer.

MARTHA SUTRO

Sutro holds an MFA in creative writing and is a university instructor and a freelance writer.

ELIZABETH VITANZA

Vitanza holds a PhD in French and Francophone studies and has been a university and a high school instructor.

GRACE WAITMAN

Waitman is pursuing a PhD in educational psychology. She holds an MA in English literature and has been a university instructor.

JOHN WALTERS

Walters is pursuing a PhD in English literature and has been a university instructor.

JOSHUA WARE

Ware holds a PhD in creative writing and has been a university instructor.

KATRINA WHITE

White is a PhD candidate in Spanish language and literature and a university instructor.

ACADEMIC REVIEWERS

JOSEPH ACQUISTO

Associate Professor of French, University of Vermont, Burlington.

ANN MARIE ADAMS

Professor of English, Morehead State University, Kentucky.

RAPHAEL ALLISON

Assistant Professor of English, MAT Program, Bard College, Annandale-on-Hudson, New York.

JOHN ALVIS

Professor of English and Director, American Studies Program, University of Dallas, Irving, Texas.

NAOMI ANDREWS

Assistant Professor of History, Santa Clara University, California.

PETER ARNADE

Dean, College of Arts and Humanities, University of Hawaiapos;i at Manoa, Honolulu.

BERNARDO ALEXANDER ATTIAS

Professor and Chair, Department of Communication Studies, California State University, Northridge.

SYLVIA BAKOS

Associate Professor of Fine Arts, SUNY Buffalo State, New York.

J. T. BARBARESE

Associate Professor of English and Creative Writing, Rutgers-Camden, New Jersey.

ROANN BARRIS

Associate Professor of Art History, Radford University, Virginia.

ADAM BARROWS

Associate Professor of English, Carleton University, Ottawa, Ontario, Canada.

WILLIAM BAUER

Associate Professor of History, University of Nevada-Las Vegas.

ROSALYN BAXANDALL

Retired Distinguished Teaching Professor, SUNY Old Westbury, New York, and Professor, Bard Prison Project and CUNY Labor School, New York.

JEREMY BEAUDRY

Assistant Professor and Director, Master of Industrial Design Program, University of the Arts, Philadelphia, Pennsylvania.

THOMAS OLIVER BEEBEE

Edwin Erle Sparks Professor of Comparative Literature and German, Pennsylvania State University, University Park.

STEPHEN BEHRENDT

University Professor and George Holmes Distinguished Professor of English, University of Nebraska, Lincoln.

JUSTYNA BEINEK

Assistant Professor of Slavic Languages and Literatures and Director, Polish Language, Literature, and Culture Program, Indiana University-Bloomington.

WILLIAM BELDING

Professorial Lecturer, School of International Service, American University, Washington, D.C.

EVGENII BERSHTEIN

Associate Professor of Russian, Reed College, Portland, Oregon.

ALEX BLAZER

Assistant Professor of English and Coordinator, Teaching Fellows,

Georgia College & State University, Milledgeville.

DAVID BLITZ

Professor of Philosophy and Director, Honors Program, Central Connecticut State University, New Britain.

JULIA BLOCH

Assistant Professor of Literature, MAT Program, Bard College, Annandale-on-Hudson, New York.

SAM BOOTLE

Teaching Fellow in French, University of St. Andrews, Fife, Scotland, United Kingdom.

MARK CAMERON BOYD

Professor of Fine Arts and Academics, Corcoran College of Art and Design, Washington, D.C.

MICHAEL P. BREEN

Associate Professor of History and Humanities, Reed College, Portland, Oregon.

DANIEL H. BROWN

Assistant Professor of Spanish, Western Illinois University, Macomb.

JAMES BROWN

Assistant Professor of English, University of Wisconsin-Madison.

ERNESTO CAPELLO

Associate Professor of History and Latin American Studies, Macalester College, St. Paul, Minnesota.

MICHAEL CARIGNAN

Associate Professor of History, Elon University, North Carolina.

TERRELL CARVER

Professor of Political Theory, University of Bristol, United Kingdom.

MALCOLM CHASE

Professor of Social History, University of Leeds, United Kingdom.

EWA CHRUSCIEL

Associate Professor of Humanities, Colby-Sawyer College, New London, New Hampshire.

ANN CIASULLO

Assistant Professor of English and Women's and Gender Studies, Gonzaga University, Spokane, Washington.

CURT CLONINGER

Assistant Professor of New Media, University of North Carolina, Asheville.

RUSSELL COOK

Professor of Communications, Loyola University Maryland, Baltimore.

RAYMOND CRAIB

Associate Professor of History, Cornell University, Ithaca, New York.

JANE CRAWFORD

Faculty, History and Political Science Department, Mount St. Mary's College, Los Angeles, California.

LESLEY CURTIS

Visiting Lecturer in French, Humanities, and Women's Studies, University of New Hampshire, Durham.

VICTORIA ESTRADA BERG DECUIR

Assistant Director and Registrar, UNT Art Gallery and Art in Public Places, and Adjunct Faculty, Department of Art History, College of Visual Arts and Design, University of North Texas, Denton.

GABRIELE DILLMANN

Associate Professor of German, Denison University, Granville, Ohio.

EDUARDO DE JESÚS DOUGLAS

Associate Professor of Art History, University of North Carolina at Chapel Hill.

ELLEN DUBOIS

Professor of History, University of California, Los Angeles.

HUGH DUBRULL

Associate Professor of History, St. Anselm College, Manchester, New Hampshire.

ELIZABETH DUQUETTE

Associate Professor of English, Gettysburg College, Pennsylvania.

MICHAEL J. DUVALL

Associate Professor of English, College of Charleston, South Carolina.

TAYLOR EASUM

Assistant Professor of Global Histories; Faculty Fellow of Draper Program, New York University.

LORI EMERSON

Assistant Professor of English, University of Colorado-Boulder.

ALEŠ ERJAVEC

Professor of Philosophy, Aesthetics, and Contemporary Art History, Institute of Philosophy, Slovenian Academy of Sciences and Arts, Ljubljana, Slovenia.

SEBASTIAAN FABER

Professor of Hispanic Studies, Director, Oberlin Center for Languages and Cultures, and Chair, Latin American Studies, Oberlin College, Ohio.

BREANNE FAHS

Associate Professor of Women and Gender Studies, Arizona State University, Glendale.

DANINE FARQUHARSON

Associate Professor of English, Memorial University of Newfoundland, St. John's, Canada.

JIMMY FAZZINO

Lecturer in the Literature Department and Writing Program, University of California, Santa Cruz.

ODILE FERLY

Associate Professor of Francophone Studies, Clark University, Worcester, Massachusetts.

JOSHUA FIRST

Croft Assistant Professor of History and International Studies, University of Mississippi, University.

LEONARDO FLORES

Associate Professor of English and Fulbright Scholar in Digital Culture, Universidad de Puerto Rico, Mayagüez.

LISA FLORMAN

Associate Professor, History of Art, Ohio State University, Columbus.

WILLIAM FRANKE

Professor of Comparative Literature and Religious Studies, Vanderbilt University, Nashville, Tennessee, and Professor of Philosophy and Religions, University of Macao, China.

SUSAN GALLAGHER

Associate Professor of Political Science, University of Massachusetts Lowell.

JAMES GIGANTINO

Assistant Professor of History, University of Arkansas, Fayetteville.

DAWN GILPIN

Assistant Professor of Journalism, Walter Cronkite School of Journalism and Mass Communication, Arizona State University, Phoenix.

DALE GRADEN

Professor of History, University of Idaho, Moscow.

PATRICK RYAN GRZANKA

Honors Faculty Fellow at Barrett, the Honors College, Arizona State University, Tempe.

ANDREW P. HALEY

Associate Professor of American Cultural History, University of Southern Mississippi, Hattiesburg.

M. SÜKRÜ HANIOGLU

Garrett Professor in Foreign Affairs, Chair, Near Eastern Studies Department, and Director, Near Eastern Studies Program, Princeton University, New Jersey.

MARK HARRISON

Professor of Theatre and Performance Studies, Evergreen State College, Olympia, Washington.

CHENE HEADY

Associate Professor of English, Longwood University, Farmville, Virginia.

MICHAEL C. HICKEY

Professor of History, Bloomsburg University, Pennsylvania.

STEPHEN HICKS

Professor of Philosophy, Rockford College, Illinois.

BENEDIKT HJARTARSON

Adjunct Professor of Comparative Literature, University of Iceland, Reykjavik.

TAMARA HO

Assistant Professor of Women's Studies, University of California, Riverside.

WALTER HÖLBLING

Professor of American Studies, Karl-Franzens-Universität, Graz, Austria.

PIPPA HOLLOWAY

Professor of History and Program Director, Graduate Studies, Middle Tennessee State University, Murfreesboro.

MARYANNE HOROWITZ

Professor of History, Occidental College, Los Angeles, California. Editor-in-Chief, New Dictionary of the History of Ideas.

BOZENA KARWOWSKA

Associate Professor of Polish Language and Literature, University of British Columbia, Vancouver, Canada.

ANTHONY KEMP

Associate Professor of English, University of Southern California, Los Angeles.

ALICIA A. KENT

Associate Professor of English, University of Michigan-Flint.

MATTHEW KINEEN

Professor of Comparative Literature, St. Louis University-Madrid, Spain.

JASMINE KITSES

PhD candidate in English, University of California, Davis.

SCOTT KLEINMAN

Professor of English, California State University, Northridge.

CHRISTOPHER KNIGHT

Professor of English, University of Montana, Missoula.

ANDREAS KRATKY

Assistant Professor of Media Arts and Interim Director, Media Arts and Practice

PhD Program, University of Southern California, Los Angeles.

CHARLES KURZMAN

Professor of Sociology, University of North Carolina at Chapel Hill.

JOSÉ LANTERS

Professor of English, University of Wisconsin-Milwaukee.

SHARON LARSON

Visiting Instructor of Modern Languages, University of Central Florida, Orlando.

KEITH LAYBOURN

Diamond Jubilee Professor, University of Huddersfield, West Yorkshire, United Kingdom.

BRENT LAYTHAM

Professor of Theology and Dean, Ecumenical Institute of Theology, St. Mary's Seminary and University, Baltimore, Maryland.

KAREN J. LEADER

Assistant Professor of Art History, Florida Atlantic University, Boca Raton.

ESTHER LESLIE

Professor of Political Aesthetics, University of London-Birkbeck, United Kingdom.

ESTHER LEVINGER

Professor of Art History, University of Haifa, Israel.

MARK LEVY

Professor of Art, California State University-East Bay, Hayward.

MARTIN LOCKSHIN

Professor of Humanities and Chair, Humanities Department, York University, Toronto, Ontario, Canada.

XIAOFEI LU

Gil Watz Early Career Professor in Language and Linguistics, as well as Associate Professor of Applied Linguistics, Pennsylvania State University, University Park.

CARY MAZER

Associate Professor of Theatre Arts and English, University of Pennsylvania, Philadelphia.

WILLIAM MCBRIDE

Associate Professor of English, Illinois State University, Normal.

KEVIN MCCOY

Associate Professor of Art and Art Education, New York University-Steinhardt.

PETER MCPHEE

Professorial Fellow of History, University of Melbourne, Australia.

GREGORY METCALF

Adjunct Professor of Art History and Theory & Criticism, University of Maryland; Maryland Institute College of Art, Baltimore.

DARREN MIDDLETON

Professor of Religion, Texas Christian University, Fort Worth.

GRÜNFELD MIHAI

Associate Professor of Hispanic Studies, Vassar College, Poughkeepsie, New York.

GAVIN MURRAY-MILLER

Adjunct Professor of History, Virginia Commonwealth University, Richmond.

DAVID N. MYERS

Professor of History and Chair, Department of History, University of California, Los Angeles.

WENDY NIELSEN

Assistant Professor of English, Montclair State University, New Jersey.

DRAGANA OBRADOVIC

Assistant Professor of Slavic Languages and Literatures, University of Toronto, Ontario, Canada.

ELAINE O'BRIEN

Professor of Modern and Contemporary Art History and Criticism, California State University, Sacramento.

JENNIFER PAP

Associate Professor of French, University of Denver, Colorado. Sanja Perovic Lecturer in French, King's College, London, United Kingdom.

EMMANUEL PETIT

Associate Professor of Architecture, Yale University, New Haven, Connecticut.

MICHEL PHARAND

Director, Disraeli Project, Queen's University, Kingston, Ontario, Canada.

JANET POWERS

Professor Emerita of Interdisciplinary Studies and Women, Gender, and Sexuality Studies, Gettysburg College, Pennsylvania.

EPHRAIM RADNER

Professor of Historical Theology, Wycliffe College, University of Toronto, Ontario, Canada.

MICHAEL RAPPORT

Professor of History and Politics, University of Stirling, Scotland, United Kingdom.

HOLLY RAYNARD

Lecturer in Czech Studies, University of Florida, Gainesville.

JONATHAN REES

Professor of History, Colorado State University-Pueblo.

JOHN RIEDER

Professor of English, University of Hawaii at Manoa, Honolulu.

PATRICIO RIZZO-VAST

Instructor in Spanish and Portuguese, Northeastern Illinois University, Chicago.

HUGH ROBERTS

Associate Professor of English, University of California, Irvine, California.

MOSS ROBERTS

Professor of Chinese, New York University.

LETHA CLAIR ROBERTSON

Assistant Professor of Art and Art History, University of Texas at Tyler.

AARON ROSEN

Lecturer in Sacred Traditions and the Arts, King's College-London, United Kingdom.

ELI RUBIN

Associate Professor of History, Western Michigan University, Kalamazoo.

GREGORY SHAYA

Associate Professor of History and Chair, History Department, College of Wooster, Ohio.

NOAH SHUSTERMAN

Assistant Professor of Intellectual Heritage, Temple University, Philadelphia, Pennsylvania.

JOEL SIPRESS

Professor of History, University of Wisconsin-Superior.

ADAM SITZE

Assistant Professor of Law, Jurisprudence, and Social Thought, Amherst College, Massachusetts.

CRAIG SMITH

Associate Professor of Art, University of Florida, Gainesville.

ROGER SOUTHALL

Honorary Professor in SWOP (Southwest Organizing Project) and Head, Sociology Department, University of the Witwatersrand, Johannesburg, South Africa.

ROBERT SPAHR

Assistant Professor of Media and Media Production, Southern Illinois University, Carbondale.

ANIA SPYRA

Assistant Professor of English, Butler University, Indianapolis, Indiana.

MARY ZEISS STANGE

Professor of Women's Studies and Religion, Skidmore College, Saratoga Springs, New York.

ELIZABETH STARK

Visiting Fellow, Yale Information Society Project, and Lecturer in Computer Science, Yale University, New Haven, Connecticut.

JANET WRIGHT STARNER

Associate Professor of English, Wilkes University, Wilkes-Barre, Pennsylvania.

R. VLADMIR STEFFEL

Professor Emeritus of History and Director, Honors Programs, Ohio State University-Marion.

SARAH STOECKL

PhD, Department of English, University of Oregon, Eugene.

MASON STOKES

Associate Professor of English and Chair, English Department, Skidmore College, Saratoga Springs, New York.

MATTHEW STRATTON

Assistant Professor of English, University of California, Davis.

WOODMAN TAYLOR

Associate Professor of Art History, American University of Dubai.

CHARISSA TERRANOVA

Assistant Professor of Aesthetic Studies, University of Texas at Dallas, Richardson.

DOUGLASS THOMSON

Professor of English, Georgia Southern University, Statesboro.

LARRY THORNTON

Professor of History, Hanover College, Indiana.

JOHN G. TURNER

Assistant Professor of Religious Studies, George Mason University, Fairfax, Virginia.

THOMAS UNDERWOOD

Senior Lecturer (Master Level), College of Arts and Sciences Writing Program, Boston University, Massachusetts.

ELIZABETH VITANZA

French Instructor, Marlborough School, Los Angeles, California.

ALICIA VOLK

Associate Professor of Art History and Director, Graduate Studies, University of Maryland, College Park.

DONALD WELLMAN

Professor of Literature and Writing, Daniel Webster College, Nashua, New Hampshire.

E. J. WESTLAKE

Associate Professor of Theatre, University of Michigan, Ann Arbor.

RACHEL WILLIAMS

Associate Professor of Studio Art and Gender, Women's, and Sexuality Studies, University of Iowa, Iowa City.

SIMONA WRIGHT

Professor of Italian, College of New Jersey, Ewing Township.

RALPH YOUNG

Professor of History, Temple University, Philadelphia, Pennsylvania.

PIERANTONIO ZANOTTI

Adjunct Professor of Japanese Language, Università Ca' Foscari Venezia, Italy.

Avant Gardes

THE ABSOLUTELY NEW: FUTURISM

ART AND REVOLUTION. SOCIALIST MODERNISMS

FROM DADA TO SURREALISM

THE FUGITIVE AND THE IDEAL: SYMBOLISM AND IMPRESSIONISM

SOUL AND FORM: ACMEISM, EXPRESSIONISM, CUBISM, VORTICISM, CREATIONISM, IMAGISM

UTOPIAN MODERNISMS: CONSTRUCTIVISM, SUPREMATISM, BAUHAUS, PURISM

APHORISMS ON FUTURISM

Mina Loy

OVERVIEW

Composed by poet Mina Loy, *Aphorisms on Futurism*, first published in the renowned American arts journal *Camera Work* in 1914, describes a process for psychic and artistic reawakening and reinvention through the opening of consciousness and the rejection of convention. Many of the manifesto's tenets were adopted from the futurists, an Italian artistic movement that argued that the conditions of modern industrial culture necessitated new forms of cultural expression. Loy was closely involved, both personally and intellectually, with the movement's founder, Filippo Tommaso Marinetti, when she composed *Aphorisms on Futurism*. Although she was profoundly influenced by the movement's new ideas about art, Loy's manifesto does not simply reiterate the futurist message. Rather, it appropriates futurism's embrace of revolutionary artistic forms while recasting the movement's macho, collective, and declarative tone as a dialogue about personal and aesthetic renewal. Addressed to an unspecified "You," *Aphorisms on Futurism* takes the form of brief maxims and fragments that interrogate the preconceptions and prejudices of both the author and the reader.

Aphorisms on Futurism created a stir among readers, who were shocked by Loy's masculine audacity and tone. With its valuation of speed, strength, and even violence, futurism was regarded as a distinctly male artistic movement. Loy's manifesto complicated that conception. Drawing on unconventional typography and syntax, she used the tools of futurism to deconstruct popular preconceptions about femininity. Readers and critics alike were scandalized by her refusal to adhere to accepted female decorum. As Loy's first publication, the manifesto introduced a radical new voice in English-language letters. Today, *Aphorisms on Futurism* is considered a central document in the futurist movement and a key to understanding the artistic project of one of modernism's most important poets.

HISTORICAL AND LITERARY CONTEXT

Aphorisms on Futurism responds to the fraught cultural and artistic moment in Europe at the turn of the twentieth century, when the innovations of modernism clashed with growing nostalgia for Victorian tradition. The roots of this conflict can be traced to the mid-nineteenth century, when new scientific discoveries and social arguments began to challenge Enlightenment ideas about the inevitability of cultural improvement and economic progress. The publication of Charles Darwin's *On the Origin of Species* in 1859 introduced the theory of evolution and upended traditional beliefs about man's place in the world. Karl Marx's *The Communist Manifesto* (1848) and *Capital* (1867) challenged the accepted notion that capitalism creates true economic prosperity. At the end of the nineteenth century, the art of the Impressionists and Cubists rejected traditional artistic practice and invented new ways of viewing the world. Meanwhile, thinkers such as Friedrich Nietzsche continued the critique of traditional Western thought. Then, in the early 1900s, Marinetti launched the futurist movement in response to cultivated Europeans' nostalgic return to the premodern era.

✢ *Key Facts*

Time Period:
Early 20th Century

Movement/Issue:
Futurism

Place of Publication:
United States

Language of Publication:
English

MINA LOY: FORGOTTEN FOR TOO LONG

Young, beautiful, and brilliant, Mina Loy burst onto the arts scene in 1914 with *Aphorisms of Futurism* and quickly earned admiration from such luminaries as T. S. Eliot and Gertrude Stein. When she began to publish poetry later that same year, she introduced a free and urgent style that overturned everyone's idea of what a woman poet could be. She was central to the art scene for two decades, but by the mid-1930s her work was out of print, and she had all but disappeared. Loy was forgotten but not gone, living in a series of cheap communal boarding houses rather than associating with sculptors and publishers and poets. As she became increasingly reclusive and ceased publishing, her reputation continued to recede.

Poet Kenneth Rexroth waged the first battle to restore Loy's reputation in the 1940s. In 1958 poet and publisher Jonathan Williams issued a collection of her out-of-print work. This initiated renewed interest from Black Mountain poets such as Robert Creeley but did not lead to a wider revival of her reputation. Another version of her work came out in 1982, but it, too, was largely overlooked. Only at the turn of the twenty-first century, after Loy's death, was she returned to her place in the modernist canon. Still, much of her work remains out of print—and the project of exhuming Loy's full literary contribution continues.

Dynamism of a Cyclist (1913), by Mina Loy's fellow Futurist, artist Umberto Boccioni. © AISA/ EVERETT COLLECTION

By the time *Aphorisms on Futurism* was written in 1914, Loy was closely involved with the futurists. She was living in Florence, Italy, and was romantically involved with Marinetti, who was actively working to provoke artistic revolution. He encouraged Loy's experimentation with both poetry and painting. Although Loy was repelled by futurism's machismo, she was enlivened by its liberating message and by Marinetti's "words-set-free," a poetic form that sought to disengage language from the strictures of linearity. In *Aphorisms on Futurism,* she co-opted futurism in order to critique it.

Aphorisms on Futurism is a response to *Manifesto of Futurism* (1909), the movement's foundational text, in which Marinetti argues that the industrial age demands a new art defined by "aggression, feverish sleeplessness, the double march, the perilous leap, the slap and the blow with the fist." Loy's tract echoes this urgent call for courage and immediacy while rejecting its bravado and violence. It also responds to a pair of manifestos by the French poet Valentine de Saint-Point, *Manifesto of the Futurist Woman* (1912) and *Futurist Manifesto of Lust* (1913). Roger L. Conover, editor of *The Lost Lunar Baedeker: Poems of Mina Loy,* explains that Saint-Point's work "announced the birth of a strong and instinctive superwoman and affirmed the rights of female sexual desire." Similarly, Loy's manifesto examines the place of femininity in futurism but offers a more nuanced and subtle response. The aphoristic form of Loy's manifesto derives from a long tradition of aphoristic writing that can be traced back to the Roman poet Hippocrates, who wrote circa 400 BCE, and was employed in the late nineteenth century by such varied writers as Nietzsche, Oscar Wilde, and Lautrémont.

Aphorisms on Futurism subsequently inspired Loy's *Feminist Manifesto* (November 1914), a vociferous cry for a radical form of women's liberation that was not published until 1982, after her death. Whereas *Aphorisms on Futurism* obliquely alludes to the female role in the futurist project and explores the process of psychic liberation, the *Feminist Manifesto* is a direct response to the sexism inherent in futurism and explicitly rebukes the feminist movement. The *Feminist Manifesto* also represents a progression in Loy's stylistic and formal experimentalism. Today, *Aphorisms on Futurism* commands significant scholarly interest for its role as the origin of Loy's radical and lifelong artistic project.

THEMES AND STYLE

The central theme of *Aphorisms on Futurism* is that psychic rejuvenation is imperative and can only be accomplished through the unflinching interrogation of convention. With the urgency of the *Manifesto of Futurism* pushing it forward, Loy's manifesto opens: "DIE in the Past. Live in the Future." These maxims immediately and forcefully introduce Loy's affinity with the futurist project by exalting speed and immediacy in pursuit of self-renewal and artistic reinvention. As this theme develops through the essay, Loy gradually distances her argument from that of Marinetti and his male adherents. "FORGET that you live in houses, that you may live in yourself—" she writes. In this way, she locates her argument in the home, in the domestic, and appeals implicitly to women, an audience ignored and alienated by the dominant strain of futurist rhetoric. As Loy's manifesto proceeds, it continues to radically rethink conventional conceptions of everything from love to time to independence.

The manifesto achieves its rhetorical effect through its dialogic form. Loy rejects the collective first-person plural point of view of the *Manifesto of Futurism* in favor of the more intimate second person. She addresses a "you" that is at once herself and her reader. This is implicit in the imperative syntax of the manifesto's opening lines, and it becomes increasingly explicit as the essay proceeds. "You prefer to observe the past on which your eyes are already opened," Loy writes. Elsewhere, she instructs this "you" to "UN-SCREW your capability of absorption and grasp the elements of Life—*Whole.*" In place of pronouncements and certainty, Loy offers ambivalence and dialogue, which she holds in tension with her spare, self-assured, and aphoristic style.

Stylistically, *Aphorisms on Futurism* is distinguished by its pithiness. Loy does not offer the reader a comprehensive and cogent argument. Rather, she dispenses with a series of forceful and concise expressions that are loosely linked together. "LOVE the hideous in order to find the sublime core of it," she writes. The next line reads, "OPEN your arms to the dilapidated; rehabilitate them." While these statements are assertive and blunt, the connection between them is loose and associative. As a result, Loy's text is able to assume the strength of a manifesto while maintaining the lyrical quality of poetry. *Aphorisms on Futurism* simultaneously espouses and critiques the futurist project. When she commands her implied "you" to "ACCEPT the tremendous truth of Futurism," it is unclear whether she is addressing the reader or herself. The aphoristic nature of the manifesto provides Loy with the rhetorical room to question her convictions.

CRITICAL DISCUSSION

When *Aphorisms on Futurism* was first published in 1914, it received mixed reactions within the artistic circles in which it circulated. Its appearance in the

PRIMARY SOURCE

APHORISMS ON FUTURISM

DIE in the Past

Live in the Future.

THE velocity of velocities arrives in starting.

IN pressing the material to derive its essence, matter becomes deformed.

AND form hurtling against itself is thrown beyond the synopsis of vision.

THE straight line and the circle are the parents of design, form the basis of art; there is no limit to their coherent variability.

LOVE the hideous in order to find the sublime core of it.

OPEN your arms to the dilapidated; rehabilitate them.

YOU prefer to observe the past on which your eyes are already opened.

BUT the Future is only dark from outside.

Leap into it—and it EXPLODES with *Light*.

FORGET that you live in houses, that you may live in yourself—

FOR the smallest people live in the greatest houses.

BUT the smallest person, potentially, is as great as the Universe.

WHAT can you know of expansion, who limit yourselves to compromise?

HITHERTO the great man has achieved greatness by keeping the people small.

BUT in the Future, by inspiring the people to expand to their fullest capacity, the great man proportionately must be tremendous—a God.

LOVE of others is the appreciation of oneself.

MAY your egotism be so gigantic that you comprise mankind in your self-sympathy.

THE Future is limitless—the past a trail of insidious reactions.

LIFE is only limited by our prejudices. Destroy them, and you cease to be at the mercy of yourself.

TIME is the dispersion of intensiveness.

THE Futurist can live a thousand years in one poem.

HE can compress every aesthetic principle in one line.

THE mind is a magician bound by assimilations; let him loose and the smallest idea conceived in freedom will suffice to negate the wisdom of all forefathers.

LOOKING on the past you arrive at "Yes," but before you can act upon it you have already arrived at "No."

THE Futurist must leap from affirmative to affirmative, ignoring intermittent negations—must spring from stepping-stone to stone of creative exploration; without slipping back into the turbid stream of accepted facts.

THERE are no excrescences on the absolute, to which man may pin his faith.

TODAY is the crisis in consciousness.

CONSCIOUSNESS cannot spontaneously accept or reject new forms, as offered by creative genius; it is the new form, for however great a period of time it may remain a mere irritant—that molds consciousness to the necessary amplitude for holding it.

CONSCIOUSNESS has no climax.

LET the Universe flow into your consciousness, there is no limit to its capacity, nothing that it shall not re-create.

UNSCREW your capability of absorption and grasp the elements of Life—*Whole.*

American journal *Camera Work,* which was published by renowned photographer Alfred Stieglitz, lent the manifesto a certain amount of prestige by association, and it was widely read in artistic circles. According to critic Rob Sheffield in the *Literary Review,* "It became a sensation, the first major English-language manifesto of Italian Futurism, and it made Loy the last word on the hottest subject in New York." Readers, however, were not unanimously convinced of the manifesto's merit. Many questioned it in sexist terms. Scholar Natalya Lusty writes in *Women: A Cultural Review,* "Loy's American audience was shocked by [the manifesto's] conscious assimilation of masculine energy and audacity." Loy's editor Alfred Kreymborg summed up the popular opinion, saying, "If she could dress like a lady, why couldn't she write like one?"

Although Loy began to move away from the futurist movement after the publication of *Aphorisms on Futurism,* the manifesto remained a significant text in her oeuvre, establishing her as one of modernism's most important and innovative voices. "After *Aphorisms on Futurism* came out," writes Sheffield, "Loy had no trouble getting her poems published in New York. She was famous now…. [A]s a genuine European, a New Woman, a modern iconoclast who flouted social conventions more outrageously than the sweet young dandies of New York could if they tried, and they did, she had a voice that commanded attention." In the near century since it was written, *Aphorisms on Futurism* has been the subject of an extensive body of criticism that has considered it in feminist, futurist, and modernist terms.

Much scholarship has been focused on the manifesto's relationship to futurism, feminism, and ethnicity. In "Eugenicist Mistress & Ethnic Mother," scholar Aimee L. Pozorski writes, "Via Futurism, Loy challenged the conventions of poetry; via feminism, at times through an appeal to futuristic ideology, she challenged the conventions of womanhood. In unmasking the racial underpinnings of the avant-garde, Loy's mediation among Futurism, ethnicity, and feminism speaks to the complexity of motherhood in the first decades of the twentieth century and beyond." Commentators have also examined the manifesto's role in establishing the terms of Loy's later poetic project. As Lusty writes, "The manifesto's address to 'You' thus becomes a self-admonishing reminder that Loy herself must overcome the constraints of decorum, both personal and aesthetic, if she is to reach her goal as one of the most original women, if not distinctive voices, of her generation. In this sense 'Aphorisms' stands as an important testing ground for both the 'Feminist Manifesto' and her long poem, 'Songs to Johannes.'"

BIBLIOGRAPHY

Sources

Burke, Carolyn. *Becoming Modern: The Life of Mina Loy.* New York: Farrar, Straus and Giroux, 1996. Print.

Lenarduzzi, Thea. "The Many Face of Mina Loy." *Times Literary Supplement* 26 Sept. 2011. Web. 4 July 2012.

Loy, Mina. *The Lost Lunar Baedeker: Poems of Mina Loy.* Ed. Roger L. Conover. New York: Farrar, Straus, Giroux, 1996. Print.

Lusty, Natalya. "Sexing the Manifesto: Mina Loy, Feminism, and Futurism." *Women: A Cultural Review* 19.3 (2008): 245-60. Web. 3 July 2012.

Pozorski, Aimee L. "Eugenicist Mistress & Ethnic Mother: Mina Loy and Futurism, 1913-1917." *MELUS* 30.3 (2005): 41-69. Web. 3 July 2012.

Sheffield, Rob. "Mina Loy in Too Much Too Soon." *Literary Review* 22 June 2003. Print.

Shreiber, Maerra, and Keith Tuma, eds. *Mina Loy: Woman and Poet.* Orono: The National Poetry Foundation, 1998.

Further Reading

Fields, Kenneth. "The Poetry of Mina Loy." *Southern Review* 3.2 (1967): 597-607. Print.

Jaskoski, Helen. "Mina Loy Outsider Artist." *Journal of Modern Literature* 28.4 (1993): 349-68. Print.

Kouidis, Virginia M. *Mina Loy: Modern American Poet.* Baton Rouge: Louisiana State UP, 1980. Print.

Loy, Mina. *Stories and Essays of Mina Loy.* Ed. Sara Crangle. Urbana: Dalkey Archive, 2011. Print.

Schaum, Melita. "'Moon-flowers Out of Muck': Mina Loy and the Autobiographical Epic." *Massachusetts Studies in English* 10.4 (1986): 254-76. Print.

Stauder, Ellen Keck. "On Mina Loy." *Modernism/Modernity* 4.3 (1997): 141-46. Print.

Vondeling, Johanna E. "The Manifest Professional: Manifestos and Modernist Legitimation." *College Literature* 27. 2 (2000): 127-45. Web. 9 June 2012.

Theodore McDermott

THE ART OF NOISES

Luigi Russolo

OVERVIEW

Penned in 1913 as a letter to Italian composer Francesco Balilla Pratella, "The Art of Noises" (*L'Arte dei rumori*) by Luigi Russolo became the manifesto for musical futurism in Italy, calling for composers to embrace the profuse variety of industrial noises and to create new instruments for a new sonic landscape. At the time the essay was written, the futurist movement had already infiltrated various genres of Italian art, including poetry, sculpture, and painting. Russolo sought the extension of its aesthetic into the medium of music, in which the speed and forcefulness of machines could be orchestrated into complex networks of "noise sounds." Further, the composer considered futurist music a natural complement to the giddy, violent energy seen in the poems of founding futurist F. T. Marinetti, whom he quoted at length in "The Art of Noises."

As a privately circulated document, "The Art of Noises" inspired a small group of futurists to construct and orchestrate "noise instruments," but their first and only concert was marred by a violent confrontation between rival groups of avant-garde artists. The essay was republished in book form in 1916; however, the work had little immediate impact outside its original futurist context, as it arrived in print after the movement had reached its peak. Nevertheless, Russolo's thinking continued to influence the careers of a small group of musicians in the twentieth century. "The Art of Noises" has since secured its place in music history as a watershed for the avant-garde. Today, Russolo's observations on the interplay of technology and music also are applied to the relatively young field of computer and electronic music, where "The Art of Noises" remains an oft-cited source of inspiration.

HISTORICAL AND LITERARY CONTEXT

The futurist movement was inaugurated in 1909 with the publication of "The Futurist Manifesto" by Marinetti. In the manifesto, the Italian poet declares the birth of a new art that will glorify the sounds and shapes of a rapidly evolving technological age. Soon afterward, the composer Francesco Balilla Pratella extended the futurist aesthetic to music in a series of essays, beginning with the 1910 *Manifesto of Futurist Musicians*. Here, he calls on young Italian musicians to escape the stifling atmosphere of conservatories

and to jettison the musical forms of the past, especially as represented by Italian folk and sacred music. This attempt to break free of tradition would come to characterize Italian futurism in all its varied manifestations.

By 1913 the futurists had laid the groundwork in most of the major genres of art in Italy, with urban landscape paintings (such as those of Carlo Carrà and Umberto Boccioni) perhaps their most notable specialty. Russolo had been involved with the futurists from 1910, primarily as a painter. By the time he wrote "The Art of Noises," he was well connected with artists of various disciplines and factions within futurism—a fact that the essay spares few opportunities to emphasize. The piece opens with a reference to a concert attended by no fewer than seven of Russolo's "futurist friends," including Marinetti, Boccioni, Carrà, and the painter Giacomo Balla.

Russolo's manifesto reflected the commonplaces of futurist aesthetics while acknowledging, atypically for a futurist tract, the value of a select few pre-futurist composers. In keeping with Marinetti's desire to escape the past, Russolo disparaged the concert halls of his day as "hospitals for anemic sounds." However, where Marinetti enjoined his comrades to demolish libraries and museums, Russolo conceded that such artists as Ludwig van Beethoven and Richard Wagner had genuine emotional significance for the young futurists. In terms of the specific style of music he advocated, Russolo had relatively few predecessors, though Thaddeus Cahill's electronic telharmonium (invented in 1897) is occasionally considered a progenitor to the futurists' novel instruments.

While Russolo calls upon "young musicians of talent" to lend their "Futurist ears" to his enterprise, it was Russolo himself who ensured that his ideas were put into action: he participated in the construction of such instruments as "noise intoners" (*intonarumori*) and exhibited them in an April 1914 concert. However, this performance came at the height of factional disagreements within the futurist movement; concertgoers were more impressed by the riot that ensued than by any quality of the music. Subsequent noise instrument concerts by Russolo and other Italian artists were uninterrupted by violence and influenced a French school of music known as *bruitisme* (literally, "noise-ism"), which Marinetti cofounded.

Key Facts

Time Period:
Early 20th Century

Movement/Issue:
Futurism

Place of Publication:
Italy

Language of Publication:
Italian

NOISE AND CHANCE IN THE WORKS OF JOHN CAGE

The American composer John Cage (1912-92) has often been considered a successor to Luigi Russolo's project in "The Art of Noises," though his work extends well beyond the incorporation of "noise sounds" into instrumental music. Cage not only elided the distinction between noise and music in some compositions; he also frequently introduced elements of chance and completely nonmusical gestures into his work. His early composition *The Wonderful Widow of Eighteen Springs* (1942) exemplifies the latter tendency: it is scored for voice and closed piano, meaning that the person "playing" the piano is restricted to striking parts of the instrument other than the keys. Cage would return to that set of ideas in *Nowth upon Nacht* (1984), in which the pianist produces sound by shutting the lid of the piano. The composer's *Variations* series (1958-67) exemplifies an even further departure from the "sound hospitals" that Russolo derided. *Variations II* (1961) is scored "for any number of players and any sound producing means," as is *Variations IV* (1963); *Variations III* (1962), exhibiting even greater indeterminacy, calls for "one or any number of people performing any actions." Each number also is distinguished by a combination of random events and mathematical algorithms, which determine the pitch, tempo, and amplitude of the instruments (if used) or the number and nature of the actions to be performed (if instruments are not used).

Still, musical futurist movements in both Italy and France were brief and largely overshadowed by technically innovative work for more traditional instruments and drew little comment from music critics.

THEMES AND STYLE

"The Art of Noises" builds upon a basic dichotomy between the mannered "sounds" typically associated with music and the much more varied "noises" found especially in industrial settings. According to Russolo, musicians and composers from ancient times have been engaged in a process of evolution toward an ideal "noise sound" that will combine the tonal attributes and organization of musical sound with the sheer variety of available noises. He maintains that the contemporary collection of orchestral instruments and mathematical strictures of written music are an unnecessary handicap on musical expression; furthermore, compositions for such instruments are growing both more tiresome and more desperate. Russolo delineates six numbered "families of noises" (including among them such items as "whistles," "mumbles," and "shrieks") that will enrich music—once futurist musicians construct new instruments to produce them.

Russolo situates his noise sound as a specifically futurist phenomenon by identifying it as a product of the industrial age. He asserts that prior to the nineteenth century, noises were virtually absent from human life: "ancient life," as Russolo terms all of pre-industrial history, "was all silence." Moreover, he describes the tremendous opportunity that noise sounds present for an innovative and exciting form of art, one that will grant the world a "new and unexpected sensual pleasure." Rather than exhausting itself, as the music of purely alien sounds has done, a music founded on noise will "keep innumerable surprises in reserve." In short, Russolo's manifesto is built on the visionary promise of an art form not yet created. Perhaps for this reason, the author is cautious to disclaim any expertise as a musician. Instead, he appeals to his colleague Pratella and to all the "young musicians of talent" who might serve the futurist cause.

Drawing on the futurist penchant for treating matters of art with militant patriotism, Russolo repeats the injunction to rebel against the constraints of traditional music—to "break out!" In the essayist's view, the music produced by a conventional orchestra not only is boring, but it also perpetuates an "idiotic religious emotion" that must be cleared away with "resonant slaps in the face"—delivered, naturally, by the futurists. Moreover, Russolo displays an enthusiasm for noises that transcend the material conditions that produce them: even war, properly seen, is a great "orchestra." The centerpiece of Russolo's essay is, in fact, a lengthy quotation from Marinetti's "Zong Toomb Toomb," an ecstatic free-verse description of the siege of Adrianople during the Balkan Wars of 1912-13. Marinetti's poem illustrates Russolo's point with its liberal onomatopoeia. The "*ZANG-TUMB-TUUMB*" of siege cannons and the "*taratatata*" of machine guns are just a few of the noises to be enshrined by Russolo's new art.

CRITICAL DISCUSSION

Russolo's essay was received with enthusiasm among futurists, though it had little immediate influence beyond that small circle of artists. Along with a few of the colleagues named in "The Art of Noises," Russolo soon put the manifesto's principles into practice by assembling orchestras of noise-generating machines, though the futurists' concerts were interrupted by the onset of World War I. Contemporary reviewers wrote off the noise intoner performances as novelties; William Austin, in "The Idea of Evolution in the Music of the 20th Century" (1953), gives a brief survey of such responses. When futurist musicians reconvened in the early 1920s, critics continued to regard them with tolerant amusement. For example, in his 1929 essay taking stock of contemporary music, André Coeuroy jocularly termed Russolo one of the "slam-bang futurists" and described the instruments of a 1921 *bruiteur* concert as "howlers, growlers, creakers, and rustlers."

In the 1940s, "The Art of Noises" rose to prominence as a foundational work for avant-garde music.

In "The Antennae of the Race" (2002), Nina Colosi notes its influence on the *musique concrète* movement of the 1940s, a series of experiments with recording technology that constituted some of the first electronic music. The most famous adopter of Russolo's ideas was John Cage, whose use of chance and noise in music won critical acclaim in the 1960s and remained influential throughout the twentieth century. Cage's ascent to fame was a boon to the critical discussion of Russolo, as the composer's work came to be seen as the fulfillment of Russolo's ideals. Apart from its perceived anticipation of Cage's work, however, "The Art of Noises" is infrequently cited today.

Contemporary readings of "The Art of Noises" tend to emphasize it as the opening of a profoundly exploratory phase in musical sound, a period that some music historians consider to have concluded with Cage. Mark Sinker's article "Shhhhhh!" (1997) describes the relationship thus: Russolo allowed noise "to gambol under strict guard through music's gardens and palaces," but Cage "wished to end all such distinctions." In "John Cage: Silence and Silencing" (1997), Douglas Kahn concurs: "Russolo initiated the strategy whereby extramusical sounds and worldliness were incorporated ... into music in order to reinvigorate it. Cage exhausted this strategy.... He *opened music up* into an emancipatory endgame." Russolo's concerts were still recognizable musical performances, but Cage, in these critics' estimation, systematically removed every marker by which music might be distinguished from nonmusic. "The Art of Noises" also has served as a recurrent talking point in academic discussions of computer music. As Kim Cascone notes in "The Aesthetics of Failure: 'Post-Digital' Tendencies in Contemporary Computer Music" (2000), glitch music—a type of computer music with an emphasis on the sound of "broken" audio devices—has proven a fitting successor to Russolo's noise sounds.

Music, 1911, by Luigi Russolo. Painted two years before the publication of "The Art of Noises," this was one of only a few Futurist paintings by Russolo. © DEA PICTURE LIBRARY/ART RESOURCE, NY

BIBLIOGRAPHY

Sources

Austin, William. "The Idea of Evolution in the Music of the 20th Century." *Musical Quarterly* 39.1 (1953): 26-36. Print.

Cascone, Kim. "The Aesthetics of Failure: 'Post-Digital' Tendencies in Contemporary Computer Music." *Computer Music Journal* 24.4 (2000): 12-18.

Coeuroy, André, and Theodore Baker. "The Esthetics of Contemporary Music." *Musical Quarterly* 15.2 (1929): 246-67. Print.

Colosi, Nina. "The Antennae of the Race." *Leonardo* 35.5 (2002): 579-80. Print.

Kahn, Douglas. "John Cage: Silence and Silencing." *Musical Quarterly* 81.4 (1997): 556-98. Print.

Russolo, Luigi. *The Art of Noises.* Trans. Barclay Brown. New York: Pendragon Press, 1986. Print.

Sinker, Mark. "Shhhhhh!" *Musical Quarterly* 81.2 (1997): 210-41. Print.

Further Reading

Cox, Christopher, and Daniel Warner. *Audio Culture: Readings in Modern Music.* New York: Continuum, 2004.

Hinant, Guy-Marc. "TOHU BOHU: Considerations on the Nature of Noise, in 78 Fragments." Trans. Michael Novy. *Leonardo Music Journal* 13 (2003): 43-46. Web. 26 July 2012.

Hopkin, Bart. *Gravikords, Whirlies, and Pyrophones: Experimental Musical Instruments.* Roslyn: Ellipsis Arts, 1996. Print.

Kahn, Douglas. *Noise, Water, Meat: A History of Sound in the Arts.* Cambridge: MIT P, 1999. Print.

Lochhead, Judy. "Hearing Chaos." *American Music* 19.2 (2001): 210-46. Print.

Maróthy, János, and Márta Batári. "Banal Order vs. Rich Disorder." *Studia Musicologica Academia Scientiarum Hungaricae* 38.1-2 (1997): 143-49.

Michael Hartwell

A DROP OF TAR

Vladimir Mayakovsky

✥ **Key Facts**

Time Period:
Early 20th Century

Movement/Issue:
Aesthetics; World War I;
Futurism

Place of Publication:
Russia

**Language of
Publication:**
Russian

OVERVIEW

Written by poet Vladimir Mayakovsky in 1915, "A Drop of Tar" describes the condition of the Russian avant-garde in relation to the changes wrought by World War I. Mayakovsky was the sole writer of the manifesto, but his work represents a revival of artistic discussions among the cofounders of Russian futurism, including his mentor, David Burliuk, and writer Victor Khlebnikov. Published as the centerpiece of a futurist miscellany, the manifesto was designed to provoke and even outrage the public and also to spur futurist artists and poets to make vital art that would be a reflection of and response to the age. Addressed to a general audience, "A Drop of Tar" calls on all Russians to reject established artistic conventions in a world marked by political and industrial change.

The manifesto was a rebuttal to those who asserted that the futurist movement, which had been significant in shaping Russian arts and letters before the war, was dead. Its playfully outrageous demands gained support among various futurist artists. However, its central aesthetic and linguistic ideas struggled to gain widespread traction at a time when global conflict had diminished public interest in domestic issues and thinned the ranks of futurist adherents, many of whom were of draft age. Today, "A Drop of Tar" is seen as an enlightening document that foreshadows the career path of Mayakovsky and the direction of Russian poetry and linguistic theory in general.

HISTORICAL AND LITERARY CONTEXT

"A Drop of Tar" responds to a need for artistic works reflecting the sweeping cultural change in Russia in the early twentieth century, when the nation experienced rapid industrialization and political unrest. Before the outbreak of World War I in 1914, Russian political groups had struggled to find representation within or outside their monarchy; meanwhile, the nation's artists had been prompted to move away from the realist and symbolist traditions that reflected the concerns of the old regime. The futurist movement promoted itself through performances and public talks, which attracted crowds but also led to government censure. The onset of the war overshadowed the domestic struggles and concerns of Russia's citizens, and the futurists wound up disbanding.

By the time "A Drop of Tar" was written in 1915, a number of futurist manifestos had been published. Some of the most vocal avant-garde advocates were from the Hylaea movement, a collective of poets who were fascinated by cubism and attempted to apply its renovated vision to literature. The primitivist work of the Hylaeans attracted other writers, including Mayakovsky, Velimir Khlebnikov, and Alexei Kruchenykh. Inspired by Italian poet Filippo Marinetti's "Futurist Manifesto" (1909), the group wrote "A Slap in the Face of Public Taste" (1912), Russia's first futurist doctrine, which created a platform around which various avant-garde artists and thinkers could coalesce. The futurist movement, engendered by "A Slap" and revived by "A Drop of Tar,"

VLADIMIR MAYAKOVSKY: SUBVERSIVE POET AND ACTIVIST

Vladimir Mayakovsky was born in Baghdati, Russian Georgia, in 1893. His youth was somewhat troubled: he was arrested three times as an agitator by age fifteen. In 1911, he studied painting at the Moscow Art School, where he became acquainted with members of the avant-garde. Mayakovsky and his mentor, David Burliuk, appeared at painters' groups to promote cubism and participated in deliberately outrageous public speeches in favor of futurism. Though inflammatory, the speeches were a success and led to a series of futurist appearances in the provinces.

Mayakovsky published his first poems, "Noch" ("Night") and "Utro" ("Morning"), at the end of 1912 in a futurist almanac. He wrote "The Backbone Flute" in 1916 as an expression of his love for Lilya Brik, the wife of his publisher. Believing the October Revolution would bring a sympathetic environment for progressive art, Mayakovsky created aggressively revolutionary poetry. He later made agit-prop posters for the communist government and edited the Left Art Front's communist futurist journal. However, he became disillusioned with Soviet communism and wrote satirical plays addressing his change of heart, including *The Bedbug* (1929). The circumstances surrounding his suicide in 1930 are a continuing source of speculation.

Because Mayakovsky's works were widely available during Joseph Stalin's reign, he exerted a strong influence on other twentieth-century Russian poets. Louis Aragon, Pablo Neruda, and Frank O'Hara have also cited Mayakovsky as an influence.

УКРАИНЦЕВ и РУССКИХ КЛИЧ ОДИН –

РОСТА

ДА НЕ БУДЕТ ПАН НАД РАБОЧИМ ГОСПОДИН!

An agitprop poster created by Vladimir Mayakovsky in 1920, during the Russian Civil War. It reads, "The rallying-cry of the Ukrainian and Russian: The white Poles will never lord it over the workers!" MARY EVANS PICTURE LIBRARY/EVERETT COLLECTION

did not last, but its members did have a significant influence on the artistic and literary development of post-revolutionary Russia.

"A Drop of Tar" draws on a series of aesthetic decrees that can be traced to Marinetti's "Futurist Manifesto." Published in France's *Le Figaro* newspaper, Marinetti's doctrine advocates for futurism as an approach to all spheres of life, from art to politics. His ideas—praising technology, urbanism, and dynamic action—gained widespread notice and inspired similar futurist declarations throughout Europe. Mayakovsky's "A Drop of Tar" built on the ideas put forth in "A Slap in the Face of Public Taste," which urges artists to disregard the established Russian literary canon, including the works of Anton Chekhov, Leo Tolstoy, and Fyodor Dostoevsky.

In the decades that followed its publication, "A Drop of Tar" inspired a significant body of literature. Beginning with Mayakovsky's poems "A Cloud in

Trousers" (1915) and "The Backbone Flute" (1916), futurist ideas sparked a new generation of Russian poets, including Boris Pasternak. Velimir Khlebnikov's "War in a Mousetrap," a series of short poems written during World War I, became a key text for antiwar protestors. In addition, Khlebnikov's experiments with *zaum,* a nonsense language, were a notable source of linguistic theory and debate. Mayakovsky, initially a proponent of the Soviet regime, was not censored under Joseph Stalin's rule. His works continued to have an influence following the end of the Stalin regime in 1953, informing the work of such poets as Yevgeny Yevtushenko. Because of its primitivist and formalist concerns, futurist literature still attracts scholarly interest.

THEMES AND STYLE

The central theme of "A Drop of Tar" is that tumultuous world events and uncertainty within Russia continue to demand a futurist approach from the

PRIMARY SOURCE

"A DROP OF TAR"

'A speech to be delivered at the first convenient occasion'

Ladies and Gentlemen!

This year is a year of deaths: almost every day the newspapers sob loudly in grief about somebody who has passed away before his time. Every day, with syrupy weeping the brevier wails over the huge number of names slaughtered by Mars. How noble and monastically severe today's newspapers look. They are dressed in the black mourning garb of the obituaries, with the crystal-like tear of a necrology in their glittering eyes. That's why it has been particularly upsetting to see these same newspapers, usually ennobled by grief, note with indecent merriment one death that involved me very closely.

When the critics, harnessed in tandem, carried along the dirty road — the road of the printed word — the coffin of Futurism, the newspapers trumpeted for weeks: 'ho, ho, ho! serves it right! take it away! finally!' (Concerned alarm in the audience: 'What do you mean, died? Futurism died? You're kidding.')

Yes, it died.

For one year now, instead of Futurism, verbally flaming, barely manoeuvring between truth, beauty and the police station, the most boring octogenarians of the Kogan-Aikhenvald type [literary critics with official positions] creep up on the stage of auditoriums. For one year now, the auditoriums present only the most boring logic, demonstrations of trivial truths, instead of the cheerful sound of glass pitchers against empty heads.

Gentlemen! Do you really feel no sorrow for that extravagant young fellow with shaggy red hair, a little silly, a bit ill-mannered, but always, oh! always, daring and fiery? On the other hand, how can you understand youth? The young people to whom we are dear will not soon return from the battlefield; but you, who have remained here with quiet jobs in newspaper offices or other similar businesses; you, who are too rickety to carry a weapon, you, old bags crammed with wrinkles and grey hair, you are preoccupied with figuring out the smoothest possible way to pass on to the next world and not with the destiny of Russian art.

But, you know, I myself do not feel too sorry about the deceased, although for different reasons.

Bring back to mind the first gala publication of Russian Futurism, titled with that resounding 'slap in the face of public taste'. What remained particularly memorable of that fierce scuffle were the three

nation's artists. With the same force as "A Slap in the Face of Public Taste," the manifesto makes an appeal to Russians who have grown disinterested in matters at home due to the war that is raging abroad: "The war, by expanding the borders of the nations and the brain, forces one to break through the frontiers of what yesterday was unknown." To this end, the manifesto recalls the ambition of futurists to destroy the "old language" and to throw out old masters of literature in order to envision a new language and a new future.

The manifesto achieves its rhetorical effect through humorous appeals to older critics of futurism and to younger artists who might adopt the movement's principles. The power of Mayakovsky's message is both in his irreverent provocation of outmoded Russian life and in his acknowledgement of the disruption of the country during World War I. "A Drop of Tar" envisions an audience of Russians who remained at home while much of the younger generation was off at war. While Mayakovsky admits the futurist movement was interrupted by the global conflict—"Yes, it died," he writes—the manifesto suggests that its principles live on in the disorder, thus creating an opening for a new artistic reality. Notably, the manifesto's suggestions are theoretical and emphasize a change in which the approach would emphasize form over content. These ideas complemented Russian formalism's linguistics, which sought, in part, to eliminate "automatized" perceptions through the technique of defamiliarization of language (for example, by separating word-as-object from the word's meaning).

Stylistically, "A Drop of Tar" is distinguished by its colloquial language and informality. Written as a "speech to be delivered at the first convenient occasion," the manifesto undermines the work of other kinds of literature (newspaper critics, for example, traverse the "dirty road ... of the printed word"), thereby establishing Mayakovsky's sincere and uncorrupted goals. Simultaneously, in detailing the shortcomings of the established literary regime, Mayakovsky demonstrates the demand for futurist writers and artists. Although its aggressive stance renders "A Drop of Tar" somewhat inflammatory, the manifesto furthers its aesthetic goals by linking Russia's emerging reality to the ideals of futurism.

blows, in the form of three vociferous statements from our manifesto.

1. Destroy the all–canons freezer which turns inspiration into ice.

2. Destroy the old language, powerless to keep up with life's leaps and bounds.

3. Throw the old masters overboard from the ship of modernity.

As you see, there isn't a single building here, not a single comfortably designed corner, only destruction, anarchy. This made philistines laugh, as if it were the extravagant idea of some insane individuals, but in fact it turned out to be 'a devilish intuition' which is realized in the stormy today. The war, by expanding the borders of nations and of the brain, forces one to break through the frontiers of what yesterday was unknown.

Artist! Is it for you to catch the onrushing cavalry with a fine net of contour lines? Repin! Samokish! [Realist painters] Get your pails out of the way – the paint will spill all over!

Poet! Don't place the mighty conflict of iambs and trochees in a rocking chair – the chair will flip over!

Fragmentation of words, word renewal! So many new words, and first among them Petrograd, and conductress! Die, Severyanin [cult Egofuturist poet]! Is it really for the Futurists to shout that old literature is forgotten? Who would still hear behind the Cossack whoop the trill of Bryusov's mandolin [precious Symbolist writer]! Today, everyone is a Futurist. The entire nation is Futurist.

FUTURISM HAS *SEIZED* RUSSIA IN A DEATH GRIP

Not being able to see Futurism in front of you and to look into yourselves, you started shouting about its death. Yes! Futurism, as a specific group, died, but like a flood it overflows into all of you.

But once Futurism had died as the idea of select individuals, we do not need it anymore. We consider the first part of our programme of destruction to be completed. So don't be surprised if today you see in our hands architectural sketches instead of clownish rattles, and if the voice of Futurism, which yesterday was still soft from sentimental reverie, today is forged in the copper of preaching.

SOURCE: *Words in Revolution: Russian Futurist Manifestoes 1912-1928* (New Academia Publishing, 2005), edited and translated by Anna Lawton and Herbert Eagle, by permission of Anna Lawton.

CRITICAL DISCUSSION

When "A Drop of Tar" appeared in the futurist miscellany *Took: A Futurists' Drum* in 1915, it did little to reverse the decline of the movement. Though some contemporaries, including critic and writer Viktor Shklovsky, lamented the censorship of part of the poem "The Backbone Flute," the book was designed as a showcase for Mayakovsky's futurist tract. Still, Mayakovsky himself acknowledged the widespread claim that futurism was in decline. And although contemporaries such as Khlebnikov and Roman Jakobson published literary works in accordance with futurist principles, the last volume of purely formalist work, *Four Birds* (a collection of verse by Burliuk and Khlebnikov), appeared in 1916. Nevertheless, futurist ideas were a vital part of the postwar constructivist movement. As Vladimir Markov states in *Russian Futurism: A History,* "individual poets … continued to develop," including Mayakovsky, who "considered himself a futurist all his life."

Although the futurist movement dispersed because of the war, the manifesto and its resulting literature remained a source of inspiration for Russian writers and members of the international avant-garde.

Perhaps divided by their diverse interests, the group's members nonetheless produced works containing elements of the cultural movement. In her introduction to *Russian Futurism Through Its Manifestoes,* Anna Lawton observes that in "A Drop of Tar," "Mayakovksy [wrote] a funeral oration to Futurism, which is at the same time a prophecy of Futurism's Second Coming." Mayakovsky was the central inspiration for a Lithuanian futurist movement called the Four Winds, which was active from 1924 to 1928. When Soviet literature emerged from Stalin's restrictive control in the 1960s, younger Soviet writers, including Yevtushenko and Leonid Martinov, adopted Mayakovsky's accessible style. In 1967, the Taganka Theatre in Moscow debuted its drama *Listen! Mayakovsky!,* a drama that takes the poet from Stalin's pedestal and depicts the lonely man betrayed by politics. In the decades since the manifesto was written, it has been the focus of criticism that considers its legacy in historical, biographical, political, and linguistic terms.

Today, "A Drop of Tar" attracts scholarly interest primarily for its biographical importance, particularly within the context of Mayakovsky's work as a poet and theorist. Scholars have noted the evolution of his work beyond the parameters of the futurist movement. Discussing the impact of futurism on Mayakovsky, Edward J. Brown states in his essay "Mayakovsky's Futurist Period" that "we witness the monstrous birth from the Futurist womb ... of a poet who bears some of the characteristic features of his parent, but combines them with others that are passing strange."

BIBLIOGRAPHY

Sources

Beumers, Birgit. *Yury Lyubimov: Thirty Years at the Taganka Theatre (1964-1994).* Amsterdam: Harwood Academic, 1997. Print.

Brown, Edward James. *Mayakovsky: A Poet in the Revolution.* Princeton: Princeton UP, 1973. Print.

Gibian, George, and H. W. Tjalsma, eds. *Russian Modernism: Culture and the Avant-Garde, 1900-1930.* Ithaca: Cornell UP, 1976. Print.

Lawton, Anna, ed. *Russian Futurism Through Its Manifestoes, 1912-1928.* Ithaca: Cornell UP, 1988. Print.

Markov, Vladimir. *Russian Futurism: A History.* Berkeley: U of California P, 1968. Print.

Proffer, Ellendea, and Carl R. Proffer. *The Ardis Anthology of Russian Futurism.* Ann Arbor: Ardis, 1980. Print.

Stapanian, Juliette R. *Mayakovsky's Cubo-Futurist Vision.* Houston: Rice UP, 1986. Print.

Further Reading

Bowlt, John E. *Russian Art of the Avant-Garde: Theory and Criticism, 1902-1934.* New York: Viking, 1976. Print.

Brown, Edward J. *Mayakovsky: A Poet in the Revolution.* Princeton: Princeton UP, 1973. Print.

Lahti, Katherine, and I. G. Vishnevetsky. "Vladimir Vladimirovich Maiakovsky." *Russian Writers of the Silver Age, 1890-1925.* Ed. Judith E. Kalb, J. Alexander Ogden, and I. G. Vishnevetsky. Detroit: Gale, 2004. *Dictionary of Literary Biography.* Vol. 295. *Literature Resource Center.* Web. 7 Aug. 2012.

Shklovsky, Victor. *Mayakovsky and His Circle.* New York: Dodd, 1972. Print.

Terras, Victor. "Vladimir (Vladimirovich) Mayakovski." *European Writers: The Twentieth Century.* Ed. George Stade. Vol. 11. New York: Scribner's, 1990. *Scribner Writers Series.* Web. 7 Aug. 2012.

Karen Bender

FUTURIST MANIFESTO

Filippo Tommaso Marinetti

OVERVIEW

Composed by Filippo Tommaso Marinetti, the *Futurist Manifesto* (1909) announced the founding of the Italian artistic movement known as futurism and outlined its principles, which consisted mainly in the exaltation of things fast, new, industrial, and aggressive. The manifesto heralded war, modern machinery, literary experimentation, and above all a complete break with history and tradition. As the first major European avant-garde of the twentieth century, futurism emerged in a climate of militant nationalism prevalent in many European nations and especially pronounced in Italy. Marinetti (1876-1944) called not only for a militant political perspective but also for a complete break with existing literary forms, opting instead for pithy, experimental language that he saw as corresponding to his political ideals. The manifesto first appeared in several minor Italian journals early in 1909 before being published on the front page of the major French newspaper *Le Figaro* on February 20 of that year. Central to the manifesto is a list of eleven pronouncements of Marinetti's philosophy of aggression, daring, and newness.

Public reaction to the manifesto was mixed. The appearance of the *Futurist Manifesto* in *Le Figaro* represented a direct challenge to the emergent French avant-garde to take a more confrontational stance vis-à-vis the public, and it quickly garnered Marinetti international attention. Many literary and art critics expressed hostility, while others praised the innovative content in the manifesto. At the time, Marinetti was the only member of the futurist movement he was christening, but within a year he had attracted a number of prominent Italian artists, largely due to the buzz created by the manifesto. The intentionally provocative piece is now considered one of the major works of early twentieth-century European avant-gardism.

HISTORICAL AND LITERARY CONTEXT

The *Futurist Manifesto* seeks to destroy what Marinetti saw as the sentimentalism and pedantry of nineteenth-century intellectual and artistic tradition. He declares at the heart of the manifesto, "It is in Italy that we are issuing this manifesto of ruinous and incendiary violence, by which we today are founding Futurism, because we want to deliver Italy from its gangrene of professors, archaeologists, tourist guides and antiquarians." Although it had a rich literary and cultural tradition, Italy had become a unified nation only in 1871 after a decades-long period of optimistic political struggle called the Risorgimento (c. 1815-71), or "uprising." Many Italians were subsequently disillusioned when, after unification, Italy was still culturally and linguistically fragmented, a collection of disparate regions unified only in name, technologically and culturally backward compared to most of its neighbors to the north. Marinetti believed that Italy could only achieve a strong identity through extreme measures and in combat both with other nations and its own complacent elite.

By the time the *Futurist Manifesto* appeared in 1909 there was already considerable unrest among Italy's youth and a growing sense that the classical, oratory literary style had run its course. Although the futurist philosophy rejected the rhetorically florid aspects of the work of Gabriele D'Annunzio (1863-1938)—at that time arguably the most influential Italian poet—it embraced and amplified D'Annunzio's vision of the *superuomo,* or superman, which in turn is derived from certain aspects of the thought of Friedrich Nietzsche. This vision of the superuomo shows up in the *Futurist Manifesto* as a vitalistic, heroic attitude exalting unbridled energy and the immediate impulses of the irrational side of the psyche.

Marinetti's vision of futurism as presented in the manifesto privileges direct, psychological experience as the only valid source of art. The author declares: "We have been up all night, my friends and I ... and trampling underfoot our native sloth on opulent Persian carpets, we have been discussing right up to the limits of logic and scrawling the paper with demented writing." In this orientation toward the nonrational and the impulsive, Marinetti's vision was influenced (somewhat indirectly) by psychologist Sigmund Freud's theory of the unconscious, which was becoming widely known in the first decades of the twentieth century. Breaking with tradition and condemning the literary and cultural past in all its forms, the manifesto glorifies the dynamic over the static, public action over private contemplation, and brashness over elegance of expression.

In the years following its publication, the *Futurist Manifesto* inspired related manifestos by Marinetti's followers. These include the *Manifesto of the Futurist*

✦ Key Facts

Time Period:
Early 20th Century

Movement/Issue:
Aesthetics; Futurism

Place of Publication:
Italy

Language of Publication:
Italian

FUTURISM AND FASCISM

Marinetti took his agenda to the streets by organizing frequent *serate,* or "nights out," during which the futurists put on riotous performances. In 1914 and 1915 Marinetti organized a number of serate in Milan to support Italy's entry into World War I. In such a demonstration in May 1915, Marinetti and Benito Mussolini, eventual leader of the National Fascist Party, were arrested. Taking his pro-war views beyond the realm of literary expression and street demonstrations, Marinetti formed the Futurist Political Party in 1918.

Although the exact nature and extent of the rapport between futurism and fascism is debated by scholars, it seems clear that Marinetti was influential in the founding of the National Fascist Party. Marinetti knew Mussolini well, and although he broke with the fascist leader in 1920, Marinetti continued to support the regime and remained loyal to it until his death in 1944. After the 1922 March on Rome, Marinetti claimed that fascism had actualized at least some of the demands outlined by the futurists. He became secretary of the Fascist Writers' Union in 1929. With its appeals to ancient Roman history and its drive toward conformity, fascism was in some ways discordant with the anti-traditional, individualist philosophy of Marinetti's futurist agenda; nonetheless, the two movements enjoyed a mutually beneficial alliance for many years.

Painters and the *Technical Manifesto of Futurist Painting,* both published collectively by artists Umberto Boccioni, Carlo Carrà, Luigi Russolo, Giacomo Balla, and Gino Severini early in 1910. These were followed in 1912 by the *Technical Manifesto of Futurist Sculpture* by Boccioni and the *Manifesto of Futurist Musicians* by Balilla Pratella. Although directly influenced by Marinetti, these authors generally distanced themselves from Marinetti's glorification of violence, focusing instead on the shared futurist fascination with speed, movement, urbanity, and technology. Marinetti published numerous subsequent manifestos, the most important being the *Technical Manifesto of Futurist Literature* (1912) and *After Free Verse and Words in Freedom* (1913), both of which elaborated the linguistic particulars of the futurist literary style. Today Marinetti's manifestos are often considered his most important work, as he exploited the potentials of the genre in an innovative and highly influential way.

THEMES AND STYLE

The central theme of the *Futurist Manifesto* is that Italy's literary and intellectual establishment has failed to keep abreast of the gritty, technological world of the twentieth century, the "future," which had already arrived. This rebellion against the antiquated can be seen, for instance, in the third of the manifesto's eleven central pronouncements: "Until today, literature has exalted pensive immobility, inner ecstasy, and dreaminess. We plan to exalt aggressive movement, feverish insomnia, running on the double, daredevil leaps, the slap and the punch." The manifesto's vandalistic attitude toward the establishment is especially pronounced in the tenth of the eleven pronouncements, which begins: "We want to destroy the museums, the libraries, and academies of every sort." The pronouncements are intended to shock the establishment and incite the young to action, and their inflammatory rhetoric correlates to the theatrical and sensationalistic orientation of the movement overall.

One of the most apparent rhetorical features of the manifesto is its use of the plural first-person pronoun "we" throughout, which gives the sense that the movement is already formed and galvanized, when in fact Marinetti was its only member at the time of the manifesto's publication. The text opens with a "we" statement ("We had been up all night...") and maintains this point of view through its entirety. Most notable is that all of the eleven central proclamations are expressed in the plural first person, and seven of them begin with the word "we" (*noi* in Italian). It could be said that Marinetti was speaking on behalf of a zeitgeist already in the air but not yet organized in such a way that it could forcefully confront the public. Marinetti thus situates himself as spokesperson for a generation of disenfranchised Italians who came of age in a nominally unified but culturally stagnant nation in need of radical new art and politics.

Stylistically, the *Futurist Manifesto* stands out for its exuberance and its optimistic (almost to the point of naïveté) expression of a liberating, new ideology. Combining narrative (in its opening and concluding sections) and enumerated declarations (as its centerpiece), the manifesto presents its demands as, in a sense, already accomplished, with the formal proclamation and public dissemination of its worldview the only remaining tasks. It achieves this effect partly though its collective first-person point of view. This rhetoric of excited collectivity confronts the reader with a group already active and in certain ways prefigures the rhetoric of fascism, with which futurism was aligned in the early years of the totalitarian regime.

CRITICAL DISCUSSION

The *Futurist Manifesto* initially received mixed reactions in literary, avant-garde, and working-class circles. Its ideas were debated in leading journals, especially the Italian *Lacerba,* an experimental journal that had wide influence in the 1910s. Many in the literary establishment saw Marinetti and his followers as a threat to good taste and erudition or dismissed them as bombastic upstarts. For others, particularly young and working-class citizens, the *Futurist Manifesto* (like fascism after it) offered hope of rejuvenation during a bleak time in Italy's history. A distinctive feature of futurism that appealed to a diverse array of radicals was its involvement of the public in the artistic process. Marinetti encouraged his audience to dispute directly with him in the public *serate,* or "nights out," that he organized in support of his movement. These events included theatrical performances provoking the audience and often culminating in riots. His agitating stance earned Marinetti friends and enemies during the arc of futurism's prominence (c. 1909-20).

In addition to providing inspiration for later European avant-gardes, including surrealism and Dadaism, futurism interested proletarian activists in the years following the publication of the *Futurist Manifesto.* Political philosopher Antonio Gramsci reported that the factory workers he was organizing in Turin during the 1910s responded favorably to Marinetti's seditious form of expression. The *Futurist Manifesto* also had significant resonance in revolutionary Russia. These positive identifications by left-wing factions are ironic given Marinetti's avidly right-wing orientation. The proletarian groups identified with not a specific political agenda but rather a more general antiestablishment attitude.

Because of its official alliance with fascism, futurism fell into disfavor in Italy after World War II, and contemporary critics are divided on the question of literary futurism's merit. In *Letteratura Italiana: Testi e critica con lineamenti di storia letteraria,* leading Italian literary critic Mario Pazzaglia says that Marinetti's work "had value primarily as a transitional movement; it served, for example, to supplant a nineteenth-century emphasis that had run its course to initiate the push toward new forms of expression." Pazzaglia and others consider futurism to have been most fruitful in the visual arts, with which Marinetti was not directly involved. In contrast, a number of Anglo-American critics connected to the avant-gardes of the 1960s and 1970s, such as Caroline Tisdall and Angelo Bozzolla, have given a more sympathetic appraisal of Marinetti's writing, celebrating its bold spirit of defiance and experimentation. From the early 1990s many scholars have focused on the relationship between futurism and fascism, while others have explored the connections between futurism and other European avant-gardes such as surrealism.

BIBLIOGRAPHY

Sources

Berghaus, Günter. *Futurism and Politics: Between Anarchist Rebellion and Fascist Reaction, 1909-1944.* Providence: Berghahn Books, 1996. Print.

Gentile, Emilio. *The Struggle for Modernity: Nationalism, Futurism, and Fascism.* Westport: Praeger, 2003. Print

Marinetti, Filippo Tommaso. *Manifesto del futurismo.* Project Gutenberg. Web. 10 June 2011.

Orban, Clara E. *The Culture of Fragments: Words and Images in Futurism and Surrealism.* Amsterdam: Rodopi, 1997. Print.

Pazzaglia, Mario. *Letteratura Italiana: Testi e critica con lineamenti di storia letteraria.* Bologna: Zanichelli, 1992. Print.

Tisdall, Caroline, and Angelo Bozzolla. *Futurism.* London: Thames and Hudson, 1977. Print.

Umberto Boccioni's bronze sculpture *Unique Forms of Continuity in Space* (1913) is considered to be one of the most important Futurist works of art. MATTIOLI COLLECTION, MILAN, ITALY/THE BRIDGEMAN ART LIBRARY

Further Reading

Bru, Sascha. *Democracy, Law and the Modernist Avant-Gardes: Writing in the State of Exception.* Edinburgh: Edinburgh UP, 2009. Print.

Drucker, Johanna. *The Visible Word: Experimental Typography and Modern Art, 1909-1923.* Chicago: U of Chicago P, 1994. Print.

Humphreys, Richard. *Futurism.* Cambridge: Cambridge UP, 1999. Print.

Marinetti, Filippo Tommaso. *Les mots en liberté futuristes (The Futurist Words in Freedom).* Reed Digital Collections: Artists Books. Reed College. Web. 10 June 2012.

Nänny, Max, and Olga C. M. Fischer. *Form Miming Meaning: Iconicity in Language and Literature.* Amsterdam: J. Benjamins, 1999. Print.

Rainey, Lawrence S., Christine Poggi, and Laura Wittman. *Futurism: An Anthology.* New Haven: Yale UP, 2009. Print.

Webster, Michael. *Reading Visual Poetry after Futurism: Marinetti, Apollinaire, Schwitters, Cummings.* New York: P. Lang, 1995. Print.

Lisa Barca

FUTURIST SYNTHESIS OF WAR

Filippo Tommaso Marinetti, et al.

⁜ Key Facts

Time Period:
Early 20th Century

Movement/Issue:
Aesthetics; Futurism

Place of Publication:
Italy

Language of Publication:
English

OVERVIEW

The "Futurist Synthesis of War"—created by a cadre of futurists, most notably Filippo Tommaso Marinetti—appeared in late 1914 and furthered the movement's embrace of violence and war as a great cleanser of civilization. By September 1914 Italy had not joined World War I, also known as "the Great War." In their founding manifesto of 1909, the futurists had proclaimed: "We want to glorify war—the only cure for the world—militarism, patriotism, the destructive gesture of the anarchists, the beautiful ideas which kill, and contempt for woman." As World War I raged in Europe, the futurists prepared a new manifesto that would use their developing assemblage style to signal their continued support of bloodshed. The "Futurist Synthesis of War" employs the group's typographical, fiery, and word-poem styles to further explain why they, the futurists, "glorify war."

The futurists celebrated war and violence, a vision of reality they espoused in theatrical readings and in self-aggrandizing gestures that made them the agents of a self-proclaimed modern artistic movement. They were driven by the desire to modernize artistic production and by the urge to dismantle traditional aesthetic values; they became the champions of "modern" art in the early twentieth century. When combined, the futurists' notoriety and calls for war gave their new, wartime manifesto additional weight. Marinetti and the other futurists viewed the document as a way to encourage Italy to enter the war on the side of the Allies (rather than the Triple Alliance, of which Italy was part). The "Synthesis of War" creates a hierarchy of nations that situates countries such as France, Belgium, England, and Japan on the side of Italy and futurism while placing Germany, Austria, and Turkey on the side of the past, irremediably "passé." In both narrative and visual artifacts, the "Synthesis of War" asserts the artistic and cultural benefit of the Great War for Italy and the rest of the world.

HISTORICAL AND LITERARY CONTEXT

People came to view the Great War as one of the catastrophes of history, a horror of technological innovation that killed more than nine million soldiers, devastated the countryside of France and Flanders, brought unprecedented physical and psychological harm to both soldiers and civilians, and destroyed the myth of an advanced Western civilization. The Great War created the concept of "total war"—violence wrought not only on combatants but also on civilians and cultural artifacts—an ideology made feasible by the first military use of dehumanizing technologies, including barbed wire, machine guns, airplanes, shells, poison gas, and tanks, all combined with the miseries of trench warfare. However, in the months preceding the war, and in the conflict's early days, a majority of people seemed to believe that a war would revitalize national cultures and overthrow the perceived decadence that had supposedly weakened European societies. This belief goes to the heart of futurist ideology and, specifically, to "Synthesis of War," which seeks to transform war into a tool that will wipe away decadence.

The need to energize and invigorate society through the war held particular fascination for Marinetti, who believed Italy was on the cusp of sitting side by side with the greatest European imperialist regimes. Tim Benton argues in his 1990 essay in *Journal of Design History* that Marinetti's well-known enthusiasm for automobiles, airplanes, and other technology came about not only from the machines' newness and speed but also from Italy's significant increase in automobile and airplane production in the first decades of the twentieth century. Thus, concludes Benton, the futurists' "romantic attitude towards cars and aeroplanes" signaled their belief that Italy was becoming an innovative, modern state. In their 1909 manifesto, the futurists conflate speed, technology, war, and violence as the recreators of art and society. The "Futurist Synthesis of War" reaffirms the group's beliefs within a wartime setting.

The futurists popularized manifestos among the early modernist movements—all of which sought to revitalize art by breaking with its historical conventions. Other early modernist movements distinguished themselves from nineteenth-century art—and, tellingly, from the futurists—through the production of manifestos. Indeed, several movements, including the futurists, remain better known for their manifestos than their art. The futurists created texts that mingle visuals with words (an early iteration of graphic design). This combined with Marinetti's performances declaiming futurist ideologies elevated their words, including the "Synthesis of War," to art works in their own right.

The "Futurist Synthesis of War" confirms not only the futurists' commitment to war and violence, but it also codifies the artistic drive within the movement's manifestos. Its graphic lines visually create two factions, while its references to "Passéism" and "Futurism" define those groups in terms that the futurists themselves had fashioned. In a way, this meta-artistic move foreshadows the playful, fractured self-awareness of postmodernism. Furthermore, critics such as Alan Bartram and Estera Milman have pointed out how advertising co-opted the graphic visual style of the futurists only to have that approach reappropriated in protest posters of the Vietnam War era. As with all avant-garde ideologies, the "Synthesis of War" no longer seems artistically radical. Instead, its legacy can be seen in the increasingly entangled areas of advertising, politics, and art.

THEMES AND STYLE

The primary mission of the "Futurist Synthesis of War" is to distinguish whom and what the futurists are against and signal why this division justifies war. Most boldly, the manifesto declares "Futurism against Passéism," or the forward focus of futurism against the outdated attributes of "passéism," in both historical and social terms. The subhead "8 people-poets against their pedantic critics," however, highlights the more localized battle at play as the futurists use this new manifesto to answer perceived misrepresentations. These disagreements might signal that the futurists feel misunderstood; on the other hand, they also hint at the argument that Italy should (as it ultimately did) fight on the side of the Allies rather than on that of the Triple Alliance led by Germany. The "Synthesis of War" combines the related issues (at least from the futurists' perspective) of art and war. It synthesizes the movement's call for a cathartic violence that will provide space for new creations within the historical realities of the actual war.

At first glance, the "Synthesis of War" operates as a visual piece. Its triangular central lines not only establish barriers between the various categories, but they also mimic an airplane, a rocket, a bullet, or a train engine—a propulsive image backed by the representatives of futurism, who are about to run over the advocates of passéism. Upon closer inspection, however, there is a series of positive attributes given in list format, featuring words such as "ELASTICITY," "INTUITIVE SYNTHESIS," and, in bold, **CREATIVE GENIUS.** These are separated "AGAINST" negative attributes, including "RIGIDITY," "ADDITION OF IDIOCIES," and "**GERMAN CULTURE.**" Visually and stylistically, all of the representatives of futurism align with the positive attributes, while the passéists fit with the negatives. In its primary verbal clusters, nations fall on either side of the explosive triangle, each defined by a cluster of words: "PRACTICAL, SPIRIT, SENSE OF DUTY," and others for England; "SHEEPISHNESS,"

FILIPPO TOMMASO MARINETTI AND FASCISM

Radical nationalism was a cornerstone of the Italian futurist worldview. In the "Futurist Synthesis of War," Filippo Tommaso Marinetti may see value in other nations, but he remains convinced of the superiority of Italy. Indeed, the manifesto's segregation of countries signals the futurists' belief in essential national character. Marinetti asserts the artistic vitality and iconoclasm of Italian futurism. Further, according to the document, this vigor makes the Italians the only artists worthy of destroying the old structures and generating new ones. This intense nationalism drew Marinetti to the first stirrings of Italian fascism.

Marinetti saw the influence of futurism waning after the war, which led him to found a futurist political party—with a bold, unrealistic platform—and then to dissolve it into the nascent fascist party of Benito Mussolini. Mussolini found Marinetti's fame to be a useful means to his political ends, but he ultimately ignored the futurist militant and took the party in the direction he desired. Eventually, Marinetti rejected fascism in disgust over the brutishness and ultraconservative attitudes of the Mussolini regime. Richard Bach Jensen maintains in *History Today* that "the violence of the Futurists was not in the same league as the violence of the Fascists and a distinction between these two kinds of violence deserves emphasis." Indeed, history might judge Marinetti poorly for embracing fascism, but it cannot erase his artistic contributions.

"BRUTALITY," "CONSTIPATION OF INDUSTRIAL CAMELOTS," and others for Germany; and only a "0" for Turkey. The "Synthesis of War" mingles the futurists' brash, aggressive verbal style with graphics to create a unique prose-poem.

The directness of the prose and the sense of being "run over" that is rendered by the layout formally sustain the violence advocated by the futurists. This presentation leaves no room for diplomacy or tolerance—instead, it calls for the annihilation of everything related to passéism. Such aggressiveness would have found many advocates before a belief in the Great War's futility became widespread. Similarly, a declaration such as the "right to destroy works of art … belongs solely to the Italian creative Genius, capable of creating a new and greater beauty on the ruins of the old," seemed less naive and callous before the truth about trench warfare was generally known. Indeed, the futurists' problematically idealistic view of war and violence contributed to their decline in the postwar years.

CRITICAL DISCUSSION

Initially, the futurists were considered *the* avant-garde movement of the modern era, and their artistic and political attitudes profoundly influenced

other avant-garde groups. The "Futurist Synthesis of War" was received as an extension of their already-established ideology. The futurists' shadow loomed so large in the prewar years that other movements—including the vorticists, imagists, and Dadaists—wrote their own manifestos distinguishing their approaches and beliefs from those of their predecessors. Between World War I and World War II, however, Marinetti sensed that the relevance of futurism was waning, and he became increasingly conservative in his politics. He involved himself in Italian fascism, becoming a strong supporter of Benito Mussolini, a decision that tainted his reputation—and the legacy of the futurists—for decades after World War II.

More recently, scholars have tried to place pre–World War I futurism in a historical context, arguing that there were glimmers of thinking that might have led to an embrace of fascism but disagreeing with the notion that Marinetti and futurism itself were inherently pre-fascist. In "Futurism, Seduction, and the Strange Sublimities of War," for example, Lucia Re studies the experiences of Marinetti and others in combat and argues that while they were not insensitive to the horrors of the Great War, they did not suffer the sharp disillusionment of their British, French, and American counterparts: "War—especially in view of the unprecedented scale of World War I—represented for the Futurists violence and destruction brought to a transcendent peak." Such analyses shed light on how the futurists evolved before, during, and after the war.

Other contemporary critics cite the futurists' influence on modernism and subsequent art ranging from advertising and graphic design to Vietnam War protest posters. As Milman points out, "There is little question that Futurism was capable of providing subsequent avant-garde communities with proof of the value inherent in the polemical presentation of a radical 'public face.'" Writing in *University of Toronto Quarterly,* Charles Ferral emphasizes the radical artistry of futurist manifestos: "Futurist manifestos actively attempt to combine all the arts by means of their performative aspects," and "the Futurists experiment with various kinds of synaesthesia as a way of breaking down the boundaries between the arts." Such experimentation with the limits of visual art, poetry, and manifesto signifies the important legacy of the futurists.

BIBLIOGRAPHY

Sources

Adamson, Walter L. "How Avant-Gardes End and Begin: Italian Futurism in Historical Perspective." *New Literary History* 41.4 (2010): 855-74. *Project Muse.* Web. 28 Aug. 2012.

Benton, Tim. "Dream of Machines: Futurism and l'Esprit Nouveau." *Journal of Design History* 3.1 (1990): 19-34. *JSTOR.* Web. 28 Aug. 2012.

Ferral, Charles. "'Melodramas of Modernity': The Interaction of Vorticism and Futurism before the Great War." *University of Toronto Quarterly* 63.2 (1993-94): 347-68. Print.

Jensen, Richard Bach. *History Today* 45.11 (1995): 35.

Marinetti, Filippo Tommaso, et al. "Futurist Synthesis of War." *Milanese Cell* 20 Sept. 20 1914. Print.

Milman, Estera. "Futurism as a Submerged Paradigm for Artistic Activism and Practical Anarchism." *South Central Review* 13.2-3 (1996): 157-79. *JSTOR.* Web. 28 Aug. 2012.

Re, Lucia. "Futurism, Seduction, and the Strange Sublimities of War." *Italian Studies* 59 (2004): 83-111. Print.

Further Reading

Bartram, Alan. *Futurist Typography and the Liberated Text.* New Haven: Yale UP, 2005. Print.

Humphreys, Richard. *Futurism.* Cambridge: Cambridge UP, 1999. Print.

Lupton, Ellen, and Elain Lustig Cohen. *Letters from the Avant-Garde: Modern Graphic Design.* New York: Princeton Architectural P, 1996. Print.

Peppis, Paul. *Literature, Politics, and the English Avant-garde: Nation and Empire, 1901-1918.* Cambridge: Cambridge UP, 2000. Print.

Somigli, Luca. *Legitimizing the Artist: Manifesto Writing and European Modernism, 1885-1915.* Toronto: U of Toronto P, 2003. Print.

Tisdall, Caroline, and Angelo Bozzolla. *Futurism.* New York: Oxford UP, 1978. Print.

Sarah Stoeckl

MANIFESTO OF MURAL PAINTING

Mario Sironi

✥ *Key Facts*

Time Period:
Early 20th Century

Movement/Issue:
Modernism; Italian
nationalism; Fascism

Place of Publication:
Italy

**Language of
Publication:**
Italian

OVERVIEW

Modernist painter Mario Sironi's *Manifesto of Mural Painting* (1933) names the mural as the form most conducive to the public expression of fascist ideals, valuing style and form over content in the process. Published in the December 1933 issue of *La Colonna,* the manifesto was signed by Sironi, Massimo Campigli, Carlo Carrá, and Achille Funi. Refuting conservative critics who defamed murals as an art form, the manifesto calls for a return to nationalist Italian aesthetic ideals, the rejection of "art for art's sake," the removal of the division between "high" and "low" art mediums, and the replacement of the public's perception of artists as indulgent bohemians with the idea that they are skilled craftsmen who make valuable cultural and social contributions. Sironi's document was devised as a reaction against the egocentrism of mainstream modernist culture and proposes an approach to the production and distribution of art that would reconcile reverence for the past with progress toward the fascist vision of a more collective future.

The conservative criticism Sironi refuted in the manifesto persisted after its release, and a general public disinterest in the mural as an art form limited the movement's cultural relevance in post-1933 Italy to the fascist artistic sphere. Sironi soon found his own work—which naturally enforced the ideals of his muralist vision—excluded from Italy's most prominent exhibits, though he remained active as an exhibit designer into the 1940s. Sironi's career mirrored that of the political revolution it was intended to bolster. The success of his exhibitions and the success of fascist ideology both peaked around the time of the text's release and then declined steadily thereafter until they each reached an effective demise—in 1941 and 1943, respectively. Today, the vision proffered by Sironi's manifesto is viewed as contributing more to the understanding of art's role in public consciousness than to the understanding of fascist ideology itself.

HISTORICAL AND LITERARY CONTEXT

The *Manifesto of Mural Painting* was a response to the decadence and indulgence of the bohemian influence on mainstream modernism and to the materialism espoused by futurists under the guidance of Filippo Tommaso Marinetti. Marinetti's *Futurist Manifesto* (1909) had promoted the embrace of all things fast, mechanical, new, and violent, stating outright, "We want no part of it, the past … we the young and strong Futurists!" Though the group claimed to possess and promote a great deal of national pride, Sironi equated its dismissal of all past styles and themes with a denunciation of and affront to all things Italian.

Sironi's manifesto was released at the height of Benito Mussolini's—and, by extension, fascism's—reign in Italy. The very past dismissed by the futurists, Sironi felt, represented the shared heritage of an entire race. This heritage, especially in the arts, was steeped in discipline and pride in craft. The primary contention of Sironi's muralist vision was that to dismiss that heritage wholesale was to relegate to sociopolitical irrelevance the culture from which its body of art sprang, an end he saw as irreversibly detrimental to the fascist cause. Therefore, by couching his arguments in the fascist rhetoric of conservative, nationalist revolution, Sironi offered a means by which to reconcile a reverence for the past with a vision of restored glory in a progressive Italian future.

The *Manifesto of Mural Painting* is in part a direct response to Marinetti's *Futurist Manifesto,* and it works closely from its model. Being a poet and critic, Marinetti was able to lend a certain fluid, stylized manner to his prose that was not typical of manifestos to that point, a tendency in keeping with the futurist credo: "we want no part of it, the past." The only break in Marinetti's prose was a brief enumeration of the guiding principles and aims of the futurist movement. Sironi, who had once been a futurist, explicitly resists this gesture in his own manifesto, making clear the severance of his ties not only with futurism but with all other modernist schools of thought.

Released some fourteen years after Marinetti's manifesto, at the apex of fascist control in Italy, Sironi's document refuses to enumerate and thereby narrowly define the direction of fascist art. Sironi insists that "fascist art will delineate itself only gradually" and only by the discipline and dedication to craft of Italy's finest artists. What follows, Sironi thus implies, are merely guidelines for recognizing those elements that characterize the finest artists and the works they produce. Unfortunately for Sironi, his vision was shared by only a very limited portion of the Italian public. Though muralism carried a great deal of significance elsewhere (particularly in Mexico), its impact on the direction of Italian art thereafter was minor.

THEMES AND STYLE

The governing theme of the *Manifesto of Mural Painting* is that of forming a genuinely "Italian" artistic aesthetic, one that recognizes its heritage while remaining forward-looking. Sironi begins by asserting that "fascism is a way of life" and that "no formula will ever succeed in fully defining or containing it" or what he refers to as fascist art. However, since "art assumes a social function in the Fascist state," he does allow that the locations ("public buildings, places endowed with civic functions") of mural paintings and the paintings' valuation of style over emotional content create artistic processes and products that are more conducive than are other forms to the transmission of fascist ideals. In Sironi's estimation, no other form upholds the previously unwritten mandate that "Fascist painting must be both ancient and ultra-new for it to achieve consonance with the spirit of the revolution."

Concerned first and foremost with promoting the fascist vision of a collective nationalist future, Sironi's primary rhetorical strategy is to highlight the various shortcomings of other modernist art theories in aligning with that vision. Most inadequate in Sironi's eyes is the tendency, especially of futurist art, to produce works informed more "by whim, by the cult of anomaly" and individuality than by the collectivity esteemed by fascist ideology. Such experimental works are characterized by Sironi as "trial balloons," all of which, regardless of diversity in style and form, "are rooted in a shared materialistic conception of life characteristic of the past century." Sironi contends that this conception precludes the works produced from performing any sort of social function, placing the conception in direct opposition to the Italian nationalist vision.

The arguments in the manifesto are driven by Sironi's defiant national pride and confidence in the virtues of the mural as the most appropriate form for state art. He seeks to restore art to the station it held "during the greatest epochs and within the greatest civilizations," the implication being that these were periods of Italian cultural prominence. To that end, Sironi sees mural painting as working "upon the popular imagination more directly than any other form of painting." In other words, because murals are more publicly and permanently visible than any other form, they more effectively "frame the question of Fascist art." The aims of that framework, as Sironi sees them, are simply to "free ... art from subjective and arbitrary elements, as well as from a specious originality that is desired and fed by vanity alone."

CRITICAL DISCUSSION

Little to no critical attention was paid to the manifesto itself, but a sense of the public response can be gathered from reactions to the works produced under its guidance. The muralist ideal as Sironi presented it favored modern interpretations of traditional forms

MARIO SIRONI: A NEARLY NON-MURALISTIC MURALIST

Although Mario Sironi did produce several series of murals, often in collaboration with his fascist colleagues, the majority of his body of work is devoted to other art forms. In international exhibitions—namely, the biennales and triennials of the 1920s and 1930s—Sironi's contributions tended toward large-scale architecture and installation art. The infamous murals at the 1933 triennial were purportedly only minor accompaniments to his *Series of Six Arches,* a group of ultra-modern clean-lined marble statues installed on the lawn of the exhibition site in Milan.

After 1933 Sironi worked even less in the mural form. His most successful works thereafter were typified by massive installation pieces more akin to constructivism than to his own conception of muralism. At the 1934 Exposition of Italian Aeronautics he filled Giovanni Muzio's Palace of Art with actual warplanes arranged in diagonal formations. The aircraft, whose irregular architecture contrasted heavily with the clean, modern lines of the space, were suspended from the ceiling, and a few stylized geometric figures (abstract podiums, display cases, etc.) populated the floor below. Installments of this type were characteristic of his lifelong emphasis on large-scale exhibit design over the production and display of individual works.

and mediums such as the fresco, and Sironi and several of his cohort contributed a series of collaborative frescos to the 1933 triennial exhibition. However, the modest heat of May was sufficient to cause severe paint loss and pigment alteration in the frescos, a debacle that Jeffrey T. Schnapp, in an article for the *South Central Review,* states "added fuel to the critical firestorm provoked by the murals." Sironi's methods, and by extension his muralist vision, came under attack from the public and from critics for failing to uphold the permanence Sironi so ardently demanded of Italian artwork.

Although the mural would persist, and even grow, as a culturally relevant form, the Italian muralist movement would dissolve less than a year after the manifesto's release. Schnapp observes a strain of criticism that found fault in Sironi's vision of art for being not only publicly produced and exhibited but also publicly funded. He notes that Ugo Ojetti was but one critic who found revolting the fact that Sironi "rendered thinkable an integral replacement of private patronage by public commissions," effectively establishing an official "state art" in the process. Yet some believe that this very accomplishment, and others like it, led at least indirectly to the formation of such organizations as the National Endowment for the Arts, a major source of artistic funding in the United States since 1965. It is speculation of this nature that fuels contemporary scholarship of the manifesto.

Like many Italian fascists, Mario Sironi found inspiration in the artistic works of ancient Rome. Here, Italian dictator Benito Mussolini stands beside a classical Roman statue in a still from the film *The Yellow Caesar.* THE ART ARCHIVE AT ART RESOURCE, NY

cultivated by style." In Eide's estimation, Sironi's professional decline was virtually assured by his insistence on working in traditional media in an era increasingly engaged in capitalist consumerism and the mechanical reproduction necessary to meet its demands.

Most of that scholarship examines the role of art in public consciousness or reexamines previous assessments of this role. Charles Harrison and Paul Wood, in the introduction to the manifesto in their anthology *Art in Theory, 1900-2000,* hint that Sironi's preoccupation with the formation of a wholly public art was more in line with ideas of public obedience than public consciousness. They assert that he employed classical themes merely to "bolster Fascist values through an implied equation with" the legacy of ancient Rome, with the hope that the public would then unconsciously transpose its reverence for Rome's former glory to current perceptions of Mussolini's Italy. In an article for the same issue of *South Central Review* containing Schnapp's assessment, Marian Eide argues that Sironi's "didactic purposes are as much undercut by the formal properties of their media as they are

BIBLIOGRAPHY

Sources

Eide, Marian. "The Politics of Form: A Response to Jeffrey T. Schnapp." *South Central Review* 21.1 (2004): 50-53. *JSTOR.* Web. 4 Oct. 2012.

Harrison, Charles, and Paul Wood. *Art in Theory, 1900-2000: An Anthology of Changing Ideas.* Malden: Blackwell, 2003. Print.

Lazzaro, Claudia, and Roger J. Crum. *Donatello Among the Blackshirts: History and Modernity in the Visual Culture of Fascist Italy.* Ithaca: Cornell UP, 2005. Print.

Further Reading

Affron, Matthew, and Mark Antliff. *Fascist Visions: Art and Ideology in France and Italy.* Princeton: Princeton UP, 1997. Print.

Anreus, Alejandro, Diana L. Linden, and Jonathan Weinberg. *The Social and the Real: Political Art of the 1930s in the Western Hemisphere.* University Park: Pennsylvania State UP, 2006. Print.

Baldacci, Paolo, and Philippe Daverio. *Futurism, 1911-1918: Works by Balla, Boccioni, Carrà, Severini, Prampolini, Depero, Sironi, Marinetti.* Milan: Philippe Daverio, 1988. Print.

Braun, Emily, and Mario Sironi. *Mario Sironi and Italian Modernism: Art and Politics Under Fascism.* New York: Cambridge UP, 2000. Print.

Humphreys, Richard. *Futurism.* Cambridge: Cambridge UP, 1999. Print.

Schnapp, Jeffrey T., Olivia E. Sears, and Maria G. Stampino. *A Primer of Italian Fascism.* Lincoln: U of Nebraska P, 2000. Print.

Clint Garner

MANIFESTO OF THE FUTURIST WOMAN

Valentine de Saint-Point

OVERVIEW

Composed by French artist Valentine de Saint-Point, "Manifesto of the Futurist Woman" (1912) replies to F.T. Marinetti's "Futurist Manifesto" (1909) from an explicitly female perspective. Like the "Futurist Manifesto," Saint-Point's work adheres to the futurist philosophy, including a celebration of the dynamic potential of war. However, she emphasizes the contributions of women in fostering a spirit of militancy, thus decrying Marinetti's framing of war as a masculine endeavor in which females are an impediment. "Manifesto of the Futurist Woman" also centers on the notion that humans of both sexes contain elements of masculinity and femininity. Saint-Point portrays gender as a continuum of traits, with the truly creative and heroic individual exhibiting the right balance of the feminine and the masculine. Addressed primarily to futurists and other avant-gardists of the time, "Manifesto of the Futurist Woman" calls on women to embrace war and for men to respect the creative, warlike spirit that females can embody.

Both "Manifesto of the Futurist Woman" and Saint-Point's "Futurist Manifesto of Lust" (1913) received wide attention when they were first published, largely because they were the only futurist manifestos besides those of artist Mina Loy to be written by a woman and the only ones to deal exclusively with questions of gender and sexuality. In addition, because the words "contempt for women" ("*il disprezzo della donna*") in Marinetti's 1909 work had become a catch phrase, a futurist manifesto proclaiming the rights of women was sure to excite attention. Despite her concern with the female condition, however, Saint-Point distanced herself from organized feminism. With her aristocratic origins—combined with an attitude influenced by Friedrich Nietzsche's notion of the "superman," or the extraordinary individual apart from the crowd—Sainte-Point had no interest in advancing the political rights of women in general. Nevertheless, her text is viewed as a strong rebuttal to the misogyny of the "Futurist Manifesto."

HISTORICAL AND LITERARY CONTEXT

"Manifesto of the Futurist Woman" and "Futurist Manifesto of Lust" deal centrally with questions of sexuality. Consequently, they stand in stark contrast to the overt masculine bias undergirding futurism

as Marinetti had presented it. Marinetti's seminal "Futurist Manifesto" had been published in Paris in the widely circulated *Le Figaro*, an international forum. It produced a great commotion, and much attention—both serious and ironic—was given to the "contempt for women" line. Marinetti's phrase even seeped into the period's visual art, such as with Arturo Martini's *Méprisez la femme* ("Despise women"). Saint-Point saw this as an injustice toward the contributions women had made to the emergent avant-garde.

"Manifesto of the Futurist Woman" was published just prior to World War I. Marinetti and his futurist peers strongly favored the eruption of war and Italy's entry into it, and Saint-Point agreed. Militant nationalism was not uncommon in many European nations in the early twentieth century. It was especially pronounced in Italy, which had become a politically unified country only in 1871 and remained fragmented both linguistically and culturally. The epigraph to "Manifesto of the Futurist Woman" includes the following quote from Marinetti's "Futurist Manifesto": "We want to glorify war—the only hygiene of the world—militarism, patriotism, anarchic and destructive actions, great ideas worth dying for, and contempt for women." By using this passage, Saint-Point sets up her argument in favor of militarism and patriotism and in opposition to the disparaging view of women.

In 1906, three years before Marinetti founded futurism with the "Futurist Manifesto," a number of Saint-Point's symbolist poems were published in his literary magazine, *Poesia*, which often featured the work of women poets. Thus, Saint-Point contributed to the creation of futurism, making her condemnation of the antiwoman statements in the "Futurist Manifesto" especially understandable. In "Manifesto of the Futurist Woman," Saint-Point places herself in the then-established tradition of manifestos stemming from the futurist movement, including "Manifesto of the Futurist Painters" and "Technical Manifesto of Futurist Painting," both published early in 1910 by artists Giacomo Balla, Umberto Boccioni, Carlo Carrà, Luigi Russolo, and Gino Severini.

Of Saint-Point's two manifestos—"Manifesto of the Futurist Woman" and the closely related "Futurist Manifesto of Lust"—the latter was arguably the more influential. For instance, in 1917 Marinetti himself

Key Facts

Time Period:
Early 20th Century

Movement/Issue:
Futurism; Avant-gardism

Place of Publication:
Italy

Language of Publication:
Italian

An illuminated manuscript from the fifteenth century depicting Joan of Arc. Valentine de Saint-Point cites Joan of Arc as an example of warrior women "who fight more ferociously than males."
© RMN-GRAND PALAIS/ART RESOURCE, NY

grew geniuses and heroes of both sexes." The idea of feminine and masculine elements intermingling in the heroic individual undergirds the entire text. Ultimately, she replaces Marinetti's dichotomy between men and women with a division between heroes (the futurists) and common people, writing, "Every superman, every hero … every genius, to the degree that he is powerful, is the prodigious expression of a race and of an epoch only because he is composed of feminine elements and masculine elements at the same time: he is a complete being."

The document achieves its rhetorical effect through appeals to a warlike notion of heroism that transcends gender differences. Saint-Point believes her historical era is marked by an excess of femininity, which prompts her to write, "In order to bring a certain virility back to our race corrupted by its femininity, one needs to force the race to become virile, even to the point of brutality." Saint-Point's main strategy for vindicating women is to catalogue and contrast "weak" and "strong" female stereotypes. She denigrates "women nurses who perpetuate weakness and old age" and "vampires of the hearth, who suck the blood of men," and celebrates women "destroyers who, breaking the weak, contribute to natural selection … the most fruitful conquest you can make."

Saint-Point's language echoes the rhetoric of political activism, but she discourages women from taking feminist actions. After presenting her "weak" and "strong" female types, she writes: "Feminism is a political error. Feminism is a cerebral error of woman, an error that her instinct will recognize. *Women should not be granted any of those rights claimed by Feminism. Granting them these rights would not produce any of the disorder hoped for by Futurists, but would cause, instead, an excess of order.*" As illustrated by this passage, Saint-Point employs a theatrical, often inflammatory style to encourage a vague idea of aggressive, anarchic action while also condemning feminism, which was the main means of activism for women at the time. The text also relies on the common idea of women as primarily intuitive rather than rational: the "cerebral error" of feminism will be corrected when females start following their instincts rather than their intellects.

published "Against Love and Parliamentarianism," in which he calls love a mere confluence of "sentimentalism and lust," a statement that recapitulates one of the main premises of "Futurist Manifesto of Lust." As contemporary scholar Mirella Bentivoglio puts it in *The Women Artists of Italian Futurism* (1997):

> While Valentine de Saint-Point in her manifesto had limited her considerations to the sexual sphere, without commenting on its related sentiments, here Marinetti launched, straight from the title, into the theme of "love," denying its existence. Moreover, the word "lust," which Valentine had hoisted right into the title itself as a flag and a challenge to morality, is repeated here.

THEMES AND STYLE

The central themes of "Manifesto of the Futurist Woman" are that the futurist movement cannot thrive without the contributions of women and that both sexes must access the ideal balance of masculine and feminine traits. Saint-Point opens by saying, "Humanity is mediocre. The majority of women are neither superior to nor inferior to the majority of men. They are equal. Both deserve the same contempt. The majority of humanity has never been anything other than the fertile soil from which

CRITICAL DISCUSSION

When "Manifesto of the Futurist Woman" was first published, it gained notice because of its unique focus on the relationship of gender to the avant-garde. It received mixed reactions both within and outside of futurist circles. Futurist critic Augusto Hernet defended it, as well as "Futurist Manifesto of Lust," in the March 1913 issue of the prominent Italian journal *Lacerba,* but other futurists denounced him for this. "Futurist Manifesto of Lust" and "Manifesto of the Futurist Woman" were included in *Lacerba*'s 1914 anthology of futurist manifestos and were also published in several different languages.

Saint-Point was, in many ways, an outsider in the futurist movement. In her essay in *Fascist Visions: Art and Ideology in France and Italy* (1997), Nancy Locke describes the ways in which Saint-Point differed ideologically from the majority of futurists:

> Whereas they wanted to burn the art of the museums, she … argued that the art of the future could be rooted only in knowledge of the art of the past. Whereas they celebrated the machine and the airplane, she clung to a Parisian symbolist vocabulary of mysticism and ancient mythology. Whereas they had "nothing but scorn for women," Saint-Point made woman the focal point of her art.

Thus, "Futurist Manifesto of Lust" and "Manifesto of the Futurist Woman" made an impact mainly as novelty pieces. Following the decline of futurism in the early 1920s, they were largely forgotten until the feminist literary critics of the 1970s rediscovered them.

Most contemporary scholarship has focused on the significance of Saint-Point's works in the context of women's literary history. The consensus among critics has been that while the writings are important to understanding both historical notions of gender and the range of the futurist movement, they are ultimately too riddled with contradictions to be regarded as coherent statements of women's experiences and status. Locke emphasizes the ultimately male-centered ideology expressed in Saint-Point's work, concluding that "despite all the ways in which Saint-Point could have fashioned a critique of futurism, and despite the fact that at times she did fashion such a critique, her notion of woman remained embedded in a language of male domination." Nevertheless, Locke notes that Saint-Point "reacted against the futurist exclusion and indictment of woman … by reclaiming the territory of woman's sexuality as the source of power and activism." This may be the most significant and enduring contribution of Saint-Point's work.

BIBLIOGRAPHY

Sources

Bentivoglio, Mirella, and Franca Zoccoli. *The Women Artists of Italian Futurism: Almost Lost to History.* New York: Midmarch Arts, 1997. Print.

Locke, Nancy. "Valentine de Saint Point and the Fascist Construction of Woman." *Fascist Visions: Art and Ideology in France and Italy.* Ed. Matthew Affron and Mark Antliff. Princeton: Princeton UP, 1997. Print.

Saint-Point, Valentine, and Giovanni Lista. *Manifeste de la femme futuriste: Suivi de manifeste futuriste de la luxure; le théatre de la femme; la Métachorie.* Paris: Séguier, 1996. Print.

Saint-Point, Valentine. "The Manifesto of the Futurist Woman." *The Women Artists of Italian Futurism: Almost Lost to History.* Ed. Mirella Bentivoglio and Franca Zoccoli. New York: Midmarch Arts, 1997. 163-166. Print

Further Reading

Adamson, Walter L. "Futurism, Mass Culture, and Women: The Reshaping of the Artistic Vocation, 1909-1920." *Modernism/modernity* 4.1 (1997): 89-114. Print.

Affron, Matthew, and Mark Antliff. *Fascist Visions: Art and Ideology in France and Italy.* Princeton: Princeton UP, 1997. Print.

Apollonio, Umbro. *Futurist Manifestos.* Boston: MFA, 2001. Print.

Berghaus, Gunter, and Valentine de Saint-Point. "Dance and the Futurist Woman: The Work of Valentine de Saint-Point (1875-1953)." *Dance Research: The Journal of the Society for Dance Research* 11.2 (1993): 27-42. Print.

Perloff, Marjorie. *The Futurist Moment: Avant-Garde, Avant Guerre, and the Language of Rupture.* Chicago: U of Chicago P, 2003. Print.

Poggi, Christine. *Inventing Futurism: The Art and Politics of Artificial Optimism.* Princeton: Princeton UP, 2008. Print.

Lisa Barca

MARY NETTIE

Gertrude Stein

✢ *Key Facts*

Time Period:
Early 20th Century

Movement/Issue:
Modernism

Place of Publication:
Mallorca

Language of Publication:
English

OVERVIEW

Gertrude Stein's "Mary Nettie" (1916) responds to the machismo-laden celebration of violence in Filippo Marinetti's *Futurist Manifesto* (1909). Stein wrote and published the piece during a sojourn to the Mediterranean island of Majorca with Alice Toklas at the height of World War I. Although Stein claims that the title is only a pun on Marinetti's name, the styles and themes in "Mary Nettie" produce an intimate portrait of domestic life in contrast to the *Futurist Manifesto*'s enshrinement of industry, masculinity, aggression, and war. In particular, Stein's prose poem relies on idiosyncratic wordplay and a series of non sequiturs to create a retreat from the chaos of wartime Europe to the daily activities of the two women. Whereas Marinetti's manifesto attacked feminism, Stein's "Mary Nettie" articulates a way in which women not only interact with their surroundings but also create and give meaning to their environment.

Stein's experimental style and the seemingly innocuous narrative of the poem caused many to overlook the manifesto as anything beyond mere wordplay. However, "Mary Nettie" signals a retreat to the quotidian activities of domestic life and offers a subtle counter to the bravado of Marinetti's manifesto. Rather than calling for revolutionary turmoil, Stein looks to care and relationships in order to combat the upheaval of the early twentieth century. The stark contrast between the two manifestos provides for a telling spectrum of modernist aesthetics and concerns; however "Mary Nettie" failed to garner a significant audience and to this day is rarely reprinted or included in anthologies.

HISTORICAL AND LITERARY CONTEXT

Indirectly responding to Filippo Marinetti's *Futurist Manifesto,* Stein crafts an antimanifesto that illustrates a tellingly different vision of the celebratory confidence that Marinetti placed in technology and industrial progress. Although Marinetti could not have foreseen the nightmares that would be associated with large-scale industrial war, his manifesto held revolution as an ideal. Stein, on the other hand, develops a thoughtful meditation on domesticity that serves as a compelling counter narrative to the disappointment that many artists faced in the wake of World War I. In a typical modernist trope, Stein relies upon the aesthetic sphere of language to make sense of a world locked in turmoil. "Mary Nettie" provides a respite from the war and serves to linguistically remake the world under a new vision that places the fragments into a newly unified whole.

At the time of the poem's publication, modernist artists were faced with a seemingly open-ended set of possibilities in the face of the technological and cultural changes of the early twentieth century. While many of her contemporaries responded to the uncertainties caused by the second industrial revolution, mass urban migration, and the horrors of large-scale war, Stein's poem calls attention to the calmness of everyday life in the face of such atrocities. However, "Mary Nettie" represents a refreshingly feminist perspective within an artistic scene dominated by male voices and a variety of aesthetic positions that celebrated the destructive force of revolution. Stein, along with luminaries such as Mina Loy and Djuna Barnes, established a rhetoric that greatly contrasted with their male counterparts such as Marinetti, Ezra Pound, and Ernest Hemingway. Although "Mary Nettie" did not reach as large an audience as Stein's other writing, the subtlety of the work points toward a greater concern with the ability of human beings to peacefully craft and change their world by participating in simple pleasures such as shopping, cooking, and conversing.

"Mary Nettie" relies on Stein's avant-garde and experimental aesthetics to erect a space in which the female narrator can actively manipulate the political, aesthetic, and social landscapes via an innovative process that strips language down to its base and then reinvigorates it with new meaning. Similar to her other Majorca pieces, "Mary Nettie" explores the experimental techniques she first used in "Tender Buttons" (1914) by jettisoning traditional syntax and grammar in favor of a series of juxtapositions, reflections, and conversations concerning the seemingly trivial aspects of shopping, walking, and eating. Additionally, "Mary Nettie" pursues an intimate portrayal of what life could be like for the two lovers, Stein and Toklas. In a sense, the manifesto solidifies the multiple moments by placing the various happenings in a narrative that allows Stein to explore her consciousness.

Although the poem resembles much of Stein's experimental writing, it is difficult to judge its impact. Similar to much of her work, Stein pays close attention to language, playing with its circularity. "Mary Nettie" revolts against futurism's infatuation with war and violence by supplanting Marinetti's rhetoric with one that finds comfort in everyday objects and their potential significance. Stein's focus on ordinary objects and everyday events, however, infuses the pedestrian with greater significance and elevates it to the realm of aesthetic concerns. Her careful selection of details allows her to subtly invert not only the traditional social norms by celebrating intimacy and domesticity but also aesthetic concerns by replacing typical objects of high art with mundane activities thought to be beneath the realm of aesthetics. "Mary Nettie," then, can be read as a precursor to many contemporary feminist aesthetics as it celebrates common experience and calls attention to an often-neglected and marginalized identity.

THEMES AND STYLE

The guiding theme of "Mary Nettie" is the primacy of the private sphere shared by two women in the midst of the chaotic world around them. In the face of the devastation caused by World War I, "Mary Nettie" offers a brief respite from the mechanical world. In stark contrast to the excessiveness of Marinetti, Stein pens a quiet, meditative piece in which the carefulness of the language is as important as the meaning. Early in the manifesto, Stein remarks, "If you care to talk to the servant do not talk to her while she is serving at table." The remark follows a curious set of observations in which a cane falls from a window. The window is a transparent barrier between the inside and outside worlds, a division that the fallen cane violates. The imperative to not talk to the server while she is serving maintains a public and private division, but it also suggests that if one wishes to truly speak with the servant, then one should speak to her with more intimacy and duration than is afforded by the temporary dialogue between patron and servant.

"Mary Nettie" establishes its meaning through the subtle turns of phrase that invert traditional structures of power. Stein's narrator remarks, "[W]e are pleased because we have an electric fan" and follows this by noting, "we took a fan out of a man's hand." The electric fan merges the worlds of industry and domesticity, and Stein's narrator removes the power of industry from the sphere of masculinity. Rather than serving as a mechanism of war, the fan symbolizes a move into the more tranquil sphere of commodities. Additionally, the transposition of meaning pushes up against the futurists' fascination with electricity. While Marinetti's manifesto is steeped in misogyny, Stein's antimanifesto elevates the feminine and the domestic over the celebration of violence. Unlike the artillery officer who self-servingly remarks, "artillery is very important in war," Stein's polyvalent narrator illustrates the importance of common objects in a variety of contexts.

As an antimanifesto to Marinetti's *Futurist Manifesto*, Stein relies on simple prose that manipulates standard forms of grammar and syntax in order to

GERTRUDE STEIN: INNOVATION AND CONTRADICTION

Gertrude Stein (1874-1946) remains one of the most studied women writers of modernism. Born in Allegheny, Pennsylvania, she studied at both Radcliffe College and Johns Hopkins Medical School before expatriating to Paris in 1903. During this time, she was a prolific writer, composing fiction, nonfiction, poems, essays, dramas, and novels. Her time in Paris exposed her to the likes of Pablo Picasso, Henri Matisse, and James Joyce, as well as to fellow expatriates F. Scott and Zelda Fitzgerald and Ernest Hemingway. The apartment that Stein and her life partner, Alice B. Toklas, shared became an artistic hub where some of modernism's profound aesthetic ideas blossomed. Stein's influence on modernism is difficult to overlook. She remains a hallmark figure of modernist aesthetic experiments, and she coined the defining phrase "the lost generation" to describe the postwar milieu.

Although Stein maintains an almost unimpeachable artistic legacy, her historical and political reputation was drastically altered after World War II. At the height of the war, Stein and Toklas retreated to southern France during the German occupation, despite the fact that they were both Jewish and lesbians. Critics have noted that not only did the couple retain their priceless art collection, but they also remained silent about the Jews who suffered under the Vichy government. Pointing to Stein's friendships with high-ranking officials, recent scholarship has focused on this time in Stein's life. It is noted that she was sympathetic to fascist politics and possibly a collaborator under the Nazi-backed French government. In spite of the political criticisms, Stein's innovative work and experimental approach to language have influenced much of contemporary writing, most notably including that of confessional poet Sylvia Plath, language poet Susanne Howe, and conceptual poet Vanessa Place, in addition to avant-garde writers such as Maxine Hong Kingston, Theresa Hak Kyung Cha, and Harryette Mullen.

achieve a fractured narrative that elicits a continuum of meaning in which play and possibility are given precedence over rigidity and stasis. Stein utilizes her experimental style to explore a variety of strategies that seek to look to the significance of objects abandoned by traditional aesthetics in order to represent not only a direct challenge to the masculine-dominated canon but also a rich, complex portrait of two women attempting to come to terms with their relationship. Framed by the sections "We Had an Exciting Day" and "Papers," the section "Not Very Likely" illustrates the dilemma Stein faces. The narrator remarks that "we were frightened. We were so brave and we never allow it. We do not allow anything at last. That's the way to say we like ours best." On its face, the passage feels resigned, but the subtle resistance built in—the glaring omissions of what "it" is—opens up a space for deeper meaning to take hold. The manifesto dwells in contradiction, playing with the delicate space between silence and resistance.

Gertrude Stein's "Mary Nettie" can be considered a tongue-in-cheek criticism of Italian Futurist Filippo Tommaso Marinetti, pictured here. PRIVATE COLLECTION/THE BRIDGEMAN ART LIBRARY

CRITICAL DISCUSSION

Although "Mary Nettie" was largely overlooked, the style and theme of the Majorcan works incorporated Stein's autobiography with a fluid narrative perspective that pushed against the boundaries between fiction and nonfiction and inserted an artistic perspective that pursued the effects of war on people's everyday lives. According to Richard Bridgman in *Gertrude Stein in Pieces* (1970), Stein's contemporaries noticed that in "Mary Nettie," along with the other Majorcan pieces, "normal speech and an increasing number of personal details entered Gertrude Stein's writing." Although World War I may feel like it sits at the periphery of "Mary Nettie," it is in fact at the very center of the work. The presence of war haunts the piece, and as David Owens notes in a 1998 essay in *Modern Fiction Studies,* the Majorcan pieces are peppered with what appears to be "a reaction to some sort of war news." "Mary Nettie" evidences a continued sense of anxiety and a building movement toward the improbability of reconciliation.

Scholars and critics have noted that the poem breaks away from Stein's earlier works because its style and subject matter are more accessible to a general audience, and although it retains the subtlety of wordplay, the work is far less abstract than her experimental poems. "Mary Nettie" provides valuable insight into the progression of Stein's talents. In an introduction to *The Stein Reader* (1993), Ulla E. Dydo remarks that focusing on Stein's development "is to discover the world in words we had never known until she used them." As such, "Mary Nettie" serves as an important bridge between Stein's early and later works. Written before her literary fame, the Majorcan pieces shed light on the process whereby Stein moved away from traditional grammar and syntax and fine-tuned her experimental style that would form her legacy.

Much of the scholarship surrounding "Mary Nettie" and the accompanying Majorcan works centers on Stein's focus on the ordinary objects she encounters and how they relate to the public and private ways individuals coped with the ever-present effects of World War I. Owens notes that the Majorcan works "convey a sense of concern and anxiety for the events in Europe. The lovers portrayed in this Mallorcan Movement have their love and affection for one another ... however, beyond the banalities of everyday living, the speaker portrays little else other than the uncertainty and anxiety of life in a time of war." Other scholars have drawn attention to the focus of lesbian love and how Stein's experimental style paved the way for other artists to express relationships that were marginalized by society. In *A Vocabulary of Thinking: Gertrude Stein and Contemporary North American Women's Innovative Writing* (2007), Deborah Mix argues, "[T]o recognize the ways in which Stein and her work both authorize and impel the responses of contemporary North American women writers is to begin the important work of revealing and articulating a feminist experimentalist community." Such an understanding allows for a deeper insight into modern avant-garde aesthetics.

BIBLIOGRAPHY

Sources

Bridgman, Richard. *Gertrude Stein in Pieces.* New York: Oxford UP, 1970. Print.

Dydo, Ulla E. *A Stein Reader.* Evanston: Northwestern UP, 1993. Print.

Mix, Deborah M. *A Vocabulary of Thinking: Gertrude Stein and Contemporary North American Women's Innovative Writing.* Iowa City: U of Iowa P, 2007. Print.

Owens, David. "Gertrude Stein's 'Lifting Belly' and the Great War." *Modern Fiction Studies* 44.3 (1998) 608-18. Print.

Stein, Gertrude. "Mary Nettie." *A Stein Reader.* Ed. Ulla E. Dydo. Evanston: Northwestern UP, 1993. 308-13. Print.

Further Reading

Cope, Karin. *Passionate Collaborations: Learning to Live with Gertrude Stein.* Victoria: U of Victoria P, 2005. Print.

Daniel, Lucy. *Gertrude Stein.* London: Reaktion, 2009. Print.

Mitrano, G. F. *Gertrude Stein: Woman without Qualities.* Burlington: Ashgate, 2005. Print.

Peterson, Becky. "Experimentation, Identification, Ornamentation: Avant-Garde Women Artists and Modernism's Exceptional Objects." Diss. U of Minnesota, 2010. Print.

Will, Barbara. *Gertrude Stein: Modernism and the Problem of "Genius."* Edinburgh: Edinburgh UP, 2000. Print.

———. *Gertrude Stein: Unlikely Collaboration: Gertrude Stein, Bernard Faÿ, and the Vichy Dilemma.* New York: Columbia UP, 2011. Print.

Josh Harteis

WHY WE PAINT OURSELVES

A Futurist Manifesto

Mikhail Larionov, Ilya Zdanevitch

OVERVIEW

Composed by Mikhail Larionov and Ilya Zdanevich, "Why We Paint Ourselves: A Futurist Manifesto" (1913) describes a movement in the Russian arts that embraced the dynamism of a new era and offered an innovative way of propagating artistic truths. The treatise represents a culmination of the aesthetic ideas and work of avant-garde poet and propagandist Zdanevich and painters Larionov and Natalia Goncharova. As the alliance between the three suggests, the manifesto addresses artistic expression in many forms. Although its authors were skilled provocateurs, their essay was not printed as a tract; it appeared in the middle-class publication *Argus,* explaining that they painted rayonist (in which "rays of force" emanate from the subject) and futurist symbols on their faces in order to bring radical artistic expression to the public. The manifesto expounds on how the act reflected major aspects of their beliefs about what contemporary Russian art should embrace: the championing of dynamism and the new; a synthesis of avant-garde ideas and forms; and the vitality of primitive artwork and symbols.

Although his tactics caused public outrage, by the time the manifesto was published Larionov and his artistic colleagues were well-known members of the Russian avant-garde, particularly as the advocates of a Russian futurist theater. Appearing in public with dramatic facial decorations was part of Larionov's stratagem to reject theatrical traditions and move theater to the streets. His faction supported several movements in the arts, including neo-primitivism, rayonism, and *Vsechestvo* ("everythingism"—the theory that almost anything can constitute art). Larionov's views of futurist aesthetics had a notable effect on the growth of Russian avant-garde and constructivist theater (which used artistic practices to utilitarian ends) and on rayonist, primitivist, and nonobjective art. The practice of face painting became a popular novelty in Russia and a fashionable practice internationally. Today, "Why We Paint Ourselves" is considered among the most important documents of the Russian pre-World War I avant-garde and is recognized as a significant influence on later aesthetic movements around the world.

HISTORICAL AND LITERARY CONTEXT

In the early 1900s industrialization and aesthetic innovation were altering the Russian political and artistic landscapes. The Russian working classes, who endured poverty, hunger, terrible working and living conditions, and high taxes, agitated and created political movements to advance their causes. In the arts, new concepts and arguments flourished. Italian poet and editor Filippo Tommaso Marinetti had published his *Futurist Manifesto* in 1909, exhorting artists and writers to abandon old traditions and create works that reflected the vitality of the new age. Futurist groupings sprang up throughout Europe. Marinetti's manifesto was not published in Russia until 1912, but various avant-garde circles espousing cubism and primitivism had already been labeled "futurists." Like the Italians, they wrote provocative manifestos to garner support, and they planned public events to attract attention. The Russian groups had differing views, however, whether to incorporate artistic trends from the West. When Marinetti visited Russia in 1914, Larionov published an essay urging Russian futurists to turn away from the Italian avant-garde leader, whose ideas, he asserted, were out of date. Whereas some Russian futurists still followed ideas from French painting, Larionov's set looked to Russian popular art and ancient and Eastern works for inspiration.

By the time "Why We Paint Ourselves" was written in 1913, Larionov had already issued an almanac and manifesto ("On the Other Hand") to distinguish his movement from Western art trends and other Russian avant-garde factions. These earlier statements supported a synthesis of cubism, futurism, and Orphism (a precursor to abstract art), as well as a strong belief in incorporating images that blended Fauvist colors with Russian folk motifs. The inclusion of the latter was hugely important as the country sought to establish an artistic identity independent of the West.

"Why We Paint Ourselves" relies on Italian futurism's bold praise of motion, dynamism, and the machine as symbols and subjects of the new age—what Tim Harte, in *Fast Forward: The Aesthetics and Ideology of Speed in Russian Avant-Garde Culture, 1910-1930,* calls "a corporeal approach to modernity's pace." When these ideas reached Russia, avant-garde artists there quickly followed suit with their

✣ *Key Facts*

Time Period:
Early 20th Century

Movement/Issue:
Aesthetics; Avant-gardism; Futurism

Place of Publication:
Russia

Language of Publication:
Russian

MIKHAIL LARIONOV: THE INCLUSIVE FUTURIST

In 1898 Mikail Larionov, a student from Tiraspol, entered the Moscow Institute of Painting, Sculpture, and Architecture. There he met Natalia Goncharova, a painter with whom he maintained a lifelong creative partnership. Larionov had a wide-ranging curiosity about artistic practices and theories. A 1906 trip to Paris in connection with the Salon d'Automne inspired him to work in a neoimpressionist style. In 1908 he began to contribute to the Golden Fleece exhibitions, which also featured the works of avant-garde artists Marc Chagall and Kazimir Malevich, Larionov's eventual rival in abstraction.

With Goncharova and others, Larionov formed the first avant-garde art societies: the Jack of Diamonds (1909-11), the more radical Donkey's Tail (1912-13), and the Target Group (1913), with whom he exhibited his initial rayonist paintings. He pursued somewhat contradictory aesthetic movements simultaneously, pioneering rayonism while maintaining an interest in neoprimitivism, which was inspired by cubism, futurism, and Russian folk art.

Larionov became a master of futurist propaganda tactics. His conception of a futurist theater inspired his group to appear in public with painted faces. Subsequently, he worked in cinema and then left Russia to pursue his most widely known career path—making sets and stage décor for Sergei Diaghilev's Ballets Russes. He never returned to Russia, but his rayonism and everythingism were crucial steps in the Russian development of abstract and constructivist art forms.

own theatrically assertive pronouncements. The poets David Burliuk, Velimir Khlebnikov, Alexander Kruchenykh, and Vladimir Mayakovsky produced "A Slap in the Face of Public Taste" (1912), imploring artists and writers to throw out their old traditions. The document's aggressive and confrontational tone became de rigueur for nascent avant-garde movements. In composing their manifesto, Zdanevich and Larionov also drew from their own earlier essays on rayonism and everythingism, which applauded a synthesis of various art movements.

In the years following the manifesto's publication, the aesthetics it espoused inspired important developments within the Russian avant-garde. The authors' theories influenced new developments in the Ballets Russes (1909-29), which director Sergei Diaghilev described as a synthesis of all the arts. The like-minded Diaghilev attributed his theater's intellectual and aesthetic origins to Russian peasant objects and design motifs. Larionov himself wanted to introduce the brazen practice of body painting into the world of fashion design; he proposed that women should go topless and paint their breasts, a suggestion so inflammatory that a Larionov impersonator managed to incite a riot. Larionov's confrontational stage performances—and those of his group—led to

participation in futurist film projects with director Vladimir Kasayov, including *Drama in the Futurists' Cabaret No. 13*. According to some critics, the film was an attempt to restore art to its proper place in human existence, an idea that "Why We Paint Ourselves" expresses in the statement: "We have loudly summoned life, and life has invaded art." Larionov's everythingism was part of a trend that nurtured both cubo-futurism and suprematism (an attempt to express pure feeling through geometric forms), all of which established a specifically Russian tradition of art. Today, the manifesto attracts scholarly attention in the context of the varied community of Russia's avant-garde history.

THEMES AND STYLE

The central theme of "Why We Paint Ourselves" is that the vibrant new age required a new community of creators and a fresh means of disseminating its artistic expressions. The opening proclaims the authors' enthusiastic entrance into the dubious achievements of modernity they celebrate: "To the frenzied city of arc lamps, to the streets bespattered with bodies, to the houses huddled together, we have brought our painted faces; we're off and the track awaits its runners." The treatise proclaims that the face and body serve as mediums on which to display an art that can keep pace with the fleeting experiences of urban modern life. In the pursuit of an innovative form of "propagation," the writers embrace a confrontational approach and an impermanent format. Notably, the manifesto does not side with a particular aesthetic; this catholicism of taste was significant as a step toward the synthesis of cubist and futurist ideas in rayonist and constructivist art.

Written as an explanation and a provocation to middle-class readers, "Why We Paint Ourselves" demands that its audience acknowledge the authors' credibility by emphasizing the positive and creative goals behind their behaviors: "Creators, we have not come to destroy construction, but to glorify and affirm it." With this sentence and others, the essay anticipates and persuasively addresses the potential criticisms of the uninitiated. Simultaneously, by arguing for the merging of diverse, even unrelated media, the writers explain their unique means of reflecting the new, anarchic, and vigorous age.

Stylistically, the treatise is distinguished by the exultation in its tone and the exaltation of its subject. The allure of modernity is conveyed through the glorification of fleeting experiences and impulsive deeds: "We join contemplation with action and fling ourselves into the crowd." The fast-paced, kinetic quality of the writing reflects the speed and rush of sensation that the futurists applauded and exhorted the public to embrace. The authors express themselves in extreme statements, insisting that the best way to herald the unknown is to discard automated reactions and long-held traditions and to "know no half measures" in doing so. They use lavishly descriptive language, declaring that "the telescope discerned constellations lost in space, painting will tell of lost ideas. We paint ourselves ... to bear man's multiple soul to the upper reaches of reality." Its style renders the manifesto somewhat grandiose in tenor, in the tradition of Russian avant-garde doctrines.

CRITICAL DISCUSSION

"Why We Paint Ourselves" received mixed reactions within and outside of artistic circles. At venues where futurist performances incorporating face painting took place, such as the Pink Lantern cabaret in Moscow, some audience members were entertained and others were scandalized, particularly when Larionov insulted the spectators as "jack-asses of the present day." From the stage, symbolist poet Konstantin Balmont and others hailed the face-paint wearers as heroes, shouting "Long live Larionov" and hurling insults at the crowd. Goncharova and the cubofuturist poets supported Larionov's ideas, though public unrest eventually caused the cabaret to close. The cessation of the face- and body-painting performances was in a large sense a success for the artist. According to Anthony Parton's *Mikhail Larionov and the Russian Avant Garde* (1993), "This [censure] cannot have disappointed [them], since the many reports in the Russian press provided maximum exposure for themselves and Russian futurism."

Although Larionov's futurist group dispersed after he and Goncharova moved to Paris in 1914 as set designers for the Ballets Russes, the manifesto remained an important record of avant-garde history as well as a source of pride for Russian artists, and Larionov's name still stands for important artistic and political innovation. Reflecting on the group's synthetic futurist ideas in a 1998 issue of *Art Bulletin,* Maria Gough writes, "Larionov's interests ... [were] an early articulation of what became, in the 1920s, the most radical wing of the Russian crusade against the West." In the century since its composition, the manifesto has been the subject of criticism that has addressed its legacy in historical and aesthetic terms.

Recent scholarship has focused on the artistic significance and cultural notoriety of "Why We Paint Ourselves," which were notable at the time of its publication despite the short duration of the artistic movements Larionov initiated. Parton quotes Gallerist Giuseppe Sprovieri discussing the artist's impact: "Larionov explained that the definition of 'futurism' was much too wide to be limited to one specific movement alone." Commentators have identified the face-painting manifesto as a notable example of an aesthetic belief system that, in Parton's words, "not only blurred the distinctions between traditional media ... but that aspired to everythingism rather than the dogmatic practice of the futurist aesthetic." In "Goncharova, Larionov and the Limits of Cubism" (2011), Jane A. Sharp elaborates on the multiple bridges the

authors' theories built: "In 1913-1914, at the height of their Russian careers, when both artists theorized *Vsechestvo* (everythingism), their most radically inclusive approach to painting—we see a process that ... is motivated by dialogues across cultures, and by life's tangential course." Other scholars have focused on the resonance between Larionov's futurism and the writings of Italian futurists, all of which differ from the ideas of such Russian practitioners as Burliuk, Velimir Khlebnikov, and Mayakovsky. In addition, great attention has been directed to the later work of both Larionov and Goncharova in the world of theater arts and ballet, where they built their international reputations.

Promenade, Venus of the Boulevard, painted by Mikhail Larionov in 1913, the year his manifesto "Why We Paint Ourselves" was published. CNAC/ MNAM/DIST. RMN-GRAND PALAIS/ART RESOURCE, NY

BIBLIOGRAPHY

Sources

Barron, Stephanie, and Maurice Tuchman. *Avant-Garde in Russia, 1910-1930: New Perspectives.* Los Angeles: LA County Museum of Art, 1980. Print.

Caws, Mary Ann, ed. *Manifesto: A Century of Isms.* Lincoln: U of Nebraska P, 2000. Print.

Chilvers, Ian, ed. *The Oxford Dictionary of Art.* Oxford: Oxford UP, 2004. Print.

Gough, Maria. "Mikhail Larionov and the Russian Avant-Garde." *Art Bulletin* 80.4 (1998): 752+. *Academic OneFile*. Web. 15 Aug. 2012.

Harte, Tim. *Fast Forward: The Aesthetics and Ideology of Speed in Russian Avant-Garde Culture, 1910-1930.* Madison: U of Wisconsin P, 2009. Print.

Parton, Anthony. *Mikhail Larionov and the Russian Avant-Garde.* Princeton: Princeton UP, 1993. Print.

Sharp, Jane A. "Goncharova, Larionov and the Limits of Cubism." *Chagall et L'Avant-Garde Russe.* Ed. Angela Lampe. Paris: Centre Pompidou, 2011. 74-98. Print.

Further Reading

Cohen, Milton. *Movement, Manifesto, Melee: The Modernist Group, 1910-1914.* Lanham: Lexington, 2004. Print.

Goldberg, RoseLee. *Performance Art: From Futurism to the Present.* 3rd ed. London: Thames, 2011. Print.

Gray, Camilla. *The Russian Experiment in Art, 1863-1922.* Rev. and expanded ed. London: Thames, 1986. Print.

Kolocotroni, Vassiliki, Jane Goldman, and Olga Taxidou, eds. *Modernism: An Anthology of Sources and Documents.* Chicago: U of Chicago P, 1998. Print.

Malmstad, John E. "The Sacred Profaned: Image and Word in the Paintings of Mikhail Larionov." *Laboratory of Dreams: The Russian Avant-Garde and Cultural Experiment.* Ed. John E. Bowlt and Olga Matich. Palo Alto: Stanford UP, 1996. Print.

Markov, Vladimir. *Russian Futurism: A History.* Berkeley: U of California P, 1968. Print.

Karen Bender

ACTUAL NO. 1, A STRIDENT PRESCRIPTION

Manuel Maples Arce

OVERVIEW

Written by Manuel Maples Arce, *Actual No. 1, A Strident Prescription* (1921) demands the overthrow of antiquated literary and artistic forms and champions a "strident" art that is commensurate to the beauty of the new century. The manifesto was first issued as a poster that Maples Arce pasted on the walls of downtown Mexico City. With its iconoclastic views and emphasis on artistic production, the text was aimed at the cultural elite, a group familiar with the development of the European avant-garde. The manifesto is organized into fourteen numbered sections that lay out the philosophy of "stridentism." It concludes with a list of more than two hundred avant-garde writers, artists, and intellectuals from Europe and Latin America, a directory of the avant-garde.

Maples Arce originally published the manifesto as part of a solitary effort. The text quickly became influential amongst writers and painters in Mexico City. Within less than a year, the manifesto had engendered an aesthetic movement known as stridentism. The movement included writers and visual artists from Mexico and Europe, and it remained active for the greater part of the 1920s. According to its founder, the group "was the first intellectual subversion to take place in America." *Actual No. 1* explained the goal that undergirded the group's diverse projects: to overturn outdated aesthetic forms and create an art that engaged with twentieth century life. Today, *Actual No. 1* can be viewed as an important document in the development of Mexico's first national avant-garde literary movement.

HISTORICAL AND LITERARY CONTEXT

Actual No. 1 is a response to the state of Mexican art and literature in the early twentieth century, a time when academic conservatism was beginning to give way to a Latin American vanguard, a parallel development to the European avant-garde. In the early 1920s anthropological and archaeological discoveries led to an increase in appreciation for Mexican heritage, which in turn pushed Mexican painting away from the European academy and toward indigenous and popular forms. Progress in literature occurred when writers associated with the group Ateneo de la Juventud sought to "move the country out of the nineteenth century philosophically and artistically."

By 1921 the effects of the recently ended Mexican Revolution were apparent in the cultural realm. According to Elissa Rashkin in her book, *The Stridentist Movement in Mexico,* "Those who had fought for the overthrow of repressive social and political institutions and found themselves victorious now had to ask what kind of institution they were prepared to create."

By the time *Actual No. 1* was written, the literary and artistic ferment in the New World had given rise to numerous avant-garde movements throughout Latin America, such as the Argentine Ultraists, the Brazilian Modernists, and the Peruvian Amauta group. In Mexico painters like Diego Rivera and David Alfaro Siqueiros had returned from Europe "with the explicit aim," according to Rashkin, "of revitalizing their national cultures." Other writers, still living abroad, such as Rafael Lozano, published articles about the European avant-garde in Mexican periodicals such as *Revista de Revistas, Zig-Zag,* and *El Univeral Ilustrado,* many of which Maples Arce would read and appreciate. When *Actual No. 1* first appeared in 1921, it assimilated many of the ideas of the European avant-garde while placing them in a Mexican context, thereby serving as the first articulation of the Mexican avant-garde's goal to create a new twentieth-century art.

Actual No. 1 draws on a long history of avant-garde art manifestos, including those of Russian and Italian futurism, Spanish ultraism, and Dadaism. Maples Arce envisions that stridentism could be "a quintessential synthesis" of the previous vanguards. Along with those well-known avant-garde manifestos, Maples Arce found inspiration in David Alfaro Siqueiros's tract, "Three Appeals for a Modern Direction to the New Generation of American Painters and Sculptors." Written in May 1921, Siqueiros's manifesto, much like Maples Arce's, calls for a "new generation" of artists who can topple the decadent influence of European academicism. Although Maples Arce's *Actual No. 1* focuses more on poetry and does not share Siqueiros's emphasis on Mexico's indigenous roots, it echoes—like all other avant-garde manifestos—the desire for a renewal and a modern direction for Mexican Art.

In the decades following the publication of *Actual No. 1,* many critics insisted that stridentism

✜ *Key Facts*

Time Period:
Early 20th Century

Movement/Issue:
Aesthetics; Avant-gardism; Mexican Revolution

Place of Publication:
Mexico

Language of Publication:
Spanish

THE MEXICAN REVOLUTION

In 1910, in the midst of dictator Porfirio Díaz's three-decade rule, Francisco I. Madero led a rebellion that overtook Ciudad Juarez and initiated the Mexican Revolution, a series of disparate conflicts, coups, and battles that would continue for more than a decade. Madero assumed the presidency but soon found himself caught between the political extremes. Emiliano Zapata and his campesino forces declared war on Madero because of his failure to initiate agrarian reform, but it was the right-wing general Victoriano Huerta who overthrew the government. Huerta was soon driven into exile by opposition forces, and Venustiano Carranza assumed the presidency, which he would hold, despite continued violence, until the constitutionalists deposed him. The election of Álvaro Obregón as president in 1920 brought an end to the conflict.

Manuel Maples Arce and the other stridentists were too young to fight in the revolution, but they all experienced, to a greater or lesser degree, the interruptions and upheaval of war. The ideals of the revolution also had an influence on Maples Arce. Indeed, while at the Escuela Libre de Derecho, he composed a thesis on agrarian law.

left no heirs, but recent scholarly inquiry has noted its literary and cultural influence. The poetry of Baja California, specifically that of Pedro Pérez y Ramírez, exhibits stridentist influences. Roberto Bolaño's 1998 novel, *Los Detectives Salvajes,* depicts the stridentists as the founders of the Mexican avant-garde, and his inclusion of long lists of obscure writers and poets is perhaps a nod to *Actual No. 1.*

THEMES AND STYLE

The central theme of *Actual No. 1* is that Mexican poetry and visual art have grown stale and that the avant-garde must transcend the old forms to create a new modern art. The hitherto dominant trend in Mexican art, the manifesto claims, is driven by traditionalists, "retrograde academics, specialists in obfuscation," and "bilious critics," who uphold a "stinking authoritarian intellectual environment," and thus attempt to "circumscribe" Maples Arce and the avant-garde's "heavenly horizons." Maples Arce argues that "every artistic technique fulfills a spiritual function at a given moment." If certain antiquated forms of expression are "awkward or inadequate ways of transmitting our personal emotions" then we need to "pull out the plug." Instead of those forms, the artists and poets should embrace the themes and images of their century, "the reign of great, throbbing, industrial cities."

The manifesto achieves its rhetorical effect through appeals, often in overwrought language, to the young poets, painters, and sculptors of Mexico. A shared sense of antagonism aids in the creation of solidarity, and the manifesto engenders its sense of unity through the oppositional stance it takes toward the public, who, according to Maples Arce, is "lacking in intellectual resources," and the traditionalists, who seek to circumscribe artistic possibilities. This collectivity is further aided through Maples Arce's use of "we" and his calls to Mexicans to join the stridentist movement. Similarly, the "directory of the avant-garde," which lists more than two hundred writers, artists, and intellectuals in Europe, Latin America, and Mexico, posits a plurality of voices and historical continuity, which belies the fact that stridentism was as yet an incipient movement. According to Rashkin, the "et cetera" that ends the directory "serves to extend an invitation to the reader."

Actual No. 1 is divided into numbered sections, suggesting systematized thinking or practical and specific goals, but the order of the fourteen sections of *Actual No. 1* evince no discernible logic. Indeed, the concepts presented in these sections often overlap, which contributes to the chaotic feel of the manifesto. This disorder is further developed through Maples Arce's use of neologisms and his declamatory poetic language, wherein he seeks to illuminate himself in the "marvelous incandescence" of his "electric nerves." Although this chaotic prose can make the manifesto a challenge to read, the style reflects Maples Arce's idea that emotion is the font of creative energy and "a form of supreme arbitrariness and specific disorder."

CRITICAL DISCUSSION

When *Actual No.1* appeared, it caused a stir in intellectual and artistic circles but the public virtually ignored it. Aside from a brief note in the January 8, 1922, issue of *Revista de Revistas,* it received no coverage in Mexican newspapers—this despite the manifesto's professed desire to incite the bourgeoisie and the manifesto's performative "publication" on the streets of Mexico City. For the younger artists and writers in Mexico, however, the stridentist manifesto was a call to arms and an opportunity to create meaningful and iconoclastic art. Soon a group of "stridentists" formed. According to Rashkin, poets and writers, including Germán List Arzubide, Luis Quintanilla, and Arqueles Vela, along with visual artists Ramón Alva de La Canal and Leopolo Méndez, "sought to transform not only written and visual language but also everyday life through the creation of new aesthetic spaces and new approaches to the urban environment."

After the stridentist movement ended in the late 1920s, *Actual No. 1,* along with subsequent stridentist manifestos, remained an important document in the history of the Mexican avant-garde and an influence on its ensuing movements. According to Rashkin, the avant-garde painting group, ¡30-30!, which issued its first manifesto in July 1928, and the Marxist-Leninist November Group, which formed in 1932, are evidence that the "'scandalous gesture' initiated at the end of 1921 with *Actual No. 1* did not disappear but rather persisted in other forms well into the 1930s and beyond." In the ninety years since its publication, the manifesto has been the subject of a small body of criticism that has considered its legacy in literary, historical, and political terms.

In the first five decades after its publication, there was a dearth of scholarly interest in *Actual No. 1.* "In the preamble to a 1968 interview with Jean Charlot, Stefan Baciu noted the absence of any substantive scholarship on stridentism." This would change in 1970 with the publication of Luis Mario Schneider's *El estridentismo o una literatura de la estrategia,* a work that focused primarily on the group's literary output, which, according to Rashkin, most scholars conceived of as "a flash in the pan, an isolated outburst with little resonance in the larger cultural or literary landscape." Recent scholarly interest, such as Rashkin's work, *The Stridentist Movement in Mexico,* has sought to place stridentism in a broader historical context and trace its influence on a larger cultural landscape.

BIBLIOGRAPHY

Sources

Danchev, Alex. "A Stridentist Prescription." *100 Artists' Manifestos: From the Futurists to the Stuckists.* London: Penguin, 2011. Print.

Flores, Tatiana. "Clamoring for Attention in Mexico City: Manuel Maples Arce's Avant-garde Manifesto Actual No. 1." *Literature and Art of the Americas.* 37.2 (2004): 208-20. Taylor & Francis Online. Web. 20 Aug 2012.

Monahan, Kenneth Charles. *Manuel Maples Arce and "Estridentismo."* Northwestern University, 1972. Proquest. Web. 20 Aug 2012.

Rashkin, Elissa J. *The Stridentist Movement in Mexico: The Avant-Garde and Cultural Change in the 1920s.* Plymouth, MD: Lexington, 2009. Print.

Further Reading

Ault, Ann Warner. *Masked Men: Staging Identity in Mexican Experimental Prose, 1921-1929.* New York: Columbia UP, 2007. Print.

Bohn, Willard. *Apollinaire and the International Avant-Garde.* Albany: State University of New York P, 1997. Print.

Caplow, Deborah. *Revolutionary Art and the Mexican Print.* Austin: U of Texas P, 2007. Print.

Flores, Tatiana. *Estridentismo in Mexico City: Dialogues between Mexican avant-garde art and literature 1921-1924.* New York: Columbia University, 2003. Print.

Foster, David William. *Mexican Literature: A History.* Austin: U of Texas P, 1994.

Torres-Rioseco, Arturo. *New World Literature: Tradition and Revolt in Latin America.* Berkeley: U of California P, 1949. Print.

Frontispiece to Metropolis (1929), a work by Manuel Maples Arce. Arce founded the strident (estridentismo) artistic movement and wrote the manifesto *Actual No. 1, A Strident Prescription* (1921). PRIVATE COLLECTION/THE STAPLETON COLLECTION/ THE BRIDGEMAN ART LIBRARY

Gregory Luther

ART, REVOLUTION, AND DECADENCE

José Carlos Mariátegui

❖ *Key Facts*

Time Period:
Early 20th Century

Movement/Issue:
Aesthetics; Marxism;
Avant-gardism

Place of Publication:
Peru

**Language of
Publication:**
Spanish

OVERVIEW

Composed by Peruvian Marxist José Carlos Mariátegui, "Art, Revolution, and Decadence" (1926) describes revolutionary art and its relationship to politics. When Mariátegui wrote his essay, Peru was under the rule of dictator Augusto B. Leguía and both workers and students were beginning to organize around revolutionary demands. Around the time of its publication, Peru was home to a burgeoning Latin American vanguardism, which had been influenced by Europe's avant-garde. The movement came to Latin America via Peruvian intellectuals who had spent time in Europe, including Mariátegui. Published in Mariátegui's journal *Amauta,* "Art, Revolution, and Decadence" aimed to reach Peruvians of all social and economic classes, but it had a limited working-class readership. The essay describes the link between politics and art, the need for a revolutionary spirit, and the importance of eliminating bourgeois decadence from truly new art.

"Art, Revolution, and Decadence" was well received by vanguardists in Peru and in other Latin American countries, but it failed to reach its intended working-class audience because of *Amauta's* avant-garde slant and relatively high price. *Amauta* sought to encourage a revolutionary intellectual group to complement the radical, and growing, class movement of indigenous peoples and workers in Peru. To that end, the essay outlines the task of the revolutionary intellectual. Upon its publication, it drew interest from a number of Peruvian writers whose work soon found a home in *Amauta,* including Abelardo Solís, Luis Valcárcel, and Eudocio Ravines. "Art, Revolution, and Decadence" remains an important essay in Mariátegui's oeuvre and is a significant contribution to his views of ethics and aesthetics and Peruvian literature as vital aspects of the revolutionary project.

HISTORICAL AND LITERARY CONTEXT

"Art, Revolution, and Decadence" outlines Mariátegui's beliefs on the relationship between politics and art and constitutes an important part of his position against the political and economic suppression of Peru's working-class and indigenous peoples. Mariátegui responds to the marginalization of these groups from cultural institutions by calling for the creation of art devoid of bourgeois influence. He sees the potential for true artistic advancement but cautions the reader to evaluate even avant-garde art for signs of decadence, which he feels must be eliminated to achieve a truly new art.

When the essay was published in 1926, Mariátegui was settling back into Peru following his exile in Europe from 1919 to 1923, a punishment imposed by Leguía as a result of Mariátegui's support for revolutionary Peruvian students and workers. During his exile, Mariátegui had come into contact with leading figures in the European postwar avant-garde in France, Italy, and Germany, including Henri Barbusse, Filippo Tommaso Marinetti, and Herwarth Walden. He read Italian futurist manifestos and was particularly influenced by French surrealism. Upon his return to his native country, Mariátegui and other transcontinental intellectuals advanced the revolutionary possibilities of the avant-garde and brought those ideas to relationships with Peruvian writers such as José María Eguren and César Vallejo. "Art, Revolution, and Decadence" was a key component in Mariátegui's Peruvian socialist project; he saw the revolutionary, inclusive potential of the avant-garde spirit and worked to advance its influence.

"Art, Revolution, and Decadence" draws on both political and aesthetic forms of the manifesto. As an avowed Marxist, Mariátegui was familiar with Karl Marx and Friedrich Engels's seminal *The Communist Manifesto* (1848), which addresses the shortcomings of capitalism and its effect on the classes. In Europe, Mariátegui read the key futurist manifestos and came into contact with avant-garde theorists from diverse movements, including Dadaism, surrealism, and cubism, all of which made extensive use of the manifesto as a vehicle for the dissemination of revolutionary artistic ideas. "Art, Revolution, and Decadence" also taps into and expands upon ideas Mariátegui broached in his *Maxim Gorky and Russia* and *Man and Myth,* both published in 1925.

Following its publication, "Art, Revolution, and Decadence" inspired Peruvian vanguardists and aided in the advancement of the artistic and literary avant-garde in Latin American intellectual circles. In addition to being a great influence on Vallejo, Mariátegui's writings were of interest to subsequent generations of Latin American thinkers. Mariátegui continued to write about literature and aesthetics in essays such as "On Explaining Chaplin" (1928) and "A Balance Sheet on Surrealism" (1930). Today, "Art, Revolution, and Decadence" is noted for its role in the development of Mariátegui's own political and aesthetic concerns and in the formation of the avant-garde in Latin America.

THEMES AND STYLE

The essay's main theme is that the revolutionary artist must operate within a political context and shed bourgeois decadence to achieve a new artistic effect. Mariátegui describes the tools of this new art, stating, "Two spirits coexist in the modern world, that of revolution and that of decadence. Only the presence of the first gives a poem or painting value as new art." He then stresses the necessity of abandoning decadence, as "images of decadence are often present in vanguard art until it sets truly revolutionary goals, overcoming the subjectivism that weakens art at times." It is not enough, in Mariátegui's view, to work in the context of the avant-garde; the artist must consciously abandon decadence and move toward a revolutionary, political goal.

The text makes use of inclusive language and an idealized vision of new art to achieve its rhetorical effect. Mariátegui makes the reader part of his project, writing that "we cannot accept as new any art that merely brings us new technique. This would mean amusing ourselves with one of the most fallacious modern illusions." The reader is called to action as Mariátegui speaks of the new artist in this new world and pronounces that a revolutionary abandonment of the bourgeois will be "the passage from the darkness on one side of the mountain to dawn." Notably, Mariátegui does not claim allegiance to any single artistic movement—instead, he urges the artist to cater only to a revolutionary spirit.

Stylistically, "Art, Revolution, and Decadence" is significant for its poetic language, cultural referents, and declarative sentences. In order to illustrate his meaning, Mariátegui includes discussions of specific artists (Massimo Bontempelli, Vicente Huidobro, and André Breton, to name a few) and their respective successes or failures. He notes that even vanguard artists can fall prey to the allure of subjectivity and decadence. He also makes use of powerful, imagistic language in the essay, as when he describes the battle between revolution and decadence: "In the end, one of the two spirits prevails. The other is left strangled in the arena." With this metaphor, he highlights the seriousness of his revolutionary pronouncement. His images work to propel the artist toward a new and politically charged space.

CRITICAL DISCUSSION

When "Art, Revolution, and Decadence" was first published, it did not reach at least half of its intended audience: the working-class and indigenous populations of Peru. It did, however, connect with members

JOSÉ CARLOS MARIÁTEGUI: PERUVIAN MARXIST

José Carlos Mariátegui (1894-1930) was a Peruvian socialist and one of his country's most significant philosophers and political activists. He was born into poor circumstances, which he later claimed allowed him to interact with all levels of Peruvian society, including proletarian miners and laborers, mestizos, and indigenous peoples. Early in his career, he worked as a journalist for the newspaper *La Prensa,* for which his writings showed socialist leanings. With friend César Falcón, he launched two newspapers of his own. The pro-labor stance of these papers resulted in Mariátegui's exile to Europe from 1919 to 1923, but it was during this period that he came into contact with schools of thought that would be significant in his intellectual development.

In France, Italy, and Germany, Mariátegui met members of the Italian Communist Party, as well as revolutionaries from France's *Clarté* group. After his return to Peru, he declared himself a Marxist. Mariátegui worked to develop a brand of Marxism that would cater to the unique social and political situations of Latin American countries. Specifically, he asserted that the indigenous populations and proletariat classes would be necessary to a successful revolution. He was arrested twice for his organizational activities and his teaching at the González Prada Popular University. Though he was only thirty-six when he died, he left behind a body of work that has had a lasting impact on politics in Latin America.

of the avant-garde in Peru and Latin America. The magazine in which the essay was published, *Amauta,* was an essential part of Mariátegui's project of creating a vanguard movement of revolutionary intellectuals in Peru. In their introduction to *José Carlos Mariátegui,* Marc Becker and Harry E. Vanden note that "if *Amauta* had its tactical aspects, it was simultaneously a superb vehicle for disseminating ideas. Further, it was one of the most outstanding literary magazines that Latin America produced during the first part of this century." Latin American artists rushed to participate in the journal, including Uruguayan poet Juana de Ibarbourou and Peruvian poets Magda Portal and Vallejo. As Becker and Vanden assert, "a whole generation of Peruvian writers found expression in *Amauta*'s pages," a development that Mariátegui's aesthetic and political discussions promoted.

Although it is not considered one of Mariátegui's most important essays, "Art, Revolution, and Decadence" remains relevant for its discussion of the link between politics and art in the Latin American world. The essay outlines the importance of politics to the Latin American artist's development, a reality that is clearly reflected in the works of artists such as Peru's Mario Vargas Llosa. In a preface to *The Oxford Book of Latin American Essays,* Ilan Stevens writes that the essay "illuminates Mariátegui's views on art and politics.

Although José Carlos Mariátegui is critical of many artists and art movements in his time period in his manifesto, he praises Irish playwright George Bernard Shaw, pictured here. © LEBRECHT MUSIC AND ARTS PHOTO LIBRARY/ALAMY

epochs, in which politics was limited to the administration or parliament, with the romantic epochs, in which politics was at the forefront."

BIBLIOGRAPHY

Sources

Becker, Marc, and Harry E. Vanden. "Introduction." *José Carlos Mariátegui: An Anthology.* Ed. and Trans. Marc Becker and Harry E. Vanden. New York: Monthly Review, 2011. 11-61. Print.

Löwy, Michael. "Communism and Religion: José Carlos Mariátegui's Revolutionary Mysticism." Trans. Mariana Ortega Breña. *Latin American Perspectives* 35.2 (2008): 71-79. *Sage Publications.* Web. 2 Oct. 2012.

Löwy, Michael. "Marxism and Romanticism in the Work of José Carlos Mariátegui." Trans. Penelope Duggan. *Latin American Perspectives* 25.4 (1998): 76-88. *JSTOR.* Web. 2 Oct. 2012.

Mariátegui, José Carlos. "Art, Revolution, and Decadence." *José Carlos Mariátegui: An Anthology.* Ed. and Trans. Marc Becker and Harry E. Vanden. New York: Monthly Review, 2011. 423-26. Print.

Stevens, Ilan. "Preface." *The Oxford Book of Latin American Essays.* Ed. Ilan Stevens. Oxford: Oxford UP, 1997. 123-26. Print.

Further Reading

Becker, Marc. *Mariátegui and Latin American Marxist Theory.* Athens: Ohio University Center for International Studies, 1993. Print.

Garrido, J. M. "The Desire to Think: A Note on Latin American Philosophy." *CR: The New Centennial Review* 7.3 (2007): 21-30. *Project MUSE.* Web. 2 Oct. 2012.

Goldemberg, Isaac, and Miguel Angel Zapata. "An Infinite Country: A View of Peruvian Literature and Culture from the Learned Provinces." *Review: Literature and Arts of the Americas* 42.2 (2009): 200-32. Routledge. Web. 2 Oct. 2012.

Grijalva, Juan Carlos. "Paradoxes of the Inka Utopianism of José Carlos Mariátegui's *Seven Interpretative Essays on Peruvian Reality.*" *Journal of Latin American Cultural Studies* 19.3 (2010): 317-44. Routledge. Web. 2 Oct. 2012.

Sharman, Adam. "Latin American Modernity ... and Yet." *Bulletin of Latin American Research* 30.4 (2011): 488-501. *Blackwell Publishing.* Web. 2 Oct. 2012.

The link between these two subjects is at the heart of the Latin American literary tradition, and few others have been able to articulate so successfully the challenge of bringing them together." Scholarship on the work, while extensive in the Spanish-speaking world, has only recently become common in English.

Contemporary scholars have focused on the influence of surrealism on the essay and the work's spiritual treatment of politics. In *Marxism and Romanticism in the Work of José Carlos Mariátegui,* Michael Löwy notes Mariátegui's fascination with surrealism: "He followed with the greatest interest the initiatives of the surrealist movement.... What attracted him to the followers of André Breton (he published several of his texts in *Amauta*) was their categorical condemnation 'en bloc' of bourgeois rationalist civilization." Löwy analyzes the inclusion of Breton and the surrealists in the essay, which "counterposes the classical

Kristen Gleason

MANIFESTO OF THE UNION [OR SYNDICATE] OF MEXICAN WORKERS, PAINTERS, AND SCULPTORS

David Alfaro Siqueiros

OVERVIEW

The *Manifesto of the Union [or Syndicate] of Mexican Workers, Painters, and Sculptors* (1923), composed principally by the social realist painter David Alfaro Siqueiros, sought to reclaim mural painting and other art forms "for the people" from the Mexican government. In 1921, after the end of the Mexican Revolution (1910-ca. 1920), minister of education José Vasconcelos commissioned works of art for display in public buildings as a means of educating a largely illiterate people. By 1922 the hired artists, Siqueiros and his colleagues, had tired of serving the interests of the government, which, they felt, was using art as a tool for reinforcing its own brand of nationalist values. They established the Union of Mexican Workers, Painters and Sculptors to reposition their art as truly representing the public. Originally published in Mexico City in the union's newspaper, *El Machete*, the manifesto was signed by Siqueiros, Diego Rivera, Jose Clemente Orozco, and five other artists. Like the government, the artists embraced Mexico's collective native roots in pre-Columbian culture and myth, but their ideology diverged: they reinforced their own Communist values by addressing historically oppressed sectors of the Mexican population, including workers, peasants, and indigenous peoples. The goal of the manifesto was to combat the threat of bourgeois interests with the true expression of the people.

In promoting native arts, Siqueiros and his colleagues were initially successful in uniting artistic and political interests, but their superficial understanding of indigenous culture and their attempt to impose socialist values regardless of local beliefs eventually alienated them and the working class from the indigenous community. Forty years later, however, in the mid-1960s, the manifesto inspired the Chicano Movement that arose in the U.S. Southwest, out of which emerged Chicano muralism. The twenty-first century's new generation of Chicano muralists still participates in the tradition established by the muralist union's manifesto in the 1920s.

HISTORICAL AND LITERARY CONTEXT

The *Manifesto of the Union of Mexican Workers, Painters, and Sculptors* responded to what the union felt was an overbearing governmental influence in cultural and artistic spheres. After the revolution, the new administration sought to reestablish stability and realize its stated values, among them general education. Along with creating a symphony, rural schools, libraries, a census of the country's indigenous regions and languages, and other initiatives, the state employed folk art and artists, most notably the "Big Three" muralists—Siqueiros, Rivera, and Orozco—to nurture cultural pride and identity. In the union's view, the government aspired to glorify Mexico's past without addressing the reality or needs of the people, including expanded public services and equal access to them, legal protection against civil and human rights violations, and land redistribution. In addition to describing these needs, the manifesto calls for the abandonment of the esoteric aims of European "easel art" and all artistic endeavor that "springs from ultra-intellectual circles, for it is essentially aristocratic." The document advocated a more vibrant, truly American model: "the monumental expression of art because such art is public property."

The formation of the Union of Mexican Workers, Painters, and Sculptors in 1922 marked the muralists' ideological disassociation from Vasconcelos's project to pursue more radical goals. According to Joe Cummings in his 1999 article "Diego, Frida and the Mexican School," Orozco was the most faithful to the manifesto's principles; he "destroyed all his earlier canvases and devoted himself to the ideals of social art for the remainder of his life." Orozco later lamented that Siqueiros and Rivera did not respect the manifesto's postulates. The union disbanded, and its members pursued their separate careers; in "Caricaturing the Gringo Tourist" (2006), Jeffrey Belnap states that "although the fragile consensus among Mexican muralists gave way to disparate creative and political agendas, their work after this early activity was permanently marked by the fusion of Mexican popular and European fine art practices."

In structuring the manifesto, Siqueiros drew heavily on the revolutionary discourse employed in earlier Mexican political manifestos, including territorial governor of California José Figueroa's 1835 *Manifesto to the Mexican Republic,* which denounces the greed of the Spanish colonizers who controlled the region at the time. The *Manifesto of the Mexican*

Key Facts

Time Period:
Early 20th Century

Movement/Issue:
Aesthetics; Socialism; Nationalism

Place of Publication:
Mexico

Language of Publication:
Spanish

MEXICAN MURALIST ICON: DAVID ALFARO SIQUEIROS

David Alfaro Siqueiros was born José de Jesús Alfaro Siqueiros in Mexico City on December 29, 1896. A veteran of the Spanish Civil War as well as the Mexican Revolution, Siqueiros was known for his radical ideals. In 1940 he participated in a failed plot to assassinate Leon Trotsky. He spent several years in the United States and actively participated in the Chicano Moratorium—a coalition of anti-Vietnam War protesters active from 1969 to 1971—contributing several artworks to the movement.

Siqueiros saw his political and aesthetic interests as inextricably intertwined. During his travels throughout Europe in the early twentieth century, he was most influenced by the Italian-based futurist movement, which focused on portrayals of youth, violence, speed, and other aspects of an envisioned future. In addition to painting, Siqueiros wrote many essays and lectures reflecting his commitment to a pan-American vanguard that would combine classical painting techniques with the new artistic values of modernity. Along with Rivera and Orozco, he was commissioned to paint numerous murals on the facades of government buildings. Well-known and influential works by Siqueiros adorn the Edificio del Sindicato Mexicano de Electricistas (*Retrato de la burguesía,* 1939-40); the Palacio de Bellas Artes (*La Nueva Democracia,* 1944-45); the Museo Nacional de Historia (*Del porfirismo a la Revolución,* 1957-66); and the Poliforum Cultural Siqueiros, a building designed by the artist and embellished with his sculpture and the mural *La Marcha de la Humanidad* (1971). Siqueiros died in Cuernavaca, Mexico, in 1974 after battling prostate cancer for several years.

Liberal Party (1911), issued during the Mexican Revolution, and the artists' union's treatise both reaffirm fundamental Communist values, echoing in turn the *Communist Manifesto* (1848) of Karl Marx and Friedrich Engels. It is very likely that Siqueiros was also influenced by the 1906 manifesto of Mexican artist Dr. Atl (Gerardo Murillo), which called for the development of a Mexican national art inspired by ancient indigenous cultures. More substantially, the Mexican artists' statement also closely followed a literary and artistic tradition of important European and Latin American avant-garde manifestoes. These formed the context for, provided models for, and possibly influenced Siqueiros and the other muralists. Two significant European examples are the Italian poet Filippo Tomasso Marinetti's *Futurist Manifesto* (1909) and the Romanian-French poet and performance artist Tristan Tzara's (antimanifesto) *Dada Manifesto* (1918). By 1923 avant-garde groups in other Latin American countries—most notably, Argentina, Chile, Cuba, and Brazil—had produced manifestoes that inspired Siqueiros and his colleagues.

Orozco's *Autobiografía,* published in 1945, criticizes the manifesto's ideals, asserting that many of its tenets were simply not practical because they focused on aesthetic cultural production rather than concrete political and social changes. Vasconcelos's four-volume autobiographical series *Ulises criollo* (1935) and Rivera's *Confesiones de Diego Rivera* (1962) also include critiques of the manifesto. The Chicano Movement's defining 1969 manifesto *Spiritual Plan of Aztlan* followed the artists' union document in associating Mexican indigenous culture with Mexican and Mexican American identity. Today, the *Manifesto of the Union of Mexican Workers, Painters, and Sculptors* is often used to define the values of the Mexican muralist movement.

THEMES AND STYLE

The main theme of the *Manifesto of the Union of Mexican Workers, Painters, and Sculptors* is a call for the socialization of art, especially murals, as a public form of cultural expression. It begins with an appeal to "the indigenous races humiliated through centuries; to the soldiers converted into hangmen by their chiefs; to the workers and peasants who are oppressed by the rich; and to the intellectuals who are not servile to the bourgeoisie." Siqueiros's immediate identification of the issue as one of class struggle, involving several different groups of oppressed people, positions the work squarely in the public realm, which is where the union believed art should be situated.

The artists' manifesto compresses its messages into only 326 words. Employing Marxist rhetoric of class struggle similar to that used in the original *Communist Manifesto,* it achieves a distinct tone through the use of the collective first-person "we," indicating the syndicate, and the second-person "you," which represents the working and underprivileged masses. In order to individualize the message, it speaks specifically to representatives of various sectors; for example, the farmers are told, "We are with those who seek the overthrow of an old and inhuman system within which you, worker of the soil, produce riches for the overseer and politician, while you starve." The phrase "within which you" is repeated several times as workers from different sectors, including factory workers and "Indian soldiers," are addressed. In addition to identifying the union's allies, the manifesto lists its opponents, the presumed "they"—the bourgeoisie, aristocrats, overseers, politicians—creating a binary that reflects the nature of class struggle as understood within Communist ideology.

The manifesto establishes its revolutionary tenor by using such verbs as "overthrow" and "liberate" to incite emotion in its audience. Although its language is formal, the manifesto draws on the common experience of oppression to unify the working classes, the indigenous peoples, and all artists, insisting that the art of Mexico "is great because it surges from the people; it is collective, and our own aesthetic aim is to socialize artistic expression, to destroy bourgeois individualism."

CRITICAL DISCUSSION

The *Manifesto of the Union of Mexican Workers, Painters, and Sculptors* was widely read, and public reaction was extremely positive; readers identified with its revolutionary fervor because most of them had lived through the Mexican Revolution and many had fought in it. Vasconcelos and the rest of the Obregón administration were displeased by the rebellious, clearly oppositional tone of the artists they had been funding. The document's emergence was one of the factors that prompted Vasconcelos's resignation as minister of education in 1924. According to Jean Charlot, a contemporary muralist, Vasconcelos "felt that the painters had gotten out of hand and refused to work in the line of pure art that he had requested. Instead, the painters were lifting the masses with their murals, expressing their political ideas" (paraphrased in Leticia Alvarez's "The Influence of the Mexican Muralists in the United States"). Intellectuals of the period saw the muralist movement and its 1922 manifesto as inextricably linked to, and an extension of, the

Mexican Revolution, praising it exactly for its radical nature and its representation of the working classes.

As the clearest statement of the ideology of the Mexican muralist movement, the manifesto has had a lasting impact on the international art world. The murals and revolutionary ideology that the "Big Three" brought to the United States in particular have been recognized as one of the sources of inspiration for the Chicano Movement of the 1960s, which demanded equality and access to higher education, among other rights. As Antonia Castaneda and her colleagues acknowledge in "A History of Mexican Americans in California: The Chicano Movement" (2004), Chicano "muralism harks back to the tradition of the great Mexican muralists of the post-Revolution era. Mural themes run from dramatizations of the Mexican Revolution to depictions of the Chicano experience." Indeed, in 1932 Siqueiros painted the first public mural in downtown Los Angeles, one of the centers of Chicano activism, although it was quickly whitewashed because its central image

Radical painter David Alfaro Siqueiros, primarily known for his murals, was one of the authors of this manifesto. Pictured is a detail from his mural in the National History Museum in Mexico City, depicting a people's army from the Mexican Revolution. GIANNI DAGLI ORTI/THE ART ARCHIVE AT ART RESOURCE, NY

was a crucified native under the symbol of an eagle. Called *América Tropical,* the mural served as an inspiration for Chicano muralists when it was rediscovered during the 1960s. In the decades since the publication of the manifesto, the document has been studied and reproduced mainly by scholars interested in the Mexican muralist movement, its national and international legacy, and the history of Mexican art in general.

In "Social Realism in Mexico: The Murals of Rivera, Orozco and Siqueiros" (1979-80), the Mexican writer, poet, and diplomat Octavio Paz noted, "The Revolution revealed Mexico to us. Or better, it gave us eyes to see it. And it gave eyes to the painters." Paz and others believe that the manifesto's Communist revolutionary ideology moved beyond the scope of the artists' union, serving also to motivate the mobilization of the working class. Scholars such as Jeffrey Belnap have recognized the combination of European and Mexican influences as a central aspect of the union's manifesto. Additionally, the legacy of the union and the Mexican muralists has been recalled in recent years by both the NeoMexicanist (postmodern Mexican art movement of the new millennium) and Chicano muralist movements, as Mariana Botey discusses in "On Populist Reason and Chicano Modernisms" (2011). In the words of Elissa Rashkin (*The Stridentist Movement in Mexico*; 2009), the *Manifesto of the Union of Mexican Workers, Painters, and Sculptors* is remembered today as "an important vehicle for collective expression and protest [...] based on the idea of art as struggle."

BIBLIOGRAPHY

Sources

Alvarez, Leticia. "The Influence of the Mexican Muralists in the United States. From the New Deal to the Abstract Expressionism." MA thesis, Virginia Polytechnic Institute and State U, 2001. Print.

Belnap, Jeffrey. "Caricaturing the Gringo Tourist: Diego Rivera's *Folkloric and Touristic Mexico* and Miguel Covarrubias's *Sunday Afternoon in Xochimilco.*" *Seeing High & Low: Representing Social Conflict in American Visual Culture.* Ed. Patricia A. Johnston. Berkeley: U. of California P, 2006. Print.

Castaneda, Antonia, et al. "A History of Mexican Americans in California: The Chicano Movement." *History.* ParkNet, National Park Service, 17 Nov. 2004. Web. 21 June 2012.

Cummings, Joe. "Diego, Frida and the Mexican School." *MexConnect Online Magazine.* MexConnect, 1 Jan. 1999. Web. 21 June 2012.

Greeley, Robin Adele. "Painting Mexican Identities: Nationalism and Gender in the Work of Maria Izquierdo." *Oxford Art Journal* 23.1 (2000): 51-72. Print.

Paz, Octavio. "Social Realism in Mexico: The Murals of Rivera, Orozco and Siqueiros." *Artscanada* 36 (1979-80): 56-65. Print.

Rashkin, Elissa. *The Stridentist Movement in Mexico: The Avant-Garde and Cultural Change in the 1920s.* Lanham: Lexington, 2009. Print.

Siqueiros, David Alfaro, et al. "Manifesto of the Union [or Syndicate] of Mexican Workers, Painters, and Sculptors by David Alfaro Siqueiros." Trans. Laurence E. Schmeckebier. *Modern Mexican Art.* By Schmeckebier. Minneapolis: U of Minnesota P, 1939. Print.

Further Reading

Barnitz, Jacqueline. "The Avant-Garde of the 1920s: Cosmopolitan or National Identity?" *Twentieth-Century Art of Latin America.* Austin: U of Texas P, 2001. 42-74. Print.

Botey, Mariana. "On Populist Reason and Chicano Modernisms / Sobre la razón populista y los modernismos chicanos." *Mex/LA: "Mexican" Modernism(s) in Los Angeles, 1930-1985.* Ed. Selene Preciado. Ostfildern: Hatje Cantz, 2011. Print.

Folgarait, Leonard. *Mural Painting and Social Revolution in Mexico, 1920-1940: Art of the New Order.* Cambridge: Cambridge UP, 1998. Print.

Ittmann, John, et al. *Mexico and Modern Printmaking: A Revolution in the Graphic Arts, 1920 to 1950.* Philadelphia: Philadelphia Museum of Art; New Haven: Yale UP, 2006. Print.

Orozco, Jose Clemente. *Autobiografia.* Mexico City: Era, 1945. Print.

Osorio, Nelson. *Manifiestos, proclamas y polémicas de la vanguardia literaria hispanoamericana.* Caracas: Ayacucho, 1988. Print.

Rivera, Diego. *Confesiones de Diego Rivera.* Ed. Luis Suarez. México: Grijalbo, 1962. Print.

Siqueiros, David Alfaro. *Art and Revolution.* Trans. Sylvia Calles. London: Lawrence, 1975. Print.

Schwartz, Jorge. *Las vanguardias latinoamericanas. Textos programáticos y críticos.* Madrid: Cátedra, 1991. Print.

Vasconcelos, José. *Ulises criollo.* Mexico: Botas, 1935. Print.

Katrina White

ON LITERARY REVOLUTION

Chen Duxiu

OVERVIEW

Written and published by Chen Duxiu in 1917, "On Literary Revolution" (*Wenxue Geming Lun*) advocates rejection of the forms and themes of classical Chinese literature as well as a renovation of Chinese intellectual production. The essay appeared in the highly influential journal edited by Chen, *Xin Qingnian,* (*New Youth,* or *La Jeunesse*) and is generally considered one of the foundational works of Chinese modernist literary theory in the period leading up to the May Fourth Movement (1917-21), a cultural and political reform movement that promoted Chinese nationalism. Like other essays in *New Youth,* the piece was addressed to a young and reform-minded urban intelligentsia and argued that national strength and prosperity in the modern period was tied to intellectual openness and innovation. This argument is proposed, however, in the traditional terms of Chinese literary-critical debate.

Initially, the essay did not receive a reaction noticeably stronger than other pieces in *New Youth,* which in early 1917 was still a small (if rapidly growing) periodical. As the journal's readership was largely composed of young students and scholars who had studied abroad, it did not provoke a response from older, more established intellectuals. However, the essay did continue a dialogue with other writers such as Hu Shi, in which extensive theorization of the relationship of modernity to national culture eventually became a main topic of debate across China, especially in the wake of the 1919 May Fourth incident. Today, the essay is recognized as one of the first important theoretical statements of the "New Culture" movement.

HISTORICAL AND LITERARY CONTEXT

"On Literary Revolution" was written during a period when China had just undergone a political revolution—overthrowing the old monarchy and establishing a new government—but it remained seriously weakened due to internal division and imperialist encroachment by the West and Japan. The new government was riven by factionalism to the point of low-grade civil war, and there were de facto splits into regions controlled by local warlords; meanwhile, significant portions of Chinese territory had been ceded to foreign powers, and all were subject to unequal trade treaties that had been agreed to by the former imperial government. Among intellectuals, there was a broad recognition that the millennia-old civilization of China had reached an unprecedented crisis and a consensus that the political, economic, and military chaos was unacceptable and required radical change. However, there was no agreement as to whether or how cultural and educational reform was a necessary component of Chinese modernization.

From the time of its founding in 1915, *New Youth* was one of the strongest voices in favor of a wholesale reworking of traditional Chinese literary culture and the eager adoption of internationalist modernism as a necessary component of Chinese national renovation. Chen Duxiu, the founder of the journal, had received a traditional Confucian education in the late nineteenth century before going on to study in Japan and France; he returned to his native Anhui province to teach high school before moving to Shanghai and founding the journal. Its immediate success and growing influence resulted in Chen's being hired as a faculty member of Peking University in 1917; after relocating to Beijing, the journal became more integrated with the academic elite, and it was soon recognized as the foremost periodical advocating cultural reform.

One of the main planks of cultural reform was use of the vernacular for writing—rather than classical Chinese, which was still the accepted standard for official documents—and Chen encouraged the use of vernacular by contributors to *New Youth.* However, writers were still experimenting with the use of vernacular Chinese for formal prose composition, and Chen's own style in "On Literary Revolution" is noticeably conservative compared with pieces published just a few years later. Perhaps even more importantly, Chen's rhetorical structures and mode of argumentation are deeply influenced by the Chinese literary-critical tradition, even while he argues for abandoning traditionalism. He surveys the course of classical Chinese literary history, arguing that those moments in the tradition most open to innovation were also the most successful.

Following the publication of "On Literary Revolution," the same topic was addressed by several other contributors to *New Youth.* In fact, the scholar Hu Shi, who had just returned to China to teach at

✥ *Key Facts*

Time Period:
Early 20th Century

Movement/Issue:
Chinese modernism; Aesthetics

Place of Publication:
China

Language of Publication:
Chinese

CHEN DUXIU: A FOUNDER OF CHINESE COMMUNISM

Chen Duxiu is primarily remembered today not as the author of "On Literary Revolution" but as one of the founding members of the Chinese Communist Party. Born in 1879 to a family of scholar-officials in Anhui province, Chen was given a traditional Confucian education and passed civil-service exams at the county and provincial levels. However, he became disillusioned with the examination system and enrolled in a more modern and foreign-oriented course of study at a university in Hangzhou in 1898. After graduation, he moved to Japan and then later to France, during which time he first became acquainted with Marxism. Later, while a professor at Peking University, he began to use the journal *New Youth* to promote the study of Marxism, and he jointly founded a study group at the university focused on Marx's works. Together with Li Dazhao, he was one of the two leaders in the official founding of the Chinese Communist Party in Shanghai in 1921; that year, Chen was elected as the national party's first general secretary.

As the leader of the Communist Party, Chen pursued a policy of strategic alliance with the ruling Nationalist Party, but the Nationalists turned on the Communists in 1927, and Chen was ousted first from his leadership position and then from party membership. After supporting a Trotskyite alternative to the Communist Party, he was jailed by the Nationalist government for several years. He died in poverty and obscurity near Chongqing in 1942.

Peking University after earning his PhD under John Dewey at Columbia University in New York City, had already brought up the concept of a "literary reform" prior to Chen's essay. Afterward, Hu continued to write a series of longer essays elaborating on the idea. These and other essays in *New Youth* helped to infuse movements toward political reform with a strongly intellectual and cultural component. Protests against Chinese weakness at the Treaty of Versailles, which ratified Japanese control over formerly German colonies in China, culminated in brief violence on May 4, 1919; the protestors' famous call for "Science and Democracy" is one example of how Chen's and others' calls for a broad cultural renovation had by then deeply influenced the form of Chinese nationalism.

THEMES AND STYLE

The main theme of the essay is that Chinese literature must cast off its elitism, classicism, and eremitism. As Chen explains near the climax of the work, "Aristocratic literature embellishes according to traditional practice and has lost its independence and self-confidence. Classical literature is pompous and pedantic and has lost the principles of expressiveness and realistic description. Eremitic literature is highly obscure and abstruse and is self-satisfied writing that

provides no benefit to the majority of its readers." This general distance from popular usage is the source of numerous problems that are traditionally ascribed to bad literature: overreliance upon hackneyed phrases and worn-out allusions, the falsification of emotions in order to satisfy genre conventions, and weak structures and lack of a driving spirit. These faults spring from literary self-removal from the social world into the world of pure letters; however, it is this removal that paradoxically causes literature to atrophy.

Initially, the essay takes a canny political stance. In the sixth year of chaos after the 1911 revolution (during which there had been two further violent seizures of power, also called "revolutions"), Chen was aware that calls for yet more "revolution" would naturally meet with a skeptical and exhausted intellectual audience. Because of this, he frames the failure of political revolution as due to the insufficient provision of cultural and ideological foundations for revolution: "The greater reason [for the failure of the revolution] is the ethics, morality, and culture, layered in darkness and mired in shameful filth, that have occupied the very core of our people's spirit and have prevented the emergence of revolutions with either bangs or whimpers." In this respect, Chen is foreshadowing the kind of ideological critique that would become stronger in the 1920s, after he helped to found the Chinese Communist Party.

For such a thoroughgoing critique of Chinese tradition (one which several times flat-out declares the inferiority of Chinese to European literature), Chen's essay is remarkably deferent to the rhetorical standards of traditional argumentation. The work is written in a relaxed late-classical style rather than in a true vernacular; it makes a very familiar survey of Chinese literary history, which subtly and selectively adapts a number of traditional judgments on the literature of various eras; and it uses the standard terms of literary critical debate in traditional China, rather than importing the standards of the European literature that it purports to praise. There is relatively little emotion or stylistic exuberance compared to some of the other pieces published in *New Youth*. On the contrary, even though it was initially read mostly by the reform minded, it employs a style that seems (like its political contextualization) calculated to reassure cultural conservatives.

CRITICAL DISCUSSION

"On Literary Revolution" has always been less important and influential as a single stand-alone essay than as a primary example of several related works calling for intellectual reform in the pages of *New Youth*. Hence, the most important immediate "reaction" to the essay is the series of complementary contemporary essays on literary revolution by Hu Shi, also appearing in *New Youth*. In general, Hu arrives at the same conclusions as Chen: Chinese literature is failing because it is stuck in a classical idiom that is divorced from modernity and inaccessible to the masses. However, there are deeper ideological divisions between Hu and Chen: unlike Chen, who had already developed an affinity for leftist thought, Hu was an American-style pragmatist who rejected ideology in favor of empiricism. Hence, while Chen's essay argues for literary revolution as an ideological foundation for effective political revolution, Hu sees literary revolution as primarily important for enabling intellectual culture to deal effectively with the actualities of modern life and to enable continual adaptation.

Through the immediate aftermath of the May Fourth Incident in 1919, these tensions were relatively subdued; in the early 1920s there was a fair amount of consensus among young intellectuals that literary reform was an immediate need, regardless of where it led. However, after Chen assisted in the establishment of the Communist Party in 1921, he and other leftists began to place more emphasis on the need for literary reform to be directed toward explicitly ideological ends. Chen himself was not a major participant in this debate; the seminal leftist position was articulated by Cheng Fangwu in his 1928 essay "From Literary Revolution to Revolutionary Literature." As Chen himself had lost his position in the party by then, "On Literary Revolution" was generally dismissed together with Hu Shi's works and grew less influential in mainland China following the communist victory. On Taiwan, where Hu Shi continued to play a major role in the intellectual life of the Republic of China after 1949, his own essays on literary revolution became canonical, while Chen's essay was largely marginalized.

There has been much valuable English-language scholarship on the May Fourth period in general. However, the only recent scholarship to discuss "On Literary Revolution" in particular has been in Chinese. In general, whether in English or Chinese, the general trend of recent scholarship of Chinese modernism has been to downplay the novelty of manifestos such as Chen's and to emphasize the ways in which literature and criticism of the late Qing period prepared the way for modernism to emerge.

BIBLIOGRAPHY

Sources

Benton, Gregor. "Chen Duxiu, 1879-1942." *Encyclopedia of Modern China*. Vol. 1. Ed. David Pong. Detroit: Cengage Learning, 2009. 197-199. Print.

Chen, Duxiu. "On Literary Revolution." Trans. Timothy Wong. *Modern Chinese Literary Thought: Writings on Literature, 1893-1945*. Stanford: Stanford UP, 1996. 140-45. Print.

Chen, Duxiu. "Wenxue Geming Lun." *Chen Duxiu Wenzhang Xuanbian*. Beijing: Sanlian, 1984. Print.

Cheng, Fangwu. "From a Literary Revolution to Revolutionary Literature." Trans. Michael Gotz. *Modern Chinese Literary Thought: Writings on Literature, 1893-1945*. Stanford: Stanford UP, 1996. 269-75. Print.

Qiao, Guoqiang, and Yuqin Jiang. "Faguo Qimeng Sixiang yu Chen Duxiu de Wenxue Guan." *Zhongguo Xiandai Wenxue Yanjiu Congkan* 3 (2005): 217-28. *China Academic Journals Full-Text Database*. Web. 8 Oct. 2012.

Tang, Xiaolin. "Zhongguo Xiandai Wenxueshi Xushu de Zhishixing Weiji—'Wenxue Geming Lun' zhi Geming Huayu Kaolun." *Shehui Kexue Yanjiu* 3 (2005): 164-70. *China Academic Journals Full-Text Database*. Web. 8 Oct. 2012.

Wang, Guimei. "Chen Duxiu Wusi Wenxue Geming Lun Neihan Pouxi." *Wenxue Lilun Yanjiu* 1 (2002): 45-51. *China Academic Journals Full-Text Database*. Web. 8 Oct. 2012.

Further Reading

Chen, Jianhua. "Revolution: From Literary Revolution to Revolutionary Literature." *Words and Their Stories: Essays on the Language of the Chinese Revolution*. Ed. Ban Wang. Leiden: Brill, 2011. Print.

Chen, Pingyuan. *Touches of History: An Entry into "May Fourth" China*. Trans. Michel Hockx, et al. Leiden: Brill, 2011. Print.

Feigon, Lee. *Chen Duxiu: Founder of the Communist Party*. Princeton: Princeton UP, 1983. Print.

Furth, Charlotte. "Intellectual Change: From the Reform Movement to the May Fourth Movement, 1895-1920." *Cambridge History of China, Volume 12: Republican China 1912-1949, Part 1*. Ed. John K. Fairbank. Cambridge UP, 1983. 322-405. Print.

Schwarcz, Vera. *The Chinese Enlightenment: Intellectuals and the Legacy of the May Fourth Movement of 1919*. Berkeley: U of California P, 1986. Print.

Wang, David Der-Wei. "Chinese Literature from 1841 to 1937." *The Cambridge History of Chinese Literature, Volume 2: From 1375*. Ed. Kang-I Sun Chang. Cambridge UP, 2010. 413-564. Print.

Weston, Timothy B. "The Formation and Positioning of the New Culture Community, 1913-1917." *Modern China* July 1998: 255-84. *JSTOR*. Web. 8 Oct. 2012.

Daniel Fried

Chen Duxiu was a leading figure of the May Fourth Movement, a Chinese political, intellectual, and cultural movement that began on May 4, 1919. This plaque in Beijing commemorates the movement. © IDS PHOTOGRAPHY/ALAMY

OUR AMERICA

Waldo Frank

✢ *Key Facts*

Time Period:
Early 20th Century

Movement/Issue:
Utilitarianism;
Freudianism;
Avant-gardism

Place of Publication:
United States

**Language of
Publication:**
English

OVERVIEW

Novelist and social historian Waldo Frank's *Our America,* published in November 1919, is a cultural manifesto decrying the loss of spiritual values and social cohesion to industrial progress, a centuries-old devotion to a materialist ethos that has left the United States bereft of "wholeness." According to critic Casey Blake in his biography of Frank, "In the best jeremiad tradition, *Our America* combined a scathing indictment of the moral shallowness of modern American life with a call to retrieve and revive the religious and democratic impulses frustrated by American capitalism." An alternative history to prevailing foundation myths that glorify the American pioneering spirit and rugged individualism, *Our America* is distinguished by Frank's mysticism, which was central to his vision of the United States as an organic community, as well as by his positioning of a young generation of writers and artists as the heralds of the country's renaissance.

Our America resonated with the new generation to whom it was addressed—Frank's contemporaries who shared his disillusionment with the fragmentation of modern culture and the evils of industrialization, made all the more apparent by the horrifying consequences of the mechanized combat of World War I. *Our America* went through three editions in six months and made Frank the leading voice of New York's intellectual avant-garde. In 1929 he published a sequel, titled *The Re-discovery of America,* which placed even greater emphasis on the religious and populist dimensions of American life. By the time this work appeared, however, Frank's vision for an integrated United States had already lost favor in a more racially and ethnically divided climate that had been given added momentum by government immigration quotas. Although his ideas of cultural pluralism, espoused in his social criticism as well as in a series of novels, were popular in Latin America in later decades, Frank was virtually unknown to U.S. audiences at the time of his death in 1967.

HISTORICAL AND LITERARY CONTEXT

Our America revealed Frank to be profoundly pessimistic about the progress of American civilization but hopeful for its future. He charted a course of utilitarianism from the time of the original colonists, whose struggle for survival had dulled their spiritual senses:

"[Every] narrowing instinct of self-preservation and acquisition tended to make them intolerant, materialist, unaesthetic." The decay characterized the settlement of the Western frontier as well, relieved only by Native American and Mexican cultures, which, though doomed to extinction, had once existed in spiritual harmony with the universe. Frank called on his contemporaries to expand the base of the national character to include subdued cultures and cited his own Jewish heritage, repressed by his assimilationist parents, as the source of his deep mysticism. *Our America* ends on a note of optimism, entrusting a new breed of writers and artists with recovering the country's dynamic and life-giving spiritual forces: "In a dying world, creation is revolution."

Our America calls on like-minded intellectuals to reject the stodgy New England legacy of commercialism and pragmatism that has infected American middle-class life. Frank's appeal struck a chord with members of his generation eager to participate in the "revolt against the academies and institutions which would whittle America down to a few stale realities current fifty years ago … that organized anarchy today expressed in Industrialism which would deny to America any life—hence any unity at all—beyond the ties of traffic and the arteries of trade." In addition, as a dissection of the American collective consciousness, *Our America* benefited from the emerging interest in Freudian theory at the time and was even marketed by its publisher, Boni & Liveright, as a psychoanalytic treatment of the various geographic regions of the country.

The origins of *Our America* can be traced to Frank's appreciation for the coalescence of art and revolution in French culture. He introduced these ideas to American readers through his essays and reviews in *Seven Arts,* a journal that, though short-lived (1916-17), formed the principal outlet for the radical synthesis of politics, religion, and art that Frank and his coeditors, James Oppenheim and Van Wyck Brooks, had made fashionable among New York intellectuals even prior to the appearance of *Our America.* Frank followed *Our America* in the 1920s with a series of what he called "lyric novels," which were fictional embodiments of the thesis of *Our America* featuring characters in search of mystical union with the cosmos. Neither these nor his later social criticism, much of which looked to the preindustrial societies of Latin America and Spain as models of cultural organicism, generated the enthusiasm sparked by *Our America*. However, Frank remained well known to American radicals in the 1930s through his socialist political agitation and regular contributions to the progressive journal the *New Republic*.

Our America gradually fell into obscurity amid complaints that Frank's subsequent output was mystically charged to the point of incomprehensibility, written in an obtuse style that Edmund Wilson, as quoted in Blake's work, characterized as a mingling of "James Joyce with the Hebrew prophets." The legacy of *Our America* in the twenty-first century rests mainly on what it reveals about the intensity of the disillusionment among liberal intellectuals of the time, some of whom seized upon its words for inspiration and went on to achieve lasting literary fame, notably the poets Hart Crane and Jean Toomer.

THEMES AND STYLE
According to Paul J. Carter in his 1967 biography of Frank, "The quest for consciousness gives [*Our America*] its unifying theme; the object of the quest is a richer, fuller life, one which will embrace all experience and at the same time bring man an awareness of his link with the cosmos." For Frank, the key to realizing this wholeness of experience is the recovery of spiritual awareness. In an approach that is both historical and geographic, he describes an accumulation of social and economic forces that have made the United States a sterile and materialistic culture devoted to industrialization and commercial progress. American studies scholar Ned Paynter explains the theme of *Our America* in his dissertation "American Writers and the Machine Age": "America, Frank thought, had been bewitched by the machine, and was in thralldom to the many forms of self-delusion which result from such idolatry: the lie of the conquest of nature, the lie of success, the lie of pragmatism, of progress, and of the self-sufficiency of the isolated ego."

Frank's strategy in *Our America* is twofold: to illustrate both the failure of the United States and the promise of its future. The book is a type of cultural geography that summarizes key regions of the country on the basis of its artists and political leaders. Frank enlists these examples, good and bad, in his project to reconcile the American ideal of self-sufficiency with the democratic ideal of community. In this task he claims as his master literary writer Walt Whitman, whose poem "Starting from Paumanok" forms an epigraph to the volume: "I say that the real and permanent grandeur of These States must be their religion." Frank praises the nineteenth-century transcendentalists for their flight from materialism and finds the same creative spiritual values among certain members of his own generation: from Chicago, writers Carl Sandburg and Sherwood Anderson; from New England, writers Robert Frost and Amy Lowell;

POLITICAL AGITATION

Waldo Frank's literary campaign against capitalist excess drew him into leftist politics in the 1930s. Though he rejected orthodox Marxism for its contempt of religion, he nonetheless allied himself with the Communist Party of America and traveled and lectured with the League of American Writers on its behalf. In 1935 he represented the league at a Paris congress of antifascist and communist intellectuals. Frank wrote articles for the American leftist publications *New Masses* and the *Daily Worker*, and he supported the Bonus Marchers, veterans who descended on Washington, D.C., in 1932 demanding full payment for their service in World War I. That same year he headed the relief effort for striking miners in Harlan County, Kentucky. The mine owners threatened the lives of Frank and his companions, local deputies overturned their truckloads of food, and Frank and lawyer Allan Taub were badly beaten by a mob.

Frank officially broke with the Communist Party of America in the late 1930s in protest over the purges of Joseph Stalin, general secretary of the Communist Party of the Soviet Union. Frank was himself denounced at the time as a Trotskyite by Earl Browder, secretary of the Communist Party of America.

and from New York, several Jewish artists whose works embody the mystical unifying vision of Whitman's poetry, including the photographer Alfred Stieglitz, composer Leo Ornstein, and poet James Oppenheim.

The language of *Our America* is alternately ominous and idealistic. It is dense with poetic prose describing the fading beauty of the vast American landscape and seeks to capture in this grandeur some idea of the magnitude of the creative revolution that will be necessary to secure the transcendence of the United States. Frank entrusts his generation, the first "spiritual pioneers," with the heady task of reversing the country's downward spiral. Paynter notes, "In being drawn to so large and even grandiose a theme, Frank was, of course, hardly alone among American writers. His concern with an American destiny conceived in these terms unites him most obviously with Whitman … but it also places him in the company of a long line of writers in the American prophetic tradition."

CRITICAL DISCUSSION
Our America enjoyed breakthrough success upon its first appearance. Applauded in the contemporary press—Gilbert Cannan of the *New York Times* called it "a modern miracle, a Mystery of America"—it was embraced by the intellectual avant-garde. As biographer Carter noted, it arrived "at just the right time to attract the various postwar groups concerned with

new ideas in opposition to the stereotyped thinking of the so-called 'practical men' of a materialistic society." Among the fledgling writers *Our America* inspired was Gorham Munson, who went on to become a well-known literary critic and one of the academics early associated with New York's New School for Social Research (now New School University). Munson wrote of *Our America* in his 1985 book *The Awakening Twenties*: "The book dazzled my immediate generation…. We were then two or three years out of college and more recently out of military service…. We felt obstructed by puritanism in expression of our vision and interpretation of life…. Waldo Frank came swiftly to proclaim promise and dream."

Frank never achieved the dominance as a cultural critic that *Our America* seemed to predict. Blake discusses the subsequent neglect of the book in terms of the "cultural limbo" that its author occupied as his career progressed: "Too radical for his apolitical or conservative countrymen, too religious for liberals and radicals, and ultimately too strong-willed a personality for most people who had contact with him." Yet Frank established important mentoring relationships as a result of the publication of *Our America*. In addition, Carter points out the book's importance "as an introduction to the religious and esthetic principles which appear throughout Frank's subsequent writing, especially in his cultural studies."

Assessments of the legacy of *Our America* generally focus on its philosophy of cultural pluralism. Onita Estes-Hicks writes in the article "Jean Toomer and the Politics and Poetics of National Identity":

> The moderns—heralded by Van Wyck Brooks, Randolph Bourne, and Waldo Frank—called for a 'deprovincialization of the arts' and for a literature which reflected a more inclusive national character. The younger generation of writers, spurred on by the heavy waves of immigration which changed the face of America, succeeded in moving American letters from its New England base, making way for the depiction of other regions and other cultures.

But almost as soon as *Our America* was published, its call for diversity and an end to cultural elitism began to lose sway to the anti-immigration fervor of the 1920s. For this reason, in his book Our America: *Nativism, Modernism, and Pluralism* (2002), literary theorist Walter Benn Michaels describes *Our America* as "oddly transitional": "the model of the America it proclaims as struggling to be born was dying, the model it describes as dead was being reborn." Still, the valorization of buried cultures in *Our America* is known to have had a profound effect on the work of poet Crane and Harlem Renaissance luminary Toomer. Critics have written at length on Toomer's identification, as an African American, with Frank's protest against the degradation of Jews in *Our America,* especially as it is revealed in Toomer's novel *Cane.* Crane was moved by Frank's notion of organicism. In a letter dated February 27, 1923, and quoted by Adam Kirsch in the article "The Mystic Word," Crane wrote to Frank: "I am certain that a number of us at least have some kind of community of interest. And with this communion will come something better than a mere clique.... It is vision, and a vision alone that not only America needs, but the whole world."

BIBLIOGRAPHY

Sources

Blake, Casey. "Waldo (David) Frank." *Modern American Critics, 1920-1955.* Ed. Gregory S. Jay. *Dictionary of Literary Biography.* Vol. 63. Detroit: Gale, 1988. Literature Resource Center. Web. 8 Sept. 2012.

Carter, Paul J. *Waldo Frank.* New York: Twayne, 1967. Print.

Estes-Hicks, Onita. "Jean Toomer and the Politics and Poetics of National Identity." *Analysis and Assessment, 1980-1994.* Vol. 2. Ed. Cary D. Wintz. New York: Garland, 1996. 298-320. Print.

Frank, Waldo. *Our America.* New York: Boni & Liveright, 1919. Print.

Kirsch, Adam. "The Mystic Word." *New Yorker.* Condé Nast, 9 Oct. 2006. Web. 9 Sept. 2012.

Michaels, Walter Benn. *Our America: Nativism, Modernism, and Pluralism.* Durham, NC: Duke UP, 2002. 135-42. Print.

Munson, Gorham B. *The Awakening Twenties.* Baton Rouge: Louisiana State P, 1985. Print.

Paynter, Ned. "American Writers and the Machine Age." Diss. U of California Berkeley, n.d. Print.

"Waldo Frank." *The House of Boni & Liveright, 1917-1933, A Documentary Volume.* Ed. Charles Egleston. *Dictionary of Literary Biography.* Vol. 288. Detroit: Gale, 2004. *Dictionary of Literary Biography Complete Online.* Web. 7 Sept. 2012.

Further Reading

Bittner, William. "*Our America.*" *The Novels of Waldo Frank.* Philadelphia: U of Pennsylvania P, 1958. 56-60. Print.

Blake, Casey Nelson. *Beloved Community: The Cultural Criticism of Randolph Bourne, Van Wyck Brooks, Waldo Frank, and Lewis Mumford.* Chapel Hill: U of North Carolina P, 1990. Print.

Frank, Waldo. *The Re-discovery of America: An Introduction to a Philosophy of American Life.* New York: Scribner's, 1929. Print.

———. *Memoirs of Waldo Frank.* Ed. Alan Trachtenberg. Amherst: U of Massachusetts P, 1973. Print.

Munson, Gorham. *Waldo Frank.* New York: Boni & Liveright, 1923. Print.

Terris, Daniel Stern. *Waldo Frank and the Rediscovery of America, 1889-1929.* Cambridge: Harvard UP, 1992. Print.

Yellin, Michael. "Visions of Their America: Waldo Frank's Jewish Modernist Influence on Jean Toomer's 'Fern.'" *African American Review* 43.2-3 (2009): 427-42. Print.

Janet Mullane

POETISM MANIFESTO

Karel Teige

✧ *Key Facts*

Time Period:
Early/Mid-20th Century

Movement/Issue:
Avant-gardism

Place of Publication:
Czechoslovakia (Czech
Republic)

**Language of
Publication:**
Czech

OVERVIEW

Authored by Karel Teige, central theoretician of the Czech avant-garde movement Devĕtsil, the *Poetism Manifesto* (1928; originally published in a shorter version in 1924 as *Poetism*) rejects formal approaches to poetry represented by art's dominant "isms" and advocates for a new art—a fusion of poetry and life. The *Poetism Manifesto* was published as Czech president Tomáš Masaryk's First Republic began to take hold in the city of Prague; young intellectuals were able to draw upon international influences from within a newly independent Czechoslovakia, free from Austrian influence, and were able to infuse their work with the positive, capricious spirit of poetism. At the time of the manifesto's publication, the Czech avant-garde was splitting into factions. Teige and members of Devĕtsil criticized the ideological orientation of other radicals and their proletariat project and called, instead, for a more spontaneous, international, and inclusive art. The *Poetism Manifesto* is directed at both artists holding traditional views of art and those using art to promote an ideological platform. It asks artists to move beyond the institution of art, to conceive of poetry as a style of living, and to create from a sense of playfulness and cheer.

Conservative critics reacted negatively to the publication of the *Poetism Manifesto,* rejecting the poetists as trifling, unserious, and antinationalistic. More critically, the manifesto deepened the rift between poetists and other young, proletariat radicals. Many politically oriented artists saw the poetists as having abandoned the communist project of social commitment. Eventually, Devĕtsil considered itself the most left wing and the only truly modern faction of the avant-garde movement. The *Poetism Manifesto* presents the definitive definition of poetism, which has come to define the Czech avant-garde of the 1920s and marks a radical departure from Czech literary tradition.

HISTORICAL AND LITERARY CONTEXT

The *Poetism Manifesto* urges the artist to break free of art's various institutions, to regain the sensuousness of the word, and to conceive of poetry as a life philosophy rather than a form. At the end of World War I, six years before the manifesto's publication, Czechoslovakia had become an independent state, and the end of Austro-Hungarian occupation brought the optimism of a new era. Previously isolated from many outside influences, Czech artists and writers found themselves able to access literature and art from Western Europe, the United States, and postrevolutionary Russia. Members of Devĕtsil, including Teige, began traveling, and they came into contact with the Paris avant-garde. Czech poets, such as future Nobel Prize winner Jaroslav Seifert, drawing upon Dadaism, Italian futurism, and the beginnings of surrealism, moved away from politically oriented art toward a poetry of sensuousness and synthesis. The Devĕtsil avant-garde had as its project the liberation of art from formal, political use. Thus poetism was born, set to supplement constructivism—a movement promoting the process of constructing art, which was fueled by Utopian beliefs in science, reason, and progress.

Although Devĕtsil and the Czech avant-garde established themselves as proletariat and communist artists, by the time the *Poetism Manifesto* was published, members of the group had come to feel that proletariat art belonged to the bourgeois and that true revolution would require the destruction of the barrier between highbrow and lowbrow art. Poetists, after all, believed that individuals had their own needs beyond that of the masses. The first of the Devĕtsil poets to express discomfort with the group's proletariat orientation was Vítězslav Nezval, who felt that revolution should be individual and instinctive. Nezval, Teige, Seifert, and Jiří Voskovec, a theater and film actor, are all mentioned as collaborators in the text of the *Poetism Manifesto.* With the publication of the manifesto, Czech literature was able to incorporate a new orientation, one more international and less action-driven. The manifesto's insistence on art as life and interdisciplinary practice paved the way for the Czechoslovak Surrealist Group and the Czech New Wave.

Over the years, Teige and the Devĕtsil movement authored a number of manifestos outlining the artistic project of the Czech avant-garde. In 1920 Teige and fourteen other artists signed the first declaration made by the Devĕtsil Art Association, with none of the signatories claiming leadership. Teige later emerged as the leading theorist of the group, publishing manifestos and essays in various literary magazines such as *Host, Pásmo,* and *ReD,* which served as vehicles essential to the dissemination of the Devĕtsil project.

The *Poetism Manifesto*'s preoccupation with the senses recalls nineteenth-century French poets, such as Arthur Rimbaud and Charles Baudelaire, romantic poets who had worked to liberate poetry from its form in order to achieve sensual power. In seeking to revolutionize poetry into life, the manifesto set Czech literature toward modernism.

Following the publication of the *Poetism Manifesto*, Czech literature underwent some changes. Proletariat writers such as Jiří Wolker lost their popularity, Dadaism and Italian futurism gained stronger footholds, and members of Devětsil published subsequent theories on poetry and art influenced by these movements. In 1930, as surrealism took hold in Czechoslovakia, a Czech journal entitled *Zvěrokruh* published French writer Andre Breton's *Second Surrealist Manifesto* (1929). Subsequently, the Italian futurist Filippo Marinetti published *The Futurist Cookbook* (1932), part poetry anthology, cookbook, and political manifesto. Essential to the early modernist movement was an outline of the intended poetic project, even if such a project eschewed definition. Modern literature in general owes much to the poetist's manipulation of form and tradition.

THEMES AND STYLE

The central theme of the *Poetism Manifesto* is the necessity of abandoning the institutions of art. It advocates for a more casual, spontaneous relationship with art that goes outside the bounds of constructivism. The manifesto asserts: "Professionalism in art cannot continue. If the new art, and that which we shall call poetism, is an art of life, and art of living and enjoying, it must become, eventually, a natural part of everyday life, as delightful and accessible as sport, love, wine, and all manner of other delectations." In order to achieve this new art, the manifesto calls for the artist to experience life as poetry, to look for art in the "the refreshing greenery of parks, in the bustle of seaports." It introduces the concept of poetism as free from philosophy or denomination and speaks of poetry as the "animating heart" of life.

The manifesto works to persuade its audience through its use of broad, inclusive statements about the nature of art. It achieves its project of freeing art from a derived, constructivist format by finding art in the everyday scenes of life. The reader is able to feel like a poet, as "the modern poets are clowns, dancers, acrobats, and tourists." The manifesto then reminds the reader that "socialism means that the world should be controlled by reason and wisdom," but that "reason would cease to be wise if it were to suppress the domain of sensibility in the process of its rule over the world." The reader, awash in ideology in postwar Czechoslovakia, is then reassured that "it is here that poetism intervenes and comes to the rescue of our emotional life, our joy, and our imagination." In distancing itself from the tension of a wrought political climate, the *Poetism Manifesto* persuades by its insistence on humor, play, and sense.

KAREL TEIGE: IN PURSUIT OF *ARS UNA*

The author of the *Poetism Manifesto*, Karel Teige (1900-51), was an architectural theorist, typographer, graphic artist, and photographer. As a member of the Czech avant-garde, he was a proponent of modernism who helped pave the way for a new age in Czech art and literature. He was a member of the Czech avant-garde group Devětsil, editing and contributing to its literary magazine, *ReD (Revue Devětsilu)*. Teige worked to bring the international arts community to Prague, sponsoring exhibitions that drew artists such as American photographer Man Ray and Swiss painter Paul Klee to Czechoslovakia. He believed in an *ars una*, an art free of constraint and definition. Driven by this belief, Teige promoted inter-media art forms and worked across genres himself.

As a progressive, Teige welcomed the Soviet army's invasion, but after communism took hold of Czechoslovakia in 1948, he was silenced by the Communist Party and forbidden to publish. He died of a heart attack in 1951 following a Soviet press campaign that was leveled against him. Teige's work was recovered after the nationwide protests of the Velvet Revolution of 1989, and his work has regained popularity in Europe and the United States.

Teige maintains a poetic style in the *Poetism Manifesto*. Although it borrows some tone and language from the political arena, the *Poetism Manifesto* often gives way to bright and surprising imagery. Teige says that authors mentioned in the manifesto "wish to savor all the fruits of poetry, cut loose from a literature destined for the scrap heap, a poetry of Sunday afternoons, picnics, luminous cafés, intoxicating cocktails, lively boulevards, spa promenades, but also the poetry of silence, night, quiet, and peace." The language itself accomplishes the project of delivering art from seriousness. In addition, the manifesto makes use of repetition to deliver its message. For example, Teige writes that "Poetism is not literature," "Poetism is not painting," and, finally, "Poetism is not an -ism." Contained within the language itself is the radical contradiction of the poetist project and its break with Czech literary tradition.

CRITICAL DISCUSSION

Following its publication, the *Poetism Manifesto* was dismissed by some literary critics in Czechoslovakia since it called for a break from orthodox ideologies. Alfred French, in his book *The Poets of Prague* (1969), notes that "conservative critics received the challenge with sarcasm and contempt, branding the poetists as café idlers playing at revolution, and dubbing them a disgrace to Czech literature." Poetism's other target, the proletariat faction of the avant-garde, also reacted negatively to the manifesto. As French states, poets

A 1936 photograph of Jaroslav Seifert, a friend of Karel Teige and one of the founding members of Devětsil and poetism. Seifert would later win the 1984 Nobel Prize for Literature. © CTK/ALAMY

century criticism examines the *Poetism Manifesto*'s legacy in regard to the Central European avant-garde, iconicity, and its relationship to symbolists and semiotics.

Much of the scholarship discussing the *Poetism Manifesto* focuses on its significance to the development of the Czech avant-garde in its move away from formalism and toward modernism. Teige scholar Peter Zusi focuses on poetism's relation to functionalism and movement toward modernism in his essay "Tendentious Modernism: Karel Teige's Path to Functionalism" (2008), in which he states,

> Karel Teige's theoretical texts on constructivism, for example, represent an important point of contact between Prague structuralism and Czech modernist architecture or the avant-garde in general. Clearly, this emphasis on function is not unique to the Czech avant-garde and to a large extent reflects modernist trends developing elsewhere, particularly in France, Germany, Holland, and (somewhat later) the Soviet Union.

Critical scholarship mentioning the impact of the *Poetism Manifesto* also points to its importance in discussion of semiotics. Malynne M. Sternstein, in her essay "Sensuous Iconicity: The Manifestoes and Tactics of Czech Poetism" (1998), asserts that the poetist's interest in reendowing the word with sense meant

> not only freeing it from servitude to alternate (arguably "communicative") purposes by rendering it autotelic, but also liberating it from dependence on any other definition to substantiate its being; that is, the word is set truly free by making its being its own. An attempt was made to establish what might be called the word as thing—a semiotic revolution to rival the social revolutions consuming Europe at the time.

Sternstein understands the *Poetism Manifesto* to mirror and complement the political and linguistic environment in which it was published.

"who clung to the Proletarian conception of socially committed literature … regarded the poetists as deserters from the truth path of Communist art." The publication of the manifesto caused some members of the avant-garde, such as S. K. Neumann, to adopt more extreme positions. Ultimately, the *Poetism Manifesto* served to further split the already divided Czech avant-garde.

The *Poetism Manifesto* paved the way for a new Czech literature, the incorporation of the influence of Dadaism, futurism, and, eventually, surrealism into Czech art, and the rise of discourse surrounding the project of poetics. Although Lenka Bydžovská's essay in *Karel Teige, 1900-1951* (1999) states that "the spring of 1927 saw a rise in the Czech press of a fairly forceful critical wave disclaiming Karel Teige and Vítězslav Nezval's poetism as obsolescent and exhausted," the poetists persisted in their project, eventually creating successful art that was "free of their earlier dependence on foreign avant-garde models." In *Central European Avant-Gardes* (2002), Bydžovská demonstrates the internationalizing influence of the new avant-gardes, writing that the group "organized the Bazar moderniho umeni [Bazaar of Modern Art], promoting a new perception of the world." The poetist project proved its expansive nature, as the bazaar featured "a broad architectural section, documented theater activity, and exhibited compositions of 'colored music' (watercolors whose color relationships could be interpreted analogously with musical notes), photograms, pictorial poetry, photomontage, and book graphics." Twenty-first-

BIBLIOGRAPHY

Sources

Bydžovská, Lenka. "The Avant-Garde Ideal of Poiĕsis: Poetism and Artificialism during the Late 1920s." Trans. Karolina Vočadlo. *Karel Teige, 1900-1951: L'Enfant Terrible of the Czech Modern Avant-Garde.* Eds. Eric Dluhosch and Švácha Rostislav. Massachusetts: MIT, 1999. 46-63. Print.

———. "Prague." *Central European Avant-Gardes: Exchange and Transformation, 1910-1930.* Ed. Timothy Benson. Los Angeles: MIT, 2002. 81-89. Print.

French, Alfred. *The Poets of Prague: Czech Poetry between the Wars.* London: Oxford UP, 1969. Print.

Sternstein, Malynne M. "Sensuous Iconicity: The Manifestoes and Tactics of Czech Poetism." *Mosaic* 31.2 (1998): 77-100. *ProQuest.* Web. 26 July 2012.

Teige, Karel. "Poetism." Trans. Alexandra Büchler. *Karel Teige, 1900-1951: L'Enfant Terrible of the Czech Modern Avant-Garde.* Eds. Eric Dluhosch and Švácha Rostislav. Massachusetts: MIT, 1999. 64-71. Print.

Zusi, Peter. "Tendentious Modernism: Karel Teige's Path to Functionalism." *Slavic Review* 67.4 (2008): 821-39. *JSTOR.* Web. 26 July 2012.

Further Reading

Benson, Timothy, ed. *Between Worlds: A Sourcebook of Central European Avant-Gardes, 1910-1930.* Los Angeles: MIT, 2002. Print.

Bojtár, Endre. *East European Avant-Garde Literature.* Trans. Pál Várnai. Budapest: Akadémiai Kiadó, 1992. Print.

Di Mauro, Laurie. "Czechoslovakian Literature." *Twentieth-Century Literary Criticism* 42. Detroit: Gale, 1991. 103-96. Print.

Levinger, Esther. "Karel Teige on Cinema and Utopia." *Slavic and East European Journal* 48.2 (2004): 247-74. *JSTOR.* Web. 26 July 2012.

Zusi, Peter. "The Style of the Present: Karel Teige on Constructivism and Poetism." *Representations* 88.1 (2004): 102-24. *JSTOR.* Web. 26 July 2012.

Kristen Gleason

PROLETARIAN REALISM

Mike Gold

✢ *Key Facts*

Time Period:
Mid-20th Century

Movement/Issue:
Communism; Aesthetics

Place of Publication:
United States

**Language of
Publication:**
English

OVERVIEW

Written by Mike Gold, "Proletarian Realism" (1930) decries the sentimentalities of bourgeois literature and calls for a new movement that portrays the worker's experience. The essay was published in *The New Masses,* a leftist magazine that Gold cofounded in 1926. As its publication in *The New Masses* suggests, the work's focus is on working-class artists and writers. Addressed simply to "the Workers," it demands that proletarian writers create a type of literature that serves a social function: to portray the suffering of the hungry and the persecuted, as opposed to the "silly little agonies" of the bourgeois.

Whereas Gold's autobiographical novel *Jews without Money* (1930) garnered critical interest and considerable sales following its appearance, "Proletarian Realism," published in a magazine with a circulation of only 25,000, received little attention. Nevertheless, it helped to articulate the theoretical concerns of a burgeoning literary movement: proletarian realism, whose aesthetic was typified by Gold's novel, as well as by works by writers as diverse as Jack Conroy, Agnes Smedley, Josephine Herbst, James T. Farrell, and others. Along with providing prescriptions for content, the essay dictates stylistic and formal constraints for proletarian realist texts. Today, "Proletarian Realism" is viewed as an important document in the emergence of the mid-twentieth-century literary left.

HISTORICAL AND LITERARY CONTEXT

"Proletarian Realism" responds to the state of literature and politics in the late 1920s, when high modernism was ascendant and a radical political left had formed in the United States. Although it is not possible to posit an exact date for the birth of literary modernism, the 1920s saw the publication of numerous modernist texts that embrace formal experimentation, including James Joyce's *Ulysses* (1922), T. S. Eliot's *The Waste Land* (1922), and Virginia Woolf's *Mrs. Dalloway* (1925). On the American political scene, the Socialist Party was formed in 1902, nearly three decades prior to the publication of "Proletarian Realism." Furthermore, according to scholar Erin Jean Sagerson in "Art and Bread: Mike Gold, Proletarian Art, and the Rhetoric of American Communism, 1921-41" (2009), the success of the

Bolshevik Revolution of 1917 and a series of leftist revolts in Europe in 1918 and 1919 caused American radicals to feel "confident that revolutionary fever would spread to America."

By the time "Proletarian Realism" was published in 1930, the United States was entering the Great Depression. The hardships brought on by the depression reinvigorated a variety of leftist revolutionary movements, which viewed the economic collapse as a sign that capitalism was in decline. Meanwhile, *The New Masses* was under the direction of Walt Carmon, who wanted to publish a piece of Marxist criticism in the magazine. When "Proletarian Realism" appeared, it provided a critical foundation for proletarian writers seeking a literature of and for the working class. In fact, proletarian literature, the aesthetic that the essay helped to engender, would remain an important literary movement until the beginning of World War II.

"Proletarian Realism" draws on a wide array of political writing, including *The Communist Manifesto* (1848) by Karl Marx and Friedrich Engels, which analyzes the class struggle between the exploited proletariat and the landowning bourgeois. *The Communist Manifesto* contends that the contradictions of capitalism are so fundamental that the system contains the seeds of its own destruction. Gold was also influenced by more-contemporary political writers, such as Max Eastman, whose pieces in the magazine *The Masses* (not to be confused with *The New Masses*) were among the first radical essays that Gold encountered.

In the years following the essay's publication, "Proletarian Realism" inspired a large body of literature reflecting its radical ideas. Beginning with the publication of critical essays and literary texts in leftist publications such as *The New Masses,* proletarian writers quickly developed a broad range of outlets. Gold's *Jews without Money* is an important artistic realization of the critical aims espoused in "Proletarian Realism." Proletarian literature also made an impact on African American literature, such as Richard Wright's *Native Son* (1940), and although, strictly speaking, it would be inaccurate to label John Dos Passos and John Steinbeck as proletarian writers, the movement undoubtedly influenced their respective American classics, *U.S.A.* (1930-1936) and *The Grapes of Wrath* (1939). With so many esteemed writers connected to the movement, proletarian literature continues to command significant scholarly interest today.

THEMES AND STYLE

The central theme of "Proletarian Realism" is that literature must abandon the "sickly mental states" of bourgeois writing and engage more directly with the experience of the worker. According to the essay, much modern writing—embodied by authors such as Marcel Proust, whom Gold characterizes as the "master-masturbator" of bourgeois fiction—strips literature of its social function, which is to engender a "revolutionary élan" that will sweep away the economic disparities of capitalism. To this end, the text outlines a literary aesthetic that is accessible to the masses, avoids verbal acrobatics, expresses the "courage of the proletarian experience," and unflinchingly portrays the "mud puddle" of the worker's life while expressing a hope for revolutionary change.

The essay achieves its rhetorical force through appeals to a sense of unity among the working class. This effect comes primarily through the use of the term "the Workers" and the word "we," which implies that both the author and the readers are part of a single, inclusive body whose shared interest in overthrowing an unjust capitalist system underpins a desire to create proletarian realist literature. The vilification of the bourgeois writer—whose literature speaks of "spiritual drunkards and super-refined Parisian émigrés," experiences ostensibly alien to the lives of the Workers—reinforces the solidarity of the proletariats and urges them to create literature that matters to the "suffering of hungry, persecuted and heroic millions."

Stylistically, "Proletarian Realism" is distinguished by its declarative prose. The text is organized into nine numbered paragraphs, giving the impression of a simple set of logical rules and achievable goals. By following the call for "swift action, clear form, [and] the direct line," the text asserts that the proletarian writer can create a literature that will inspire a successful revolution. The language is accessible to the masses and thus in concert with its stylistic exhortations: "As few words as possible. We are not interested in the verbal acrobats—this is only another form of bourgeois idleness. The Workers live too close to reality to care about these literary show-offs, these verbalist heroes."

CRITICAL DISCUSSION

Initial reaction to the work was mixed, both inside and outside proletarian circles. Although many of those involved in mass struggle responded favorably, a number of intellectually inclined Marxist theorists—including Phillip Rhav and Wendell Phillips, who wrote for the *Partisan Review*—felt that Gold's outright rejection of "bourgeois writers" was

MIKE GOLD: COMMUNIST VOICE

Remembered primarily as the author of the proletarian realist novel *Jews without Money* (1930), Mike Gold dedicated much of his life to the communist cause. Born to immigrant parents in 1893, Itzok Granich, as Gold was christened, was forced because of poverty to quit school at the age of twelve and to work at a gas mantle factory and then at the Adams Express Company. By 1914 he had encountered the influential leftist magazine *The Masses,* to which he submitted a Walt Whitman-esque poem about the death of three anarchists. After receiving admission to Harvard University as a provisional student in 1916, he wrote a daily column in the *Boston Journal.*

His academic career ended abruptly in early 1917 when he suffered a nervous breakdown. He fell into a deep depression and soon found himself in poverty, wandering the streets in dirty rags and scrounging money for food. He emerged from this period with greater artistic focus and wrote several pieces for the theater before crossing into Mexico to avoid the draft. While there, he raised money to purchase a translation of the Soviet constitution. Upon returning to the United States, he published many of his proletarian tracts in the leftist newspaper *The New Masses.*

too simplistic and one-sided. In *The Literary Wars of Mike Gold, A Study in the Background and Development of Mike Gold's Literary Ideas, 1920-1941* (1979), scholar Azar Naficy calls the attempt to "boycott the bourgeoisie" a theoretical shortcoming. Even Marx and Engels, writes Naficy, "developed their own theories from bourgeois thinkers such as [Georg Wilhelm Friedrich] Hegel, [Ludwig] Feuerbach, [Jean-Jacques] Rousseau, [Adam] Smith, Richard Saint Simon and others ... nor did they forget its great literature ... the works of [William] Shakespeare, [Johann Wolfgang von] Goethe, [Charles] Dickens, [Elizabeth] Gaskell and above all the royalist [Honoré de] Balzac."

After the end of the proletarian realist movement—and the historical context that gave birth to it—with the dawn of World War II, "Proletarian Realism" remained an important document in the history of working-class literature and the revolutionary movement. Discussing Gold's influence on both politics and literature, Naficy writes, "The most important contributions of Gold lie in his persistent efforts to create a genuinely revolutionary literature, one which would be democratic and popular, but not commercial and vulgar, one which would follow in the footsteps of men like Whitman, Twain, and London, but also embrace the essence of its own times." In the decades since the essay was written, it has been the subject of an extensive body

Proletarier aller Länder vereinigt Euch! (Proletarians of the World, Unite!), an engraving in a 1904 issue of *Neuen Postillon*. Mike Gold's 1930 essay "Proletarian Realism" discusses proletarian literature, the literature of workers. DIETMAR KATZ/ART RESOURCE, NY

of criticism that has evaluated its legacy in historical, political, and literary terms.

Much scholarship has focused on proletarian literature's relationship with the Communist Party and its nature as propaganda. In a 1938 *Southern Review* essay, Phillip Rahv maligns proletarian literature, saying it "is the literature of a party disguised as the literature of a class." Sagerson writes that proletarian literature was "largely ignored by scholars" owing to its association with communism. Some contemporary scholarship, such as Alan M. Wald's *Exiles From*

a Future Time (2002), attempts to compensate for proletarian literature's political bias and oversights.

BIBLIOGRAPHY

Sources

Folsom, Michael Brewster. "The Education of Michael Gold." *Proletarian Writers of the Thirties.* Ed. David Madden. Carbondale: Southern Illinois UP, 1968. 222-51. Print.

Gold, Mike. "Proletarian Realism." *New Masses* 6.4 (1930): 5. Web. 17 Sept. 2012.

Naficy, Azar. *The Literary Wars of Mike Gold, A Study in the Background and Development of Mike Gold's Literary Ideas, 1920-1941.* Norman: U of Oklahoma P, 1979. *ProQuest.* Web. 17 Sept. 2012.

Rahv, Phillip. "Proletarian Literature: A Political Autopsy." *Southern Review* 4.3 (1938): 616-28. Web. 18 Oct. 2012.

Sagerson, Erin Jean. "Art and Bread: Mike Gold, Proletarian Art, and the Rhetoric of American Communism, 1921-41." Diss. Texas Christian University, 2009. *ProQuest.* Web. 17 Sept. 2012.

Wald, Alan M. *Exiles from a Future Time: The Forging of the Mid-Twentieth-Century Literary Left.* Chapel Hill: U of North Carolina P, 2002. Print.

Yancey, Peter W. "Steinbeck's Relationship to Proletarian Literature." *Steinbeck Review* 9.1 (2012): 39-55. Wiley Online Library. Web. 17 Sept. 2012.

Further Reading

Gold, Michael. *Jews without Money.* New York: Carrol and Graf, 1930. Print.

Hancuff, Rich. "John Dos Passos, Mike Gold, and the Birth of the New Masses." *Reconstruction* 8.1 (2008): n. pag. Web. 17 Sept. 2012.

Hanley, Lawrence. "Cultural Work and Class Politics: Re-reading and Remaking Proletarian Literature in the United States." *Modern Fiction Studies* 38.3 (1992): 715-32. Project Muse. Web 17 Sept. 2012.

Ledbetter, Kenneth Lee. *The Idea of a Proletarian Novel in America, 1927-1939.* Urbana: U of Illinois P, 1963. *ProQuest.* Web. 17 Sept. 2012.

Khader, Jamil. "Transnationalizing Aztlan: Rudolfo Anaya's *Heart of Aztlan* and US Proletarian Literature." *MELUS* 27.1 (2002): 83-106. JSTOR. Web. 17 Sept. 2012.

Rabinowitz, Paula. "Domestic Labor: Film Noir, Proletarian Literature, and Black Women's Fiction." *Modern Fiction Studies* 47.1 (2001): 229-54. Web. 17 Sept. 2012.

Gregory Luther

A Short Organum for the Theatre

Bertolt Brecht

OVERVIEW

Bertolt Brecht's "A Short Organum for the Theatre" argues that the modern age demands a new dramatic aesthetic governed by empirical principles, and demonstrates how this aesthetic is supplied by Brecht's revolutionary socialist theater. Consisting of a prologue and a collection of short, epigrammatic fragments, "Organum" articulates the following claims: that Aristotle's dramatic theory is woefully outdated and must be supplanted by a modern, scientific theater; that the theater's highest purpose is entertainment and pleasure; that because instruction is the greatest source of pleasure, the modern theater must endeavor to educate its audience; that the particular subject of its instructions should be the Marxist philosophy of dialectical materialism; and that such instruction can be best accomplished using a technique called the "alienation effect" that Brecht himself has developed. Formulated, in large part, as a set of practical instructions for directors and playwrights, "Organum" is also an influential work of aesthetic philosophy that has had a significant impact on the fields of theater, opera, literature, film, and the visual arts.

The title of Brecht's text derives from Aristotle's *Organum* and Francis Bacon's *Novum Organum,* both foundational works of natural philosophy that are integral to the history of science. In citing these two works, Brecht emphasizes the "social-scientific" basis of dialectical materialism, even as he asserts that science itself is grounded in aesthetic principles. In addition, the use of the word *organum,* which literally means "instrument," frames the text as a conceptual tool with a pragmatic social value. By blurring the line between art and empiricism, Brecht is able to formalize his dramatic approach while simultaneously arguing for the practical and political necessity of the theater. When "Organum" was first published in 1948, Brecht had moved to eastern Berlin, which was administered by the recently formed socialist state known as the German Democratic Republic, and such bold cultural assertions had the potential to inflame postwar sensitivities. Brecht defends the revolutionary basis of his dramatic project while tempering his claims according to the complex cultural politics of the time.

HISTORICAL AND LITERARY CONTEXT

Brecht's "Organum" formulates the parameters for a dramatic aesthetic that is structured by scientific thinking. Brecht, one of the most renowned dramatists of the twentieth century, was continually developing and recasting the terms for his revolutionary approach to the theater. At the same time, the way in which he theorized this approach, and the relative priority he assigned to various aspects of his dramatic theory, shifted with the political moment and according to his intended audience. In particular, Brecht's exile from Germany for a thirteen-year period bracketing World War II—during which time he lived successively in Denmark, Sweden, Finland, the United States, and Switzerland—required him to continually rearticulate his aesthetic aims to new national audiences that were relatively unfamiliar with his work. "Organum" is the last major theoretical text that Brecht completed; his theoretical magnum opus, *The Messingkauf Dialogues,* remained unfinished upon his death in 1956. As such, "Organum" has often been read as the culminating exposition of Brecht's aesthetic, although it should be remembered that this text was addressed to a particular audience and historical moment—that of Brecht's fraught return to his homeland on the heels of a decade of ideological disputation in which socialism, fascism, and capitalism battled for the upper hand.

Brecht got his start as a playwright and director in the Weimar Republic during the 1920s. The runaway success of his *Threepenny Opera,* cowritten with Kurt Weill and first produced in 1928, catapulted Brecht to fame and installed him as a prominent fixture of the interwar German cultural scene. He participated in a series of influential debates about the expressionist movement, in which he tended to favor the dispassionate pragmatism of the "New Objectivity" against the utopian mysticism of the expressionists. In the course of these debates, Brecht distinguished himself by presenting an alternative to the doctrine of socialist realism expounded by György Lukács and other critics.

Brecht's early writings called for a forceful rejection of Aristotelian dramatics, which he identified with the decadent complacency of the nineteenth-century bourgeois theater. In the most important

✢ *Key Facts*

Time Period:
Mid-20th Century

Movement/Issue:
Marxist aesthetics

Place of Publication:
Germany

Language of Publication:
German

Gerard Murphy as Oedipus and John Shrapnel as Creon in a 1992 Royal Shakespeare Company production of the "Oedipus plays of Sophocles." In "A Short Organum for the Theatre," Bertolt Brecht uses such plays to describe his philosophy of theater. © ARENAPAL/TOPHAM/THE IMAGE WORKS

"Organum," together with Brecht's earlier work, is closely associated with the critical theory of the Frankfurt School, especially the writings of Walter Benjamin, Theodor Adorno, and Siegfried Kracauer. These theorists are known for bringing a dialectical-materialist perspective to their analysis of the mass cultural phenomena (such as cinema, radio, and musical revues) that grew in popularity beginning in the 1920s and were broadly associated with the negative forces of American capitalism. Brecht's practical methods for the theater often tested, challenged, and complicated Frankfurt School theories as he reimagined modern drama in productive opposition to mass culture. At the same time, Brecht's legacy has extended far beyond the reach of modernity, radically altering the landscape of contemporary drama in Europe, the United States, and around the world. Heiner Müller (of Germany), Tony Kushner (of the United States), Dario Fo (of Italy), and Athol Fugard (of South Africa) are only a few of the many notable dramatists whose aesthetic achievements are deeply indebted to Brecht.

THEMES AND STYLE

Brecht's "Organum" is framed as an extended reflection on dramatic innovations that Brecht had worked out in practice during his years in exile. First and foremost, Brecht argues for the productive value of the modern theater, which is intended for an audience of workers "who live hard and produce much." The theater, like its ideal audience, must draw its inspiration from a "great passion for producing." Indeed, "self-production"—that is, the improvements to the self that are brought about through pleasurable instruction—is among the modern theater's highest aims. In service of this goal, Brecht's stage represents society as a kind of game, enabling the audience to be "entertained with the wisdom that comes from the solution of problems, with the anger that is a practical expression of sympathy with the underdog, with the respect due to those who respect humanity." The audience, therefore, ought to be intellectually engaged with the events of the play and to take pleasure in this active engagement.

Brecht goes on to describe the "alienation effect" in relation to acting and to discuss the utility of this technique. The "a-effect" is essentially a process of defamiliarization: the subject of the representation is recognizable but is made to seem foreign or strange. For the actor, this involves a certain self-conscious presentation that draws attention to the art of acting—as an example, Brecht suggests that an actor might smoke a cigar, then put it down to reenter the narrative of the play—such that the performer must never appear wholly transformed into the character he represents. The alienation effect is meant to arouse a state of attentive suspicion in the spectator, a condition that is linked to scientific observation. Brecht specifies that the spectator should cultivate "that detached eye with

theoretical text of his early period, "Notes to the Opera *The Rise and Fall of the City of Mahagonny* (1930)," Brecht set out the terms for an "epic theater" that would generate a critical distance between the performers and the audience. The purpose of this distance, which Brecht called the "alienation effect" or "a-effect," was to train the audience to become better "readers" of the historical and ideological conditions represented onstage and thus equip them to assimilate the lessons of dialectical materialism. By the time Brecht wrote "Organum," however, socialist realism—which was firmly grounded in Aristotelian ideas—had emerged as the dominant aesthetic of socialist East Germany. Brecht thus uses "Organum" to soften his previous critiques and to rehabilitate Aristotle, cleverly casting him as a figure sympathetic to Brecht's own dramatic project by focusing on the pleasure-giving functions of the theater. Tellingly, the phrase "epic theater" does not appear anywhere in "Organum"; instead, Brecht favors the terms "dialectical" and "scientific" to describe his art.

which the great Galileo observed a swinging chande-lier. He was amazed by this pendulum motion, as if he had not expected it and could not understand its occurring, and this enabled him to come on the rules by which it was governed." This condition of wonder and estrangement, a state that is "disconcerting but fruitful," is precisely that "which the theatre must provoke with its representations of human social life." The a-effect thus provides Brecht's theater with its po-litical efficacy, because, he argues, the rules of society must be made unfamiliar before they can be changed.

Brecht goes on to argue that just as character must be demonstrated through "something approach-ing experimental conditions; i.e., that a counter-experiment should now and then be conceivable," so too should episodes in the dramatic story call atten-tion to the way they are "knotted together." The seams of the dramatic narrative should be exposed for the audience's examination, suggesting that the alteration of any individual event would affect the whole plot. The theoretical text of "Organum" could be said to replicate something of the "knotted" style Brecht pre-fers for the modern theater: its short fragments trace recurring themes but seldom flow seamlessly from one to the next, rather developing their argument through a process of complication and contradiction. In this way, Brecht causes his readers to engage in the same "terrible and never-ending labour" he intends for his spectators—that is, to participate in a struggle of un-ceasing inquiry, inference, and doubt.

CRITICAL DISCUSSION

Having risen to cultural prominence before the war, Brecht returned to Germany as one of the most respected dramatists in Europe. "Organum" was published shortly before Brecht founded his own theater company, the Berliner Ensemble, in 1949, and implicitly served as a mission statement for this new theater, which achieved great popularity in East Germany and abroad. In the decades following its publication, "Organum" has been widely read and translated into multiple languages. Its clear distilla-tion of what is now recognized as the author's sig-nature "Brechtian" aesthetic has found an audience among theater practitioners as well as within the academy, where critics such as Loren Kruger have described "Organum" as Brecht's most systematic presentation of his method and have remarked on the sophistication and originality of its critique of bourgeois culture.

Brecht's socialism was crucial in the development of his aesthetic. His aim was to harness the theater as an ideological training ground, effecting change in the material world by altering his audience's opinions about the world represented onstage. John White has observed the shades of logical contradiction inherent in this project, and he writes that "an intervention-ism that both precedes and legitimates Epic Theater while at the same time being the goal and end product

of Epic Theater is something of a viciously circular conception." Because Brecht conceived of his aes-thetic as having an expressly political purpose, how-ever, critics should resist the temptation to reduce the "epic" to a mere set of formal characteristics. As Peter Brooker remarks, "Organum" implies that "a theatre which employed the techniques of 'epic' without its objectives would be an idealist and aestheticized ver-sion of his own intentions." Even as Brecht's method, as presented in "Organum," takes its cues from dia-lectical materialism, it in turn constitutes an innova-tive interpretation of the dialectical tradition and thus succeeds in advancing a theory of the theater located squarely at the crosscurrents of dramatic modernism and socialist aesthetics.

BIBLIOGRAPHY

Sources

Brecht, Bertolt. "A Short Organum for the Theatre." *Brecht on Theatre: The Development of an Aesthetic.* Ed. and trans. John Willett. New York: Hill and Wang, 1966. Print.

Brooker, Peter. "Key Words in Brecht's Theory and Prac-tice of Theatre." *The Cambridge Companion to Brecht.* Ed. Peter Thomson and Glendyr Sacks. New York: Cambridge UP, 1994. 185-200. Print.

Kruger, Loren. *Post-Imperial Brecht: Politics and Perfor-mance, East and South.* New York: Cambridge UP, 2004. Print.

White, John J. *Bertolt Brecht's Dramatic Theory.* Rochester: Camden, 2004. Print.

Further Reading

Bentley, Eric. *Bentley on Brecht.* Evanston: Northwestern UP, 2008. Print.

Bloch, Ernst, et al. *Aesthetics and Politics.* London: Verso, 1980. Print.

Esslin, Martin. *Brecht: A Choice of Evils. A Critical Study of the Man, His Work and His Opinions.* London: Eyre Methuen, 1980. Print.

Fuegi, John. *Brecht and Company: Sex, Politics, and the Making of the Modern Drama.* New York: Grove, 1994. Print.

Jameson, Frederic. *Brecht and Method.* New York: Verso, 1998. Print.

Mews, Siegfried, ed. *A Bertolt Brecht Reference Companion.* Westport: Greenwood, 1997. Print.

———. "Brecht, Bertolt." *The Columbia Encyclopedia of Modern Drama.* Ed. Gabrielle H. Cody and Evert Sprinchorn. Vol. 1. New York: Columbia UP, 2007. Print.

Puchner, Martin. "Bertolt Brecht: The Theater on a Leash." *Stage Fright: Modernism, Anti-Theatricality, and Drama.* Baltimore: Johns Hopkins UP, 2002. Print.

Thomson, Peter, and Glendyr Sacks, eds. *The Cambridge Companion to Brecht.* New York: Cambridge UP, 1994. Print.

Rebecca Kastleman

CANNIBAL MANIFESTO

Oswald de Andrade

❖ *Key Facts*

Time Period:
Early/Mid-20th Century

Movement/Issue:
Aesthetics; Avant-gardism; Artistic nationalism

Place of Publication:
Brazil

Language of Publication:
Portuguese

OVERVIEW

Written by Brazilian poet and novelist Oswald de Andrade, the "Manifesto Anthropófago" ("Cannibal Manifesto," 1928) articulates the desire among the Brazilian avant-garde to define cultural and national identity outside of a hegemonic European paradigm. Noted for its irreverence, Andrade's manifesto satirizes the influence of Europe on the development of Brazilian culture. Primarily a literary manifesto, the text expresses unwillingness to unconditionally accept and implement European modernism, suggesting instead the figurative cannibalization of European influences. The manifesto introduced a new theory and motif of postcolonial experience: neither blind acceptance nor total rejection of its European predecessors, Andrade's idea of cannibalization means intentional consumption of the colonizer to merge with the colonized. The "Cannibal Manifesto" became a guiding text for the Brazilian modernist movement, called *modernismo,* and initiated its own short-lived movement.

Published in the first edition of *Revista de Antropofagia* in May 1928, the manifesto was enthusiastically received by members of the Brazilian avant-garde. It engendered a brief cultural and literary movement known as the Cannibalist movement, which was active for fourteen months before internal rifts divided the group. Comprising poets, novelists, and artists, the Cannibalists were concerned with achieving a hybridized national identity, encompassing both colonial European traditions and the indigenous heritage of Brazil. By the 1930s the Cannibalist movement had been absorbed into the broader modernist movement, but Andrade's manifesto remained significant for its iconoclastic theory of Brazilian modernism and has been widely recognized as "a paradigm for the creation of a modern and cosmopolitan, but still authentically national culture" in Brazil.

HISTORICAL AND LITERARY CONTEXT

The "Cannibal Manifesto" responds to the imposition of European modernism onto Brazilian cultural development at a time when the Latin American avant-garde was attempting to define itself outside of a colonial system. Early twentieth-century modernism initiated a worldwide change in thinking, destabilizing long-held values and systems like colonialism. Yet the movement was not without limitations; for example, modernist

interest in the primitive seemed to simply reaffirm colonial domination. In response to this international movement, the "Cannibal Manifesto" is at once a statement against the noble-savage ideal projected onto Latin Americans and an assertion of Latin American cultural and intellectual autonomy. The manifesto resists mimicking European models of modernism but proposes a methodology for creating an autonomous cultural identity that instead emphasizes contradictions between Europe and Brazil: cannibalism.

By the time the "Cannibal Manifesto" was written in 1928, modernism had been percolating in Brazil for nearly five years. Modernism was first introduced during the February 1922 *Semana de Arte Moderna* (Modern Art Week) in São Paolo, which included art exhibits, readings, and musical performances that emphasized modernization and "Brazilianization." Organizers "conceived of [the week] as a manifesto of cultural autonomy" and aspired to a national modernism with roots in Brazil's postcolonial, Latin soil. At the same time, a renewed interest in Brazil's indigenous history—instigated in part by the modernist preoccupation with the primitive—led some to see Brazil's history of miscegenation as proof of the nation's cultural unity, recasting diversity as a national strength. The "Cannibal Manifesto" expands on the topics introduced in the *Semana,* using the metaphor of the cannibal to reevaluate and reshape national identity in light of Brazil's profound diversity.

The early twentieth century witnessed prolific artistic and literary production among the avant-garde, upon which the "Cannibal Manifesto" draws heavily. Often cited as Andrade's inspiration, Tarsile do Amaral's painting *Abaporu* depicts a combination of the primitive and the cosmopolitan that informed the manifesto. An active member of the *modernismo,* Andrade wrote earlier manifestos, including "Manifesto a Poesia Pau Brasil" (1924), treating such themes as the reconciliation of the earthly and surreal. Francis Picaba's *Manifeste Cannibale* (1920), a performance piece associated with the Dadaist movement, influenced not only Andrade's title but also the idea of consuming the past to make something new. The manifesto's theoretical underpinnings derive in large part from internationally significant texts such as Marx's *Communist Manifesto,* Freud's *Totem and Taboo,* and Rousseau's concept of the noble savage.

Immediately following its publication, the "Cannibal Manifesto" gained momentum as a foundational theory for *modernismo*. The manifesto also initiated the Cannibalist movement, a subset within the avant-garde dealing with the Brazilian experience of "colonization and translation." Although the Cannibalists disbanded by 1930, the theory and themes of cannibalism continued to influence Brazilian literature, including Andrade's own subsequent texts. Concrete poet Haroldo de Campos grapples with cannibalism in "The Rule of Anthropophagy: Europe under the Sign of Devoration" (1986). The theory was later incorporated into postcolonial discourse and connected to ideas such as transculturation. Continuing into the twenty-first century, the "Cannibal Manifesto" remains a seminal text in Brazilian art and literature.

THEMES AND STYLE

The central theme of the "Cannibal Manifesto" is that by "digesting" European influences and mixing those with indigenous traditions, Brazilian culture can engender an authentic and validated national identity. The central trope used throughout the manifesto is that of the cannibal, a metaphor that satirizes the relationship between Brazil and Portugal. Opening with the declarative statement "Only Cannibalism unites us," the manifesto asserts that what connects the colonizer and the colonized is consumption of the other, equating colonization with ritualistic killing. Paradoxically, Andrade also avers that cannibalism is the "disguised expression of all individualisms," resisting social, economic, and philosophical domination. The cannibal metaphor allows Andrade to at once undermine Portugal's position of power and valorize Brazil's hybridized history.

The manifesto achieves its rhetorical effect through assertions of the superiority of precolonial Brazil. This sense of superiority is primarily achieved by discrediting the country's colonial history and by an emphasis on contradictions between Europe and Brazil throughout the manifesto. Through satire and deconstruction, Andrade undermines the colonizer:

Sixteenth-century engraving by Theodor de Bry depicting cannibalism by native Brazilian people, from *Americae Tertia Pars* (1592). Brazilian writer Oswald de Andrade's "Manifesto Antropófago" references such tales, championing Brazil's history of "cannibalizing" other cultures. SERVICE HISTORIQUE DE LA MARINE, VINCENNES, FRANCE/GIRAUDON/THE BRIDGEMAN ART LIBRARY

PRIMARY SOURCE

CANNIBAL MANIFESTO

We want the Carib Revolution. Greater than the French Revolution. The unification of all productive revolts for the progress of humanity. Without us, Europe wouldn't even have its meager declaration of the rights of man.

The Golden Age heralded by America. The Golden Age. And all the *girls.*

* * *

Heritage. Contact with the Carib side of Brazil. *Où Villegaignon print terre.* Montaigne. Natural man. Rousseau. From the French Revolution to Romanticism, to the Bolshevik Revolution, to the Surrealist Revolution and Keyserling's technicized barbarian. We push onward.

* * *

We were never catechized. We live by a somnambulistic law. We made Christ to be born in Bahia. Or in Belém do Pará.

* * *

But we never permitted the birth of logic among us.

* * *

...

We already had justice, the codification of vengeance. Science, the codification of Magic. Cannibalism. The permanent transformation of the Tabu into a totem.

* * *

Down with the reversible world, and against objectified ideas. Cadaverized. The stop of thought that is dynamic. The individual as victim of the system. Source of classical injustices. Of romantic injustices. And the forgetting of inner conquests.

* * *

Routes. Routes. Routes. Routes. Routes. Routes. Routes.

* * *

The Carib instinct.

* * *

Death and life of all hypotheses. From the equation "Self, part of the Cosmos" to the axiom "Cosmos, part of the Self." Subsistence. Experience. Cannibalism.

* * *

Down with the vegetable elites. In communication with the soil.

* * *

We were never catechized. What we really made was Carnaval. The Indian dressed as senator of the Empire.

Making believe he's Pitt. Or performing in Alencar's operas, full of worthy Portuguese sentiments.

* * *

We already had Communism. We already had Surrealist language. The Golden Age.

* * *

Catiti Catiti
Imara Notiá
Notiá Imara
Ipejú.

* * *

Magic and life. We had the description and allocation of tangible goods, moral goods, and royal goods. And we knew how to transpose mystery and death with the help of a few grammatical forms.

* * *

I asked a man what the Law was. He answered that it was the guarantee of the exercise of possibility. That man was named Galli Mathias. I ate him.

* * *

Only where there is mystery is there no determinism. But what does that have to do with us?

* * *

Down with the histories of Man that begin at Cape Finisterre. The undated world. Unrubrified. Without Napoleon. Without Caesar.

* * *

The determination of progress by catalogues and television sets. Only machinery. And blood transfusers.

* * *

Down with the antagonistic sublimations. Brought here in caravels.

* * *

Down with the truth of missionary peoples, defined by the sagacity of a cannibal, the Viscount of Cairu:—It's a lie told again and again.

* * *

But those who came here weren't crusaders. They were fugitives from a civilization we are eating, because we are strong and vindictive like the Jabuti.

SOURCE: Translated by Leslie Bary, *Latin American Literary Review,* vol. 19, no. 38, July–Dec 1991, pp. 39, 40, 41. Copyright © 1991 by Latin American Literary Review Press. All rights reserved. Reproduced by permission.

"We already had communism. We already had a surrealist language. The golden age." Deconstructing the cannibal trope, Andrade reappropriates the term's pejorative associations with the savage to be a source of strength. In the manifesto's best-known line, "Tupi or not tupi that is that question," Andrade plays on Hamlet's well-known soliloquy, substituting the name of an indigenous Brazilian tribe known for its cannibalism in order to pose the question of whether or not to be a cannibal. Using the literal and figurative implications of the term, Andrade in effect cannibalizes Shakespeare by recontextualizing the canonical phrase—precisely what he is advocating throughout the manifesto.

Stylistically, the "Cannibal Manifesto" presents numerous challenges for readers. Lacking meter and rhyme scheme, and without consistently complete phrases, the manifesto cannot be classified as poetry or prose. There is not a clear sense of logic, as the text does not follow a linear progression and is instead marked by unexpected juxtapositions. Although replete with esoteric insider references and mysterious metaphors, at times the tone is playful: "I asked a man what was Right. He answered me that it was the assurance of the full exercise of possibilities. That man was called Galli Mathias. I ate him." Satirical critiques of European institutions such as colonialism also emerge: "Before two Portuguese discovered Brazil, Brazil discovered happiness." The manifesto achieves its rhetorical force through its rejection of valorized modes of thought (linear rationality) and irreverent treatment of European institutions.

CRITICAL DISCUSSION

When the "Cannibal Manifesto" was first published, the Brazilian avant-garde received it enthusiastically. Although some found Andrade's notion of cannibalism shocking and others even perceived the whole venture as a joke, the manifesto was a defining text of the *modernismo* movement. Among the avant-garde, the manifesto was a "powerful intellectual declaration" that Brazil remained "culturally colonized." Its implications were parsed out among the Cannibalists in subsequent issues of the *Revista de Antropofagia,* such as in Mario de Andrade's criticism "Antropofagos?" Yet such squabbles did not detract from the importance of the theoretical approach presented in the manifesto. With the first English translation of the manifesto, critic Leslie Bary introduced cannibalism to English-speaking audiences in 1991, many of whom were scholars invigorated by the refreshing perspective on postcolonialism.

The Cannibalist movement continued for roughly one year following the publication of the "Cannibal Manifesto," dissolving in 1929 with the final edition of the *Revista de Antropofagia. Modern-*

ismo also fell out of favor by the end of the 1930s due to reactions against the avant-garde, but modernism had by then already left its mark on Brazil. Latin literary groups concerned with representing cultural diversity such as the Concretists and Tropicalists rediscovered and repopularized the manifesto in the 1960s, when its theoretical force was again acknowledged. Bary asserts that the manifesto has been "canonized as a theoretical basis of Brazilian cultural identity," which itself "hinges on the emphasis of hybridization." It has since become a key text in Brazilian cultural analysis. The manifesto and the brief Cannibalist movement inspired later literary works and writers with their blend of indigenous and civilized, primitive and cosmopolitan.

Scholarship concerning the "Cannibal Manifesto" has proliferated in the decades since its "rediscovery" in the middle of the twentieth century. Dominant threads include the analysis and reconsideration of the cannibalism trope, particularly in terms of postcolonial studies. Sara Castro-Klarén has explored in her genealogical reading of the text in which she claims that the manifesto offers "a vantage point from which to examine the gaps created by the aphoristic structure of the 'Manifesto.'" Other critics, including Bary, have reconsidered how effectively it subverts the power it purports to criticize. Another predominant trend is to apply the cannibal trope to areas left untreated in the manifesto, such as the role of women in Brazilian identity. In recent years, the metaphor has even been applied to technological development. The collective Design Livre sees in cannibalism a representation of the collaborative process through which technological innovations are made and cites the "Cannibal Manifesto" as a source of inspiration.

BIBLIOGRAPHY

Sources

Amstel, Frederick van, CaioVassão, and Gonçalo Ferraz. *Design Livre: Cannibalistic Interaction Design.* 3rd International Forum Design as Process, Nov. 2011, Turin, Italy. Unpublished conference paper, 2011. Print.

Andrade, Oswald de. "Cannibal Manifesto." Trans. Leslie Bary. *Latin American Literary Review* 19.38 (1991): 38-47. Print.

Bary, Leslie. "Oswald de Andrade's 'Cannibalist Manifesto.'" *Latin American Literary Review* 19.38 (1991): 35-37. Print.

Castro-Klarén, Sara. "A Genealogy for the 'Manifesto Anthropófago,' or the Struggle between Socrates and the Caraibe." *Nepantla: Views from South* 1.2 (2000): 295-322. Print.

Jackson, Kenneth David. "A View on Brazilian Literature: Eating the 'Revista de Antropofagia.'" *Latin American Literary Review* 7.13 (1978): 1-9. Print.

"Manifesto Anthropófago." *Encyclopedia Itaú Cultural Visual Arts* 23 Nov. 2005. Web. 20 Aug. 2012.

Further Reading

Applegate, Matt. "Gastronomic Solutions to Imperial Problems: Oswald de Andrade's 'Cannibal Manifesto.'" *Prodigies & Monsters.* Wordpress, 29 Mar. 2011. Web. 21 Aug. 2012.

Bary, Leslie. "The Tropical Modernist as Literary Cannibal: Cultural Identity in Oswald de Andrade." *Chasqui* 20.2 (1991): 10-19. Print.

Jackson, Kenneth David. "Literary Criticism in Brazil." *Brazilian Literature: Bibliographies.* Eds. Roberto González Echevarría and Enrique Pupo-Walker. Vol. 3. The Cambridge History of Latin American Literature. Cambridge: Cambridge UP, 1996. 329-44. Web. 28 Aug. 2012.

Madureira, Luís. *Cannibal Modernities: Postcoloniality and the Avant-Garde in Caribbean and Brazilian Literature.* Charlestown: U of Virginia P, 2005. Print.

———. "A Flat Carnivalesque Intention of Being a Cannibal; or, How (Not) to Read the 'Cannibal Manifesto.'" *Ellipsis* 9 (2011): 13-33. Print.

Tosta, Antonio Luciana de Andrade. "Modern and Postcolonial: Oswald de Andrade's Antropofagia and the Politics of Labeling." *Romance Notes* 51.2 (2011): 217. Print.

Vinkler, Beth Joan. "The Anthropophagic Mother/Other: Appropriated Identities in Oswald de Andrade's 'Manifesto Antropófago.'" *Luso-Brazilian Review* 34.1 (1997): 105-11. Print.

Wujcik, Stacey. "An Anthropophagic Legacy: Oswald de Andrade's 'Manifesto Anthropófago' in Brazilian Anti-Art and the Works of Cildo Meireles." Diss. Temple University, 2011. Print.

Elizabeth Boeheim

Dada Cannibalistic Manifesto

Francis Picabia

OVERVIEW

French painter Francis Picabia wrote the "Dada Cannibalistic Manifesto" (1920) in opposition to cubism, which was then the dominant art movement in Paris. Picabia had painted in the cubist style until 1915, when he underwent a major transformation in New York and adopted a machinist sensibility. The cubist philosophy was itself a resistance to realism that attempted to redefine the relationship between viewers and art. Dadaists, however, insisted that this new definition was not a radical enough position and called for a rejection of art in general. Whereas cubist manifestoes had been critical of artistic practice, Picabia used his text to directly attack the daily experiences and value systems of the cubists and of the French viewing public in general. The dadaists believed that the various states resulting from their profanity—whether hilarity or disgust—were more productive than complacent reactions to art. In his "Dada Manifesto 1918," Tristan Tzara had declared in visceral but less offensive terms that "Dada Means Nothing," an assertion echoed by Picabia two years later.

Picabia did not seek to win the approval of anyone other than dadaists with his "Dada Cannibalistic Manifesto." He wanted to shock the public and the art world, and he succeeded in creating space for his movement mainly through its growing notoriety. When surrealism effectively replaced Dada by 1924, its adherents attempted to match the energy and controversy of the preceding movement while also allowing guidelines to structure their aesthetics. André Breton ended *Nadja* (1928), his surrealist novel, by proclaiming in a constructive way what dadaists would have framed deconstructively: "Beauty will be CONVULSIVE or will not be at all."

HISTORICAL AND LITERARY CONTEXT

Picabia served briefly on the front in World War I and then moved to New York City in 1915 on military business. He was critical of the nationalism that the war created, which existed to a lesser degree overseas. The "Dada Cannibalistic Manifesto" is not a direct response to the war; rather it addresses the dissatisfaction some artists felt with the attitudes of repatriation that were prevalent at the conflict's end. Picabia had traveled to New York in 1913, made connections with artists at the Armory Show, and showed his cubist paintings at 291, a gallery associated with Alfred Stieglitz. He had already rejected cubism as static when he returned to New York during the war. The industrial atmosphere of New York prompted him to make paintings based on the inner workings of machines.

When Picabia went back to Paris after the war, he had befriended Tzara, who was theorizing the aesthetics of Dada in Zurich. Tzara and poet Hugo Ball had founded Cabaret Voltaire in 1916, showcasing the spontaneous, absurdist antiart that grew out of the antinationalist reaction many artists had to World War I. Meanwhile, the poets Breton and Paul Eluard were attempting to transform literary perceptions in France, but they avoided the growing Dada movement until they encountered Picabia's "Thoughts Without Language" (1919). By this time, Picabia had begun an international journal, *391*, which featured his own and other polemical writings and would become integral in publicizing dadaist events.

In the twelfth edition of *391*, appearing just before the event at which the "Dada Cannibalistic Manifesto" was delivered, Picabia printed his "Dada Manifesto." This first manifesto contains the same themes as the second, as well as a similar rhetorical strategy. In both pieces, Picabia addresses art collectors, belittling their lack of taste and sarcastically suggesting that they should be purchasing dadaist work. In the "Dada Cannibalistic Manifesto," however, Picabia details even more concretely the problems he has with the cubist pieces that had come to be so popular with collectors. He derides the dominant art style, finding it simplistic and appropriative, as it has only "cubed primitive paintings, cubed Negro sculpture … cubed guitars … and the profiles of young girls."

For the next two years after the publication of the "Dada Cannibalistic Manifesto," Picabia and other dadaists continued their performances and their manifestoes. The succeeding surrealist movement was largely based on the views introduced in dadaism and was also grounded in nonrational, counterculture sentiments. Surrealist texts differ, however, in that they are often more positive and less self-destructive than their dadaist counterparts. The influence of dadaism can still be felt today. In 2006, for example, the Museum of Modern Art in New York and the Centre Georges Pompidou in Paris staged dadaist exhibitions.

❖ *Key Facts*

Time Period:
Early 20th Century

Movement/Issue:
Aesthetics; Dadaism; Avant-gardism

Place of Publication:
France

Language of Publication:
French

bia critiques the cubist philosophy of rules and discipline, he shows contempt for French culture as well, asking "What are you doing here, parked like serious oysters—for you are serious, right?" Picabia and the other dadaists felt that being too serious and setting up intransigent value systems led to an artistic culture based on greed and a world culture based on war.

The antisystematic approach that Picabia champions results in his text purposefully and comically contradicting itself. After putting to "death, death, death" the "money which doesn't die … [but] just leaves on trips," Picabia concludes that the dadaists will soon "sell [their] paintings for several francs." His antiart philosophy is meant to offend the public and thus rouse it from its stupor. Following Breton's reading, Picabia came on stage with a stuffed monkey tacked to a frame. The monkey's tail was pulled between its legs as though it was pointing an accusatory finger at the audience. Around the "still life" were the words *Portrait de Cezanne, Portrait de Rembrant, Portrait de Renoir*—referring to the three masters. To accompany the performance, a program was printed featuring Picabia's drawing *La Sainte Vierge* (The Blessed Virgin), simply a splash of black ink on a white page. These performative additions enhanced the text's polemical aims.

CRITICAL DISCUSSION

The audience reacted to Breton's performance of the "Dada Cannibalistic Manifesto" by booing and hissing. According to Picabia's biographer, William Camfield, in *Francis Picabia: His Art, Life and Times* (1979), this culminated with "coins, handkerchiefs, umbrellas and assorted objects" being thrown onstage. Reviewers of the event called for Dada to end or be ignored. Camfield was able to unearth only one contemporary critic, Renée Dunan, who connected the ideas of Dada to other philosophies shaping Parisian life in 1920. She predicted that a "new psychology [would] correspond to a renewed aesthetic." Responding to the confounded reaction to the "Dada Cannibalistic Manifesto," Dunan explained: "Dada is not mystification: it is the entire human mystery."

In keeping with his nondogmatic approach to aesthetics, Picabia, along with most of the rest of dadaism's practitioners, renounced the movement by 1924 and embraced surrealism. In Breton's first "Manifesto of Surrealism," also written in 1924, he concedes, "There remains madness, 'the madness that one locks up,' as it has aptly been described." The resistance to the "madness," however, takes a more hopeful tone. Still in opposition to a market-driven system, he proclaims, "The time is coming when it [poetry] decrees the end of money and by itself will break the bread of heaven for the earth!"

Modern-day scholars have acknowledged the unprecedented success of the "Dada Cannibalistic Manifesto" in rejecting previous movements and in

L'Oeil cacodylate, a 1921 work of art by Francis Picabia, an artist who wrote about the Dada movement in "Manifeste Cannibale Dada" (1920). CNAC/MNAM/DIST. RMN-GRAND PALAIS/ART RESOURCE, NY

THEMES AND STYLE

The "Dada Cannibalistic Manifesto" is one of the most scathing critiques to emerge from the dadaist movement. It calls artists and art lovers together so that they can be "accused" of greed, "snobism," superficiality, and allowing the market to dictate their tastes. Denouncing the influence of money, Picabia asserts that those associated with the art world love only idolatrous religion, "death for others," and nationalism. The work was originally delivered in a darkened hall during a much-anticipated "Dadaist Manifestation." Breton read the text, while Picabia waited backstage with Tzara.

The rhetorical strategy of the "Dada Cannibalistic Manifesto" is evident in its first demand: a call for the audience to "stand up" that creates an atmosphere of a formal accusation before a tribunal. Picabia then blasphemously likens the repudiated dadaism to religion, comparing the dadaist performance in a dark hall to "standing as for God save the king" and "the flag." Picabia insults the audience further when he draws a parallel between dadaism, which "is nothing" and the audience's hopes, which are "nothing," as are its "political men," "heroes," and "artists." When Pica-

reframing the perspective of artists. There is also a general view that the collective atmosphere of the dadaist movement—which included collaborations such as that of Breton and Picabia on "Dada Cannibalistic Manifesto"—contributed to the modernist and then postmodernist view that authorship is a sort of farce. George Baker illustrates this in his 2012 essay "The Artwork Caught by the Tail." In addition, Katharine Conley has found Picabia's use of *The Blessed Virgin* alongside his text to be appropriate and restorative. In a 2002 essay for *French Review,* she writes that his female figure manages to touch "both the irrational and the rational, articulating the inexpressible."

BIBLIOGRAPHY

Sources

Breton, André. "Manifesto of Surrealism" *Manifestos of Surrealism.* Trans. Richard Seaver and Helen R. Lane. Ann Arbor: Ann Arbor Paperbacks, 1972. 1-48. Web. 6 Nov. 2012.

Camfield, William A. *Francis Picabia: His Art, Life and Times.* Princeton: Princeton UP, 1979. Print.

Césaire, Aimé. "Breaking with the Dead Sea." *Surrealist Painters and Poets.* Ed. Mary Ann Caws. Cambridge: MIT, 2001. Print.

Conley, Katharine. "Writing the Virgin's Body: Breton and Eluard's *Immaculée Conception.*" *French Review* 67.4 (1994): 600-608. Rpt. in *Poetry Criticism.* Ed. Elisabeth Gellert. Vol. 38. Detroit: Gale, 2002. *Literature Resource Center.* Web. 12 Oct. 2012.

Picabia, Francis. "Dada Manifesto." *The Dada Reader: A Critical Anthology.* Ed. Dawn Ades. Chicago: Chicago UP, 2006. Print.

Further Reading

Baker, George. "The Artwork Caught by the Tail." *October* 97 (2001): 51-90. *JSTOR.* Web. 12 Oct. 2012.

Erickson, John D. "The Apocalyptic Mind: The Dada Manifesto and Classic Anarchism." *French Literature Series: Manifestoes and Movements* 7 (1980): 98-109. Rpt. in *Twentieth-Century Literary Criticism.* Ed. Thomas J. Schoenberg. Vol. 168. Detroit: Gale, 2005. *Literature Resource Center.* Web. 13 Oct. 2012.

Erickson, John D. *Dada: Performance, Poetry and Art.* Boston: Twayne, 1984. Print.

Foster, Steven C. *Dada Dimensions.* Ann Arbor: UMI Research, 1985. Print.

Thompson, Jan. "Picabia and His Influence on American Art, 1913-17." *Art Journal* 39.1 (1979): 14-21. Print.

Caitie Moore

DADA EXCITES EVERYTHING

Tristan Tzara, et al.

⊹ Key Facts

Time Period:
Early 20th Century

Movement/Issue:
Aesthetics; Dadaism;
Avant-gardism

Place of Publication:
France

**Language of
Publication:**
French

OVERVIEW

The two-page treatise "*Dada Soulève Tout*" ("Dada Excites Everything" or "Dada Lifts Up Everything)" was written in Paris on January 12, 1921; signed by Tristan Tzara, Max Ernst, Marcel Duchamp, André Breton, and several other artists; and published in the avant-garde journal *Little Review.* One of several high-profile Dada manifestos, it begins with the proclamation that "Dada knows everything. Dada spits everything out." The document is both a defense of what Dada is and an attack on what it is not in relation to the art and literary movements of the day. In true Dada fashion, the text is nonsensical, nonlinear, and absurdist in both its declarations and its irreverent assaults, particularly on the Italian arts movement known as futurism, which celebrated both violence and technology.

"Dada Excites Everything" was distributed at the Théatre de l'Ouevre in Paris on January 15, 1921, during a Dadaist disruption of a lecture given by Filippo Tommaso Marinetti, a leading Italian futurist poet and author of the *Futurist Manifesto* (1909). In combination with shouts and jeers from attending Dadaists and other audience members caught up in the spirit of the sabotage, the document succeeded in derailing not only the afternoon's lecture program and annoying the speaker but also in rebutting Marinetti's suggestion that Dada was an inheritor of futurism. "Dada Excites Everything" is included in most surveys of Dada literature and serves as an excellent example of the movement's simultaneous definition and questioning of its own tenets. This self-analytical philosophy greatly influenced French, German, and American theorists throughout the twentieth century.

HISTORICAL AND LITERARY CONTEXT

Dada was an international artistic and literary movement born as a response to the horrors of World War I. It began in 1916 at the Cabaret Voltaire in Zurich as an artistic celebration of chaos and irrationality, as opposed to the logic and capitalism its members believed had launched the world into war. "Dada Excites Everything" responds to the increasing number of artistic and literary movements of the day that claimed purity, originality, and avant-garde tendencies. It also promotes its own revolutionary counterattack through an arsenal of provocative questions and criticizes established and conventional art and literary practices. Like many other treatises of its time, "Dada Excites Everything" was about the direction of art and literature; in particular, it refers to the place of Dada within the art and literary worlds and the distinctions between Dada and other modern art and literary movements in Europe, including cubism, futurism, and expressionism.

In 1921 Paris was the epicenter of Western art and literature. With the arrival of the charismatic and energetic leader of Dada, Tristan Tzara, a Romanian-born artist, writer, and critic, the city became a pivotal center for Dada activity. Significant Dada movements also cropped up in various forms in Germany, Holland, and the United States. A central characteristic of Dada was celebrating transnationalism by rejecting nationalism, which was an ominous and increasingly dire aspect of European society between the First and Second World Wars. The writers of the manifesto make clear and direct reference to the transnationalism of Dada by stating that "the signatories of this manifesto live in France, America, Spain, Germany, Italy, Switzerland, Belgium, etc. but have no nationality." In addition, the writers target Italian nationalism by naming heroes with fascist associations, such as Decadent poet and soldier Gabriele d'Annunzio, and linking those associations to futurism.

"Dada Excites Everything" was written only one year after the arrival in Paris of Dada hero Tzara and followed the spirit of both his activism and the tradition of the written manifesto within the political and cultural avant-garde as declarations and calls to action for change. Writing itself was a treasured medium of Dada artists, and most of the signatories of "Dada Excites Everything" had either collaborated on various Dada manifestos or had written their own. Independent publications that permeated Dada's literary and artistic practice, such as the French artist and poet Francis Picabia's *391*; the collective review *Littérature,* edited by André Breton, Philippe Soupault, and Louis Aragon; and the short-lived *Bleu,* based in Mantua, Italy, helped keep readers aware of Dada pronouncements and activities and published various manifestos and treatises.

"Dada Excites Everything" encourages future Dada manifestos to define and attack rival art and literary movements and helped perpetuate the practice of inflammatory writing to question and provoke. It advocates the Dada treatment of words and meaning as malleable and flexible and emphasizes the characteristic negation and nihilism of early Dada interventions and actions. The writing style perpetuates the parallel artistic technique in the use of collage and a similar style of film editing that juxtaposed unusual elements. In both their literary and artistic output, Dadaists used the technique of collage to cut up, rearrange, and recontextualize words and images and their meanings. The writers of this treatise take seemingly disparate words and sentences and list and repeat them to emphasize their meaning but also use repetition to subvert that emphasis.

THEMES AND STYLE

The central theme of "Dada Excites Everything" is a warning to its readers. In a time of continued social and cultural unrest throughout Europe, the treatise warns about the dangers of intellectual stagnation, inertia, and apathy. It warns its readers to be wary of blind belief, false prophets, fascism, and totalitarianism. In keeping with other Dada writing, "Dada Excites Everything" exhorts readers to maintain vigilance and be aware of falsehoods and truth in language. The text warns, "Beware of forgeries!" and goes on to differentiate Dada's "pure idiocy" from "dogmatism and pretentious imbecility," which is an indictment of futurism. Most fervently, "Dada Excites Everything" cautions against the dangers of reason, rationality, and seriousness.

The reader becomes involved in an absurd conversation, complete with a survey of topics encouraging him or her to conjure images of seemingly random and unassociated notions, such as accordions, women's pants, and Massachusetts. Interspersed within these banal subjects are associations to fascism and reminders of recent hard-fought rights of the working class, such as the eight-hour work day. In addition, while continuing to be satirical and absurdist, "Dada Excites Everything" retains Dada's revolutionary inclinations by insisting that "the ministry is overturned." Ultimately, the document simultaneously questions and declares Dada's influence. Toward the end, the writers offer a reward to "the person who finds the best way to explain DADA to us."

The writers of "Dada Excites Everything" address the reader directly, using "you" and "citizens, comrades, ladies, gentlemen" as a means to engage the reader in the conversation. The authors employ characteristic Dada literary techniques, including the repetition of words that, when spoken, reveal a rhythmic pattern; erratic changes in typography and size as a deliberate subversion of a linear and logical format and layout; and the intentional use of words that lend themselves to double meanings to enlist the reader's own perspective and imagination to create and reconcile meaning. The writers barrage the reader with simultaneous negations and assertions of Dada

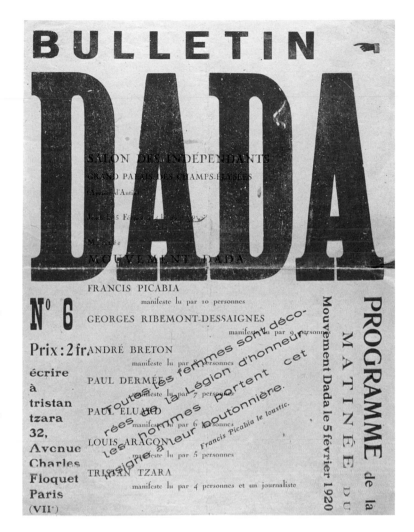

An advertisement for a Dada exhibition in Paris, France, in *Bulletin Dada*, 1920. This exhibition featured many of the writers and artists behind the 1921 manifesto "Dada Excites Everything." GALLERIA PICTOGRAMMA, ROME, ITALY/ALINARI/THE BRIDGEMAN ART LIBRARY

in relation to other contemporaneous art movements and philosophies by describing cubism as "constructing a cathedral of artistic liver paste" and stating that expressionism "poisons artistic sardines." In response to the repeated question, "What does Dada do?" the writers declare that "Dada passes everything through a net." The nonsensical and absurd descriptions of other movements is counteracted by the imagery of Dada cleansing or filtering out these movements' impurities. The use of language in this way causes a kind of disorientation in the reader that was probably meant as a self-referential parallel to the disruption of Marinetti's lecture, for which the pamphlet was produced.

CRITICAL DISCUSSION

The January 15, 1921, event at the Théatre de l'Ouevre received more acclaim in Dada publications and newspapers than did the actual text of "Dada Excites Everything." Descriptions of the event and its aftermath in the form of letters to the editors of the French art and literary review *Comoedia* suggest that the associated Dadaists would have gladly entered into fisticuffs with Marinetti based on his threat of violence in order to quash the disruption at his lecture. The Italian publication *Bleu* noted that "Futurists and Dadaists clashed" and provided its own rebuttal to the tenuous arguments made by Marinetti during his lecture and to the larger suggestion of an owed legacy to futurism. "Dada Excites Everything" was published in its entirety in the first edition of the 1921 quarterly publication *Little Review,* a "magazine of the arts" based in the United States that promoted many international surrealists and Dadaists.

The writers of "Dada Excites Everything" attempted to resurrect the unabashedly ridiculous and disruptive characteristics and motivations of early Dada in both print and action. Soon after its publication, however, a long-standing rift within the Paris Dada group ruptured and caused a permanent division between ultimately antagonistic factions. Both groups continued to pursue the agitation characteristic of Dada through interventions, displays, and manifestos. Several of the signatories of the document, including Tzara, Hans Arp, Man Ray, Ernst, and most notably Breton—who became a leader of the surrealist movement and wrote the *Manifesto of Surrealism* (1924)—went on to work in the surrealist style, often incorporating themes of reason and logic from the Dada arsenal into their work.

While "Dada Excites Everything" did not receive as much critical literary response as the poetry of the Dadaists or as much attention as the earlier and seminal "Dada Manifesto" (1918), also written by Tzara, it is included in most surveys of Dada literature and continues to serve as an important example of the type of visual and literary production of the Dada movement. "Dada Excites Everything" evokes the spirit and motivations of the European avant-garde during a fertile period of both art and literature. Copies of the manifesto are collected and sold at fine art and print auctions and housed in major libraries and museum collections. In 1989 the work was included in the exhibition "Word as Image" at the National Gallery of Australia.

BIBLIOGRAPHY

Sources

Ades, Dawn. *The Dada Reader: A Critical Anthology.* Chicago: U of Chicago P, 2006. Print.

Caws, Mary Ann, ed. *Manifesto: A Century of Isms.* Lincoln: U of Nebraska P, 2001. Print.

"Dada souleve tout." *Little Review* 7.4 (1921): 62-63. Print.

Danchev, Alex, ed. *100 Artists' Manifestos.* London: Penguin, 2011. Print.

Lippard, Lucy, ed. *Dadas on Art.* Englewood Cliffs: Prentice-Hall, 1971. Print.

Sanouillet, Michel. *Dada in Paris.* Cambridge: MIT P, 2009. Print.

Further Reading

Allen, Roy F. "Zurich Dada, 1916-1919: The Proto Phase of the Movement." *Dada/Dimensions.* Ed. Stephen C. Foster. Ann Arbor: UMI Research, 1985. *Literature Resource Center.* Web. 7 Nov. 2012.

Huelsenbeck, Richard, ed. *The Dada Almanac.* London: Atlas, 1998. Print.

Marinetti, F. T. *Critical Writings: New Edition.* Ed. Gunter Berghaus. Trans. Doug Thompson. New York: Farrar, Straus & Giroux, 2006. Print.

Motherwell, Robert, ed. *The Dada Painters and Poets: An Anthology,* Boston: G. K. Hall, 1951. Print.

October 105 (2003): 1-181. Print.

Richter, Hans. *Dada: Art and Anti-art.* New York: McGraw-Hill, 1965. Print.

Tzara, Tristan. *Seven Dada Manifestos and Lampisteries.* Trans. Barbara Wright. London: Calder, 1977.

Victoria DeCuir

DADA MANIFESTO 1918

Tristan Tzara

OVERVIEW

"Dada Manifesto 1918" is one of a series of essays in which Romanian-French poet Tristan Tzara (whose original name was Samy Rosenstock) attempts to express the nature of Dada, an art movement of the early twentieth century. First published in Zurich in 1918, Tzara's manifesto decries many of the values that determined previous artistic discourse and singles out cubism and futurism as passé and uninteresting. Tzara formulates the Dada aesthetic largely in the negative, as a rejection of beauty, perfection, and especially morality, which the artist sees as "an injection of chocolate into the veins of all men." Tzara also offers, in the phrasing and structure of the manifesto, a formal recapitulation of Dadaist ideas. The author injects the manifesto with lines of free verse, jumbled phrases, and bold, sometimes grotesque images, and he fluctuates in tone between serious essayist and experimental, ecstatic poet.

The manifesto was one element of a comprehensive campaign by Tzara to establish Dada both within its Zurich outpost and internationally. In this effort, critics largely concur that Tzara succeeded, though Dada as a distinct movement was soon overtaken by the demurring surrealists. Over the course of the twentieth century, "Dada Manifesto 1918" became one of the most influential documents of its kind, serving as a point of reference to be imitated or rejected by the founders of several succeeding cultural movements. Moreover, Tzara's insistence on the manifesto as an art form in itself infused later manifesto writers with a degree of artistic self-consciousness. Today, the work is a focal point in academic discussions about the nature and efficacy of manifestos in general.

HISTORICAL AND LITERARY CONTEXT

"Dada Manifesto 1918" is a statement of purpose of an art movement that gained strength in the context of rapid technological and social change via new genres and aesthetics. Numerous art movements, including cubism, futurism, and (in literature) imagism, that developed during this time were variously characterized by their political outlook, their choice of subjects, and the technical properties of their work. At the same time, there was a growing sense among art and literary critics that these disparate movements represented an underlying trend that might be labeled "modernism" or "avant-garde," despite practitioners' insistence on the uniqueness of their art. World War I dimmed the hopes of many of these artists. It all but extinguished the vorticists in England, the futurists in Italy, and other pockets of innovative art throughout Europe.

The war gave rise to new art movements, including Dada, that reacted not only against the horror of industrialized warfare, but also against the styles of art that had come to emblematize confident militarism. Tzara had witnessed the encroachment of the war on his home country of Romania before seeking refuge in Zurich in 1915. He was disgusted by the futurist celebration of mechanized warfare and by the perceived pandering of contemporary art to bourgeois sensibilities. Tzara recognized the potential for an art that would sublimate rather than glorify violence, directing it toward those he saw as the real perpetrators of the war. In a 1998 piece for Art Bulletin, S.A. Mansbach writes that Tzara "exhorted his contemporaries ... to replace pencils with knives and substitute for the customary editorial conventions a collection of weapons with which to bomb bourgeois hearths." This "assault on rationality and conventional aesthetic expectations" is developed at length in the 1918 manifesto.

As Martin Puchner notes in *Poetry of the Revolution: Marx, Manifestos, and the Avant-Gardes* (2006), Tzara was one of many avant-garde artists to participate in the "manifesto culture" of the early twentieth century. Futurists, vorticists, and imagists had produced series of essays announcing their work, asserting its political relevance, and trumpeting its superiority to prior movements. Dadaists themselves were active manifesto writers, with Hugo Ball penning the first "Dada Manifesto" in Zurich in 1916. Tzara wrote numerous tracts for the movement, which together with his 1918 essay, were collected as *Seven Dada Manifestos and Lampisteries*.

"Dada Manifesto 1918" came as the Dada movement was approaching its height, having achieved a degree of local fame in Zurich in 1916 and proceeding to a brief period of international interest around 1920. Dadaists, Tzara among them, pushed the nihilistic element of Dada "anti-art," delivering performances and exhibitions that jettisoned any resemblance to traditional art. Despite (or perhaps,

Key Facts

Time Period:
Early 20th Century

Movement/Issue:
Dadaism; Avant-gardism

Place of Publication:
France

Language of Publication:
French

THE GAS HEART AND THE END OF DADA

The Gas Heart (1921) is a short play that encapsulates Tzara's major expression of Dada aesthetics. The drama offers a compressed but vivid portrait of the Dada insistence on flouting audience (and especially critical) expectations: Its own stage directions announce it as "the only and greatest three-act hoax of the century," and the first character to speak, Eye, begins his monologue with "Statues jewels / roasts statues jewels…" Such decontextualized repetition is the mainstay of the play, with the characters Nose and Neck later carrying on an entire conversation of adjectives: "Huge. / Fixed. / Cruel. / Broad."

First performed June 10, 1921, in Paris, *The Gas Heart* was extremely poorly received. This in itself was not so ominous—after all, Tzara believed that real artists "rejoice[d] at the venom of the masses." The play's repetitive and nihilistic style, however, galled Tzara's longtime collaborator, poet André Breton. Nursed by inflammatory pamphlets on both sides, this tension went beyond the aesthetic and exploded in an outright brawl when Tzara reprised the performance as part of a 1923 show. Within two years, Breton and associates had resuscitated a dormant surrealism into a recognizable movement, complete with headquarters (the Bureau of Surrealist Research), a dedicated periodical (*The Surrealist Revolution*), and, of course, its own manifesto.

in part, owing to) the enthusiasm of its proponents, the Dada movement eventually gave in to factional conflicts. Many consider Tzara's play *The Gas Heart* (1921) to be the last major Dada production, though works labeled as Dada were produced as late as 1924.

THEMES AND STYLE

In "Dada Manifesto 1918," Tzara takes an iconoclastic approach to art, arts movements, and even the act of manifesto writing: "To put out a manifesto you must want ABC to fulminate against 1, 2, 3." Tzara takes pains to demonstrate that he wishes to demolish, rather than replace, the false idols of earlier art; he explains that the term *Dada* itself is so laden with potential meanings as to be meaningless. At once (allegedly) a term used by the Kru (an ethnic group of Liberia and the Ivory Coast) to describe a sacred cow's tail, the Italian word for "cube," and the Russian and the Romanian word for "hobby horse," *Dada* is Tzara's first and most resonant example of the over-determined signs from which art is constructed. Yet Tzara remains circumspect about Dada's status as a movement: "I speak only of myself since I do not wish to convince, I have no right to drag others into my river."

Tzara alternately explains his own position relative to other art movements and demonstrates the Dada approach to writing. Under headings such as "Dada Means Nothing" and "Active Simplicity," he

makes it evident that he is not interested in providing a political argument for the movement. "I am writing a manifesto and I don't want anything," the author insists, paradoxically declaring himself "on principle against manifestos" and, for that matter, "against principles." Tzara lays out a series of somewhat self-contradictory aphorisms regarding what art should and should not be—including "art is never beautiful by decree" and "beauty is dead"—interspersed with lines that enact rather than promote Dada. For example, Tzara offers the cry:

> Ideal, ideal, ideal
> Knowledge, knowledge, knowledge,
> Boomboom, boomboom, boomboom

as "a pretty faithful version" of human progress in general. The poet loosely and tentatively associates art with class struggle, as when he sarcastically asks if "the aim of art [is] to make money and cajole the nice nice bourgeois," but in the 1918 essay this is a secondary motif, symptomatic of the larger philosophical forces constraining artistic freedom.

Tzara's manifesto draws on startling imagery to show his dissatisfaction with the mannered quality of earlier art movements. Brief passages on the sublimity of art invoke chrysanthemums, archangels, and a "luminous waterfall," but these are frequently associated with diseases and bodily fluids, seemingly to undermine the notion of the sublime. The manifesto draws to a close with a litany of sorts, not so much defining Dada as extending the term to include a huge range of social and artistic reactions: "Dada: abolition of memory; Dada: abolition of archaeology; Dada: abolition of prophets; Dada: abolition of the future…" In the end, Tzara abandons even this politicized language, leaving "a roaring of tense colors, an interlacing of opposites and of all contradictions, grotesques, inconsistencies: / LIFE."

CRITICAL DISCUSSION

Tzara's manifesto found a ready audience in Zurich, if a less enthusiastic one than had greeted the announcements of Dada in 1916. "Dada Manifesto 1918" formed an important part of the poet's transnational efforts at promoting Dada. Writing for *American Scholar* in 2000, Jacques Barzun notes that this and other manifestos "made their way across frontiers, so that by 1920, Dadaism … was one of the new schools that critics treated with respect." Nowhere were Dada principles (or anti-principles) more in evidence than in Tzara's own poetry, which reached Swiss, German, and French audiences through a network of Dada periodicals. Further Dada manifestos, such as a 1920 essay by Louis Aragon, attempted to extend Tzara's claims into a realm of total nihilism, declaring (or demanding), "enough of all these imbecilities, no more, no more, no more…"

While not contesting its place in the history of the manifesto genre, critics have reassessed the extent to which Tzara's ironic use of the manifesto form was truly a novel development. In the article "The Manifesto as Art Form" (1984), Marjorie Perloff notes that the transition from futurism to Dada "is a shorter step than the Dadaists would have liked to have us think"—many of the devices that made Tzara's manifesto memorable have clear precedents in the "1909 Futurist Manifesto" of F. T. Marinetti, despite Tzara's forceful rejection of futurist ideals. Gavin Grindon, writing in *Oxford Art Journal* (2011), further suggests the continuity of the 1918 document with earlier movements by noting in Tzara's work the centrality of protest, an element that the critic traces (despite the poet's own anti-Marxist performances) as far back as the *Communist Manifesto* (1848).

"Dada Manifesto 1918" has been upheld as a point of reference for latter-day manifesto writers, primarily within the arts, where its aestheticized irony is generally more welcome than in political debates. Writing for *Design Issues* (2002), Sharon Helmer Poggenpohl and Sang-Soo Ahn note the echoes of Dada in successive movements such as Fluxus, which, indeed, was briefly known as "neo-dadaism." Moreover, Poggenpohl and Ahn show that the influence of Tzara's contentious work has percolated into the manifestos of not only artists but also professional associations of educators. In a sense, Tzara's work has come full circle: Announced as shocking and bizarre in 1918, the elements of Dada have become classic talking points of twentieth-century art history.

Exquisite Corpse, a 1929 drawing by Valentine Hugo, Tristan Tzara, and Greta Knutsen. One of the leading figures of Dada, Tzara wrote about the movement in works such as "Dada Manifesto 1918." CNAC/MNAM/DIST. RMN-GRAND PALAIS/ART RESOURCE, NY

BIBLIOGRAPHY

Sources

Barzun, Jacques. "The Artist as Prophet and Jester." *American Scholar* 69.1 (2000): 15-33. Web. 31 July 2012.

Grindon, Gavin. "Surrealism, Dada, and the Refusal of Work: Autonomy, Activism, and Social Participation in the Radical Avant-Garde." *Oxford Art Journal* 34.11 (2011): 79-96. Web. 31 July 2012.

Mansbach, S.A. "The Foreignness of Classical Modern Art in Romania." *Art Bulletin* 80.3 (1998): 534-54. Web. 31 July 2012.

Further Reading

Garner, Stanton B., Jr. "The Gas Heart: Disfigurement and the Dada Body." *Modern Drama* 50.4 (2007): 500-16. Web. 30 July 2012.

Hage, Emily. "The Magazine as Strategy: Tristan Tzara's Dada and the Seminal Role of Dada Art Journals in the Dada Movement." *Journal of Modern Periodical Studies* 2.1 (2011): 33-53. Web. 30 July 2012.

Jaussen, Paul. "'Allow Intelligence to Survive': Life's Language in Williams and Tzara." *William Carlos Williams Review* 28.1-2 (2008): 17-33. Web. 30 July 2012.

Melzer, Annabelle. *Dada and Surrealist Performance.* Baltimore, MD: Johns Hopkins UP, 1994.

Perloff, Marjorie. "'Violence and Precision': The Manifesto as Art Form." *Chicago Review* 34.2 (1984): 65-101. Web. 31 July 2012.

Poggenpohl, Sharon Helmer and Sang-Soo Ahn. "Between Word and Deed: The ICOGRADA Design Education Manifesto, Seoul 2000." *Design Issues* 18.2 (2002): 46-56. Web. 31 July 2012.

Puchner, Martin. *Poetry of the Revolution: Marx, Manifestos, and the Avant-Gardes.* Princeton: Princeton UP, 2006. Print.

———. "Manifesto = Theatre." *Theatre Journal* 54.3 (2002): 449-65. Web. 30 July 2012.

Tzara, Tristan. "Dadaist Manifesto." Trans. Mary Ann Caws. *Manifesto: A Century of Isms.* Ed. Mary Ann Caws. Lincoln: U of Nebraska, 2001. Print.

———. *The Gas Heart.* Trans. Michael Benedikt. *Emory University Dept. of English,* 10 March 1999. Web. 30 July 2012.

———. *Seven Dada Manifestos and Lampisteries.* Trans. Barbara Wright. London: Calder, 1997. Print.

Yanoshevsky, Galia. "The Literary Manifesto and Related Notions: A Select Annotated Bibliography." *Poetics Today* 30.2 (2009): 287-315. Web. 30 July 2012.

Michael Hartwell

IN THE GUISE OF A LITERARY MANIFESTO

Aimé Césaire

❖ *Key Facts*

Time Period:
Mid-20th Century

Movement/Issue:
Colonialism; Négritude;
Surrealism

Place of Publication:
Martinique

**Language of
Publication:**
French

OVERVIEW

Martinican writer and politician Aimé Césaire's 1942 surrealist poem "In the Guise of a Literary Manifesto" (En guise de manifeste littéraire) challenges European hegemony to demand recognition of black writers. Written at a time of international upheaval, the manifesto is indicative of imminent political and social changes in the Caribbean. The manifesto announces the entrance of nonwhite voices into the Western literary arena. Deftly employing avant-garde, surrealist stylings, "In the Guise of a Literary Manifesto" censures the very culture it mimics. Although the poem broadly addresses colonialism, Césaire's critique targets Eurocentric intellectual and literary communities that had historically marginalized black writers and black experience.

The poem received little attention upon its publication, but it has come to be regarded as emblematic of anticolonial stirrings in mid-twentieth century Martinique. Published in the fifth volume of Césaire's surrealist literary journal, *Tropiques,* "In the Guise of a Literary Manifesto" is a reworked excerpt from Césaire's celebrated epic poem and first published work, *Notebook of a Return to My Native Land* (*Cahier d'un retour au pays natal*) (1939), which recounts an expatriate's return to a homeland devastated by colonial rule. The longer work has received significant attention for its assertion of black Caribbean identity and for coining the term "négritude." Scholars look to "In the Guise of a Literary Manifesto" as a model of avant-garde manifestos and a demonstration of black Caribbean unrest.

HISTORICAL AND LITERARY CONTEXT

"In the Guise of a Literary Manifesto" articulates the discontent felt by nonwhite colonial subjects in the mid-twentieth century, a time when many colonies were attempting to become more politically and culturally autonomous. Responding to nearly three centuries of colonial rule, the manifesto seeks to end the marginalization of blacks by their European colonizers. Almost one hundred years after the abolishment of slavery in Martinique, racial tensions remained high, and black West Indians continued to suffer prejudicial treatment at the hands of whites. Preceded by artists and writers involved in movements—such as the Harlem Renaissance in the 1920s and 1930s—that affirmed and celebrated black culture,

black West Indians began to seek a new collective identity and validation of their culture and heritage. "In the Guise of a Literary Manifesto" is a testament to that search.

By the time "In the Guise of a Literary Manifesto" was published, Martinique—still a French colony—was fast becoming a center of intellectual and cultural revolution. Spurred on by international black-centric movements, Césaire collaborated with other Caribbean thinkers to found the 1930s négritude movement, which looked to Africa as the primary source for developing a black West Indian identity. Significantly, négritude enabled nonwhite colonial subjects to divorce their identities from a history of subjugation. Surrealism, a 1920s artistic movement started by André Breton, further cultivated anticolonial sentiment and the interest in Africa. Eschewing the European emphasis on the value of reason and tradition, surrealists instead found truth in the instinctual and irrational, thus offering Martinicans validation in their rejection of their colonizers' worldview.

The manifesto's dedication to Breton, author of the *Manifesto of Surrealism,* reveals much about the text's literary context. Having escaped the French Vichy government, Breton allegedly encountered Césaire's work in passing during a short visit to Martinique in 1941. The first issue of *Tropiques* had just been published, and Breton's interest in the journal led to international recognition of Césaire and Martinican surrealism. The journal had an international list of contributors, but its perspective was decidedly Martinican and helped to galvanize a secondary movement, black surrealism. The imagery of "In the Guise of a Literary Manifesto" demonstrates a surrealist influence, but its anticolonial message and colloquial phrases convey a uniquely Martinican take on the European movement. The manifesto's assertive pro-black stance also demonstrates the influence of black movements and thinkers in other countries, including poet Langston Hughes of the Harlem Renaissance and pan-Africanism proponent Marcus Garvey.

"In the Guise of a Literary Manifesto" encapsulates the malaise experienced by many in Martinique and throughout the French Antilles prior to decolonization, which occurred in Martinique in 1946. While not a direct cause, the increased sense of solidarity and self-determination promoted in the text may have contributed to the desire for change. Soon after the manifesto's publication, though, Caribbean intellectuals abandoned avant-garde modes of resistance, of which Césaire's work is an example, turning instead to communism. Although forceful and resonant, "In the Guise of a Literary Manifesto" has not been as influential as the longer poem in which the piece originally appeared. *Notebook on a Return to My Native Land* has come to be regarded as a seminal postcolonial text and integral to the development of black Martinican identity.

THEMES AND STYLE

The central theme of "In the Guise of a Literary Manifesto" is the rejection of colonial domination and intellectual marginalization. The poem echoes many of the same themes and concerns found in the longer work from which it was taken. Prompted by Césaire's return to Martinique after eight years abroad in Europe, *Notebook* depicts a speaker returning to his homeland to find pervasive complacency with regard to racialized aspects of colonialism. Initially, the speaker mourns the cultural demise brought about by colonial rule; later, he undertakes to reinvigorate his people and to articulate an independent sense of self through a celebration of the Caribbean. Distilling these ideas, "In the Guise of a Literary Manifesto" directly refutes myths of black Caribbean racial inferiority: "Who and what are we? Admirable question! Haters. Builders. Traitors. Hougans. Especially Hougans." The speaker does not directly answer this question yet asserts his autonomy throughout the remainder of the poem, declaring, "And so we sing."

The manifesto achieves its rhetorical effect through an appeal to black Caribbean solidarity. This call to unity is made via invocations of the violent subjugation of blacks under colonial power, imagery that equates colonialism with disease, and affirmations of self-determination. In a veiled reference, Césaire describes colonial incursion as "poisonous flowers bursting across furious prairies" and "skies of love slashed with embolism." Equating the arrival of Europeans with pestilence sets up a diametric opposition between the speaker and his presumably European audience. The repetition of "I, only I" later in the poem underscores the speaker's difference from his audience and significantly affirms his sovereignty.

"In the Guise of a Literary Manifesto" is a free-verse poem replete with disjointed imagery. Its confusing metaphors are often considered opaque and challenging for lay readers, but the poem's tone is unambiguous. Aggressive language permeates the manifesto; in a declaration of self-validation, the speaker states, "Make room for me. I will not get out of your way." Critic Gregson Davis has pointed out the sardonic choice of title as "a welcome signpost for the interpreter who is interested in clues to that elusive critical grail, the 'intention of the author.'" Davis's implication is that Césaire's poem imitates the style of a literary manifesto with the intention to undermine

AIMÉ CÉSAIRE: ACTIVIST POLITICIAN

Writer Aimé Césaire's legacy rests largely on his foundational role in the Caribbean literary scene and his contribution to the négritude movement. However, Césaire's politics were not limited to his literary work. Throughout his life, Césaire was an internationally recognized political figure. As one critic put it, "One of the singular achievements of this towering Black figure … was his ability to combine these usually contradictory roles, that of reflective writer and activist politician." First elected mayor of the Martinican capital, Fort-de-France, in 1945, Césaire held that position for fifty-six years. He also served as a deputy in the French National Assembly, representing his island in the Parisian metropole. As a representative, Césaire ardently advocated for the departmentalization of the Lesser Antilles. The act, which passed in 1946, granted the island official "state" status within the French government.

However, rather than encouraging development and cultural independence as was hoped, departmentalization engendered economic dependence and institutionalized assimilation. Critics decried the move and denounced Césaire for his role in it. Abandoning the Communist Party, Césaire founded the Martinican Progressive Party in 1958, advocating for a reversal of the "assimilating, deculturalizing process that statehood unleashed." At the time of his death in 2008, Césaire still had not accomplished this goal, yet he maintained a staunch anticolonial position to the end. On one infamous occasion, Césaire refused to meet then-Minister of the Interior Nicolas Sarkozy because of the latter's endorsement of pedagogical emphasis on colonialism's positive effects. In tribute to his significant and lasting impact, Césaire was honored with a state funeral in Martinique, the third ever for a writer and the only one to take place outside of France.

the supposed universality of the genre. By dealing intensively with race in his manifesto, Césaire emphasizes the ability of black West Indians to create literature in their own image and thus assert their independence from their white European counterparts.

CRITICAL DISCUSSION

When "In the Guise of a Literary Manifesto" was first published in 1942, little fanfare accompanied its incendiary language and politics. Its readership was limited to Caribbean and European intellectuals associated with *Tropiques,* many of whom were presumably already aligned with Césaire's position. Moreover, the manifesto had been previously published as part of *Notebook* three years earlier, again with little acknowledgment. Nonetheless, *Notebook* was heralded by Breton as "the greatest lyrical monument of this time" and "a poem with a subject if not with a thesis." Even if the work was not widely known, its message was clearly received by readers. Not until a 1956 reissue of *Notebook* generated widespread interest in Césaire's literary works did "In the Guise of a Literary Manifesto" become better known.

Aimé Césaire's surreal "anti-manifesto" attacked the universalizing assumptions of the manifesto as a literary form. © PIMENTEL JEAN/ COLLECTION CORBIS KIPA

exploring its role in establishing racial difference and black francophone solidarity. Winkiel writes, "With the words 'So we're singing,' Césaire self-reflexively comments on his poetic that renders Afro-Caribbean and black diasporic experience plural, remembered, and in contemporaneous conflict with metropolitan centers of modernity." Regardless of the terms in which analysis of the poem is couched, however, "In the Guise of a Literary Manifesto" offers a valuable record of black intellectual thought and the appropriation of surrealism in mid-twentieth-century Martinique.

BIBLIOGRAPHY

Sources

"Aimé Césaire (1913-2008)." *Literary Movements: Manifesto.* 10 Feb. 2011. Web. 9 July 2012.

Davis, Gregson. *Aimé Césaire.* Cambridge: Cambridge UP, 1997. Print.

Kruidenier, Julie-Françoise. "Francophone Manifestos: On Solidarity in the French-Speaking World." *International Journal of Francophone Studies* 12.2-3 (2009): 271-87. Print.

Puchner, Martin, ed. *Poetry of the Revolution: Marx, Manifestos, and the Avant-Gardes.* Princeton: Princeton UP, 2006. Print.

Rosemont, Franklin, and Robin D. G. Kelley, eds. *Black, Brown, & Beige: Surrealist Writings from Africa and the Diaspora.* Austin: U of Texas P, 2009. Print.

Winkiel, Laura. *Modernism, Race and Manifestos.* Cambridge: Cambridge UP, 2011. Print.

Further Reading

"Aimé Césaire, Martinique Poet and Politician, Dies at 94." *New York Times.* New York Times, 18 Apr. 2008. Web. 8 July 2012.

Arnold, A. James. "Césaire is Dead: Long Live Césaire!: Recuperations and Reparations." *French Politics, Culture & Society* 27.3 (2009): 9-18. Print.

———. "Césaire's Notebook as Palimpsest: The Text Before, During, and After WWII." *Research in African Literatures* 35.3 (2004). 133-40. Print.

———. *Modernism and Negritude: The Poetry and Poetics of Aimé Césaire.* Cambridge: Harvard UP, 1981. Print.

Britton, Celia. "How to be Primitive: *Tropiques,* Surrealism and Ethnography." *Paragraph* 32.3 (2009): 168-81. Print.

Dash, J. Michael. "Aimé Césaire: The Bearable Lightness of Becoming." *PMLA* 125.3 (2010): 737-42. Print.

Hale, Thomas. *Critical Perspectives on Aimé Césaire.* Three Continents, 1980. Print.

Miles, William F. S. "Introduction: Aimé Césaire as Poet, Rebel, Statesman." *French Politics, Culture & Society* 27.3 (2009): 1-8. Print.

Winkiel, Laura. "The Rhetoric of Violence: Avant-Garde Manifestoes and the Myths of Racial Community." *Avant-Garde Critical Studies: The Intervention of Politics in the European Avant-Garde (1906-1940).* Ed. Sascha Bru and Gunther Matens. New York: Rodopi, 2006: 65-90. Print.

"In the Guise of a Literary Manifesto" appeared to diminish in relevance as political and cultural movements shifted. As a result of waning Martinican and global interest in surrealism, "In the Guise of a Literary Manifesto" came to be regarded as a relic of mid-century avant-garde thought. While the 1946 departmentalization of Martinique officially ended the island's colony status, this bureaucratic change did little to resolve issues of racial inequality, economic dependence, and cultural assimilation, instead merely shifting the terms of the colonial conversation, which would be taken up by later writers. Today, the poem stands as testimony to the time and place in which it was created—pre-departmental Martinique—and offers a better understanding of black intellectualism, anticolonial activism, and nonwhite manifestations of the avant-garde.

Abetted by the rising popularity of postcolonial criticism and a renewed interest in the poet following his death, Césaire's works have received increased scholarly attention since the turn of the twenty-first century. Much scholarship has focused on the text as a self-proclaimed manifesto; critics have considered its genre conventions, its deployment of those conventions, and its goals. In his book *Poetry of the Revolution: Marx, Manifestos, and the Avant-Gardes,* Martin Puchner considers Césaire's poem foremost as an avant-garde text and looks to the intersection of revolution and art therein. Alternately, Laura Winkiel, in her book *Modernism, Race and Manifestos,* and Julie-Françoise Kruidenier, writing in the *International Journal of Francophone Studies,* treat the poem as an anticolonial text,

Elizabeth Boeheim

LÉGITIME DÉFENSE

Etienne Léro, Réne Menil, Jules Monnerot

OVERVIEW

The first and only issue of the radical journal *Légitime défense* (Self-defense) was published in France in 1932 by a group of Martinican students studying in Paris, including Réne Menil, Jules Monnerot, and Etienne Léro. The preface to the journal is regarded as a militant declaration of a new generation of Afro-Caribbean poets, attacking assimilationist tendencies of the previous generation of poets. The journal emerged around the same time that the Négritude movement was formed in Paris by the likes of Aimé Césaire and other Caribbean intellectuals, although the authors of *Légitime défense* did not share much of the Négritude ideology but rather espoused Marxist and surrealist ideals. Addressed directly to the Martinican bourgeoisie and members of the older intellectual generation on the island, the journal advocated an anti-imperialist struggle that incited colonial peoples against the colonial powers and the bourgeoisie.

The French elite rejected and French authorities suppressed *Légitime défense* because of its vicious attack on colonial and French bourgeoisies and aristocracies. While the publication did not directly spark any anti-imperialist revolutionary acts, it did have a significant impact on the Négritude movement and the formation of modern Francophone black literature. In the journal, Léro and his fellow authors present a "legitimate defense" against the politics of oppression and colonial domination. They focus on two main issues: the need for the liberation of colonized peoples and the development of a literary style based in black culture. Nevertheless, the development of "black values" took a backseat to the work's primary focus on social transformation. Today, *Légitime défense* is recognized for the historic role it played in the birth of modern Francophone literature.

HISTORICAL AND LITERARY CONTEXT

The recent history of Martinique and other French colonies in the Caribbean informed the actions of the writers of the *Légitime défense.* Slavery had been abolished in 1848, but abolition did little to relieve racial tensions on the island. At the turn of the twentieth century, there remained rigid class boundaries largely determined by race, which greatly limited opportunities for social mobility of blacks, Indians, and other recent immigrants to the island. The exploitation of the predominately black and brown labor force was made apparent in the construction of the Panama Canal, which began in 1905. The financial greed of investors and the colonial elite who would benefit from the canal greatly devalued the lives of the laborers. The Martinican students who authored the 1932 journal were children of elite Creole families who also benefited from the oppression and exploitation of their own people and who tended to deny or ignore their own African roots.

Growing unrest among lower and middle class colonists in Martinique informed the anti-imperialist ideology of Léro and his fellow Martinicans in Paris. Léro, Minel, and Monnerot were among the members of the young generation of colonial Martinique bourgeoisie of color who had received government grants to study in Paris between the two world wars. The surrealist and communist movements in Europe during the period directly influenced the group's ideology. Around the time that *Légitime défense* was published, European surrealists strove to dissolve the boundaries between surrealism and communism in an attempt to gain momentum for their shared anti-imperialist politics. Several prominent surrealists, including André Breton,

❖ *Key Facts*

Time Period:
Mid-20th Century

Movement/Issue:
Anti-assimilationism;
Anticolonialism;
Afro-Caribbean
aesthetics

Place of Publication:
France

**Language of
Publication:**
French

A harbor in Martinique, homeland of the three students who published *Légitime défense.* JAKE RAJS/PHOTODISC/GETTY IMAGES

PRIMARY SOURCE

LÉGITIME DÉFENSE

THIS IS JUST a foreword. We consider ourselves totally committed. We are sure that other young people like us exist prepared to add their signatures to ours and who – to the extent that it remains compatible with continuing to live – refuse to become part of the surrounding ignominy. And we've had it with those who try, consciously or not, with smiles, work, exactitude, propriety, speeches, writings, actions, and with their very being, to make us believe that things can continue as they are. We rise up against all those who don't feel suffocated by this capitalist, Christian, bourgeois world, to which our protesting bodies reluctantly belong. All around the world the Communist Party (Third International) is about to play the decisive card of the 'Spirit' – in the Hegelian sense of the word. Its defeat, however impossible it might be to imagine that, would be the definitive end of the road for us. We believe unreservedly in its triumph because we accept Marx's dialectical materialism freed of all misleading interpretation and victoriously put to the test of events by Lenin. In this respect, we are ready to accept the discipline such conviction demands. In the concrete realm of means of human expression, we equally unreservedly accept surrealism with which our destiny in 1932 is linked. We refer our readers to Andre Breton's two manifestos and to all the works of Aragon, Andre Breton, Rene Crevel, Salvador Dali, Paul Eluard, Benjamin Peret and Tristan Tzara. We consider it to be one of the disgraces of our age that these works are not better known wherever French is read. And in Sade, Hegel, Lautreamont and Rimbaud – to mention just a few – we seek everything surrealism has taught us to find. We are ready to use the vast machinery that Freud has set in motion to dissolve the bourgeois family. We are hell–bent on sincerity. We want to see clearly into our dreams and we are listening to what they have to tell us. And our dreams allow us to clearly perceive the life they claim to be able to impose on us for such a long time. Of all the filthy bourgeois conventions we despise more than anything humanitarian hypocrisy that stinking emanation of Christian decay. We despise pity. We don't give a damn about sentiments. We intend to shed a light on human psychic concretions similar to that which illuminates Salvador Dali's splendid convulsive paintings, in which it sometimes seems that lovebirds, taking wing from assassinated conventions could suddenly become inkwell or hoe or small morsels of bread.

This little journal is a provisional tool, and if it collapses we shall find others. We are indifferent to the condition of time and space which, defining us in 1932 a people of the French Caribbean, have consequently established our initial

---

Louis Aragón, and Antonin Artaud, joined the French Communist Party in 1927. In 1925 France was at war with the colonized people of Morocco, who were fighting for freedom under the leadership of Abd-el-Krim. Martinican intellectuals were clearly influenced by the African colony's revolutionary ideals, which were backed by the surrealist community and the French Communist Party.

Légitime défense draws on several different literary and ideological traditions, namely the black expressionism emerging from the Harlem Renaissance, as well as radical labor journals in France and early twentieth-century surrealist and communist writing. The 1932 journal was viewed by many as the sequel—albeit more militant in nature than the original—to the journal *Revue du monde noir* (Review of the black world), which was published between 1931 and 1932 and had introduced its readers to the work of Harlem Renaissance writers, including Langston Hughes and Alain Locke. *Légitime défense* clearly follows in the tradition established in the writings of several anticolonial organizations that were active in Paris beginning in the late 1920s, including the Comité de défense de la race negré (Committee for the defense of the black race), which published the journal *La voix des Nègres* (The voice of the negro). This has been recognized as the prelude to the Négritude movement in its organization of blacks throughout the French Empire.

Légitime défense clearly influenced the work of many black French and Afro-Caribbean intellectuals in the early to mid-twentieth century. Many scholars have acknowledged the journal's impact on the work of André Breton and Aimé Césaire, particularly related to their attention to the experience of blacks in the Caribbean. This influence is evident in Césaire's 1939 book-length poem *Cahier d'un retour au pays natal* (Return to my native land), which reads as a poetic revolt against the oppressive French crown. René Menil was a major influence for Césaire, with whom he collaborated on the Martinique-based periodical *Tropiques* in the early 1940s. The influence of *Légitime défense* also is evident in the 1934 literary magazine, *L'Etudiant noir* (The black student), associated with the Négritude movement, which militantly opposed assimilation by valorizing the singularity of the black cultural experience. Today *Légitime défense*, while not as well known as the work of Césaire or other later Négritude writers, continues to receive significant scholarly interest.

boundaries without in the least limiting our field of action. This first collection of text is devoted particularly to the Caribbean question as it appears to us. (The following issue, without abandoning this question, will take up many others.) And if, by its content, this collection is primarily addressed to young French Caribbeans, it is because we think it opportune to aim our first effort at people whose capacity for revolt we certainly do not underestimate. If it is especially aimed at young blacks, it is because we consider that they in particular suffer from the effects of capitalism (apart from Africa, witness Scottsboro) and that they seem to offer—in having a materially determined ethnic personality – a generally higher potential for revolt and joy. For want of a black proletariat, from which international capitalism has withheld the means of understanding us, we are addressing the children of the black bourgeoisie. We are speaking to those who are not already branded as killed established fucked–up academic successful decorated decayed provided for decorative prudish opportunists. We are speaking to those who can still accept life with some appearance of truthfulness.

…

Emerging from the French mulatto bourgeoisie, one of the most depressing things on earth, we declare (and we shall not retract this declaration) that, faced with all the

administrative governmental, parliamentary industrial commercial corpses and so on, we intend—as traitors to this class—to take the path of treason so far as possible. We spit on everything they love and venerate, on everything that gives them sustenance and joy.

And all those who adopt the same attitude, no matter where they come from, will find a welcome among us.

Etienne Léro, Thélus Lero, René Menil, Jules–Marcel Monnerot, Michel Pilotin, Maurice–Sabas Quitman, Auguste Thésée, Pierre Yoyotte

1 June 1932

Note

1. If our critique is purely negative here, if we put forward no positive proposals against what we irrevocably condemn, we apologize for the necessity to make a start, something that has not allowed a certain maturity. From the next issue, we hope to develop our ideology of revolt.

THEMES AND STYLE

The declaration that prefaces the essays and poetry in *Légitime défense* reads as a virulent condemnation of the oppressive colonial structure of the French Empire and its engrained racism. The authors write, "Emerging from the French mulatto bourgeoisie, one of the most depressing things on earth, we declare (and we shall not retract this declaration) that, faced with all the administrative governmental, parliamentary industrial commercial corpses and so on, we intend—as traitors to this class—to take the path of treason so far as possible." The manifesto's authors not only identify their enemies but also fully embrace their militant stance against the French government. The manifesto declaration also expounds on its ideology, noting both the surrealist and communist thinkers who inspired their composition of *Légitime défense*.

The journal achieves its forceful message through a defiant, militant rhetoric that aims to establish the serious nature and legitimacy of its cause. By writing in the collective "we," the authors demonstrate the unity and solidarity of their group and invite other young people to join them: "We are sure that other young people like us exist prepared to add their signatures to ours, and who … refuse to become part of the surrounding ignominy." The

authors continue, "We intend—as traitors to this class—to take the path of treason so far as possible. We spit on everything that they love and venerate, especially those things that give them sustenance and joy." The authors' self-identification as "traitors" highlights the revolutionary nature of their message, distancing their work from a purely literary or aesthetic declaration. Yet the message also has a very personal element—they are traitors not just to the French crown but to their class—Léro and his peers declare their hostility toward the values and principles of their own bourgeois parents.

Légitime défense relies on a hostile, impassioned tone to communicate the urgency of its cause. Although written in a relatively formal style, the journal does not veil its denunciatory message but rather illustrates the authors' strong feelings through descriptive prose. "It is only by horribly gritting our teeth that we are able to endure the abominable system of constraints and restrictions, the extermination of love and the limitation of the dream, generally known by the name of western civilization.… We spit on everything that they love and venerate, especially those things that give them sustenance and joy." The image of gritting one's teeth and spitting on the cherished possessions of one's enemies enhances the force

DEVELOPING A DIASPORIC BLACK CONSCIOUSNESS: THE NÉGRITUDE MOVEMENT

A literary and ideological movement, Négritude was developed in France in the 1930s by black Francophone writers, intellectuals, and politicians whose founders included Martinican poet Aimé Césaire, future Senegalese President Léopold Sédar Senghor, and Léon Damas from Guiana. Négritude writers shared a black heritage and identity that directly renounced the French colonial racism that they were forced to endure daily. The group saw the common African heritage shared by members of the African diaspora as the best weapon with which to oppose French intellectual and political power. With this identity as its foundation, proponents of Négritude established a literary and political movement influenced by Marxist ideology, simultaneously creating a realistic literary style.

Guianan Damas published a book of poetry titled *Pigments* in 1930 that many have regarded as the manifesto of the Négritude movement, which called for European and New World society to cure its ills. The three movement founders, known as *les trois péres* (the three fathers), came together in Paris in 1931 where they began discussing their ideas, many of which were embodied in *La revue du monde noir* (1931–32), a literary journal that discussed the ideology of this growing group of Caribbean and African intellectuals in the city. Négritude gained international recognition in 1939 with Césaire's publication of his book-length poem *Cahier d'un retour au pays natal* (Notebook of a Return to My Native Land). There is a close parallel between Négritude and the *negrismo* movement of the Hispanic Caribbean that emerged around the same period and championed many of the same ideas of black solidarity and the denunciation of the racism of colonial politics.

of the declaration. *Légitime défense* highlights, above all, the problems that its authors found vital to their cause—colonialism and the complicity of the bourgeoisie in allowing this oppressive system to continue.

CRITICAL DISCUSSION

French authorities at home and in the colonies immediately censured and suppressed *Légitime défense* when it was published in Paris in 1932. As René Ménil explains in *Refusal of the Shadow: Surrealism and the Caribbean* (1996), "*Légitime défense* was to remain practically unrecognized by Martiniquan society … for more than four decades …. Doubtless we must blame the ban it received from the colonial power when it was published. But beyond this, the reason for what has to be considered a rejection lies within Martiniquan social consciousness itself." The majority of the responses to the journal were from within the circle of black intellectuals residing in Paris at the time of its publication. Both Césaire and Léopold Sédar Senghor regarded the declaration in *Légitime défense* as too assimilationist, while Négritude writer León Damas, according to Dale Tomich (1979) in *Review,* regarded it as the representation of "the will of a generation of men of color to denounce the

bankruptcy of three centuries of French colonization in the West Indies."

Légitime défense marks an interesting moment in the development of anti-imperialism on the one hand and the creation of an unapologetic form of black expression on the other. While much has been written about the manifesto's influence on Négritude, scholars such as Carole Sweeney clarify that its influence was much broader. In *From Fetish to Subject: Race, Modernism, and Primitivism, 1919-1935* (2004), Sweeney writes, "The genealogy of [Négritude's] influence is undeniable, but we should be wary of assigning *Légitime défense* an overprivileged place in black intellectual history as the singular catalyst for a new black diasporic consciousness. Rather, *Légitime défense* is part of a wider trajectory of metropolitan diasporic activities" that encompassed radical labor movements and communist activities. In the decades since its first publication, *Légitime défense* has been the subject of extensive scholarship that has considered its legacy in diverse political and cultural arenas.

Many scholars have focused on the peculiar combination of communist and surrealist notions presented in *Légitime défense*. Shireen Lewis examines this incongruity in *Race, Culture, and Identity: Francophone West African and Caribbean Literature and Theory from Négritude to Créolité* (2006): "*Légitime défense* marks the historical period of coexistence and collaboration between communists and surrealists. To these Martinican intellectuals, colonized and assimilated by the French, both organizations helped them to see bourgeois culture as artificially constructed and provided them with the theoretical tools to subvert, parody, and transgress bourgeois hegemony." Other scholars have examined the cultural impact of the journal. Tomich writes, "*Légitime défense* was important initially for proposing a set of solutions to the problems of racial and cultural identity raised by colonialism. Yet, to a large degree, these solutions remained abstract and problematic in the work of Léro and his companions. The Negro's condition as a proletarian was emphasized over his condition as a Black."

BIBLIOGRAPHY

Sources

Breton, André. *What Is Surrealism?: Selected Writings.* Ed. Franklin Rosemont. New York: Monad, 1978. Print.

Hale, Thomas A. "From Afro-America to Afro-France: The Literary Triangle Trade." *French Review* 49.6 (1976): 1089-96. Print.

Lewis, Shireen K. *Race, Culture, and Identity: Francophone West African and Caribbean Literature and Theory from Négritude to Créolité.* Lanham: Lexington, 2006. Print.

Ménil, René. "1978 Introduction to *Légitime défense.*" *Refusal of the Shadow: Surrealism and the Caribbean.* Ed. Michael Richardson. Trans. Krzysztof Fijałkowski. New York: Verso, 1996. 37-43. Print.

Rosemont, Franklin. Introduction. *Martinique: Snake Charmer.* El Paso: U of Texas P, 2008. 1-42. Print.

Sweeney, Carole. *From Fetish to Subject: Race, Modernism, and Primitivism, 1919-1935.* Westport: Praeger, 2004. Print.

Tomich, Dale. "The Dialectic of Colonialism and Culture: The Origins of the Négritude of Aimé Césaire." *Fernand Braudel Center Review* 2.3 (1979): 351-85. Print.

Further Reading

Kesteloot, Lilyan. *Black Writers in French: A Literary History of Négritude.* Trans. C. Kennedy. Philadelphia: Temple UP, 1974. Print.

Moore, David Chioni. "Local Color, Global 'Color': Langston Hughes, the Black Atlantic, and Soviet Central Asia, 1932." *Research in African Literatures* 27.4 (1996): 49-70. Print.

Noland, Carrie. "Red Front / Black Front: Aimé Césaire and the Affaire Aragon." *Diacritics* 36.1 (2006): 64-85. Print.

Rabbitt, Kara M. "'Our Ancestors …': Cultural Genealogies and Pre-Négritude Africanicity in *Légitime défense.*" *SORAC Journal of African Studies* 2 (2002): 1-16. Print.

Steins, Martin. "Brown France vs. Black Africa: The Tide Turned in 1932." *Research in African Literatures* 14.4. (1983): 474-97. Print.

Katrina White

Manifesto for an Independent Revolutionary Art

André Breton, Leon Trotsky

✣ Key Facts

Time Period:
Mid-20th Century

Movement/Issue:
Aesthetics; Artistic
production; Trotskyist
Communism

Place of Publication:
Mexico

**Language of
Publication:**
French

OVERVIEW

Written jointly by French surrealist writer André Breton and exiled Bolshevik revolutionary leader Leon Trotsky, "Manifesto for an Independent Revolutionary Art" (1938) asserts that all artists are natural revolutionaries who can best serve the communist revolutionary effort by subjectively assimilating the spirit of communism and freely expressing it in their art. The manifesto was written in Mexico and was signed by Breton and Trotsky's host in Mexico City, painter Diego Rivera. The manifesto was first published in Mexico City in French as a broadside and appeared a few months later in an English translation in the *Partisan Review.* In support of free artistic expression, the manifesto calls on artists to use their creations to oppose reactionary political regimes that the authors contend censor artistic production.

"Manifesto for an Independent Revolutionary Art" was not received enthusiastically by artists, and its goals were never fully realized. Breton returned to France and, following one of the precepts of the manifesto, formed the International Federation of Independent Revolutionary Art (FIARI). Several prominent surrealists joined the French chapter, but FIARI found weak support among the artistic community, and at its peak FIARI numbered only sixty members. *Clé,* a monthly magazine about the activities of the federation, folded in February 1939 after only two issues, and its passage marked the failure of the movement that the manifesto had attempted to establish. In a 1939 letter to Trotsky, Breton acknowledged that he was "not very talented as an organizer," and he blamed the advent of World War II, among other "enormous obstacles," for FIARI's failure. Although the manifesto's aesthetic and practical impact was limited, it remains of interest to scholars for its insights into Trotsky's views on the role of artists in a communist state.

HISTORICAL AND LITERARY CONTEXT

The manifesto offers a means of judging social freedom by considering the conditions of artistic production in the context of increasing anti-Semitism, the deadly rivalry between Trotsky and Joseph Stalin, and the rise of fascism in Spain, Italy, and Nazi Germany. By the time of publication, Breton had also carried forth a decade long effort to convince the French

Communist Party (PCF) of the revolutionary potential of surrealism, which the PCF had declared to be inherently bourgeois. A succession of attacks on surrealism at literary congresses led by communist writers and artists as well as state censorship of art under Stalin had convinced Breton that art—and artists—were universally under siege. The authors' pledge to "find a common ground on which all revolutionary writers and artists may be reunited, the better to serve the revolution by their art" reflects the political instability of the time, as Trotskyists, anarchists, and communists battled for supremacy on the literary and political fronts.

Nearly a decade of disputes between the Breton-led surrealists and the Stalin-led Communist Party preceded the publication of "Manifesto for an Independent Revolutionary Art." In the mid-1920s Breton had engaged in a lengthy public debate over the revolutionary potential of surrealism with a colleague, Pierre Naville, who subsequently joined the leadership of the Communist Party. Surrealist poet Louis Aragon, a friend of Breton, was coerced in 1930 into signing a repudiation of surrealist philosophy (including Breton's *Second Surrealist Manifesto*) at the Congress of Revolutionary Writers in Kharkov, Ukraine. Three years later, Breton was expelled from the board of directors of the communist-led Association of Revolutionary Writers and Artists (AEAR) for publishing, in a surrealist magazine, a letter by a contributor that denounced "the wind of systematic cretinism blowing from the U.S.S.R." By 1935, when the communist-sponsored First International Congress of Writers for the Defense of Culture was held in Paris, relations between surrealists and communists had degenerated even further, following a violent altercation between Breton and Soviet writer Ilya Ehrenburg. The sham Moscow Trials (1936-1938), a purge of Stalin's political rivals, horrified Breton, who undertook his visit to Mexico partly with the objective of forming a political alliance with Trotsky.

"Manifesto for an Independent Revolutionary Art" is one of many political and aesthetic tracts authored or coauthored by Breton during the 1920s, 1930s, and 1940s. Trotsky, a noted political theorist, published an even larger body of work on political subjects, but only one other major work on aesthetics, *Literature and Revolution* (1924). Two earlier manifestos, the *Dada Manifesto* (1918) by Tristan Tzara and the *Manifesto of Surrealism* (1924) by Breton, were important precursors, as was *The Communist Manifesto* (1848) by Karl Marx and Friedrich Engels. In 1939, shortly after his return from Mexico, Breton published an essay in the surrealist magazine *Minotaure* titled "Souvenir du Mexique" ("Remembrance of Mexico"). The journal *Clé* provides additional information about the activities of FIARI.

Because the manifesto was not reprinted in French until 1953 in a volume of Breton's selected essays, it failed to have a resounding literary impact, and its immediate political impact ended with the 1939 dissolution of FIARI. The manifesto appeared in an English translation in the anti-Stalinist periodical *Partisan Review* in fall 1938 and has been reprinted in English several times since the 1970s.

THEMES AND STYLE

The theme of "Manifesto for an Independent Revolutionary Art" is the oppression of artists and writers by authoritarian political regimes. The opening paragraph invokes the horror of the impending war (World War II), comparing it to the invasions of the Vandals that toppled the Roman Empire in the fifth century CE, obliterating the advanced cultures of classical antiquity. Using a combination of emotional and logical appeals, the authors paint a grim picture of censorship under Stalin in the Soviet Union and Hitler in Germany, where they claim that artists had been "reduced … to the status of domestic servants of the regime, whose task it is to glorify it on order, according to the worst possible aesthetic conventions." The authors encourage artists and writers to band together across national borders to oppose, discredit, and overthrow these regimes.

The manifesto achieves its rhetorical effect by appealing to a feeling of solidarity among artists and writers that transcends aesthetic and political differences to combat a common threat: government censorship. "The aim of this appeal is to find a common ground on which all revolutionary writers and artists may be reunited, the better to serve the revolution by their art and to defend the liberty of that art itself against the usurpers of the revolution." The authors make an impassioned plea to "every friend and defender of art" to stand with them against "reactionary persecution" by joining FIARI, which Breton was about to form: "To those who urge us, whether for today or for tomorrow, to consent that art should submit to a discipline which we hold to be radically incompatible with its nature, we give a flat refusal and we repeat our deliberate intention of standing by the formula: complete freedom for art."

Because the audience they addressed was diverse and divided on political, philosophical, and aesthetic matters, Breton and Trotsky emphasized the third-person plural "we" and stated categorically that under

FRIDA KAHLO AND LEON TROTSKY: A COMPLICATED RELATIONSHIP

Although textual evidence and anecdotal accounts show that "Manifesto for an Independent Revolutionary Art" was drafted by Breton and heavily revised and added to by Trotsky, Trotsky was not one of the cosigners of the document. Instead, the manifesto was cosigned by Diego Rivera, Trotsky's host in Mexico City, because Trotsky had been forbidden by Lázaro Cárdenas, Mexico's president, to write on political subjects while seeking asylum in the country and Trotsky felt that the manifesto should be signed by two artists. At the time, Trotsky and his wife, Natalia, were staying at the home of Frida Kahlo in the Mexico City suburb of Coyoacán. Kahlo, who was married to Rivera, was a celebrated painter of biracial descent (her father was German and her mother Mexican).

Upon seeing Kahlo's self-portraits, Breton declared her a surrealist, a label Kahlo openly rejected. He included her work in the 1940 International Surrealist Exhibition and organized an exhibit of her paintings in Paris, which Kahlo traveled to attend. The break between Rivera and Trotsky, which occurred in January 1939 and contributed to the demise of the FIARI, may have been aggravated by an extramarital affair between Trotsky and Kahlo. Within two years of the manifesto's publication, Trotsky was murdered in Coyoacán by an agent of Stalin.

communism, artists and writers would not be persecuted: "The communist revolution is not afraid of art." The authors incorporate quotations from earlier works, including a quotation from Marx: "The first condition of freedom of the press is that it is not a business activity," suggesting that in a Trotskyist state, the "inalienable" right of artists to free creative expression would be safeguarded. By using inclusive language, Breton and Trotsky hoped to bring artists, writers, and other creative minds to the conclusion that refusal to conform their art to meet a propagandist agenda set by the government would help to topple totalitarian states.

CRITICAL DISCUSSION

The publication of "Manifesto for an Independent Revolutionary Art" as a broadside in Mexico City led directly to the founding of the journal *Clé* and FIARI, an international association with branches in Paris, London, Mexico, and New York. However, shortly after he founded FIARI, Breton was drafted by the French Army, and in Mexico a deep rift formed between Rivera and Trotsky, inflicting "serious misfortunes" on the activities of FIARI, according to a letter Breton wrote to Trotsky. The coming of World War II was perhaps the greatest hindrance to FIARI and to the manifesto's success as a motivational cry, but fighting within the surrealist group between artists who were PCF members and Breton, who had been

At a fair in Paris circa 1923, French surrealist poets Paul Éluard, André Breton, and Robert Desnos pose in a photographic set featuring an airplane. © STEFANO BIANCHETTI/ CORBIS

expelled from the party, also limited its influence. A translation published in *Partisan Review* brought the manifesto to the attention of a contemporary English-speaking audience, but it was not published in book form until 1953 in French, and 1978 in English.

Though its immediate impact was limited, the manifesto continues to stand as one of the few examples in history of a joint statement by a poet and a political theorist and offers insight into Trotsky's views on art. Robin Adele Greeley, a critic who has investigated the historical and ideological impact of Trotsky's thinking on surrealism, suggests that Trotsky's understanding of aesthetic issues and knowledge of Breton's work may have been merely superficial.

Although few critics have focused on the aesthetic and political ideas in the manifesto itself, several have written about the circumstances that attended its creation, specifically the eight to ten meetings that took place between Trotsky and Breton in various locations in Mexico between May and July 1938. Textual examination of the manuscript has been conducted by Gerard Roche (in French), but the best anecdotal discussion of the essay in English is in Mark Polizzotti's *Revolution of the Mind: A Life of André Breton. Free Rein* (1995), a translation of Breton's *La Clé des Champs* by Michel Parmentier and Jacqueline D'Amboise, includes an annotated complete translation of the manifesto, which was abridged in earlier English versions.

BIBLIOGRAPHY

Sources

Breton, André, Michel Parmentier, and Jacqueline D'Amboise. *Free Rein: La Clé Des Champs.* Lincoln: U of Nebraska P, 1995. Print.

Breton, André, and Diego Rivera. "Manifesto for an Independent Revolutionary Art." *Marxists Internet Archive.* Marxists.org, 2001. Web. 1 July 2012.

Breton, André, and Franklin Rosemont. "Declaration d'André Breton a propos du second process de Moscou." *What Is Surrealism?: Selected Writings.* New York: Monad, 1978. Print.

Greeley, Robin Adele. "For an Independent Revolutionary Art: Breton, Trotsky and Cárdenas's Mexico." *Surrealism, Politics and Culture.* Eds. Raymond Spiteri and Donald LaCoss. Aldershot, UK: Ashgate, 2003. Print.

Polizzotti, Mark. *Revolution of the Mind: The Life of André Breton.* New York: Farrar, Straus, and Giroux, 1995. Print.

Tzara, Tristan. *Seven Dada Manifestos and Lampisteries.* Oxford: Oneworld Classics, 2011. Print.

Van Heijenoort, Jean. *With Trotsky in Exile: From Prinkipo to Coyoacán.* Cambridge: Harvard UP, 1978. Print.

Further Reading

Lewis, Helena. *The Politics of Surrealism.* New York: Paragon, 1988. Print.

Lyon, Janet. *Manifestoes: Provocations of the Modern.* Ithaca, NY: Cornell UP, 1999. Print.

Marx, Karl, Friedrich Engels, and E. J. Hobsbawm. *The Communist Manifesto: A Modern Edition.* London: Verso, 1998. Print.

Montagu, Jemima. *The Surrealists: Revolutionaries in Art & Writing 1919-35.* London: Tate, 2002. Print.

Puchner, Martin. *Poetry of the Revolution: Marx, Manifestos, and the Avant-Gardes.* Princeton, NJ: Princeton UP, 2006. Print.

Terraroli, Valerio. *1920-1945: The Artistic Culture between the Wars.* Milan: Skira, 2006. Print.

Trotsky, Leon. *Literature and Revolution.* Chicago: Haymarket Books, 2005. Print.

Cristina Brown Celona

MANIFESTO OF SURREALISM

André Breton

OVERVIEW

Written by André Breton in 1924, the *Manifesto of Surrealism* calls on its readers to unfetter their imaginations from traditional aesthetics and daily routine, invoking a poetics that would do no less than portray "the actual functioning of thought." Strongly influenced by the antitraditionalist aesthetics of the poets Guillaume Apollinaire, Paul Valéry, and Charles Baudelaire and, later, the dadaists, Breton's manifesto carries on their tradition of subverting contemporary social and literary conventions. (It was Apollinaire who coined the term *surrealism* in 1917.) The *Manifesto of Surrealism,* however, weds similar revolutionary aesthetics to a notion—influenced by Sigmund Freud's psychoanalytic theory—of a subconscious reservoir of dreamlike beauty, accessible through automatic, unedited artistic production "in the absence of any control exercised by reason."

The *Manifesto of Surrealism* sparked interest in the movement beyond its initial circle of Parisian writers. The first surrealist art exhibition debuted in Paris in 1925, and a permanent surrealist gallery opened a year later. Throughout the late 1920s and well into the 1930s, the surrealist movement continued to gain momentum, in many ways defining artistic production during the interwar period, especially in France. In her article "The Avant-garde, Madness and the Great War," Annette Becker reports that during World War II, Breton himself claimed, "Surrealism in effect was the only intellectual movement which succeeded in covering the distance separating" the two world wars. Although Breton, along with several other surrealists, wrote the *Second Manifesto of Surrealism* in 1929 and even drafted a third in 1942, it was the initial manifesto that inspired artists all over the world.

HISTORICAL AND LITERARY CONTEXT

Breton's *Manifesto of Surrealism* appeared amid a wave of disillusionment with inherited political, social, and aesthetic values following the devastation of World War I. In her aforementioned article, Becker suggests, "If the Great War was not the creator of the surrealist movement, it was certainly its catalyst" in cultivating distaste for and distrust of the previous generation's cultural values. In addition to spawning antitraditionalist sentiments that came to influence surrealism, the war was personally formative for Breton. While serving as a doctor in a psychiatric hospital during the war, he not only witnessed the devastation wrought by the fighting but also spent an extensive amount of time studying and utilizing the psychoanalytic methods developed by Sigmund Freud, which were then largely unknown in France. Freud's theories about the subconscious were especially significant for the manifesto, influencing Breton's thoughts on automatic writing and the surrealist synthesis of dream and reality.

On October 15, 1924, when the *Manifesto of Surrealism* was published, Europe was still extricating itself from the aftermath of the Great War. France had withdrawn its last troops from Germany only two months earlier. Although France had a new, progressive, and comparatively popular president in Gaston Doumergue, who was elected on June 13, 1924, Breton and his friends and fellow surrealists Philippe Soupault, Louis Aragon, and Paul Éluard remained suspicious of the establishment. After World War I, the scorched French soil, heavy with corpses, provoked grisly memories of the fighting, and Breton and his Parisian circle determined that looking toward politics would not free their minds from these shackles. Thus, they opted to push their minds, through surrealist writing, toward "the limitless expanses" of pure thought.

Breton and his surrealist cohort were not alone in their mistrust of established modes of thought and political life. In his article "Surrealism's Unnamed Manifesto," Serge Gavronsky calls the *Manifesto of Surrealism* "a reaffirmation of the anti-rationalist evolution of French thought begun in the Romantic period and carried through into Symbolism and its psychoanalytic counterpart." This subversive trend reached a particularly poignant moment in the wake of World War I in the form of dadaism, an artistic movement that had originated in 1916. Dadaism rejected rationalism and logic on the grounds that their exploitation by bourgeois capitalist society had precipitated the Great War and that their implementation in art would mark the artist as complicit in the barbarities of modernity. Breton—himself an organizer of the Dada exhibit in Paris in 1920—continued to oppose rationality and instrumental logic, but he combined this antirational approach with a systematic search for a Freudian subconscious, a pristine realm of thought

❖ Key Facts

Time Period:
Early 20th Century

Movement/Issue:
Surrealism; World War I

Place of Publication:
France

Language of Publication:
French

BRETON'S DADAIST BACKGROUND: SURPASSED LIMITATION OR CRUCIAL FORMATION?

Although Dada is inarguably an important precursor to surrealism, there has been some debate about André Breton's relationship with the dadaist movement. In *Conversations: The Autobiography of Surrealism,* a chronicle based on a series of interviews from 1952, Breton reflects that Tristan Tzara's 1918 *Dada Manifesto* "seemed to throw the doors wide open, but you discovered that these doors led to a corridor that turned around in circles." Similarly, E. San Juan, Jr. claims that surrealism rose "from the nihilistic ruins of Dada to lay the groundwork for building a society founded on liberty and justice."

On the other hand, Matthew S. Witkovsky suggests that Breton's belief in dadaism was more than a passing fancy. In his article "Dada Breton," Witkovsky argues that "retrospective judgments" made by Breton—after surrealism's fame was cemented—led scholars to incorrectly devalue the importance of dada for the writer. Witkovsky claims that "Breton's initial sincerity and fervor for a Dadaist rebellion" ought not be disregarded as simply a preliminary stage that he later transcended. If Breton moved beyond dada in his *Manifesto of Surrealism,* Witkovsky suggests that it was not because he had rejected dadaism as a past folly but, rather, because his thought was so thoroughly imbued with dadaism. After all, as Witkovsky points out, "Dada bred a desire to pass judgment on all societal formations, including that of Dada itself."

and artistic potential free from the tyranny of reason. While Surrealism shared Dada's disillusionment with conventional aesthetics and logic, it sought a more programmatic approach to dispelling rationality from art than did Dada; in contrast to the amorphous and nonsensical nature of Dada, Breton utilized specific, systematic techniques, such as automatism, in order to better access the creativity he believed was hidden within the subliminal mind.

The *Manifesto of Surrealism* inaugurated a major global movement in myriad forms of art. It not only affected poetry, Breton's primary focus in the manifesto, but also reached beyond literature to influence film, the visual arts, and music. Immediately following the publication of the manifesto, Breton and his circle began circulating the journal *The Surrealist Revolution,* the twelve issues of which were published from 1924 through 1929. The final issue contained Breton's *Second Manifesto of Surrealism.* The surrealist movement gave rise to some of the early twentieth century's iconic works of art, including René Magritte's *The Treachery of Images* (1929) and Salvador Dalí's *The Persistence of Memory* (1931). Indeed, few assertions of artistic vision have made an impact as powerful and long-lasting as Breton's *Manifesto of Surrealism.*

THEMES AND STYLE

The central problem Breton expresses in the *Manifesto of Surrealism* is how to extricate ourselves from "the reign of logic," how to emancipate the imagination from its woeful "state of slavery." Drawing on Freudian psychoanalysis, Breton locates "the key to this corridor" in dream states, or, more specifically, in the synthesis of dreams and reality "into a kind of absolute reality, a *surreality.*" Breton claims that we may access this "absolute reality" through automatic writing, in which we let thoughts flow to the page with "no effort whatsoever to filter" and become "simple receptacles of so many echoes, modest recording instruments" for that "marvelous" reservoir of "surreality." This state of pure poetic production is, for Breton, fundamentally irrational, a state in which reason's role is "limited to taking note of, and appreciating, the luminous phenomenon."

Although Breton celebrates the virtues of escaping instrumental logic, his manifesto is decidedly analytical in style. He includes a surrealistic example of jarringly juxtaposed images—newspaper headlines collaged into a poem—but his prose reads almost like a medical diagnosis. In fact, the use of medical terminology is an important rhetorical strategy in Breton's manifesto, as he not only couches the surreal in the psychoanalytic terms of the "discoveries of Sigmund Freud" but also cites "certain pathological states of mind" as being indestructible within our speech patterns, arguing that "there is no conversation in which some trace of this [speech] disorder does not occur." By medicalizing the surrealist synthesis of the dream state and reality as a pre-existent, Freudian subconscious, Breton casts surrealism not as a new and radical innovation on the part of the artist but instead as the removal of all obstacles to pure thought, a process that allows the imagination to be unobstructed by "the incurable mania" of instrumental reason.

Despite its analytical bent, the *Manifesto of Surrealism* is suffused with an immediate, pressing, emancipatory tone. As Breton utilizes the medical vocabulary he gained in his psychiatric training to paint surrealism as a natural state of the imagination, he concurrently calls on us to recognize, with all due urgency, that we are living "a dog's life," blind to the beautiful, "limitless expanses" within us. By attending to the flame fed by surreal images, one finds that "the mind is ripe for something more than the benign joys it allows itself in general." Throughout the manifesto, Breton's tone is that of a man trying to wake his readers from a dream, or rather, trying to wake his readers *to* the dream.

CRITICAL DISCUSSION

Surrealism would grow to be a great global movement, but initial reactions to Breton's 1924 manifesto were mixed. In his *History of the Surrealist Movement,* Gérard Durozoi recalls the suspicious views of some contemporary critics: Edmond Jaloux initially feared

that surrealist literature would be perhaps more "artificial" than that which it critiqued, and Henri Michaux, in 1925, suggested that, with regard to automatism in art, it "won't be that easy to reach such a complete letting go." Perhaps most critically, Durozoi summarizes Henri Poulaille's view of surrealism as "nothing more than a useless and sterile restlessness." Although these initial doubts dispersed as the movement achieved success in Europe, the surrealists also encountered resistance in the United States; in his article "'An Amusing Lack of Logic': Surrealism and Popular Entertainment," Keith L. Eggener quotes art critic and curator Jeffrey Wechsler's reflection that surrealism in interwar America "had terrible timing … Surrealism was an irritation to those with growing perceptions of a national art with meaning and dignity."

Breton's *Manifesto of Surrealism* inaugurated a movement that grew to be influential not only in the realm of literature, but also in visual arts, as well as politics. In "A Metaphorical Reading of Breton's Theory of the Image," Nicola Gardini discusses the literary legacy of Breton's work, arguing that "Breton's understanding of poetic imagery and creation remains among the most fruitful and clever pieces of contemporary literary theory." The manifesto also inspired many visual artists, such as René Magritte, Man Ray, Max Ernst and Salvador Dalí, who endeavored to portray the pure dreamscapes of the subconscious mind. In the political sphere, surrealism's influence was

momentous but fraught. After the inaugural *Manifesto of Surrealism,* the movement became increasingly politicized—drawn especially to the revolutionary politics of Marx and Communism—but its politicization not only alienated some former surrealists but also failed to fall perfectly in sync with the French Communist Party. These problems proved so prickly that they ultimately occasioned the publication of the *Second Surrealist Manifesto,* in which Breton both calls on his fellow surrealists to embrace a new radical politics and publicly denounces the "decline in the ideological level" of the French Communist Party. In his tripartite career as a poet, playwright, and politician in Martinique, Aimé Césaire embodied this multiform legacy of surrealism. In *Antonio Gramsci on Surrealism and the Avant-garde,* author E. San Juan, Jr. opens with a quote from Césaire about the breadth, and the power, of Breton's movement: "Surrealism provided me with what I had been confusedly searching for …. It was a weapon that exploded the French language. It shook up absolutely everything."

Much of the scholarship on the *Manifesto of Surrealism* focuses on its political impact. Gavronsky suggests that simply by calling the work a manifesto, Breton "explicitly set up a sequence of references, guiding the reader, politically, back to the 1848 *Communist Manifesto.*" In his article "Breton and Trotsky: The Revolutionary Memory of Surrealism," Pierre Taminiaux notes that despite the fact that one might "argue that the political discourse of surrealism was often overshadowed by the aesthetic perspective" in Breton's first manifesto, a great number of surrealists turned to the Communist Party. A related focus in scholarship—also harkening back to the "specter haunting Europe" in Karl Marx's *Communist Manifesto*—is the role of ghosts in the *Manifesto of Surrealism*. In "Haunting Transcendence: The Strategy of Ghosts in [Georges] Bataille and Breton," Kendall Johnson discusses the functions of ghosts and haunting in the two writers' work. In a similar vein, Katharine Conley's article, "Surrealism's Ghostly Automatic Body," examines the "ghostly aspect" of surrealism's artistic automatism.

BIBLIOGRAPHY

Sources

Becker, Annette. "The Avant-Garde, Madness and the Great War." *Journal of Contemporary History* 35.1 (2000): 71-84. Print.

Breton, André. *Manifestoes of Surrealism.* Trans. Richard Seaver and Helen R. Lane. Ann Arbor: U of Michigan P, 2000. Print.

———. *Conversations: The Autobiography of Surrealism.* Trans. Mark Polizzotti. Washington, DC: Marlowe, 1995. Print.

Conley, Katharine. "Surrealism's Ghostly Automatic Body." *Contemporary French and Francophone Studies* 15.3 (2011): 297-304. Print.

Durozoi, Gérard. *History of the Surrealist Movement.* Chicago: U of Chicago P, 2002. Print.

Eggener, Keith L. "'An Amusing Lack of Logic': Surrealism and Popular Entertainment." *American Art* 7.4 (1993): 30-45. Print.

Gardini, Nicola. "A Metaphorical Reading of Breton's Theory of the Image." *French Forum.* 21.1 (Jan. 1996): 61-77. Print.

Further Reading

Gavronsky, Serge. "Surrealism's Unnamed Manifesto." *Manifestoes and Movements.* Columbia: U of South Carolina, Dept. of Foreign Langs. and Lits., 1980. 88-98. Print.

Johnson, Kendall. "Haunting Transcendence: The Strategy of Ghosts in Bataille and Breton." *Twentieth Century Literature* 45.3 (1999): 347-70. Print.

Lewis, Helena. "Surrealists, Stalinists, and Trotskyists: Theories of Art and Revolution in France between the Wars." *Art Journal* 52.1 (1993): 61-68. Print.

San Juan, E., Jr. "Antonio Gramsci on Surrealism and the Avant-garde." *Journal of Aesthetic Education* 37.2 (2003): 31-45. Print.

Taminiaux, Pierre. "Breton and Trotsky: The Revolutionary Memory of Surrealism." *Yale French Studies* 109 (2006): 52-66. Print.

Witkovsky, Matthew S. "Dada Breton." *October* 105 (2003): 125-36. Print.

Elliott Niblock

THE MECHANICS FOR A LITERARY "SECESSION"

Gorham B. Munson

OVERVIEW

Gorham B. Munson's essay "The Mechanics for a Literary 'Secession'" (1922) appeared in the November issue of the literary magazine *S4N* and proposes a new approach to aesthetics in letters that would assign precedence to "form," "simplification," "strangeness," "respect for literature," and "abstraction"—ideas that had been put forth by Munson's editorial partner Malcolm Cowley. Munson, a literary critic, called for a movement among American writers that would serve as a "secession" from the literary arts of the era. For Munson, this action did not need to occur with the ferocity of revolution but rather as a "calm intelligent resolute swerving aside." The most direct audience for his manifesto was the readership of *S4N*. However, the forum also provided Munson an opportunity to articulate the philosophy behind his own publication, *Secession*.

Reaction to the essay was linked to perceptions of Munson and what he had come to represent in the literary community following the appearance of the first three issues of *Secession* earlier in 1922. His magazine openly criticized similar publications of the time, including the *Dial* and the *Little Review,* for various and seemingly unrelated reasons. *Secession* would play an important, if rather dramatic and buffoonish, role in advocating the tenets of modernism (which rejected realism and reason) and Dada (which embraced chaos), as well as the varying views of its editorial staff. If Munson was perhaps unjustified for writing in a "Post Mortem" published after *Secession*'s final issue that the magazine "will perhaps be known as the magazine that introduced the twenties," he was certainly, through his essay "The Mechanics for a Literary 'Secession'" and his prolific expression during that period, a vital figure of that time.

HISTORICAL AND LITERARY CONTEXT

Munson's essay is structured around what he describes as the fundamentals for secession. First, he asserts that secession requires something to separate from, and for Munson this is an American literary environment still overly focused on the "permanent expatriate type," which was embodied by Ezra Pound. (Despite this view, and in keeping with his often inconsistent criticisms, Munson would publish several authors and works from abroad.) Second, Munson asserts that secession is necessary because of a literary reliance on

outdated modes (such as naturalism and realism) and "good taste" that are accompanied by a passivity (or politeness) in criticism and a negative attitude toward industrial innovation. Munson then invokes his third fundamental element: a group of artists willing and ready to secede. Here he highlights writers ("chaps") in their early twenties who are interested in the five listed concerns of Cowley, beginning with "form" and ending with "abstraction." Munson closes by referring to other requisites, such as the "new primitiveness," and by naming his first troops: William Carlos Williams, E.E. Cummings, and others.

Munson's article was published when modernism was at its height and numerous magazines existed that, like *Secession*, aimed to capture its spirit in letters. In October 1922 T.S. Eliot began his own publication, the *Criterion,* in which he released "The Waste Land" for the first time. Dada had already begun to decline—though *Secession* would include representatives from the movement in its first issues—and surrealism was taking hold in Europe. Munson's four major editorial partners (Matthew Josephson, Cowley, John Brooks Wheelwright, and Kenneth Burke) held different views on these currents, which led to a series of theatrical conflicts within the magazine's pages. Further, as Munson observed in *The Awakening Twenties: A Memoir-History of a Literary Period* (which appeared after his death), the early 1920s was a time of American "awakening": from a mostly rural aesthetic to an awareness of world culture, from Puritanism to more liberal ideals, and finally, toward a distinct literary identity for the United States.

A 1921 article of Cowley's in the "Literary Review" of the *New York Evening Post* was the most direct inspiration for the founding of *Secession* by Munson. The article, "This Youngest Generation," in which Cowley enumerated the five tenets that would appear in Munson's manifesto, was a call for young writers to abandon all previous literary forms and look toward French writers (both contemporary and classical) rather than English writers for inspiration. Cowley's ideas resonated with Munson (then age twenty-five and only five years out of college), as he had observed the power of this school of young writers "diffused into the corners of various magazines." Munson further remarked "it would be a good thing to concentrate the new impulses in a single review."

Key Facts

Time Period:
Early 20th Century

Movement/Issue:
Aesthetic secession;
Avant-gardism

Place of Publication:
United States

Language of Publication:
English

SPOTLIGHT ON A SECESSIONIST: HART CRANE

Although American poet Hart Crane became inadvertently central to the conflict among editors of *Secession,* Crane's life outside the magazine was full of its own contradictions. Crane was born in Ohio in 1899, son of a candy manufacturer who begged him to forgo an early inclination toward writing. Crane did not finish high school or attend college, but his move to New York City in 1916 and a personal dedication to the study of Elizabethan and French poets afforded him ample familiarity with writers who would shape his verse.

Crane became part of the modernist scene in New York that included E.E. Cummings and Jean Toomer. He worked at a number of odd jobs before sailing to Mexico in 1931 with the goal of writing about the Spanish conquest. Crane was best known for a long poem *The Bridge,* whose fifteen sections examine and synthesize the United States, geographically and historically, with an emphasis on modern technology reminiscent of T.S. Eliot and with a tone akin to Walt Whitman. Crane struggled with alcoholism and instability that marred his friendships and contributed to an early demise. Crane ended his life at thirty-three by jumping off a steamship returning from Mexico to New York.

Unfortunately, Munson's ambition and enthusiasm led him to select writers not only from the "youngest generation" but also those of varying aesthetics; he published several French writers, as well. For this reason, it was difficult to discern what the magazine aimed to do or whether it met these aims.

Munson's essay in *S4N* allowed him to address *Secession*'s identity and present a more unified view of its philosophy than editorial comments in the magazine had allowed. His publication was not the first to issue a manifesto of this kind. Many of *Secession*'s contemporaries issued statements that spoke to their purpose and aesthetic, including *Broom* and the *Little Review.* Whether it was Munson's manifesto or his magazine that gained more attention for Munson, his comments drew editorial comment from a range of publications. *Secession* and the tenets intended to guide it contributed to the literary careers of Hart Crane, Waldo Frank, Wallace Stevens, Tristan Tzara, and Cummings, among others. *Secession* is today regarded as an integral part of the "little magazine" movement that indelibly shaped American letters by giving voice to postwar writers.

THEMES AND STYLE

The central theme of "The Mechanics for a Literary 'Secession'" is that American letters need to be changed by a group of literary artists who remove themselves from the norm, and he declares: "I begin with a general call to writers to secede." Munson then differentiates his proposed movement from the "direct violent opposition we mean by revolt," calling instead for "an emotional sloughing off of irrelevant drains … and a prompt deviation into purely aesthetic concerns." To this end, the manifesto outlines Munson's four main concerns regarding writing by his contemporaries (and those they esteem), and he counters them with Cowley's five proposed remedies.

Munson's argument is developed systematically. First, he describes the need for secession, then the reasons for it, and finally, how it will occur. He assures readers at the opening that, rather than "an isolated personal venture," he was proposing a movement (embodied by *Secession*) that was "predicated by American literary activity at large, and … may link up with possible important developments in American letters." His address is a "general call" rather than an invitation exclusive to certain parties, and Munson's closing asserts that he founded the magazine for writers already engaged in the movement, such as Crane and Slater Brown. He "invite[s] the readers of *S4N* to partake as they see fit in a necessary movement," implying humbly that they may participate in their own fashion, though secession itself is clearly required.

Although there are moments of "clean" argumentation in Munson's essay, Munson often exhibits the kind of biting, name-calling criticism for which he became known both in *Secession* and through harsh reviews he published elsewhere. His rhetoric seems to imply that one would be completely foolish to disagree with Munson's view. He pointedly attacks Sinclair Lewis, Sherwood Anderson, and Theodore Dreiser, claiming that they create "more or less duplicate effects … laboring within exhausted forms." Munson goes on to insult Robert Frost for his attentions to the canon of "good taste." He accuses American criticism of "general flabbiness … united and vigorous toward a stupid reactionaryism," particularly as it relates to critic Paul Rosenfield, whom he deems "an inflated windbag of premature ejaculations no one, apparently, thinks of dredging or pricking."

CRITICAL DISCUSSION

Munson's essay emerged in a literary climate already electrified by the appearance of *Secession* and its attack on contemporaries. The *Little Review* had perceived *Secession*'s first issue (which included harsh attacks of the *Review*) as the publication's actual "manifesto," and editor Jane Heap accused Munson of "acrid scholastic stink." Heap also asked why Munson did not "join the laugh and incidentally the epoch," implying that the "new epoch" he proposed was already in existence. Critical remarks about *Secession* also appeared in the *New Republic* and the *Freeman,* where Munson's vision was indicted with the statement that it "will never constitute a literature." The *Dial,* also attacked by *Secession,* was a bit more reserved in its criticism, but it called for less "manifesto" and fewer limitations, as "enjoyment follows its own laws … and the creative artist is the most potent when he discovers his laws within himself."

Secession, and Munson, struggled to hold fast to any stringent set of guidelines but ultimately failed, perhaps because of the harsh assessments of those outside Munson's realm, an overly ambitious scope, and the widely varying designs of editors, some of whom were outside the United States. Controversy began in issue three, before the "Mechanics" had even appeared, when editor Wheelwright printed his own story despite Munson's having voted it down. From there on, Secession became a conflicted terrain, in which content was edited, radically altered, and printed abroad without Munson's approval, including a version of Crane's "The Marriage of Faustus and Helen" that enraged the author. By the seventh issue, Munson was running the magazine alone, and the eighth—comprised solely of a complex essay on poetics by Yvor Winters—was the last issue of Secession.

Munson's manifesto represents the lofty goals of a literary group that was mostly modernist but also influenced by Dada during a vibrant period in American letters. Secession, and the tenets it aimed to espouse, played an important role among the modernist journals shaping literature at that time, both by publishing new authors and also for the dogma of its editors. In a comprehensive study of magazines during this period in The Little Magazine, Secession was described as "indispensable to an understanding of the twenties." The newly released online archive to all eight issues of Secession on Jacket2's website, wherein the publication is esteemed for displaying "a critical attention to the literary politics of little magazines in the early twenties," indicates the value of Munson's vision to this day.

BIBLIOGRAPHY

Sources

Brooker, Peter, and Andrew Thacker, eds. The Oxford Critical and Cultural History of Modernist Magazines. Oxford: Oxford UP, 2009. Print.

Lehmann-Haupt, Christopher. Rev. of The Awakening Twenties: A Memoir-History of a Literary Period, by Gorham Munson. New York Times. New York Times, 15 July 1985. Web. 2 Oct. 2012.

Munson, Gorham Bert. "The Mechanics for a Literary 'Secession.'" S4N 4 (1922). Web. 5 Oct. 2012.

Poet E.E. Cummings, whom Gorham Munson championed as a "Secessionist" writer.
© PICTORIAL PRESS LTD/ ALAMY

———. Dir. Secession, 1922-1924. Jacket2. Jacket2, n.d. Web. 26 Sept. 2012.

Rosenfeld, Alvin H. "John Wheelwright, Gorham Munson, and the 'Wars of Secession.'" Editorial. Michigan Quarterly Review. Michigan Quarterly Review, Winter 1975. Web. 5 Oct. 2012.

Toomer, Jean. Jean Toomer: Selected Essays and Literary Criticism. Ed. Robert B. Jones. Knoxville: U of Tennessee, 1996. Print.

Further Reading

Cowley, Malcolm. Exile's Return: A Literary Odyssey of the 1920s. New York: Viking, 1951. Print.

Fisher, Clive. Hart Crane: A Life. New Haven: Yale UP, 2002. Print.

Hoffman, Frederick John, Charles Albert Allen, and Carolyn F. Ulrich. The Little Magazine: A History and a Bibliography. Princeton, NJ: Princeton UP, 1946. Print.

Munson, Gorham Bert. The Awakening Twenties: A Memoir-History of a Literary Period. Baton Rouge: Louisiana State UP, 1985. Print.

———. Robert Frost: A Study in Sensibility and Good Sense. New York: George H. Doran, 1927. Print.

Rachel Mindell

THE MODEST WOMAN

Baroness Else von Freytag-Loringhoven

❖ **Key Facts**

Time Period:
Early 20th Century

Movement/Issue:
Modernism; Avant-
gardism; Freedom of
speech

Place of Publication:
United States

**Language of
Publication:**
English

OVERVIEW

"The Modest Woman" by the poet and actress Baroness Elsa von Freytag-Loringhoven is a prose poem, initially published in the July 1920 issue of the *Little Review,* that chastises the American reading public—and American culture in general—for its hypocritical views toward modesty in literature, dress, and manners. Occasioned by allegations of obscenity in James Joyce's *Ulysses,* von Freytag-Loringhoven's manifesto asserts that the book's imminent banning speaks to the vulgarity and pretentiousness of American readers. Writing in an emphatic, deliberately fractured English that serves to symbolize her Europeanness (and thereby cultural authority), the baroness further argues that prudishness of any sort betrays a lack of intellectual depth. Her declaration that "artists are aristocrats" would become one of the defining statements of her literary career.

Although eclipsed by such major poems as "Cast-Iron Lover" and by the baroness's own larger-than-life public persona, "The Modest Woman" contributed to public impressions of von Freytag-Loringhoven as a "tragically neurotic" artist. Moreover, its peculiarities of syntax and imagery reaffirm the author's connection with Dada, a primarily European avant-garde movement, then at its peak. It did little, however, to affect the debate surrounding *Ulysses,* which would not become legally available in English until 1934. For much of the twentieth century, appraisals of "The Modest Woman," favorable or otherwise, tended to emphasize the author's eccentricities of personality rather than the specific claims of the poem itself. This perception has changed gradually, with twenty-first-century historians of avant-garde art treating the poem as a reflection of von Freytag-Loringhoven's preoccupations as an artist. These scholars see "The Modest Woman" not only as a timely commentary on literary censorship but also as a more troubling and complex display of the baroness's attitudes on race, class, and nationalism.

HISTORICAL AND LITERARY CONTEXT

"The Modest Woman" responds to the legal and literary controversy attending the publication of *Ulysses.* The *Little Review,* a mainstay of American avant-garde literature in the 1910s and early 1920s, had serialized Joyce's novel since 1918, but American literary critics were largely ambivalent to initial installments of the book, inured by the abundance of experimental poetry and fiction after World War I. Margaret Anderson, editor and publisher of the *Little Review,* hoped to cultivate readers' interest in *Ulysses,* a work she personally admired, by running von Freytag-Loringhoven's sometimes incendiary remarks alongside new chapters of the novel.

In 1920, however, *Ulysses* attracted publicity of an unwelcome sort when the *Little Review* printed the allegedly obscene thirteenth chapter (or "episode"). Outraged by the sexually suggestive material, members of the New York Society for the Suppression of Vice promptly filed suit against the *Little Review.* The journal, which presented itself as "A Magazine of the Arts: Making No Compromise with the Public Taste," would eventually lose the case but continued to publish additional chapters until 1921, when the *Review* was declared obscene and its circulation seized by court order. A longtime favorite of the *Little Review,* von Freytag-Loringhoven published "The Modest Woman" alongside the second half of the offending chapter, introducing Joyce in laudatory terms to a readership she considered unworthy of the great novelist.

In crafting her manifesto, the baroness had many contemporary precedents to draw upon. Her own poetry shares with *Ulysses* a stream of consciousness quality, which von Freytag-Loringhoven applies to her manifesto and to her less polemical works. Moreover, in the same issue of the *Little Review* as "The Modest Woman" is an essay by the poet John Rodker that speaks directly to the question of von Freytag-Loringhoven's influences. He lists a wide assortment of literary figures in connection with her style, including the Romanian-French Dadaist Tristan Tzara, the Italian futurist F. T. Marinetti, and the American poet Ezra Pound, who at various points championed imagism, vorticism, and Dada. In the decade preceding the *Ulysses* controversy, each of these authors had penned a manifesto blending characteristics of poetry and essay, providing possible models for von Freytag-Loringhoven's approach.

"The Modest Woman" had little effect on the progress of the Joyce obscenity trial; indeed the author undercuts her own authority on the matter by claiming never to have read *Ulysses* and by characterizing her assumed audience as a pack of unruly, unsophisticated children who ought to keep silent before European literary talent. Its serialization suspended, *Ulysses* would be published in French in 1922, but English editions would remain largely unavailable until 1934, seven years after von Freytag-Loringhoven's death. Nevertheless, scholarly interest in the work persists, examining the poem in terms of the author's persona and her political views.

THEMES AND STYLE

"The Modest Woman" is concerned foremost with establishing that a belief in "modesty" is a specifically American instrument of self-repression and is therefore a symptom of cultural inferiority. In the poem, von Freytag-Loringhoven delineates the characteristics—at the barbershop, at the table, and elsewhere—of unhealthy prudishness, citing these as evidence of a shameful relationship to one's own body. Americans, whom she deems "smart aleck[s]," "countrylout[s]," and "parvenus," are vulgar in proportion to the effort they expend on "smoothness–smugness–sanitation–cleanliness." She contrasts these qualities with the expansive, uncensored thinking of Joyce and of European artists in general. "In Europe—," the poet explains, "when inferiors do not understand superiors—they retire modestly." This ignorance, she suggests, is the true reason for the negative response to *Ulysses* and to her own poetry published in the *Little Review*.

While the *Ulysses* scandal was triggered by the book's sexual content, von Freytag-Loringhoven's poem focuses first on other bodily functions not usually mentioned in polite company: "if I can eat I can eliminate—it is logic—it is why I eat!" she maintains, adding, "as aristocrat—with my ease of manner can afford also to mention my ecstasies in toilet room!" She further explains her attitude toward shame via repeated comparisons of the human body to "machinery:" "Why should I—proud engineer—be ashamed of my machinery—part of it?" It is this machine metaphor that connects her discussion of eating and elimination to Joyce, a master "engineer" for whom "to talk shop is his sacred business." In his candor regarding the human body, then, Joyce not only shows himself as an "aristocrat" but also displays his "love" for the "engine that carries him through flashing glades to his grave."

Stylistically, von Freytag-Loringhoven's poem closely resembles her other printed poetry, including much of the work to appear in the *Little Review*. She favors long, exclamatory utterances and rhetorical questions held together as much by a succession of dashes as by the words themselves: "America's comfort:—sanitation—outside machinery—has made American forget own machinery—body!" Her pattern of speech eschews articles, possessives, and other short words, possibly to lend an air of "foreignness" to her admonition of American readers. Some later

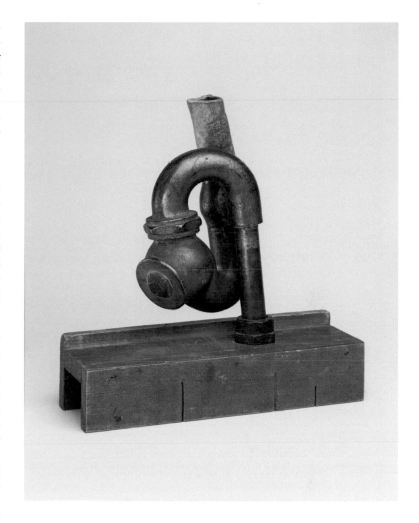

appraisers of von Freytag-Loringhoven's work have considered these instead to be the simple errors of a poet lacking a firm command of English; however an examination of von Freytag-Loringhoven's other *Little Review* poems suggests that such calques as "makes me difficulty" are largely for effect, depicting exasperation, perhaps, but hardly ignorance.

CRITICAL DISCUSSION

Von Freytag-Loringhoven's contributions to the *Little Review* were tremendously controversial, though it remains unclear what immediate influence "The Modest Woman" had on the baroness's numerous writings. Rudolf E. Kuenzli in *Women in Dada: Essays on Sex, Gender, and Identity* (2001) outlines the debate surrounding the poet's late work, noting the disgusted letters the *Little Review* periodically received. *Poetry* magazine editor Harriett Monroe likewise expressed a chilly opinion of von Freytag-Loringhoven. Kuenzli notes that in a terse appraisal of the *Little Review*, Monroe writes that she "could forgive" the magazine's avant-garde enthusiasm if only "it would drop Else von Freytag-Loringhoven." Nevertheless, the poet found ardent defenders in *Little Review* editors

God, a sculpture attributed to Elsa von Freytag-Loringhoven and Morton Livingston Schamberg (circa 1917). Artist and poet von Freytag-Loringhoven created sculptures and paintings as well as writings such as the poem "The Modest Woman" (1920). THE PHILADELPHIA MUSEUM OF ART/ART RESOURCE, NY

PRIMARY SOURCE

"THE MODEST WOMAN"

Artists are aristocrats.

Artists who call themselves artists—not aristocrats—are plain working people, mixing up art with craft, in vulgar untrained brain.

Who wants us to hide our joys (Joyce?)

If I can eat I can eliminate—it is logic—it is why I eat! My machinery is built that way. Yours also—though you do not like to think of—mention it—because you are not aristocrat.

Your skirts are too long—out of "modesty," not decoration—when you lift them you do not do it elegantly—proudly.

Why should I—proud engineer—be ashamed of my machinery—part of it?

Joyce is engineer! one of boldest—most adventurous—globetrotter—! to talk shop is his sacred business—we want him to—to love engine that carries him through flashing glades to his grave—his glorious estate.

If your ears are too vulgar—put white cotton into—in tufts—bunches! fitting decoration! Afflicted people should stay home—with family—friends. You are immodest—because you are not healthy.

America's comfort:—sanitation—outside machinery—has made American forget own machinery—body! He thinks of himself less than of what should be his servant—steel machinery.

He has mixed things! For: he has no poise—no tradition. Parvenu—ashamed

of his hide—as he well might.

That is American! it is truly disgusting to imagine him in any "physical functions"—eating not excluded.

Eats stupidly also.

Has reason to hide—feels that—and:—because newly rich—in vast acquisition—feels also he has something to say—everything—everybody.

Smart aleck—countrylout—in sunday attire—strutting!

Yawning—all teeth—into space—sipping his coffee with thunder noise—elbow on table—little finger outspread stiffly—he knows how to behave in society!

Why—America—can you not be modest? stay back—attentive—as wellbred child? You have so much to learn—just out of bushes!

But—you are no wellbred child—you are noisy—nosey—bad-mannered

— assumptive.

... Goethe was grandly obscene—what do you know about it? Flaubert—Swift—Rabelais—Arabian Nights—Bible if you please! only difference—Bible is without humour—great stupidity! So: how dare you strut—step out—show yourself with your cotton-tuft in ear?

Anderson and Jane Heap, and just a few pages prior to "The Modest Woman," Rodker praises her as one of the great minds of Dadaist literature.

At mid-century von Freytag-Loringhoven's reputation suffered somewhat, with critics and supporters often more interested in the details of her eventful life than in the literary merit of her work. G. Robert Stange in a 1954 review for *Poetry* deemed her an "interestingly, tragically neurotic" character but dismissed her poetry as merely "an extreme form of Imagism written by someone who had not yet learned the language." Those who had appreciated her work during her lifetime were more sympathetic. Writer Djuna Barnes, the late poet's friend and benefactor, gave a nod to her ideal of self-fashioned aristocracy in the verse play *The Antiphon* (1958), whose heroic Miranda is an improbable combination of "aristocrat, pauper, artist, beggar!"

While biographical interest in von Freytag-Loringhoven continues to thrive, several studies in recent years have taken up the political dimensions of "The Modest Woman," especially its emphasis on the author's status as foreign aristocrat. Adam McKible (2005), writing in *American Periodicals,* suggests that the manifesto, when read alongside "Mefk Maru

Mustir Daas" (another *Little Review* poem), "echoes a concern about the body that was shared by many Americans, particularly its 'Nordic' population: that its best 'race' was becoming too weak to defend itself against whole hordes of inferior, primitive people." Irene Gammel, in *Pioneering North America: Mediators of European Culture and Literature* (2000), questions the consistency with which von Freytag-Loringhoven held such views, observing that the poet participated in a strident debate "regarding Europe's involvement in the building of an American civilization." Gammel writes that W. C. Williams, among others, often conflated von Freytag-Loringhoven with an antagonistic Europe. As a response to this treatment, the high-handed posture of "The Modest Woman" appears as theatrical a statement as any of the baroness's stage appearances or public "happenings."

BIBLIOGRAPHY

Sources

Gammel, Irene. "German Extravagance Confronts American Modernism: The Poetics of Baroness Else." *Pioneering North America: Mediators of European Culture and Literature.* Ed. Klaus Martens. Würzburg, Königshausen & Neumann, 2000. 60-75. Print.

In Europe—when inferiors do not understand superiors—they retire modestly—mayhap baffled—but in good manner. By that fact—that they do not understand—they know their place. They are not invited—of class inferior—the dance is not theirs.

They can not judge—for: they lack real manners—education—class.

If they are desirous of judging—sometime—they must think—study—rise —

slowly! So society is made in Europe slowly—! so: culture—so: aristocratic public.

That attitude of the learner—the inferior—you should feel in regard to James Joyce.

That you do not—shows you have less inherent culture than European washer-lady.

Here—madame—every bank clerk meddles.

Ancient Romans had proverb—one of few great principles of world-structure—culture: *Quod licit Jovi, non licit Bovi.*

To show hidden beauty of things—there are no limitations! Only artist can do that—that is his holy office. Stronger—braver he is—more he will explore into depths.

Do not eat the *Little Review.*

Therein all strong angels are!

I have not read "Ulysses." As story it seems impossible—to James Joyce's style I am not yet quite developed enough—makes me difficulty—too intent on my own creation—no time now.

Sometime I will read him—have no doubt—time of screams—delights—dances—soul and body—as with Shakespeare.

From snatches I have had shown me it is more worth while than many a smooth coherent story by author of real genuine prominence.

The way he slings "obscenities"—handles them—never forced—never obscene—vulgar! (thank Europe for such people—world will advance.)

Shows him one of highest intellects—with creative power abundant—soaring!

Such one you dare approach—little runt?

Whatever made you read him—*Little Review*—anyway?

Back to my astonishment!

You see how ridiculous you are?

Well—if not—others will.

That is why I wrote this—!

SOURCE. *Manifestos. A Century of Isms,* edited by Mary Ann Caws, University of Nebraska Press, 2001. Pp. 324-326.

Kuenzli, Rudolf E. "Baroness Elsa von Freytag-Loringhoven and New York Dada." *Women in Dada: Essays on Sex, Gender, and Identity.* Ed. Naomi Sawelson-Gorse. Cambridge: MIT, 2001. 442-475. Print.

McKible, Adam. "'Life is Real and Life is Earnest': Mike Gold, Claude McKay, and the Baroness Elsa von Freytag-Loringhoven." *American Periodicals* 15.1 (2005): 56-73. *JSTOR.* Web. 6 Sept. 2012.

Rodker, John. "'Dada' and Else von Freytag-Loringhoven." *Little Review* 7.2 (1920): 33-36. *Modernist Journals Project.* Web. 6 Sept. 2012.

Stange, G. Robert. "The 'Lost' Renaissance." Rev. of *The Little Review Anthology,* ed. Margaret Anderson. *Poetry* 83.5 (1954): 290-294. *JSTOR.* Web. 6 Sept. 2012.

Von Freytag-Loringhoven, Elsa. "The Modest Woman." *Little Review* 7.2 (1920): 37-40. *Modernist Journals Project.* Web. 1 Sept. 2012.

Further Reading

Barnes, Djuna. *The Antiphon.* Los Angeles: Green Integer, 2000. Print.

Cavell, Richard. "Baroness Elsa and the Aesthetics of Empathy: A Mystery and a Speculation." *Politics of Cultural Mediation.* Ed. Paul Hjartarson and Tracy Kulba. Edmonton: U of Alberta P, 1999. 25-39. Print.

Gammel, Irene. *Baroness Elsa: Gender, Dada, and Everyday Modernity—A Cultural Biography.* Cambridge: MIT, 2002. Print.

Gammel, Irene, and Suzanne Zelazo, eds. *Body Sweats: The Uncensored Writings of Elsa von Freytag-Loringhoven.* Cambridge: MIT, 2011. Print.

Golding, Alan C. "*The Dial, The Little Review,* and the Dialogics of Modernism." *American Periodicals* 15.1 (2005): 42-55. *JSTOR.* Web. 6 Sept. 2012.

McKenna, Bernard. *James Joyce's* Ulysses: *A Reference Guide.* Westport: Greenwood, 2002. Print.

Michael Hartwell

POETRY IS VERTICAL

Eugene Jolas

✛ **Key Facts**

Time Period:
Mid-20th Century

Movement/Issue:
Aesthetics; Avant-
gardism; Utopianism

Place of Publication:
France

**Language of
Publication:**
French

OVERVIEW

Poet and translator Eugene Jolas is the primary author of the manifesto "Poetry Is Vertical" (1932), which he published in the literary journal *transition*—a journal he also edited. Others added their signatures to the manifesto, though some would later reject its proposed aesthetic, and Jolas also signed the name of his alter ego, Theo Rutra. As with other works of the time, including Jolas's "The Revolution of the Word" (1929), the piece proclaimed the sovereignty of poets and poetry, asserting that they should not be constricted by the borders of language or linguistic convention. What made this proclamation different from others was its articulation of the word *vertical,* a label meant to convey a poetry that rises from darkness toward a utopian light.

As with many of the works Jolas published in his experimental literary journal *transition,* "Poetry Is Vertical" created controversy. Written at a time when many poets were turning toward politics to find a more concrete framework for critical thought, Jolas's essay argued for a more spiritual solution to social upheaval. Fascism and communism were the main parties in which artists sought refuge; however Jolas felt both placed constraints on the imagination and subconscious. His vision of a broader, more open resolution was shaped by his unique history. Jolas was born in the United States but raised in a bilingual community on the German-French border. He eventually returned alone to New York at the age of fifteen. His migrations and his insider-outsider status enabled him to imagine a community united around the written word, which would transcend the borders of nationalities and polarizing political views.

HISTORICAL AND LITERARY CONTEXT

Although World War I had ended years before, it was not until 1932 that Jolas felt literary movements had fully regained their ability to influence culture. However, by then fascism was gaining a firm foothold in Europe, especially in the tense border region of Alsace-Lorraine, where Jolas was raised. "Poetry Is Vertical" celebrates the newly reclaimed freedom to debate aesthetics and warns against the extreme nationalism promoted by the Nazi Party. In Jolas's other home, the United States, the general public was recovering from the Great Crash of 1929 and undergoing a program of what he referred to as a delusion "into beliefs in progress." Urbanites were left feeling "confused" by their subjection to "mechanical conformity." Having worked as a newspaper journalist in Pittsburgh, New York, and Paris, Jolas was highly sensitive to the pitfalls of the particular sociopolitical climates of those cities and rejected them all.

In Paris, Jolas had inherited Ford Maddox Ford's column *Rambles through Literary Paris,* written for the *Chicago Tribune,* which detailed the goings-on of the Parisian literati. His journalism led Jolas to cafés and salons where he crossed paths with many writers whose work he would later publish in *transition,* which began publication in 1927. These artists have been loosely grouped as the so-called Lost Generation, a term coined by Gertrude Stein and popularized by Ernest Hemingway to refer to writers living in Paris after World War I. Jolas, in "Poetry Is Vertical,"

TRANSITION'S REVOLUTIONARY CURATION

Eugene Jolas's magazine, *transition,* published the most difficult and experimental work of the 1920s and 1930s, incorporating the work of a few key visual artists. The magazine was printed with relative regularity from 1927 to 1936 and showcased the writings of Gertrude Stein, André Gide, Samuel Beckett, James Joyce, Paul Claudel, Kay Boyle, and others. Jolas and his wife, Maria, undertook the task of translating everything into English, hoping that *transition* would expose poets of many different backgrounds to each other, lending his magazine a feeling of international citizenship. To this end he placed special significance on publishing work in translation and work laced with multilingual puns and portmanteaus, such as James Joyce's.

The magazine was hailed as an open forum for modernists to place their work in the context of international contemporaries. Consistent with the ideals laid out in "Poetry Is Vertical," Jolas felt that *transition* stood for "the evocation of the distinctive personal and collective universe," and he eventually added the subtitle "An International Experiment for Orphic Tradition." When World War II broke out in Europe, he suspended publication and eventually handed the magazine over to Georges Duthuit.

promotes the strengths of this community, including their regenerative myths, general revolutionary tone, and occasionally hermetic language.

Hermeticism was central to literary debate in the early 1930s, referring to works that the public deems inaccessible or difficult. James Joyce had by this time established himself as a major figure of the avant-garde and was living in Paris. He was close with Jolas and his wife, Maria, both of whom were committed to including him in *transition,* in which early installments of *Finnegans Wake* (1939) garnered contentious reactions. Part of the difficulty of Joyce's later work is its multilingualism, which many English speakers at the time found offensive and insular. Jolas wanted to challenge this view by calling attention to the positive aspects of an enriched language, which for him reflected a deep "inner life." Joyce's resistance to the boundaries of English served to deepen Jolas's faith that an Atlantic language could do justice to his multinational community and unite it.

"Poetry Is Vertical" draws on another important trend of that era. Psychiatry, in the approaches of Sigmund Freud and Carl Jung, emphasized the valuable attributes of dreams and viewed them as vehicles into the subconscious. Such notions were in keeping with Jolas's theories that the individual's imagination

was beneficial to humanity, and he explicitly refers to "the psychiatric condition" in point seven of the manifesto. The phrase was by then part of the common vernacular of virtually all artists in Paris, and psychiatry's new perspective shaped their work.

THEMES AND STYLE

The term *vertical* was key to Jolas's thinking about aesthetics and to readers grappling with his metaphors. His general idea is that poetry should travel from the darkness of dreams and secrets up into a transcendental light. The concept of verticality is explained in a work he published earlier that year, "Night-Mind and Day-March" (1932), in which he writes that "mystic action proceeds from the lower strata toward a higher region…. It is vertical motion and seeks a final synthesis in a world beyond a world." He echoes this idea in point six of "Poetry Is Vertical," which states "the reality of depth can be conquered" by moving "from the irrational to a world beyond a world." This natural progression of darkness toward light, as he sees it, cannot exist without obscurity and irrationality. He worries that a "melioristic dementia" had "seized the world" and urges poets to work against it.

The manifesto calls for the "disintegration" of the individual into the "collective." Touting the

PRIMARY SOURCE

"POETRY IS VERTICAL"

On a été trop horizontal, j'ai envie d'être vertical.

LÉON PAUL FARGUE

In a world ruled by the hypnosis of positivism, we proclaim the autonomy of the poetic vision, the hegemony of the inner life over the outer life.

We reject the postulate that the creative personality is a mere factor in the pragmatic conception of progress, and that its function is the delineation of a vitalistic world.

We are against the renewal of the classical ideal, because it inevitably leads to a decorative reactionary conformity, to a factitious sense of harmony, to the sterilisation of the living imagination.

We believe that the orphic forces should be guarded from deterioration, no matter what social system ultimately is triumphant.

Esthetic will is not the first law. It is in the immediacy of the ecstatic revelation, in the a-logical movement of the psyche, in the organic rhythm of the vision that the creative act occurs.

The reality of depth can be conquered by a voluntary mediumistic conjuration, by a stupor which proceeds from the irrational to a world beyond a world.

The transcendental "I" with its multiple stratifications reaching back millions of years is related to the entire history of mankind, past and present, and is brought to the surface with the hallucinatory irruption of images in the dream, the daydream, the mystic-gnostic trance, and even the psychiatric condition.

The final disintegration of the "I" in the creative act is made possible by the use of a language which is a mantic instrument, and which does not hesitate to adopt a revolutionary attitude toward word and syntax, going even so far as to invent a hermetic language, if necessary.

Poetry builds a nexus between the "I" and the "you" by leading the emotions of the sunken, telluric depths upward toward the illumination of a collective reality and a totalistic universe.

The synthesis of a true collectivism is made possible by a community of spirits who aim at the construction of a new mythological reality.

HANS ARP, SAMUEL BECKETT, CARL EINSTEIN, EUGÈNE JOLAS, THOMAS McGREEVY, GEORGES PELORSON, THEO RUTRA, JAMES J. SWEENEY, RONALD SYMOND

SOURCE: *transition* 21, 1932, pp. 148-149. Reprinted in *Manifestos: A Century of Isms,* edited by Mary Ann Caws, University of Nebraska Press, 2001. © 2001 by Alma Classics. All rights reserved. Reproduced by permission.

qualities of myths as well as "orphic" or "mantic" poetry (that is, poetry that privileges sonority and intuition over logic), the manifesto suggests that the creative act leads the poet outside the self. The poetic, aural qualities that Jolas calls for are set in opposition to straightforward narration and description, which he states only end in a mundane suppression of the imagination. However, the collective that he refers to is not one of blind nationalism or a "decorative reactionary conformity," and he does not wish the imagination to serve the "pragmatic conception of progress" prevalent in both the United States and Europe.

The new world that is continuously mentioned in "Poetry Is Vertical" is meant to be literal. Jolas supports Dadaism, futurism, and surrealism—all major literary movements of modernism. Yet he criticizes the surrealists for stopping short of their goal to utilize art to construct a new reality. In language that is at once clear and mystical, he attempts to manifest that new world through prose. The concrete reality he envisions is called "a vitalistic world" that will be accessed by "the living imagination." Furthermore, this new world is "made possible by a community of spirits who aim at [its] construction."

CRITICAL DISCUSSION

Initially the publication of the manifesto was lauded by modernist writers and disparaged by the wider public for the hermetic qualities it valued. Writer Samuel Beckett, though he was an original cosigner of the document, later critiqued it in an essay published in 1949 with the writer Georges Duthuit. Contemporary scholar David A. Hatch notes that Beckett's dissatisfaction with the essay is based on the fact that it contradicted itself, failing to show how the creation of a new reality would be possible in conjunction with Jolas's "disintegration of the 'I.'" Furthermore, "Poetry Is Vertical" seemed to Beckett and Duthuit to repeat aesthetic theories proposed by earlier movements, without resolving their flaws.

More recently, literary theorist Marjorie Perloff in a 1999 essay for *Kunapipi* noted that the dreamlike character of the manifesto was simply no match for the growing fascism in Europe. Jolas was advancing a literary revolution that was largely theoretical and "ran into the very real political revolution that brought the Nazis to power in 1932." However, Perloff argues that his ideas of the collective and his clear vision of the potential of multilingualism are now being addressed in contemporary poetry. She notes that Jolas's values are evident in the work of Kamau Brathwaite and Theresa Hak Kyung Cha, who stretch their readers' vocabulary and imagination by adding Jamaican Creole or French to their English-language poems. This type of mixed-language, sound-based poetry was even more necessary, Jolas notes, after "the international migrations, which the apocalyptic decade has unleashed, bring in their wake a metamorphosis of communication." The collective that he envisions has become more crucial to poets attempting to communicate in a globalized context.

With Yale University's acquisition of the Eugene and Maria Jolas papers, scholars in the United States have had greater opportunity to analyze the poet's work as a whole. The critical writings and correspondence contained in the collection have been lauded for their foresight and clarity, and the theories of "Poetry Is Vertical" have come to be seen as having a largely Jungian conception of creativity and the arts. Scholar Craig Monk argues in *Mosaic* (1999) that Jolas's insistence on invention and his objective of creating a new reality is paralleled by Jung's work in the field of the subconscious and the assertion that "nothing would be more erroneous than to assume the poet creates from the material of tradition."

BIBLIOGRAPHY

Sources

Hatch, David A. "Beckett in Transition: 'Three Dialogues,' Little Magazines, and Post-War Parisian Aesthetic Debate." *Samuel Beckett Today* 15 (2005): 43-56. *JSTOR*. Web. 24 Sept. 2012.

Jolas, Eugene. *Critical Writings: 1924-1951*. Evanston: Northwestern UP, 2009. Print.

———. *Man from Babel*. New Haven: Yale UP, 1998. Print.

Monk, Craig. "Eugene Jolas and the Translation Policies of *transition*." *Mosaic* Dec. 1999: 17. *Literature Resource Center*. Web. 24 Sept. 2012.

Perloff, Marjorie. "'Logocinéma of the Frontiersman': Eugene Jolas's Multilingual Poetics and Its Legacies." *Kunapipi* 20 (1999): 145-163. *Electronic Poetry Center*. Web. 24 Sept. 2012.

Further Reading

Apter, Emily S. *The Translation Zone: A New Comparative Literature*. Princeton: Princeton UP, 2006. Print.

Brathwaite, Kamau. *D.S. (2): Dreamstories*. New York: New Directions, 2007. Print.

Cha, Theresa Hak Kyung. *Dictee*. Berkeley: U of California P, 2009. Print.

Scobie, Stephen. "Eugene Jolas." *American Poets, 1880-1945: First Series*. Ed. Peter Quartermain. Vol. 45. Detroit: Gale Research, 1986. *Dictionary of Literary Biography*. Web. 24 Sept. 2012.

Caitie Moore

PROUST

Samuel Beckett

✥ *Key Facts*

Time Period:
Mid-20th Century

Movement/Issue:
Aesthetics; Absurdism

Place of Publication:
England

**Language of
Publication:**
English

OVERVIEW

Composed in 1930 and published in 1931, Samuel Beckett's essay *Proust* is a critical discussion of the novel *À la recherche du temps perdu* by French writer Marcel Proust and also a discussion of Beckett's own theories about the human condition and its representation in literature. The piece was commissioned by the publishing house Chatto and Windus for inclusion in their Dolphin Books series of popular literature and was intended for an intellectual but otherwise nonacademic audience. Although the original purpose of the essay was to present a critical discussion of Proust's work, it became the foundation upon which Beckett established the absurdist theories he later explored as a playwright.

The essay was initially met with a lukewarm reception. Some critics found insight in Beckett's theories, but the majority of scholars ultimately felt that his convoluted language and pessimistic conclusions detracted from both his theory and criticism. Despite its initial lack of success, the work did inspire the ideas about human essence and purpose—or lack thereof—that would heavily influence Beckett's later works, which became esteemed contributions to both French and English theater. Because Beckett focused on his philosophical theories in the essay and—sometimes forcibly—applied those theories to Proust's writing, the work was initially seen as somewhat of an embarrassment to the academic community; only later was it viewed as crucial to the development of Beckett's playwriting genius. Thus, *Proust* ultimately proved to be an influential founding theoretical text for the theater of the absurd movement that continues to inspire critical responses from scholars today.

HISTORICAL AND LITERARY CONTEXT

Proust's novel was highly influential and generated popular and critical acclaim, although it had a reputation for being long and unwieldy. It was considered revolutionary for its ability to combine scientific thought with the artistic medium of novel writing. Beckett, like Proust to some degree, believed that the human essence could not be accurately captured through any artistic medium because it existed as a result of daily habits and memory that were affected by time. As such, the human self was constantly changing and could never be captured in a static representation.

Also like Proust, Beckett is concerned with the nature of memory and how memories change depending on when and why they are recalled. He incorporates Proust's division of voluntary and involuntary memory—or the memory recalled intentionally and that recalled through association with a smell, sound, or other external stimuli. This leads Beckett to ask if the essential human self is still the same self at a different time, or if it is a different self altogether.

Beckett wrote *Proust* during his final year as a lecturer at École Normale Supérieure in Paris, about nine months before he decided against pursuing his academic career and gave up his newly acquired teaching position at Trinity College in Dublin. Beckett had been commissioned to write the essay because of the critical acclaim of his earlier poetry, particularly *Whoroscope* (1930). The essay shows Beckett's disillusionment with academic writing and foreshadows his decision to abandon the academic community in order to pursue his novel- and play-writing career.

Although the essay was intended as a critical academic piece about Proust's novel, it turned into a document in which Beckett worked out his own philosophical ideas about the essence of humanity and its relation to time and memory. These ideas were influenced by Beckett's stay in Paris and his exposure to surrealist artwork and theories, including works by French proto-surrealist writer Alfred Jarry and existentialist theories such as those proposed by German philosopher Friedrich Nietzsche. He was also directly influenced by his friend and mentor, Irish poet Thomas MacGreevy, who had previously published an essay on T. S. Eliot for the same series.

Despite its lukewarm reception, Beckett's essay eventually generated a substantial body of criticism and was eventually seen as a foundational text for Beckett's absurdist theories that he explored in his later plays. Through the process of writing the essay and developing his ideas about the essence of humanity in the literary medium—and the complete lack of meaning he found therein—Beckett came to the realization that he was acting as nothing more than a middleman between the text and the reader. As such, he believed that he was only contributing another layer of information and theoretical discussion that he felt was based on meaningless ideas. He continued to develop these theories in his theatrical productions, such as *Waiting for Godot* (1953) and *Not I* (1972), which became classified as "theater of the absurd." These plays developed from the application of existentialist theories in the wake of the brutality of two world wars. Other plays influenced by Beckett's theories that fell into the absurdist category include Tom Stoppard's *Rosencrantz and Guildenstern Are Dead* (1966) and Eugène Ionesco's *The Bald Soprano* (1950).

THEMES AND STYLE

The central theme of Beckett's *Proust* is the failure of the literary medium to represent the true essence of a human being, because that essence is composed of a multitude of constantly changing essences that exist through time and the ever-changing practices of habit and memory. Beckett believes that the self is in constant flux and exists as a memory in time and, consequently, is continuously reconstructed so that it never truly exists as a singular entity but instead as an ever-changing state. Because time is always changing and altering our perceptions and memories of the world around us, Beckett suggests that human beings rely on habits—or the mundane occurrences of everyday life—in order to impose a sense of meaning on memory. Therefore, literary characters, exemplified by the characters in Proust's *À la recherche du temps perdu* are only momentary representations of people in constant flux: "Proust's creatures, then, are victims of this predominating condition and circumstance—Time," Beckett writes.

Beckett develops his argument by using obtuse language and circuitous logic while discussing the properties of time, memory, and habit. Beckett quotes nineteenth-century German philosopher Arthur Schopenhauer in order to define the artistic procedure as "the contemplation of the world independently of the principle of reason." This separation of the composition of art from the reality of life necessitates the impossibility of understanding the human condition through representations within artistic mediums. For example, Beckett describes a scene in Proust's novel opaquely: "And he realises that his grandmother is dead, long since and many times, that the cherished familiar of his mind, mercifully composed all along the years by the solicitude of habitual memory, exists no longer, and that this mad old woman, drowsing over her book, overburdened with years, flushed and coarse and vulgar, is a stranger whom he has never seen." In this analysis, Beckett believes that Proust's character cannot know his dead grandmother because the truth does not align with his memories of her as a warm and caring person. She is thus neither dead nor alive—without purpose or meaning—and exists solely as a memory of the protagonist.

Stylistically, the language of Beckett's *Proust* is notoriously convoluted and difficult to navigate; his tone is one of sardonic attachment. His choice of words only complicates the situation. For example,

SAMUEL BECKETT

Born to a wealthy Protestant bourgeois family in the suburbs of Dublin, Beckett was properly educated for someone of his class, attending distinguished institutions such as Portora Royal School—one of five Royal Schools founded in 1608 by James I that held onto their status as English "free schools"—and Trinity College, Dublin. He went to École Normale Supérieure in Paris as a lecturer of English, where he met Thomas MacGreevy and James Joyce, two men who would prove highly influential to Beckett's writing career. During his time in Paris, Beckett also frequented art museums where he developed an interest in avant-garde and surrealist art.

Beckett is perhaps best known for his theatrical writing, which dominated his interests during the later portion of his career. His first major success, *En Attendant Godot,* was performed in 1953 in Paris, but it quickly attracted international attention, especially from American publishers. The play, translated as *Waiting for Godot,* was an accumulation of his intellectual and theoretical experiences. It generated both praise and disapproval from literary and theater critics, which skyrocketed Beckett to the top of the Western world's list of leading intellectual playwrights. It also placed him among the founding writers of the theater of the absurd, a movement that explored the meaninglessness of human existence.

Playwright Samuel Beckett in Paris, 1986. PHOTO BY REX USA/COURTESY EVERETT COLLECTION

he describes the wrongful association of an image or sound as the "non-logical statement of phenomena in the order and exactitude of their perception, before they have been distorted into intelligibility in order to be forced into a chain of cause and effect." The language was also designed to reflect the novelist who is supposedly at the center of the entire document: Marcel Proust. "The Proustian equation is never simple," Beckett writes, and Beckett's language can be interpreted as a reflection of the complications in Proust's literature.

CRITICAL DISCUSSION

The initial reaction to *Proust* was generally one of confusion, with many scholars rejecting his complicated thought processes and untraditional interpretation of Proust's cherished novel. A student of Beckett at École Normale Supérieure once complained "I wish he would explain his explanations," a comment that many critics, including James Acheson in his essay "Beckett, Proust and Schopenhauer" (1978), apply to *Proust*. Celine Surprenant in "An Occult Arithmetic" (2007) also notes how *Proust* was initially derided "as an inappropriate academic work" because of the way it alters Proust's meaning in order to develop Beckett's own ideas.

Despite the initial cynicism, however, the essay has generated a wave of critical scholarship that continues into the present. With the development of the theater of the absurd, including Beckett's influential *Waiting for Godot* (1953), the essay can be seen in hindsight as the document that initiated Beckett's theories of time, absurdity, and the inability to capture the human essence in literature and art. Nicholas Zurbrugg, in *Beckett and Proust* (1988), explains that Beckett's essay is "even more interesting as a record of the 'turning points' at which Beckett rejected many of Proust's ideas and, in the process, manifested the first substantial signs of his own originality." Zurbrugg goes on to describe the work as an "eccentric essay" that "repeatedly offers an extremely heretical account of what one might think of as the Proustian 'faith.'"

The general trends when discussing *Proust* tend to be expressions of Beckett's confusing writing style and his use of Proust's work to explore his own theoretical ideas. Steven Rosen in *Samuel Beckett and the Pessimistic Tradition* (1976) surmises the critical trends surrounding Beckett's *Proust* by writing that "both style and content of *Proust* have come in for sharp attack, the former for various excesses, the latter for triteness." Following this trend, James Acheson defines *Proust* as "obscurely worded and seriously underargued," and claims that "the effect of Beckett's argument is weakened by the obscurity of his language." Not all scholars regard *Proust* in a negative light, however. Celine Surprenant claims that "Beckett's particular paraphrasing, transposition and translation of Proust's text seizes upon something essential about the novel" and that his use of mathematical and musical theorists such as Schopenhauer is metaphorically connected to Proust's work. As such, Surprenant views *Proust* as "an essay written precisely according to those aesthetic prescriptions that Proust's novel sets out."

BIBLIOGRAPHY

Sources

Acheson, James. "Beckett, Proust, and Schopenhauer." *Contemporary Literature* 19.2 (1978): 165-79. *JSTOR.* Web. 3 Oct. 2012.

Beckett, Samuel. *Proust.* New York: Grove, 1957. Print.

Rosen, Steven J. *Samuel Beckett and the Pessimistic Tradition.* New Brunswick: Rutgers UP, 1976. Print.

Surprenant, Celine. "An Occult Arithmetic: The 'Proustian Equation' According to Beckett's *Proust.*" *Journal of Romance Studies* 7.3 (2007): 47+. *Literature Resource Center.* Web. 4 Oct. 2012.

Zurbrugg, Nicholas. *Beckett and Proust.* Totowa: Barnes and Noble, 1988. Print.

Further Reading

Ben-Zvi, Linda. *Samuel Beckett.* Boston: Twayne, 1986. *The Twayne Authors Series.* Web. 4 Oct. 2012.

Bryden, Mary, and Margaret Topping, eds. *Beckett's Proust/ Deleuze's Proust.* New York: Palgrave Macmillan, 2009. Print.

Cronin, Anthony. *Samuel Beckett: The Last Modernist.* London: Harper, 1996. Print.

Esslin, Martin. *The Theatre of the Absurd.* New ed. London: Methuen, 2001. Print.

Fletcher, John. *About Beckett: The Playwright and the Work.* London: Faber & Faber, 2003. Print.

Gibson, Andrew. *Samuel Beckett.* London: Reaktion, 2010. Print.

Kenner, Hugh. *A Reader's Guide to Samuel Beckett.* New York: Farrar, 1973. Print.

Nixon, Mark, and Matthew Feldman, eds. *The International Reception of Samuel Beckett.* London: Continuum, 2009. Print.

Pothast, Ulrich. *Metaphysical Vision: Arthur Schopenhauer's Philosophy of Art and Life and Samuel Beckett's Own Way to Make Use of It.* New York: Peter Lang, 2008. Web. 4 Oct. 2012.

Wilcher, Robert. "What's It Meant to Mean?: An Approach to Beckett's Theatre." *Critical Quarterly* 18.2 (1976): 9-37. Rpt. in *Contemporary Literary Criticism.* Ed. Dedria Bryfonski. Vol. 11. Detroit: Gale, 1979. *Literature Resource Center.* Web. 4 Oct. 2012.

Katherine Barker

SECOND SURREALIST MANIFESTO

André Breton

OVERVIEW

Originally published on December 15, 1929, in the twelfth issue of the journal *La Révolution surréaliste* (The Surrealist Revolution), André Breton's *Second Surrealist Manifesto* praises surrealism's "true" path in beautiful poetic passages and issues ruthless, vitriolic diatribes against those whom Breton viewed as enemies of the movement. With many thematic parallels to the *Manifesto of Surrealism,* which Breton had published five years earlier, the *Second Surrealist Manifesto* is distinctly more politicized. In the years separating the two texts, many advocates of surrealism, including Breton, had joined the Communist Party, splintering many formerly allied artists along political lines. With the *Second Surrealist Manifesto,* Breton intended not only to denounce the movement's defectors but also to explain its newly political character, all while reiterating surrealism's guiding principles.

Because of its explicitly political and polemical nature, the *Second Surrealist Manifesto* found a number of vocal critics, especially among those Breton so stringently derides in the manifesto. Despite the critics, however, the manifesto cemented Breton's position as the standard-bearer of surrealism. In her book *Investigating Modern Art,* Liz Dawtrey notes that throughout the 1930s, "Breton increasingly dominated the movement, shaping almost every ideological twist and turn." As an official statement of the political position of surrealism, the *Second Surrealist Manifesto* rallied supporters both of the movement and of Breton as its leader.

HISTORICAL AND LITERARY CONTEXT

The Communist Party in France was not yet ten years old when the *Second Surrealist Manifesto* was published. Throughout the 1920s communism had garnered the support of an increasing number of French intellectuals. Breton himself was a member and had a long, complicated relationship with the party. Stuart Kendall, in his book *Georges Bataille,* explains that the politicization of surrealism in the latter half of the 1920s "at once galvanized the group and tore it apart," and thus the divisive yet solidifying presence of communism within its ranks meant that "the movement was simultaneously at its height and in tatters." In this atmosphere, in which surrealism was both fraught with division and gifted with a flourishing vitality, Breton's *Second Surrealist Manifesto* attempts

concurrently to capitalize on the movement's momentum and to dictate its direction. For Breton, surrealism's "tenet of total revolt" would be violated were it not extended to embrace political revolution; nevertheless, the shift into party politics was viewed by many as a betrayal of the movement's core values.

In addition to responding to the growth of communism within surrealism, Breton drafted his manifesto to address several recently published critiques of him and his movement. Breton was deeply interested in mental health issues and studied the work of the psychoanalyst Sigmund Freud. The *Second Surrealist Manifesto* opens with excerpts from the journals *Annales médico-psychologiques* and *Société médico psychologique,* both accusing Breton and other "authors who call themselves Surrealists" of "slander and libel" against metal health professionals, even suggesting that Breton's novel *Nadja,* the story of a mad young woman, goes so far as to be "tantamount to inciting murder." With his former colleagues calling him a slanderous proponent of murder and the members of his movement increasingly at odds over political issues, Breton saw the need to publish a second manifesto in December 1929. Although Breton would later write another tract titled *Prolegomena to a Third Surrealist Manifesto or Not* (1942), its tentative tone is bespoken by its title, and it failed to eclipse the influence exacted by the *Second Surrealist Manifesto.*

In the five years following the publication of the *First Surrealist Manifesto,* Breton saw great success with the publication of *Nadja* and *Surrealism and Painting,* but the *Second Surrealist Manifesto* bears most vividly the imprint of the first manifesto. The more political, combative tone of the second manifesto might be partially credited to the influence of Salvador Dalí's *Catalan Anti-Art Manifesto,* or *Yellow Manifesto,* which had been published the previous year. Although the primary influence for Breton's first manifesto had been Dadaism, with a concurrent desire to set himself apart from it, by the second manifesto Dadaism was less of a concern for Breton and he took the opportunity to reach out to Tristan Tzara, the founder of Dada, suggesting that past misunderstandings between them "be forgotten."

The fiery *Second Surrealist Manifesto* proved a productive crucible for the movement, galvanizing a newly unified front within surrealism while

Key Facts

Time Period:
Early 20th Century

Movement/Issue:
Surrealism; Communism

Place of Publication:
France

Language of Publication:
French

KOJÈVE, HEGEL, AND TWENTIETH-CENTURY FRENCH THOUGHT

In the decade following the publication of André Breton's *Second Surrealist Manifesto,* interest in Hegelian philosophy blossomed among French intellectuals. Hegel's increasing influence on French thought in the 1930s and beyond is widely credited to Russian émigré Alexandre Kojève. Between 1933 and 1939, Kojève taught a series of profoundly influential seminars in Paris. In those seminars, by nearly all scholarly accounts, especially through his reinterpretation of Hegel's famous "master-slave" dialectic, Kojève single-handedly changed the trajectory of philosophy in France—Hegel's importance was on the rise.

The list of mid-twentieth-century French intellectuals whose work was strongly influenced by Kojève's lectures is remarkable; it includes Jean-Paul Sartre, Jacques Lacan, Raymond Queneau, and Breton's rival Georges Bataille. Subsequent to Breton's Hegelian attacks against him in the *Second Surrealist Manifesto,* Bataille attended Kojève's seminars, and throughout the course of the late 1930s, Bataille proved himself to be at the forefront of Kojève's astonishing array of promising pupils. As Stuart Kendall reports in his book *Georges Bataille,* the seminars brought to fruition the Hegelian seed sown in Bataille by Breton's attacks. After attending Kojève's seminars, "Hegel became Bataille's favorite foe, the privileged enemy against whom he constantly fought."

also influencing even its detractors. Breton ridicules fellow surrealists, such as Antonin Artaud, who had supported the first manifesto but had since diverged in their philosophies, as tensions between art and politics increased. In "The Futures of Surrealism: Hegelianism, Romanticism, and the Avant-Garde," David Cunningham notes that despite the fact that the second manifesto sparked a series of "spectacularly bad-tempered exchanges" between Breton and another prominent French surrealist, Georges Bataille (whom Breton bitterly condemns at length in the manifesto's conclusion), Bataille himself was nevertheless profoundly influenced by the manifesto and his ensuing acerbic exchange with Breton. It was only after these arguments in which, according to Cunningham, "Breton is already wielding [Georg Wilhelm Friedrich] Hegel against Bataille," that Bataille came seriously to study the work of Hegel, a philosopher who came to play a crucial role in the development of Bataille's intellectual life.

THEMES AND STYLE

The *Second Surrealist Manifesto* is primarily concerned with articulating how surrealism's initial aim of liberating the creative imagination from the shackles of rationality connects with and perhaps even demands an embrace of revolutionary politics. Breton emphasizes that although his sympathies are "wholeheartedly with those who will bring about the social Revolution," at the same time the "problem of social action ... is only

one of the forms of a more general problem which Surrealism set out to deal with," namely, the total liberation of human expression in all its forms." If the second manifesto's chief goal is officially to place surrealism in the camp of those who will strive "to bring about the day of that Revolution"—despite a lamentable "decline in the ideological level" of the Communist Party—Breton also takes care to caution his fellow surrealists against losing their roots: "let us not lose sight of the fact that the idea of Surrealism aims quite simply at the total recovery of our psychic force by means which is nothing other than the dizzying decent into ourselves, the systematic illumination of hidden places ... the perpetual excursion into the midst of forbidden territory." Breton envisions an artistic avant-garde working in tandem with a political vanguard.

While Breton often relies on grand rhetorical flourish to glorify the surrealist release of the mind into itself—into "the light that will cease to fail"—he also deploys vicious and violent rhetoric against those whom he views as enemies of surrealism, such as Bataille and Georges Limbour. In these diatribes Breton demands the theoretical use of "the avenging arm of the idea against the bestiality of all beings," calling out a number of enemies by name. From the outset Breton makes his violently combative stance apparent, even going so far as to suggest that "the simplest Surrealist act consists of dashing down the street, pistol in hand, and firing blindly" and that anyone who stubbornly resists "putting an end to the petty system of debasement" in either art or politics "has a well-defined place in that crowd, with his belly at barrel level."

As the aforementioned murderous metaphor attests, the emotional tenor of the *Second Surrealist Manifesto* is not plaintive but pugilistic and even paranoid—much less collaborative than the first manifesto. With the notable exception of Tzara, Breton extends no olive branches in his second manifesto; he is quick to praise those "blessed with violence" so long as they struggle to help "arrest the spread of this cancer of the mind which consists of thinking all too sadly that certain things 'are,' while others, which well might be, 'are not.'" In both alienating his enemies and rousing his surrealist allies, Breton achieves his goal of carving out what he felt was the "true" surrealism and removing it, under his own leadership, from the dead wood of those who resisted its emancipatory aims.

CRITICAL DISCUSSION

Immediately following the publication of the *Second Surrealist Manifesto* in December 1929, Breton's violent rhetoric earned him just as much ire as admiration from opposite sides of his now sharply drawn line in the sand. In the volley of insults that followed, perhaps the most striking, symbolic response was a box of human feces left on Breton's doorstep. In the manifesto Breton denounces Bataille at great length, calling him an "excremental philosopher," and, as Nikolaj Lübecker points out in *Community, Myth and Recognition in*

Twentieth-Century French Literature and Thought, "Breton (rightly?) suspected that Bataille was responsible for sending him a box of human excrements."

The *Second Surrealist Manifesto* proved a successful rallying cry, both for the movement in general as an official statement of its political position and for Breton personally as a reassertion of himself as its leader. Dawtrey notes that Breton dictated "almost every ideological twist and turn" after his second manifesto's publication, even striking a tentative truce with his recently bitter rival Bataille in 1935, when both became members of the political group Counterattack. Although surrealism has been interpreted and reinterpreted numerous times, Breton's *Second Surrealist Manifesto* remains the most successful attempt at redefining the movement and its direction.

Much of the recent scholarship on Breton's second manifesto discusses the tract's often violent rhetoric as well as its clearly political character. In his essay "Breton and Others: The Power of the Insult," Robert Short interprets Breton's equation of the "simplest Surrealist act" with firing a gun blindly into a crowd through the lens of the insult as the antithesis of "rational argument," a form of rhetorical violence that is meant to close the gap "between the word and the act" in hopes of restoring "a lost immediacy to language." In a similar vein, in "'Avant-Garde of What?': Surrealism Reconceived as Political Culture," Kirsten Strom also views the violence in this "simplest Surrealist act" as "strategically inflammatory rhetoric" but foregrounds its place—along with the second manifesto as a whole—within "a seemingly incessant battle against public misinterpretation" of the surrealists' political and aesthetic aims. Martin Puchner, in his book *Poetry of the Revolution: Marx, Manifestos, and the Avant-Garde,* argues that Breton believed "that the foundational act of a manifesto must be preserved at all costs in order for this act to retain its force over time" and that, consequently, because any "subsequent manifesto would threaten to undermine a first, foundational manifesto," his decision to publish the *Second Surrealist Manifesto* constitutes a remarkably "major change of direction" for himself and for the movement.

BIBLIOGRAPHY

Sources

Breton, André. *Manifestoes of Surrealism.* Trans. Richard Seaver and Helen R. Lane. Ann Arbor: U of Michigan P, 2000. Print.

Cunningham, David. "The Futures of Surrealism: Hegelianism, Romanticism, and the Avant-Garde." *SubStance* 34.2 (2005): 47-65. Print.

Dawtrey, Liz. *Investigating Modern Art.* New Haven, CT: Yale UP, 1996. Print.

Kendall, Stuart. *Georges Bataille.* London: Reaktion, 2007. Print.

Lübecker, Nikolaj. *Community, Myth and Recognition in Twentieth-Century French Literature and Thought.* London: Continuum International, 2009. Print.

Puchner, Martin. *Poetry of the Revolution: Marx, Manifestos, and the Avant-Garde.* Princeton, NJ: Princeton UP, 2006. Print.

Short, Robert. "Breton and Others: The Power of the Insult." *Andre Breton: The Power of Language.* Ed. Ramona Fotiade. Exeter, UK: Elm Bank, 2000. 75-82. Print.

Strom, Kirsten. "'Avant-Garde of What?': Surrealism Reconceived as Political Culture." *Journal of Aesthetics and Art Criticism* 62.1 (2004): 37-49. Print.

Further Reading

Breton, André. *Conversations: The Autobiography of Surrealism.* Trans. Mark Polizzotti. New York: Paragon, 1993. Print.

Chénieux-Gendron, Jacqueline, and Andrew Eastman. "Surrealists in Exile: Another Kind of Resistance." *Poetics Today* 17.3 (1996): 437-51. Print.

Durozoi, Gerard. *History of the Surrealist Movement.* Chicago: U of Chicago P, 2002. Print.

Lomas, David. *The Haunted Self: Surrealism, Psychoanalysis, Subjectivity.* New Haven, CT: Yale UP, 2000. Print.

Taminiaux, Pierre. "Breton and Trotsky: The Revolutionary Memory of Surrealism." *Yale French Studies* 109 (2006): 52-66. Print.

Elliott Niblock

Poster for *L'Age d'Or*, a 1930 film by Surrealists Salvador Dalí and Luis Buñuel, who were among the artists who signed André Breton's *Second Surrealist Manifesto* in 1929. VICOMTE CHARLES DE NOAILLES/THE KOBAL COLLECTION/ART RESOURCE

SEVEN DADA MANIFESTOS

Tristan Tzara

✢ *Key Facts*

Time Period:
Early 20th Century

Movement/Issue:
Dadaism; Aesthetics;
Avant-gardism

Place of Publication:
France

**Language of
Publication:**
French

OVERVIEW

Seven Dada Manifestos (1924) is a collection of texts composed by Tristan Tzara that makes an unconventional, and often absurdist, case for the antiart agenda of the Dadaist movement. Each manifesto was individually published between 1916 and 1921 in various French journals and anthologies. When the texts were collected in 1924, illustrations by the Dada artist Francis Picabia were added. These doodle-like drawings only increased the sense of whimsy and playfulness that already imbued the text. "Logic is a complication," Tzara declares in "Dada Manifesto 1918." "Logic is always false." Throughout the manifestos, Tzara maintains suspicion of reason and embraces the productive potential of play. This attitude embodies the outlook of Dadaism, which began in 1916 in response to the senseless brutality of World War I. While Tzara and his compatriots were influenced by cubism and futurism, Dadaism led directly to surrealism and indirectly to Fluxus and other late twentieth-century antiart movements.

Although Dadaism was essentially over by the time *Seven Dada Manifestos* appeared in print, the manifestos were formative and influential statements when they were originally published. "Dada Manifesto 1918," in particular, is credited with helping to catalyze the movement's revolutionary avant-garde innovations. As the movement spread from Zurich, Switzerland, where Tzara and other Dada founders lived, it rapidly moved around the world. In New York, Paris, Berlin, and elsewhere, artists and writers such as Marcel Duchamp and André Breton embraced calls by Tzara and others for a new art that embraced contradiction, chaos, and chance. Today *Seven Dada Manifestos* is considered among the most important collections of Dadaist writings and is recognized as having a significant influence on later international art movements.

HISTORICAL AND LITERARY CONTEXT

The texts collected in *Seven Dada Manifestos* respond to the brutality of World War I and to the trappings of European civilization, which had engendered the violent conflict and were incapable of ending it. As Richard Sheppard writes in *Modernism—Dada—Postmodernism* (2000), "Tristan Tzara was quite adamant that Dada was born out of a sense of disgust

at the war." The global conflict began in 1914, two years before the first of Tzara's seven manifestos appeared. Due to advances in weapons technology, the war was bloodier than previous conflicts, and it soon devolved into a war of attrition, with many men dying to accomplish seemingly trivial military gains. For Tzara and the other early Dadaists, the war's senselessness was an indictment of contemporary modernity. Thus, they aimed to undermine modernity's underlying values, particularly the conception that reality is intelligible and orderly.

By the time "Monsieur Antipyrine's Manifesto," the first of the seven manifestos, was issued in 1916, the Dadaist movement had begun to take shape in Zurich. Its leader was Hugo Ball, a poet and theorist who opened a cabaret bar called the Cabaret Voltaire in February 1916. There the Romanian-born Tzara and other artists and writers initiated the Dadaist movement. Inspired by the formal innovations of cubism, expressionism, and futurism, they gave readings and put on exhibitions that confronted audiences with a new kind of art that used collage, assemblage, and found objects to undermine the conventional assumption that art should be beautiful, mimetic, and refined. While the texts contained in *Seven Dada Manifestos* were issued during the movement's heyday, the collected volume appeared just as Dadaism was giving way to surrealism.

Seven Dada Manifestos draws on a history of polemical avant-garde writing, in particular on Filippo Tommaso Marinetti's *Futurist Manifesto.* Issued in 1909, the *Futurist Manifesto* announces the emergence of a new artistic movement in Italy known as futurism. Like Dadaism, futurism was a response to rapid technological and cultural change in the early twentieth century. However, Marinetti's manifesto embraced the speed and aggression of modernity and advocated a radical break with artistic convention and the cultural assumptions that undergirded tradition. The influence of other futurist manifestos can also be detected in Tzara's texts. The poet Mina Loy's *Aphorisms on Futurism* (1914), for example, utilizes unconventional typography, as does Tzara throughout the *Seven Dada Manifestos.*

After its publication in 1924, *Seven Dada Manifestos* influenced various avant-garde polemical writings. The same year that the collection appeared,

Breton, a writer who had been affiliated with Dadaism, published his *Manifesto of Surrealism,* which responded in part to Tzara's texts. While Breton furthered Tzara's assault on artistic convention and faith in rationality, he rejected Tzara's comprehensive skepticism and embraced a systemic probing of subconscious thought. The influence of *Seven Dada Manifestos* could also be felt decades later in the *Fluxus Manifesto* (1963) of George Maciunas. His call for a new form of antiart that embraced chaos and chance was directly influenced by the Dadaist theorizing of Tzara.

THEMES AND STYLE

The central theme of *Seven Dada Manifestos* is a call for a new artistic movement that rejects convention and embraces absurdity, contradiction, and play in response to the senseless chaos of the contemporary world. In "Dada Manifesto 1918," Tzara writes, "A work of art shouldn't be beauty *per se,* because it is dead." In this formulation, both the work of art and beauty are dead. Their death, according to Tzara, compels the artist to create something other than "a sober, definitive, irrefutable work. The new artist protests: he no longer paints (symbolic and illusionistic reproduction) but creates directly in stone, wood, iron, tin, rocks, or locomotive structures capable of being spun in all directions by the limpid wind of the momentary sensation." Tzara's argument is about more than art; it has a moral dimension. In the 1918 manifesto, he writes, "Goodness is lucid, clear and resolute, and ruthless towards compromise and politics." Thus, he advocates "active simplicity" as an antidote to the cruel complexity of the modern world.

Tzara achieves the manifestos' rhetorical effect by enacting his message of radical artistic and moral openness to contradiction and senselessness rather than by plainly declaring it. Throughout the collection, Tzara employs associative paradoxes and non sequiturs in order to make a case for Dada while rejecting the idea that Dada stands for anything. The collection's first manifesto, "Monsieur Antipyrine's Manifesto," begins, "DADA is our intensity: it erects inconsequential bayonets and the Sumatral head of German babies." The long first sentence continues, "it is against and for unity and definitely against the future … that we cry liberty but are not free." Through this combination of absurdity and inconsistency, Tzara's texts embody his argument and demonstrate his vision of Dada technique.

Stylistically, *Seven Dada Manifestos* is distinguished by its radical unconventionality. In each manifesto, Tzara experiments with form, syntax, and typography as a means of disrupting the possibility of logic and demonstrating the creative potential of play. "Unpretentious Proclamation" (1919), for example, is composed of absurd and often fragmented aphorisms that feature inconsistent spacing and are displayed in a variety of fonts. "Manifesto of Monsieur AA the Antiphilosopher" (1920) is formatted like a free-verse

TRISTAN TZARA: DADAIST PROPAGANDIST

Tristan Tzara was born Sammy Rosenstock in Bucharest, Romania, in 1896. He fled his homeland in 1915 in order to avoid military service in World War I, and he arrived in Zurich, Switzerland, to study philosophy and math. Although Zurich was not as cosmopolitan as major European cities such as Paris and Rome, Switzerland's neutrality made the city a haven for radical, young, and disillusioned artists and thinkers. While the war raged, Tzara encountered Hugo Ball at the bar Ball had founded, the Cabaret Voltaire. Together with Hans Arp, Richard Huelsenbeck, and others, these fiery radicals founded Dadaism.

An enthusiastic promoter of the movement, Tzara authored his numerous manifestos and edited the magazine *Dada* as a means of propagandizing a constructively anarchic cultural revolution. In addition to his polemical writings, Tzara wrote poetry and published *Vint-cinq poèmes* ("Twenty-five poems") in 1918. Two years later he left Zurich for Paris, where Francis Picabia and other Dadaists had begun to convene. While there, he became involved in the nascent surrealist movement and eventually switched his allegiance from Dadaism to surrealism. He wrote poetry and essays in the surrealist vein but eventually fell out with the group due to his growing allegiance to communism. During World War II he was active in the French Resistance. Until his death in 1963, he collected Stalinist memorabilia and wrote essays on art and literature.

poem. Nearly a full page of "Dada Manifesto on Feeble Love and Bitter Love" is filled with eight columns of the word "howl." These and other strange, nontraditional stylistic choices emphasize Tzara's commitment to the invention of new forms that reflect new, illogical modes of thinking and creating.

CRITICAL DISCUSSION

When *Seven Dada Manifestos* was published in 1924, it was largely overlooked, due to the declining activity of, and general interest in, Dadaism. However, the individual texts received a greater response upon their initial appearance between 1916 and 1921. The most prominent of these texts was "Dada Manifesto 1918." When it appeared in the third issue of the movement's journal, *Dada,* it was widely read and appreciated among Dadaists and other members of the avant-garde. Philippe Soupault, a French Dadaist, typified that response in a letter he sent to Tzara early in 1919: "I would also like to send you my compliments on the really remarkable manifesto which I greatly liked. I read it out to many friends, André Breton, Louis Aragon, and Jacques Vaché."

After the Dadaist movement died out in the early 1920s, Tzara's manifestos remained an important source of inspiration to other artistic movements. The surrealists, in particular, built on the innovations

A 1927 portrait of Tristan Tzara by Hungarian painter Lajos Tihanyi. PRIVATE COLLECTION/THE BRIDGEMAN ART LIBRARY

a 2002 essay for *Theatre Journal,* the scholar Martin Puchner writes of "Dada Manifesto 1918," "This manifesto declares that it wants 'nothing' and that its central cause is 'nothing.'" Puchner goes on to note, "Tzara's strategy of entangling his manifesto in the impossible position of being against the manifesto in principle and being against principles. Between these two contradictory statements, Tzara's manifesto oscillates between continuing to be a manifesto and becoming a parody of one." Commentators have also discussed the significance of the manifestos' appearances in Dadaist journals. According to scholar Emily Hage, "The journal was an essential tool in Tzara's drive to set the Dada movement apart from these other groups that had, he proposed, devolved into 'academies.' …Rather than simply producing paintings, drawings, poems, and essays to be chosen and reviewed by outside critics, Dadaists such as Tzara became editors themselves, thus challenging proscribed roles."

BIBLIOGRAPHY

Sources

Hage, Emily. "The Magazine as Strategy: Tristan Tzara's *Dada* and the Seminal Role of Dada Art Journals in the Dada Movement." *Journal of Modern Periodical Studies* 2.1 (2011): 33-53. Print.

Puchner, Martin. "Manifesto=Theatre." *Theatre Journal* 54.3 (2002): 449-65. *Project Muse.* Web. 7 Sept. 2012.

Sanouillet, Michel. *Dada in Paris.* Trans. Sharmila Ganguly. Cambridge: MIT, 2009. Print.

Sheppard, Richard. *Modernism—Dada—Postmodernism.* Evanston: Northwestern UP, 2000. Print.

Tzara, Tristan. *Seven Dada Manifestos and Lampisteries.* Trans. Barbara Wright. New York: Riverrun, 1992. Print.

Further Reading

Blythe, Sarah Ganz, and Edward D. Powers. *Looking at Dada.* New York: Museum of Modern Art, 2006. Print.

Brill, Dorothée. *Shock and the Senseless in Dada and Fluxus.* Hanover: Dartmouth College P, 2010. Print.

Coutts-Smith, Kenneth. *Dada.* London: Studio Vista, 1970. Print.

Hemus, Ruth. *Dada's Women.* New Haven: Yale UP, 2009. Print.

Hopkins, David. *Dada and Surrealism: A Very Short Introduction.* New York: Oxford UP, 2004. Print.

———. *Dada's Boys: Masculinity after Duchamp.* New Haven: Yale UP, 2007.

Theodore McDermott

and arguments implicit in Tzara's writings. Of the early surrealist writers, Michel Sanouillet writes, "Everything leads us to believe that for these young minds despairing of being able to give a form to their revolt, Dada—in this case the 'Dada Manifesto 1918' and Tzara himself—acted like one of those elements called catalysts in chemistry, whose role is to facilitate a reaction without participation themselves." Since *Seven Dada Manifestos* first appeared, Tzara's writings have been the subject of a small but growing body of criticism that has considered them in literary, historical, and political terms.

Much scholarship has focused on Tzara's manifestos within the context of avant-garde writing. In

THEATER OF CRUELTY

Antonin Artaud

OVERVIEW

Written by Antonin Artaud in 1932 and published in *La Nouvelle Revue Française,* a prominent French literary magazine, the First Manifesto of the *Theater of Cruelty* lays out a plan for a new model of theatrical performance that will reunite spectators with their subconscious feelings as well as with their bodily, as opposed to intellectual, experience of the world. When the manifesto was published, Artaud was struggling both creatively and financially, and he addressed the piece to established writers and financiers as well as to the readers of the literary periodicals in which his writing appeared. Artaud subsequently attempted to realize his vision for a more authentic, embodied, and visceral theater, but the few plays he directed were critically and commercially unsuccessful. Three decades after the publication of the manifesto, avant-garde directors in Europe and the United States began to stage productions that more successfully enacted Artaud's demands. The ideas developed in the manifesto have since become a cornerstone of the twentieth-century avant-garde.

Artaud's concept of a Theater of Cruelty was initially met with hostility. Benjamin Crémieux, a writer and former supporter of Artaud's Alfred Jarry Theater, threatened to resign from the staff of *La Nouvelle Revue Française* if Artaud ever published with them again. Readers found Artaud's rejection of primarily language-based theater, which engaged the intellect instead of the body, threatening to the aesthetic values of much of the European cultural canon. Today, however, *Theater of Cruelty* is immediately recognizable to scholars of twentieth-century experimental theater, philosophy, literary criticism, and art history.

HISTORICAL AND LITERARY CONTEXT

The *Theater of Cruelty* is primarily concerned with recovering the primal, ritualistic function of theater. In it, Artaud rejects the primacy of the script, hoping to realign the spatial, auditory, and visual conventions of the theater to emphasize nonverbal signs and to excite physiological responses in the audience. The manifesto argues that "instead of continuing to rely upon texts considered definitive and sacred, it is essential to put an end to the subjugation of the theater to the text, and to recover the notion of a kind of unique language half-way between gesture and thought." By developing this new language, Artaud sought to escape the traditional demand that the theater represent a recognizable version of real life.

Artaud was writing the *Theater of Cruelty* in France between World War I and World War II, during the rise of fascism in Europe. Although he lived through both wars, he was often incarcerated in sanatoriums or mental hospitals, and his experience with what he saw as a brutal system shaped his writing about the body and the psyche. Artaud underwent electroshock therapy, which was a common practice at the time. Although violence, totalitarianism, and human suffering characterized the political atmosphere of the 1930s, Artaud also lived in a time and place of extreme creative and artistic output. The work of Cubist painters such as Pablo Picasso and Georges Braque and writers such as André Gide, Georges Bataille, and André Breton helped shape the cultural climate that produced the *Theater of Cruelty.*

Artaud had broken from the surrealist movement by the time he wrote the *Theater of Cruelty,* but the manifesto is clearly indebted to the surrealists' attempts to access the deep, and often absurd, recesses of the human psyche. Artaud was also profoundly influenced by a performance of Balinese theater at the 1931 Paris Colonial Exhibition; he mistook the choreographed performance for involuntary, shamanistic gestures and strove to reproduce what he saw as an authentic primitivism in his own Theater of Cruelty. In addition, Artaud was a film and radio actor, and he was specifically influenced by the Marx Brothers, whose comic films he viewed as celebrations of the anarchic quality of laughter and the disruptive possibility of humor.

Artaud's writing was especially influential to the post-structuralist school of thought that emerged in the 1960s and 1970s. Philosophers such as Jacques Derrida and Julia Kristeva referred to the *Theater of Cruelty* when developing their own theories of language and the body. In particular, Artaud's critique of language influenced Derrida's idea that textuality displaces and defers meaning. Although in his own day Artaud failed to put the Theater of Cruelty effectively into practice, his manifesto influenced many important figures in the avant-garde theater, notably Peter Brook, Jerzy Grotowski, Sam Shepard, and John Cage, whose experimental orchestral pieces often

❖ *Key Facts*

Time Period:
Mid-20th Century

Movement/Issue:
Aesthetics; Avant-gardism; Modernism

Place of Publication:
France

Language of Publication:
French

ANTONIN ARTAUD: THE MAD POET

Throughout his life, Artaud struggled to find rewarding acting work and was often impoverished. He was also addicted to opiates and was repeatedly institutionalized for symptoms of schizophrenia, delirium, and paranoia. Stephen Barber suggests that Artaud's writing specifically approaches the subject of madness, which becomes "raw material to be treated with great irony and great anger." Even as Artaud discussed his own symptoms, he also critiqued the institution of psychiatry. He was an important figure for Michel Foucault, whose *Madness and Civilization* (1961) is perhaps the seminal critique of the modern mental institution.

After his failed attempt, with *The Cenci,* to bring the Theater of Cruelty to life, Artaud visited Mexico in 1935, participating in a peyote ritual with the Tarahumara Indians and further developing his romantic idealization of so-called "primitive" groups of people. After a visit to Ireland in 1937, Artaud was placed in asylums for the next nine years of his life, where he went through fifty-one electric shock comas but also wrote profusely on the subjects of evil, god, scatology, and the body. After World War II Artaud came to be celebrated within the Paris literary scene and hailed as the romantic ideal of a suffering, mad poet. Artaud's image as a spiritual sufferer and mad genius continues to shape the criticism of his work.

manipulated the performance space to make the audience an unwitting, but central, participant in his performances.

THEMES AND STYLE

In the *Theater of Cruelty,* Artaud presents his vision for a "total" theater, an experience that would overwhelm audiences by engaging or assaulting the sensory perceptions normally put aside when watching a play and relying instead on a logic more akin to that of dreams or drug-induced hallucinations than everyday life. Artaud believed that a traditional play—one in which all of the elements were ultimately subordinate to the script—distanced audiences from their own sensory and emotional experiences. Artaud argues that the "language of sounds, cries, lights, onomatopoeia" has a superior ability to work in tandem with the physical space of the theater to affect audiences by "acting upon the sensibility." Artaud rejects not only the traditional script, but also the traditional theater space, favoring use of a "single site, without partition or barrier of any kind," which would enable a "direct communication" between the actors and spectators.

Artaud's first statement in the manifesto decries the theater's current allegiance to realistic representation onstage and to verbal expression at the expense of a range of sensory experiences. In the first pages of the manifesto, Artaud redefines the terms "reality" and "language." His new language of the theater describes the physical "language" of the actors' presence, not the words spoken in the play. The manifesto continues by laying out guidelines for "technique" and "themes," and it ends with a list of works that the Theater of Cruelty will "stage, without regard for text," including "the story of Bluebeard" and stories by the Marquis de Sade "in which the eroticism will be transposed, allegorically mounted and figured, to create a violent exteriorization of cruelty."

Artaud uses "cruelty" to express multiple ideas: the disciplines of performing and directing should be cruel in their rigor; the nonverbal, emotionally powerful "language" of the theater should render audiences powerless in the face of a performance; life and art must become indistinguishable through the theater; and force—an attack on the senses—must take precedence over form—the recognizable ways the theater communicates ideas. The use of cruelty allows the theater to furnish "the spectator with the truthful precipitates of dreams, in which his taste for crime, his erotic obsessions, his savagery, his chimeras, his utopian sense of life and matter, even his cannibalism, pour out, on a level not counterfeit and illusory, but interior." When spectators undergo the cruelty of the theater, they can also tap into their subterranean, contradictory, and cruel desires. Artaud values this possibility because it puts the audience "in a state of deepened and keener perception, [which] is the very object of the magic and the rites of which the theater is only a reflection."

CRITICAL DISCUSSION

Readers initially rejected the theory proposed by the *Theater of Cruelty.* Although previous avant-garde groups, notably the Dadaists, had also experimented with theatrical spectacles designed to provoke the audience into active engagement with the performance and contemplation of their own lives, many readers were unable to accept the manifesto's refusal of Western performance conventions. The manifesto was intended to attract investors to Artaud's plan to create a Theater of Cruelty, yet financiers were largely apathetic. In 1933 Artaud published a second manifesto of the *Theater of Cruelty,* which expanded upon his initial concept and outlined a proposed performance. Five years later, Artaud published his collected writing on the theater as *The Theater and Its Double.* The *Theater of Cruelty* was introduced to the United States in 1958, when Grove Press published Mary Caroline Richards's translation of *The Theater and Its Double.* The manifesto quickly won the widespread interest of countercultural groups in the 1950s and 1960s, particularly the Beats and performance-art collectives.

Artaud's manifesto has been widely influential across the fields of theater, performance art, music, literature, and philosophy. In the 1960s numerous French and American writers were drawn to Artaud and strove in their own work to produce a "total art" that spoke in its own language. Martin Puchner has noted in *New Literary History* that scholars "from Plato to Hegel" have relied on the theater to illustrate their main ideas and that in the twentieth century some of the most important philosophers gravitated toward Artaud as a theorist not only of theatrical production but also of the way language contains and shapes everyday human experience. Aside from Bertolt Brecht's theory of alienation, the ideas developed in the *Theater of Cruelty* have been perhaps the greatest influence on contemporary theater.

For many contemporary critics, it has become important to see in the *Theater of Cruelty* a prescription for shocking spectators into radical political action. Leo Bersani, Maggie Nelson, and Stephen Barber interpret Artaud's theory as a method for breaking down everyday experience and forcing spectators to recognize their own capacity for cruelty. By contrast, Kimberly Jannarone argues in *Artaud and His Doubles* that the *Theater of Cruelty,* and Artaud's oeuvre in general, has been misread by leftist thinkers who want to see Artaud's call for aesthetic revolution aligned with their own politics. Instead of seeing the *Theater of Cruelty* as a shock that prods an audience toward empathy or personal growth, Jannarone argues that the manifesto rejects the romantic linking of suffering and enlightenment, pointing readers instead toward a definition of freedom that "is found through loss and immersion rather than individual liberty and self-realization."

BIBLIOGRAPHY

Sources

Artaud, Antonin. *The Theater and its Double.* Trans. Mary Caroline Richards. New York: Grove, 1958. Print.

Barber, Stephen. *Antonin Artaud: Blows and Bombs.* London: Faber, 1993. Print.

Innes, Christopher. *Avant-garde Theatre, 1892-1992.* London: Routledge, 1993. Print.

Jannarone, Kimberly. *Artaud and His Doubles.* Ann Arbor: U of Michigan P, 2010. Print.

Puchner, Martin. "The Theater in Modernist Thought." *New Literary History* 33:3 (2002): 521-32. *Project MUSE.* Web. 21 Aug. 2012.

Scheer, Edward, ed. *Antonin Artaud: A Critical Reader.* New York: Routledge, 1994. Print.

Poet and actor Antonin Artaud in a scene from the 1928 film *The Passion of Joan of Arc,* directed by Carl Dreyer. HENRY GUTTMANN/GETTY IMAGES

Further Reading

Baker, Geoffrey. "Nietzsche, Artaud, and Tragic Politics." *Comparative Literature* 55:1 (2003): 1-23. *JSTOR.* Web. 21 Aug. 2012.

Bermel, Albert. *Artaud's Theatre of Cruelty.* New York: Taplinger, 1977. Print.

Gorelick, Nathan. "Life in Excess: Insurrection and Expenditure in Antonin Artaud's Theater of Cruelty." *Discourse* 33:2 (2011): 263-79. *Project MUSE.* Web. 21 Aug. 2012.

Greene, Naomi. "Antonin Artaud: Metaphysical Revolutionary." *Yale French Studies* 39 (1967): 188-97. *JSTOR.* Web. 21 Aug. 2012.

Jamieson, Lee. *Antonin Artaud: From Theory to Practice.* London: Greenwich Exchange, 2007. Print.

Monje, David. "Force over Form: Resistance, Method, Theory, and Artaud's 'Theory of Cruelty.'" *Cultural Studies, Critical Methodologies* 12:3 (2012): 213-19. *Sage Publications.* Web. 21 Aug. 2012.

Nelson, Maggie. *The Art of Cruelty: A Reckoning.* New York: Norton, 2011. Print.

Savarese, Nicola, and Richard Fowler. "1931: Antonin Artaud Sees Balinese Theatre at the Paris Colonial Exposition." *TDR* 45:3 (2001): 51-77. JSTOR Web. 21 Aug. 2012.

Schumacher, Claude. *Artaud on Theatre.* London: Methuen, 1999. Print.

Anna Ioanes

YELLOW MANIFESTO

Salvador Dalí

OVERVIEW

Published jointly by painter Salvador Dalí, literary critic Luis Montanyà, and art critic Sebastian Gasch in March of 1928, the *Yellow Manifesto,* or *Catalan Anti-Art Manifesto,* is the definitive defense of avant-garde art in early twentieth-century Catalonia. Although all three signatories contributed to the text, and the concluding list of artists endorsed in the *Yellow Manifesto* was a synthesis of their interests, according to Fèlix Fanés in his book *Salvador Dalí: The Construction of the Image 1925-1930,* "its authorship must be largely attributed to Dalí…. In the last analysis, Dalí decided on the outcome of the text." All three, however, were equally concerned with the manifesto's primary target: denouncing the state of official culture in Catalonia and, in its stead, advocating for artists associated with Dadaism, surrealism, cubism, and futurism. Although the manifesto was eventually distributed far beyond Catalonia, it was quite explicitly addressed to a Catalan audience. Initially supportive of the manifesto—and listed among its endorsed artists—poet Federico García Lorca ultimately decided against contributing to its composition, citing the fact that he himself was not a Catalan.

If, as Spanish writer Ernesto Giménez Caballero has stated, the *Yellow Manifesto* "fell like a bomb in the Catalan literary world," the blast drove its readers in diametrically opposed directions. The openly polemical tenor of the tract polarized its readers' reactions, and in the weeks following its release it was praised, and condemned, with verve. In the long run, however, the *Yellow Manifesto* has proved profoundly influential: not only did it provide a crucial rallying cry for progressive artists within Catalonia, but it also influenced modernism much farther afield, featuring, for example, in André Breton's *Second Manifesto of Surrealism.*

HISTORICAL AND LITERARY CONTEXT

The *Yellow Manifesto*'s primary goal is to jar its Catalan audience to reject what its authors saw as the stagnant state of art in Catalonia. Fanés cites Gasch—who Dalí identified as the initial instigator of the project, though Dalí himself drove the composition—retrospectively reflecting on the group's motives, saying they "were more and more irritated by the absolute lack of preparation with which certain of our intellectuals treated artistic issues" and that a "constant state of confusion and eclecticism" had limited artistic production in Catalonia, even to the point of a rigid, reactionary "pseudo-Hellenism." As Dalí wrote in a letter prior to the manifesto's publication, with characteristic eccentricity, "We discovered Greece in the antiseptic folds of the lady golfer's pullover, in the repugnant folds of Aurea's fat flesh, pestilent with veils and bronze paint!"

Despite Spain's neutrality in World War I, when the *Yellow Manifesto* was released a decade later in 1928, the Great War's presence was still felt. Within artistic communities throughout Europe, the fallout of disillusionment, especially in the form of Dadaism—a movement initiated in 1916, fervently rejecting reason on the grounds that it had precipitated the war—continued to be felt throughout the late 1920s. Another important contemporary cultural influence clearly visible in the manifesto was the early twentieth-century proliferation of industry and technology. As Robert S. Lubar points out in *Art and Anti-Art: Miró, Dalí, and the Catalan Avant-Garde,* "Dalí's generation witnessed a vast expansion of media technologies," and these new artistic media such as film, photography, and recorded music were all consequently championed in the *Yellow Manifesto* over and "against the entrenched parochialism of the Catalan bourgeoisie."

Although the *Yellow Manifesto* differs in some respects from its predecessors, it was nevertheless composed in the same vein as earlier modernist manifestos. In *The Persistence of Memory: A Biography of Dalí,* Meredith Etherington-Smith claims that the manifesto was "written and laid out in a manner obviously derived from Marinetti's *Futurist Manifesto.*" In crafting the manifesto, Dalí was also clearly influenced by the Dadaists and surrealists and, in particular, Breton's 1924 *Manifesto of Surrealism.* In 1926 Dalí made his first trip to Paris, where he met Pablo Picasso and Joan Miró—both of whom Dalí endorsed in the *Yellow Manifesto*'s conclusion two years later—and, as Nicholas Philip James notes in *Salvador Dalí in Formation,* they were the ones who "subsequently introduced him to Dadaists and Surrealists," marking a crucially influential moment in the life of the budding Catalan artist.

The themes of Gasch, Montanyà, and Dalí's manifesto were carried through to ensuing assertions of artistic vision, both in manifestos by other artists as well as in the later work of the authors themselves. A few months after the manifesto's publication, Dalí and Montanyà took part in a meeting of avant-garde artists at the Ateneu in Sitges, in which, according to Fanés, Dalí's speech stole the show and "might be considered a continuation" of the *Yellow Manifesto*. The manifesto also influenced Breton's issuing of the *Second Manifesto of Surrealism*, which Dalí himself also signed, though this was far from the only mention of the manifesto; indeed, as Aránzazu Ascunce Arenas points out in *Barcelona and Madrid: Social Networks of the Avant-Garde*, Gasch, Montanyà, and Dalí's "manifesto is one of the most frequently referenced documents of the artistic and literary revolutionary moment" of the early twentieth century.

THEMES AND STYLE

The *Yellow Manifesto*'s chief concern is to "DENOUNCE" the classical, traditionalist, parochial culture of Catalan artistic and intellectual life and, in lieu of this "sickly sentimentality" and obstinate imitation of the past, to promote the growth of modernism across the board. The three authors are keen to declare to their fellow Catalans that "WE LIVE in a new era, of unforeseen poetic intensity" and that to cling fast to the art forms of the past is to blindly shut out the truly "revolutionized" world of the modern era. They define themselves and their allies in art as, in fact, "anti-artistic," unfettered by the art forms of the past. In contrast to the ossified bourgeoisie, the manifesto suggests that "a sportsman, free from artistic notions and all erudition is nearer and more suited to experience the art of today and the poetry of today than myopic individuals, burdened by negative training."

The most immediately striking rhetorical feature of the manifesto is, quite simply, how it appears on the page, laid out with capitalized assertions on the left margins, followed by explications of those assertions of various lengths along the right side of the page. The left side begins each sentence with statements such as "WE HAVE ELIMINATED," "WE DECLARE," "THERE ARE," or "WE DENOUNCE," with subsequent lists and expansions of these assertions, of varying lengths, following down the right margin. The stylized presentation of the manifesto not only lends it a feeling of listing a litany of grievances, as it appears itemized rather than in standard paragraph form, but also, by snubbing that form, the manifesto enacts the very thing it calls for: a rejection of literary forms from the past.

The emotional tenor of the language deployed in the *Yellow Manifesto* is fiery and divisive. The text opens with an assertion that its authors "have eliminated … all courtesy in our attitude," suggesting that it was "useless to attempt any discussion with the representatives of present-day Catalan culture." The openly hostile descriptions of "the grotesque and extremely sad spectacle of the Catalan intelligentsia"

SALVADOR DALÍ AND WALTER BENJAMIN

In many ways, Walter Benjamin's famous 1936 essay *The Work of Art in the Age of Mechanical Reproduction* echoes themes expressed by Salvador Dalí in the *Yellow Manifesto*. The manifesto asserts that, thankfully, "MECHANIZATION has revolutionized the world," bringing about myriad new means of mass-producing art, such as the gramophone or the camera. Benjamin, likewise, sings the praises of mechanical reproduction and its impact on the arts, arguing that a work of art's "aura," its air of authenticity begotten by being a *singular* object incapable of authentic reproduction, precludes it from being accessed in an egalitarian manner—one might think of the large crowds, who must pay an entrance fee, thronging to catch a glimpse of the *Mona Lisa* at the Louvre.

Despite their similar attitudes toward mechanization's potentially positive impact on the arts, Dalí and Benjamin could not have had more contradictory political views. While Benjamin concludes his essay with a strong condemnation of fascism, which he claims attempts to turn politics and war into art rather than, as he would have it, mechanical reproduction "politicizing art" in service of the revolution, Dalí was deeply sympathetic with fascism. He was on friendly terms with Spain's fascist dictator Francisco Franco, and his admiration for authoritarianism was diametrically opposed to Benjamin's revolutionary politics, which wholly decried fascism in all its forms. Although, as Robin Adele Greeley reports in *Surrealism and the Spanish Civil War*, when André Breton accused Dalí of idolizing Adolf Hitler due to his comments about the great innovative "novelty" of Nazism, Dalí confidently countered, "I am Hitlerian neither in fact nor intention."

Salvador Dalí on the set of Alfred Hitchcock's film *Spellbound*, 1945. Dalí was a principal author of the *Yellow Manifesto*, which attacked the Catalan art establishment. COURTESY EVERETT COLLECTION

PRIMARY SOURCE

YELLOW MANIFESTO

We have eliminated from this MANIFESTO all courtesy in our attitude. It is useless to attempt any discussion with the representatives of present-day Catalan culture, which is artistically negative although efficient in other respects. Compromise and correctness lead to deliquescent and lamentable states of confusion of all values, to the most unbreathable spiritual atmospheres, to the most pernicious of influences. An example: *La Nova Revista*. Violent hostility, in contrast, clearly locates values and positions and creates a hygienic state of mind.

WE HAVE ELIMINATED

all reasoning   There exists an enormous

WE HAVE ELIMINATED

all literature   bibliography

WE HAVE ELIMINATED

all poetry   and all the effort

WE HAVE ELIMINATED

all philosophy   of artists of today

in favour of to replace all this.

our ideas

…

WE WARN

those still uncontaminated of the risk of infection. A matter of strict spiritual asepsis.

WE KNOW

that we are not going to say anything new. We are certain, however, that it is the basis of everything new that now exists and everything new that could possibly be created.

WE LIVE

in a new era, of unforeseen poetic intensity.

MECHANIZATION

has revolutionized the world.

MECHANIZATION

— the antithesis of circumstantially indispensable futurism — has established the most profound change humanity has known.

A MULTITUDE

anonymous — and anti-artistic — is collaborating with its daily endeavours towards the affirmation of the new era, while still living in accordance with its own period.

…

ARTISTS

of today have created a new art in accordance with this state of mind. In accordance with their era.

HERE, HOWEVER, PEOPLE GO ON VEGETATING IDYLLICALLY

THE CULTURE

of present-day Catalonia is useless for the joy of our era. Nothing is more dangerous, more false or more adulterating.

WE ASK CATALAN INTELLECTUALS:

'What use has the Bernat Metge Foundation [for the study of the classics] been to you, if you end up confusing Ancient Greece with pseudo-classical ballerinas?'

WE DECLARE

that sportsmen are nearer the spirit of Greece than our intellectuals.

WE GO ON TO ADD

that a sportsman, free from artistic notions and all erudition is nearer and more suited to experience the art of today and the poetry of today than myopic intellectuals, burdened by negative training.

FOR US

Greece continues in the numerical precision of an aeroplane engine, in the anti-artistic, anonymously manufactured English fabric meant for golf, in the naked performer of the American music-hall.

WE NOTE

that the theatre has ceased to exist for some people and almost for everybody.

WE NOTE

that everyday concerts, lectures and shows taking place among us now, tend to be synonymous with unbreathable, crushingly boring places.

IN CONTRAST

new events, of intense joy and cheerfulness, demand the attention of the youth of today.

THERE IS

the cinema

THERE ARE

stadia, boxing, rugby, tennis and a thousand other sports

THERE IS

the popular music of today: jazz and modern dance

THERE ARE

motor and aeronautics shows

THERE ARE

beach games

THERE ARE

beauty competitions in the open air

THERE IS

the fashion show

THERE IS

the naked performer under the electric lights of the music-hall

THERE IS

modern music

THERE IS

the motor-racing track

THERE ARE

art exhibitions of modern artists

THERE ARE

moreover, great engineering and some magnificent ocean liners

THERE IS

an architecture of today

THERE ARE

implements, objects and furniture of the present era

THERE IS

modern literature

THERE ARE

modern poets

THERE IS

modern theatre

THERE IS

the gramophone, which is a little machine the camera, which is another little machine

THERE ARE

newspapers with extremely quick and vast information

THERE ARE

encyclopaedias of extraordinary erudition

THERE IS

science in great action

THERE IS

well-documented, guiding criticism

THERE ARE

etc., etc., etc.

THERE IS

finally, an immobile ear over a small puff of smoke.

WE DENOUNCE

the sentimental influence of [the poet] Guirnerà's racial clichés

WE DENOUNCE

the sickly sentimentality served up by Orféo Català, with its shabby repertoire of popular songs adapted and adulterated by people with no capacity whatsoever for music, and even, of original compositions. (We think optimistically of the choir of American Revellers.)

WE DENOUNCE

the total lack of youth in our youth

WE DENOUNCE

the total lack of decision and audacity

WE DENOUNCE

the fear of new events, of words, of the risk of the ridiculous

WE DENOUNCE

the torpor of the putrid atmosphere of clubs and egos mingled with art

WE DENOUNCE

the total unawareness of critics with regard to the art of the present and the past

WE DENOUNCE

young people who seek to repeat painting of the past

WE DENOUNCE

young people who seek to imitate literature of the past

WE DENOUNCE

old, authentic architecture

WE DENOUNCE

decorative art, unless it is standardized

WE DENOUNCE

painters of crooked trees

WE DENOUNCE

present-day Catalan poetry, made with stale Maragallian clichés

WE DENOUNCE

artistic poisons for the use of children like: *Jordi.* (For the joy and understanding of children, nothing is more suitable than Rousseau, Picasso, Chagall…)

WE DENOUNCE

the psychology of little girls who sing: 'Rosó, Rosó …'

WE DENOUNCE

the psychology of little boys who sing: 'Rosó, Rosó … '

FINALLY WE DEDICATE OURSELVES TO THE GREAT ARTISTS OF TODAY, within the most diverse tendencies and categories:

PICASSO, GRIS, OZENFANT, CHIRICO, JOAN MIRÓ, LIPCHITZ, BRANCUSI, ARP, LE CORBUSIER, REVERDY, TRISTAN TZARA, PAUL ÉLUARD, LOUIS ARAGON, ROBERT DESNOS, JEAN COCTEAU, GARCÍA LORCA, STRAVINSKY, MARITAIN, RAYNAL, ZERVOS, ANDRÉ BRETON, ETC., ETC.

SOURCE: © Salvador Dalí, Fundació Gala-Salvador Dalí, Figueres, 2012.

were aimed not at reconciliation with the artistic establishment but were rather a rallying cry, a call to arms for young Catalans to throw out the forms of their forefathers in order to embrace the modern era and all the new art it had to offer. Gasch, Montanyà, and Dalí were quite content to burn their bridges to the past, placing their faith in "THE GREAT ARTISTS OF TODAY" to blaze a trail into the future.

CRITICAL DISCUSSION

With its repeated invectives against the "putrefied atmosphere" of the Catalan intelligentsia, the *Yellow Manifesto* proved to be profoundly and unsurprisingly polarizing. As Etherington-Smith writes, the manifesto "provoked raucous partisanship on both sides," attracting many progressive Catalan intellectuals to the "anti-art" it advocated while concurrently alienating many members of the established intelligentsia in Catalonia, who were deeply insulted. This, however, was exactly what its authors intended.

While in the *Yellow Manifesto* Gasch, Montanyà, and Dalí were able to compromise on their differing aesthetics in service of denouncing the traditionalism in Catalonia they all agreed was hindering artistic progress, in the years that followed that unified aesthetic front crumbled considerably. According to Etherington-Smith, Lorca was among the first to dissociate himself from the group, striking his name from the list of artists when he published the manifesto, translated from Catalan into Spanish, in *Gallo*. By 1932 Gasch and Dalí had butted heads over surrealism so frequently that the two had, in Arenas's terms, "parted ways indefinitely." Only two years later Dalí was the one to split with surrealism, as he was officially expelled from the Surrealist Group in 1934 over disagreements with Breton. If, as Caballero said, the manifesto "fell like a bomb in the Catalan literary world," it seems that its shrapnel of vitriol boomeranged back, severing even the bonds between its own authors.

Although most scholars see Gasch, Montanyà, and Dalí's manifesto as an important moment in art and intellectual history, English scholarship on the *Yellow Manifesto* is comparatively scarce. Most anglophone scholars tend to situate the manifesto within the intellectual and artistic trajectory of Dalí's life; the aforementioned texts *Salvador Dalí in Formation* by James, *Salvador Dalí: The Construction of the Image 1925-1930* by Fanés, and *The Persistence of Memory: A Biography of Dalí* by Etherington-Smith are all prime examples of such a treatment of this tract. Alternatively, other authors often place the text in the context of Catalan and Spanish artistic evolution, exemplified by Arenas's *Barcelona and Madrid: Social Networks of the Avant-Garde,* as well as the essay collection *Barcelona and Modernity: Picasso, Gaudi, Miró, Dalí.*

BIBLIOGRAPHY

Sources

Arenas, Aránzazu Ascunce. *Barcelona and Madrid: Social Networks of the Avant-Garde.* Lanham: Bucknell UP, 2012. Print.

Breton, André. *Manifestoes of Surrealism.* Trans. Richard Seaver and Helen R. Lane. Ann Arbor: U of Michigan P, 2000. Print.

Dalí, Salvador, Sebastian Gasch, and Luis Montanyà. "Yellow Manifesto." *100 Artists' Manifestos: From the Futurists to the Stuckists.* Ed. Alex Danchev. New York: Penguin, 2011. Print.

Etherington-Smith, Meredith. *The Persistence of Memory: A Biography of Dalí.* Cambridge: Da Capo, 1995. Print.

Fanés, Fèlix. *Salvador Dalí: The Construction of the Image 1925-1930.* New Haven: Yale UP, 2007. Print.

Greeley, Robin Adele. *Surrealism and the Spanish Civil War.* New Haven: Yale UP, 2006. Print.

James, Nicholas Philip. "Salvador Dalí in Formation: A Hallucinogenic Journey." *CV/Visual Arts Research Series 37,* 2004. Print.

Lubar, Robert S. "Art and Anti-Art: Miró, Dalí, and the Catalan Avant-Garde." *Barcelona and Modernity: Picasso, Gaudi, Miró, Dalí.* New Haven: Yale UP, 2006. Print.

Further Reading

Ades, Dawn. *Dalí.* New York: Thomas and Hudson, 1995. Print.

Cate-Arries, Francie. "Salvador Dalí, Federico Garcia Lorca, and the Persistence of Memory: Revealing Hidden Faces." *Anales de la literatura espanola contemporanea* 20.1 (1995): 11-28. Print.

Finkelstein, Haim. *Salvador Dalí's Art and Writing 1927-1942: The Metamorphosis of Narcissus.* Cambridge: Cambridge UP, 1996. Print.

Jenny, Laurent, and Thomas Trezise. "From Breton to Dalí: The Adventures of Automatism." MIT Press 51 (1989): 105-14. Print.

Kachur, Lewis. *Displaying the Marvelous: Marcel Duchamp, Salvador Dalí, and the Surrealist Exhibitions.* Cambridge: MIT Press, 2001. Print.

Elliott Niblock

ANIMA HOMINIS

William Butler Yeats

OVERVIEW

Composed by William Butler Yeats, "Anima Hominis" (1918) outlines its author's idiosyncratic poetic vision and describes his theory of the origin of artistic inspiration. Yeats was among the twentieth century's most celebrated poets and playwrights and was a prominent advocate for the revival of Gaelic language and culture in his native Ireland. When he composed his artistic manifesto, he was in the midst of a transition from the late-Romanticism of his early work to the poetic modernism of his later period. A longstanding interest in occultism and theosophy undergirded his evolving ideas about poetry. Borrowing from his spiritual belief, "Anima Hominis" argues that artists derive insight and creativity from the tragedy and tumult of the inner life but that artistic achievement depends on escaping individual nature and experience. Central to the essay are Yeats's esoteric conceptions of the "mask" and the "antithetical self," terms that refer to the true artist's requisite ability to create a false identity that serves as both an ideal to aspire to and a shield against psychic injury. The essay originally appeared in *Per Amica Silentia Lunea,* a "philosophical book," according to Yeats, that offers a key to understanding the foundation of his artistic project.

Initially, "Anima Hominis" was greeted with confusion. In general, reviewers wrote that *Per Amica Silentia Lunea* contained a wealth of compelling ideas that were imprecisely worded and difficult to follow. In response to early feedback, Yeats had rewritten and expanded the essay before it appeared in print. After his 1917 marriage to Georgie Hyde-Lees, a student of religions and the occult, the philosophy that animated his manifesto became increasingly mystical and inspired by the tenets of automatic writing, which ostensibly proceeds directly from the subconscious. In 1925, eight years after "Anima Hominis" first appeared, Yeats published *A Vision,* an extended treatise on the occult philosophy underlying his poetry. Today, "Anima Hominis" is considered valuable in understanding the poet's position on the cusp of two great literary movements. It is also read by scholars as a precursor to *A Vision,* one of Yeats's most studied works.

HISTORICAL AND LITERARY CONTEXT

The origins of Yeats's idiosyncratic and mystical belief system can be traced to the mid-1880s, when, in his twenties, he began to study psychology, magic,

mysticism, fairy and folk tales, and Eastern religions. His growing conviction that the poetic tradition was a kind of religion later animated much of his argument in "Anima Hominis." Yeats was initiated into the Theosophical Society, an influential occult organization founded on beliefs in pantheism and reincarnation, in 1890. In 1896 he began performing Celtic rituals with the ardent nationalist Maud Gonne and others, thus combining his esoteric and nationalist convictions. The poetry of this early period drew on his spiritual and folk interests, exploring supernatural and occult themes in symbolic, stylized verse that looks nostalgically back to the Romantics of the early and middle 1800s. He considered Gonne his muse and was deeply influenced by her feminist poetry and ardent devotion to Irish causes. At the turn of the twentieth century, however, after Gonne rejected a marriage proposal from him, he turned away from Romanticism, embracing realism and directness in his work while holding onto his occult interests.

Although Yeats was already a renowned poet when he produced "Anima Hominis," his poetic output had been in decline for a full fifteen years as he focused on creating an Irish national theater. Since 1900, he had published only three brief volumes of verse, *In the Seven Woods* (1903), *The Green Helmet* (1910), and *Responsibilities* (1914), which are widely considered his weakest works. During this period, he reinvented himself as a realist, replacing the ornament and mythology of his early poems with the style and subjects of the commonplace contemporary world. The worsening political situation in Europe in the years leading up to World War I greatly concerned him. In 1909 he met the poet Ezra Pound and began to "modernize" his work, employing ordinary language in increasingly elaborate formal structures, which, despite the influence of Pound and T. S. Eliot, remained fairly conservative. Within his participation in modernist poetic circles, Yeats's interest in the occult continued to grow. He was aware, however, that his mystical perspective was difficult for many readers to access. "Anima Hominis," along with the other materials included in *Per Amica Silentia Lunea* (a prologue, a poem, a companion essay called "Anima Mundi," and an epilogue, all of which were closely interrelated), were meant to remove this

✛ *Key Facts*

Time Period:
Early 20th Century

Movement/Issue:
Aesthetics; Mysticism; Artistic inspiration

Place of Publication:
England

Language of Publication:
English

W. B. YEATS: POET, PLAYWRIGHT, AND POLITICIAN

Although he is best remembered as one of the twentieth-century's principal English-language poets and playwrights, W. B. Yeats had a long and varied career that involved activities as disparate as founding a national theater and serving in the Irish Senate. Born in 1865 in Sandymount, a suburb of Dublin, and raised in rural County Sligo, Yeats was a dreamer as a child and an indifferent student. Rather than attend Trinity College, as was traditional in his family, he chose to go to art school in Dublin. There, he studied painting and wrote poetry. When he had finished school, he delved into occult and esoteric thought, wrote verse, and published his first collections of poetry.

In the late 1800s, Yeats began writing plays, and in 1899 he helped establish an Irish national theater. Five years later, it opened its doors as the Abbey Theatre, soon becoming an important Irish artistic institution. This endeavor marked the beginning of Yeats's official involvement with the state. In 1922 he was appointed to the first Irish senate, where he worked to design a new national currency, modify the education system, and form the Irish Academy of Letters. He won the Nobel Prize for Literature in 1923 and continued to serve in the senate until 1928. In the late 1930s, he became attracted to, and even advocated, Fascism. Yeats died in France in 1939.

impediment. As Yeats wrote in a 1917 letter to his father, he conceived of the volume "as a kind of prose backing to my poetry."

"Anima Hominis" draws on the poetic thought of William Blake and Percy Bysshe Shelley; on the poetry of Dante Alighieri, who exercised a tremendous influence on both the Romantics and the modernists; and on the ideas of late-nineteenth-century occult philosophers such as Madame H. P. Blavatasky, the cofounder of the Theosophical Society. The two Romantic poets provided a metaphysical conception of poetry. Shelley's interest in ideal esoteric wisdom and his use of recurrent symbolic patterns in his poems particularly influenced Yeats. In its arguments, "Anima Hominis" uses quotes from Dante and other Italian poets of the thirteenth-century Dolce Stil Novo movement, which itself drew inspiration from Provençal troubadour, Tuscan, and Sicilian poetry. Dante is a "brooding presence" in "Anima Hominis," according to Yeats biographer Roy Foster. Yeats also quotes from two English poets, Walter Savage Landor, a classicist, and Edwin Ellis, a Blakean. Blavatsky's *Secret Doctrine* (1888) offered another source of inspiration for Yeats's manifesto. A comprehensive mystical cosmology, the book relies on three foundational principles: that the universe is bound by an organizing idea (rather than a deity), an "Immutable Principle on which all speculation is possible"; that the world is the site of a great conflict between good and evil; and that all souls are

part of a "Universal Oversoul." These creeds formed a foundation for Yeats's essay, which fused the Romantic and occult with his new interest in the innovations of modernism.

"Anima Hominis" served as a framework for the further development of its author's mystical and poetic thought and output. In 1919 he published *The Wild Swans at Coole*, a volume of verse that explores his ideas of the mask and antithetical self. He elaborated and modified the ideas of his essay in *A Vision*. Though Yeats's poetry remains an important source of inspiration for contemporary poets, particularly Irish poets such as Seamus Heaney, the influence of "Anima Hominis" is difficult to detect outside his own oeuvre. Critics and scholars, however, continue to study the essay as a key to Yeatsian thought.

THEMES AND STYLE

The central theme of "Anima Hominis" is that artistic achievement is born of intense personal struggle that leads the artist to assume a mask: an invented self that provides him with a heroic ideal. The pursuit of artistry is a divine quest—indeed, a search for God: "He only can create the greatest imaginable beauty who has endured all imaginable pangs, for only when we have seen and foreseen what we dread shall we be rewarded by that dazzling, unforeseen, wing-footed wanderer." Since suffering alone cannot produce beauty, the artist must aspire to be what he is not in order to push his art forward: "If we cannot imagine ourselves as different from what we are, and try to assume that second self, we cannot impose a discipline upon ourselves though we may accept one from others." While it constitutes a false identity, the mask conceals the artist from his imperfect self as well as from others, thereby protecting him from judgment and allowing him to become something greater than his character would otherwise allow: "We make out of the quarrel with others, rhetoric, but of the quarrel with ourselves, poetry. […] The other self, the anti-self or the antithetical self, as one may choose to name it, comes to those who are no longer deceived, whose passion is reality."

Organized as a series of brief, enumerated sections, "Anima Hominis" achieves its rhetorical aim of defending Yeats's idiosyncratic artistic project through the use of a first-person narrator and an acknowledgment of the difficulty of its arguments. This self-awareness is announced in the opening sentences: "When I come home after meeting men who are strange to me, and sometimes even after talking to women, I go over all I have said in gloom and disappointment. Perhaps I have overstated everything from a desire to vex and startle, from hostility that is but fear; or all my natural thoughts have been drowned by an undisciplined sympathy." His sentences often begin "I think" or "I remember." This helps tether his often abstract argument to the figure of the author and keeps the reader grounded in the movement of his thought.

Among manifestos, "Anima Hominis" is distinguished by its lyricism. Yeats builds his argument as a poet rather than a polemicist through imagery, metaphor, aphorism, and other lyric devices. His diction and syntax are as lofty and abstract as the ideas he is aiming to convey. When he imagines what poetic achievement would be like, he writes, "I shall find the dark grow luminous, the void fruitful when I understand I have nothing, that the ringers in the tower have appointed for the hymen of the soul a passing bell." In this way, the essay illustrates the argument that the quest for artistic creation must travel beyond the self.

CRITICAL DISCUSSION

When "Anima Hominis" first appeared as part of *Per Amica Silentia Lunea,* many readers found the essay as difficult to understand as the poetry it was meant to explicate. A reviewer for the *Times Literary Supplement* wrote on February 7, 1918, "Where we can follow [Yeats], he is a guide to be trusted; and then suddenly he leaves us in a cloud. Suddenly he talks a language we do not understand; we do not know whether it is a language at all or gibberish." According to the critic Elizabeth T. Lickindorf, writing in 1982, this response to the essay was typical, as contemporary commentators were left "nonplussed" by the volume and perplexed by its arguments. According to a review included in *W. B. Yeats: The Critical Heritage,* even Yeats's fellow poet and admirer Eliot wrote in 1919 of his difficulty in comprehending the work, commenting that Yeats "as much in his prose as in his verse, is not 'of this world'—*this* world, of course, being our visible planet with whatever theology or myth may conceive as below or above it."

In the years following its publication, the essay failed to accomplish Yeats's goal. While readers and critics initially looked to it and the other works in the volume for insight into the poet's complex verse, the treatise was largely replaced in this exegetical capacity by the more thorough but no less esoteric *Vision.* The past century has confirmed "Anima Hominis" as the subject of a small body of criticism devoted to its relationship to occultism, Romanticism, modernism, and psychology.

Among the strands of scholarship on the essay is the study of Yeats's conflation of artistic and mystic pursuits in "Anima Hominis." According to the literary scholar Harold Bloom, the essay contains a "true visionary argument ... Yeats makes a hieratic withdrawal from life and finds himself as the poet-visionary proper, enjoying a heroic condition." Commentators have also examined the obscurity of the work's mystical language. Richard Ellmann has argued that it is a "trick of evasion"—that Yeats's "prose is almost as metaphorical as verse," and this "makes it impossible to object to his theory of the supernatural mask." For such critics as David Lynch, the poet's argument about

Portrait of W. B. Yeats, 1886, painted by his father, John Butler Yeats. DUBLIN CITY GALLERY, THE HUGH LANE, IRELAND/THE BRIDGEMAN ART LIBRARY

the antithetical self and the mask can be viewed in psychological terms: "To feel as Yeats does about "Anima Hominis" is to feel that being 'somebody' is like being imagined by somebody else, and that the somebody you might imagine yourself being is nobody at all."

BIBLIOGRAPHY

Sources

Bloom, Harold. *Yeats.* New York: Oxford UP, 1970. Print.

Eliot, T. S. "A Foreign Mind." Review of *The Cutting of an Agate,* by W. B. Yeats. *Athaneum* 4633 (1919): 553. *W. B. Yeats: The Critical Heritage.* Ed. A. Norman Jeffares. Boston: Routledge, 1977. 230-32. Print.

Ellmann, Richard. *Yeats: The Man and the Masks.* New York: Macmillan, 1948. Print.

Foster, Roy. *W. B. Yeats: A Life.* 2 vols. Oxford: Oxford UP, 1998-2003. Print.

Lickindorf, Elizabeth. "W. B. Yeats's 'Per Amica Silentia Lunae.'" *English Studies in Africa* 25.1 (1982): 39-52. Web. 20 June 2012.

Lynch, David. *Yeats: The Poetics of the Self.* Chicago: U of Chicago P, 1979. Print.

Yeats, W. B. *Mythologies.* London: MacMillan, 1959. Print.

Further Reading

Bornstein, George. "Yeats's Romantic Dante." *Colby Quarterly* 15.2 (1979): 1-21. Print.

Devine, Brian. *Yeats, The Master of Sound: An Investigation of the Technical and Aural Achievements of William Butler Yeats.* Gerrards Cross: Smythe, 2006. Print.

Donoghue, Denis. "Yeats, Trying to Be Modern." *New England Review* 31.4 (2010): 131-44. Web. 20 June 2012. Print.

Ellman, Richard. *Eminent Domain: Yeats among Wilde, Joyce, Pound, Eliot, and Auden.* New York: Oxford UP, 1967. Print.

Engelberg, Edward. *The Vast Design: Patterns in W. B. Yeats' Aesthetic.* 2nd ed. Washington, DC: Catholic U of America P, 1988. Print

Greaves, Richard. *Transition, Reception and Modernism in W. B. Yeats.* New York: Palgrave, 2002. Print.

Maddox, Brenda. *Yeats's Ghosts: The Secret Life of W. B. Yeats.* New York: Harper, 1999. Print.

Wenthe, William J. "'It Will Be a Hard Toil': Yeats's Theory of Versification, 1899-1919." *Journal of Modern Literature* 21.1 (1997): 29-48. Web. 21 June 2012.

Theodore McDermott

A GREEN SUN

Takamura Kōtarō

OVERVIEW

Composed by the Japanese poet Takamura Kōtarō, "A Green Sun" (1910) claims that Japanese painting—and to a lesser extent, its Western counterpart—is stuck and incapable of moving forward, a situation that can only be remedied by granting absolute freedom to the artist. The essay was first issued in *Subaru,* a magazine that published poetry and translations, as well as art criticism on Japanese works and those by Westerners, such as Kōtarō's 1909 article on Henri Matisse, which evinced Japan's and Kōtarō's growing interest in Western art. "A Green Sun" is not addressed to a specific audience, and—according to Hiroaki Sato, who quotes from leading scholar Kitagawa Taichi in the notes to his translation of "A Green Sun"—it reads less as an aesthetic declaration and more as an attempt "to clarify his own principles."

While some of Kōtarō's poetry, especially that published in his early collection *Dōtei,* provoked criticism and outrage for its dismissal and mockery of Japanese cultural and aesthetic values, "A Green Sun," with its less incendiary tone, made less of an initial impact. The essay did, however, serve as an early articulation of Kōtarō's aesthetic aims. Along with his growth as a poet, as demonstrated by Makoto Ueda's claim in *Modern Japanese Poets and the Nature of Literature* that many would come to consider him "the father of contemporary Japanese verse," Kōtarō continued to publish criticism about European avant-garde art. These works include his 1912 article "The Scream of the Futurists," which helped to catalyze Japanese interest in Italian futurism. Today, "A Green Sun" is considered to be an important aesthetic document in the development of contemporary Japanese poetry.

HISTORICAL AND LITERARY CONTEXT

"A Green Sun" responds to an early twentieth-century trend in which many Japanese artists began to incorporate Western elements into their work. During the first two decades of the Meiji Era (1868-1912), Japan witnessed rapid Westernization, as the country implemented Western technologies such as the telegraph, railways, and steamships. Literature soon followed, but, according to Sukehiro Hirakawa in *Japan's Love-Hate Relationship with the West* (2005), "by the 1880's a reaction had set in," and although this "return to Japan" was "not a reversion to the blind xenophobia of late Tokugawa times," it did slow the incorporation of Western aesthetics in Japanese art.

By the time "A Green Sun" was issued in 1910, Japan was on the cusp of discovering the European avant-garde. That same year, White Birch, a literary organization in which Kōtarō was a member, held its first exhibitions, including one devoted to the sculpture of Auguste Rodin. In the pages of White Birch's literary magazine, *Shirakaba,* the Japanese artist Arishima Ikuma published an article extolling the virtues of Paul Cézanne; according to Ikuma, Cézanne opposed any system of rules and "listened to his inner voice in order to satisfy himself." In 1906, with only $250, Kōtarō left for New York, where he spent a year before traveling to Paris and becoming deeply influenced by the art of the European avant-garde. He returned to Japan in 1908, and two years later he drafted and published his seminal text.

Although "A Green Sun" was not explicitly conceived of as a manifesto, it is generally considered one today. Only the symbolist and futurist manifestos predate it, and the impact of those texts would not be felt in Japan until two years after Kōtarō's essay was published. Thus, the primary influences on "A Green Sun" were the pieces of art criticism published in Japan's literary journals. In 1909 Kōtarō completed a translation of Matisse's *Notes of a Painter* (1908), which defines Matisse's aesthetic. Along with his notes on his use of color, his belief in "felt experience," and his criticisms of author artists, Matisse's claim that "rules have no existence outside of individuals" calls to mind Kōtarō's emphasis on the "freedom" of the individual artist's personality.

In the years after its publication, "A Green Sun" provided the theoretical principles that underpinned Kōtarō's poetic oeuvre. Although he took on painting as the essay's explicit topic, the emphasis on the freedom of the artist and the incorporation of Western color translated well into his poetry. According to Hiroaki Sato in the introduction to *A Brief History of Imbecility* (1992), Kōtarō's first collection of poetry, *Journey* (1914), "went on to become one of the two landmarks in Modern Japanese poetry, showing a mastery of colloquial language for the first time." This use of "colloquial language" was derived from European and American influences that Kōtarō freely incorporated into his work, just as his text encouraged.

✣ *Key Facts*

Time Period:
Early 20th Century

Movement/Issue:
Aesthetics;
Westernization

Place of Publication:
Japan

Language of Publication:
Japanese

The Cathedral (1908) by Auguste Rodin. Takamura's sculptural work drew upon both Japanese traditions and the work of Western artists, especially Rodin. MUSÉE RODIN, PARIS, FRANCE/PETER WILLI/THE BRIDGEMAN ART LIBRARY

direct appeals to a rising Westernized avant-garde in Japan, his criticism of more traditional painters—such as Kuroda Seiki, an important representative of impressionism who "appears to be striving to Japanize himself"—frames them as a group against which the existence of this avant-garde can be posited. The mentions of seminal Western painters such as Paul Gauguin, James McNeill Whistler, and Claude Monet serve both as models for these nascent Japanese artists and as examples of the relative freedom that Western painters, as opposed to those in Japan, are afforded.

Stylistically, "A Green Sun" is distinguished by its rigid, self-conscious style and its use of French, English, and German words. According to Kōtarō's translator, Sato, the "surprisingly awkward" prose exists "because the public stance he [Kōtarō] took made him unduly self-conscious." Much of the eloquence of Kōtarō's idea is undermined by the stilted style of the text. The inclusion of numerous foreign language words, from "local color" to *allgemeine uebereinstimmung"* ("universal concord" in German), contribute to this the effect, but the poor stylistic decision does have some beneficial consequences. First, the use of foreign words narrows the audience of the text to one that is familiar with Western languages (the group most likely to be appreciative of Western painting) and creates a sense of solidarity with the author. Second, these words can be viewed as the prosaic embodiment of Kōtarō's aesthetic principle that painting must move beyond the strictures of Japanese "local color."

CRITICAL DISCUSSION

When "A Green Sun" was first issued in 1910, it garnered little notice from the Japanese press, though it did resonate with young artists. His poetry from that period—such as "The Country of Netsuke" (1911), which is, in essence, a derogatory description of the Japanese—stirred up considerably more ire than his essay did. The relatively limited response to "A Green Sun" can also be explained, in part, by its publication in *Subaru,* a magazine that had acquired a reputation for unbridled sensuality, which primarily appealed to, according to the scholar Atsumi Ikuko in "The Poetry of Takamura Kotaro," a "coterie ... interested in European *art nouveau,*" a relatively small group in Japan. The document did, however, provoke some reaction, and according to Sato in his notes from *A Brief History of Imbecility,* the text was often considered Japan's first impressionist manifesto.

In the years following its appearance, the essay remained an important statement about the influence of the West on Japanese art. Although Taichi claims that the document was Kōtarō's attempt to define his own aesthetic, it also served as an impressionist manifesto in that it brought ideas about freedom of individual expression, personality, and color to Japanese art. Kōtarō's reputation as a promulgator for the European avant-garde grew with his continued publications on figures such as Gauguin, Émile Zola, Henri

Today, scholarly criticism continues to recognize "A Green Sun" as an important influence on the development of modern Japanese art and poetry.

THEMES AND STYLE

The central theme of "A Green Sun" is that Japanese painting has hitherto been restricted by its emphasis on the use of only "local color" and that personal freedom to paint—even if it is a "green sun"—is important for the development of contemporary Japanese art. Writing about many traditional artists in Japan, Kōtarō claims, "There also seem to be not a few people who take a step or two, then hesitate, thinking that nature in Japan has a certain inviolable set of colors peculiar to it, so that if they infringe on it, their works will immediately lose their *raison d'etre."* According to Kōtarō, this restrictiveness is, in part, derived from the desire for Japanese artists to "Japanize" themselves in order to avoid colors or aesthetics that lead to a "Western smell." Out of his desire to free Japanese painting from these shackles, Kōtarō advocates for recognition of "the infinite authority in the artists personality."

The essay achieves its rhetorical effect through its subtle diagnosis and denunciation of traditional Japanese aesthetics. While Kōtarō does not make

de Toulouse-Lautrec, and Claude Debussy. In his introduction to "A Green Sun" in *100 Artists' Manifestos* (2011), Alex Danchev notes that Kōtarō's screed marks an early fascination with European art and that continued interest in the text "lies in its cross-cultural transmission." "A Green Sun" has attracted limited scholarly interest in the West for its influence on modern Japanese aesthetics.

Some scholarship has focused on the discrepancies between Kōtarō's reputation in Japan and internationally. According to Ueda, "Kotaro's poetry seems uninspiring to many Western readers. In the context of world literature his imagination appears limited, his ideas simplistic, and his style prosaic." Indeed, Kōtarō anticipates such a reaction in his poem "My Verse," which claims that the physique of Western poetry is "built on flour, butter, and beef [and] would not translate into my Japanese." Hirakawa's *Japan's Love-Hate Relationship with the West* focuses on Kōtarō's vacillating opinions on the West—from the admiration expressed in "A Green Sun" to the claim that the Japanese will "smash up the enemy" in his pro-war poem "To General Kuribayashi" (1942).

BIBLIOGRAPHY

Sources

Atsumi, Ikuko. "The Poetry of Takamura Kotaro." *Japan Quarterly* 20.1 (1973): 308. Print.

Danchev, Alex. *100 Artists' Manifestos: From the Futurists to the Stuckists*. New York: Penguin Modern Classics, 2011. Print.

Emiko, Yamanashi. "Japanese Encounter with Western Painting in the Meiji and Taisho Eras." *Japan & Paris: Impressionism, Postimpressionism, and the Modern Era.* Ed. Stephen Little. Honolulu: Honolulu Academy of the Arts, 2004. 29-37. Print.

Sukehiro Hirakawa. *Japan's Love-Hate Relationship with the West.* Kent: Global Oriental, 2005. Print.

Takamura Kōtarō. *A Brief History of Imbecility.* Introduction by Hiroaki Sato. Honolulu: U of Hawaii P, 1992. Print.

Volk, Alicia. "A Unified Rhythm: Past and Present in Japanese Modern Art." *Japan & Paris: Impressionism, Postimpressionism, and the Modern Era.* Ed. Stephen Little. Honolulu: Honolulu Academy of the Arts, 2004. 39-55. Print.

Further Reading

Keene, Donald. *Dawn to the West: Japanese Literature of the Modern Era.* New York: Columbia UP, 1999. Print.

Makoto, Ueda. *Modern Japanese Poets and the Nature of Literature.* Stanford: Stanford UP, 1983. Print.

Morton, Leith. *Modernism in Practice: An Introduction to Postwar Japanese Poetry.* Honolulu: U of Hawaii P, 2004. Print.

Murphy, Patrick. *Literature of Nature: An International Source Book.* Chicago: Fitzroy Dearborn, 1998. Print.

Takamura Kōtarō. *Chieko's Sky.* New York: Kodansha America, 1978. Print.

Toshiharu, Omuka. "Futurism in Japan, 1909-1920." *International Futurism in Arts and Literature.* Ed. Gunter Berghaus. Berlin: Walter de Gruyter, 2000. Print.

Gregory Luther

MODERN FICTION

Virginia Woolf

❖ *Key Facts*

Time Period:
Early 20th Century

Movement/Issue:
Modernism; Aesthetics

Place of Publication:
England

Language of Publication:
English

OVERVIEW

"Modern Fiction," an essay included in the *Common Reader* (1925), is one of Virginia Woolf's most widely known and frequently cited essays. Often referred to as her "manifesto of literary modernism," the essay contrasts materialist "Edwardian" fiction with that of the more "spiritual" modernists. It was first published years earlier, in 1919, as "Modern Novels," appearing anonymously in the *Times Literary Supplement*. It later reemerged as "Modern Fiction" after Woolf had made a name for herself with such works as *An Unwritten Novel* (1920) and *Jacob's Room* (1922). Woolf's stature would only increase when *Mrs. Dalloway* (1925) was published just a month after "Modern Novels" was resurrected as "Modern Fiction."

"Modern Fiction" initially garnered little attention as part of the warmly received *Common Reader*. But in its earlier, anonymous form, several critics maintain that "Modern Novels" attracted the unhappy attention of the prolific novelist Arnold Bennett, whom Woolf critiques alongside his fellow Edwardians H. G. Wells and John Galsworthy for "disappoint[ing]" contemporary readers with fact-laden social realism that fails to represent the "consciousness" of its characters. Indeed, although "Modern Novels" was unsigned, Samuel Hynes argues in his essay "The Whole Contention between Mr. Bennett and Mrs. Woolf" that a somewhat bitter Bennett was well aware of its "bluestocking" author's identity when he wrote disparagingly of *Jacob's Room* in *Cassell's Weekly*.

Bennett's counterattack only seems to have emboldened Woolf, who challenged him further in her 1923 essay "Mr. Bennett and Mrs. Brown." She more forcefully condemned the Edwardians in "Modern Fiction" for being more concerned with the "body" than the "spirit," for obeying the "unscrupulous tyrant" of convention, and for writing of "unimportant things" that make "the trivial and transitory appear the true and the enduring." Thus, although "Modern Fiction" has long been used to discuss Woolf's fictional method—with its most famous lyrical passages so suggestive of her "impressionism"—the essay was clearly rooted in the literary journalism of the time. It continues to be cited in scholarship on literary modernism as a work that helped solidify the oppositional terms "materialist" and "spiritualist" for a growing audience of critics debating postwar fiction's purpose from the early 1920s forward.

HISTORICAL AND LITERARY CONTEXT

When Woolf composed "Modern Novels," Bennett was already regarded as one of the greatest novelists of the day. This fact did not inhibit Woolf from challenging his fictional methods, partly because she knew Bennett had questioned them himself years earlier. In Bennett's essay "Neo-Impressionism and Literature" (1910), he posits what might happen if "some writer were to come along and do in words" what Paul Cézanne and the other abstract artists had done in paint. He goes on to imagine how he might react if a "young writer turned up" one day and "forced" him and his contemporaries to "admit that [they] had been concerning [them]selves unduly with inessentials." As fate would have it, Woolf would effectively come to be that "young writer" when she called Bennett and his peers to task for their formally stunted conventional realism.

Although Woolf was clearly responding to Bennett's earlier self-critique in "Modern Novels," she was more likely inspired by her closer contemporary T.S. Eliot when she decided to transform "Modern Novels" into "Modern Fiction" and to revisit her "quarrel" with Edwardian social realism in the *Common Reader*. Just five months after noting in her diary that her friend and fellow *Athenaeum* contributor Eliot had earned both public and private praise from her husband, Leonard, and several of their acquaintances for a volume of criticism derived from his journalism (*Sacred Wood*, 1920), Woolf announced in another diary entry that she intended to "shape" several essays she had published in periodicals into the "Reading book" that was to become the *Common Reader*. However, the more she read of "other peoples [sic] criticism"—Eliot's included—the more, Woolf confessed, she hesitated as she struggled to compile her own. Despite a delay of five years, the *Common Reader* would feature near its center a previously published essay—"Modern Fiction"—that many have come to consider its author's "personal manifesto," effectively explaining how to read Woolf's creative work.

Yet "Modern Fiction" was not simply a critical product meant to illuminate Woolf's existing and forthcoming fictional products. It was also a product of its time—so much so that it inspired "Mr. Bennett and Mrs. Brown" and "Character in Fiction" (1924), which Woolf carefully crafted for different audiences. Taken together with "Modern Fiction," these works help articulate how many early twentieth-century writers and readers—impacted by the Great War, newly interested in the "dark places of psychology," and intrigued by Russian literature (thanks, in part, to Bennett himself)—felt conventional English literature no longer resembled the "vision" in their "minds."

"Modern Fiction," however, stands apart from "Mr. Bennett and Mrs. Brown" and "Character in Fiction" because of its language. Only "Modern Fiction" metaphorically evokes "innumerable atoms" that "shower" the "ordinary mind" on an "ordinary day," imaginatively describing "life" as "a luminous halo" and dramatically calling for modern writers to "record the atoms as they fall upon the mind in the order in which they fall." Reminiscent of art critic Walter Pater's notoriously passionate conclusion to *The Renaissance* (1873) and suggestive of the modernist "stream of consciousness" narrative technique that earned its name from philosopher William James's *Principles of Psychology* (1890), "Modern Fiction" is a literary manifesto that, like the finest prose, approaches poetry. Its appearance marked a turning point in Woolf's career: her criticism began to appear in a more diverse array of English and American venues, and she started earning more than her prolific husband did from writing, thus securing her position as a major modernist writer and theorist.

THEMES AND STYLE

At its core, "Modern Fiction" is about resisting convention. Conventions such as "plot," "love interest," and "catastrophe in the accepted style" are the tools of the Edwardians, whose "materialist" worldview Woolf contrasts with the more "spiritual" outlook that Russian writers had long exhibited. James Joyce evokes this spiritual outlook in *A Portrait of the Artist as a Young Man* (1916) and was beginning to explore it in *Ulysses* (1918-20) as well.

But even as "Modern Fiction" abides by the conventions of the early twentieth-century manifesto form in its blatant rejection of "convention," it refuses to follow the unwritten "rules" of effective twentieth-century manifesto writing as it slowly and tentatively proceeds. For example, what manifesto would begin by suggesting that new art does *not* necessarily improve upon the art of the past? Woolf emphasizes the limited nature of her first-person-plural vision by making "no claim to stand, even momentarily, upon that vantage ground" from which a past might be understood and a future might be glimpsed. She does not simply hesitate and apologize but also makes a "confession of vagueness which afflicts all criticism of novels."

Indeed, to make her case, presumably for the kind of innovative art she and other English authors

MANIFESTOS MULTIPLIED

Although "Modern Fiction" is probably the Woolfian work that has most often been called a "manifesto"—whether "personal," "aesthetic," "modernist," or all three—it is hardly Virginia Woolf's only work to have been so labeled. Given the qualities it shares with "Modern Fiction," "Mr. Bennett and Mrs. Brown" might also be deemed a manifesto. It effectively out-asserts "Modern Fiction"—and possibly every other Woolfian essay for that matter—with its outrageously bold declaration that "on or about December 1910 human character changed." Likewise, it is not unusual that *A Room of One's Own* should be called Woolf's feminist manifesto, since its influence has been felt over the course of several waves of feminist criticism.

However, it is *Three Guineas* (1938), as Laura Winkiel persuasively shows in *Modernism, Race, and Manifestoes* (2008), that represents Woolf's most complicated engagement with the manifesto form, as it "criticizes the flurry of manifestos" that were "littering the public sphere" by the late 1930s not only for their "empty rhetoric" and "abstract language" but also for their signatories' obvious desires for "money, publicity, and fame."

aim to practice themselves, Woolf surprisingly focuses specifically on an Irish contemporary about whose writing she remains ambivalent (Joyce) and a Russian author (Anton Chekhov) who died nearly fifteen years before her essay's first appearance—all in a tone that suggests not only nostalgia and uncertainty but also some English national pride. Woolf argues that Joyce's *Ulysses* presents "life itself" but still "fails to compare" with Joseph Conrad's *Youth* (1898) or Thomas Hardy's *Mayor of Casterbridge* (1886) for several reasons she fails to define. Furthermore, though the work of Chekhov and his fellow Russians expresses an "understanding of the soul" and "reverence for the human spirit" that English writing still lacks, Woolf adds "perhaps we see something that escapes" the inconclusive Russian mind—"comprehensive" and "compassionate" though it may be. After all, she continues, "English fiction from [Laurence] Sterne to [George] Meredith bears witness to [a] natural delight in humour and comedy, in the beauty of the earth, in the activities of the intellect, and in the splendour of the body." In spite of this assertion's bold generalization and backward glance, however, Woolf concludes "Modern Fiction" both inconclusively and prophetically, saying: "But any deductions that we may draw from the comparison of two fictions so immeasurably far apart are futile save indeed as they flood us with a view of the infinite possibilities of the art and remind us that there is no limit to the horizon, and that nothing—no "method," no experiment, even of the wildest—is forbidden, but only falsity and pretence."

A portrait of Virginia Woolf by Roger Eliot Fry. Woolf criticized the writers she called "materialists," instead championing the "spiritual" fiction of James Joyce. ON LOAN TO LEEDS MUSEUMS AND GALLERIES (CITY ART GALLERY)/THE BRIDGEMAN ART LIBRARY

CRITICAL DISCUSSION

Biographer John Mepham explains that in the early 1920s, "the word that critics grasped hold of" in their efforts to categorize Woolf's fiction and "make it seem more approachable" was "impressionist." It is for this reason that the famous metaphorical passages in "Modern Fiction" earned their long-lasting notoriety even as Woolf's related anti-Edwardian essays inspired lively periodical debates. However, this image of Woolf, Mepham insists in *Virginia Woolf: A Literary Life* (1991), is too simple because it fails to present her as an uncertain novice novelist still trying to "clear a way for her own writing" between 1919 and 1925. Writing more than a decade after Mepham, in *Virginia Woolf, the Intellectual, and the Public Sphere* (2003), Melba Cuddy-Keane continues to challenge the still-persistent commonplace belief that, taken together with "Mr. Bennett and Mrs. Brown," "Modern Fiction" represents Woolf's definitive modernist statement, showing her "theme" to be the "subjective inner world" and her approach to be "impressionistic, poetic, and lyrical." Unlike Mepham, Cuddy-Kean emphasizes the veteran essayist Woolf's deliberate interrogation of the very labels she is forced to use

rather than attributing her apparent critical hesitancy to neophyte confusion.

Although "Modern Fiction" may be said to serve partly as a "modernist manifesto" because it explains modernism's break from the "materialist" novel, Cuddy-Keane makes clear that it does not simply champion modernist practices at the expense of traditional realism. Instead, the essay carefully "assesses the strengths and weaknesses of each mode" because "in setting out her materialist/spiritual opposition, Woolf significantly qualifies and redefines both terms." Even more recently, as interest in the manifesto genre has continued to increase, Laura Winkiel, in *Modernism, Race, and Manifestoes* (2008), draws attention to the ways in which Woolf engaged throughout her career with the manifesto form upon which so many of her male contemporaries throughout Europe relied to broadcast their aesthetic credos in a radicalized art world.

Although Winkiel focuses on "Mr. Bennett and Mrs. Brown" in her discussion of Woolf's early uses of certain manifesto conventions, she emphasizes a key message that the essay shares with "Modern Fiction" when she notes how Woolf "describes a disconnection between Edwardian writers such as Arnold Bennett and the myriad impressions and experiences that beset ordinary readers and their everyday lives," before appealing to her audience's "inherent sense" of "life itself." Though Woolf is well aware, Winkiel argues, of the manifesto's "shortcomings," she nevertheless "borrows from the genre several of its revolutionary qualities." Thus "Mr. Bennett and Mrs. Brown," like "Modern Fiction," prophesies a new era of literature, calls its audience to action, and takes an "iconoclastic approach to literary history." Yet what Cuddy-Keane calls its "dialogic evaluative" style is perhaps what makes "Modern Fiction" seem particularly iconoclastic as countless binary oppositions persist in spite of today's increasing globalization.

BIBLIOGRAPHY

Sources

Cuddy-Keane, Melba. *Virginia Woolf, the Intellectual, and the Public Sphere.* New York: Cambridge UP, 2003. Print.

Hussey, Mark. *Virginia Woolf A-Z.* New York: Syracuse UP, 1991. Print.

Lee, Hermione. "'Crimes of Criticism': Virginia Woolf and Literary Journalism." *Grub Street and the Ivory Tower: Literary Journalism and Literary Scholarship from Fielding to the Internet.* Ed. Jeremy Treglown and Bridget Bennett. Oxford: Clarendon, 1998. 112-34. Print.

Majumdar, Robin, and Allen McLaurin, eds. *Woolf: The Critical Heritage.* Boston: Routledge & Kegan Paul, 1975. Print.

Mepham, John. *Virginia Woolf: A Literary Life.* New York: St. Martin's, 1991. Print.

Winkiel, Laura A. *Modernism, Race, and Manifestoes.* New York: Cambridge UP, 2008. Print.

Woolf, Virginia. *The Diary of Virginia Woolf.* Ed. Anne Olivier Bell. Vol. 2. London: Hogarth, 1978. Print.

———. *The Essays of Virginia Woolf.* Ed. Andrew McNeillie and Stuart N. Clarke. Vols. 2, 3, and 4. New York: Harcourt, n.d., 1988, and 1994. Print.

Further Reading

Bell, Quentin. *Virginia Woolf: A Biography.* 2 vols. London: Hogarth, 1972. Print.

Bennett, Arnold. *Books and Persons: Being Comments on a Past Epoch, 1908-1911.* London: Chatto and Windus, 1917. Print.

———. *The Common Reader.* 1925. Ed. Andrew McNeillie. New York: Harcourt, 1989. Print.

Churchill, Suzanne W., and Adam McKible. *Little Magazines and Modernism: New Approaches.* Burlington: Ashgate, 2008. Print.

Daugherty, Beth Rigel. "The Whole Contention between Mr. Bennett and Mrs. Woolf, Revisited." *Virginia Woolf Centennial Essays.* Ed. Elaine K. Ginsurg and Laura Moss Gottlcib. New York: Troy, 1983. 269-94. Print.

Dubino, Jeanne, ed. *Virginia Woolf and the Literary Marketplace.* New York: Palgrave Macmillan, 2010. Print.

Eliot, T.S. *The Sacred Wood: Essays on Poetry and Criticism.* London: Methuen, 1960. Print.

Hynes, Samuel. "The Whole Contention between Mr. Bennett and Mrs. Woolf." *Novel: A Forum on Fiction* 1 (1967): 34-44. Web. 9 Aug. 2010.

James, William. *Principles of Psychology.* 1890. New York: Dover, 1950. Print.

Lee, Hermione. *Virginia Woolf.* New York: Vintage, 1996. Print.

Meisel, Perry. *The Absent Father: Virginia Woolf and Walter Pater.* New Haven: Yale UP, 1980. Print.

Pater, Walter. *Studies in the History of the Renaissance.* 1873. Oxford: Oxford UP, 2010. Print.

Woolf, Leonard S. "Back to Aristotle." Rev. of *The Sacred Wood,* by T.S. Eliot. *Athenaeum* 17 Dec. 1920: 834-35. Print.

Hannah Soukup

ON THE ARTIST'S CALLING AND THE TASKS OF ART

Jacek Malczewski

✢ *Key Facts*

Time Period:
Early 20th Century

Movement/Issue:
Aesthetics; Polish
nationalism

Place of Publication:
Poland

**Language of
Publication:**
Polish

OVERVIEW

Initially presented as a lecture, Jacek Malczewski's "On the Artist's Calling and the Tasks of Art" (1912) depicts artists as prophets for whom an understanding of God's creations is more important than mastery of technique and whose works are among the highest forms of prayer. Malczewski gave the lecture at the Krakow Academy of Fine Arts in Galicia, the part of Poland then occupied by Austria, during a time when direct reference to Polish reunification was banned. Thus, the lecture contains only oblique references to the theme that defined Malczewski's career as a painter: the dream of an autonomous Poland. Cloaked in religious language, "On the Artist's Calling and the Tasks of Art" tries to impress upon young polish artists the importance of their role and the inevitable hardships they will face in helping to forge a glorious future.

Polish artists in the early 1900s operated in a climate of censorship. Consequently, they deliberately avoided making political statements. Malczewski would not have been able to continue working as a painter, a teacher, and an art school administrator had he characterized his speech as a manifesto. Foreign occupation of Poland began in 1772 and lasted until 1918. Banned from political expression, Polish people turned to their writers and artists for leadership, and images and stories from the nation's history were woven into literature and art to teach successive generations about cultural identity and to pass on the fervor for reunification. By 1912, however, the young artists addressed by Malczewski had begun to chafe at the limited style and subject matter of their elders. Malczewski's work continued to command respect, but his message of resistance to foreign powers became obsolete when Poland gained its independence six years after the lecture was delivered.

HISTORICAL AND LITERARY CONTEXT

"On the Artist's Calling and the Tasks of Art" responds to more than a century of Polish subjugation, the failed insurrections of 1863-64, and the lessening of patriotic fervor among the new generation of artists. In the decade leading up the lecture, Russian-occupied parts of Poland had experienced relative autonomy. The Russo-Japanese War (1904-05) turned Russia's attentions elsewhere. For a brief period, Polish was once again taught in the schools, the Roman Catholic Church was given more freedom to minister to its followers in former Polish territory, and artists and intellectuals were allowed to use Polish symbolism more openly in their work. However, censorship was still a consideration.

At the same time, younger Polish artists were exhibiting a desire for change. Many of these artists traveled to Vienna, Paris, and other art-oriented cities and became interested in the avant-garde movements of their European peers. They wanted to work with subjects besides Polish history and martyrdom. A group calling itself the Polish Independents mounted three shows between 1911 and 1913 that dealt with non-narrative, ahistorical works in a range of styles, including cubism and recidivist classicism. Though Malczewski was one of the few older artists whose work was included in the Independents' shows, he was undoubtedly aware that his vision of art as a sacred calling and an expression of patriotism was not being carried forward. Malczewski's effort to unite a new generation of Polish patriots with "The Artist's Calling" was largely unsuccessful. Polish artists branched out during World War I and experimented with a variety of European avant-garde styles. Then Poland achieved reunification in 1918.

Malczewski delivered his speech three years after Italian painter and fascist Filippo Tommaso Marinetti published his *Futurist Manifesto,* which is considered to be the first avant-garde artists' manifesto of the twentieth century. "The Artist's Calling" contains echoes of that work, with its calls for patriotism and rebellion and its romantic, elitist notion of the artist as the world's last best hope. In both works, the artist is presented as uniquely capable of charting the right course for the future. Unlike "The Artist's Calling," however, Marinetti's text derides tradition, embraces hatred, and places man rather than God at the center of the universe. Malczewski's sharp departure from the futurists on these points raises the following questions: Had Malczewski been living in a sovereign nation, would he have chosen religion as the vehicle for his message? And would he have been so tied to history as a subject matter? Whereas Marinetti concludes his work with a stirring injunction to rebel, Malczewski is confined to opaque and symbolic statements that scarcely hint at his desire for freedom.

Between 1909 and World War II, numerous artist-related manifestos appeared, though none in direct response to Malczewski's. In the late 1940s, socialist realism became the official policy in Poland. Based on Joseph Stalin's 1930s-era "principles" on art, socialist realism art celebrated the Soviet regime and created a repressive artistic environment not unlike that of Malczewski's lifetime. Polish artists rediscovered Malczewski, finding a kindred spirit through his coded messages of Polish nationalism. Avant-garde theater director Tadeuz Kantor was one of the artists who experienced censorship under Stalin in the 1950s and acknowledged Malczewski's influence on his work. Kantor wrote several art manifestos of his own, including the *Manifesto of the Theater of Death* (1976).

THEMES AND STYLE

The central themes of "The Artist's Calling" are that the Polish artist is a martyr to the cause and that art is a higher calling. This calling, though cloaked in religious terms, involves promoting Polish nationalism. In choosing this path, the artist has agreed to continue the sacred work of his predecessors, and the ostensible tasks are to recreate the glory of God's universe and to preserve history. Malczewski opens by reassuring artists that they are not alone, "for here we are a family." He reminds them that they have chosen to "strive for ideals in art, art which for the rest of society is above all a form of entertainment, before becoming, with the passage of time, history and a very special form of knowledge." The lecture promises young artists that, in addition to receiving a technical education, they will be shown how to look for evidence of God's glory in all things and how to be "proud in spirit, and humble in every moment of life." In other words, they will learn to serve their cause.

The document succeeds rhetorically through appeals to artists as members of a select group. Artists are praised as belonging to "a sect of the initiated"—they are "sons of God" who possess the God-like ability to create. Ultimately, then, artists "shall become immortal" through their works. Malczewski draws heavily on biblical language, likening the artist to a martyr or prophet. When artists pray, they should follow Jesus's advice in the Gospel of Matthew and "not pray so that your neighbor will see you." Equally important, however, is what Malczewski leaves unsaid. Because of censorship, he does not mention his true goal of Polish reunification. Thus, the audience must decipher his symbolic language.

On the surface, "The Artist's Calling" is a rarity among modern art manifestos. It does not advocate for change or revolution, and it scrupulously avoids mentions of politics. Malczewski places a high value on history and religion, two subjects often derided in manifestos of the early twentieth century. Unlike the upstarts responsible for the futurist manifestos that advocate for doing away with elders, Malczewski is himself an elder, one who is attempting to pass the torch

JACEK MALCZEWSKI: A PAINTER OF MANIFESTOS

The oeuvre of Jacek Malczewski (1854-1929) consists of an estimated two thousand paintings. His canvases draw parallels between Poland's struggle for independence and the artist's own search for identity. One of his most fundamental works, *Melancholia* (1890-94), sometimes referred to as his "manifesto," is better known than his written manifesto, "On the Artist's Calling and the Tasks of Art," and far more influential.

The painting portrays a dreamlike scene of the artist in a drab studio, slumped over his desk, seemingly fighting off a teeming vision of the Polish masses. These figures filling the room—heroes, peasants, old men, priests, Poles from every station in life—represent various aspects of one hundred years of occupation and failed uprisings. Outside the artist's studio window is a bright, vibrant world guarded by the title figure, Melancholia, who is dressed in black and is looking inside. *Melancholia* combines Malczewski's signature symbolism with the realism of his predecessor and mentor, Jan Matejko. It touches on many of the major themes in Malczewski's work: nationalism, the role of the artist in interpreting signs, the process of creation, and the personification of death. *Melancholia* is rich in symbols and myths from Polish culture and history. The work continues to be a source of debate, as scholars do not agree on the meanings of particular figures and objects.

to the next generation. However, there is more to his text than meets the eye. The revolutionary message of "The Artist's Calling" is disguised, making clever use of two traditional forces—history and Christianity—to undermine the foreign powers occupying Poland. By employing history to represent Polish nationalism and the struggle for independence and by urging artists to answer only to God, Malczewski undercuts the authority of any temporal government. Given a symbolist reading, the lecture's message is closer to that of its contemporaries than it first appears.

CRITICAL DISCUSSION

Malczewski delivered "The Artist's Calling" at the Krakow School of Fine Arts as the opening speech during his term as rector. The aim was to bring new artists into the fold and remind returning students of their role in society and the difficult task ahead of them. In Austrian-controlled Krakow, publishing a manifesto urging Poles to resist foreign domination would have been dangerous. According to Elizabeth Clegg in her 1989 essay in *Apollo*, "The expression of patriotic sentiment was more likely to be indulged if it appeared to be illustrating the world of literary imagination rather than commenting on that of political reality." The Polish artists and students in his audience would have understood the hidden messages, because,

Self-Portrait (1905)
by Jacek Malczewski.
PRIVATE COLLECTION/THE
BRIDGEMAN ART LIBRARY

continues to be felt in present-day Poland. Known as the chief representative of symbolism in Polish painting, he is credited with inspiring several painters, including Janusz Lewandowski and Jerzy Duda-Gracz, as well as artists within theater and film. For example, Malczewski's work is the subject of the film *The Phantom of the Fieldpass* (1961). In 1991 the Polish government named an art school after him, the Jacek Malczewski Complex of Schools of Fine Arts.

On the international stage of art history, recent scholarship about Malczewski has focused on his extensive oeuvre of paintings and, to a lesser extent, his influence on later Polish artists. Much of the writing examines the historical significance of the work within philosophical, literary, and religious contexts. Malczewski's canvases are also discussed in the context of Polish fin-de-siècle landscape painting. Some scholarship has moved beyond the political and historical significance of his work, homing in on its artistic merit.

BIBLIOGRAPHY

Sources

Clegg, Elizabeth. "The Siberian Tea Party: Jacek Malczewski and the Contradiction of Nationalist Symbolism." *Apollo* 129.324 (1989): 254-59. Print.

———. "Paris: Jacek Malczewski." *Burlington Magazine* 142.1165 (2000): 252-54. *JSTOR*. Web. 1 Sept. 2012.

Lawniczakowa, Agnieszka. "The Naked Soul: Polish Fin-de-Siècle Painting." *Malczewski: A Vision of Poland.* Ed. Agnieszka Lawniczakowa. London: Barbican Art Gallery, 1990. Print.

"Malczewski, Jacek." *Grove Art Online.* Web. 4 Sept. 2012.

Mansbach, S.A. *Modern Art in Eastern Europe: From the Baltic to the Balkans ca. 1890-1939.* Cambridge: Cambridge UP, 1997. 88-91, 96-97. Print.

Miklaszewski, Krzysztof. *Encounters with Tadeuz Kantor.* Ed. George Hyde. New York: Routledge, 2002. Print.

Further Reading

Benson, Timothy. *Behind the Obscurity of the Central European Avant-Garde.* Cambridge: Cambridge UP, 2002. Print.

Clegg, Elizabeth. *Art, Design & Architecture in Central Europe: 1890-1920.* New Haven: Yale UP, 2006. Print.

Czeczot-Gawrak, Zbigniew. "Polish Film on Art and the Problem of a Synthesis of the Artistic Vision." *Artibus et Historiae* 1.2 (1980): 157-65. *JSTOR.* Web. 4 Sept. 2012.

Rosenblum, Robert. *Art at the Crossroads.* New York: Harry N. Abrams, 2000. Print.

Szydlowski, Tadeusz. "Jacek Malczewski: The Polish Painter-Poet." *Slavonic & Eastern European Review* 10.29 (1931) 274-84. *JSTOR.* Web. 12 Sept. 2012.

Kristin King-Ries

as Clegg also notes, "Malczewski's application of this lesson [inserting fantastic elements into realism], with its religious context, to nationalist ends was a characteristically Polish response." Two years later, World War I broke out, and the tripartite nature of occupation served to increase tensions among Polish people from the different occupied regions. S.A. Mansbach explains the move away from patriotic subjects in the volume *Modern Art in Eastern Europe* (1997): "And yet during the midst of deadly destruction, a new national state and new forms of cultural expression were being gestated." Thus, Polish artists drew from an ever-widening field during the war, embracing fauvism, futurism, and expressionism.

The influence of Malczewski's paintings and his role as a historical figure waned during the early years of Polish reunification. However, the artist whose paintings themselves have often been described as manifestos took on relevance due to renewed censorship during the Soviet era. Malczewski's influence

THE SYMBOLISM OF POETRY

William Butler Yeats

OVERVIEW

Poet William Butler Yeats's "The Symbolism of Poetry," which first appeared in *The Dome* in April 1900, reacts against the depredations of modern industrial society, Enlightenment rationalism, genteel Victorian verse, and literary and philosophical realism, establishing a new aesthetic of mystical expressivism. The essay represents the culmination of Yeats's thoughts about the condition and concerns of poetry, inspired by his connection with the London Rhymers group and by French Symbolist poets and dramatists. Ambivalent about the rise of realism, Yeats published his essay, in part, to assert the primacy of symbolism over other aesthetic schools of thought, including the decadent movement. Addressed to the art community in general, the essay asserts that central to the power of poetry is the primacy of the symbol, which has "supra-rational" powers of evocation and suggestion to help poets discover and communicate powerful universal meanings.

Initially members of the press criticized Yeats for championing an aesthetic that sought to escape reality rather than to reflect it. Yeats, however, maintained that poetry was not for the masses and cited French symbolist Villiers de L'Isle-Adam's idea that poetry should separate the arts from their historical moment in order to reveal hidden truths. Over time, this new aesthetic proved compelling, and the essay helped to introduce English-speaking writers to symbolism, changing the course of modern literature. American poet T. S. Eliot became an adherent to the modes and ideals of symbolism's French practitioners, particularly with respect to their use of free verse. Today Yeats's essay is known for promoting the author's unique variety of symbolism, which fused aesthetics with Irish nationalist doctrine.

HISTORICAL AND LITERARY CONTEXT

"The Symbolism of Poetry" responds to literary movements provoked by the discoveries of Charles Darwin, the empirical philosophies of René Descartes and John Locke, and the industrial and commercial revolutions. Whereas realism and naturalism used scientific approaches to character and reality, symbolism approached subjects with idealized, even supernatural, treatment. By the late nineteenth century, continental European writers were moving away from objective description. In 1886 poet Jean Moréas published the Symbolist manifesto ("Le Symbolisme") in *Le Figaro*, and in 1896 poet Stéphane Mallarmé wrote "Crise de vers," in which he attempts to liberate poetry from the burden of representation and communication. For symbolists such as Mallarmé, poetry is meant to be outside of everyday experience so that words can take on new and ambiguous meanings.

By the time Yeats wrote his essay on symbolism, British poets and writers had developed two new artistic movements: aestheticism and the decadent movement. Famous decadents include writer Oscar Wilde, who objected to the notions of a moral imperative in the creation of art. Yeats resisted prosaic meaning and behavior in art and moreover sought mystical understanding through poetry. "The Symbolism of Poetry" crystallizes ideas he had tested in his early poetic and dramatic works, helping to make symbolism a significant movement in the evolution of modernist writing. Moreover, in Yeats's home country of Ireland, symbolism came to serve as a nationalist tool rejecting the authority of the dominant aesthetic of realism.

Yeats's essay owes a debt to the work of the English Romantic poets, particularly to the aesthetic theories offered by poet William Blake in *The Marriage of Heaven and Hell* (1790). In the book, the prophets Isaiah and Ezekiel speak to the author and impart the idea that "all Gods would at last be proved to originate in ours & to be the tributaries of Poetic Genius." Therefore, to Blake, art is prophetic in a religious sense because it discloses the secret pattern to human life. Blake's empowerment of the artist was a compelling aesthetic and spiritual alternative for Yeats, a clergyman's son who rejected religion and swore off journalistic and scientific trends in writing.

The legacy of Yeats's essay "The Symbolism of Poetry" is inextricably tied to that of his career and larger body of work. His later works are part of a canonical oeuvre with which modern poets in general, and Irish writers in particular, must grapple. Because subsequent generations of Irish poets admired his work but resisted his example, he is most often cited as a primary influence on American modernist poet T. S. Eliot, along with less totemic Irish poets Louis MacNeice and Patrick Kavanaugh. Yeats's symbolist example is also evident in the work of Northern Irish poets, including Medbh McGuckian and Michael

✣ *Key Facts*

Time Period:
Early 20th Century

Movement/Issue:
Aesthetics; Symbolism

Place of Publication:
Ireland

Language of Publication:
English

WILLIAM BUTLER YEATS AND THE FRENCH SYMBOLISTS

Although William Butler Yeats was deeply inspired by the French symbolists, his limited grasp of the French language made his interpretation of symbolist poetry and drama unique. In the late nineteenth century, he completed a translation of *Axël* (1890) by Villiers de L'Isle-Adam, remarking in his introduction to the play that the translation was "all the more profound because I was never quite certain that I had read a page correctly." The process had such a profound influence on him that his play *The Shadowy Waters* (1900) is said to be *Axël* translated into nautical terms.

Yeats's essays and reviews also reveal that he read Maurice Maeterlinck and other French symbolists in translation. During an 1894 visit to Paris, he met Paul Verlaine but had to speak with the poet in English. He acknowledges Arthur Symons's translation of Stéphane Mallarmé's *Heriodade* (1887) "may have given elaborate form" to verses in his *Wind among the Reeds* (1899). Given the poverty of Yeats's French, his brand of symbolism is distinct from that of the French poets and is indebted to English writers such as William Blake, Percy Bysshe Shelley, and Dante Gabriel Rossetti, as well as to the occult texts he read as part of the Theosophical Society in London.

Longley, who addressed cultural conflicts that divided the Irish population. Today Yeats's brand of symbolism is known for its potent expression of nationalism, inextricably linking the poet to politics.

THEMES AND STYLE

The central theme of "The Symbolism of Poetry" is that poetry should be created in the service of a larger transcendent aim: to communicate secret truths through the elegant and powerful use of the symbol. With the force of Blake's *The Marriage of Heaven and Hell* and Mallarmé's "Crise de vers," Yeats's essay connects great poets through their use of timeless symbols. He asserts that poems move readers through symbolism and that artists should effect "a casting out of descriptions of nature for the sake of nature, of the moral law for the sake of the moral law, a casting out of all anecdotes and of that brooding over scientific opinion." Thus, he describes the ways in which symbols exceed reason and intellect to achieve sincerity in poetry: "[poetry] must have the perfections that escape analysis, the subtleties that have a new meaning every day."

A persuasive aesthetic tract, Yeats's essay unfolds in five sections. Written in response to writer Arthur Symons's book on symbolism, which Symons dedicates to Yeats, "The Symbolism of Poetry" acknowledges that it is part of a de facto conversation among Yeats and his contemporaries, their spiritual and cultural forefathers, and current practitioners of the arts. In the essay, Yeats laments that "the scientific movement brought with it a literature, which was always tending to lose itself in externalities of all kinds." He suggests that a solution can be found by examining past aesthetic theories to recover the "pure inspiration of earlier times." For the author, timeless poetry communicates through symbols, as in the works of Blake, Robert Burns, and William Shakespeare. Therefore, Yeats uses quotations from these writers as aesthetic models so that "the arts [can] overcome the slow dying of men's hearts that we call the progress of the world."

Stylistically, "The Symbolism of Poetry" is notable for its sweeping analysis of history and its use of hypnotic language. Although Yeats disparages the analysis present in realist literature, he uses analytic techniques, such as chronology, linguistic critique, and logic, to establish the necessity of a mystical art form that evokes rather than communicates or represents. He writes, "The form of sincere poetry, unlike the form of the popular poetry, may indeed be sometimes obscure, or ungrammatical as in some of the best of [Blake's] *Songs of Innocence and Experience,* but it must have the perfections that escape analysis, the subtleties that have a new meaning every day." By linking great writers of the past in a continuum connected to the use of symbolism, Yeats ennobles the aesthetic path he champions. In addition, by despairing of the effects of "progress," he makes the symbolists' "return to imagination" a welcome refuge.

CRITICAL DISCUSSION

Upon publication, Yeats's essay met with resistance. In *Vale* (1914) novelist and critic George Moore accused the poet of writing obscure symbolist works: "Mallarmé could not be darker than this." However, with the death of Queen Victoria in 1901 and further developments in the social sciences, Yeats's embrace of symbolism became increasingly relevant—politically and psychologically—though at times he produced literature that was difficult for the average reader. Some observed that his grafting of symbolism onto national concerns demonstrates the movement of symbolism from aesthetic poetry toward writing that addresses harsh realities. Although symbolism proved a phase of modernist poetic development, for Yeats and for other writers, it offered potent solutions for individual aesthetic concerns.

In terms of symbolist aesthetics, Yeats had the greatest impact on Irish writers who were participating in a national literary revival focused on the nature and concerns of poetry. Critics view the dramatic and poetic work of J. M. Synge as an immediate outgrowth of Yeats's variety of symbolism. In fact, Yeats encouraged Synge to leave Paris, even though Synge was enamored of French symbolist works, in order to return to Ireland to address Irish concerns. Fellow London Rhymers Lionel Johnson and Ernest Dowson also adopted Yeats's brand of poetic symbolism. As Richard Ellmann in *The Identity of Yeats* (1954) states, Yeats "found support in sharing an iconography" with his London contemporaries.

In the century since it was written, Yeats's essay has been studied in several historical, aesthetic, literary, and biographical contexts. Much scholarship has been focused on the influence of earlier poets, particularly Blake and the Romantics. Some scholars have examined Yeats's symbolism from a biographical and political perspective with regard to the poet's complex identity as an Irishman and as a member of the British Empire during decolonization. Still others have looked at Yeats and his symbolism in regards to literary trends in changing Ireland. Novelist James Joyce's literary resistance to Yeats is particularly notable with respect to symbolism: Ellman writes of an encounter Yeats had with Joyce, in which Joyce questioned why the poet concerned himself "with politics, with folklore, [and] with the historical settings of events." When Yeats responded that all good art depends on tradition, Joyce replied, "Generalizations aren't made by poets; they are made by men of letters. They are no use."

BIBLIOGRAPHY

Sources

Adams, Hazard. *Blake and Yeats: The Contrary Vision.* New York: Russell & Russell, 1968. Print.

Ellmann, Richard. *The Identity of Yeats.* New York: Oxford UP, 1954. Print.

Moore, George. *Vale.* New York: D. Appleton, 1914. Print.

O'Driscoll, Robert. *Symbolism and Some Implications of the Symbolic Approach: W.B. Yeats during the Eighteen-Nineties.* Dublin: Dolmen, 1975. Print.

Schuchard, Ronald. "The Legacy of Yeats in Contemporary Irish Poetry." *Irish University Review: A Journal of Irish Studies* 34.2 (2004): 291-307. *Literature Resource Center.* Web. 2 Aug. 2012.

Villiers de L'Isle-Adam, Auguste, comte de. *Axël.* Trans. W.B. Yeats. London: Soho Book, 1986. Print.

Vlasopolos, Anca. *The Symbolic Method of Coleridge, Baudelaire, and Yeats.* Detroit: Wayne State UP, 1983. Print.

Yeats, W.B. *Ideas of Good and Evil.* 2nd ed. London: A.H. Bullen, 1903. Print.

Further Reading

Antonielli, Arianna. "William Butler Yeats's 'The Symbolic System' of William Blake." *Estudios Irlandeses* 3 (2008): 10-28. *Literature Resource Center.* Web. 2 Aug. 2012.

Auden, W.H. "Yeats as an Example." *Kenyon Review* 10.2 (1948): 187-95. *LitFinder for Schools.* Web. 1 Aug. 2012.

Bloom, Harold, ed. *William Butler Yeats.* New York: Chelsea, 1986. Print.

Donoghue, Denis. "Yeats, Trying to Be Modern." *New England Review* 31.4 (2010): 131-44. *Literature Resource Center.* Web. 1 Aug. 2012.

O'Neill, Michael. *The Poems of W.B. Yeats: A Routledge Study Guide and Sourcebook.* New York: Routledge, 2004. Print.

Rose, Margaret. *The Symbolist Theatre Tradition from Maeterlinck and Yeats to Beckett and Pinter.* 1st ed. Milano: Edizioni Unicopli, 1989. Print.

Scott, Clive. "The Poetry of Symbolism and Decadence." *Symbolism, Decadence, and the Fin de Siècle: French and European Perspectives.* Ed. Patrick McGuinness. Exeter: U of Exeter P, 2000. Print.

William Blake's frontispiece to *Songs of Experience* from his *Songs of Innocence and Experience* (circa 1808). W.B. Yeats analyzes the poetry of Blake and others in the essay "The Symbolism of Poetry" (1900). FITZWILLIAM MUSEUM, UNIVERSITY OF CAMBRIDGE, UK/THE BRIDGEMAN ART LIBRARY

Joshua Ware, Karen Bender

THE ABCS OF CINEMA

Blaise Cendrars

❖ Key Facts

Time Period:
Early 20th Century

Movement/Issue:
Aesthetics; Avant-gardism; Cinematic modernism

Place of Publication:
France

Language of Publication:
French

OVERVIEW

Composed by Blaise Cendrars between 1917 and 1921, "The ABCs of Cinema" offers a swirling, lyric vision of the revolutionary possibilities afforded by the then-new technology of film. At the time of the essay's initial composition, Cendrars was writing at the cutting edge of the European avant-garde. Influenced by cubism, futurism, and other international modernist art movements, he sought new forms for encapsulating the chaotic multiplicity of the rapidly changing modern world. Written in the inventive style that characterizes his various poetic and prose experiments, "The ABCs of Cinema" offers not a logical argument but an associative stream of imagery and possibility. In a characteristic passage, Cendrars writes, "And here's Daguerre, a Frenchman, who invents photography. Fifty years later, cinema was born. Renewal! Renewal! Renewal!" The essay ends with four speculations (labeled A, B, C, and Z) on the radical power of cinema.

Though originally designed to be a book-length treatise on the poetic origins and potential of cinema, the text Cendrars originally published in 1919 offered only a one-page treatment of his subject. Four years later, he expanded the text and published it again. At the time, Cendrars was a major figure in the European avant-garde but was popularly obscure. Though he is widely considered a vital influence on the course of modernist and postmodern writing in the twentieth century, scholarly appreciation and criticism of Cendrars's work has been minimal, particularly in English. Among the few critics who have treated "The ABCs of Cinema," however, it is considered an important text that emerged during the flowering of one of the most important avant-garde writers of the twentieth century.

HISTORICAL AND LITERARY CONTEXT

"The ABCs of Cinema" responds to the flowering of modernism in Europe, when new aesthetic modes proliferated in response to rapid social and technological change. During a peripatetic childhood and youth, Cendrars was exposed to various strains of an artistic revolution that would upend longstanding aesthetic conventions. He was a child in Italy during the beginnings of futurism, a movement that embraced the rapid technological change of the early twentieth century. From time spent in Germany, Cendrars knew of expressionism, a varied avant-garde movement that rejected traditional notions of beauty. In St. Petersburg, he was present for the first waves of Russian futurism. After leaving Russia, he went to New York just as Dadaism and conceptualism were emerging. As the scholar Monique Chefdor writes in her introduction to Cendrars's *Modernities and Other Writings,* Cendrars "had already been exposed to the revolutions in art and literature which had burst on other parts of Europe long before they shook the Parisian literary world."

By the time "The ABCs of Cinema" first appeared in 1919, Cendrars was a prominent figure in Paris's growing avant-garde community. He had published his first poem in 1912. Titled "Les Pâques" ("Easter"), it featured a number of modernist innovations and, according to Chefdor, is considered today a "breakthrough of twentieth-century French poetry." The next year, Cendrars published *La Prose du Trans-sibérien (The Prose of the Transsiberian),* a long poem that included a number of formal innovations and helped secure his reputation as a vital, young avant-garde writer. Cendrars then served in World War I and lost his arm during combat. In 1917, after returning to Paris, he began work on a long project about the poetics of film. Though he never finished his planned book-length study, Cendrars did complete a much shorter essay on the subject, which he called "The ABCs of Cinema" and first published two year later.

In addition to beginning what would become "The ABCs of Cinema," Cendrars initiated and completed numerous experiments in poetry, prose, and criticism in 1917. Chefdor argues that these disparate works are united by "one of the fundamental characteristics of the age: the compulsive proclamation of the simultaneous perception of things multiple and diversified through the perpetually whirling gyres of consciousness." In *The End of the World Filmed by the Angel of Notre Dame,* for example, Cendrars offers a vision of the kind of film called for in "The ABCs of Cinema." Written as a hybrid form of fiction that combines elements of a screenplay and a novel, *The End of the World* borrows the staccato style and fragmented form of "The ABCs of Cinema": "The glaciers are liquefied. The sun solidifies. The vapors thin out, rise halfway up. It's hot."

Following its publication, "The ABCs of Cinema" proved inspirational among early French modernist and avant-garde filmmakers. This influence can be seen most explicitly in the writing and directing of Jean Epstein. Widely considered one of the most significant French filmmakers of the silent era, Epstein authored an essay in 1921 called "Bonjour Cinéma" that echoed and elaborated Cendrars's call for a new kind of cinema. (In fact, Cendrars, then an editor at *Les Editions de la Sirène*, was responsible for publishing Epstein's essay.) Cendrars's argument about cinema was also an important influence on the French writer Antonin Artaud, who worked as a scriptwriter, an actor, and a film theorist in the 1920s.

THEMES AND STYLE

The central theme of "The ABCs of Cinema" is that cinema represents the revolutionary new art form for a profoundly new era of humanity. As Cendrars writes, "The latest advancements of the precise sciences, world war, the concept of relativity, political convulsions, everything foretells that we are on our way toward a new synthesis of the human spirit, toward a new humanity and that a race of new men is going to appear. Their language will be the cinema." Cendrars traces the historical and artistic developments that have led to this new paradigm as means of illustrating that film represents the apotheosis of a long process. Now that cinema has arrived, he writes, "the floodgates of the new language are open." The result will be a revolution of anyone who envisions being "on the screen among the convulsions of the crowd, who shouts and cries out, protests and struggles."

Cendrars makes his case for cinema's grand possibility by thoroughly, albeit hurriedly, placing it within a larger aesthetic and historical context. His text begins urgently: "Cinema. Whirlwind of movement in space." In this way he introduces the connection between film and our human relationship to reality—a relationship that is rapidly changing under the terms of technological, economic, and aesthetic development. "New civilization. New humanity," Cendrars writes. "The digits have created an abstract, mathematical organism, useful gadgets intended to serve the senses' most vulgar needs and that are the brain's most beautiful projection." He charts the trajectory of this new paradigm all the way back to the invention of "writing and the book" in ancient Greece. From there he marks the various revolutions in the means of recording human civilization over time. By the essay's end, Cendrars has arrived at the future: "Watch the new generations growing up suddenly like flowers. Revolution. Youth of the world. Today."

Stylistically, "The ABCs of Cinema" is distinguished by its lyricism. Written in a series of fragmented sentences, the text's prismatic style reflects Cendrars's vision of cinema's potential to encapsulate a world in which "everything opens up, tumbles down, blends in today, caves in, rises up, blossoms." The text also employs vivid imagery that allows Cendrars's argument to exceed the narrow limitations of the merely logical. Of the bullet points that end the essay, the third is "C On Earth," and it reads, "At the same time, in all the cities of the world, the crowd which leaves the theaters, which runs out into the streets like black blood, which extends its thousand tentacles like a powerful animal and with a tiny effort crushes the palaces, the prisons." This kind of poetic liberty lends "The ABCs of Cinema" a greater rhetorical range and power.

CRITICAL DISCUSSION

When "The ABCs of Cinema" was published—first in the journal *La Rose Rouge* in 1919 and then in expanded form in *Promenoir* in 1921—it made a powerful impression on members of the Parisian avant-garde. This impression can be detected in the movies of the French film director Abel Gance, whose work Chefdor observes "strikingly echoes" the ideas laid out in Cendrars's essay. In 1920 Cendrars worked with Gance on his film *La Roue,* which helped introduce the innovations in filmic language that "The ABCs of Cinema" suggested. Gance also took up Cendrars's argument in a 1927 essay of his own, titled "Le Temps de l'image est venu." Though appreciation for Cendrars's writing was strongest in France, he was known elsewhere as well. The English writers Richard Adlington and Aldous Huxley, for example, wrote approvingly of his work as early as 1920.

BLAISE CENDRARS: A PERIPATETIC LIFE IN FICTION

Blaise Cendrars was famous for inventing for himself an absurd and elaborate past. He claimed to have hunted whales, smuggled jewels, and worked as a juggler. Even his name was a fiction: Cendrars was born Frédéric Sauser. The truth of his life, however, was nearly as fantastical as his lies about it.

Born in 1887 in Switzerland, he was the son of a former math teacher who had taken up inventing and business. When the writer was young, his father moved the family to Egypt. After two years spent operating a hotel there, his father moved the family back to Europe. As Cendrars bounced from Egypt to Naples to Germany, he did poorly in school but read widely on his own. At seventeen Cendrars (still known then as Frédéric) moved to Russia, which was on the cusp of revolution. He did not, as he claimed, smuggle jewels along the Transsiberian railroad, but he did work for a watchmaker in St. Petersburg for three years. Afterward he resumed his wandering. He went to Switzerland, Belgium, and America, among many other places. In 1915 he served in the French Foreign Legion. While in battle, his arm was shattered by a bombshell. To save himself, Cendrars amputated his own arm. Though based in Paris after the war, Cendrars continued to travel throughout the rest of his life.

Portrait of Blaise Cendrars
by Amedeo Modigliani,
1918. © AISA/EVERETT
COLLECTION

Following the appearance of "The ABCs of Cinema." Cendrars remained an important force in the development of modernist aesthetics. Writers as diverse as John Dos Passos and Henry Miller were influenced by Cendrars's formal and stylistic innovations. In 1960 Miller praised him for his ability to "reassemble the multitudinous and contradictory elements which constitute the essential character of our time," as quoted in Chefdor's introduction to *Complete Postcards of the America* (1976). In his 2004 overview of Cendrars, Jeff Bursey notes that other critics, including Marjorie Perloff, have argued that Cendrars's work anticipates and informs not only modernism but postmodern movements such as the Black Mountain school and the Beats. While numerous commentators have argued for Cendrars's integral role in the history of twentieth-century literature, very little criticism has been written in English about "The ABCs of Cinema."

Of the few scholars who have considered the significance of "The ABCs of Cinema," Chefdor has written most admiringly on it. According to her, "*ABC* is so perceptive in its grasp of the artistic

potential of film that it is both a literary work of art and a historical document." Other commentators have drawn attention to the essay's place within Cendrars's oeuvre. In her essay "Blaise Cendrars: A Cinema of Poetry," scholar Mary Ann Caws notes the relationship between Cendrars's poetic and filmic interest: "The spiral of the whirlwind is a primary image both in his lyric appreciation of the modern spirit … and in his homage to the cinema."

BIBLIOGRAPHY

Sources

Bursey, Jeff. "Blaise Cendrars." *Review of Contemporary Fiction* 24.1 (2004): 58-93. *Academic Search Elite.* Web. 5 Oct. 2012.

Caws, Mary Ann. "Blaise Cendrars: A Cinema of Poetry." *Kentucky Romance Quarterly* 17.4 (1970): 345-56. Print.

Cendrars, Blaise. *Complete Postcards from the Americas: Poems of Road and Sea.* Berkeley: U of California P, 1976. Print.

———. *Modernities and Other Writings.* Lincoln: U of Nebraska P, 1992. Print.

Kogan, Steve. "The Pilgrimage of Blaise Cendrars." *Literary Imagination* 3 (2001): 254-76. *Oxford Journals.* Web. 5 Oct. 2012.

Further Reading

Bochner, Jay. *Blaise Cendrars: Discovery and Re-creation.* Toronto: U of Toronto P, 1978. Print.

———. "Blaise without War: The War on Anarchy in Blaise Cendrars's Moravagine." *Modernism/Modernity* 2.2 (1995): 49-62. Print.

Bordwell, David. *On the History of Film Style.* Cambridge: Harvard UP, 1997. Print.

Breton, André. *Manifestoes of Surrealism.* Trans. Richard Seaver and Helen R. Lane. Ann Arbor: U of Michigan P, 1969. Print.

Caws, Mary Ann. "From Prose to the Poem of Paris to Cendrars's *Tour*" in *Dada Surrealism* 9. New York: Wittenborn, 1979. Print.

Chefdor, Monique. *Blaise Cendrars.* Boston: Twayne, 1980. Print.

Horrex, Susan. "Blaise Cendrars and the Aesthetics of Simultaneity." *Dada Surrealism* 6. New York: Queens College P, 1976. Print.

Manoll, Michael. "Blaise Cendrars: The Art of Fiction, No. 38." Trans. William Brandon. *Paris Review* 37 (1966). Web. 5 Oct. 2012.

Vertov, Dziga. *Kino-Eye: The Writings of Dziga Vertov.* Ed. Annette Michelson. Trans. Kevin O'Brien. Berkeley: U of California P, 1984. Print.

Wolf, Matt. "A Cubist Vision of Theater as Sculpture in Motion." *New York Times.* The New York Times Company, 13 Sept. 1998. Web. 5 Oct. 2012.

Theodore McDermott

AXIOMATA

Ezra Pound

OVERVIEW

First published on January 13, 1921, in the socialist periodical the *New Age,* Ezra Pound's "Axiomata" laid out his stance toward religion and spirituality in a confident and defiant way. His propositions provided a contentious redefinition of many common terms of religious discourse, declaring belief "a cramp, a paralysis, an atrophy of the mind in certain conditions" and dogma "bluff based upon ignorance." In place of formal creeds, which Pound perceived as oppressive and misguided, the poet asserted as axioms (principles advanced for the sake of argument) the unknowability of God and the personal nature of all mystical experiences. In doing so Pound aligned himself with a larger socialist tendency toward secularism. His attitude toward religion, however, was by no means universally accepted among British socialists, even by his *New Age* colleagues.

In fact, the magazine's editor, A.C. Orage, was among the first to critique Pound's collection of axioms, including a pseudonymous reply in the very same issue. This rejoinder, however, belies the half century of relative neglect that would follow. In the 1930s and 1940s Pound came to be associated with Italian fascism, and it is on these grounds, if any, that his philosophical positions were generally analyzed. Eclipsed on the one end by Pound's earlier artistic declarations as an imagist and a vorticist and on the other by the complex and controversial views presented throughout the *Cantos,* the "Axiomata" now occupies an almost ephemeral position in the literary biography of the great modernist poet. Nevertheless, some Pound scholars have seen in the document a trace of the essential philosophical elements of the poet's work as a whole, projecting the ideas treated there backward in time to his earliest poems and forward to the notoriously difficult *Cantos.* Others have worked to illuminate the specific philosophical influences, both classical and modern, that informed Pound's attack on dogmatism and, by extrapolation, his critique of organized religion in general.

HISTORICAL AND LITERARY CONTEXT

The "Axiomata" came from a long line of philosophical writings that had posited the existence of an abstract, impersonal, or unknowable deity in contrast to the personal, epiphanically revealed God of the major theistic religions. According to Peter Liebregts in *Ezra Pound and Neoplatonism* (2004), Pound was writing in a tradition at least as old as Plato and appears, particularly in his insistence on a nondogmatic approach, to have been especially influenced by the Neoplatonist thinker Plotinus. Much later the seventeenth-century Dutch philosopher Baruch Spinoza would assert a similarly impersonal God and elaborate the consequences of this belief in his *Ethics.* Pound, a reader and admirer of Spinoza, adopted an axiomatic style similar to that of the Renaissance rationalist, though much abbreviated.

Since its origins in the nineteenth century, the British socialism championed in the *New Age* had likewise borne a vexed relationship to religion, especially to Christianity. The German thinker Karl Marx, whose observations laid the groundwork for many nineteenth- and twentieth-century socialist movements, had notoriously declared religion the "opium of the people" and critiqued it for disguising the suffering of those exploited by capitalism. However, Victorian Britain had also seen the rise of a Christian socialist movement whose proponents maintained that there was no essential conflict between the two ideological systems. These Christian socialists composed a significant minority of the nascent Labour Party, whose 1900 foundation marked a milestone for socialism in Britain. Pound and his fellow *New Age* writers thus addressed an audience for whom the compatibility of Christian and socialist worldviews was still heavily debated.

Born in 1885, Pound was no stranger to expressing his beliefs through movements and manifestos. In 1913 he had written the essay "A Few Don'ts by an Imagiste" as an expression of his affiliation with the imagist school of poetics; only a few years later he would contribute some important early poems to the vorticist movement, which he cofounded with painter Wyndham Lewis. It was in a sense natural, then, that Pound's views regarding religion and the socialist cause, to say nothing of his sometimes contentious relationship with the *New Age* milieu, would take the form of an abstract and authoritative statement.

Apart from immediate reactions among the *New Age* circle, Pound's "Axiomata" would not prove a very influential document. All but forgotten in the

Key Facts

Time Period:
Early 20th Century

Movement/Issue:
Socialism; Theology

Place of Publication:
England

Language of Publication:
English

SPINOZA'S *ETHICS* AND POUND'S "AXIOMATA"

That Ezra Pound read Baruch Spinoza is evident from an examination of his literary essays, in which he periodically cites the Renaissance philosopher; Pound was especially fond of Spinoza's statement that "the intellectual love of a thing consists in understanding its perfections," a remark he would apply repeatedly to his own work of literary criticism. The full extent of Spinoza's influence on Pound, however, remains an open question. Certainly there are some striking formal and methodological similarities between Pound's "Axiomata" and Spinoza's much longer *Ethics,* published 250 years earlier.

Spinoza's basic approach in this treatise is to state a conservative set of axioms regarding the nature of God, reality, and human emotion and then to extend the results to their necessary logical conclusions. This has sometimes been characterized as a "geometric" model because of its resemblance, in turn, to the works of early Greek mathematicians and their successors in Renaissance Europe. Pound's approach is transparently less tidily "geometric" than Spinoza's but shares with *Ethics* a reliance on a progression from basic axioms to their obvious (in Pound's opinion) consequences. Like his predecessor, Pound purports to treat complex matters of human behavior using the formal metaphor of mathematical reasoning.

wake of his World War II-era writings, the early work has retained importance for scholars chiefly as a record of the poet's philosophical outlook at the time he left England for France. Certain basic elements of the "Axiomata," such as its metaphor of mathematical rigor, have proved mainstays of the manifesto genre before and since, but no later writing (save Pound's own) has been identified as specifically drawing upon his list of axioms.

THEMES AND STYLE

The primary point of Pound's "Axiomata" may be found in the very first axiom, which states that "the intimate essence of the universe is *not* of the same nature as our own consciousness." For Pound it follows that the common belief in a personal deity, along with many other traits of widely practiced religions, are harmless fictions at best and exploitative schemes at worst: human consciousness is unable to grasp the kinds of information that would rationally justify such a belief. Pound's definition of God is an abstract and impersonal Spinozian deity: "there is no reason for not applying the term God, *Theos,* to the intimate essence [of the universe]." Pound notes the historical association between organized religion and a series of "ulterior purpose[s]," including "exploitation, control of the masses, etc."

Pound's claims, as Orage was quick to point out, are boldly stated, but the poet offers them as axioms—that is, as unproved assertions assumed as the basis for further reasoning—professing here, as in his other writings, a horror of dogmatism. However, unlike the geometric or logical axioms that Pound's term invokes, the "Axiomata" bear some rather explicit value judgments about the people who disagree with them. Those who attempt "to contain the *theos* in consciousness" are "foolish," and, somewhat more acerbically, it is axiomatic for Pound that both "savages and professed believers in religion" lack a "concept of common decency." Moreover, rather than bearing a strictly logical relation to each other, many of the axioms are restatements of the same essential point: that human consciousness and the inferences to be made from it are limited. While it would be unproductive to hold the poet to the standard of rigor his term suggests, Pound certainly avails himself of the authority (and the deniability) of a philosopher proposing axioms rather than venturing personal identification with his beliefs.

Such judgments notwithstanding, Pound lays out his argument in a more or less unemotional manner, rarely indulging in the lyricism or passion that would characterize so much of his other work. Occasionally an axiom blossoms into a particularly poetic flourish of language, as when Pound, seeking to explain the problem of attributing mystical experiences to a deity, notes that the sensations of such experiences do not "[differ] intellectually from the taste of a lemon or the fragrance of violets or the aroma of dung-hills, or the feel of a stone or of tree-bark." On balance, however, Pound's work aims to appeal to its reader more through its adoption of a philosophical position than through the force of its language.

CRITICAL DISCUSSION

Orage's essay immediately following the "Axiomata" in *New Age* gives perhaps the clearest contemporary reaction to the work. He praised the work but took issue with some of its points, suggesting an ironic duplicity in Pound's attack on religious creeds. Orage regarded the document as Pound's "intellectual will and testament" and maintained the usefulness of such a work as a "table of contents" of the mind of its writer. Such a reference might serve as a basis, the editor maintained, for evaluating the work of any poet or critic; Pound had already established his reputation as both. In an unusual interpretive gesture, Orage then proceeded to label the axioms a "Creed" in their own right and to locate in them "the two most serious defects in Mr. Pound's work … his enmity to Religion and his lack of psychological depth."

Few, if any, early readers responded to the "Axiomata" with such force as Orage; by 1969 the well-known modernist scholar Hugh Witemeyer would declare the essay both "very important and almost unknown."

As Witemeyer would go on to explain in *The Poetry of Ezra Pound: Forms and Renewal, 1908-1920,* the importance of the work for his project (and for many Pound scholars since) lay in its reflection of "some of the unchanging philosophical assumptions behind all of Pound's work" rather than in its efficacy as a manifesto. Critics since Witemeyer have further demonstrated the place of "Axiomata" in a tentative timeline of Pound's philosophical and political development. In a 1989 essay in *English Literary History,* Patricia Rae noted that the "Axiomata" expresses ideas already at work in Pound's earliest poems; Rae also joined Witemeyer in detecting the axioms' influence through the *Cantos,* a project that ran to the end of Pound's career.

In recent decades critics have also attempted to situate the "Axiomata" in the context of Pound's numerous philosophical and literary influences. Kimberly Kyle Howey, in a dissertation describing Pound's "extended extra-poetic interest" in science, observed that the specific language of the "Axiomata," especially its formulation of religion as a problem of "consciousness," may be seen to derive in part from the French poet Remy de Gourmont, whose work Pound translated. Additional influences, though speculative, include Friedrich Nietzsche and the psychologist William James. While only a minor contribution to the discourse of socialism and religion in the post–World War I era, Pound's brief list of axioms does, as Orage suggested nearly a century ago, shed light on a set of early influences that would shape the poet's work for many years to come.

BIBLIOGRAPHY

Sources

Howey, Kimberly Kyle. *Ezra Pound and the Rhetoric of Science, 1901-1922.* Diss. University College London, 2009. Web. 20 July 2012.

Liebregts, Peter. *Ezra Pound and Neoplatonism.* Lanham: Farleigh Dickinson UP, 2004. Print.

Pound, Ezra. "Axiomata." *New Age* 28.11 (1921): 125-26. *Modernist Journals Project.* Web. 20 July 2012.

Rae, Patricia. "From Mystical Gaze to Pragmatic Game: Representations of Truth in Vorticist Art." *ELH* 56.3 (1989): 689-720. Print.

R. H. C. (Orage, A. C.). "Readers and Writers." *New Age* 28.11 (1921): 126-27. *Modernist Journals Project.* Web. 20 July 2012.

Riddell, Joseph N. "Pound and the Decentered Image." *Georgia Review* 29.3 (1975): 565-91. Print.

Witemeyer, Hugh. *The Poetry of Ezra Pound: Forms and Renewal, 1908-1920.* Berkeley: U of California P, 1969. Print.

Further Reading

Cookson, William, ed. *Ezra Pound: Selected Prose, 1909-1965.* New York: New Directions, 1975. Print.

Cotsell, Michael. "*The New Age,* Volume 28 (November 4, 1920 to April 28, 1921): An Introduction." *Modernist Journals Project.* Web. 20 July 2012.

Rae, Patricia. *The Practical Muse: Pragmatist Poetics in Hulme, Pound, and Stevens.* Lewisburg: Bucknell UP, 1997. Print.

Wilhelm, J. J. *Ezra Pound in London and Paris, 1908-1925.* State College: Penn State UP, 1990. Print.

Michael Hartwell

Bust of Ezra Pound (circa 1909-1914) by Henri Gaudier-Brzeska. © DAVID LEES/CORBIS

BANG FIST MANIFESTO

John Cage

✣ *Key Facts*

Time Period:
Mid-20th Century

Movement/Issue:
Aesthetics;
Avant-gardism

Place of Publication:
United States

**Language of
Publication:**
English

OVERVIEW

Composed by John Cage, the *Bang Fist Manifesto* (1937) denies that silence exists and insinuates that even incidental noise can be equivalent to music. Composed of only eight brief lines of text that are interspersed and surrounded with pauses and that conclude with the banging of a fist, the manifesto offers a lyrical statement of Cage's radical theory and practice of musical composition. Cage emphasized in the *Bang Fist Manifesto* and elsewhere the importance of chance, randomness, and spontaneity in artistic creation. His conception of musical composition was influenced by the innovative composers Henry Cowell and Arnold Schoenberg, both of whom mentored Cage in the mid-1930s. At the time of the manifesto's creation, Cage's apprenticeship had ended and he had begun experimenting with the use of unconventional objects in musical composition. The manifesto's integration of text, silence, and nonmusical sound (a banged fist) were indicative of the radical style of artistic creation that Cage employed throughout his lengthy and diverse career.

Although Cage's *Bang Fist Manifesto* was composed in 1937, it did not receive public attention for another seventeen years, when it was included as one of many elements in his 1954 piece *45' for a Speaker*, which was assembled from previous writings as well as from new elements and was delivered as a lecture at the Composers' Concourse in London. *Bang Fist Manifesto* was then collected in Cage's seminal 1961 text *Silence*. Today the *Bang Fist Manifesto* can be viewed as a brief, idiosyncratic encapsulation of the thought of one of the twentieth century's most innovative, influential, and controversial composers.

HISTORICAL AND LITERARY CONTEXT

The *Bang Fist Manifesto* responds to the state of classical music in the 1930s, when modernism was booming and composers were seeking new techniques and forms for creating musical works. Cage's artistic interest was wide-ranging: he studied architecture, writing, and painting before turning to music. As a result he was influenced greatly not only by Cowell and Schoenberg but also by writers such as Gertrude Stein and James Joyce, painters such as Piet Mondrian, and conceptual artists such as Marcel Duchamp. Though these influences were diverse, all of them shared a commitment to reinventing artistic form and process. Schoenberg expanded and altered the fundamental conventions of classical music by embracing dissonance, eliminating traditional tonality, and inventing the twelve-tone system of composition.

By the time the *Bang Fist Manifesto* was composed in 1937, Cage had been studying with Schoenberg in Los Angeles for approximately two years. However, Cage had begun to move away from his mentor's powerful influence and toward a looser style of composition inspired by futurism. The futurists were a group of Italian artists who embraced the speed and chaos of mechanized and industrialized modernity. The group's leader, Philippo Marinetti, experimented with sound in his poems and play. Luigi Russolo, a futurist composer, invented machines that created an "art of noises." Cage was also increasingly interested in music from outside the European sphere. Indonesian gamelan music, Balinese music, and Caribbean music all helped drive Cage beyond the conventions of classical form and past even the innovations of Schoenberg and other modernist composers.

The *Bang Fist Manifesto* draws on a history of avant-garde manifesto and, in particular, on Russolo's *The Art of Noises* (1913). According to Cage, Russolo's manifesto was "a great encouragement to me in my work." In it Russolo outlined "a new art" that he imagined emerging from the futurist music. He traced a kind of brief history of sound, noise, and music, and he declared that "today music, as it becomes continually more complicated, strives to amalgamate the most dissonant, strange and harsh sounds. In this way we come ever closer to *noise-sound*." This interest in incidental noise (rather than traditional instrumentation) as a component of composition heavily influenced the *Bang Fist Manifesto*.

The *Bang Fist Manifesto* served as an important template for a career's worth of writing on music and composition by Cage. In 1937, the same year the manifesto was issued, Cage delivered a talk titled "The Future of Music: Credo." In it he fleshed out the manifesto's argument about the omnipresence of noise, the absence of sound, and the ways in which composition is the arrangement of these elements. Like the manifesto, Cage's 1937 credo takes an unconventional, lyrical form. Over the next twenty-plus years, Cage continued to write experimental texts and speeches that furthered his exploration of compositional processes through innovative poetic and prose forms. Many of these texts, including *45' for a Speaker*, were assembled as the collection *Silence*. As Cage's career continued for another three decades, so did his textual explorations. Today Cage's writings, although not as influential as his musical compositions, command significant scholarly interest.

THEMES AND STYLE

The central theme of the *Bang Fist Manifesto* is that sound is omnipresent and that it can be arranged as a kind of music. The manifesto opens with an eighteen-second pause. This pause is followed by a blunt, seemingly paradoxical, declaration: "There is no such thing as silence." By opening his manifesto with apparent silence and then declaring that such silence does not exist, Cage demonstrates the idea that he states in his next sentence: "Something is always happening that makes a sound." The "something" that is happening to make sound, the manifesto implies, may be someone speaking or playing an instrument—or it may be the incidental noise that fills any apparent silence. For Cage, composition is not limited to the arrangement of musical notes. Rather it is "the organization of sound," as he puts it in an essay version of "The Future of Music: Credo," also included in *Silence*. His *Bang Fist Manifesto* offers a curt, open statement of this philosophy of composition.

The manifesto achieves its rhetorical effect by demonstrating, rather than merely stating, its argument. Cage does so by including pauses in his manifesto—and by emphatically breaking the seeming silence of those pauses. He breaks them with speech and with his parenthetical instruction for the performer to "bang fist" at the end of the manifesto. Though the manifesto opens with a pair of authoritative declarations about the nature of silence, the text's sense of certainty quickly unravels. The third sentence undermines the sense of authority that undergirds the manifesto's opening. "No one," Cage writes, "can have an idea once he starts really listening." This inability to form coherent thought amidst the chaos of sound becomes evident in the manifesto's closing lines, which are fragmentary and unfinished.

Stylistically the *Bang Fist Manifesto* is distinguished by its performative and poetic nature. Rather than presenting a discursive argument about composition, Cage offers instructions for a one-minute-long performance. As a result the text includes along its left margin measurements of time in ten-second intervals. In instructions that precede *45' for a Speaker* Cage informs the reader that each line should be read in two seconds. There are long pauses at the beginning and end of the manifesto, and there are two-second pauses between each two-second-long line. This alternation of pause and text creates rhythm and structure from speech and silence. The text itself becomes

JOHN CAGE: ARTISTIC INVENTOR

When asked what he thought of his former student John Cage, Arnold Schoenberg answered, "Of course he's not a composer, but an inventor—of genius." Cage's inventiveness was not something he manifested entirely of his own volition. It was something he inherited. His paternal grandfather, Gustavus Cage, was an amateur inventor who had patented a touch-key finder for typewriters. His father, John Cage, Sr., was a professional inventor who designed everything from a submarine to an inhaler that treated colds. As Cage biographer David Revill writes, "John senior taught [Cage] the pioneer urgency of innovation."

This spirit of innovation can be seen throughout Cage's expansive oeuvre and, more concretely, in an invention of his own: the prepared piano. Inspired by the experiments of his teacher Henry Cowell, who had composed pieces that called for plucking and striking the strings inside a piano, Cage first altered a piano by placing objects on its strings in 1940. He installed a screw, a bolt, and weather-stripping. The effect was a piano that produced novel pitches and timbres and provided an unpredictable succession of sounds. For the next decade, pianos prepared in various ways were the principal instruments used in Cage's compositions.

increasingly lyrical and indeterminate. It ends, "It is very simple but extra-urgent / The Lord knows whether or not / the next," followed by a blank space that represents a pause.

CRITICAL DISCUSSION

While the *Bang Fist Manifesto* was barely noticed when it was first written in 1937, it came to greater popular and critical attention in 1961, when it was included in Cage's book *Silence*. It appeared there as an element of *45' for a Speaker*, a piece for two pianos and a speaker. According to Cage biographer David Revill, *Silence* was published "to interested but often puzzled review." In a 1962 review included in *Writings about John Cage*, the scholar John Hollander wrote, "Even if one is kindly disposed toward John Cage's book, it is hard to decide upon a justly suitable response to it." Hollander wrote that Cage's writings, including *45' for a Speaker*, "confuse systematically the musical and the meta-musical."

The ideas expressed and implied in Cage's manifesto went on to inform his nearly sixty-year career as a composer. The idea that "there is no such thing as silence" was central to nearly all of Cage's compositions. As Revill writes in *The Roaring Silence*, silence had been "an important facet of Cage's music" since the beginning of his career. This interest reached its peak on August 29, 1952, when Cage premiered his latest work, *4' 33'*, which was composed entirely of silence. "Since no sounds are to be intentionally produced in

John Cage (left) working with experimental composer David Tudor at the Royal Festival Hall, May 22, 1972. © HULTON-DEUTSCH COLLECTION/ CORBIS

the piece," Revill writes, "the structure is illuminated only by the sounds which accidentally occur." This was the ultimate demonstration of the manifesto's claim that "something is always happening that makes a sound." Cage continued to experiment with silence in his work, and his interest spread to other musicians and composers such as La Monte Young. Yoko Ono and John Lennon recorded a track called "Two Minutes Silence" in 1969. Since the manifesto's composition in 1937, Cage's ideas about the relationship between silence and music have been the subject of an extensive body of criticism.

Much scholarship has focused on the wide-ranging implications of Cage's valuation of silence, chance, and unmusical sounds in his compositions. Many scholars have noted Cage's revolutionary adoption of a wide gamut of nonmusical sound in his compositions. However, some commentators have questioned that inclusiveness. In his essay "John Cage: Silence and Silencing," the scholar Douglas Kahn examines the "social, political, poetic, and ecological" implications of Cage's interest in non-Western music. "What

becomes apparent in general," Kahn writes, "is that while venturing to the sounds outside music, his ideas did not adequately make the trip; the world he wanted for music was a select one, where most of the social and ecological noise was muted and where other more proximal noises were suppressed." Other commentators have argued that while Cage's compositions were profoundly influential and innovative, his writings on music represent his most important work. In *Writing about John Cage* the critic Petr Kotik states that Cage's "most lasting contribution, however, is the introduction of his musical ideas and compositional concepts." "Silences," Kotik continues, "became equally important to sounds, and tones produced on instruments became equally important to noises."

BIBLIOGRAPHY

Sources

Cage, John. *Silence: Lectures and Writing.* Middleton: Wesleyan UP, 1961. Print.

Gann, Kenneth. *No Such Thing as Silence.* New Haven: Yale UP, 2010. Print.

Kahn, Douglas. "John Cage: Silence and Silencing." The *Musical Quarterly* 81.4 (1997): 556-98. *JSTOR.* Web. 20 Aug. 2012.

Kostelanetz, Richard, ed. *John Cage.* New York: RK, 1970. Print.

———. *Writings about John Cage.* Ann Arbor: U of Michigan P, 1993. Print.

Revill, David. *The Roaring Silence: John Cage, A Life.* New York: Arcade, 1992. Print.

Russolo, Luigi. *The Art of Noises.* Ubuweb. Web. 21 Aug. 2012.

Further Reading

Cage, John. *Musicage: Cage Muses on Words, Art, Music.* Middleton: Wesleyan UP, 1996. Print.

Fleming, Richard, and William Duckworth, eds. *John Cage at Seventy-Five.* Lewisburg: Bucknell UP, 1989. Print.

Kostelanetz, Richard. *John Cage (Ex)plain(ed).* New York: Schirmer, 1996. Print.

Nicholls, David. *John Cage.* Urbana: U of Illinois P, 2007. Print.

Perloff, Marjorie, and Charles Junkerman, eds. *John Cage: Composed in America.* Chicago: U of Chicago P, 1994. Print.

Silverman, Kenneth. *Begin Again: A Biography of John Cage.* New York: Knopf, 2010. Print.

Theodore McDermott

BLAST
Wyndham Lewis

OVERVIEW

"Blast," published in the magazine of the same name in July 1914 and written by painter and novelist Wyndham Lewis in collaboration with poet Ezra Pound, is an influential text on the British arts movement known as Vorticism. Several other Vorticist artists put their names on the essay, signaling their shared advocacy of this distinctly British brand of modern art. "Blast," like many Vorticist documents, is both aesthetically and rhetorically aggressive: it adopts an eye-catching, heavily capitalized typographic style reminiscent of newspaper advertisements and provides lists of items, people, and nations to be "blessed" or "blasted"—sometimes both—under the principles of the new movement. With "Blast," Lewis attempted to establish that the Vorticists had different ideals and aesthetics than their precursors, especially the Italian futurists, to whom their work was more than superficially similar. Nonetheless, the Vorticists would be hounded for their brief collective life by a critical culture unable or unwilling to make this distinction.

Vorticism as a movement of any significance did not survive World War I. In this sense, "Blast" was a document of limited efficacy, reaching few contemporary readers and motivating fewer. However, the subsequent careers of its coauthors have secured "Blast" a place in literary history; the essay set the terms of an aesthetic project in which both Lewis and Pound would engage, if sometimes nostalgically, throughout their lives. This was particularly true of Lewis, who is now considered to be a major exponent of the manifesto as an art form in its own right, with "Blast" serving as his early masterpiece. More generally, critics have seen "Blast" as a milestone for the arts manifesto in English, one that expands on the work begun by Continental writers only a few years prior.

HISTORICAL AND LITERARY CONTEXT

Vorticism announced itself as the inauguration of great and overdue change in British arts and letters. Queen Victoria had died in 1901, marking a literal end to the era that bore her name, but in many ways British literature was slow, as the Vorticists would have it, to leave behind Victorian gentility and conservatism. An exclusive and very influential "Bloomsbury set" of authors and critics had risen to power in the early twentieth century, and the magazine *Blast* would ridicule their work as mannered and unimaginative. In the years immediately preceding World War I, an overlapping group of poets known as the Georgians (after King George V, who reigned from 1910 to 1936) also enjoyed popular and critical approval; they were known for their aristocratic, formally conservative, and often pastoral verse. Modernism, as heralded by such works as T. S. Eliot's *The Waste Land* (1922), would not arrive in force for some years yet.

In the meantime, artists and writers who wished to break with tradition and explore boldly experimental forms or taboo subjects were often drawn to modern Continental styles. In painting, including Lewis's own, both cubism (Franco-Spanish in origin) and Italian futurism were major influences; in literature, too, the futurists played a significant role, producing several works that today would be identified with such practices as concrete poetics and stream-of-consciousness narrative. At the same time, Lewis expressed his unease at the importation of these "foreign" movements, especially futurism, which captured the spirit of the industrial age but bore with it a militaristic enthusiasm that struck him as sentimental. The artist's personal dissatisfactions—both with the staidness of British contemporary art and with the ideological trappings of futurism—are inscribed in numerous passages from "Blast."

Yet if "Blast" rejects futurism on philosophical grounds, it retains much of the precursor movement's style. As with several other items in *Blast* magazine, the essay draws explicitly upon the rhetorical gestures that characterize F.T. Marinetti's "Futurist Manifesto" (1909). Indeed, Lewis's praise of a hairdresser's "systematic mercenary war" on the "wildness" of beards seems almost a brief homage to the futurist fascination with youth and warfare. The arresting and forceful typography of "Blast" was unusual for a British literary journal, but it too has an antecedent in futurist art, such as the sprawling, crisscrossing profusion of fonts and figures in Marinetti's poem "Zang Tumb Tumb" (1912-14).

Like its contentious older siblings, Vorticism was short-lived, with World War I virtually disbanding the group of British artists. Several major Vorticist figures, including the sculptor Henri Gaudier-Brzeska, were

❖ *Key Facts*

Time Period:
Early 20th Century

Movement/Issue:
Aesthetics; Vorticism; Modernism

Place of Publication:
England

Language of Publication:
English

PRIMARY SOURCE

"BLAST"

BLESS ENGLAND!
BLESS ENGLAND

FOR ITS SHIPS

which switchback on Blue, Green and
Red SEAS all around the PINK
EARTH-BALL,
BIG BETS ON EACH.
BLESS ALL SEAFARERS.

THEY exchange not one LAND for another, but one
ELEMENT
for ANOTHER. The MORE against the LESS ABSTRACT.

****

BLESS the vast planetary abstraction of the OCEAN.

****

BLESS THE ARABS OF THE ATLANTIC.
THIS ISLAND MUST BE CONTRASTED WITH THE BLEAK
WAVES.

****

BLESS ALL PORTS.

PORTS, RESTLESS MACHINES of

- scooped out basins
- heavy Insect dredgers
- monotonous cranes
- stations

- lighthouses, blazing
- through the frosty
- starlight, cutting the
- storm like a cake
- beaks of Infant boats,
- side by side,
- heavy chaos of
- wharves,
- steep walls of
- factories
- womanly town

BLESS these MACHINES that work the little boats across
clean liquid space, in beelines.
BLESS the great PORTS

- HULL
- LIVERPOOL
- LONDON
- NEWCASTLE-ON-TYNE
- BRISTOL
- GLASGOW

BLESS ENGLAND,
Industrial Island machine, pyramidal
workshop, its apex at Shetland, discharging itself on
the sea.
BLESS

- cold
- magnanimous
- delicate
- gauche
- fanciful
- stupid

killed in action, and others lost interest in Vorticism by the war's end. Lewis returned from his own tour of duty to find only the merest ember of the movement he had founded in 1914, but he proceeded to enjoy an eclectic career in print and paint over the next four decades. "Blast" would remain important to appraisals of his oeuvre. As Julian Hanna states in "Blasting after *Blast*: Wyndham Lewis's Late Manifestos," the document helped to establish Lewis as "the figure most closely associated with the manifesto in British twentieth-century art and literature."

THEMES AND STYLE

Perhaps the strongest message of "Blast" is that Vorticists are artistic mercenaries, willing to temporarily support whoever happens to share their values. Lewis gives ample space to the image of the mercenary in his "blasts" and "blessings," including some figures whose placement in the essay may otherwise seem peculiar. Consider the hairdresser who occupies second place among those "blessed" by Lewis: "he attacks Mother Nature for a small fee," but his mercenary behavior has a salutary effect on the world, shaping a present

ENGLISHMEN.
CURSE
WITH EXPLETIVE OF WHIRLWIND
THE BRITANNIC AESTHETE
CREAM OF THE SNOBBISH EARTH
ROSE OF SHARON OF GOD-PRIG OF SIMIAN VANITY
SNEAK AND SWOT OF THE SCHOOL-ROOM
IMBERB (or Berbed when in Belsize)-PEDANT

- PRACTICAL JOKER
- DANDY
- CURATE

BLAST all products of Phlegmatic cold
Life of LOOKER-ON.
CURSE
SNOBBERY
(disease of femininity)
FEAR OF RIDICULE
(arch vice of Inactive, sleepy)
PLAY
STYLISM
of this LYMPHATIC finished
(we admit in every sense finished)
VEGETABLE HUMANITY.
OH BLAST FRANCE

- pig plagiarism
- BELLY
- SLIPPERS
- POODLE TEMPER
- BAD MUSIC

SENTIMENTAL GALLIC GUSH
SENSATIONALISM
FUSSINESS.

PARISIAN PAROCHIALISM.

Complacent young man,
so much respect for Papa
and his son !—Oh !—Papa
is wonderful: but all papas
are!

BLAST

APERITIFS (Parnots, Amers picon)
Bad change
Naively seductive Houri salon-
picture Cocottes
Slouching blue porters (can
carry a pantechnicon)
Stupidly rapacious people at
every step
Economy maniacs
Bouillon Kub (for being a bad pun)
PARIS.

- Clap-trap Heaven of amative German professor.
- Ubiquitous lines of silly little trees.
- Arcs de Triomphe.
- Imperturbable, endless prettiness.
- Large empty cliques, higher up.
- Bad air for the individual.

BLAST
MECCA OF THE AMERICAN
because it is not other side of Suez Canal, instead of an
afternoon's ride from London.

SOURCE: *Manifestos: A Century of Isms,* edited by Mary Ann Caws. University of Nebraska Press, 2011. Copyright © 1914 Wyndham Lewis, © 2008 Whyndham Lewis Memorial Trust (a registered charity).

that is "scour[ed]" and "trim[med]" free from the past. In a gesture that recalls the role of hired German soldiers in the American Revolutionary War, the barber is a specifically "Hessian (or Silesian) expert" who "correct[s] the grotesque anachronisms of our physique."

Lewis reinforces this sense of nonpartisan art-for-hire by both blessing and blasting many of the same targets. England is blasted first for the "sins and infections" of its weather, which conspires with global climate patterns "to make us mild." A few pages later, England is blessed for its seafarers, the "restless machines" of its numerous ports, and its "cold magnanimous delicate gauche fanciful stupid Englishmen." Typical of "Blast," the stance taken on England depends not on any allegiance to the nation as such but to the degree to which each of the two Englands mentioned reflects Vorticist ideals. Here, as elsewhere, states William C. Wees in "Ezra Pound as a Vorticist," the essay juxtaposes an "attack" on "mildness, softness, compromise, nature" with a celebration of "harshness, extremes, violence, the present, machinery" in the same object.

and Vorticism, Archie Loss observes in "*Vile Bodies,* Vorticism, and Italian Futurism" that for many critics circa World War I, "Cubism, Futurism, and Vorticism blended together to form a common aesthetic vision." The Vorticist penchant for glibly violent imagery was another chilling factor for contemporary audiences, as World War I followed the publication of "Blast" by only a year. For example, Lewis's call for "a laugh like a bomb" was sharply rebuked in "The Death of Futurism" by John Cournos, who, in announcing the death of futurism (and thereby perpetuating its conflation with Vorticism), considered the "masculomaniac" aggressiveness of "Blast" to be a blithe expression of peacetime ignorance.

At a greater historical remove, "Blast" assumed importance as the prototypical example in Lewis's own long line of manifesto writings, which (as for few artists since) constituted a vital and significant portion of his work. Hanna notes that Lewis had effectively turned the manifesto into a genre of its own for British authors and artists of his time. However, as he also observes, Lewis kept "blasting" well after the initial manifesto and, in fact, referred to many of his subsequent polemical writings as "blasts." Lewis seldom used the term "manifesto" for his work after Vorticism, but his chilly exchanges throughout the late 1920s with editors of the Paris-based *transition* are, for Hanna, just one instance of the genre's recurring importance to the painter and novelist.

"Blast" has also come to be seen as a watershed for the manifesto form in the English language. In "The Manifest Professional: Manifestos and Modernist Legitimation," Johanna E. Vondeling calls the essay a crucial vehicle for the "legitimation" of modernist arts movements and suggests that "Blast" serves as a means of establishing the professionalism and critical authority of the Vorticists. Moreover, Vondeling notes the document's importance in differentiating Vorticism (for its adherents) not only from movements of the past but also from contemporary rivals, whom Lewis criticized as either undisciplined reactionaries or plagiarists of earlier ideas. In "'Chaos Invading Concept': *Blast* as a Native Theory of Promotional Culture," Paige Reynolds sheds light on a different relationship between "Blast" and print culture, calling to readers' attention the text's complicated stance toward commercial advertisements. Reynolds acknowledges Lewis's sometimes heavy-handed "blasting" of the bourgeois "art" of self-promotion, but she also sees "Blast" as being grounded in the style of the newspaper ad, as a prescient appropriation of a commonplace visual language. For Lewis and his contemporaries, Reynolds suggests, such typographical choices were a means of reasserting agency in the face of an increasingly market-driven artistic culture.

Front cover of issue no. 2 of *Blast* magazine, featuring a woodcut by Wyndham Lewis. © THE WYNDHAM LEWIS MEMORIAL TRUST/THE BRIDGEMAN ART LIBRARY

The language of "Blast" is often gleeful, bordering on manic. The text appears in many places to be a conscious and ironic reworking, sometimes a parody, of the enthusiasm of the futurists. This is evident in the many lists Lewis employs, which often jump from abstract qualities to objects to personal names, demanding of the reader both interpretive and literal saccades. A similar energy is on display in the strangeness of Lewis's proposed response to England's (blasted) climate: "Let us once more wear the ermine of the north. WE BELIEVE in the existence of this USEFUL LITTLE CHEMIST in our midst!" In a further example, taken from Lewis's blessing of English humor, anaphora also contributes to the essay's sense of dynamism: "Bless this hysterical WALL built round the EGO. Bless the solitude of LAUGHTER. Bless the separating, ungregarious BRITISH GRIN."

CRITICAL DISCUSSION

Preliminary reactions to "Blast" were limited by confusion among literary and art critics as to the difference between Vorticism and other movements. Examining the relationship between Italian futurism

BIBLIOGRAPHY

Sources

Cournos, John. "The Death of Futurism." *Egoist* 4.1 (1917): 6-7. *Modernist Journals Project.* Web. 21 Aug. 2012.

Hanna, Julian. "Blasting after *Blast*: Wyndham Lewis's Late Manifestos." *Journal of Modern Literature* 31.1 (2007): 124-35. *JSTOR.* Web. 21 Aug. 2012.

Loss, Archie. "*Vile Bodies,* Vorticism, and Italian Futurism." *Journal of Modern Literature* 18.1 (1992): 155-64. Print.

Reynolds, Paige. "'Chaos Invading Concept': *Blast* as a Native Theory of Promotional Culture." *Twentieth Century Literature* 46.2 (2000): 238-68. Print.

Vondeling, Johanna E. "The Manifest Professional: Manifestos and Modernist Legitimation." *College Literature* 27.2 (2000): 127-45. *JSTOR.* Web. 21 Aug. 2012.

Wees, William C. "Ezra Pound as a Vorticist." *Wisconsin Studies in Contemporary Literature* 6.1 (1965): 56-72. *JSTOR.* Web. 21 Aug. 2012.

Further Reading

Dasenbrock, Reed Way. *The Literary Vorticism of Ezra Pound and Wyndham Lewis: Towards the Condition of Painting.* Baltimore: Johns Hopkins UP, 1985. Print.

Edwards, Paul, ed. *Blast: Vorticism 1914-1918.* Burlington: Ashgate, 2000. Print.

Henkle, Roger B. "The 'Advertised' Self: Wyndham Lewis' Satire." *NOVEL: A Forum on Fiction* 13.1 (1979): 95-108. *JSTOR.* Web. 21 Aug. 2012.

Materer, Timothy. *Vortex: Pound, Eliot, and Lewis.* Ithaca: Cornell UP, 1979. Print.

Morrisson, Mark. "*Blast*: An Introduction." *Modernist Journals Project.* Brown University, n.d. Web. 21 Aug. 2012.

Rae, Patricia. "From Mystical Gaze to Pragmatic Game: Representations of Truth in Vorticist Art." *ELH* 56.3 (1989): 689-720. *JSTOR.* Web. 21 Aug. 2012.

Michael Hartwell

The Business of Poetry

Marsden Hartley

❖ *Key Facts*

Time Period:
Early 20th Century

Movement/Issue:
Aesthetics; World War I

Place of Publication:
United States

Language of Publication:
English

OVERVIEW

"The Business of Poetry," published in the December 1919 issue of *Poetry* magazine, is a brief essay in which American poet and painter Marsden Hartley disavows the emotional, autobiographical tendencies he sees as weakening contemporary verse. In their place, Hartley argues for an art reliant on intellect and a focused, deliberate application of technique. The author draws several comparisons between the poetry he finds effective and the finely engineered technological structures of his time, noting that in both cases great precision is essential to make the work "go." Connecting the work to be done in literature with the accomplishments of modern painters, Hartley declares that technical expertise—"an eye with a brain"—is the essential quality for strong poetry.

Hartley's essay missed inclusion in *Adventures in the Arts* (1921), his major collection of nonfiction from the post-World War I years, and evidently attracted little notice during the author's lifetime. In posthumous criticism, "The Business of Poetry" was initially overshadowed by Hartley's numerous essays on painting but, in the late twentieth century, the essay came to be regarded as a significant milestone in Hartley's literary life. Still, as the manifesto of an artist better known as a painter than as a poet, "The Business of Poetry" is now generally critiqued (in an association the author himself repeatedly suggests) in the context of Hartley's painting career. Scholarly discussions of Hartley's essay have varied widely in their claims for its importance to his later work: some see the "machine aesthetic" it espouses as a fleeting phase for Hartley, while others regard the essay's concern with clear-sightedness as a lifelong ideal toward which the artist strove.

HISTORICAL AND LITERARY CONTEXT

"The Business of Poetry" critiques an expressionistic tendency that, prior to World War I, had been widespread and fully accepted in both literature and painting. In the early 1910s, an emphasis on personality and originality could be seen among thriving metropolitan communities of avant-garde artists; arts circles in New York, Paris, Berlin, and elsewhere represented a variety of movements that generally privileged artists' subjectivity over fidelity to fact. In painting, this tendency was noticeable in the works of the cubists and expressionists, who each in their way sought to capture the emotional reality of a subject. In literature, the experimental poet Gertrude Stein and her Paris salon, for example, attracted writers who expressed the moment with emotion.

World War I caused many artists, including Hartley, to rethink their relationship to the highly subjective work of their prewar years. Hartley had himself participated in these earlier trends, having spent time in Stein's Paris circle and later, in Berlin, with such figures as Russian-born abstract painter Wassily Kandinsky. Indeed, Hartley produced "Portrait of a German Officer" (1914), arguably his most famous painting, at the height of his own expressionist phase. He returned from Germany in 1915, with the war already under way, and his friend the American photographer Alfred Stieglitz quickly organized a showing of the painter's new work. Its militaristic German themes, coupled with the tepid reactions of art critics, however, made for a mediocre reception at best. This disappointing experience, and Hartley's subsequent wish to suppress subjective interpretation of his work, appears to have been a main trigger for Hartley's shift in aesthetic, as well as for his departure to the American Southwest—albeit with some of his colleagues—where he would spend years painting not abstract portraits but expressionist desert landscapes. "The Business of Poetry" was written, as Hartley relates, while "riding through Arizona in the Pullman," en route to the beginning of his Southwestern period.

Compared to the exuberant manifestos that characterized prewar arts movements such as vorticism and Italian futurism, Hartley's work is sedate in tone and modest in its claims. "The Business of Poetry" establishes its place in history not by reference to a manifesto tradition per se but by drawing on famous poets who had served as a similar bridge for their own time. For instance, Hartley invokes a maxim, set down by the Austrian poet Rainer Maria Rilke, that "the poet, in order to depict life, must take no part in it"; while the quotation itself transparently serves Hartley's purpose, it also links his proposals to a major poetic mediator between late romanticism and early modernism. Reaching further back, Hartley also mentions the nineteenth-century English poet Francis Thompson as one who "had a wing in his brain, but he had feet also." Hartley's call for a "mechanics" of poetry thus seems contiguous with great literary voices of the past.

Nonetheless, there is little evidence that "The Business of Poetry" had any great impact on the course of literary modernism, though Hartley redoubled his claims in a 1928 essay on "Art and the Personal Life." Indeed, some of Hartley's predictions, read in hindsight, seem to have been thwarted utterly: witness his confident declaration that "the age of confession perished with the [mid-nineteenth-century] Parnassians." Hartley himself, at the end of his career, turned back toward the emotional expressionism that had been present in his early artistic works. In the twenty-first century, the essay is important chiefly to specialists in Hartley scholarship.

THEMES AND STYLE

"The Business of Poetry" posits an essential dichotomy between two broad styles of poetry (and of art more generally): an emotional, intuitive poetics predicated on "personality," which Hartley advises readers to avoid, and a more intellectual approach to craft that aims "to have an eye with brain in it." Hartley explains this distinction in a variety of ways throughout the essay's seven pages, making the aphoristic claim that "[The poet] must see first and feel afterward, or perhaps not feel at all" and maintaining that "real art comes from the brain, as we know, not the soul." Hartley also suggests that painters have preceded poets in their understanding of this fact and that writers stand to learn a great deal from studying painters' approaches to their subjects.

Rhetorically, Hartley delineates the artistic landscape as one of conflict between nostalgia for the romantic past, which is impossible to recover, and immersion in the present. The virtues of the latter approach are symbolized throughout the essay by Hartley's invocation of mechanical and industrial imagery. He insists that the "art of the time is the art of the mechanism of the time" and that, consequently, "we cannot feel as we do and attempt [English romantic poet John] Keats's simplicities, or Keats's lyricism even." But the problem of creating better art is, for Hartley, neither simply one of subject matter nor generational changes in style: Hartley wishes to liberate even "hackneyed words, like 'rose' and 'lily'," from their "Swinburnian encrustations," in which melodiousness and emotional imagery was honored. The poets Hartley champions produce works that are "structured" like industrial fans or airplane motors; they are "master mechanics in the business of poetry." Hartley even suggests that technology itself has set the terms of the new poetics, closing with the claim that "we are not moonlit strummers now: we are gunpointers and sky-climbers."

Hartley's roll call of successful modern artists emphasizes painters as well as poets; moreover, painterly images and a concern for the pictorial pervade

Marsden Hartley, author of "The Business of Poetry."
© EVERETT COLLECTION INC/ALAMY

Hartley's essay in spite of its title. One major line of Hartley's argument is that, despite a contemporary critique by American author Louis Untermeyer, an emphasis on visual imagery is a legitimate element of poetry, not a "brutal" or unimaginative step backward; the alternative, Hartley warns, is recourse to the "old-fashioned stimuli" of "preoccupation [and] blocked introspection." Speaking of American poet Walt Whitman's tendency toward "simple frankness," Hartley says that one "finds him presenting the picture" of his poetic subject. The books of American poet and novelist Edgar Lee Masters are, likewise, described as "shades of the same powerful grey" as his *Spoon River Anthology* (1915). For Hartley, finally, it is the "eye" and not the ear that matters most.

CRITICAL DISCUSSION

"The Business of Poetry" was largely unremarked upon in the years after its publication and even throughout Hartley's life. By the time of the author's death in 1943, history had confirmed what many of Hartley's contemporaries had suspected: that he would be much better known as a painter than as a poet. Perhaps as a consequence, this early essay was lost—for many scholars—in the sheer volume of later nonfiction works that treated painting more directly. Major early biographies of Hartley, such as Elizabeth McCausland's 1952 study, tend to mention the work mainly in the interest of bibliographic completeness.

In the late twentieth century, critical reappraisals of Hartley began to relate his literary essays to the stylistic trajectory of his paintings, while extending comparatively little attention to his poetry. Consequently,

PRIMARY SOURCE

"THE BUSINESS OF POETRY"

I am riding through Arizona in the Pullman. I am thinking of the business of poetry. Every other man attends to the details of business, if he is a good business man. A train is mostly business men....

Poets must, it seems to me, learn how to use a great many words before they can know how to use a few skillfully. Journalistic verbiage is not fluency. Alfred Kreymborg agrees with me that poets do not write prose often enough. I speak mostly of the poets who do not write with the sense of volume in their brevities. Brevity of all things demands intensity, or better say tensity. Tensity comes from experience. The poet must see the space for the word, and then see to it the word occupies it. It is almost mechanical science these days, it would seem—the fitting of parts together so the whole produces a consistent continuity. Subjects never matter, excepting when they are too conspicuously autobiographical. *"Moi–même, quand même"* is attractive enough, but there are so many attractive ways of presenting it.

Personal handling counts for more than personal confessions. We can even learn to use hackneyed words, like "rose" and "lily", relieving them of Swinburnian encrustations. We can relieve imagery from this banality.

Poets cannot, as aspiring poets, depend, it seems to me, ever upon the possible natural "flow" that exists in themselves. Poets have work to do for the precision of simplicity, and for the gift of volume in simplicity. It is the business of good poetry to show natural skill as well as natural impetus. Some poets would like to say the former is more important. It surprises one a deal how much even the better poets effuse, or rely upon their momentary theories. The subject calls for handling, not for enthusiams. Painters of this time have learned this; or ought to have learned it by now, with the excellent examples of the time. Personality is a state, it is not the consummate virtue. It begins, but it does not finish anything. We have eventually to insert in the middle spaces all we can of real ability. What is much needed is solidity,

postmodern interpretations of "The Business of Poetry" frequently transpose its claims for writing to the realm of the visual. Dickran Tashjian, in his article "Marsden Hartley and the Southwest" (1980), takes what now appears as a moderate stance on "The Business of Poetry," noting that Hartley's emphasis on unemotional "seeing" was an essential value for Hartley's Southwestern period, in which he produced work more realistic and less abstract than he had in Europe during the 1910s. Gail R. Scott, in her 1988 biographical study of the painter, makes a much larger claim for the essay: she suggests that Hartley "encapsulated his goals as an artist" in "The Business of Poetry" and that he "articulat[ed] in words what would take him another twenty years to achieve in paint." Robert Creeley, introducing Hartley's *Collected Poems* in 1989, provides a rare assessment of "The Business of Poetry" in its original literary context, citing the work as an example of the "apparent ambivalence as to whether one's art is deliberately or intuitively made," a theme that Hartley would develop in subsequent essays.

Recent scholarly claims for "The Business of Poetry" as a key to Hartley's paintings are much more attenuated, when they are offered at all.

Heather Hole, whose book *Marsden Hartley and the West* (2007) focuses on Hartley's Southwestern landscape art, exemplifies this cautious approach. She considers "The Business of Poetry" evidence of just one of the many "postures" that Hartley "tried on" throughout his lifetime, often concomitant with shifts in both his visual style and his choice of subject. Viewed in this way, the early essay is no more or less definitive than Hartley's preoccupation with Native American ceremony in 1920, his declarations as a Dadaist in 1921, or his subsequent, strident return to the "eye with a brain" aesthetic in 1928.

BIBLIOGRAPHY

Sources

Creeley, Robert. "Foreword to *The Collected Poems of Marsden Hartley.*" *The Collected Essays of Robert Creeley.* Berkeley: U of California P, 1989. Web. 16 August 2012.

Hole, Heather. *Marsden Hartley and the West: The Search for an American Modernism.* New Haven: Yale UP, 2007. Print.

Scott, Gail R. *Marsden Hartley.* New York: Abbeville, 1988. Print.

even of sentiment, combined with efficacy of form. This might be served as an injunction to some of the "girl" poets. Poets have not so much to invent themselves as to create themselves, and creation is of course a process of development.

…

The fierce or fiery spaciousness is the quality we look for in a real poem, and coupled with that the requisite iron work according to the personal tastes of the poet. The mere gliding of musical sequences is not sufficient. Poetry is not essentially or necessarily just vocalism. It may have plot or it may be plotless—that is for the poet to decide: what is wanted is some show of mechanistic precision such as the poet can devise. He must know his motive as well as himself, and to invent the process of self–creation is no little task. That is the first principle to be learned by the versifiers. Poetry is not only a tool for the graving of the emotions; nor is it an ivory trinket. It calls for an arm. We need not be afraid of muscularity or even of "brutality."

…

There is no less need of organization even if we do not employ the established metre and rhyme. Likewise, if a poet must state his or her personal history, he or she may be asked to be as brief as possible. It is easier to read epigrams than to read the diary, no matter how short the latter may be. The age of confession perished with the Parnassians. We are a vastly other type of soul—if we are soul at all, which I keenly doubt. The poet's attitude then, for today, is toward the outside. This does not necessarily imply surface. We present ourselves in spite of ourselves. We are most original when we are most like life. Life is the natural thing. Interpretation is the factitious. Nature is always variable. To have an eye with brain in it—that is, or rather would be, the poetic millenium. We are not moonlit strummers now: we are gun–pointers and sky–climbers.

SOURCE: *Poetry,* vol. 15, no. 3, December 1919, 152–158.

Tashjian, Dickran. "Marsden Hartley and the Southwest: A Ceremony for Our Vision, a Fiction for the Eye." *Arts Magazine* 54 (1980): 127-31. Print.

Further Reading

Hartley, Marsden. *Adventures in the Arts: Informal Chapters on Painters, Vaudeville, and Poets.* New York: Boni and Liveright, 1921. *Project Gutenberg.* Web. 16 August 2012.

Kaladjian, Walter, ed. *The Cambridge Companion to American Modernism.* Cambridge: Cambridge UP, 2005. Print.

Kornhauser, Elizabeth Mankin, ed. *Marsden Hartley: American Modernist.* New Haven: Yale UP, 2002. Print.

McCausland, Elizabeth. *Marsden Hartley.* Minneapolis: U of Minnesota P, 1952. Print.

McDonnell, Patricia. *Marsden Hartley: American Modern.* Seattle: U of Washington P, 1997. Print.

Tashjian, Dickran. *William Carlos Williams and the American Scene.* Berkeley: U of California P, 1979. Print.

Weinberg, Jonathan. *Speaking for Vice: Homosexuality in the Art of Charles Demuth, Marsden Hartley, and the First American Avant-Garde.* New Haven: Yale UP, 1995. Print.

Michael Hartwell

COMPOSITION AS EXPLANATION

Gertrude Stein

✛ *Key Facts*

Time Period:
Early 20th Century

Movement/Issue:
Aesthetics; Avant-
gardism; Cubism

Place of Publication:
England

**Language of
Publication:**
English

OVERVIEW

Written by Gertrude Stein, "Composition as Explanation" (1926) explores the relationship between time, narrative, and technique, and argues for art that invents new forms to inhabit and express the present moment. Although Stein had been publishing fiction since 1909, when her novel *Three Lives* appeared, "Composition as Explanation" was her first work of criticism. Initially read aloud as a lecture to a Cambridge University literary society, the essay explains Stein's idiosyncratic writing style. Deeply informed and inspired by the innovations of cubism, her prose is marked by its repetitive syntax, plain diction, and extreme fragmentation. Her work was widely considered strange and difficult, but it became increasingly well known in the mid-1920s. The essay offers an argument that composition is "what is seen" and that prose must find forms in which to capture that composition.

When it was first read aloud, "Composition as Explanation" generated divided responses from Stein's audience. While many were impressed by the originality of her thought and style, others were suspicious of her seemingly paradoxical and nonsensical argument. Soon after it was delivered, the essay was published in the United States and Europe, and there was a rapid growth in interest in Stein's writings. Over the next two decades, as she published numerous works to widespread acclaim, her reputation soared. By the early 1930s she had become an unlikely literary celebrity. Today, "Composition as Explanation" is considered a key to the revolutionary prose innovations that made her so highly regarded. Although not a conventional manifesto, the work is a cogent declaration of her literary vision and ambition.

HISTORICAL AND LITERARY CONTEXT

"Composition as Explanation" responds to the European artistic milieu in the early twentieth century, when cubism and other modernist movements were radically questioning and rethinking artistic convention in response to rapidly changing economic, social, and technological realities. Although Stein grew up in the United States and studied medicine at Johns Hopkins University, she left for Paris in 1903 to pursue writing. While there, she became personally involved with many of France's leading painters, including Pablo Picasso, Henri Matisse, Juan Gris, and Paul Cézanne. She became an important collector of their pieces and was deeply influenced by their compositional, formal, and technical innovations, applying them to her own work as a writer of poetry and prose. According to Bettina L. Knapp in the biography *Gertrude Stein* (1990), "As Picasso, George Braque, and Gris created their collages, so Stein generated her own reality in the word, which she viewed as a *thing* in and of itself."

At the time "Composition as Explanation" was written in 1926, Stein's renown as a writer was beginning to grow. While she had already published several books that would later be recognized as seminal, including *Three Lives* and *Tender Buttons* (1914), it was in 1925 that Stein's masterpiece, *The Making of Americans,* appeared in its complete form. She had worked on the nine-hundred-page novel for nearly a decade, completing it in 1911. When the book was finally published, it brought her newfound fame and critical acclaim, which led to invitations to lecture at the literary societies of Cambridge and Oxford. She was reluctant to accept these offers but did so at the insistence of friends and admirers who argued that the lectures would help her expand her audience.

"Composition as Explanation" draws on the innovations of various modernist writers, but the work of pragmatist philosopher William James had the greatest influence on Stein's theory of writing. As scholar Robert Bartlett Hass writes in his introduction to *What Are Masterpieces* (1970), "Composition as Explanation" "is no mere exposition of Stein literary methods; here, rather, is a vital and uncompromising commentary upon the change in categories wrought within that Mind which has grown naturally to conceive and accept the Pragmatic attitude." This pragmatic attitude, as described by James, entails accepting the transitory, fluctuating nature of reality. The notion that everything is in a state of change informs Stein's central premise that composition is way of seeing life as an ongoing event.

"Composition as Explanation" provided the foundation for Stein's later writings on the theory and process of writing. In 1931 she published *How to Write,* a volume of essays, continuing the exploration of composition, language, and grammar that begin in "Composition as Explanation." Five years later, her essay "What Are Master-Pieces and Why Are There So Few of Them?" was delivered as a lecture. In this essay, she furthers her thoughts on the nature of important and enduring writing, arguing that a masterpiece "may be un-welcome but it is never dull." Today she is considered one of modernism's most important prose writers, and "Composition as Explanation" commands significant scholarly interest as a key to the radical style she developed over her long career.

THEMES AND STYLE

The central theme of "Composition as Explanation" is that composition is a way of seeing the ever-changing present and that writing is a means of recording the flux of reality. Written in a refracted style that is the signature of all Stein's prose, "Composition as Explanation" explores the relationship between the time in which something is composed and the time within the composition. She writes, "The time of the composition is a natural thing and the time in the composition is a natural thing it is a natural thing and it is a contemporary thing." In the essay, time is "a continuous present a beginning again and again and again and again." She defends her method of fragmentary and repetitive composition as a faithful rendering of the "continuous present" in which she lives. Further, this rendering is not merely accurate but also "wonderfully beautiful."

The essay achieves its rhetorical effect by employing its compositional technique rather than merely explaining it. Throughout the essay, Stein writes in a fragmentary and repetitive way that demonstrates her vision of the contemporary present she inhabits. She argues, "The composition is the thing seen by every one living in the living that they are doing, they are the composing of the composition that at the time they are living is the composition of the time in which they are living." By insistently repeating the words "living" and "composition" in this long, sinuous sentence, Stein intertwines these concepts, thereby illustrating her point that composition is a mode of inhabiting life's continuous present.

Stylistically, "Composition as Explanation" is distinguished by its effusive openness. Although initially delivered as a university lecture, the essay overturns the expectations accompanying an academic context. Rather than offering a formal disputation of her process and theory of writing, Stein creates a text that bursts through the boundaries of conventional argumentation. In so doing, she provides an implicit critique of convention while also presenting a radical alternative to it. She does not ignore literary precedent as much as she confronts it. Without apologizing for her iconoclasm, she acknowledges the challenges posed by her style: "If every one were not so indolent they would realize that beauty is beauty even

GERTRUDE STEIN: LITERARY INNOVATOR

Gertrude Stein was born in 1874 in Allegheny City, Pennsylvania, a town that is now part of Pittsburgh. As an infant, she lived in Europe, but she grew up in Oakland, California, and Baltimore, Maryland. In 1893 she enrolled in Radcliffe College, then the women's college of Harvard University. While there, she studied with philosopher and psychologist William James, whose pragmatic ideas about the nature of reality would prove central to her later artistic vision. In 1896 she published her first work, a psychology paper titled "Normal Motor Automatism." After completing her undergraduate work, she enrolled in the Johns Hopkins Medical School but did not graduate.

She then turned her attention toward the arts and began writing fiction. In 1903 she moved to Paris, where she lived with her brother Leo. They started buying the paintings of local artists such as Pierre-Auguste Renoir, Paul Gauguin, Paul Cézanne, and other impressionists before the artists were widely recognized. The artists, and their compositional innovations, profoundly influenced Stein's writing. Although she had written several traditional stories, she began to change her approach. The result was her first book, *Three Lives* (1909), a collection of novellas that began her lifelong project of demolishing the conventions of fiction as narrative and point of view.

when it is irritating and stimulating not only when it is accepted and classic." Stein's style serves both as an argument for and evidence of her work's validity.

CRITICAL DISCUSSION

When "Composition as Explanation" was first delivered in 1926, it received mixed reaction. According to an anonymous reviewer in the *Times Literary Supplement,* as presented by Kirk Curnutt in *The Critical Response to Gertrude Stein* (2000), "[I]n many ways her essay is of great interest, though as an explanation and justification of the writings which follow it, it may be deficient." According to John Malcolm Brinnin in *The Third Rose: Gertrude Stein and Her World* (1959), the Cambridge lecture was "a resonant success," while the response at Oxford was somewhat more contentious. Brinnin includes an account from writer Osbert Sitwell, who attended Stein's talk and recalled "a certain commotion rising" during it. When the essay appeared in print, it garnered a glowing review from Elliot H. Paul in the *Chicago Tribune*'s Paris edition. As conveyed by Curnutt, Paul writes that the essay "makes important contributions to the literature of aesthetics" and recommends it as "good to be studied."

Stein's published output grew considerably, as did her reputation, following her reading of "Composition as Explanation" in Cambridge and Oxford. Soon after

Sir Edward Grey, 1st Viscount Grey of Fallodon, who was Britain's foreign secretary from 1905 to 1916. In *Composition as Explanation,* author Gertrude Stein refers to a remark by Lord Grey about war, which she relates to composition and sense of time. PRIVATE COLLECTION/ THE BRIDGEMAN ART LIBRARY

Much recent scholarship has focused on the essay's place in the development of semiotics. In a 1978 essay for *Twentieth Century Literature,* Bruce Bassoff writes that "Composition as Explanation" "is a kind of premonitory condensation of some of the salient principles of semiotic analysis from Walter Benjamin to Claude Leví-Strauss." Commentators have also examined the essay's discussion of the relationship between time and composition. Robert Barlett Hass, in his introduction to *What Are Masterpieces?* (1970), calls Stein's argument "the epoch which conditions the life of the artist also conditions the character of the art which he makes." According to Hass, a composition "is dependent upon [the artist's] moment of seeing; it is dependent upon his recognition of the particular character of the composition in which he lives his life."

BIBLIOGRAPHY

Sources

Bassoff, Bruce. "Gertrude Stein's 'Composition as Explanation.'" *Twentieth Century Literature* 24.1 (1978): 76-80. *JSTOR.* Web. 12 Sept. 2012.

Brinnin, John Malcolm. *The Third Rose: Gertrude Stein and Her World.* Boston: Little, Brown, 1959. Print.

Curnutt, Kirk. *The Critical Response to Gertrude Stein.* Westport: Greenwood, 2000. Print.

Dubnick, Randa. *The Structure of Obscurity: Gertrude Stein, Language, and Cubism.* Urbana: U of Illinois P, 1984. Print.

Hass, Robert Barlett. Introduction. *What Are Masterpieces?* by Gertrude Stein. New York: Pitman, 1970. Print.

Knapp, Bettina L. *Gertrude Stein.* New York: Continuum, 1990. Print.

Stein, Gertrude. *What Are Masterpieces?* New York: Pitman, 1970. Print.

Further Reading

Daniel, Lucy. *Gertrude Stein: Critical Lives.* London: Reaktion, 2009. Print.

Mitrano, G.F. *Gertrude Stein: Woman without Qualities.* Burlington: Ashgate, 2005. Print.

Neuman, Shirley, and Ira B. Nadel, eds. *Gertrude Stein and the Making of Literature.* Boston: Northeastern UP, 1988. Print.

Watson, Dana Cairns. *Gertrude Stein and the Essence of What Happens.* Nashville: Vanderbilt UP, 2005. Print.

Will, Barbara. *Gertrude Stein, Modernism, and the Problem of "Genius."* Edinburgh: Edinburgh UP, 2000. Print.

the lectures, the essay was published and appeared in the prestigious American journal *Dial.* Over the course of the next decade, Stein published numerous novels, plays, and other prose works, and became a literary celebrity both in the United States and in Europe. Her *Autobiography of Alice B. Toklas* became an unlikely best seller in 1933. Throughout her long career, which lasted until her death in 1967, "Composition as Explanation" continued to inform the way critics and general readers viewed her radical aesthetic project. Today the essay is the subject of a body of criticism that has considered its legacy in aesthetic, literary, and semiotic terms.

Theodore McDermott

EXPRESSIONISM

Hermann Bahr

OVERVIEW

Written by Austrian cultural critic, playwright, and artist Hermann Bahr, *Expressionism* (1914) seeks to both explain and elevate the expressionist movement. The book was published when an intellectual war was being waged over which modern art movement would define the age. Responding to the combination of excitement and angst felt during the late nineteenth and early twentieth centuries, modernist artists and thinkers saw art in a romantic light. For the modernist, art could potentially cure the world's ills—provided it combined enough innovation with true genius. Bahr had long been an observer-participant in various modernist movements, and he came to see expressionism as the vehicle with the greatest potential for transforming art and the world.

Among participants, observers, and detractors, modernist movements have never had stable definitions, and expressionism is no exception. Initially, Bahr's book was hailed in some quarters as a clarifying work. Critics, however, questioned his fitness to define a movement that some people viewed as French and others German (by far its strongest national affiliation today). Indeed, subsequent discussions of expressionism in general, and German expressionism in particular, have often ignored Bahr or mention him only in passing. His modest artistic talent, propensity to switch allegiances between various artistic movements, and Austrian origins kept him out of the established group of expressionists. Yet for those studying modernism in broader terms, particularly its continental manifestations, Bahr's work aligns with a tradition of artistic writings in modernism and provides a useful understanding of expressionism.

HISTORICAL AND LITERARY CONTEXT

The chief antagonist in Bahr's *Expressionism* is the earlier impressionist movement, which dominated modern art in the late nineteenth and early twentieth centuries. In the book's defining statement on the subject, the section subtitled "Expressionism," Bahr aligns impressionism with the problems of the modern era, those aspects of life that constrain the human soul. Here Bahr reveals the tone of the age: the prevailing belief that the modern era has profoundly limited the individual and the romantic feeling among artists that their work could improve the trajectory of civilization. Bahr's ideas on the matter came from a unique perspective. He began his career devoted to the notion of a distinct Austrian culture but was later profoundly influenced by German and French art. This experience gave him a broader perspective on modern art, enabling him to see expressionism in more expansive terms that crossed national boundaries.

Despite his international outlook, Bahr's primary influences were Austrian and German, an important attribute given the book's publication under the shadow of World War I. Impressionism was largely viewed as a French movement, and France was among Germany's opponents in the war. Thus, Bahr traces impressionism's countermovement, expressionism, from German philosophers Friedrich Nietzsche and, in particular, Johann Wolfgang von Goethe. Bahr's perspective is not militaristic or pro-war; nevertheless, *Expressionism* emphasizes the importance of German cultural and artistic production to modern art. Notably, Bahr admits limitations in expressionism as well, revealing the complicated, often bleak perspective shared by Germans and Austrians on their contemporary cultures and the modern world.

Expressionism follows a trend of artistic writings in the modernist era. However, unlike Wyndham Lewis, Filippo Tommaso Marinetti, or Ezra Pound, Bahr propounded a movement he did not found and to which he had only tangential connections. On the one hand, *Expressionism* appears less biased by a desire to promote the author's own artistic movement. On the other, Bahr sometimes seems like an artistic dilettante, hopping from novelty to novelty. Noting the cluster of "isms" epitomizing modern art—for example, vorticism, futurism, and imagism—particularly prior to World War I, *Expressionism* traces a trajectory of art that strives to move ever closer to an innovative way of representing human experience. Appearing as it did at the beginning of the war, a borderline in modernism, Bahr's work not only touts expressionism but also characterizes a profound transition away from impressionism and realism and toward this new depiction of reality.

Among scholars of expressionism, particularly in the United States and Britain, Bahr's critical and artistic works often seem to be an aberration unworthy of inclusion in analyses of the movement. His long

Key Facts

Time Period:
Early 20th Century

Movement/Issue:
Expressionism; Modernism; Aesthetics

Place of Publication:
Austria

Language of Publication:
German

JOHANN WOLFGANG VON GOETHE: THE ORIGINAL EXPRESSIONIST?

Johann Wolfgang von Goethe (1749-1832) is generally considered to be one of the world's great writers. American transcendentalist Ralph Waldo Emerson even included Goethe with William Shakespeare, Plato, and Napoleon Bonaparte in his list of "representative" men. Raised in a comfortable, bourgeois family, Goethe was encouraged by his mother to pursue his artistic ambitions, and he studied art and law. He had a prolific career, not only as an author but also as a naturalist, lawyer, and bureaucrat. His best-known literary works are the novels *The Sorrows of Young Werther* (1774) and *Wilhelm Meister's Apprenticeship* (1795-96) and the two-part play *Faust* (1808, 1832), wherein Goethe expresses his interest in alchemy and adds to the legacy of one of Western civilization's great stories. He is often attributed with beginning the genre of the *bildungsroman,* or novel of development. Goethe was also affiliated with the romantic Sturm und Drang movement, which celebrated Promethean restlessness in contrast to enlightenment rationality.

Rhetorically, when Bahr singled out Goethe as the original expressionist, he claimed a long and impressive artistic legacy for the movement. He also emphasized the importance of German literature and art to civilization and the modern world. Bahr's allegiance to expressionism ultimately waned, but his admiration for Goethe never did. Today Goethe remains a major figure in literary history.

and varied career prevents scholars from aligning him with any specific movement, style, or mode of thought, making it easy to ignore his thoughts on expressionism. Nevertheless, Bahr's treatise proves valuable to contemporary readers as a culminating definition of expressionism when following the trajectory of modern art up to that time. Further, his style exhibits some of the very tenets of expressionism his piece espouses, thereby aligning it with other modernist writings that formally represent their movement's ideologies in prose.

THEMES AND STYLE

Expressionism argues that the constraint put on the soul by modern life is reflected in its primary artistic movement at the time, impressionism. In contrast, expressionism attempts to break through modernity's barriers and express a true emotional experience. Bahr asserts: "Distress cries aloud; man cries out for his soul; this whole pregnant time is one great cry of anguish. Art too joins in, into the great darkness she too calls for help, she cries to the spirit: this is Expressionism." Expressionism emphasizes emotional truth over visual or factual truth and uses bold colors, surrealistic images, and disproportionate or abstract figures in order to shock the audience into experiencing the artist's feelings.

Bahr's piece uses several rhetorical strategies to explain the movement. First, he describes both impressionism and expressionism as physical, acting agents. Bahr argues that the "eye of the Impressionist only beholds, it does not speak; it hears the question but makes no response." In contrast, the expressionist "tears open the mouth of humanity; the time of its silence, the time of its listening is over—once more it seeks to give the spirit's reply." The physical metaphors are quite striking, making expressionism both a mirror of human experience and a sort of persona with which the reader can empathize. Second, Bahr establishes ethos and a lineage for expressionist art through frequent references to Nietzsche and Goethe. Both were recognized as geniuses of Western civilization; further, their German origins helped Bahr assert the importance of German expressionism to modern art. Third, Bahr repeats the phrase "This is the vital thing," an approach that emphasizes the importance of his argument. This repetition also serves to highlight the physical aspect of his argument about expressionism, such as when he writes, "This is the vital point—that man should find himself again…. All that we experience is but the strenuous battle between the soul and the machine for the possession of man."

Bahr's tone in *Expressionism* is impassioned. The rhetoric is sweeping, designed to stir emotion in the reader and to speak to the emotional experience of living in modernity. This style thereby fulfills the goals of expressionism to recreate an emotional response in the audience. Bahr declares: "Clouded by our earthly senses, we cannot behold [truth], but illumined by the divine spirit we can bear witness to her" through art. He breathes emotion into his prose, signaling the value he sees in expressionist art, encouraging the reader to feel as he feels and rejecting the stodgy restraints of traditional essay writing. In so doing, Bahr creates an expressionistic essay in which the style and tone illustrate his argument.

CRITICAL DISCUSSION

Because Bahr was an outside observer and proponent of expressionism rather than one of its major figures, it remains unclear what affect his text had on the movement's artists. However, his rhetorical acumen and his commitment to European avant-garde movements meant that he was uniquely situated to at least generally influence thinking on modern art. In "'Der grosse Überwinder': Hermann Bahr and the Rejection of Naturalism," Andrew Barker argues that Bahr served as a mentor and advocate for many of the younger writers and "clearly participates in the birth of German modernism as a whole." Bahr himself said that he was the first to use the term "modernism," a claim that Barker refutes while reaffirming Bahr's importance to the promotion of expressionism and other modernisms.

Opposite page:
Austrian artist Oscar Kokoschka's poster for his play Mörder, "Hoffnung der Frauen" (Murderer, Hope of Women). Kokoschka was one of the expressionist artists championed by Hermann Bahr. ERICH LESSING/ART RESOURCE, NY

Expressionism as a movement quickly became fractured, with Bahr and subsequent critics looping in older artists such as Goethe and Edvard Munch while many of the contemporary artists claimed they were not expressionists at all. Like most modernist movements, expressionism exceeds its defining characteristics. Thus, Bahr's text works less as a rubric by which we measure what is and is not expressionism and more as an expressionist statement in its own right. Reflecting Bahr's own argument in *Expressionism,* Victor Miesel asserts in *Voices of German Expressionism*: "Styles within the movement ranged from the representational to the non-objective, but all shared a common determination to subordinate form and nature to emotional and visionary experience."

Recent scholars tend to focus on resurrecting interest in Bahr as an important historical figure and critical thinker. In the most comprehensive study of Bahr to date, *Understanding Hermann Bahr,* Donald Daviau writes that with *Expressionism,* the author reveals how his transitory interest in the movement highlights his evolving engagement with artistic developments. Miesel notes how expressionism became particularly Germanic because, as he argues, "it was in Germany between 1900-1920 that subjectivity and emotionalism *in all the arts* became more widespread and accepted than anywhere else." Building on this concept, Donald Gordon contends in *Expressionism: Art and Idea* that the war profoundly impacted expressionist style through the "absurdity of the war situation itself, its destruction of commonly shared ideals, and its invasion of the personal lives of artists." Citing Bahr's hopeful call for a "miracle" that would revitalize the human experience, Gordon maintains, "But the hope for a miracle occurred precisely amid the 'great darkness.' It was the war experience itself against which any call for spiritual renewal had to be measured."

BIBLIOGRAPHY

Sources

Bahr, Hermann. "Expressionism." *Paths to the Present: Aspects of European Thought from Romanticism to Existentialism.* Ed. Eugen Weber. New York: Dodd Mead, 1960. 223-27. Print.

Barker, Andrew W. "'Der grosse Überwinder': Hermann Bahr and the Rejection of Naturalism." *Modern Language Review* 78.3 (1983): 617-30. *JSTOR.* Web. 12 Sept. 2012.

Daviau, Donald G. *Understanding Hermann Bahr.* St. Ingbert: Röhrig Universitätsverlag, 2002. Print.

Gordon, Donald E. *Expressionism: Art and Idea.* New Haven: Yale UP, 1987. Print.

Miesel, Victor H. *Voices of German Expressionism.* Englewood Cliffs: Prentice Hall, 1970. Print.

Further Reading

Barron, Stephanie, Wolfe Dieter Dube, and Palazzo Grassi, eds. *German Expressionism: Art and Society.* New York: Rizzoli, 1997. Print.

Caws, Mary Ann. *Manifesto: A Century of Isms.* Lincoln: U of Nebraska P, 2001. Print.

Daviau, Donald G. "Hermann Bahr and the Secessionist Art Movement in Vienna." *The Turn of the Century: German Art and Literature, 1890-1915.* Ed. Gerald Chapple and Hans H. Schulte. Bonn: Bouvier, 1981. 433-62. Print.

Donahue, Neil H., ed. *A Companion to the Literature of German Expressionism.* Rochester: Camden House, 2005. Print.

Elfe, Wolfgang, and James N. Hardin. *Twentieth Century German Dramatists, 1889-1918.* Detroit: Gale Research, 1992. Print.

Lloyd, Jill. *German Expressionism: Primitivism and Modernity.* New Haven: Yale UP, 1991. Print.

Segel, Harold B. *The Vienna Coffeehouse Wits, 1890-1938.* West Lafayette: Purdue UP, 1993. Print.

Sarah Stoeckl

GREEN BOX

Marcel Duchamp

OVERVIEW

Marcel Duchamp, a French-born artist, wrote the *Green Box* (1934) as a textual and diagrammatic companion to his mixed-media creation *Large Glass* (1923); together, the two components are titled *The Bride Stripped Bare by Her Bachelors, Even*. Disenfranchised with contemporary trends in the art world, particularly cubism, Duchamp sought a new mode of artistic production that would undermine both artists and critics who glorified retinal aesthetics. To this extent, the *Green Box* functions as an attack on the sensibilities of all artists, critics, and art lovers who adhere to traditional means of interacting with a work of art. Composed as a series of notes, drawings, poems, and calculations, *The Bride Stripped Bare* forces observers to engage the piece textually and conceptually as well as visually.

While traditionalists initially objected to *The Bride Stripped Bare,* several prominent figures in the art world championed the multiform artwork as a revolutionary experiment. The projects and studies that led to its final form, published as *The Box of 1914* (1914), inspired both the Dada and surrealist movements. Once completed, *The Bride*'s originality and disregard for convention found favor with abstract expressionists such as Robert Rauschenberg and Jasper Johns. Likewise, Sol LeWitt and artists associated with the conceptual art movement of the mid- to late twentieth century based their artistic theories on Duchamp's use of text and diagrams in order to outline the underlying concepts of his work. Today, *The Bride Stripped Bare* holds a place as a masterpiece of conceptual art and is considered to be a highlight of Duchamp's storied career.

HISTORICAL AND LITERARY CONTEXT

Duchamp's *Green Box,* as part of the larger work *The Bride Stripped Bare of Her Bachelors, Even,* responds to the cubist adherence to visual art forms and the manner in which they promoted an art-for-art's-sake mentality. Duchamp believed that the artists of his day had divorced their art from the religious, philosophical, and moral content that once bonded it to everyday society. However, his motives for creating *The Bride Stripped Bare* were also personal: when, in March 1912, the artist submitted his *Nude Descending a Staircase, No. 2* to a cubist exhibition at Salon des

Indépendants, Albert Gleizes of the Puteaux cubist group derided the piece for demonstrating symbolist tendencies. Duchamp's *The Bride Stripped Bare* also critiques the unfailing optimism in science and technology as progressive aspects of society that the cubist and futurist movements both shared.

In 1923 Duchamp declared *The Bride Stripped Bare* "definitively unfinished" and sold the mix-media project to American art benefactor Katherine Dreir. By the time the *Green Box* portion of *The Bride Stripped Bare* received widespread publication in 1934, the project had generated many admirers. Years later Duchamp published a series of notes he omitted from the *Green Box,* titling the additional material *A l'Infinitif* (1964), and provided the public with an even more detailed account of the project's planning and development. Specifically, the *A l'Infinitif* portion of the *Green Box* devotes considerable effort to explaining a mysterious fourth dimension in which Duchamp believed his creation exists.

One literary forbearer of the *Green Box* is the work of Alfred Jarry, a French author and dramatist who wrote during the late nineteenth and early twentieth centuries and who greatly influenced the surrealist theater of the 1920s and 1930s. Jarry's novel *Gestes et opinions du docteur Faustroll, pataphysicien* (1911) champions his pseudoscience of pataphysics, or the "science of imaginary solutions," in order to create a humorous story that combines science, theology, and art. Likewise, the author's essay "The Passion Considered as an Uphill Bicycle Race" (1903) inspired the drawing *Le Surmâle* (1902), which Duchamp embedded within the text of the *Green Box*. Finally, the wordplay found in "arrhe is to art as / shitte is to shit" echoes the opening of Jarry's play *Ubu Roi* (1896). Another source of literary inspiration for Duchamp's the *Green Box* is Raymond Roussel's *Impressions d'Afrique* (1910). Roussel, a French novelist, employed an elaborate system of homophones and puns within his novel to distort the meaning of his text.

Duchamp's *The Bride Stripped Bare,* particularly the *Green Box* portion, fostered a great deal of interest in the intersection of text and art over the course of the next several decades, inspiring an entire generation of conceptual artists. Sol LeWitt, an American artist and a founder of the conceptual art movement, responded to Duchamp's work in his essay *Artforum*

++ *Key Facts*

Time Period:
Mid-20th Century

Movement/Issue:
Aesthetics; Cubism

Place of Publication:
France

Language of Publication:
French

MARCEL DUCHAMP AND CHESS

Even in his youth, French-born artist Marcel Duchamp played chess regularly. His older brother, Villon, taught him the rules of the game when he was eleven years old, and they would play regularly throughout Marcel's childhood and early adult life. Until 1923, however, Duchamp's artistic pursuits appear to have relegated the game to a hobby.

After leaving *The Bride Stripped Bare by Her Bachelors, Even* in a state of perpetual incompletion, Duchamp returned to Europe from New York City in February 1923. Out of ideas and no longer working as a practicing artist, he moved to Brussels, where he played chess every day and qualified for the Brussels Tournament that fall, winning seven of ten matches. By 1925 he had attained the title of Chess Master of the Fédération Française des Echecs as a result of his sixth-place finish in the French national championship. In 1968, just months before he died, Duchamp performed the stage play *Reunion* with experimental musician John Cage, which consisted simply of the two men playing chess for an audience.

(1967) by declaring that "the idea become[s] a machine that makes the work of art." In addition to creating and exhibiting art-objects that directly engage textual elements and processes, LeWitt wrote more than fifty art books, many of which bear a striking resemblance to Duchamp's *Green Box.* Similarly, Joseph Kosuth, another American conceptual artist, wrote in *Art after Philosophy and After* (1969) that "all art [after Duchamp] is conceptual [in nature] because art only exists conceptually."

THEMES AND STYLE

While the *Green Box* provides directions for the creation and explanation of the *Large Glass,* it also contains a series of statements that challenge the manner in which artists, critics, and art aficionados understand and perceive works of art, language, science, the body, and their relationships to one another. For example, in the opening section "Kind of Subtitle: Delay in Glass," Duchamp writes: "Use 'delay' instead of picture or painting; picture on glass becomes delay in glass—but delay in glass does not mean picture on glass." By creating a new term ("delay") for his creation, Duchamp forces his audience to rethink the most basic precepts of an artwork when we "lose the possibility of recognizing" that with which we are most familiar. To this extent, Duchamp employs "prime words" that contain "no concrete reference" to other words and necessitate "a schematic sign" for the development of a "new alphabet" relative to an individual work. The schematic for Duchamp's new alphabet, as it relates to the *Green Box,* contains mathematical equations, photographs, drawings, musical notations, diagrams, language that is struck out, and blueprints.

Duchamp develops a pataphysics in the *Green Box* for *The Bride Stripped Bare* by conflating machines with human bodies. The artist asserts that the "bride basically is a motor" that produces a "very timid-power." In fact, Duchamp refers to the entire project as an "Agricultural machine" and an "Apparatus / instrument for farming." However, he simultaneously undermines the artwork's reliance on scientific method and technology by incorporating an overriding "Regime of Coincidence" predicated on "canned chance" that produces parameters "as it pleases" so that it "creates a new image of the unit of length" for which the entire project bases itself upon. These contradictions serve to perplex the reader. To this extent, the *Green Box* does not attempt to persuade its audience of a particular, dogmatic principle; instead, the confusion prompts those who encounter *The Bride Stripped Bare* to reevaluate their engagement with the artwork and asks them to question the nature of art in general.

Like the rhetorical thrust of the *Green Box,* Duchamp imbues the language and structure of his document with contradictions. On the one hand, the artist divides the *Green Box* into twenty-three units that lend to an overarching structure; on the other hand, the language found within each unit is fragmented and often pictorial, abjuring clarity and definitive meaning. The language that Duchamp composes for the *Green Box* exhibits these contradictions as well. In the "Laws and General Notes" section, for example, Duchamp employs scientific terms such as "solidity of construction" and "stable equilibrium," but these words are used to poetic effect, in the sense that they are "representing … new relations" that are "inexpressible by the *concrete alphabetic* forms of language living now and to come." In this sense, Duchamp takes the form of scientific inquiry and method in order to give shape to the inexpressible mysteries of human existence.

CRITICAL DISCUSSION

While some critics and art aficionados greeted *The Bride Stripped Bare* with hostility, notable figures such as André Breton, the leader of the surrealist movement, noticed the importance of the work immediately. Upon the 1934 publication of the *Green Box,* Breton composed his essay "Marcel Duchamp: Lighthouse of the Bride," wherein he claims that Duchamp is "at the very forefront of all the 'modern' movements" and calls *The Bride Stripped Bare* an "incredibly complex" and "uncompromising" work of art that "assures it an important place among the most significant works of the twentieth century." Dreir, the first owner of *The Bride Stripped Bare,* could not contain her excitement when she received her copy of the *Green Box.* A month after its formal release, she wrote Duchamp, incorrectly praising his "amazing book" as one of the "most perfect expressions of Dadaism" she had witnessed.

The *Green Box* component of *The Bride Stripped Bare* received widespread publication when French art critic Michel Sanouillet edited Duchamp's collected writing in *Marchand du sel* (1958). Fifteen years later, Elmer Peterson translated and published the English version. The Mexican poet Octavio Paz published an important study on Duchamp's *The Bride Stripped Bare* titled *Appearance Stripped Bare* (1978). Paz calls Duchamp and Pablo Picasso, a Spanish cubist, "the two painters who have had the greatest influence on our century." Furthermore, the poet highlights the conceptual thrust of Duchamp's work, arguing that "all the arts, including the visual, are born and come to an end in an area that is invisible." Duchamp's commitment to the invisible idea from which art begins and ends, to Paz's mind, imbues the work with a "wisdom and freedom, void of indifference" that resolves into a "purity" of experience.

Because of the dynamic, conceptual nature of Duchamp's *The Bride Stripped Bare,* a wide range of critical trends developed over the years. Calvin Tomkins's *The Bride & The Bachelors: The Heretical Courtship in Modern Art* (1962), for instance, traces Duchamp's influence on twentieth-century artists such as John Cage, Jean Tinguely, and Robert Rauschenberg. In "Duchamp's Etchings of the *Large Glass* and *The Lovers,*" Hellmut Wohl examines the allusions and references in the diagrams and sketches Duchamp embeds in his written passages. David Hopkins, writing in *Marcel Duchamp and Max Ernst: The Bride Shared* (1998), explores the "structural interaction and free play" between the "belief systems" of Duchamp and Ernst. And Francis M. Naumann's *Marcel Duchamp: The Art of Making Art in the Age of Mechanical Reproduction* (1999), whose title plays off of Walter Benjamin's famous essay "Art in the Age of Mechanical Reproduction," outlines the "related themes of replication and appropriation" that "underlie virtually every decision he made as an artist."

The Bride Stripped Bare by Her Bachelors, Even (The Large Glass), by Marcel Duchamp. THE PHILADELPHIA MUSEUM OF ART/ART RESOURCE, NY

BIBLIOGRAPHY

Sources

Ades, Dawn, Neil Cox, and David Hopkins. *Marcel Duchamp.* New York: Thames and Hudson, 1999. Print.

Breton, André. "Marcel Duchamp: Lighthouse of the Bride." *Surrealism and Painting.* Trans. Simon Watson Taylor. New York: Harper & Row, 1965. 85-99. Print.

Hopkins, David. *Marcel Duchamp and Max Ernst: The Bride Shared.* Oxford: Clarendon, 1998. Print.

Naumann, Francis M. *Marcel Duchamp: The Art of Making Art in the Age of Mechanical Reproduction.* New York: Harry N. Abrams, 1999. Print.

Paz, Octavio. *Appearance Stripped Bare.* Trans. Rachel Phillips and Donald Gardner. New York: Viking Press, 1978. Print.

Sanouillet, Michel, and Elmer Peterson. Introduction. *Salt Seller: The Writings of Marcel Duchamp (Marchand Du Sel).* New York: Oxford UP, 1973. Print.

Tomkins, Calvin. *Duchamp: A Biography.* New York: Henry Holt, 1996. Print.

Wohl, Hellmut. "Duchamp's Etchings of the Large Glass and The Lovers." *Dada/Surrealism* 16 (1987): 168-183.

Further Reading

Breton, André. *Manifestoes of Surrealism.* Ann Arbor: U of Michigan P, 1969. Print.

Golding, John. *Marcel Duchamp: The Bride Stripped Bare by Her Bachelors, Even.* London: Allen Lane Penguin, 1973. Print.

Hamilton, George Heard. Introduction. *From the Green Box.* New Haven: Readymade, 1957. Print.

Henderson, Linda Dalrymple. *Duchamp in Context: Science and Technology in the* Large Glass *and Related Works.* Princeton: Princeton UP, 1998. Print.

Hulten, Pontus, ed. Introduction. *Marcel Duchamp: Work and Life.* Cambridge: MIT, 1993. Print.

Kuenzli, Rudolf, and Francis M. Naumann, eds. *Marcel Duchamp: Artist of the Century.* Cambridge: MIT. 1989. Print.

Taylor, Michael R. *Marcel Duchamp: Étant donnés.* New Haven: Yale UP, 2009. Print.

Tomkins, Calvin. *The Bride & The Bachelor's: The Heretical Courtship in Modern Art.* New York: Viking, 1965. Print.

Joshua Ware

[Intersectionist] Manifesto

Fernando Pessoa

❖ **Key Facts**

Time Period:
Early 20th Century

Movement/Issue:
Intersectionism; Avant-gardism; Modernism; Aesthetics

Place of Publication:
Portugal

Language of Publication:
Portuguese

OVERVIEW

Written by Portuguese poet Fernando Pessoa in 1914, the *[Intersectionist] Manifesto* describes an artistic project that suggests a step beyond cubism and futurism to explore the intersection between the sensation of the object and the sensation of that sensation. Pessoa wrote the tract during a period of extreme political and social unrest, shortly after the failure of Portugal's constitutional monarchy and the subsequent establishment of the first Portuguese Republic in 1910. Prior to 1914 Pessoa and other Portuguese writers, such as Mário de Sá-Carneiro, had begun to hear news of European avant-garde movements from Portuguese artists who had traveled to Paris and to experiment with those new modernist ideas in their own work and within their own -isms. Although the *[Intersectionist] Manifesto* was not published until the 1990s, the Portuguese writers and artists in Pessoa's literary circles who were introduced to his ideas reacted with interest to intersectionism's creative energy, emphasis on sensation, and idea of the object as both independently real and personally constructed.

In Lisbon, the *[Intersectionist] Manifesto* was embraced by Pessoa's immediate artistic circle, which included poets Sá-Carneiro and José de Almada Negreiros and painters Santa Rita Pintor and Amadeo de Souza-Cardosa. Members of the Portuguese literary avant-garde began to demonstrate intersectionist tendencies in their work and to publish intersectionist poetry in the only two issues of their journal, *Orpheu*. About the time that Pessoa wrote the manifesto, his first heteronyms ("fake personalities" under which he wrote) appeared, including three of his most prolific: Alberto Caeiro, Ricardo Reis, and Álvaro de Campos. Caeiro and Campos, in particular, demonstrate intersectionist influence in their poetry. Despite not seeing publication until well after the twilight of the Portuguese avant-garde, the *[Intersectionist] Manifesto* is credited with helping the Grupo de Orpheu bring modernism to Portugal.

HISTORICAL AND LITERARY CONTEXT

The *[Intersectionist] Manifesto* builds on some of Pessoa's previous -isms, including Paulism, and attempts to go beyond cubism and futurism to advocate for an increased focus on sensation and an exploration of the many faces of an object, both as that object exists and as it is perceived. Pessoa had developed many private -isms (such as vertiginism, abstractionism, and fusionism) before introducing intersectionism and sensationism to his artistic circles. He also had been interested in symbolism, but prior to meeting Sá-Carneiro in 1912, Pessoa had created these -isms in ideological isolation. In Sá-Carneiro, who was based in Paris and familiar with other modernist movements such as cubism and futurism, Pessoa found an intellectual equivalent, and the two formed the nexus for the Grupo de Orpheu.

When Pessoa wrote *[Intersectionist] Manifesto* in 1914, the first Portuguese Republic was just four years old. The population of Portugal was not completely in support of the republic, with many favoring a return to the constitutional monarchy. Urban unrest and the outbreak of World War I resulted in the short-lived dictatorial reign of General Pimenta de Castro, who was overthrown in May 1915. Pessoa was a nationalist of sorts, although he did not favor a return to the monarchy; he later supported the 1917 military coup undertaken by Major Sidónio Pais and wrote in support of the national dictatorship established by President Óscar Carmona in 1928 (although he later withdrew his support for the dictatorial regime following the establishment of the New State in 1933). The *[Intersectionist] Manifesto* demonstrates a fractured vision of the object in much the same way that Pessoa's heteronyms demonstrate his varied ideological orientations and political sympathies.

The *[Intersectionist Manifesto]* draws on both the tenets of other modernist movements, primarily cubism, and Pessoa's own antecedent -isms. Early in his development, he was introduced to romantic poets such as William Wordsworth, whose *Preface to Lyrical Ballads* (1801) is often viewed as the manifesto for English romanticism. Pessoa was also greatly influenced by the French symbolists, who often made use of the manifesto (for example, Stéphane Mallarmé's *Action Restricted* [1886] and Jean Moréas's *Symbolist Manifesto* [1886]). Lead proponents of cubism, from which intersectionism takes a number of cues, also drafted manifestos, including Guillaume Apollinaire, who wrote "On the Subject of Modern Painting" (1912). In drafting the *[Intersectionist] Manifesto*, Pessoa draws on an extensive body of literary and artistic manifestos to highlight the abstract intersection between the object, the sensation of the object, and the sensation of that sensation.

When Pessoa introduced the *[Intersectionist] Manifesto* to his literary circle in Lisbon, many poets and writers of the Portuguese avant-garde began to integrate intersectionist ideas into their work, and the work's subsequent literary legacy is substantial. Poet Sá-Carneiro was already influenced by Pessoa's Paulism and sensationism when introduced to intersectionism, and his poetry, published in *Orpheu,* exhibits the influence of all three. José de Almada-Negreiros, an experimental writer, painter, and member of the Grupo de Orpheu, also created a number of works that function as demonstrations of intersectionist principles. Additionally, many of Pessoa's heteronyms made use of intersectionist theory, including Álvaro de Campos, who published another intersectionist manifesto titled *Ultimatum* (1917) in the only issue of the magazine *Portugal Futurista.* The *[Intersectionist] Manifesto,* along with the Grupo de Orpheu, secured modernism in Portugal and paved the way for the development of Portuguese poets such as Herberto Hélder and António Ramos Rosa. In the twenty-first century, the *[Intersectionist] Manifesto* has garnered scholarly interest for its contribution to Portuguese modernism and its influence on that country's literary development.

THEMES AND STYLE

The central theme of the *[Intersectionist] Manifesto* is that earlier artistic and literary movements have failed to set forth a successful method for representing a reality that should be written out of the intersection of object and sensation. As Pessoa explains, "True Reality actually consists in two things—our sensation of the object and the object. Since the object does not exist outside of our sensation—for us, at least, and that's what matters to us—it follows that true reality consists in our sensation of the object and in our sensation of our sensation." Intersectionism goes beyond romanticism, which suggests that individual sensation and aesthetic experience are the only true paths to reality, to suggest that "true reality" consists of the object as separate from sensation, sensation itself, and the sensation of that sensation.

To achieve its rhetorical effect, the *[Intersectionist] Manifesto* makes use of an "us" versus "them" division that invites the reader to join while simultaneously disparaging those who would not. For example, Pessoa states:

> Classical art was an art of dreamers and madmen. Romantic art, despite its greater intuition of truth, was an art of men who were adolescents in their notion of the reality of things but not yet adults in how they felt that reality.

> Reality, for us, is sensation. No other immediate reality can exist for us.

FERNANDO PESSOA: AUTHOR, SPLINTERED

Although barely published in his lifetime, Fernando Pessoa is now considered one of the greatest Portuguese poets. He spent a portion of his childhood in Durban, South Africa, but returned to Lisbon in 1905 and rarely left Portugal for the rest of his life. Fluent in French and English, he was highly influenced by English and French writers and wrote his first poetry in English. In Lisbon he became part of a group of writers and artists called the Grupo de Orpheu, which included Mário de Sá-Carneiro and Almada Negreiros. They created the magazine *Orpheu,* of which they were only able to publish two issues. *Orpheu,* however, helped introduce modernism to Portugal.

Pessoa's single published book of poems in Portuguese, *Mensagem (Message),* appeared in 1934. In addition to poetry, he wrote prose, philosophy, and literary criticism, often under one of his seventy heteronyms, authors whom Pessoa called "fake personalities." In addition, he was interested in the occult, spiritualism, and mediumship, all of which influenced his writing. After Pessoa died, his editor discovered thousands of pages of Pessoa's writing that had been stored in a trunk. Much of this work was not published until the 1990s; however, its publication earned Pessoa a reputation as one of the world's most fascinating poets.

> Art, whatever it is, must be founded on this element, which is the only one we have.

The manifesto uses language that is at once inclusive and aggressive. Either the reader sees the validity in the intersectionist project or risks joining the ranks of the madmen and adolescents.

The *[Intersectionist] Manifesto* makes use of repetition, a declarative tone, and strategic spaces within the text to achieve its logical but loose style. Pessoa's repeated use of the words "object," "sensation," and "intersection" ensures the reader's attention. In the final paragraph, separated from the text of the manifesto by a space break to give emphasis, Pessoa writes:

> Intersection of the Object with itself: Cubism. (The intersection, that is, of various aspects of the same Object with each other.)

> Intersection of the Object with the objective ideas it suggests: Futurism.

> Intersection of the Object with our sensation of it: Intersectionism strictly speaking, which is what we propose.

He asserts the aesthetic agenda of the intersectionists—to create out of the intersection of object and sensation—in the last line of the text in order to emphasize this idea as the culmination of other modernist movements. Making use of inclusive

language, Pessoa works to garner the support of a new breed of writers and artists devoted to the intersectionist project.

CRITICAL DISCUSSION

When Pessoa first shared the *[Intersectionist] Manifesto* with his colleagues in Lisbon, he received a largely positive response. Earlier movements of Pessoa's creation had been incorporated into the work produced by his literary friends, and the same synthesis occurred following the introduction of intersectionism. Pessoa, under his own name, published an intersectionist poem, "Chuva Oblíqua," in *Orpheu*. As Richard Zenith notes in his preface to *The Selected Prose of Fernando Pessoa* (2001), the publication of *Orpheu* "succeeded in prompting violent reactions in the press, where a number of scathing reviews and lampoons appeared, and Pessoa's genius was also noted, even if grudgingly." Although Pessoa may not have taken his various literary movements entirely seriously, he was devoted to their advancement and to *Orpheu*. Tania Martuscelli, in her essay "Between Modernism and Surrealism" (2012), explains that "Pessoa was interested in developing and expressing the aesthetics of a Portuguese modernity that would have an international dimension and resonance…. [He] only accepted the comparison between [Filippo Tommaso] Marinetti's Futurism and his intersectionism to draw the attention of Frank Palmer, a British publisher, to Orpheu."

The *[Intersectionist] Manifesto,* and its influence on literary persons in Lisbon at the time of its writing, had an important role in introducing modernism to Portugal. The activities of Pessoa and his literary circle were viewed with interest by new generations of experimental Portuguese writers. Alex Severino, in his 1979 essay in *World Literature Today,* writes about Pessoa's enduring influence, noting of the Presença ("Presence") literary group:

> As they looked for literary vocations as genuine as their own, the *Presença* group became interested in the poets from *Orpheu.* Theirs had been an authentic and sincere poetry, and as such it needed to be revived and their authors brought back from semi-oblivion into the Modernist fold. Therefore the group that called itself 'the second Modernism' set out to promote the poets from the first Modernism. In one of the journal's first issues, José Régio wrote in reference to Pessoa: 'For all these advantages, Fernando Pessoa has the makings of a Master and is the richest in outlets of the so-called Modernists' [*Presença,* 1927].

In the twenty-first century, critical interest in *[Intersectionist] Manifesto* examines its place in Pessoa's development as a writer, its influence on modernism in Portugal, and its relationship to cubism.

Although the *[Intersectionist] Manifesto* was not published until the 1990s, its influence on Pessoa's development as a writer and the development of his heteronyms is significant. In her 1997 essay in *Luso-Brazilian Review,* Darlene Sadlier examines some of Pessoa's poetry through the lens of intersectionism, symbolism, and even futurism. She observes that "Pessoa's contribution to the [second issue of *Orpheu*], the six-part 'intersectionist' poem entitled 'Chuva Oblíqua,' borrows some of its motifs from symbolism, but has a distinctly unorthodox feel. Meanwhile, Pessoa's heteronym, the 'engineer' Álvaro de Campos, writes a thirty-eight-page-long 'Ode Marítima,' which, like his 'Ode Triunfal,' breaks into onomatopoeic effects that verge on Marinetti's 'words at liberty.'" Commentators have also examined the contribution that Pessoa's -isms made to the development of modernism in Portugal and his unique interpretation of other international modernist movements. Jerome Boyd Maunsell in "The Hauntings of Fernando Pessoa" (2012) writes that "Pessoa also wanted to engage with the wider sphere of Modernism outside Portugal, and despite his relative isolation from the currents of Modernism elsewhere in Europe and America, his work resounds with extraordinarily close unconscious echoes and prefigurings of other contemporary writers." Maunsell concludes that "[Pessoa's] oeuvre reconfigures the given narratives of international Modernism, as well as providing ghost or shadow Modernisms of its own."

BIBLIOGRAPHY

Sources

Martuscelli, Tania. "Between Modernism and Surrealism: Dada in Portugal." MODERNISM/*modernity* 19.2 (2012): 277-86. *Project MUSE*. Web. 21 Sept. 2012.

Maunsell, Jerome Boyd. "The Hauntings of Fernando Pessoa." MODERNISM/*modernity* 19.1 (2012): 115-37. *Project MUSE*. Web. 21 Sept. 2012.

Pessoa, Fernando. "[Intersectionist] Manifesto." *The Selected Prose of Fernando Pessoa*. Ed. and Trans. Richard Zenith. New York: Grove, 2001. 65-66. Print.

Sadlier, Darlene J. "Nationalism, Modernity, and the Formation of Fernando Pessoa's Aesthetic." *Luso-Brazilian Review* 34.2 (1997): 109-22. Rpt. in *Twentieth-Century Literary Criticism*. Ed. Kathy D. Darrow. Vol. 257. Detroit: Gale, 2011. *Literature Resources from Gale*. Web. 21 Sept. 2012.

Severino, Alex. "Fernando Pessoa's Legacy: The *Presença* and After." *World Literature Today* 53.1 (1979): 5-9. Rpt. in *Poetry Criticism*. Ed. Carol T. Gaffke. Vol. 20. Detroit: Gale Research, 1998. *Literature Resources from Gale*. Web. 21 Sept. 2012.

Zenith, Richard. "Sensationism and Other Isms." *The Selected Prose of Fernando Pessoa*. Ed. and Trans. Richard Zenith. New York: Grove, 2001. 58-61. Print.

Further Reading

Fernando Pessoa & Co.: Selected Poems. Ed. and Trans. Richard Zenith. New York: Grove, 1998. Print.

Frier, David G., ed. *Pessoa in an Intertextual Web: Influence and Innovation*. London: Legenda, 2012. Print.

Jackson, K. David. *Adverse Genres in Fernando Pessoa*. New York: Oxford UP, 2010. Print.

Kotowicz, Zbigniew. *Fernando Pessoa: Voices of a Nomadic Soul*. London: Menard, 2008. Print.

Sadlier, Darlene J. *An Introduction to Fernando Pessoa: Modernism and the Paradoxes of Authorship*. Gainesville: UP of Florida, 1998. Print.

Zenith, Richard. *Fernando Pessoa*. Lisboa: Temas e Debates, 2008. Print.

Kristen Gleason

NON SERVIAM

Vicente Huidobro

✣ *Key Facts*

Time Period:
Early 20th Century

Movement/Issue:
Aesthetics; Creationism;
Avant-gardism

Place of Publication:
Chile

**Language of
Publication:**
Spanish

OVERVIEW

Written by Chilean poet Vicente Huidobro, "Non Serviam" (1914) calls for a new poetry that does not imitate the appearance of things but seeks to free itself from the natural world and evoke a separate realm, independent of nature. Although the essay was not published until the release of his book *Manifestos Manifest* (1925), Huidobro read "Non Serviam" at a university, Ateneo de Santiago, in 1914. The work is an early sounding of the theoretical concepts that would preoccupy Huidobro throughout his career, thus leading to the publication of subsequent manifestos, such as "Warning to Tourists" (1914-17) and "We Must Create" (1922). The movement that "Non Serviam" inspired, creationism, was explicitly poetic, but it mirrored many of the aesthetic preoccupations of visual artists at the time: self-referentiality, or art that references the art form or artist itself; nonrepresentational images; and abstraction.

Although Huidobro was considered a strong new voice on the Chilean poetry scene, "Non Serviam" received little attention at and immediately after the Ateneo de Santiago reading. It was not until 1916 that his work garnered more notice. In July of that year, Huidobro spoke at the university in Buenos Aires and published his first collection of creationist poems, *Water Mirror;* he also moved to Paris, where he quickly made connections and influenced the avant-garde poets of the day, including cubists Pierre Reverdy, Paul Durméc, and Max Jacob. In 1918 Huidobro made his first trip to Madrid, where the creationist ideas in his essay made a profound impact on the development of a Spanish creationist school, as well as Spanish ultraism. Today, "Non Serviam" is viewed as an important document in the development of Latin American and, indeed, European avant-garde poetry.

HISTORICAL AND LITERARY CONTEXT

"Non Serviam" responds to the state of representational poetry at the end of the nineteenth century, when the *Symbolist Manifesto* (Jean Moréas, 1886) had articulated an aesthetic inimical to the objective descriptions of naturalism. French symbolist poets such as Stéphane Mallarmé produced works approaching abstraction, but according to scholar Ana Maria Nicholson in *Vicente Huidobro and Creationism* (1967), Mallarme's poems "are constantly referring to

something outside themselves." Huidobro's aesthetic agreed with the symbolist stance toward naturalism but sought to make an even more significant break with representational images.

When Huidobro read "Non Serviam" at Ateneo de Santiago, the Chilean avant-garde was almost non-existent. However, the vanguard Huidobro encountered upon his arrival in Europe in 1916 was on the cusp of abstraction and self-referential art forms. In Zurich, the Dadaist Hugo Ball was constructing non-representational sound poems that share much with Huidobro's creationist aesthetic. In Paris the poet helped to fund Pierre Reverdy's *Nord-Sud,* a magazine that published vanguard poetry. According to Nicholson, many of the cubist writers of this period, including Max Jacob, insisted on "objectivity" in their poems. Huidobro's 1917 collection of poetry, *Horizon Carre,* with its staccato imagery and typographical experimentation, typifies this self-referential style, and "Non Serviam," along with Huidobro's other manifestos, offers a theoretical statement about the aims of his poetry.

"Non Serviam" draws on a long history of avant-garde art manifestos, most specifically Filippo Tommaso Marinetti's *Futurist Manifesto* (1909) and Guillaume Apollinaire's *On the Subject of Modern Painting* (1912). The *Futurist Manifesto* advocates a new-form poetry and art that will overturn tradition and embrace speed, violence, and machinery. Despite some attacks on futurism, much of Huidobro's thinking in the early 1910s reflects that movement's ideals. In *Spanish Literary Creationism* (1999), scholar Brianne von Fabrice writes that Huidobro "spoke out against the "mummified culture of museums," "rare books," and other cultural manifestations. Huidobro also subscribed to *Soiree de Paris,* the magazine that published Apollinaire's aforementioned manifesto, which contends that modern painters no longer need to copy nature, a theme later taken up by Huidobro in "Non Serviam."

In the decades following Huidobro's reading, "Non Serviam" inspired a small body of literature that adheres to the aesthetic demands of the essay. During his 1918 visit to Madrid, and with the subsequent publication of his books in Spain, Huidobro offered an example of a new kind of poetry to young Spanish poets such as Gerardo Diego and Juan Larrea, who soon began to call themselves creationists. Huidobro's desire to break with modernism and romanticism also influenced Spanish ultraism, Spain's first avant-garde poetry movement. The New World felt the influence of creationism when Jorge Luis Borges began to promote ultraism to Latin America upon his return to Buenos Aires in 1921. Today creationist poetry, although not quite as well known as that of the ultraists, continues to command significant scholarly interest.

THEMES AND STYLE

The central theme of "Non Serviam" is that poets must free themselves from their servitude toward nature and create new worlds through nonrepresentational art. Calling on his "brothers," Huidobro criticizes naturalist and realist poetry, which often seeks to imitate the world of appearances: "We have sung Nature (which did not concern her). Never have we created any proper realities, as she does and used to do when she was young and heavy with creative impulses." Creationism attempts to break from those old aesthetics, to flee the "traps" of nature and its "exaggerated claims of being old, sensual, and senile." To this end, the essay offers no exact prescription or technique, but it does attempt a poetic definition of this self-referential aesthetic in a direct address to nature: "I'll have my trees, too, which won't be like yours, I'll have my mountains, I'll have my rivers and my oceans, I'll have my sky and my stars."

The manifesto achieves its rhetorical effect through appeals to a sense of unity among young poets who have grown weary of naturalism. This is primarily achieved through the use of the first-person plural pronoun "we." In an intimate call to "his brothers" in poetry, Huidobro envisions and flatters a group of inchoate avant-garde poets of which he is also a part: "We haven't thought that we also could create realities in a world that would be ours." Group solidarity is created through shared culpability over the staid state of poetry: "*We* have accepted, without reflecting further, the fact there can be no other realities." Huidobro adds that enthusiasm is engendered through shared opportunity, writing, "A new era is beginning."

Stylistically, "Non Serviam" is distinguished by its direct address to an anthropomorphized "Nature" that has tyrannized artists and subjected them to servitude. Huidobro uses the second-person pronoun "you" in order to dramatize his opposition to this "Nature" and, in turn, representational art. "I won't serve you," he writes, or "I don't have to be your slave, Mother Nature." Indeed, he even writes lines of dialogue for "Mother Nature," in which she speaks about Huidobro's creations, saying, "This tree is not lovely, this heaven doesn't please me…. I prefer mine." This allows for Huidobro's rebuttal, which helps to define the self-referential objectivity of his poetry. Huidobro argues that the heaven and trees he has created are his, not nature's, and "that they don't have to look alike."

THE SPANISH CIVIL WAR

On July 17, 1936, a group of Spanish generals, including Francisco Franco, staged a *pronunciamiento* against the democratically elected government of the Second Spanish Republic, but its coup d'état failed and sparked a three-year war of attrition that came to be known as the Spanish Civil War. The rebels, also known as the Nationalists, were led by Emilio Mola in the north and Franco in the south. Nazi Germany and Benito Mussolini-ruled Italy supported the Nationalist cause. The left-leaning Republican Army won the support of Mexico and the clandestine assistance of the Soviet Union. In addition, it garnered the support of poet, novelist, and creationist Vicente Huidobro

Some historical records claim that Huidobro fought on the Republican side, but it is more likely that he contributed to the cause through poems, political manifestos, articles, interviews, and letters. His support of the Republicans was shared by many poets of the day. Along with Huidobro, Pablo Neruda, Cesar Vallejo, Octavio Paz, and Antonio Machado, all spoke out against the rising tide of fascism. However, the Nationalists possessed greater military strength than the Republican Army. Their victory in 1939 resulted in Franco becoming dictator of Spain, a position he held until his death in 1975.

CRITICAL DISCUSSION

When "Non Serviam" first appeared in 1914, it received little attention In isolated and provincial Chile. It was not until Huidobro's arrival in Paris in late 1916 that creationism and the manifesto underpinning it generated interest and, eventually, controversy in the realm of avant-garde poetry. The general public continued to ignore these developments, and there is almost no mention of him in newspapers of the time. The poet's involvement in the publication of Reverdy's magazine, *Nord-Sud*, suggests the inroads his work had made with the Parisian vanguard by 1917, but, according to Nicholson, "a series of quarrels and intrigues, some of them not very clear, began to darken Huidobro's reputation." This ultimately led to claims that he had not founded creationism but had simply passed off Reverdy's theories as his own and that he had falsely dated the first edition of his collection *Water Mirror* to make it look as if the Parisians had imitated him. However, these accusations ignore the 1914 reading of "Non Serviam," which is evidence of the development of Huidobro's creationist aesthetic.

After creationism died out, "Non Serviam" continued to influence the Spanish avant-garde. According to von Fabrice, creationism "had a substantial impact on numerous young poets and helped change the face of Spanish poetry." This is mostly clearly seen in the rise of the Spanish ultraists, who borrowed elements from a number of avant-garde movements, including creationism. Von Fabrice argues that Huidobro's creationism acted as a catalyst for the Spanish avant-garde. Prior to his arrival in Madrid in

Statue of writer Gerardo Diego in Santander, Spain. Vicente Huidobro considered Diego to have been a creationist poet.
© IMAGEBROKER/ALAMY

versa, Nicholson writes, "It would perhaps be closer to the truth to say that the objectification of art was a concept that originated with the cubist painters as a result of their experimentations and which affected a number of writers, including Huidobro."

BIBLIOGRAPHY

Sources

Huidobro, Vicente. *100 Artists' Manifestos: From the Futurists to the Stuckists.* Ed. Alex Danchev. New York: Penguin Adult, 2011. Print.

Nicholson, Ana Maria. *Vicente Huidobro and Creationism.* San Diego: U of California San Diego P, 1967. *ProQuest.* Web. 3 Aug. 2012.

Villalon, Fernando Perez. "Huidobro/Pound: Translating Modernism." *Hispanic Issues.* Vol. 6. Minneapolis: U of Minnesota P, 2010. *ProQuest.* Web. 3 Sept. 2012.

Silva, Maria Eugenia. *Vicente Huidobro and Pierre Reverdy in the Works.* Baltimore: Johns Hopkins UP, 2007. *ProQuest.* Web. 3 Aug. 2012.

Von Fabrice, Brianne. *Spanish Literary Creationism.* Ann Arbor: U of Michigan P, 1999. *ProQuest.* Web. 3 Aug. 2012.

Further Reading

Delvillar, A. "Ultraism and Creationism + Huidobro, Vicente Controversial Persona." *Cuadernos Hispano-americanos* 511 (1993): 25-39. Print.

De Costa, Rene. *Vicente Huidobro: The Careers of a Poet.* Oxford: Clarendon, 1984. Print.

Peridigo, Luis Marina. *The Origins of Vicente Huidobro's Creacionismo (1911-1916) and Its Evolution (1917-1947).* Lewiston: Mellen UP, 1994. Print.

Weintraub, Scott, and Luis Correa-Diaz. "Huidobro's Absolute Modernity/Futurity: An Introduction." *Hispanic Issues.* Vol. 6. Minneapolis: U of Minnesota P, 2010. *ProQuest.* Web. 3 Sept. 2012.

Willis, Bruce Dean. *Aesthetics of Equilibrium: The Vanguard Poetics of Vicente Huidobro and Mario de Andrade.* West Lafayette: Purdue UP, 2006. Print.

Gregory Luther

1918, writes von Fabrice, it had been "unaware of—or at least unconcerned by—avant-garde activity" in Paris.

Much scholarship has focused on the controversy surrounding the founding of creationism. Scholar David Bary has claimed that it was only after Huidobro's arrival in Paris that creationism as such came to fruition. In contrast, Nicholson strives to establish that, at the very least, "Non Serviam" serves as evidence that Huidobro had begun to articulate his creationist ideas prior to coming to Europe. As for the debate surrounding Reverdy's influence on Huidobro, or vice

ON BEAUTIFUL CLARITY

Mikhail Kuzmin

OVERVIEW

Written by prominent poet and prose writer Mikhail Kuzmin, "On Beautiful Clarity" (1910) marked a turning point for Russian literature, which had been previously dominated by vague and mystical symbolist imagery, with a call for clarity, economy, and logic in expression. Published in the literary journal *Apollon,* the essay was a response to dominant naturalist and symbolist trends in the Russian literary community at the start of the twentieth century. Kuzmin addresses writers of the new age, literary artists who lived and published while their country struggled with industrialization and a change of leadership. Central to the text are aesthetic suggestions: a demand for skilled architecture, action over drama, and economy and clarity over rhetorical flourishes and vagueness.

"On Beautiful Clarity" was initially praised by younger and more forward thinking members of Russia's literati, although it was dismissed by major symbolist poets of the day, including Kuzmin's colleague Vyacheslav Ivanov. The essay foretells the rise of acmeism, a short-lived but influential group of poets who rejected the vague and emotional language of symbolism in favor of concreteness and texture. Eventually, his suggestions in "On Beautiful Clarity" became widely embraced and were adopted by some of Russia's best-known poets. Today "On Beautiful Clarity" is considered to be a significant statement that heralded the evolution of Russia's literature at the start of the twentieth century.

HISTORICAL AND LITERARY CONTEXT

"On Beautiful Clarity" responds to aesthetic challenges facing Russian writers in the early twentieth century, when they sought to move away from symbolism toward a neoclassicist objective view of contemporary reality. Toward the end of the nineteenth century, Russian literature had been directed by the German-influenced romanticism practiced by Alexander Pushkin, Fyodor Tyutchev, and Mikhail Lermontov and by the moralizing realism of Leo Tolstoy. Subsequently, Russian symbolism gained sway, a genre defined by mystical content, symbols, and artistic impressionability. Influenced by the ideas of philosopher Vladimir Solovyov, Fyodor Dostoevsky wrote novels that invoked religious beliefs with an aim of transfiguring the existing world. Other symbolist

writers, such as Andrei Bely and Alexander Blok, wrote with evocative musicality and bold rhythms to conjure specific emotions in readers. At the time of the Russo-Japanese War (1904-05) and the first Russian revolution (1905-07), Russian readers prized the symbolists' garishly rendered conflicts and elaborate stylization and complex structures. However, after the first attempt at revolution, Russian fiction writers sought to bring greater clarity and narrative cohesion to their works.

By the time "On Beautiful Clarity" was published in 1910, a younger generation of writers saw a need to portray Russia with concision and accuracy, but a movement had not coalesced. Among the most vocal advocates in St. Petersburg were the poets and Ivanov and Blok, who gave public speeches on the need to address Russia's diverse and unpredictable citizenry in a simpler style. Ivanov's "On the Russian Idea" (1908) and Blok's "The People and the Intelligentsia" (1908) reflect shifts in aesthetics for these symbolist writers, who grappled with Marxist ideas as a solution to Russia's spiritual problems. When Kuzmin's "On Beautiful Clarity" appeared, it provided a platform on which young writers could create artistically and intellectually complex work in more stylistically accessible prose.

"On Beautiful Clarity" draws on earlier European aesthetic manifestos going back to German thinker Heinrich Heine's *Über die französische bühne* ("On the French Stage"). Written in 1840, Heine's work of prose criticism asserts that, according to Kuzmin biographer John E. Malmstad, countries such as France "were the cradle of the novella and novel, for there the Apollonian view of art was more developed ... exact and harmonious." Kuzmin, then a columnist for *Apollon,* which served as a forum for a wide variety of modernist writers and artists, was not attached to a particular school of literary ideas. He wrote his essay in response to the convoluted symbolist stylization, just as Heine had critiqued the excesses of German romantic writers. Malmstad notes that Kuzmin's essay emphasizes "clarity," "crystalline form," and "balance."

In the years following its publication, "On Beautiful Clarity" inspired a significant body of literature that supported its aesthetic priorities and reoriented Russian letters away from symbolism. The call for "clarism" led to the brief but important acmeism

Key Facts

Time Period:
Early 20th Century

Movement/Issue:
Aesthetics; Realism

Place of Publication:
Russia

Language of Publication:
Russian

MIKHAIL KUZMIN: PROLIFIC STYLIST

Mikhail Kuzmin did not become a published poet until his thirties, but he quickly won a unique place in Russian literature. He worked in many genres besides poetry, including prose, drama, and criticism. Kuzmin was born in 1872 in Yaroslavl, Russia, the second-youngest child in a large noble family that was not wealthy. He was influenced by French music and literature at an early age and studied music at a conservatory in St. Petersburg in the 1890s. He had an early spiritual crisis that led him to follow a Russian Orthodox sect called the Old Believers. Travel had a lasting influence on Kuzmin's writing. Two short trips to Egypt and Italy inspired his early poetry and his novel *Wings* (1906), the first Russian fiction to address homosexual relationships.

Kuzmin was a charming performer and musician, and he gained immediate popularity in the various artistic salons and communities he frequented (the Stray Dog cabaret and Vyacheslav Ivanov's Tower, for example). Though not an acmeist himself, he wrote the preface to Anna Akhmatova's volume *Evening* (1912). Kuzmin briefly supported the Russian revolution, but the Soviet Union was a hostile environment for his work. He published his late masterpiece, *The Trout Breaks the Ice,* in 1929 but spent many of his later years in poverty, earning a meager living as a reviewer and translator.

literary movement. Osip Mandelshtam wrote an essay, "The Morning of Acmeism" (1913), echoing Kuzmin's advice that writers use words like skillful building blocks. Mandelshtam's volume of poetry *Stone* (1913) is considered an acmeist masterpiece. Although acmeism was made up of poets, they did not eschew fiction. Nadezhda Mandelshtam, Osip's wife, clarified this stance and included the novelist Boris Pasternak as an acmeist. In *Hope against Hope,* Nadezhda Mandelshtam writes, "The world was no longer divided into ugly prose and sublime poetry. In this connection I think of [Anna] Akhmatova, who knew 'from what trash poetry, quite unashamed, can grow,' and of Pasternak with his passionate defense of the 'daily round' in *Dr Zhivago*." Today acmeist literature continues to command significant scholarly interest.

THEMES AND STYLE

The central theme of "On Beautiful Clarity" is that writers have diminished the meaning and effectiveness of literature by working in a style that is murky, mystical, and impressionistic as opposed to logical and clear. The essay opens with a compelling argument that the time has arrived for a new clarity in literature: "[W]e see that the creative periods striving toward clarity stand as beacons pointing the way to a single goal." To this end, Kuzmin outlines his standards for clarity in prose, imploring writers to be logical in design, construction, and syntax.

The text achieves its rhetorical effect through appeals to readers and writers who are unified in valuing logic as a guiding principal in literature. Kuzmin repeatedly uses the words "clarity" and "logic" with regard to prose writing. Addressing a broad audience, the essay imagines readers and writers who are subject to the cyclical nature of literature and art. The essay suggests that the best writing brings humans out of "chaos, bewildered horror and fragmentation of ... spirit." For Kuzmin, a master of style "preserves the logic and spirit" of a language. Notably, the essay lauds the works of French writers as examples of a clear and logical style while hesitating to bestow the same praise on Russian symbolist writers such as Bely and Aleksei Remizov, whose narrative structures are complex.

Stylistically, "On Beautiful Clarity" is distinguished by an easygoing tone that masks a nuanced understanding of literary trends of the era. Written as unpretentious professional remarks from a contributor to *Apollon,* the piece demands credibility. Kuzmin also employs other writers' interrogations of literary style to support his argument: "One would like to write out in letters of gold the scene from [Moliere's] *Le bourgeois gentilhomme* on the wall of an 'academy of prose.'" Simultaneously, by reviewing the common practices of a variety of Russian prose writers, Kuzmin demonstrates his qualification to make suggestions for the direction of his nation's literature. Although "On Beautiful Clarity" favors certain writers for achieving balance, perspective, and elegance, it achieves its rhetorical force through its careful consideration of many writers' styles and devices.

CRITICAL DISCUSSION

When "On Beautiful Clarity" was first published in 1910, it received mixed reviews within literary circles. Symbolists, including Ivanov, decried the publication of Kuzmin's essay as an attempt to appeal to the younger generation while overlooking modernist masters. *Apollon*'s editor denied that Kuzmin's "clarism" essay summarized the magazine's ideals; however, many young writers were attracted by the essay's relationist approach to literature. Though Kuzmin himself wrote in a variety of modes, "On Beautiful Clarity" was a significant contribution to the evolution of prose style. In his introduction to Kuzmin's *Selected Prose & Poetry,* Michael Green writes: "One should not belittle the significance and the effect of such a piece at a time when the mystical and metaphysical were expected qualities of a written work." Furthermore, Peter Bailey suggests in his preface to Kuzmin's novel *Wings* that the essay anticipates the "Acmeists' belief in elegance and purity in style."

The acmeist movement dispersed after the October Revolution of 1917, but "On Beautiful Clarity" remained an important source of inspiration in the aesthetically restrictive climate of the Soviet Union. In his introduction to Kuzmin's *Selected Writings,* Green describes the writer's contribution to Russian modernism: "Into the breach hacked by Kuzmin in Symbolist aesthetics and poetics poured the fresh forces that were to shape post-Symbolist poetry…. It is impossible to underestimate the service rendered by Kuzmin to those who found in themselves the strength to overcome Symbolism." In the century since the essay was written, it has been the subject of criticism that has considered its legacy in biographical, historical, and literary terms.

Recent scholarship has focused on the literary significance of "On Beautiful Clarity" as a herald of the acmeist movement. In his biography of Kuzmin, Malmstad observes that the essay was "the opening salvo in an attack on Symbolism … and a kind of 'pre-manifesto' of the rival Acmeist movement." Commentators are quick to note that Kuzmin was a writer who incorporated a variety of approaches into his own work and was, as Green points out in his introduction to *Selected Writings,* "careful to keep aloof of polemic, thus preserving … the respect of those engaged in literary skirmishing." Kuzmin, scholars note, was indebted to symbolism and later attempted to create a new literary movement called emotionalism—rooted in German expressionism—that met with little notice. The poet Anna Akhmatova rejected the notion that Kuzmin had an influence on acmeism, but commentators find that his early verse has common principles with acmeist poems. Clarism aesthetics are often analyzed to illuminate the works of Mandelshtam and Akhmatova. Patricia Pollock Brodsky writes in her essay in *Osip Mandelstam* (1988) that even when the Soviet regime began to dictate a political agenda for its writers, Akhmatova asserted that the acmeist movement would transcend time by assuming the function of "moral and aesthetic memory."

BIBLIOGRAPHY

Sources

Brodsky, Patricia Pollock. "Chapter 2: Symbolism, Acmeism, Stone." *Osip Mandelstam.* By Jane Gary Harris. Boston: Twayne, 1988. Twayne's World Authors Series 799. *The Twayne Authors Series.* Web. 24 Aug. 2012.

Kuzmin, Mikhail Alekseevich. *Wings: Prose and Poetry.* Ed. and trans. Neil Granoien and Michael Green. Ann Arbor: Ardis, 1972. Print.

————. *Selected Prose & Poetry.* Ed. and trans. Michael Green. Ann Arbor: Ardis, 1980. Print.

————. *Selected Writings.* Ed. and trans. Michael A. Green and Stanislav A. Shvabrin. Introduction by Michael A. Green and Stanislav A. Shvabrin. Lewisburg: Bucknell UP, 2005. Print.

————. *Wings.* Trans. by Hugh Aplin. Preface by Peter Bailey. London: Hesperus, 2007. Print.

Malmstad, John E., and Nikolay Bogomolov. *Mikhail Kuzmin: A Life in Art.* Cambridge: Harvard UP, 1999. Print.

Mandelshtam, Nadezhda. *Hope against Hope.* Trans. by Max Hayward. Introduction by Clarence Brown. New York: Atheneum, 1978. Print.

Further Reading

Barnstead, John C. "Mikhail Kuzmin's 'On Beautiful Clarity' and *Viacheslav Ivanov: A Reconsideration.*" *Canadian Slavonic Papers/Revue Canadienne des Slavistes* 24.1 (1982): 1-10. *JSTOR.* Web. 24 Aug. 2012.

Brown, Clarence, and Osip Mandelshtam. "Mandelshtam's Acmeist Manifesto." *Russian Review* 24.1 (1965): 46-51. *JSTOR.* Web. 24 Aug. 2012.

Dobrenko, Evgeny, and Marina Balina. *The Cambridge Companion to Twentieth-Century Russian Literature.* New York: Cambridge UP, 2011. Print.

Rosslyn, Wendy. "The Acmeist Movement in Russian Poetry: Culture and the World." *Modern Language Review* 93.2 (1998): 596+. *Literature Resource Center.* Web. 24 Aug. 2012.

Tcherkassova, Farida A., and I.G. Vishnevetsky. "Mikhail Kuzmin." *Russian Writers of the Silver Age, 1890-1925.* Ed. Judith E. Kalb, J. Alexander Ogden, and I. G. Vishnevetsky. Detroit: Gale, 2004. *Dictionary of Literary Biography.* Vol. 295. *Literature Resource Center.* Web. 24 Aug. 2012.

Karen Bender

Portrait of Mikhail Kuzmin, 1911-12, painted by Nikolaj Nikolaevič Sapunov, depicts the author shortly after he wrote "On Beautiful Clarity." BELORUSSIAN NATIONAL GALLERY, MINSK, BELARUS/ THE BRIDGEMAN ART LIBRARY

ON "CUBISM"

Albert Gleizes, Jean Metzinger

✣ *Key Facts*

Time Period:
Early 20th Century

Movement/Issue:
Aesthetics; Avant-
gardism; Cubism

Place of Publication:
France

**Language of
Publication:**
French

OVERVIEW

Composed by Albert Gleizes and Jean Metzinger, *On "Cubism"* (*Du "Cubisme"*; 1912) describes the developments that led to the cubist art movement and attempts to facilitate understanding and appreciation of this radical art form. Gleizes and Metzinger were important cubist painters, and their text is the first book-length work on the movement. Published in conjunction with the Salon de la Section d'Or, a cubist exhibition in Paris, *On "Cubism"* is addressed to artists and critics who had yet to embrace modern art. By tracing the origins of cubism through the history of painting, Gleizes and Metzinger attempt to legitimize the movement's radical innovations as inevitable outcomes and as the only means of faithfully depicting the complex reality of modernity. Ultimately, they write, "we must see it [cubism] as the only conception of pictorial art currently possible."

On "Cubism" was widely read and admired; within two months of its October 1912 publication, the text was reprinted seven times in France. Within the first year, it had been translated into English and Russian. The authors' argument resonated with readers and helped to define what was then a nascent and controversial movement. Cubist exhibitions in 1911 and 1912 had scandalized the public, and the use of government property to display the controversial works was debated in the French parliament. *On "Cubism"* succeeded in convincing readers that this art form should be taken seriously and helped popularize a radically avant-garde movement that was only just beginning. Today, *On "Cubism"* is considered the first major cubist text and is recognized as a significant influence on the development of one of the twentieth century's most important artistic movements.

HISTORICAL AND LITERARY CONTEXT

On "Cubism" responds to the cultural situation in Paris at the beginning of the twentieth century, when cubism rose to prominence. The art movement is typically traced to 1907, when Pablo Picasso composed *Les Demoiselles d'Avignon*. This depiction of five nude prostitutes was a radical departure from convention. The painting shocked audiences with its subject matter and its style of composition. The figures were angular and abstract and were presented in a flattened plane that upended longstanding conventions of spatial illusion and compositional unity. In a 1908 review of a Georges Braque exhibition, critic Louis Vauxcelles notes the use of "geometric schemes and cubes." The term "cubism" springs from this observation.

By the time *On "Cubism"* was published, cubist art had proliferated and become a source of controversy. While Picasso and Braque continued to explore the limits of three-dimensional depiction on two-dimensional canvas in the early 1910s, a new and distinct strain of cubism emerged on the city's Left Bank. In 1910 Gleizes, Metzinger, and Henri Le Fauconnier exhibited at the Salon d'Automne. Critic Roger Allard identified them as representative of new movement: salon cubism. A year later an exhibition of this group at the Salon des Indépendants elicited public outrage, as viewers were shocked and baffled by the paintings' abstraction. As the salon cubists prepared to exhibit their work at the Salon d'Automne in 1912, Gleizes and Metzinger collaborated on *On "Cubism"* as a means of preempting the scandal that their work elicited.

On "Cubism" draws on writings about art, philosophy, and even mathematics. The arguments of French philosopher Henri Bergson in *Time and Free Will* (1899) and *Creative Evolution* (1907) informed the authors' notion about the relationship between a painting and its audience. As Mark Antliff writes in *Inventing Bergson* (1993), "In Bergson's philosophy, every expressive medium, whether it be plastic, literary, or musical, is the end of a process whereby the inner, manifold self becomes spatialized through the process of self-representation." According to Antliff, Gleizes and Metzinger draw on this notion to defend "the seemingly arbitrary scale employed in Cubist works: we should read such spiritual disjunctions as the plastic equivalent to durational being." The manifesto also draws from philosopher Friedrich Nietzsche and from the cubism-inspired prose of Gertrude Stein, including her 1909 verbal portrait of Picasso.

On "Cubism" inspired other writings about cubism and proved particularly influential on Guillaume Apollinaire's book *The Cubist Painters: Aesthetic Meditations* (*Les peintres cubists: Méditations esthétiques*; 1913). Apollinaire's text examines the importance of cubism through the framework of his poetic theories and through the example of specific cubist artists. In keeping with his primary interest in poetry, Apollinaire's essay is written in a lyrical, aphoristic style that contrasts with the analytical and technical approach taken by Gleizes and Metzinger. Today, both works command significant interest for their role in shaping cubism and the scholarly approaches that have been applied to the movement since its end in the early 1920s.

THEMES AND STYLE

The central theme of On "Cubism" is that it is the artist's task to interpret rather than depict reality and that cubism offers the most apt means of so doing. After tracing the historical origins of cubism, Gleizes and Metzinger confront the notion that a painting should faithfully reflect reality. For them, mere documentation is pointless, as it reveals "nothing about the painter's talent or genius." "To dispute this," they argue, "is to deny the painters' space; it is to deny painting." Gleizes and Metzinger argue that cubism offers a glimpse into a world that exceeds the conventions of realism. Cubism sees beyond the superficialities of realism and discovers the true complexities of form. The result may seem challenging, they concede, but "it is not in the language of the crowd that painting must address the crowd; it is in its own language, in order to move, to dominate, to direct, not in order to be understood."

The text presents cubism not as a radical new artistic fad but as an accessible and useful new way of seeing the world. Gleizes and Metzinger do not argue for the novelty of cubism but for its inevitability. They do so by tracing the movement's origins to accepted styles of painting. After a brief introduction, they begin their first section, "To evaluate the importance of cubism, we must go back to Gustave Courbet." By invoking one of France's most respected nineteenth-century realist painters, Gleizes and Metzinger signal their acceptance of convention and tradition. Through the rest of the work, they chart cubism's genealogy through Édouard Manet, Paul Cézanne, and other established artists. To the same end, Gleizes and Metzinger root their argument not only in aesthetic theory and art history but in a purported spirit of generosity and openness: "We want to dazzle others with what we wrest on a daily basis from the sensible world and, in return, we want others to make their trophies known to us."

Throughout On "Cubism," Gleizes and Metzinger use a confident tone to express with certainty their ideas about the superiority of cubism to other artistic approaches. "In other words, at the present time," they write, "cubism is painting itself." Elsewhere, they declare, "For the partial freedoms achieved by Courbet, Manet, Cézanne, and the impressionists, cubism substitutes an unlimited liberty." Even doubt in the form of contemporary criticism is evidence of their argument's validity: "Some take a liking today to what exasperated them yesterday. It is

ALBERT GLEIZES: PRACTICAL IDEALIST

Though best remembered for his role in writing On "Cubism" and for the cubist paintings he made in the 1910s and 1920s, Albert Gleizes's first passion was not for the visual arts but for the theater. As a child in suburban Paris, he aspired to be an actor. Though he was allowed to pursue that interest, he was also forced to learn industrial design from his father, a successful professional who specialized in furniture fabrics. This experience—not the time he spent reciting poetry and performing in plays—proved to have a substantial and lasting effect on Gleizes's artistic development. Even as he became an innovative fine artist, Gleizes retained the workmanlike approach that he learned in his father's workshop.

In 1906 Gleizes moved into Abbaye de Créteil, an idealistic artists commune. Designed to provide artists and writers with a means of limiting their labor in order to focus on their craft, the Abbaye pursued a bucolic and utopian way of life but was ultimately untenable. Despite the fact that the experiment failed within a year, Gleizes remained committed to the idea of communal living and made multiple attempts to establish new artist communities later in his life.

a very slow transformation, and that slowness can be explained: how could comprehension evolve as rapidly as the creative faculties? It trails behind them." In this way, Gleizes and Metzinger are able to co-opt doubt as proof of cubism's farsightedness and truth.

CRITICAL DISCUSSION

On "Cubism" garnered an immediate enthusiastic response. For skeptics, the text offered a persuasive case for the seriousness of the cubist project. As David Cottington writes in Cubism and Its Histories (2004), the text "immediately became a reference work on contemporary art for commentators across Europe." For cubists themselves, the work provided, for the first time, an attempt at a self-definition of the movement's motivations and aims. In defining cubism, On "Cubism" provoked rebellion against that very definition. In A Cubism Reader (2008), Antliff and Patricia Leighten write that "the publication of Du 'Cubisme' was the product of a theoretical consensus in cubist circles that proved to be very brief, even for its authors."

On "Cubism" remains an important point of reference in the ongoing development of cubism. In the wake of the text's appearance, cubism did not calcify into the framework set out by Gleizes and Metzinger. Rather, it continued to evolve, often in response to the essay. Marcel Duchamp, a close associate of Gleizes and Metzinger prior to the publication of On "Cubism," explicitly rebelled against the text. According to Antliff and Leighten in Cubism and Culture (2001), Duchamp, in his 1914 piece Bottlerack, "attacks the notion of intuition, championed by Gleizes and

Paysage avec personnages (Landscape with Figures), a 1911 Cubist painting by Albert Gleizes. GIANNI DAGLI ORTI/THE ART ARCHIVE AT ART RESOURCE, NY

now sought to transcend." Commentators have also drawn attention to the work's "elitist" argument about the role of taste in artistic appreciation. Cottington argues that Metzinger and Gleizes use taste "as a means of sorting the sheep from the goats within the expanding menagerie of the artistic avant-garde." According to Cottington, this statement and others like it are representative of an "undisguised elitism serving to underscore the clear separation its authors wished to establish between their art and popular culture."

BIBLIOGRAPHY

Sources

Antliff, Mark, and Patricia Leighten. *A Cubism Reader: Documents and Criticism, 1906-1914.* Chicago: U of Chicago P, 2008. Print.

Brettell, Richard R. *Modern Art 1851-1929: Capitalism and Representation.* New York: Oxford UP, 1999. Print.

Cottington, David. *Cubism.* New York: Cambridge UP, 1998. Print.

———. *Cubism and Its Histories.* New York: Manchester UP, 2004. Print.

Gamwell, Lynn. *Cubist Criticism.* Ann Arbor: UMI, 1996. Print.

Further Reading

Antliff, Mark. *Inventing Bergson: Cultural Politics and the Parisian Avant-Garde.* Princeton: Princeton UP, 1993. Print.

Antliff, Mark, and Patricia Leighten. *Cubism and Culture.* New York: Thames and Hudson, 2001. Print.

Apollinaire, Guillaume. *The Cubist Painters.* Trans. Peter Read. East Sussex: Artists Bookworks, 2002. Print.

Brook, Peter. *Albert Gleizes, for and against the Twentieth Century.* New Haven: Yale UP, 2001. Print.

Cottington, David. *Cubism and the Shadow of War: The Avant-Garde and Politics in Paris, 1905-1914.* New Haven: Yale UP, 1999. Print.

Gray, Christopher. "The Cubist Conception of Reality." *College Art Journal* 13.1 (1953): 19-23. Print.

Henderson, Linda D. *The Fourth Dimension and Non-Euclidean Geometry in Modern Art.* Princeton: Princeton UP, 1983. Print.

Nash, John. "The Nature of Cubism: A Study of Conflicting Interpretations." *Art History* 3.4 (1980): 436-47. Print.

Theodore McDermott

Metzinger in *Du 'Cubisme'* (1912), both through his presentation of an unaltered 'found object' as a work of art and in the *éqouttoir*'s punning rejection of *goût* or artistic 'taste.'" In the century since the piece was written, it has been the subject of an extensive body of criticism that has considered its legacy in aesthetic, historical, and philosophical terms.

Much scholarship has centered on the aesthetic argument about pictorial space that is made in *On "Cubism."* As Antliff and Leighten write, "By associating pure 'visual space' with three-dimensional Euclidean space, and its step-child, Renaissance perspective, the cubists signaled the perceptual limitations underlying the art of the past, an art they

ON CUBISM

Pierre Reverdy

OVERVIEW

Pierre Reverdy's "Sur le Cubisme," or "On Cubism," was first published in 1917 in the inaugural issue of his journal *Nord-Sud* and articulates his views on cubism. The journal itself was named after a north-south subway line in Paris that connected the artist neighborhoods Montmartre and Montparnasse. Reverdy edited *Nord-Sud* with other experimental poets, including Guillaume Apollinaire, Vicente Huidobro, and Max Jacob. There was, by then, no dearth of cubist literature and criticism; paintings in this style had been exhibited in Paris for a decade, and most newspapers were staffed with art critics to review the work. However, few writers were as perceptive on the subject as Reverdy. He proved capable of solving the internal problems of cubism, acutely criticizing some practitioners while championing others.

Though most Parisian painters were trying out the new formal techniques of cubism by 1917, many did not fully understand its questions. Minor painters reproduced the cubist experimentations of Pablo Picasso, Georges Braque, and Juan Gris, who were reacting against the one-point perspective that had dominated painting for nearly five hundred years. In his essay, Reverdy implicitly states which artists are practicing cubism in a productive way and which are being imitative. One direct consequence of the critique was that Reverdy and Mexican painter Diego Rivera, who was newly trying out the form, came to blows outside of a café. Eventually, Reverdy's cubist theories would be taken up by poets who sought to problematize subjects, objects, and duration in their works.

HISTORICAL AND LITERARY CONTEXT

Cubism can be traced to Paul Cézanne and to the liberating influence of African and other non-European sculpture, examples of which were on display in Paris at the Musée d'Ethnographie du Trocadéro, an anthropological museum founded in 1878. The shapes and profiles of the museum's artifacts were directly incorporated into the figures of Picasso, as seen in his *Les Demoiselles d'Avignon* (1907). Cézanne, meanwhile, was the immediate predecessor to Picasso and Braque. He had narrowed the visual field of his compositions and had invented the technique of *passage,* in which one plane of a composition passes through

another. Picasso and Braque incorporated this technique into their own art. Passage is used to break the illusion of depth; its geometric shapes do not result in abstraction but rather reinforce the internal reality of the work. In general, cubist painters were highly logical and nearly scientific in form; Gris, for example, used a mathematical equation to compose his works.

"On Cubism" was published during World War I, in which many painters and poets living in France served, save Picasso and Gris, who were Spaniards. Gradually, those who were wounded, including Braque and Guillaume Apollinaire, returned from the front to Paris and resumed their work. Reverdy himself fought in World War I as well as World War II. The rigorous logic of cubism has been viewed in contrast to the illogic of warfare and politics, though it is not quite that simple. While Reverdy was a radical who would eventually have a hand in liberating Paris, "On Cubism" does not directly tie aesthetics to politics. What Reverdy argues against is using painting as a means to access something else, whether a reality external to the work or a higher power. To this end, he says, "Cubism is an eminently plastic art; but an art of creation, not of reproduction or interpretation."

Before Reverdy published his text, Apollinaire wrote many reviews of various painters, including Henri Matisse and Braque, as well as criticism of the mode itself in articles such as "The Beginnings of Cubism" (1912). Apollinaire, however, never went so far as to answer questions that the painters were posing or direct the artist to an overlooked aesthetic problem. Prior to Reverdy, only Jacques Rivière, the essayist and educator, had been so clear in his observations. Rivière noted the problem of light in cubist paintings at a time when artists were still providing the viewer with the illusion of depth using a technique called *chiaroscuro.*

Reverdy's theorization not only helped painters to notice what they had left unattended, but it also made the pictures meaningful to the non-painting public. In the essay he explains that the perceived distortion in cubism is only the result of "what is eternal and constant" being "extracted" from objects in the world. This essentialist value system can also be observed in Reverdy's poetry, though he never characterized that form as cubist. The self-referential quality of his work, fixated as it is on borders and reflections,

❖ *Key Facts*

Time Period:
Early 20th Century

Movement/Issue:
Cubism; Aesthetics

Place of Publication:
France

**Language of
Publication:**
French

PIERRE REVERDY'S RETREAT

Pierre Reverdy (1889-1960) was a famously reticent and mysterious man, even to his friends. Today, however, a few key biographical details are widely known. When Reverdy first lived in Paris, he was poor and took a job at a print shop, where he was required to work overnight shifts. He used the shop to print his first book as well as issues of *Nord-Sud.* Most of his books were illustrated by his cubist friends, and the first, *Prose Poems* (1915), was issued in an edition of one hundred and includes drawings by Juan Gris. Though he was close with many painters and poets in Paris, his solitary and spiritual qualities led him to leave that urban atmosphere in 1926 and move with his wife to live near a Benedictine monastery in Solesmes.

The retreat lent his poetry the stark and haunting qualities that are most remarked upon by critics today. His poems have emerged as some of the finest examples of modernism. Reverdy is praised for his fluency with the prose poem, his use of parataxis, and the austere and solitary position of his speaker. The prose poem "Under the Stars" could have been written today, contemporary as its syntax is with lines such as "I have in all likelihood lost the key and everyone laughs all about me, each one showing me a mammoth key hung about his neck."

gained more recognition in the 1950s and has been noted in the stylings of younger poets such as Robert Creeley and Gary Snyder.

THEMES AND STYLE

"On Cubism" makes a case for eliminating discrepancies in artists' understanding of the form. Reverdy maps out "certain essential points" in an effort to unify the cubist theory, contending that "the picture itself" is the subject and that objects within the piece should be distilled down to their constitutive properties in order to better serve the particular needs of the work. In arguing that art is all the more real when it exists "apart from the evocation or reproduction of the things of life," Reverdy reinforces the value of the cubist perspective and its aesthetic purpose. It is possible that the "superficial side" of what he deems a "profound art" is still what is seen today, as the general public regards cubism as simply representing multiple angles and perspectives at once. Reverdy, however, insists in his essay that cubism radically alters the relationship between artists and their works. By "detaching themselves from life," these works "find their way back into it" and become all the more real and relevant.

Reverdy's essay addresses the artistic community, calling for it to "come together and understand one another better." He dares to direct painters in an undertaking whose execution differs vastly from his own medium and insinuates that many minor painters are

on the wrong track. Despite its aims of unification, however, the essay wound up dividing the community by delineating who was merely painting "*in the manner*" of the genuine practitioners. Gris addressed this polarization in a letter he later wrote, saying that "painters were wrong to get worked up about Reverdy's article, which is not aggressive and does no more than set out a few ideas with which one can either agree or disagree." Either way, the controversy brought more attention to "On Cubism" than it otherwise might have received.

In his ultimate respect for the formal revolution represented by cubism, Reverdy's tone is that of a passionate intellectual. He argues that the cubist tendency to add words to compositions presents the viewer with "a facile and dangerous appearance of novelty." Though he is a poet, he is able to convince his audience that he has the authority to cover painting because of his accurate reading of what has occurred so far in the form. Furthermore, he is able to set his high expectations for painters precisely because of the high esteem in which he holds cubism, which he considers to be "painting itself."

CRITICAL DISCUSSION

Although "On Cubism" had a polarizing effect, many painters adhered to its views and subsequently refined their techniques. Six months after it was published, Braque would write "Thoughts on Painting" for *Nord-Sud,* in which he echoes what been mapped out by Reverdy. In the piece Braque theorizes that "the subject is not the object; it is the new unity" and "one does not imitate the appearance; the appearance is the result." A further reaction to Reverdy's decree can be seen in cubist paintings themselves after 1917, which became more flattened and geometric, as in Picasso's *Still Life with Pipe and Glass* (1918) and Gris's *The Man from Touraine* (1918).

Reverdy's critical involvement in the field of visual art led poet Kenneth Rexroth to ask in his translation of *Selected Poems,* "But what is the Cubism in poetry?" During World War I poets such as Gertrude Stein, André Salmon, and Blaise Cendrars had written art criticism about the form. Stein's language, which accrues meaning through its repetition, has been referred to as cubist. Reverdy's poems, however, are nothing like Stein's, relying very little on repetition or rhythm. Rexroth considers Reverdy's poems to be ultimately in keeping with his "On Cubism" due to "the conscious, deliberate dissociation and recombination of elements into a new artistic entity made self-sufficient by its rigorous architecture." The interiority of Reverdy's poetry is countered by his use of stark objects, such as hands and walls, which had also made cubist paintings legible to the public.

Recent scholarship has turned toward the lack of discussion about the war in "On Cubism." Jennifer

Pap remarks in her 2006 essay in *Modern Language Review* that although the work "can certainly be said to turn away from the contingencies of history," it is not necessarily escapist to call for the subject to be "the picture itself." Pap argues that Reverdy was transforming rather than suppressing his experience of the war. Her position is countered by Christopher Butler, who explains in his book *Early Modernism: Literature, Music and Painting in Europe 1900-1916* (1994) that the "aim then was not to provide reliable descriptions of external reality, but to produce forms which modified these in such a way as to provoke psychological responses" that would convey "subjective experience." Reverdy himself argues in his essay that there is a balance between the emotion or context "in which the work comes into being" and the emotion the work brings about, adding that "all art stands between these two poles."

BIBLIOGRAPHY

Sources

Butler, Christopher. *Early Modernism: Literature, Music and Painting in Europe 1900-1916.* Oxford: Clarendon, 1994. Print.

Fry, Edward F. *Cubism.* London: Thames & Hudson, 1978. Print.

Pap, Jennifer. "Transforming the Horizon: Reverdy's World War I." *Modern Language Review* 101.4 (2006). 966-78. *JSTOR.* Web. 24 Sept. 2012.

Reverdy, Pierre. *Selected Poems.* Trans. Kenneth Rexroth. New York: New Directions, 1969. Print.

Further Reading

Apollinaire, Guillaume. *Apollinaire on Art: Essays and Reviews 1902-1918.* Ed. Leroy C. Breunig. Trans. Susan Suleiman. Viking, 1972. Print.

Green, Christopher. *Juan Gris.* New Haven: Yale UP, 1993. Print.

Greene, Robert W. "Pierre Reverdy, Poet of Nausea." *PMLA* 85.1 (1970): 48-55. *JSTOR.* Web. 24 Sept. 2012.

Krauss, Rosalind E. *The Originality of the Avant-Garde.* Cambridge: MIT P, 1986. Print.

North, Percy. "Bringing Cubism to America: Max Weber and Pablo Picasso." *American Art* 14.3 (2000): 58-77. *JSTOR.* Web. 24 Sept. 2012.

Reverdy, Pierre. *Roof Slates and Other Poems of Pierre Reverdy.* Trans. Mary Ann Caws and Patricia Terry. Boston: Northeastern UP, 1981. Print.

Caitie Moore

Pierre Reverdy *(left)* with Cubist painter Pablo Picasso and artists Jean Cocteau and Brassaï, in Paris in 1944. PRIVATE COLLECTION/ ARCHIVES CHARMET/THE BRIDGEMAN ART LIBRARY

ON THE SUBJECT OF MODERN PAINTING

Guillaume Apollinaire

✤ **Key Facts**

Time Period:
Early 20th Century

Movement/Issue:
Aesthetics; Modernism;
Cubism

Place of Publication:
France

**Language of
Publication:**
French

OVERVIEW

Written by French poet and critic Guillaume Apollinaire, "On the Subject of Modern Painting" (1912) describes a modern art that rejects the painting of the past—in which the subject is a reconstitution of nature—in favor of an art in which the subject is artistic expression itself. The essay was first published as the opening article in the premiere issue of *Les Soirées de Paris,* a periodical established by André Billy and others for the publication of Apollinaire's critical articles. During this period Apollinaire made weekly visits to the Paris salons, where he viewed the work of newcomers such as Giorgio de Chirico, Marc Chagall, Henri Matisse, Marcel Duchamp, and Robert Delaunay. "On the Subject of Modern Painting" arose as a response to the works of the avant-garde and more specifically to heightened levels of abstraction in the synthetic cubist paintings of 1911 and 1912.

Although *Les Soirées de Paris* did not have a large readership, one of its cofounders, René Dalize, wor-

ried that "On the Subject of Modern Painting" might affect its circulation. He protested that Apollinaire only wanted to promote the cubists, most of whom Dalize believed had no talent. Despite opposition to the article, Apollinaire did not waiver in his beliefs. Less than a year later he reused part of "On the Subject of Modern Painting" in an article titled "Esthetic Meditations," and by 1913 he published it as part of the introduction to his only book of criticism, *The Cubist Painters* "On the Subject of Modern Painting" is today considered one of the most important aesthetic statements on the development of cubism and early twentieth century avant-garde painting.

HISTORICAL AND LITERARY CONTEXT

"On the Subject of Modern Painting" responds to the development of the European avant-garde at the end of the nineteenth and beginning of the twentieth centuries. Painters of this period began to abandon traditional representational "realism" in favor of brighter palettes, heavier paint application, and increasing levels of abstraction. Five years prior to the essay's publication, a retrospective exhibition consisting of fifty-six of Paul Cezanne's paintings was held in Paris. The geometricization of forms found in Cezanne's late work had a profound influence on the Parisian avant-garde, most specifically Pablo Picasso. This geometricization and abstraction was evident in Picasso's *Les Demoiselles d'Avignon,* a proto-cubist work that so impressed Apollinaire he claimed that language could not adequately describe it, "for our words are made in advance." By 1912 several avant-garde groups, including the cubists and the futurists, were incorporating greater levels of abstraction into works that were increasingly self-referential.

By the time "On the Subject of Modern Painting" was first issued in 1912, the avant-garde art scene in Paris was rife with competing schools and aesthetics. Several years prior to the publication of his article, Apollinaire established a strong friendship with Picasso. He also introduced Picasso to Georges Braque, thereby accelerating the cross-breeding of their cubist styles. Along with cubism, other avant-garde groups were on the rise, such as Section d'Or, futurists, and Orphists. Duchamp painted his most famous work, *Nude Descending the Stairs,* in 1912 when Chagall, Matisse, and Delaunay were all living and painting in

APOLLINAIRE: THE SOLDIER

In March 1915, heartbroken by the end of his affair with Louise de Coligny-Châtillon, Guillaume Apollinaire volunteered to fight in World War I. He continued to write poetry while on the front, much of it a celebration of war—or a celebration of life in the midst of death—and he was overjoyed that he, a professional poet, could contribute as much as other men. According to biographer Margaret Davies, in her book *Apollinaire,* the objects of warfare soon became the imagery of his poems: "A burnt out shell is his heart, the love exploded and gone, the gun-flares are women dancing, the snakes in the trenches a woman's sinuous arms."

In his enthusiasm for the war, and because of his desire to become an officer, Apollinaire requested a transfer to infantry, where he discovered the real difficulties of the conflict. Now he was in the frontline trenches in a "desolation of mud and ice." There was insufficient food, no water, and no beds, but Apollinaire endured the difficulties and proved himself a brave officer. In the spring of 1916, while reading the literary gazette *Mercure de France,* a fragment of a shell pierced his helmet and wounded him on the right temple. He was sent back to Paris and died two years later of Spanish influenza.

Paris. To create a voice for art criticism in such a fecund era, Apollinaire, André Billy, Dalize, and others founded *Les Soirées de Paris,* in which "On the Subject of Modern Painting" was first published as a defense of the avant-garde against academic painting.

Although "On the Subject of Modern Painting" is often considered a manifesto, it was originally published as a piece of art criticism. Its antecedents and influences then are less modernist art manifestos and more critical works of poets-cum-critics such as Stendhal, Denis Diderot, Oscar Wilde, and Charles Baudelaire. Apollinaire's poetic description of Picasso as a surgeon reminds the reader of Baudelaire's incisive and poetic statement about Eugène Delacroix's work—that it was "a volcanic crater artistically concealed beneath bouquets of flowers." Alfred Werner's statement about Baudelaire's criticism—that his "finest pages are those on the roles of art criticism of art, and of genius"—could easily have been written about Apollinaire.

In the century since its publication, "On the Subject of Modern Painting" has continued to be one of the most important critical works on the aesthetics of modern art. Although much of the early literature surrounding the essay decried Apollinaire as an amateur, contemporary scholars recognize the historical significance of his work and the perspicacity of his judgments regarding cubism and modern art in general.

THEMES AND STYLE

The central theme of "On the Subject of Modern Painting" is that the artists of the avant-garde have freed themselves from the hindrances of the past and of representation and that the subject of modern art is "pure painting" or artistic expression itself. Hitherto it has been the skillful representation of objects found in nature that constitute pleasure art. Now, according to Apollinaire, abstract art creates these pleasures simply through "the harmony of contrasting hues and light." As a result, Apollinaire argues, modern painting will continue to embrace greater levels of abstraction and it may one day "manage to free itself entirely from the old style of painting."

The essay achieves its rhetorical effect in two ways: by drawing comparisons between modern art and music and by establishing historical authority and continuity for the avant-garde. With the use of the inclusive first-person plural, Apollinaire claims that "we are moving towards an entirely new art.... It will be pure painting, as music is pure literature." He argues that music lovers experience different joys when listening to a concert or natural sounds. Similarly, "new painters will provide their admirers" with different pleasures than those derived from viewing representations of natural phenomena. As evidence, and to lend historical authority and continuity to this position, Apollinaire retells Pliny the Elder's story of Apelle and Protogenes, in which each painter drew a finer and finer line and the viewers of the painting "gazed on it

Paysage de Ceret (Landscape, Ceret), a 1913 Cubist painting by Juan Gris. In "On the Subject of Modern Painting," Guillaume Apollinaire describes modern painters' shift toward abstraction. GIANNI DAGLI ORTI/THE ART ARCHIVE AT ART RESOURCE, NY

with as much pleasure as if, instead of showing almost invisible lines, it depicted gods and goddesses."

"On the Subject of Modern Painting" is distinguished stylistically by its blend of simple, declarative prose and poetic lyricism. Written as art criticism, Apollinaire strengthens its arguments with his poetic sensibilities. His abstractions about the pleasures of music and sound are made concrete with lyrical phrases about the "murmur of streams, the roar of a waterfall, the wind soughing through a forest, or the harmonies of human speech." His poeticism is also capable of a remarkable compression of idea, as in "Picasso studies an object like a surgeon dissecting a corpse," which not only presents the reader with a visceral image of the lines and angles of Picasso's work but also articulates one of the goals of cubism: to render familiar objects abstractly to reexamine them, to present again as yet unseen sides.

CRITICAL DISCUSSION

When "On the Subject of Modern Painting" was first published in 1912, reactions ranged from hostility to praise. Dalize, cofounder of *Les Soirées,* attacked Apollinaire, saying that the "*Soirées* was not created to support the ignorant and pretentious painters with whom you surround yourself only because they flatter you." The controversy surrounding the cubist exhibitions of the period made the publication of *The Cubist Painters* (1913), which contains the essay, a newsworthy event, even in general interest newspapers such as *Le Temps* In the premiere issue of *Montjoie!* Maurice Raynal articulated one of the period's most typical responses to Apollinaire's art criticism: that Apollinaire "does not *understand* painting, *but sees it and experiences it,*" a refrain that would later be echoed by Picasso and, with a more negative connotation, by the foremost cubist art dealer Daniel-Henry Kahnweiler. Picasso never abandoned representation, and he abhorred paintings that did. For him, the issue with "On the Subject of Modern Painting" was its presentation of cubism as nonrepresentational art. Apollinaire's essay was unquestionably important, helping to shape much of the thinking about cubism and art in general during the second decade of the twentieth century. But it is arguably not an apt account of what was going on within the cubism of Picasso and Braque.

After Apollinaire's death in 1918, "On the Subject of Modern Painting" remained an oft-disputed piece of art criticism. According to Peter Read, in the notes for his translation of *The Cubist Painters,* Kahnweiler "would rarely miss an opportunity to speak ill of Apollinaire's art criticism." Kahnweiler claimed that Apollinaire "knew nothing about painting." According to Read, these views negatively influenced the views of "notable art historians, particularly in Britain and the United States." More recently, however, art historians such as William Buckley and Peter Read have sought to reestablish Apollinaire's reputation as a critic. In the century since its initial publication, his essay has attracted broad scholarly interest for its significance as one of the first critical writings on cubism and the French avant-garde.

Much scholarship has focused on establishing the legitimacy of Apollinaire's criticism in "On the Subject of Modern Painting," despite its lack of a contemporary critical vocabulary. Discussing the aesthetic impact of the text, as well as his art criticism in general, Buckley observes in his book *Guillaume Apollinaire as an Art Critic* that "no other critic produced the quantity of material that is now available in the books and collected journalism of Apollinaire. No other critic displays for the avant-garde the interest which Apollinaire possessed." Read describes Apollinaire as a daring critic who courted controversy and gambled on "reputations which were not yet assured," yet his "choices have been validated by posterity." He also argues that "On the Subject of Modern Painting" correctly identifies "self-referentiality" as one of the most important aesthetic tendencies in modern art.

BIBLIOGRAPHY

Sources

Apollinaire, Guillaume. *The Cubist Painters.* Ed. Peter Read. Berkeley: U of California P, 2004. Print.

Buckley, Harry E. *Guillaume Apollinaire as an Art Critic.* Ann Arbor: UMI Research, 1981. Print.

Davies, Margaret. *Apollinaire.* London: Oliver & Boyd, 1964. Print.

Read, Peter. *Apollinaire and Picasso: The Persistence of Memory.* Berkeley: U of California P, 2008. Print.

Werner, Alfred. "Baudelaire: Art Critic." *Kenyon Review* 28.5 (1966): 650-52. *JSTOR.* Web. 17 Aug. 2012.

Further Reading

Apollinaire, Guillaume, Dorothea Eimert,and Anatoli Podoksik. *Cubism.* New York: Parkstone Press International, 2010. Print.

Bohn, Willard. *Apollinaire and the International Avant-Garde.* Albany: State U of New York P, 1997. Print.

———. *Apollinaire, Visual Poetry, and Art Criticism.* Lewisburg: Bicknell UP, 1993. Print.

Chicken, Adrian. *Apollinaire, Cubism, and Orphism.* Burlington: Ashgate, 2002. Print.

Samaltanos-Stenström, Katia. *Apollinaire, Catalyst for Primitivism, Picabia, and Duchamp.* Ann Arbor: UMI Research, 1984. Print.

Gregory Luther

OUR VORTEX

Wyndham Lewis

OVERVIEW

"Our Vortex," composed by English painter and author Wyndham Lewis (1882-1957), was one of several brief essays to articulate the aims of the vorticist art movement. It was first published in *Blast: Review of the Great English Vortex,* a 1914 magazine that expressed the movement's goal of capturing the vitality and forcefulness of a new technological era. Although the vorticists shared this project with the Italian futurists, Lewis and others believed that futurist movement was sentimental, even idolatrous, in its treatment of automobiles and other human-made objects. Written in four sections of roughly ten lines each, "Our Vortex" is as much a free-verse poem as it is an organized list, cataloguing vorticist articles of faith regarding time, emotion, and the political role of the artist.

"Our Vortex" was an ancillary work, written to clarify a position stated at greater length in "Long Live the Vortex!" and the "Vorticist Manifesto" (both printed in *Blast*). The bold claims of these essays were soon undercut, not by a rebuttal from a rival movement but by World War I, which disastrously thinned the ranks of the vorticists. Lewis survived his tour of duty but returned to find little left of the artistic circle he had helped to found. He briefly attempted to rekindle enthusiasm for the vorticist project, but the movement was effectively dead by 1920. Although Lewis had struggled mightily in "Our Vortex" to establish the difference between vorticism and futurism, an association between the two persisted among critics, who often elided the very distinctions the author sought to preserve. Today vorticism is considered a minor historical trend, important chiefly in connection with the later (postvorticist) work of founding members such as Lewis and the poet Ezra Pound.

HISTORICAL AND LITERARY CONTEXT

The literary critic Roger B. Henkle has characterized Vorticism as "a delayed response to the sense of change and cultural liberation that hung over England after the death of Victoria, stimulated ... by the rapid technological advances of the early century" (1979). Lewis and his fellow vorticists found themselves in a welter of such characterizations, many of them made well before 1914, and thus strove to differentiate themselves from other aesthetics that they considered inferior. As a painter, Lewis had produced work in the vein of cubism and futurism but concluded that these were infected with the same "sentimentality" as impressionism, a style he saw as sustained primarily by nostalgia. Moreover, he considered these movements to be Continental "imports" and hoped to establish an art style that responded to specifically English concerns.

Lewis's rebuttal of these trends came in the form of *Blast: Review of the Great English Vortex* (1914). *Blast* incorporated numerous specimens of vorticist painting and drawing, along with a notable selection of poetry by Pound. In editing this publication (and providing ample commentary via "Our Vortex" and other essays), Lewis hoped to distinguish vorticism from superficially similar work with a different underlying philosophy. Especially troublesome in this regard was Italian futurism, a movement inaugurated in 1909 and well under way at the time of *Blast*'s publication. Many of the points raised in "Our Vortex" are direct refutations of futurist concepts.

Indeed, Lewis's treatment of futurism in "Our Vortex" extends beyond particular issues to engage futurism on the levels of form and language. Elsewhere in *Blast*, Lewis speaks of the tendency of founding futurist poet F.T. Marinetti to "hammer away in the blatant mechanism of his Manifestos," yet Lewis evidently adopts much of this "machinery" in his own writing. "Our Vortex" in particular is built on a similar template as Marinetti's 1909 "Futurist Manifesto," and many of Lewis's points correspond directly to Marinetti's declarations therein. Lewis critiques Marinetti's emphatic and grandiose gestures, answering with an almost patronizing calm. Where the Italian poet declares "We are on the extreme promontory of the centuries!" Lewis counters that "the Future is distant, like the past, and therefore sentimental." Likewise, in opposition to Marinetti's glorification of "ruinous and incendiary violence," Lewis declares that "the Vorticist is not the Slave of Commotion, but it's [sic] Master."

Few, if any, direct literary descendants of "Our Vortex" exist. The work appeared alongside so many other manifesto-like expressions of vorticist ideals that it is difficult to separate them in retrospect. Initial supporters of vorticism—including T.S. Eliot and Pound, who coined the movement's name —went on to pursue idiosyncratic poetic projects that would be much more closely associated with modernism. Moreover,

❖ *Key Facts*

Time Period:
Early 20th Century

Movement/Issue:
Aesthetics; Vorticism

Place of Publication:
England

Language of Publication:
English

VORTICISM AND FASCISM

One possible source of the critical reticence surrounding vorticism lies in Wyndham Lewis's association with fascism, which had a chilling effect on his reception among Anglophone audiences. Lewis made little overt show of supporting fascism during his vorticist years, but persistent confusions between Italian futurism and English vorticism ensured that the claim could be made by the author's enemies—for example, members of the influential "Bloomsbury Group," whom the vorticists satirized. As the author built a later career independent of vorticist ideology, he increasingly gave vent to political opinions that scandalized the English and American literary establishments.

Lewis would first record his thoughts on fascism in the 1926 nonfiction work *The Art of Being Ruled*, but his political isolation in England would be all but confirmed with the publication of *Hitler* (1931), which presented the ascendant Nazi politician in a favorable light. The iconoclastic Lewis found much to critique in Italian fascism as the movement developed, including a fascination with the past similar to the "sentimentality" he had disparaged in futurist art; likewise, he completely revised his position on Hitler in the 1939 volume *The Hitler Cult*. The nuance and flexibility with which Lewis approached his political positions, however, did little to counteract their unpopularity among English readers.

Opposite page:
A 1913 self-portrait in the Vorticist style by Henri Gaudier-Brzeska, one of the artists who signed the manifesto "Our Vortex." SOUTHAMPTON CITY ART GALLERY, HAMPSHIRE, UK/THE BRIDGEMAN ART LIBRARY

even though many of the leading modernists had clear and highly politicized views of aesthetic questions, few of them drew up anything as frankly annunciatory as the vorticist manifestos. Several twentieth-century political manifestos share the listlike simplicity and arresting concision of "Our Vortex," but none derives from the latter to an identifiable extent.

THEMES AND STYLE

"Our Vortex," like many of the essays in *Blast,* defines vorticism primarily in terms of what the movement is not. Futurism constitutes the most obvious and sustained target of the essay and is attacked on a number of grounds. The essential difference, for Lewis, is that futurism is sentimental whereas vorticism is rational. "In a Vorticist Universe," Lewis writes, "we don't get excited at what we have invented. / If we did it would look as though it had been a fluke." Lewis further construes futurist "excitement" over human-made technologies as part of a larger philosophical perversion. Whereas futurists seem to revere machines (especially cars), vorticists "hunt machines, they are our favourite game." Finally, in place of the futurist preoccupation with dynamic movement, Lewis claims that "the Vorticist is at his maximum point of energy when stillest."

As *Blast*'s subtitle suggests, Lewis portrayed vorticism as a peculiarly English phenomenon and, in so doing, hoped to awaken the artistic spirit of his countrymen. Though not as strident as other passages from *Blast*, "Our Vortex" maintains the distinction between an intellectually rigorous English vorticism and a Continental futurism, which it often portrays as childish. Lewis extends this dichotomy to impressionism, which he portrays as an unwanted refugee "attempting to eke out a little life in these islands." Lewis, however, stops short of categorically disparaging Continental artists: at one point he invokes the idea of a "Rembrandt Vortex" as a historical precedent for his concept of artistic revolution.

"Our Vortex" proceeds in a succession of freestanding lines, each of them containing a single sentence; these are generally abstract pronouncements regarding the vorticist position on time, technology, and emotion. Lewis favors anaphora as a means of lending unity to his claims: lines throughout begin with slight variants of "Our Vortex..." or "The Vorticist..." Imagery, where used, is sparse and striking, as when the past and the future are figured as "the prostitutes Nature has provided" to distract artists. The fourth and final section is more densely populated with images and bears an intensity, even a violence, otherwise absent from the essay: the Vortex is likened to a "disastrous polished dance," endowed with "red-hot swiftness," and unleashed "like an angry dog at your Impressionistic fuss."

CRITICAL DISCUSSION

"Our Vortex" (and *Blast* in general) failed to attract much critical notice upon publication, largely because nonvorticists could not reliably distinguish the movement's products from those of its rivals. Literary historian Archie Loss notes that "to any observer of the English art scene of the mid-1910s to the mid-1920s, Cubism, Futurism, and Vorticism blended together to form a common aesthetic vision" (1992). World War I put an almost complete halt to the production of new works by vorticists and, perhaps more importantly, revealed a definitive dark side to the technological advancements celebrated by artists of the early 1910s. For Lewis's English audience, neither futurist exuberance nor vorticist self-assurance seemed an appropriate postwar stance: machines, the vorticists' "favourite game," had shown their own predatory potential.

"Our Vortex" continued to provoke relatively little discussion through the mid-twentieth century, as the polyphonic literature of modernism came to prominence. Former vorticist Pound began to view the movement with nostalgic regret but voiced this primarily in private correspondence, demoting vorticism to the status of "a private joke from childhood" (R. Lewis, 1985). Wyndham Lewis himself would declare, via subsequent publications, new aesthetic positions that bore little resemblance to vorticism except in their emphasis on satire. Thomas R. Smith wrote in 1980 that Lewis's oeuvre, including the vorticist works, had been "largely ignored by literary critics"—so much so, in fact, that Smith considered his writing a "literary time capsule" preserved from the distorting effects of a critical tradition.

Only at the end of the twentieth century, when it became clear that a postmortem analysis could at last be performed on modernism, did "Our Vortex" attain a measure of critical significance as one of the movement's forerunners. Critics have returned to "Our Vortex" partly in an effort to appreciate vorticism's impact on modernist poetics, as well as to understand the commonalities between Lewis's more highly regarded later work and his vorticist beginnings. Julian Hanna (2007) presents the view that Lewis gradually developed the manifesto form into a major component of his literary work, and Carolyn Marie Tilghman (2007) suggests that, upon reexamination, vorticism was in many ways doomed from the start. In Tilghman's estimation, the aims espoused in "Our Vortex" (and in other *Blast* works by Lewis) were "continually beset by conflict on the cultural, political, and economic fronts," leading to "a losing, anxiety-inducing competition" with better-remembered literary and arts movements.

BIBLIOGRAPHY

Sources

Hanna, Julian. "Blasting after *Blast*: Wyndham Lewis's Late Manifestos." *Journal of Modern Literature* 31.1 (2007): 124-35. Print.

Henkle, Roger B. "The 'Advertised' Self: Wyndham Lewis' Satire." *NOVEL: A Forum on Fiction* 13.1 (1979): 95-108. Print.

Lewis, Roger. Review of *Pound/Lewis: The Letters of Ezra Pound and Wyndham Lewis* by Timothy Materer. *New England Quarterly* 58.4 (1985): 607-14. Print.

Loss, Archie. "*Vile Bodies,* Vorticism, and Italian Futurism." *Journal of Modern Literature* 18.1 (1992): 155-64. Print.

Smith, Thomas R. "Opening a Literary Time Capsule." Review of *Fables of Aggression: Wyndham Lewis, the Modernist as Fascist* by Fredric Jameson. *Hudson Review* 33.2 (1980): 288-92. Print.

Tilghman, Carolyn Marie. "Lewis in Contention: Identity, Anxiety, and the London Vortex." *South Central Review* 24.3 (2007): 2-22. Print.

Wagner, Geoffrey. "Wyndham Lewis and the Vorticist Aesthetic." *Journal of Aesthetics & Art Criticism* 13.1 (1954): 1-17. Print.

Further Reading

Dasenbrock, Reed Way. *The Literary Vorticism of Ezra Pound and Wyndham Lewis: Towards the Condition of Painting.* Baltimore: Johns Hopkins UP, 1985. Print.

Edwards, Paul, ed. *Blast: Vorticism 1914-1918.* Burlington, VT: Ashgate, 2000. Print.

Lewis, Wyndham, ed. *Blast: Review of the Great English Vortex* 1 (1914): 147-49. *The Modernist Journals Project.* Web. 29 June 2012.

Materer, Timothy. "The English Vortex: Modern Literature and the 'Pattern of Hope.'" *Journal of Modern Literature* 3.5 (1974): 1123-39. Print.

Rae, Patricia. "From Mystical Gaze to Pragmatic Game: Representations of Truth in Vorticist Art." *ELH* 56.3 (1989): 689-720. Print.

Michael Hartwell

PREFACE TO *DER BLAUE REITER ALMANACH*

Wassily Kandinsky, Franz Marc

OVERVIEW

Written by artists Wassily Kandinsky and Franz Marc, the preface to the book *Der Blaue Reiter Almanach* (*The Blue Rider Almanac*), originally published in German in 1912 and edited by Kandinsky and Marc, introduces a collection of artwork from the Blue Rider art movement, as well as essays and aesthetic theories, from a range of artists, composers, and writers who were linked by the wish to express inner truths through art. As the alliance between these diversely creative personalities attests, the Blue Rider movement established a connection between art and music and between primitive, modern, and nonfigurative works of art. More than just an introduction, Kandinsky and Marc's text builds on aesthetic theories set out in *Über das Geistige in der Kunst* (*Concerning the Spiritual in Art*), Kandinsky's own treatise on abstraction that was published in 1911. It calls on artists to speak of art that advances their spiritual aesthetic and to denounce the lies of established orthodox artistic conventions.

Almost immediately a popular success, *Der Blaue Reiter Almanach* and its combination of spiritual and formal concerns heralded a turning point for a number of significant artistic movements that had a far-reaching legacy. While the Blue Rider movement only existed from 1911 to 1914, it helped coalesce German art that expressed metaphysical necessity and inner emotion. Although the movement was heavily imbued with mysticism and informed by philosophic ideas, including those presented in German philosopher Arthur Schopenhauer's *The World as Will and Representation* (1818), some of its aesthetic goals were carried on in the annihilation of materiality within abstract painting and in expressionism, a movement that rejected realism in favor of rendering psychological and emotional responses in vivid color. The works featured within *Der Blaue Reiter Almanach* represent a major artistic movement of the twentieth century and are recognized as a significant influence on avant-garde and modern movements in art, dance, film, music, cinema, and architecture.

HISTORICAL AND LITERARY CONTEXT

Kandinsky and Marc's preface to *Der Blaue Reiter Almanach* responds to the established conventions of realism and pragmatism of the early twentieth century, a time when philosophical, scientific, and artistic works began to emphasize the importance of the subjectivity of human experience. Munich, where the Blue Rider movement developed, was a major art center at the time, but modernist art found little support in that city. Five years before Kandinsky and Marc wrote their preface, a group of Fauvist painters exhibited their work in Paris, displaying simplified forms and saturated colors. In 1901 Kandinsky and others founded the Phalanx Society in order to provide young artists with a place to display their works. The Phalanx Society had limited financial resources, and its focus on international artists weakened when Kandinsky left the city to travel in Tunisia, France, and Italy. A new group of artists, inspired by the Fauvists' vibrant colors and Paul Gauguin's flattened forms, reorganized as the NKVM (Neue Künstlervereinigung, or New Artists' Association of Munich) with Kandinsky as one of its officers. The group's first traveling exhibition in 1909 met with vehement criticism. Spectators objected to the intense colors and simplified forms. The critical reception to NKVM's second exhibition in 1910, particularly to Kandinsky's painting *Composition II,* influenced Kandinsky to resign from the group.

By the time *Der Blaue Reiter Almanach* was published in 1912, groups of artists, including Die Brücke in Dresden, had already started to identify their work as expressionist in intent. Despite strong critics, Kandinsky believed that his near-abstract art was the mode of the future, and Marc was among the most vocal of his supporters. Together, they published pamphlets about their aesthetic beliefs to refute the conservative values of German art critics and museums. They withdrew from the NKVM, conceived of a new plan to advance the new cultural era they envisioned, and produced *Der Blaue Reiter Almanach,* one of modern art's key documents. The book achieved almost immediate popularity and sold out its initial print run of fifteen-hundred copies. It provided a platform around which various avant-garde movements could coalesce. Expressionism and abstract art remained a strong force in Germany, throughout Europe, and with American artists throughout the twentieth century.

The preface to *Der Blaue Reiter Almanach* draws on a history of aesthetic and philosophical tracts that

✣ *Key Facts*

Time Period:
Early 20th Century

Movement/Issue:
Aesthetics; Blue Rider movement; Expressionism; Abstract art

Place of Publication:
Germany

Language of Publication:
German

WASSILY KANDINSKY: AN ABSTRACT THEORETICIAN

Wassily Kandinsky was born in Moscow on December 4, 1866. He studied music in Odessa before returning to Moscow to pursue legal studies. In 1895 he attended an exhibition of French impressionists, which awakened in him a desire to paint. He moved to Munich, and in 1897 he became a pupil of painter Anton Azbé before joining the Munich Academy. He was influenced by the works of Vincent Van Gogh and Paul Cézanne, as well as by art nouveau developments in book design, line, and typography.

In 1908 a chance discovery of an upside-down painting led Kandinsky to think about the possibilities of nonobjective painting. He was already experimenting with Fauvism, but he now realized the powerful possibilities of communication within form and color. He wrote a theory to explain his experiments, published as *Über das Geistige in der Kunst* (*Concerning the Spiritual in Art*) in 1911. Fellow artists Paul Klee, Hans Arp, August Macke, and Franz Marc echoed his interest in abstraction, and together they formed the Blue Rider movement. When World War I ended, Kandinsky returned to Russia, where suprematism and constructivism were dominant artistic schools. Eventually, he returned to Germany and found a creative home in the Bauhaus school of design until 1933. Kandinsky's final years were spent elaborating and consolidating his abstract style in Paris.

Opposite page:
Cover of the journal
Der Blaue Reiter, 1912.
Lithograph by Wassily
Kandinsky. ERICH LESSING/
ART RESOURCE, NY

can be traced to French symbolism and the spiritual ideas of Rudolf Steiner and other theosophists, who believed in an imminent new spiritual epoch. Kandinsky drew an important theoretical justification for his shift to pure abstraction from the theosophical book *Thought Forms* (1901), written by Annie Besant and C.W. Leadbeater. In her book *Klee and Kandinsky in Munich and the Bauhaus* (1981), Beeke Sell Tower writes, "Just as an initiate to theosophy can interpret the 'fine matter' surrounding a person, Kandinsky believed that the abstract colors and forms of his paintings would communicate very subtle, nameless, inner states of emotion." In composing their preface, Kandinsky and Marc understood the need for a manifesto to convey their desire to separate themselves from the Old World and previous eras with innovative and interconnected art forms.

In the decades following its composition, the preface to *Der Blaue Reiter Almanach* inspired a considerable body of literature and artwork supporting the essay's principles, and the book itself brought together and created a dialogue among artists as varied as Paul Klee and Robert Delaunay and composer Arnold Schoenberg. Although the group dispersed because of personal differences and international political conflict, its diversely active members had a wider influence. Kandinsky's spiritual ideas did not find a home with Russian constructivist artists, but

Kandinsky and Klee eventually joined the Bauhaus movement in the 1920s. Kandinsky published theoretical tracts in which he discusses the psychological effects of various elements in abstract painting. Various European and American post-World War I movements took up the principles and enthusiasms of the Blue Rider movement, and in the early twenty-first century the Blue Rider movement and its expressionist and abstract works continued to command significant scholarly interest.

THEMES AND STYLE

The central theme of the preface to *Der Blaue Reiter Almanach* is that a new series of interconnected art forms should be created to reflect the principles of the "spiritual awakening" taking place in Europe in the early 1900s. With the force of Kandinsky's own *Concerning the Spiritual in Art* behind it, the essay opens with an appeal to the responsibilities of artists in a new age: "A great era has begun: the spiritual 'awakening,' the increasing tendency to regain 'lost balance,' the inevitable necessity of spiritual plantings, the unfolding of the first blossom." To this end, the preface outlines the role of *Der Blaue Reiter Almanach* in reporting and encouraging this new spirituality. It presents a collection of international works that reflect a personal, inner necessity on the part of artists; rejects hollow formal traditions of earlier periods; and creates a space for dialogue among these new artists.

The preface achieves its rhetorical effect through calm appeals for artistic vision at the dawning of a new "spiritual age." This ennobling sense of spirituality is created by restrained language that identifies aesthetic goals as an attempt to "regain lost balance." Addressing readers of *Der Blaue Reiter Almanach*, Kandinsky and Marc imagine a sympathetic audience of artists, critics, and spectators who are connected by a need for a spiritual life conveyed through art. The best art, the text suggests, is one that emanates from an "inner necessity." Notably, Kandinsky and Marc link diverse art forms and techniques through their reflection of an "inner voice that reflects the great change" of the era. Although Kandinsky and Marc attempt to establish their own aesthetic group, they make clear it is an international one connected "by humanity."

Stylistically, the preface to *Der Blaue Reiter Almanach* is characterized by formal and measured language. It establishes credibility as a document by artists for artists, critics, and spectators. It uses the art world's own tools to create a new discussion about art. Kandinsky and Marc write, "Because of the growth of the daily press, many unqualified art critics have stolen in among the qualified ones.... We will devote one column to this unfortunate, harmful power." Moreover, by using their essay as an introduction to a collection of resonant but diverse artists, Kandinsky and Marc assert the primacy of their own artistic tastes and vision. Although its balanced tone renders

the preface distinct from belligerent artistic manifestos of the period, it gains power through its thoughtful prioritization of artistic concerns.

CRITICAL DISCUSSION

The immediate success of *Der Blaue Reiter Almanach* encouraged Kandinsky and Marc to continue with an annual almanac "to awaken the realization … of the spiritual essence of all things," according to author Peter Selz in his book, *German Expressionist Painting*. World War I, however, interrupted these plans. Some artists who had been colleagues of Kandinsky and Marc in the NKVM objected to the spiritual and formal goals of the Blue Rider movement. Art historian Otto Fischer, quoted by Milton A. Cohen in his book *Movement, Manifesto, Melee: The Modernist Group 1910-1914,* writes, "[A picture] does not lend immediate expression to the soul; it expresses the soul within the object. A picture without an object is meaningless…. The empty-headed dreamers and charlatans are on the wrong track." For many artists, the spiritual aims of the Blue Rider movement were an inspiration. Quoted by author Peter Vergo in *The Blue Rider,* Klee writes of Kandinsky's work: "In [Kandinsky's] case, the rigor of the mind takes on productive forms…. Museums do not illuminate him, he illuminates them." In combination with Kandinsky's theoretical works, *Der Blaue Rieter Almanach* and its preface influenced generations of artists.

While the Blue Rider movement ended in 1914, *Der Blaue Reiter Almanach* and its preface remained an important source of inspiration for modern artists. Kandinsky's biographer, Hugo Zehder, believes that the book and its preface are of enormous significance:

> Probably no book on modern painting, no manifesto, has achieved similar significance, or has exercised such a great influence on the development of modern painting itself…. There is hardly an artist among the "Expressionists" who does not somehow instinctively acknowledge his writings, when it is a matter of the "inner sound" of color or the principle of forming according to "inner necessity."

Since *Der Blaue Reiter Almanach* was published, the book and its preface have been the subject of a broad body of criticism that considers its legacy in historical, biographical, and aesthetic terms.

Discussing the artistic impact of the essay, Cohen notes in that "in the whole history of the prewar period, Kandinsky's and Marc's labors may well deserve the foremost place … [due] to the modernist sensibility and achievement that they so profoundly influenced." Commentators also draw attention to the artistic differences that led, in part, to the movement's demise. Still other critics address the diverse modernist movements that found their origins in Kandinsky's spiritual abstractions. Rose-Carol Washton Long, editor of *The Life of Vasilii Kandinsky in Russian Art,* notes, "As painters like Jackson Pollock and Robert Motherwell began to move away from the geometric abstraction of the thirties and forties, they looked again at Kandinsky's pre-World War I ideas on color symbolism, movement and rhythm."

BIBLIOGRAPHY

Sources

Bowlt, John E., and Rose-Carol Washton Long, eds. *The Life of Vasilii Kandinsky in Russian Art: A Study of* On the Spiritual in Art. Newtonville: Oriental Research Partners, 1980. 43-61. *Literature Resource Center.* Web. 13 Aug. 2012.

Cohen, Milton A. *Movement, Manifesto, Melee: The Modernist Group 1910-1914.* Lanham: Lexington, 2004. Print.

Kandinsky, Wassily. *Kandinsky in Munich, 1896-1914.* New York: Guggenheim Foundation, 1982. Print.

Selz, Peter. *German Expressionist Painting.* Berkeley: U of California P, 1957. 223-33. *Literature Resource Center.* Web. 13 Aug. 2012.

Tower, Beeke Sell. *Klee and Kandinsky in Munich and the Bauhaus.* Ann Arbor: UMI Research, 1981. Print.

Vergo, Peter. *The Blue Rider.* Oxford: Phaidon, 1977. Print.

Zehder, Hugo. *Wassily Kandinsky.* Dresden : R. Kaemmerer Verlag, 1920.

Further Reading

Behr, Shulamith. *Expressionism.* London: Tate Gallery, 1999. Print.

Everdell, William R. *The First Moderns: Profiles in the Origins of Twentieth-Century Thought.* Chicago: U of Chicago P, 1997. 303-20. *Literature Resource Center.* Web. 13 Aug. 2012.

Kramer, Hilton. "The 'Blue Rider' Imbroglio." *New Criterion* 22.4 (2003): 68+. *Literature Resource Center.* Web. 13 Aug. 2012.

Lipsey, Roger. *An Art of Our Own: The Spiritual in Twentieth-Century Art.* Boston: Shambhala, 1988. 40-50. *Literature Resource Center.* Web. 13 Aug. 2012.

Mackie, Alwynne. "Kandinsky and Problems of Abstraction." *Artforum* 17.3 (1978): 58-63. *Literature Resource Center.* Web. 13 Aug. 2012.

Read, Herbert. *Art and Alienation: The Role of the Artist in Society.* Horizon Press, 1967. 138-50. *Literature Resource Center.* Web. 13 Aug. 2012.

Karen Bender

BAUHAUS MANIFESTO

Oskar Schlemmer

OVERVIEW

Penned by Oskar Schlemmer, the *Bauhaus Manifesto* (1923) describes the shifting direction of the Staatliches Bauhaus (Bauhaus School) and its project of unifying art and technology. The manifesto was published not long after the inception of the new and liberal German Weimar Republic, during a time when nationalism and anti-Semitism were on the rise in Germany. Following Germany's adoption of a democratic constitution, central and eastern European students and intellectuals interested in the international and utopian Bauhaus project had arrived at the school in force to study and work. Reflecting a new constructivist focus, the manifesto encourages artists in the Bauhaus school to achieve a fusion of art and technology through study, research, and work.

The *Bauhaus Manifesto* appealed to intellectuals interested in its description of a radical innovation in education but was received with skepticism by Weimar's local culture, which was increasingly influenced by German nationals. A movement toward constructivism took hold in the Bauhaus School in 1923 after Hungarian László Moholy-Nagy joined the faculty. This new orientation was reflected in the manifesto's focus on technology. Two years after the manifesto's publication, municipal authorities in Weimar closed the school in response to political pressure, necessitating its relocation to Dessau. The *Bauhaus Manifesto* is now considered an important document detailing the trajectory of the Staatliches Bauhaus and the internationally influential Bauhaus movement.

HISTORICAL AND LITERARY CONTEXT

Schlemmer's manifesto continued in the Bauhaus tradition of encouraging internationalism and utopian idealism while increasing dedication to the study of technology and its application to art and life in the face of growing German nationalism and conservative criticism. Instruction at the Staatliches Bauhaus became more forward-looking, and workshops included attempts to create models of objects that might be mass-manufactured. Although Germany had recently become a new, liberal republic, the city of Weimar was still largely a tradition-bound culture when the manifesto was published. The *Bauhaus Manifesto* responds to the rise of international constructivism and its focus on the utilitarian function of art. By inviting

Moholy-Nagy onto the faculty, Walter Gropius, founder of the Bauhaus School, acknowledged and supported a modern belief in the capacity of technology and the machine to effect progress.

When the *Bauhaus Manifesto* was published in 1923, Germany was governed by the new, democratic Weimar Constitution. However, the strict peace conditions dictated by the Versailles Treaty, which had been signed by the Weimar Republic, fueled the mistrust of a growing number of German nationalists. The Staatliches Bauhaus's multinational, inclusive project stood in direct contrast to a local culture that was becoming increasingly conservative, while the international and Jewish student body and faculty threatened the growing anti-Semitic movement in Germany. During the school's last years in Weimar, Gropius hired Swiss Paul Klee, Hungarian Moholy-Nagy, and German Schlemmer, remaining committed to the ideal of an educational institution and art movement that ignored political boundaries in favor of progress. This utopian idealism served to secure the Bauhaus's enduring and international influence long after the school's closure in 1933.

The *Bauhaus Manifesto* demonstrates the influence of modernism on the Bauhaus movement and continues in the tradition of earlier modernist manifestos, such as the *Futurist Manifesto* (1909), written by Filippo Marinetti and signed by a group of Italian painters. Such early modernist manifestos took as their model Marx and Engels's famous *Communist Manifesto* (1848), employing language designed to garner attention and incite the devotion of followers. The use of the manifesto to outline aesthetic concerns began with romanticism in the 1820s and continued into and beyond modernism. Notably, the *Bauhaus Manifesto* also responds to the concept of the "minimal dwelling" mentioned in the Weimar Constitution.

Schlemmer's influence as a new faculty member of the Staatliches Bauhaus was cemented by the publication of the *Bauhaus Manifesto*. His theater workshops became integral to the Bauhaus creative community, and his performance's abstract human figures reflected the manifesto's urging to abandon individuality in favor of a collective utility. Gropius composed the first Bauhaus manifesto, titled *The Program of the Bauhaus in Weimar*, in 1918. The

❖ *Key Facts*

Time Period:
Early 20th Century

Movement/Issue:
Aesthetics; Avant-gardism; International constructivism; Technological development

Place of Publication:
Germany

Language of Publication:
German

OSKAR SCHLEMMER

Born in 1888, Oskar Schlemmer was a German choreographer, painter, and sculptor best remembered for his association with the Staatliches Bauhaus (Bauhaus School). Prior to joining the faculty of the Bauhaus School, Schlemmer supported himself from an early age, working as an apprentice in both inlay and marquetry workshops. In 1920, after seeing Schlemmer's sculpture exhibited at the Berlin Gallery Der Sturm, architect and Bauhaus School founder Walter Gropius invited him to join the sculpture faculty at the school, where his work turned to theater and choreography.

Schlemmer's theater pieces often featured the human form in abstraction; stylized female figures, not unlike marionettes, appeared masked and devoid of individuality on a bare stage. His interests were central to the Bauhaus project until he left the school in 1929. Nazis forced his resignation from the Vereinigte Staatsschulen in 1933, where he was a professor, and he then left Berlin, first traveling to Eichberg and then to Sehringen. Toward the end of his life, Schlemmer withdrew from public life, creating his famous "Fensterbilder" ("Window Pictures"), which he drew while gazing from his window into the lives of his neighbors. He died in 1943.

Bauhaus school made frequent use of manifestos to transmit the Bauhaus project, including Farkas Molnár's *KURI Manifesto* (1922), Moholy-Nagy's *Production-Reproduction* (1922), and Ernö Kállai's *Herwarth Walden* (1928). The effects of the modernist manifesto are far-reaching, as evidenced by contemporary manifestations of the form such as German director Werner Herzog's manifesto on cinema verité, the *Minnesota Declaration* (1999).

THEMES AND STYLE

The *Bauhaus Manifesto*'s central theme is that the aim of the Staatliches Bauhaus should be to integrate the study of art and technology to achieve progress. Speaking directly to the members of the Bauhaus School, Schlemmer writes, "We become bearers of responsibility and the conscience of the world. An idealism of activity that embraces, penetrates, and unites art, science, and technology and that influences research, study, and work will construct the 'art-edifice' of Man, which is but an allegory of the cosmic system." The manifesto reflects the Bauhaus School's continuing concern with uniting a transnational student body and faculty in the pursuit of an idealized, utopian educational community as well as pointing toward the school's more technological reorientation: if the project is to remain relevant, it must acknowledge the machines of the future.

Appealing to Germany as a whole and to a diverse and international population, the *Bauhaus Manifesto* achieves its effect through the use of inclusive language and devotion to a utopian ideal. The manifesto caters to a radical artist group that saw itself as central to both spiritual and artistic revolution. Schlemmer states, "The Staatliches Bauhaus, founded after the catastrophe of the war in the chaos of the revolution and in the era of the flowering of an emotion-laden, explosive art, becomes the rallying-point of all those who, with belief in the future and the sky storming enthusiasm, wish to build the 'cathedral of Socialism.'" While thus addressing all artists of the Bauhaus School, Schlemmer makes a particular call to "Germany, country of the middle, and Weimar, the heart of it" to acknowledge that it is "the adopted place of intellectual decision." He invests the reader with purpose, stating, "We become bearers of responsibility and the conscience of the world." The manifesto works to inspire the devotion of artistic radicals and idealists, as well as German nationalists, to work together toward progress.

The *Bauhaus Manifesto* is written in a direct, inspirational style, while making use of poetic language and concrete, affective images to achieve its emotional resonance. The manifesto sets forth the project of the Staatliches Bauhaus in lofty language, as it states, "The Staatliches Bauhaus in Weimar is the first and so far the only government school in the Reich—if not in the world—which calls upon the creative forces of the fine arts to become influential while they are vital." As the school experienced wavering support from the Weimar Republic, which was increasingly criticized by German nationalists and Weimar's traditional culture, such elevated language worked to cement the school's position as a government institution while inspiring its artists with purpose. When Schlemmer writes, "*We exist! We have the will! We are producing!*" he includes artists from Germany and across Europe in an exhilarating project that extends beyond the classroom and works to influence both life and art.

CRITICAL DISCUSSION

The Staatliches Bauhaus, while garnering international attention and a diverse student body, had detractors both among the traditional denizens of Weimar and other avant-gardists. As Michael Müller notes in his essay "The Dictate of Coldness: Critique from the Left, 1919-1933," among the avant-garde,

> "there was doubt as to whether the Bauhaus was ready or able, through aesthetic means, not only to modernize a society of class conflict, but also to overcome it … Ernst Kállai spoke of the 'Bauhaus style' and of 'dangerous formalisms,' while Adolf Behne alluded to 'flat-roof chic.' They and others were convinced that a technologically based rationalization of everyday life only played into the hands of conforming to the imperatives of a life-dominating capitalist society."

The school, although supported by the new republic, inspired suspicion from the general public in Weimar itself. As Éva Bajkay in her essay "Weimar" explains, the school's "efforts to create a new, shared visual language remained alien and separate from the tradition-bound local culture of Weimar."

Although the school was closed because of the rising influence of Nazism, the movement's devotion to an idealized, utopian project, as demonstrated in the *Bauhaus Manifesto,* ensured its continued influence. In *Bauhaus Culture* (2006), Kathleen James-Chakraborty describes the Bauhaus School as "the site of the twentieth century's most influential experiment in artistic education … In Weimar, where it was founded in 1919, in Dessau, where it reopened in 1926, and Berlin, where it finally closed in 1933, a concrete alternative to the state-sponsored fine arts academies that had flourished during the nineteenth century finally took definitive shape." The Bauhaus school ideas have endured in art schools and technical institutions, and criticism of Schlemmer's manifesto explores the persistent legacy of its educational plan and its relation to the political climate of the time.

Criticism has examined the influence that the Staatliches Bauhaus had over methods of art instruction. Many contemporary art institutions and fine arts schools borrow heavily from the workshop model favored by the movement. Contemporary scholarship on the manifesto also examines the political divisiveness of the Bauhaus project in Germany between the wars. In his essay "Un-German Activities: Attacks from the Right, 1919-1933," Justus H. Ulbricht explores how Bauhaus threatened traditional culture: "the emphatic celebration of industrial-technological rationality and aesthetics found in many manifestos of modernism was frightening, above all to those who had suffered from the results of progress and were barely surviving the social and political dislocations of the Weimar Republic."

BIBLIOGRAPHY

Sources

Bajkay, Éva. "Weimar." *Central European Avant-Gardes: Exchange and Transformation, 1910-1930.* Ed. Timothy Benson. Los Angeles: MIT, 2002. Print.

James-Chakraborty, Kathleen. "Introduction." *Bauhaus Culture.* Ed. Kathleen James-Chakraborty. Minneapolis: U of Minnesota P, 2006. xi-xix. Print.

Müller, Michael. "The Dictate of Coldness: Critique from the Left, 1919-1933." *Bauhaus Conflicts, 1919-2009: Controversies and Counterparts.* Ed. Philipp Oswalt. New York: Museum of Modern Art, 2009. Print.

Schlemmer, Oskar. "Bauhaus Manifesto." *Between Worlds: A Sourcebook of Central European Avant-Gardes, 1910-1930.* Ed. Timothy Benson. Massachusetts: MIT, 2002. Print.

Ulbricht, Justus H. "Un-German Activities: Attacks from the Right, 1919-1933," *Bauhaus Conflicts, 1919-2009: Controversies and Counterparts.* Ed. Philipp Oswalt. New York: Museum of Modern Art, 2009. Print.

Further Reading

Droste, Magdalena, ed. *Bauhaus, 1919-1933.* London: Taschen, 2002. Print.

Feierabend, Peter, and Jeannine Fiedler, eds. *Bauhaus.* Köln: Ullmann. 2009. Print.

Fox, Nicholas Weber. *The Bauhaus Group: Six Masters of Modernism.* New York: Knopf, 2009. Print.

Koss, Juliet. "Bauhaus Theater of Human Dolls." *The Art Bulletin* 85.4 (2003): 724-45. *JSTOR.* Web. 10 Aug. 2012.

Lidtke, Vernon. "Abstract Art and Left-Wing Politics in the Weimar Republic." *Central European History* 37.1 (2004): 49-90. *JSTOR.* Web. 10 Aug. 2012.

Saletnik, Jeffrey, and Robin Schuldenfrei, eds. *Bauhaus Construct: Fashioning Identity, Discourse and Modernism.* New York: Routledge. 2009. Print.

Kristen Gleason

Three costumes for Oskar Schlemmer's *Triadisches Ballet* (1919-1922). Wuerttembergisches Landesmuseum, Stuttgart, Germany. ERICH LESSING/ ART RESOURCE, NY

THE BEAUTY OF MODERN VISUAL FORM

Josef Čapek

✤ *Key Facts*

Time Period:
Early 20th Century

Movement/Issue:
Aesthetics; Avant-
gardism; Modernism;
Czech nationalism

Place of Publication:
Austria-Hungary

**Language of
Publication:**
Czech

OVERVIEW

Written by Josef Čapek, "The Beauty of Modern Visual Form" (1913-14) instructs the modern artist to create an entirely original conception of art via conscious experimentation with form. The essay was published in Austria-Hungary in the years leading up to World War I and the Austro-Hungarian Empire's disintegration, a time in which the general population of ethnic Czechs was highly nationalistic and the Czech Realist Party was already working to achieve independence and preserve Czech history and language. In the prewar years, Prague was a hotbed of intellectual activity and host to artists working in a variety of movements, including German expressionism, Italian futurism, and French and Czech cubism. Addressed to an artistic elite, "The Beauty of Modern Visual Form" asserts that the task of the modern artist is to portray the subject's ideal essence using architectural objectivity, color, and space.

Indicative of a schism in the Czech avant-garde, "The Beauty of Modern Visual Form" was received well by some artists in Prague, including those in the art association Spolek výtvarných umělců Mánes (Mánes Association of Fine Artists), and rejected by others, such as members of Skupina výtvarných umělců (Group of Visual Artists), a collective with which Čapek had recently split to return to Mánes. The essay highlights a point of contention between the two groups, as it does not advocate strict adherence to Pablo Picasso's style, points to the success of Gothic art, and urges the modern artist to break with the past. Despite conflicting tendencies, the works of both Skupina and Mánes—including the publication of "The Beauty of Modern Visual Form"—helped situate Prague at the center of artistic activity in central Europe and paved the way for postwar Czech avant-garde groups, including the Obstinates (Tvrdošíjní) and Devětsil.

HISTORICAL AND LITERARY CONTEXT

"The Beauty of Modern Visual Form" responds to a rigid and prescriptive view of art that Čapek feared might hinder modern artistic progress. The manifesto attacks art's old guard and warns against adherence to artistic styles that fail to incorporate new conceptions of space, such as Henri Matisse's expressionism. Čapek urges modern artists not to overly philosophize or argue on behalf of their technique lest they inadvertently define their art using antiquated vocabularies. Instead, the essay asks the artist to portray the ideal essence of the subject through artificial form. Additionally, the manifesto's insistence on a revolutionary and international vocabulary for art reflects the difficulty of writing and working in a minority language.

At the time of the essay's publication, Czech artists living and working in Prague were engaging with a local Czech arts culture while at the same time interacting with international artistic movements in Paris, Munich, and Berlin. Mánes had separated into factions supporting different versions of cubism. Painter Emil Filla, sculptor Otto Gutfreund, and other members of Skupina, which had formed in 1911, rallied around a cubism that took its cues almost exclusively from Picasso and Georges Braque. Although initially Čapek, along with his brother, writer Karel Čapek, belonged to Skupina, they later formed a faction that supported what they felt was a more bohemian version of cubism, which embraced expressionism, orphism, rayonnism, and futurism. Later, Čapek would essentially abandon cubism and in 1918 join the Obstinates, who fought to refocus modern art practice on content, finding inspiration in nature and the idea of the primitive.

"The Beauty of Modern Visual Form" is a manifesto on aesthetics in the tradition of nineteenth-century romanticism. Its form and central preoccupations can be traced to other works on the artistic sensibility, such as Charles Baudelaire's *The Painter of Modern Life* (1859). Avant-garde movements in Europe made extensive use of the manifesto as a method for the dissemination of artistic ideas, beginning with Italian futurist Filippo Marinetti's *Futurist Manifesto* (1909). Members of the Czech avant-garde penned a number of manifestos, including Pavel Janák's *The Prism and the Pyramid* (1911), Gutfreund's *Surface and Space* (1912), and Filla's *On the Virtue of Neo-Primitivism* (1912). Many of these works were published in journals such as *Volné Směry* and *Umělecký Měsičnik,* which were central to the development and coherence of the Czech avant-garde.

Shortly after the publication of "The Beauty of Modern Visual Form," World War I and the disintegration of the Austro-Hungarian Empire temporarily halted the forward motion of the Czech avant-garde.

However, the document helped set the stage for the more internationalist orientation of the second wave of Czech avant-garde artists that took shape between the wars. Čapek went on to pursue illustration, theater design, painting, and journalism during the 1920s and remained relevant and involved with the Czech avant-garde until the advent of World War II. Today, the activities of the prewar Czech avant-garde are seen as important precursors to the development of later avant-garde groups in Czechoslovakia, including one influenced by cubism, Group 42 (active in the late 1930s to 1940s).

THEMES AND STYLE

The central theme of "The Beauty of Modern Visual Form" is that the modern artist must develop a new perspective from which to engage in formal experimentation to express the subject's ideal essence as distinct from its purely representational form. Čapek outlines the primary objective of this new perspective here: "*Autonomy* or *artificiality* of the modern form is the primary quality we demand of the new endeavor, as the very nature of modern art is that it seeks originality, which it wants to grasp as the highest guiding creative principle. And that happens through consistency, experimentation and conscious 'cultivation' of form." The modern artist is asked to create out of a genuine originality and to abandon strict adherence to absolute representation of the object.

The manifesto takes an aggressive stance on modern art and at times uses a tone that is dismissive of those who do not agree, achieving its rhetorical effect somewhat combatively. Čapek references principal artists and theorists of the avant-garde such as Picasso and architect Vlatislav Hoffman to lend credibility to his argument, while deriding those who might not accept his particular interpretation of the modern art movement. The essay rejects the reader who might not agree, asserting that "to those who are incapable of immediate communication with the art of the present, practical aesthetics will offer even less assistance than those speculations that place various notions applicable to all art in general without a deeper commitment, above a new formal expression. It is difficult to offer explanations to someone who represents a dead link in an environment of such electrifying intensity as the modern era." The manifesto works to point the way toward modernity by advocating a break with the dying past.

In terms of style, "The Beauty of Modern Visual Form" is notable for its logical, persuasive language; sparing but effective use of italics; and somewhat aggressive tone. From the outset of the essay, Čapek takes an antagonistic stance, beginning, "Modern art—the so-called Cubist movement—gives the initiated a rich aesthetic experience that must be incomprehensible to most people. And that is why its champions are at a disadvantage against its opponents.... For it is impossible to convince a person lacking a deeper ability to enter a spiritually and formally new area about its

JOSEF ČAPEK

Author of "The Beauty of Modern Visual Form," Josef Čapek (1887-1945) was a Czech painter, writer, and critic who is largely credited with inventing the word "robot," which first appeared in print in his brother Karel Čapek's play *R.U.R.* (Rossum's Universal Robots) in 1920. Čapek was born in Bohemia, in what is now the Czech Republic. Early in his career he studied weaving at a craft school but soon turned his attention to painting. He studied in Prague and Paris, where a meeting with poet Guillaume Apollinaire sparked his interest in cubism. When he returned to Bohemia, he continued to paint in a cubist style, although his artistic interests widened to include symbolism, expressionism, and futurism. He was also an author and illustrator of children's books, and he wrote numerous essays. Later in life he became influenced by folk art and began to paint subjects including children and scenes from country life.

An outspoken critic of national socialism and the war, he was arrested in 1939 by the Nazis during the German occupation of Czechoslovakia and imprisoned at Dachau. He was eventually relocated to Bergen-Belsen concentration camp, where he wrote *Poems from a Concentration Camp*. He died in Buchenwald concentration camp in 1945.

beauty." Here, the manifesto outlines the modern artist's task, which is to engage in a new, formal experimentation, and also disparages those who do not accept this project as deficient in artistic sensibility and spirituality.

CRITICAL DISCUSSION

When "The Beauty of Modern Visual Form" was published, members of the avant-garde received it with interest, specifically those in Mánes, although it served to further distance Čapek from Skupina because it advocated for a more generous vision of modern art not as faithfully adherent to Picasso's example. In response to a proposed Mánes-sponsored cubist exhibition in France, Filla, a member of Skupina, traveled to Paris to speak to art dealer Daniel-Henry Kahnweiler; in personal correspondence, Čapek notes "the Group wants to damage and discredit the Cubist exhibition.... This is why Filla has gone to see Kahnweiler and tried to make him believe that Mánes deliberately wants to promote Cubists (mainly Metzinger and [Albert] Gleizes) against Picasso, Derain, and Braque."

Prewar Czech cubism, although forgotten during the occupation by Germany during World War II and artistic suppression under communism, demonstrates the beginnings of a Czech avant-garde tradition that stretches into the 1920s, contributing to the development of Dadaism, futurism, and surrealism in Czech art. As Wanda Bubriski notes in her review of *Czech Cubism: Architecture and Design, 1910-1925*, "[Czech cubism] represents one effort towards reknotting

Woman Figure, 1913, by Josef Čapek. Čapek began his artistic career as a member of the Cubist school of painting. © AISA/ EVERETT COLLECTION

and sculpture, a figure conceived existentially as the fulcrum between the world of the spirit and the senses, between nature and the universe." Scholars have also noted the contribution of Viennese art theory to the development of the Czech avant-garde. Timothy Benson, in his essay "New Alternatives," asserts that Czech cubists "understood the potential of the artificiality of art in terms of a profound philosophical discourse informed by Wilhelm Worringer (whose theories were essential for the Expressionists) and the emerging Viennese art history of Alois Riegl, among others."

BIBLIOGRAPHY

Sources

Benson, Timothy O. "New Alternatives." *Between Worlds: A Sourcebook of Central European Avant-Gardes, 1910-1930.* Ed. Timothy Benson and Éva Forgács. Massachusetts: MIT P, 2002. 79-80. Print.

Bubriski, Wanda. "Czech Cubism: Architecture and Design, 1910-1925." Rev. of *Czech Cubism: Architecture and Design, 1910-1925,* by Cooper-Hewitt National Museum of Design, Smithsonian Institution. *Journal of the Society of Architectural Historians* 52.4 (1993): 483-86. *JSTOR.* Web.18 Sept.2012.

Čapek, Josef. "The Beauty of Modern Visual Form." Trans. Alexandra Büchler. *Between Worlds: A Sourcebook of Central European Avant-Gardes, 1910-1930.* Ed. Timothy Benson and Éva Forgács. Massachusetts: MIT P, 2002. 109-12. Print.

———. "Fragments of Correspondence: Josef Čapek to Jarmila Pospíšilová." Trans. Alexandra Büchler. *Between Worlds: A Sourcebook of Central European Avant-Gardes, 1910-1930.* Ed. Timothy Benson and Éva Forgács. Massachusetts: MIT P, 2002. 103-09. Print.

Hume, Naomi. "Avant-Garde Anachronisms: Prague's Group of Fine Artists and Viennese Art Theory." *Slavic Review* 71.3 (2012): 516-45. *JSTOR.* Web. 18 Sept. 2012.

Vlček, Tomáš. "Art between Social Crisis and Utopia: The Czech Contribution to the Development of the Avant-Garde Movement in East-Central Europe, 1910-30." *Art Journal* 49.1 (1990): 28-35. *JSTOR.* Web. 18 Sept. 2012.

Further Reading

Benson, Timothy, ed. *Central European Avant-Gardes: Exchange and Transformation, 1910-1930.* Los Angeles: MIT P, 2002. Print.

Bru, Sascha, and Gunther Martens, eds. *The Invention of Politics in the European Avant-Garde (1906-1940).* New York: Rodopi, 2006. Print.

Levinger, Esther. "Czech Avant-Garde Art: Poetry for the Five Senses." *Art Bulletin* 81.3 (1999): 513-532. *JSTOR.* Web. 18 Sept. 2012.

Mansbach, S.A. *Modern Art in Eastern Europe: From the Baltic to the Balkans, ca. 1890-1939.* New York: Cambridge UP, 1999. Print.

Sayer, Derek. *The Coasts of Bohemia: A Czech History.* Trans. Alena Sayer. New Jersey: Princeton UP, 1998. Print.

Czechoslovakia's long historical ties with Western Europe that were severed under communism.... Czech Cubism marks the confluence of various artistic currents, most notably from France and Germany.... The synthesis of international trends with the Czechs' own artistic heritage helped form a cultural self-identity for the Czech cubists." Current scholarship addresses the influences contributing to Czech cubism and its unique features, its influence on rondocubism, and its relation to Viennese schools of thought.

Criticism of Czech cubism and "The Beauty of Modern Visual Form" has focused on the aesthetic influence and legacy of its aesthetic project. Addressing elements contributing to its formation, historian and theorist Tomáš Vlček, in his 1990 essay in *Art Journal,* notes that Czech cubism "was shaped by a myriad of sources, from the traditional Baroque incarnations of the spiritual, which reflected the existential side of Central European art, to the novel visual and literary forms of Cubism and Futurism. As a result, the main theme of the Czech Cubists became, in both painting

Kristen Gleason

A CALL FOR ELEMENTARIST ART

Raoul Hausmann, et al.

OVERVIEW

Aufruf zur elementaren Kunst ("A Call for Elementarist Art"; 1922) represents an appeal to artists working in various traditional and modern media to "yield to the elements of form" that only they could "discover." The treatise, composed in German primarily by Raoul Hausmann in 1921, augured the birth of the interdisciplinary trans-European avant-garde movement that would come to be known as international constructivism. Signed in Berlin by Hausmann, Hans Arp, László Moholy-Nagy, and Ivan Puni, the document was published in 1922 in the Dutch journal *De Stijl*. The journal had been founded in 1917 by the artist Theo Van Doesburg to promote a multimedia avant-garde movement that bore the same name—De Stijl, meaning "the Style." Like the original 1918 "De Stijl Manifesto" (composed by Van Doesburg and his colleagues), "A Call for Elementarist Art" decries the tyranny of the "individual" in art and rejects the "styles" of the past that hinder the development of a purer collective "STYLE," universally expressive of the epoch at hand. Whereas the "De Stijl Manifesto" (published in four languages) merely announced its Dutch authors' international aspirations, however, "A Call for Elementarist Art," with its Austrian (Hausmann), French-German (Arp), Hungarian (Moholy-Nagy), and Russian (Puni) signatories, effectively signaled the imminent fulfillment of these aspirations during the 1920s.

A wide range of European artists convened at the May 1922 International Congress of Progressive Artists in Düsseldorf as well as the Congress of Constructivists and Dadaists in Weimar that September. At these meetings artists embraced the issues raised by "A Call for Elementarist Art," which was formally published later that year. At the May gathering the International Faction of Constructivists formed to oppose expressionist excesses, while the September meeting led to the foundation of the new periodical *G: Materials for Elemental Form-Creation*—"the organ of constructivists in Europe"—and to anti-expressionist reforms at the Weimar Bauhaus in 1923.

HISTORICAL AND LITERARY CONTEXT

After the Russian Revolution and World War I, artists—including painters, poets, sculptors, photographers, filmmakers, collagists, architects, and designers associated with Russian suprematism (Puni, Moholy-Nagy), Zurich Dada (Arp), Berlin Dada (Hausmann), and De Stijl (Van Doesburg)—converged in Berlin; "A Call for Elementarist Art" was the result. Disgusted by the egotistical forces that had misused technology to bring about widespread European destruction, these artists found common ground in their desire to embrace machinery in a positive way, to reject the decorative embellishment of art nouveau, to refuse the political and productivist utilitarianism of Russian constructivism, and, most importantly, to dismiss expressionism's wanton subjectivism.

Whereas Dadaists often caustically recapitulated wartime destruction with multimedia works mimicking disintegration, the suprematists, De Stijl artists, and emerging international (as opposed to solely Russian) constructivists sought to rebuild the world around them using an "elemental" aesthetic artistic language comprised of simple geometric shapes, minimalist color schemes, and basic everyday materials. In spite of these apparently contradictory motivations, however, critics agree that Dada crucially created the tabula rasa needed for the process of "constructive" reconstruction to begin in European art. Thus the fact that "A Call for Elementarist Art" is largely hopeful and nonwhimsical is not as implausible as might be expected, even though the document was drafted by the notoriously satirical "Dadasoph" Hausmann with input from Arp, Zurich Dada's whimsical cofounder.

Not long before Berlin Dada began to dissolve in 1920, Hausmann produced the assemblage *The Spirit of Our Time—Mechanical Head*. He is now best known for this work, which might be seen as an early example of art expressing the "forces" of its "epoch"—the ideal that he and his peers would claim in "A Call for Elementarist Art." Built from simply shaped found objects with latent basic functions, the *Mechanical Head* evokes a modern world in which the individual subject submits to external materials; it does this in much the same way that the artist invoked by "A Call for Elementarist Art" must yield to the "elements of form." Hausmann may have felt cynical about this inevitability when he created the empty head bedecked with objects that "chance" has glued to it; by the time he wrote "A Call for Elementarist Art," however, he seems to have become more confident that these conditions could lead to a new

⁜ *Key Facts*

Time Period:
Early 20th Century

Movement/Issue:
International constructivism;
Aesthetics;
Avant-gardism

Place of Publication:
Germany

Language of Publication:
German

ELEMENTARIST INVENTORS: IN THEIR OWN ELEMENTS

Because "A Call For Elementarist Art" insists that the "individual does not exist in isolation," it is only fitting that its authors are remembered not primarily as producers of the treatise but also for their involvement in other efforts. The Russian painter, illustrator, and designer Ivan Puni is probably best known for organizing the 1915 exhibition in St. Petersburg (The Last Futurist Exhibition of Painting "0.10") at which Kazimir Malevich launched the suprematist movement and debuted his famous *Black Square*. The following year the Alsatian painter, poet, and sculptor Hans Arp first made a name for himself as a cofounder of the Zurich Dada movement, from which Arp moved on to surrealism in Paris in 1925. A few years after Dada came to Berlin, the Austrian painter, collagist, photographer, sculptor, and poet Raoul Hausmann unveiled his *Mechanical Head* (1920); although it foreshadows some of the ideas Hausmann would express in "A Call for Elementarist Art," the artist himself (the movement's resident mock-philosopher, or "Dadasoph") regarded it as a quintessentially Dadaist creation. Finally, throughout the 1920s the Hungarian painter, photographer, sculptor, and Bauhaus professor László Moholy-Nagy was a pioneering theorist of photography, a leading advocate of the use of technology in the arts, and the creator of the *Light Space Modulator* (1930), which brought movement to light sculpture.

"regenerative [and] revolutionary art." Indeed, "A Call for Elementarist Art," with its suggestion of infinite opportunities, is an uncharacteristically sincere manifesto for Hausmann. His 1919 "What Is Dadaism and What Does It Demand in Germany?" (composed in collaboration with the poet Richard Huelsenbeck) expressly demands the unattainable, including radical pseudo-Communist goals such as unemployment through mechanization, compulsory adherence of the clergy to Dadaism, and so forth. In his "Manifesto of PREsentism" (1921), he had disparaged as nostalgic the human obsession with reaching for the impossible. Both of these represent ironic counterpoints to the earnest "Call for Elementarist Art."

Haussmann's tone and intent found its way into at least one more Dada/Constructivism-inspired platform: "The Mavo Manifesto" (1923), drafted by the artist and theorist of "conscious constructivism" Murayama Tomoyoshi. Composed in Japanese, the treatise helped broaden the international scope Hausmann and his peers had envisioned for their movement. A close friend of Van Doesburg, Murayama participated in the international congress in Düsseldorf. In the founding document of the Mavo movement, he presented his own appeal for an inclusive and unceasingly innovative aesthetic revolution. "A Call for Elementarist Art" might thus be seen as an "elemental" manifesto in that it not only cleared

ground for nearly a decade of further international constructivist work but also paved the way for the term *elementary/-ist* (which it had borrowed from Van Doesburg in the first place) to be reclaimed, resuffixed, and redefined as "elementarism" in the mid-1920s by Van Doesburg himself.

THEMES AND STYLE

With its insistence upon the production of truly "new art" that both encapsulates and emblematizes its era, "A Call for Elementarist Art," Eleanor M. Hight notes in *Picturing Modernism* (1995), resembles F.T. Marinetti's "Futurist Manifesto" (1909) and Naum Gabo and Antoine Pevsner's "Realistic Manifesto" (1920). Shorter and simpler than both of these works, "A Call for Elementarist Art" largely does away with figurative language, embraces impersonality, refuses specific reference to the past, and stands out as the most earnestly optimistic of the three.

Whereas Marinetti's poetic prewar outburst begins with an egoistic preamble and a declaration of a "love [for] danger" before celebrating the "beauty [of] speed," "glorify[ing] war," and enthusiastically envisioning "riot," Hausmann's spare and prosaic postwar "Call for Elementarist Art" presents itself anonymously, acknowledging no history, and announces a more positive and focused "love [of] brave discovery" and the orderly renewal of art in direct and coherent rhetoric. While Marinetti insists that what Hausmann later calls the "tireless interplay of the sources of power" necessarily leads to unending cycles of beautiful destruction, Hausmann alludes neither to the international annihilation nor to the Dadaist deconstruction that preceded his "A Call for Elementarist Art" other than implying that they set the stage for "art to grow as something purer, liberated from usefulness and beauty," and "elemental in everybody."

Meanwhile, although Gabo and Pevsner's "Realistic Manifesto" similarly dismisses "beauty" and celebrates art's universality, it diverges from "A Call for Elementarist Art" with its self-referentiality, its metaphoric language and rhetorical questioning, its indictments of cubism and futurism, and its demand that art be useful, renouncing much more than it affirms. Indeed, though "A Call for Elementarist Art" openly disdains "passing fashion," shuns "individual whim," and concludes with an emphatic denunciation of "reactionary art," its mood, in contrast to that of the "Realistic Manifesto," remains hopeful throughout. Perhaps most importantly, though, "A Call for Elementarist Art" does not simply demand that aspiring adherents to its program "reject the styles" in favor of a collective general "STYLE." Rather, it attempts to model that universal and elemental "STYLE" in its own basic form, from its opening sentences that pair emotion ("We love the brave discovery, the regeneration of art") with aphorism ("Art is the expression of the forces of an epoch") to its jubilant ("We proclaim elemental art!") and jibing ("Down with the reactionary in art!") end. Thus, true to its suprematist roots, "A Call for Elementarist Art" itself and the "elementarist art" it describes both begin, as the suprematist movement's founder Kazimir Malevich had insisted the new art must, with "pure feeling." True to its skeptical Dadaist origins, this manifesto and this art refuse to philosophize. On their most basic levels, therefore, both "A Call for Elementarist Art" and the art it promotes are "built up" of their "own elements alone."

CRITICAL DISCUSSION

"A Call for Elementarist Art" garnered its first public response within the very same issue of *De Stijl* in which it appeared. In *Theo Van Doesburg* (1974), Joost Baljeu points out that in a skeptical note to the text, Van Doesburg, the journal's editor and the original promoter of the "elementary/-ist" designation in the visual arts and architecture, wrote, "We are pleased to comply with the request that we publish the following manifesto in *De Stijl*, whereas it will depend on the way this is 'put into practice' whether we subscribe to or accept any responsibility for its content." While the Van Doesburg scholar Baljeu regards this note as "an early indication of the controversies between De Stijl on the one hand and the incipient Constructivist and Functionalist trends—in art and architecture in Germany on the other," the Hausmann critic Timothy O. Benson (in *Raoul Hausmann and Berlin Dada*; 1986) suggests that some last-minute changes Hausmann made to the text may have prompted Van Doesburg to withhold his "full endorsement" of "A Call for Elementarist Art" in *De Stijl*.

Given the unusually unblemished optimism "A Call for Elementarist Art" expresses at a time when most manifestos were still addressing past grievances as they laid out future plans, the Dada admirer Van Doesburg may well have wished to temper this positive proclamation with some Dadaist doubt and a hint of chance, even if his own hopes for the work's influence remained strong, as his subsequent involvement in the Düsseldorf and Weimar congresses and *G* magazine (with his article "On Elemental Form-Creation" in the first issue) indicate. Despite his divergence from Baljeu on the question of Van Doesburg's note, Benson follows the earlier scholar in deeming "A Call for Elementarist Art" "an early expression of ideas associated with Functionalism in architecture." Most art historians, however, agree with Stephen Bann, who emphasizes in *The Tradition of Constructivism* (1974) the more immediate role of "A Call for Elementarist Art" in heralding the international constructivist movement across a widening range of artistic media and throughout postwar Europe.

While "A Call for Elementarist Art" clearly put into circulation ideas that would help bring about

Dada-Cino, a 1920 collage by Raoul Hausmann. GIRAUDON/THE BRIDGEMAN ART LIBRARY

a major cultural transformation meant to heal the wounds of nationalist destruction through, quite appropriately, an internationalist and constructivist ethos, the term *elementary/-ist/ism* seems to have fallen through the cracks. It did live on, however, albeit transformed, in the pages of *G* (as Detlef Mertins and Michael W. Jennings have shown in *G: An Avant Garde Journal*; 2010) and again in *De Stijl*. Van Doesburg began using the term in the mid-1920s to champion the introduction of diagonals in visual art and architecture, which had previously favored vertical and horizontal lines along with planes joined at right angles. Although this move further separated *De Stijl*'s longtime editor from the Dutch painter Piet Mondrian, who had been involved with the De Stijl movement from the beginning, Van Doesburg ultimately saw "elementarism" as a unifying principle of dynamic balance between opposing forces. Thus, even this later elementarism had an essential optimism in common with Hausmann, Arp, Moholy-Nagy, and Puni's revolutionary "Call for Elementarist Art."

BIBLIOGRAPHY

Sources

Baljeu, Joost. *Theo Van Doesburg.* New York: Macmillan, 1974. Print.

Bann, Stephen, ed. *The Tradition of Constructivism.* London: Thames, 1974. Print.

Benson, Timothy O. *Raoul Hausmann and Berlin Dada.* Ann Arbor: UMI, 1986. Print.

Gabo, Naum. *Gabo on Gabo: Texts and Interviews.* Ed. Martin Hammer and Christina Lodder. East Sussex: Artists Bookworks, 2000. Print.

Hausmann, Raoul. "'A Call for Elementarist Art.'" *The Tradition of Constructivism.* Ed. Stephen Bann. London: Thames, 1974. 51-52. Print.

Hight, Eleanor M. *Picturing Modernism: Moholy-Nagy and Photography in Weimar Germany.* Cambridge: MIT P, 1995. Print.

Marinetti, F.T. "The Founding and Manifesto of Futurism." 1909. Rpt. in *Manifesto: A Century of Isms.* Ed. Mary Ann Caws. Lincoln: U of Nebraska P, 2001. 185-89. Print.

Mertins, Detlef, and Michael W. Jennings, eds. *G: An Avant-Garde Journal of Art, Architecture, Design, and Film, 1923-1926.* Trans. Steven Lindberg and Margareta Ingrid Christian. Los Angeles: Getty, 2010. Print.

Puchner, Martin. *Poetry of the Revolution: Marx, Manifestos, and the Avant-Gardes.* Princeton: Princeton UP, 2006. Print.

Further Reading

Beckett, Jane. "Dada, Van Doesburg and De Stijl." *Journal of European Studies* 9.1-2 (1979): 1-25. Print.

Blotkamp, Carel, ed. *De Stijl: The Formative Years, 1917-1922.* Trans. Charlotte I. Loeb and Arthur L. Loeb. Cambridge: MIT P, 1982. Print.

Elderfield, John. "On the Dada-Constructivist Axis." *Dada/Surrealism* 13 (1984): 5-16. Print.

Fabre, Gladys, and Doris Wintgens Hötte, eds. *Van Doesburg and the International Avant-Garde: Constructing a New World.* London: Tate, 2009. Print.

Jaffé, Hans L.C., ed. *De Stijl: Extracts from the Magazine.* Trans. R. R. Symonds and Mary Whithall. London: Thames, 1970. Print.

Lodder, Christina. *Russian Constructivism.* New Haven: Yale UP, 1983. Print.

Overy, Paul. *De Stijl.* London: Thames, 1991. Print.

White, Michael. *De Stijl and Dutch Modernism.* Manchester: Manchester UP, 2003. Print.

Katie Macnamara

CONSTRUCTIVISM

Ernő Kállai

OVERVIEW

Composed by Ernő Kállai in 1923, "Constructivism" outlines the basic tenets of international constructivism as interpreted by the Hungarian avant-garde. The essay was written at a time when many Hungarian artists were living in exile in Germany and Austria following the collapse of the Hungarian Soviet Republic in 1919. Kállai and other Hungarian members of the avant-garde, such as poet and painter Lajos Kassák, had been largely isolated from Western influence prior to fleeing Budapest; in the early 1920s they came into contact with Russian constructivist El Lissitzky, members of the Bauhaus, and other international members of the avant-garde in Berlin. "Constructivism" appeared in *Ma*, a literary and political journal created by Kassák, and, although published in Vienna, the piece addressed artists living inside and outside of Hungary. "Constructivism" presented a Hungarian take on the constructivist ideology that stressed the utopian possibility of art, its relation to technology, and the necessity for collective creation.

Although received with interest by the international avant-garde, "Constructivism" alienated those communist Hungarian artists in exile who desired a more politicized application of art. Although Kállai stressed a collective art in the essay, Kassák refused the idea of art as a tool for any political program, insisting on art's absolute autonomy. Already disillusioned by the lukewarm reception to their work in Vienna and motivated by this break in their ranks, many members of the Hungarian avant-garde chose to relocate to Berlin and other cities in Germany. The essay's push for utopian possibility served to further distinguish the Hungarian constructivists project, which was subsequently forgotten in the years between the wars. However, a direct link between the Hungarian artists living in exile in Vienna in the 1920s and the Hungarian neo-avant-garde of the 1960s and 1970s is evident, as is *Ma*'s influence on Romanian and Yugoslavian avant-garde journals of the late 1920s.

HISTORICAL AND LITERARY CONTEXT

"Constructivism" was penned by Kállai during a period when many Hungarian artists were living in exile following the failure of Béla Kun's communist Hungarian Soviet Republic and, for some, a period of imprisonment in Hungary under the rule of the conservative Right, led by Admiral Miklós Horthy. Although Kassák, Kállai, and many other Hungarian artists had initially supported the Hungarian Soviet Republic, they had already begun to react to the party's restrictive cultural edicts prior to being forced into exile. As a result the essay defies overt political affiliation while simultaneously calling for a collective, socialist art, and it presents art practice and the artist as agents of change. "Constructivism" matches the Russian and German constructivist projects in that it recognizes the role of the machine in the future of art while addressing particularly Hungarian concerns, such as the pursuit of an ideal future.

When the text was written in 1923, Hungarian constructivists were at the height of their influence in Vienna and Berlin, collaborating with Lissitzky, members of the Bauhaus, and Dadaists. Kassák stood at the head of the Viennese circle, and his journal, *Ma*, published art and writing by a wide variety of international avant-gardists. *Ma* served as an organizing vehicle for the Hungarian avant-garde in exile, including those living in Berlin, such as László Péri, László Moholy-Nagy, and Kállai. Kassák also maintained ties to members of the avant-garde still living in Hungary; his wife, Jolán Simon, covertly distributed issues of *Ma* to interested parties during trips to Budapest. While Kassák and Kállai also wrote for German and other international periodicals, the work they published in *Ma* spoke to specifically Hungarian interests and advocated for an artistic push toward an idealized future.

"Constructivism" recalls political manifestos, such as Karl Marx and Friedrich Engel's *Communist Manifesto* (1848), in its prescriptive and revolutionary language. Kállai's essay continues in a tradition of outlining an artistic project in manifesto form that began with romanticism in the 1820s. Prior to 1923 Kassák had published a number of manifestos himself while living in Hungary, in the journals *A Tett* and *Ma*, and while living in Vienna, including *Program* (1916); *Proclamation for Art!* (1918); *Activism* (1919); and, perhaps most notably, *Picture-Architecture* (1922). Kállai began sending Kassák essays and reviews from Berlin in 1921, and in addition to "Constructivism" he published a great deal of art criticism, including *Moholy-Nagy* (1921) and, later, after becoming disillusioned with constructivism in the mid-1920s, *The Twilight of Ideologies* (1925).

❖ *Key Facts*

Time Period:
Early 20th Century

Movement/Issue:
Aesthetics;
Constructivism

Place of Publication:
Vienna

Language of Publication:
Hungarian

LAJOS KASSÁK: WORKING-CLASS AVANT-GARDE

Lajos Kassák was a Hungarian poet, painter, and publisher and a central figure in the Hungarian avant-garde. He began his working life as an apprentice to a blacksmith and participated in the labor movement in Budapest as a young man. From 1909 to 1910 he traveled through Western Europe and began to write poetry and fiction. He began a long publishing career in 1915 with the journal *A Tett* (The deed), which was censored and banned for espousing an antimilitaristic point of view. Undeterred, he began a new journal in Budapest in 1919 titled *Ma* (Today). Although Kassák had a decidedly constructivist orientation, the journal published works by artists from a wide variety of competing movements, such as surrealism and Dadaism. After *Ma* was banned in Budapest, Kassák immigrated to Vienna, where he maintained contact with the avant-garde in Hungary and abroad.

Kassák returned to Hungary in 1926. There he served on the Hungarian Arts Council but was forced from his office in the 1950s. During this period he turned his attention from public arts work to his own artwork, creating line drawings and oil paintings that built on his 1921 concept of "picture-architecture." He exhibited his art in Hungary in 1956, but by 1957 he had been forbidden to publish, exhibit, or travel by the Social Democratic Party in Hungary, an injunction that lasted until his death in 1967, although he continued to exhibit internationally and received the Kossuth Prize in Budapest in 1965.

Following the publication of "Constructivism," the Hungarian avant-garde divided over Kassák's refusal to prioritize communism over constructivism and his distaste for Dada. However, subsequent journals of the Hungarian avant-garde, including *Ék* and *ReD* (*Revue Devětsilu*), were clearly influenced by *Ma* and some of the tenets of Kassák's constructivism. *Ma* also served as a model for other central European avant-garde journals, including the Serbian journal *Út* and the Romanian journals *Periszkop* and *Genius,* published in 1925 and 1926, respectively. Additionally, many of the geometric and rational ideals upheld in constructivism reappear in Hungarian minimalist art of the 1960s and 1970s, as well as in the work of the Hungarian neo-avant-garde, and now inspires scholarly examination.

THEMES AND STYLE

The central theme of "Constructivism" is that artists must acknowledge the connection between art and technology, create out of a collective space, and work toward a socially and morally ideal future. Clearly outlining the constructivist artist's task, the essay states that "the will toward geometric necessity and purity establishes an organic interrelation between Constructivist art and the objective working methods and technological systems of our age. Constructivist art, even given the architectonic

unity of the total vocabulary of its forms, affords opportunities for a pervasive division of labor. It is a *collective* art." "Constructivism" stresses both an engagement with a burgeoning technological age and an orientation toward a collective, utopian future. The constructivist artist is to make use of objective, realistic forms to achieve a new art and, subsequently, a new humanity.

"Constructivism," along with many of the works published by Kállai and Kassák in *Ma*, attempts to reach Hungarian artists living in Hungary and abroad as well as to engage international avant-gardists in conversation. The text achieves its rhetorical effect via its inclusive language and direct, formal tone. Using expansive language, Kállai lays out the collective utopian vision of constructivism as he writes that it "cannot tolerate the hierarchic subdivision of emphases, only their uniformity…. The consciousness responsible for its existence prevails in the unconditional readiness for action and momentum in every conceivable direction of spatial, logical and ethical expansion. Constructive consciousness is absolute expansiveness." The essay works to engage the sympathies of international constructivists with its focus on technology while appealing to the seriousness of the Hungarian artist's ideal, socialist future.

In terms of style, "Constructivism" uses logical, scientific language; a straightforward progression through ten paragraphs; and limited, but significant, use of italics for emphasis to appeal to the more rational orientation of international constructivists. Kállai employs technical language as he writes, "Each and every peripheral function of constructive consciousness is set within an immanent gravitational system in which the centrifugal and centripetal forces are in perfect balance." The language is specific and recalls the objective workings of the machine that constructivism strives to replicate. However, the essay does not shy away from making use of idealized, abstract language in its attempt to sway the Hungarian artist still working toward social and cultural revolution, as Kállai notes: "The totality of these principles is structured into a system by the ideal of the new human who is economically organized in both body and mind." "Constructivism" is at once practical and, dissatisfied with an inadequate present, forward looking.

CRITICAL DISCUSSION

The Hungarian avant-garde was experiencing its period of greatest influence abroad in 1922, one year before the publication of "Constructivism." The shifting conception of constructivism presented in the essay served to divide the Hungarian avant-garde and distinguish Hungarian constructivists from their international counterparts. In particular, writes S. A. Mansbach in *Art Journal,* Kassák's "refusal to subordinate art to the programs of any political party engendered great controversy among the Hungarian Activists in exile, just as this attitude had alienated both the former Habsburg and communist governments in Hungary. Many of the avant-garde painters and leftist art critics continued to believe dogmatically in the obligation of progressive artists to serve the needs and promote the interests of the proletariat by acting in accordance with Communist Party directives." Notably, Kállai became disillusioned with Kassák's idealistic notions shortly after authoring "Constructivism" and dedicated himself to exploring the connection between contemporary art and politics.

Hungarian constructivism's period of greatest influence ended shortly after the publication of "Constructivism," although Kassák continued to publish *Ma* until 1925. In her 1987 essay "The Theory of Hungarian Constructivism," critic Esther Levinger notes that "the very idea of Activism and constructive art meant for Kassák an eternal dissatisfaction with the present, in whatever form, and a battle for a still-better future. It was this view of the future that ultimately distanced Kassák and the Hungarian Constructivists from Russian and international Constructivism…. The memory of MA was quickly erased from collective international awareness, and the unique contribution made by the Hungarian Activists to constructive art theory went unnoticed until the last decade." Current scholarship asserts the influence of the Hungarian avant-garde on the development of surrealism, minimalism, and the Hungarian neo-avant-garde of the 1960s.

Scholarship on "Constructivism" focuses on its place in developing a Hungarian version of international constructivism and the role of the manifesto in expressing the particular position of the artist living in exile. Éva Forgács, in her 2006 essay in *Arcadia*, explains Kassák's version of constructivism when she notes that "what Kassák found in Constructivism was not quite identical with either the Russian or the Western model. He saw in the constructivist idiom a new art of redemption, the possibility to build a future from clean slate; and his interpretation of this concept materialized in a majestic seriousness of almost religious exaltation. What he created was a third, classicist version of Constructivism." Forgács also describes, in an essay titled "Between Cultures: Hungarian Concepts of Constructivism," the situation of the Hungarian artist abroad as exemplified by Kállai when she writes, "Like all of the Hungarian artists who lived in emigration and accepted the Constructivity idiom, he found an intellectual home in the new language and community of the movement, which anticipated the international world of the future. But the Hungarian version of Constructivism was also shaped by the Hungarian cultural tradition, the inner contradictions of the group and the social utopias attached to it."

BIBLIOGRAPHY

Sources

Forgács, Éva. "Between Cultures: Hungarian Concepts of Constructivism." *Central European Avant-Gardes: Exchange and Transformation, 1910-1930.* Ed. Timothy Benson. Los Angeles: MIT P, 2002. 146-64. Print.

———. "'You Feed Us So That We Can Fight against You:' Concepts of Art and State in the Hungarian Avant-Garde." *Arcadia* 41.2 (2006): 260-74. *ProQuest.* Web. 6 Sept. 2012.

Kállai, Ernő. "Constructivism." *Between Worlds: A Sourcebook of Central European Avant-Gardes, 1910-1930.* Trans. John Bákti. Ed. Timothy Benson. Cambridge: MIT P, 2002. 435-36. Print.

Levinger, Esther. "The Theory of Hungarian Constructivism." *Art Bulletin* 69.3 (1987): 455-66. *JSTOR.* Web. 6 Sept. 2012.

Mansbach, Steven A. "Confrontation and Accommodation in the Hungarian Avant-Garde." *Art Journal* 49.1 (1990): 9-20. *JSTOR.* Web. 6 Sept. 2012.

Further Reading

Botar, Oliver A. I. "From the Avant-Garde to 'Proletariat Art': The Emigré Hungarian Journals Egység and Akasztott Ember, 1922-1923." *Art Journal* 52.1 (1993): 34-45. *JSTOR.* Web. 6 Sept. 2012.

Mansbach, Steven A. *Standing in the Tempest: Painters of the Hungarian Avant-Garde, 1908-1930.* Los Angeles: MIT P, 1991. Print.

Margolin, Victor. *The Struggle for Utopia: Rodchenko, Lissitzky, Moholy-Nagy, 1917-1946.* Chicago: U of Chicago P, 1997. Print.

Neubauer, John, and Borbála Zsuzsanna Török, eds. *The Exile and Return of Writers from East-Central Europe: A Compendium.* Berlin: Walter de Gruyter, 2009. Print.

Weibel, Peter, ed. *Beyond Art: A Third Culture: A Comparative Study in Cultures, Art and Science in 20th Century Austria and Hungary.* New York: Springer Wein, 2005. Print.

Kristen Gleason

El Lissitzky's 1924 painting *Proun 93.* Lissitzky's ideas about Constructivism greatly influenced critic Ernö Kállai's own survey of the movement. STAATLICHE GALERIE, HALLE, GERMANY/GIRAUDON/THE BRIDGEMAN ART LIBRARY

MANIFESTO OF THE COMMUNE

Stanislaw Kubicki, et al.

❖ *Key Facts*

Time Period:
Early 20th Century

Movement/Issue:
Avant-gardism

Place of Publication:
Germany

Language of Publication:
German

OVERVIEW

Composed collectively by a group of Central European artists known as Die Kommune, the *Manifesto of the Commune* and the *Second Manifesto of the Commune,* written in March 1922 and May 1922, respectively, declare resistance to the patterns of the established art world by disavowing the political and financial means of advancement. Formed only a few years after the end of World War I, Die Kommune was based in Berlin, the artistic capital of Central Europe, and its members laid claim to many different nationalities at a time when national borders were particularly volatile in the region. In the manifesto, the group, led by Polish artist Stanislaw Kubicki, declares an intention to seek a purer, incorruptible form of art apart from the "frogs" and dishonest "cannibals" who comprise the rest of the Central European avant-garde movement. Addressed to the Central European avant-garde, the two manifestos are striking in their use of evocative, figurative language while still maintaining a tone of urgency.

There seems to be no recorded reaction to the first manifesto. The second manifesto, in which the members state their reasons for refusing to participate in the 1922 First International Congress of Progressive Artists, seems to have caused a minor stir among the artists at the exhibition before it was forgotten. However, the public completely ignored the work. Overall the manifestos did not have a great impact, and Die Kommune broke up after the second manifesto was published. Instead the manifestos served as a stepping-stone for the group's leaders, who went on to achieve individual prominence as artists and political figures. The manifestos are significant as a clear and moving critique of capitalist forces in the art world, as well as a statement of anxieties about internationalism in a period of emerging nation-states after World War I.

HISTORICAL AND LITERARY CONTEXT

The *Manifesto of the Commune* and the *Second Manifesto of the Commune* were written in the midst of a growing avant-garde movement that was primarily concerned with the legacy of World War I and the politics of national borders. World War I had left Central Europe in shambles, disrupting and destroying artistic communities throughout the region. Kubicki was a German-born Pole who had fought in World War I against the occupying German Empire, which denied Poles many rights. Kubicki and his wife, Margarete, were founding members of Bunt, a revolutionary group of Polish artists. Later, living in Berlin, the Kubickis, along with Otto Freundlich, another prominent member of Die Kommune, contributed art to the German revolutionary left-wing literary and artistic journal *Die Aktion* (The Action). The Kubickis' choice to embrace anarchy and revolution may have been a symptom of the crumbling political structures around them.

Die Kommune issued its first manifesto in March 1922, introducing the art world to the group and stating its members' aim to be pure artists who were not concerned with status and wealth. The First International Congress of Progressive Artists, scheduled for May 1922 in Dusseldorf, declared, "Art must become international or it will perish," prompting Die Kommune to issue its second manifesto, stating that its members would not attend the exhibition. They saw the event as politically corrupt and ignorant of the full implications of the meaning of international art.

The writing of artistic and aesthetic manifestos was common among the Central European avant-garde, with many groups issuing them as a matter of course. During the early twentieth century, there was also a flourishing of artistic organizations and literary and artistic reviews. The Kubickis and Freundlich had already expressed their views, heavily influenced by German philosopher Karl Marx and the idea of socialist revolution, in publications such as *Die Aktion* and *a bis z.* The Kubickis and Freundlich would continue to write publications, produce art, and form groups with revolutionary political leanings.

Neither the first nor second manifesto seems to have had much of a literary impact. The Kubickis and Freundlich are largely forgotten figures in the Western world, perhaps because they lived in such turbulent times (both Freundlich and Stanislaw Kubicki were eventually killed by the Nazi regime). Nevertheless, the two manifestos and subsequent writings were significant for being part of a growing question in art criticism of the time: what is the social role of art? The members of Die Kommune left behind the beginnings of a socialist theory of art that would continue to influence the many groups of the avant-garde and artists in the contemporary world.

THEMES AND STYLE

The primary theme of both manifestos is the writers' separation from the political and economic aims of other artists, which they see as inherently corrupt. In the first manifesto, the members of Die Kommune declare that they "shall have nothing to with the grubby opportunism that is prevalent in artistic groups in general, or with those who devote their lives to such groups." The manifesto states that an individual must prove "mental and moral incorruptibility" and that these concepts are "human, not artistic." In the second work, the group declares that it will not attend the international exhibition in Dusseldorf, noting that "not one of the groups" is attending the exhibition "with any purpose in mind beyond the personal advantages of its members." Furthermore, the manifesto criticizes "big artistic [mainly German] groups that live by theft from a handful of inventive talents" and compares the artists participating in the exhibition to "frogs" croaking in a crowded swamp.

Both manifestos function as admonishments of the established art world, creating a feeling of exclusivity rather than inclusivity. The repetition of "we" reinforces the sense of the writers as a superior community. The manifestos are written from the perspective of the group and never deviate from a communal voice. As the first manifesto states, "[N]one of us can become dominant within the group." Neither manifesto seems overly concerned with catering to an intended audience; presumably the main audience is other avant-garde artists, whom the manifestos criticize. The language is sharp and pointed, and the manifestos wander quickly from one idea to another, moving through extreme metaphors and resisting much explanation. As the first manifesto states, its "theses are plain" so it barely bothers to justify them.

Both manifestos use extreme and sometimes unusual language that at times teeters on the brink of absurdity. The first begins with a bold statement: "We, the undersigned, are embarking on a united stand against the historical and natural world." Both works use extreme figurative language to ridicule their rivals, as in the first manifesto's statement that members of the avant-garde "remain the reeking morass where each man devours his neighbor's maggots and rolls his eyes in ecstasy." In the second manifesto, the writers repeatedly call other artists "barren," "flabby," and "parasitic," accusing them of "preach[ing] a love you can hold on the end of the string, like a toy balloon." Despite the manifestos' bluntness, both speak often of "love," albeit "a hard love," for which it is necessary to fight. This language belies a sentimentality underneath the manifestos' hard edges.

CRITICAL DISCUSSION

There has been little critical reaction to either of Die Kommune's manifestos. In an account of the international exhibition in Dusseldorf, recently published

WHO WERE THE MAIN ARTISTS OF DIE KOMMUNE?

In the Western world, the names of the writers of the *Manifesto of the Commune* and the *Second Manifesto of the Commune* remain relatively obscure. The influence of these artists seems to have been erased by the forces of geography, politics, and time. Some interest in the Die Kommune artists, however, has been revived in recent years. Stanislaw Kubicki was born in 1889 in Grosspolen, a province of Poland that was controlled by Germany at the time. Margarete Schuster was born in Berlin in 1891. The two, who probably met at an artist's school in Berlin, married in 1916 after Stanislaw had entered the Prussian army. Their work was often collaborative and inspired by one another: Margarete painted a series in 1924 with titles such as *Stanislaw Kubicki and the Plants* and *Stanislaw Kubicki with Rocks and Insects.* However, Kubicki was exiled to Poland in 1934 and executed by the Nazis in 1943, while Margarete remained in Berlin and lived to the age of ninety-three.

Otto Freundlich was born in Pomerania, a historical region now split between Poland and Germany, in 1878 and studied art history and painting in Berlin and Munich. He was a medical orderly in World War I. Perhaps his most significant work was a mosaic titled *The Birth of Man.* His work was called "degenerate art" by the Nazi regime, and in 1943 he was exiled to Poland, where he died.

in *Between Two Worlds* (2002), Polish artist Henryk Berlewi, a member of the Novembergruppe and the International Congress on Progressive Art, may have had the *Second Manifesto of the Commune* in mind when writing the following jabs: "Antagonisms of a non-artistic nature have all but disappeared for the good of one great cause: art." Perhaps pointedly ignoring the manifesto's complaints, he states, "[T]he reason that agreement is difficult" among artists "is that while one group is more advanced in its development, another, perhaps also regarded as 'progressive,' has not managed to free itself from parochialism." He also critiques German expressionism—a stylistic category that could encompass the work of the Kubickis and Freundlich—as being out of date compared to more modern movements such as cubism and Dadaism. Even though Berlewi does not state outright opposition to Die Kommune's manifesto, his account of the exhibition seems to contain some criticisms of the group.

The *Manifesto of the Commune* and the *Second Manifesto of the Commune* are most significant for being part of a growing avant-garde movement that composed aesthetic manifestos. For the artists of Die Kommune, communal political action and artistic output were a way of life. The Kubickis, along with Freundlich, all contributed work to the revolutionary paper *a bis z,* and their writing in *a bis z* was

Composition, a painting (circa 1929) by Henryk Stazewski, a contemporary of Stanislaw Kubicki and an active member of the Constructivism movement.
© INTERFOTO /ALAMY

was able to survive"—even in spite of the manifestos' stated claims to make art for personal and aesthetic reasons and not for profit. Other scholarship has focused on the political nature of the Kubickis' art. As S. A. Mansbach writes in *Modern Art in Eastern Europe* (1999), "[T]heir commitment to political democracy might explain why they concentrated their efforts on widely distributed graphic arts rather than on individual easel paintings." Freundlich, too, is largely remembered as a political figure first and as an artist second. In *Painters and Politics* (1976), Theda Shapiro writes about his simultaneous communist ideals and interest in artistic freedom, as well as his belief that "mass art was now needed to correspond to the mass public."

BIBLIOGRAPHY

Sources

Benson, Timothy O., ed. *Between Two Worlds: A Sourcebook of Central European Avant-Gardes, 1910-1930.* Cambridge: MIT, 2002. Print.

Król, Monika. "Collaboration and Compromise: Women Artists in Polish-German Avant-Garde Circles, 1910-1930." *Central European Avant-Gardes: Exchange and Transformation, 1910-1930.* Ed. Timothy O. Benson. Cambridge: MIT, 2002. 338-56. Print.

Mansbach, S. A. *Modern Art in Eastern Europe: From the Baltic to the Balkans, c.a. 1890-1939.* Cambridge: Cambridge UP, 1999. Print.

Shapiro, Theda. *Painters and Politics: The European Avant-Garde and Society, 1900-1925.* New York: Elsevier, 1976. Print.

Further Reading

Benson, Timothy O. "Exchange and Transformation: The Internalization of the Avant-Garde(s) in Central Europe." *Central European Avant-Gardes: Exchange and Transformation, 1910-1930.* Ed. Timothy O. Benson. Cambridge: MIT, 2002. 34-67. Print.

Everett, Martyn. "Art as a Weapon: Franz Seiwert and the Cologne Progressives." *Raven* Oct. 1990. *Libcom.* Web. 24 Sept. 2012.

Hoptman, Laura J. *Beyond Belief: Contemporary Art from East Central Europe.* Lakewood: Distributed Art, 1995. Print.

Lidtke, Vernon L. "Abstract Art and Left-Wing Politics in the Weimar Republic." *Central European History* 37.1 (2004): 49-90. *JSTOR.* Web. 24 Sept. 2012.

Malinowski, Jerzy. "Poznań." *Central European Avant-Gardes: Exchange and Transformation, 1910-1930.* Ed. Timothy O. Benson. Cambridge: MIT, 2002. 307-11. Print.

Emily Jones

influenced by their work in *Die Aktion.* Prominent Polish artists were also influenced by the revolutionary leanings of the Kubickis. Thus, although the two manifestos do not seem to have a strong literary influence, their legacy is in their impact on the lives of their creators and the larger movement of the time.

Scholarship on the first and second manifestos is rare, especially in the English language. Indeed, even the artists who created the manifestos have gone largely unstudied in the Western world. Attempts to revitalize public knowledge of the Central European avant-garde have recently come into focus with an exhibit at California's Los Angeles County Museum of Art in 2002. Monika Król's essay in *Central European Avant-Gardes: Exchange and Transformation, 1910-1930* (2002) focuses on the supportive partnership of the Kubickis, writing that "thanks to Margarethe's hard work as a tutor and art school teacher, the family

MANIFESTO OF WORKERS' COUNCIL FOR ART IN BERLIN

Workers' Council for Art

OVERVIEW

Published shortly after Germany's November Revolution in 1918, *Manifesto of Arbeitsrat für Kunst in Berlin* (*Manifesto of Workers' Council for Art in Berlin*) captures the hopes of the postwar generation of young architects and artists with utopian visions of transforming their war-torn country into a socialist paradise. A group of like-minded artists formed the Workers' Council for Art (WCA) under the wing of the Spartacus League (a subgroup of the Communist Party of Germany) in an attempt to influence Germany's newly forming republican government. The group's tract urges architects and artists to unite for the important task of rebuilding the art world in Germany. Written by architect Bruno Taut and signed by fifty prominent German artists and architects, the text demands that the WCA be given official status and put in charge of designing the entire appearance of the republic—everything from cathedrals to stamps and coins. Central to the document are six demands for art in the new society, including freedom from censorship, removal of class barriers, and the eradication of false distinctions between arts and crafts.

Initially embraced as a blueprint for the future, *Manifesto of Workers' Council for Art in Berlin* garnered enthusiastic support from many prominent artists and architects. However, a small number of German expressionists criticized the group's program as naïve and romantic, and they were quickly proven correct. In January 1919 German voters rejected the radical socialist agenda backed by members of the WCA in favor of a moderate democratic socialist coalition, making it clear that the manifesto's political demands would not be met. Disenchanted, Taut handed the leadership of the group over to architect Walter Gropius, who promptly jettisoned the document's political demands and focused on the group's aesthetic and spiritual goals. That same year Gropius was named director of a new state art school, which he renamed the Bauhaus School. In his *Manifesto of the Bauhaus* (1919), Gropius borrowed concepts such as art for the masses and art as a way to create a more humane, egalitarian society from *Manifesto of Workers' Council for Art in Berlin*.

HISTORICAL AND LITERARY CONTEXT

Manifesto of Workers' Council for Art in Berlin responds to Germany's tumultuous climate following its defeat in World War I. With the economy in near collapse and the country in ruins, political factions ran the gamut from ultra right to ultra left. After decades of repression and inequality under the German imperial system, socialism had a wide appeal. Taut and his fellow WCA members saw an opportunity to change and rebuild for the better. Encouraged by the success of the Russian Revolution of 1917, many Germans, including members of the WCA, believed Soviet-style government was possible in their own country. This belief was bolstered in 1918 when the German emperor Kaiser Wilhelm II abdicated the throne. Censorship was lifted, and it was now possible to publish a document like the manifesto.

By the late winter of 1918, the workers' and soldiers' councils who had sparked Germany's November Revolution had assumed control of the country. Delegates were drafting a constitution in the city of Weimar while Taut was across town drafting *Manifesto of Workers' Council for Art in Berlin*. The text was aimed specifically at these delegates and represents the WCA's efforts to wield political influence. Taut, Gropius, and like-minded architects saw that the new government would need to rebuild housing and public spaces, and they wanted to be the ones to do so in affordable, aesthetically inspiring ways. Though the manifesto's demands were never directly met, many of its aspects came to fruition in the decades between the wars with the establishment of state-supported schools for the arts and the merger of two classical art academies to form one experimental school.

Manifesto of Workers' Council for Art in Berlin was designed to complement the Weimar Constitution. Its preamble reads, "The German people united in its tribes and inspired with the will to renew and strengthen the Reich in liberty and justice, to serve internal and external tranquility, and to promote social progress, has adopted this Constitution." Taut's document even mirrors some of the language and ideas of the constitution, such as its call for unity, renewal, and social progress. Taut framed his demands as action items in a piece of parliamentary legislation

Key Facts

Time Period:
Early 20th Century

Movement/Issue:
Aesthetics; Socialism

Place of Publication:
Germany

Language of Publication:
German

BAUHAUS IN AMERICA

The Bauhaus School moved from Weimar to Dessau to Berlin until the Nazis forced the school to close its doors in 1933. Given the growing hostilities in his native land, Walter Gropius left Germany soon after, immigrating first to England and later to the United States. In 1937 he accepted a post at the Harvard Graduate School of Design as chairman of the department of architecture, bringing the Bauhaus ideals and philosophy with him. In his writing Gropius continued to advocate for the changes he and his fellow council members aspired to during their time in the Arbeitsrat für Kunst, which had been memorialized in Taut's 1918 manifesto. Gropius wrote in 1936, "Let us together desire, conceive, and create the new building of the future, which will combine everything—architecture *and* sculpture *and* painting—in a *single form* which will one day rise to the heavens from the hands of a million workers as the crystalline symbol of the new faith." Like Taut, Gropius strove to eliminate the distinction between artists and craftspeople, and one of the goals of Bauhaus in the United States was to teach young architects to respond to the technical, economic, and social conditions of their lives rather than rely on an antiquated formula. His arrival at Harvard signaled a new era in American design.

to ensure a role for architects and artists in the new government.

In the decades following its publication, *Manifesto of Workers' Council for Art in Berlin* received little attention. After the leaders of the Spartacus League died in police custody and the coalition government turned against the Communist Party, the members of the WCA joined Gropius in shying away from the manifesto's political agenda, placing greater emphasis on their artistic dimension. By 1921 the council was defunct, but parts of Taut's work were adapted by Gropius for his Bauhaus manifesto. The ideas set forth in *Manifesto of Workers' Council for Art in Berlin* have indirectly inspired volumes of literature, both positive and negative, beginning with exhibition catalogs and art criticism in Germany starting in the 1920s. However, when members of the Bauhaus School were driven out of the country by the Nazis, Bauhaus and German modernism began attracting international attention. Works on Bauhaus still appear with regularity as architects, art historians, and cultural critics debate, dissect, applaud, and deplore the ways in which German modernism continues to shape contemporary life.

THEMES AND STYLE

Manifesto of Workers' Council for Art in Berlin has several major themes: art without censorship, the artist as creator of culture and sociopolitical leader, architecture's power to transform society, and art for the masses. The first theme has its roots in German intellectual responses to the French Revolution. The second and third themes are linked to a thread of mysticism running from philosopher Friedrich Nietzsche's "artists' metaphysics" back to the Old Testament of the Bible. Nietzsche viewed the world as a work of art and the artist as a high priest. Taut adapted this idea to his concept of architecture as the foundation of a new social order in which architects and artists serve as leaders. He also drew on a notion popularized by composer Richard Wagner in the 1800s that the art of the future will bring salvation. Finally, the theme of art in the service of the people is based on the ideas of nineteenth-century anarchists Pierre-Joseph Proudhon and Peter Kropotkin, who believed that the progressive force of socialism is not the industrial proletariat but the enlightened artist who goes back to the land and works for social reform. All of these themes were part of the post-World War I debate in Europe about the role of art and architecture.

The document achieves its rhetorical effect by recognizing the need for social reform while assigning the artist/architect a special role in the new society, thus appealing to the artists' conscience and ego simultaneously. The need for social reform is underscored by repeated references to "the people," with the injunction to transform art from "a pleasure of a few" into "joy and sustenance for the masses." The work envisions the artist as shaper of the people's sensibilities who "alone is responsible for the external appearance of the new nation." The ideal government is one that actively supports art for the masses but does not interfere with artistic creation, and one that forbids bureaucratic involvement in public art, allowing the artist freedom to transform society through his buildings and designs.

In terms of style, *Manifesto of Workers' Council for Art in Berlin* is distinguished by its use of parliamentary format. It projects legitimacy through the use of political language in phrases such as "the goals are outlined in the following program excerpt." Like the Weimar Constitution, it includes an enumerated set of demands, and its goals are in line with the objectives of the new government. By composing the document in the manner of a parliamentary decree, Taut and fellow members of the Workers' Council declared their desire to break with the old regime and support "the masses," the very people the council wished to represent and whose artistic sensibilities they hoped to shape.

CRITICAL DISCUSSION

Manifesto of Workers' Council for Art in Berlin received broad-based support in the art community when it was published in 1918. The WCA attracted more than 100 members in its three-year existence, including such renowned artists as Lyonel Feininger and Wassily Kandinsky and noted art critic Adolf Behne.

The document and its signatories won converts among architects and artists who were moved by the message that art was important and powerful but came second to meeting the basic needs of the masses. A handful of German expressionists, including Otto Dix and George Grosz, failed to embrace the ideas in the manifesto, finding them naïve and sentimental.

The document's main legacy was its influence on the more enduring *Manifesto of the Bauhaus.* After Taut resigned as leader of the council and its political demands lost relevance following the 1919 German elections, his ideas lived on in the writing and work of Gropius and the architects of the Bauhaus School, first in Germany and later around the world. Taut's manifesto was also appropriated by unexpected sources. As Kathleen James-Chakraborty writes in her 2000 book *German Architecture for a Mass Audience,* "Ironically, however, it would be industry and the church, institutions deeply threatened by the November Revolution, which would utilize Taut's Expressionist tactics in an effort to stabilize German society through the spiritualization of an overtly modern architecture." These institutions assimilated Taut's ideology during the Weimar Republic in order to appear progressive and inclusive.

Much scholarship has focused on the influence of Bauhaus style on international architecture and design. The Metropolitan Museum of Art published *The International Style* in 1932, helping launch European modernism in the United States, and followed up thirty-four years later with a harsh critique of that same style with the publication of *Complexity and Contradiction.* Commentators have drawn attention to the rigidity of Taut's utopian architecture, which architects began to chafe against in the 1960s and 1970s. James-Chakraborty describes how the modernist movement in German architecture has in recent decades become an idea discredited by its own overwhelming success. Other scholarship has pointed to the Great Depression and World War II as important factors contributing to the popularity of German modernism, at least in the United States. The most recent scholarship raises the issue of Nazism among Bauhaus teachers. According to Winfried Nerdinger in *Bauhaus-Moderne im Nationalsozialismus* (1993), even after Gropius fell out of favor with the Nazis and felt compelled to leave Germany in the early 1930s, he did not reject Nazism. Nor was he alone among his German colleagues in this regard. Bauhaus reached a different audience when it became the subject of a creative nonfiction work by Tom Wolfe in 1981, *From Bauhaus to Our House.*

The Walter Gropius-designed Bauhaus-Archiv (Bauhaus Archive/ Museum of Design) in Berlin, Germany. Gropius and others describe their artistic theories in the 1919 *Manifesto of Workers' Council for Art in Berlin (Arbeitsrat für Kunst).* © PRISMA BILDAGENTUR AG/ALAMY

BIBLIOGRAPHY

Sources

Blake, Peter. *No Place Like Utopia.* New York: Knopf, 1993. Print.

Frank, Suzanne. Rev. of *Bauhaus Culture: From Weimar to the Cold War,* ed. by Kathleen James-Chakraborty. *Journal for the Society of Architectural Historians* 67.1 (2008): 140-42. *JSTOR.* Web. 4 Oct. 2012.

Hvattum, Mari, and Christian Hermansen. *Tracing Modernity: Manifestations of the Modern in Architecture and the City.* New York: Routledge, 2004. Print.

James-Chakraborty, Kathleen. *German Architecture for a Mass Audience.* London: Routledge, 2000. Print.

Naylor, Gillian. *The Bauhaus Reassessed.* New York: Dutton, 1985. Print.

Nerdinger, Winfried. *Bauhaus-Moderne im Nationalsozialismus.* Munich: Prestel, 1993. Print.

Von Effra, Helmut. Rev. of *Walter Gropius and the Creation of Bauhaus,* by Marcel Franciscono. *Art Journal* 31.4 (1972): 480-82. *JSTOR.* Web. 2 Oct. 2012.

Weitz, Eric D. *Weimar Germany: Promise and Tragedy.* Princeton: Princeton UP, 2007. Print.

Wolfe, Thomas. *From Bauhaus to Our House.* New York: Farrar, Straus & Giroux, 1981. Print.

Further Reading

Bullen, J.B. "D.H. Lawrence and Sculpture in *Women in Love.*" *Burlington Magazine* 145.1209 (2003): 841-46. *JSTOR.* Web. 2 Oct. 2012.

Deshmukh, Marion F. "The Visual Arts and Cultural Migration in the 1930s and 1940s: A Literature Review." *Central European History* 41.4 (2008): 569-604. *JSTOR.* Web. 2 Oct. 2012.

Fitch, James Marston. *Walter Gropius.* New York: Braziller, 1960. Print.

Kaes, Anton, Martin Jay, and Edward Dimendberg, eds. *The Weimar Republic Sourcebook.* Berkeley: U of California P, 1994. Print.

Mallgrave, Harry F., and Christina Contandriopoulos. *Architectural Theory: Vol. II: An Anthology.* Malden: Blackwell, 2008. Print.

Pommer, Richard, and Christian F. Otto. *Weissenhof 1927 & the Modern Movement in Architecture.* Chicago: U of Chicago P, 1991. Print.

Schirren, Matthias, and Bruno Taut: *Alpine Architecture: A Utopia.* New York: Prestel, 2004. Print.

Wiseman, Carter. *Shaping a Nation: The Twentieth Century American Architecture and Its Makers.* New York: W.W. Norton, 1998. Print.

Kristin King-Ries

MAVO MANIFESTO

Tomoyoshi Murayama

OVERVIEW

Written by Tomoyoshi Murayama (1901-77) and published as a pamphlet in July 1923 for the first exhibition of works by Mavo—a group of Japanese avant-garde artists—the *Mavo Manifesto* announces the formation of the constructivist group and describes broad plans for future Mavo activities. The manifesto was the product of the convergence of two powerful entities in the world of Western-style Japanese art—Murayama and the Japanese Futurist Art Association (FAA), an organization inspired by the European futurist movement. The left-leaning artists, activists, and entertainers of Mavo criticized the bourgeois capitalist system but also adopted consumer culture's advertising methods to help establish a "new urban aesthetic" in Japan during the 1920s. Inviting the public to submit artworks ranging from "window displays" and "stage designs" to "book designs" and "various kinds of ornaments" for possible inclusion in future Mavo shows and soliciting donations from potential "friends" of Mavo with promises of free admission to sponsored lectures, concerts, theater performances, and exhibitions, the *Mavo Manifesto* reads like an advertisement with its direct language, straightforward plea, and overt appeal to a wide audience.

Because the Mavoist founding statement is both defiantly imprecise and consciously self-contradictory, it created less of a stir in interwar Japan than the group's other visual and textual productions—including *Mavo* magazine, which was founded in mid-1924. Indeed, the manifesto's most powerful declaration—"We stand at the vanguard..." not only is weakened by Murayama's refusal to clarify the group's guiding principles but also is tempered by language that is deliberately at odds with the sense of *sentan* (pointed edge), which the manifesto, like other Japanese avant-garde statements of the era, briefly expresses. This hint of "pointed-edginess" managed to generate significant results, inspiring Mavo's Moving Exhibition Welcoming Works Rejected from Nika, which began as an open-air art display of works rejected from a state-sponsored exhibition and involved rock throwing, Mavo flag hoisting, and art parading through Tokyo's streets. The exhibition ended in a clash with police that attracted media coverage and helped establish Mavo's reputation as a destructively constructive, aesthetically political, and commercially creative force of the future.

HISTORICAL AND LITERARY CONTEXT

The *Mavo Manifesto* presents a direct challenge to an entrenched and hierarchical art establishment in Tokyo that was closely monitored by a censorious state. An ideology of individualism grounded in Western philosophical thought had permeated political and cultural discussions in Japanese society since the Meiji Restoration (1868), and Western-style painting became common in Japan during the decade that followed. However, it was not until after the Russo-Japanese War (1904-5) that Japanese artists, inspired by emerging European modernism, began to vigorously promote abstract self-expression. Likewise, it was not until after World War I that leftist political ideas—both Marxist and anarchist—gained a foothold in Japan. In 1920 the abstraction-endorsing and "anarchist-inclined" FAA—Mavo's immediate precursor—was formed.

Japanese artists had been interested in the futurist movement's dynamism and subjectivism since its inception in Italy in 1909. They replaced futurism's militant nationalist ethos with a revolutionary internationalist one that embraced some aspects of Russian futurism (via Ukrainian David Burliuk). When Murayama returned to Tokyo after a year of witnessing dadaism, futurism, expressionism, constructivism, anarchism, and Marxism in action and fraternizing in Berlin with a number of prominent Western artists and social critics—including Theo van Doesburg, Kurt Schwitters, Tristan Tzara, and George Grosz—he found that his new theory of "conscious constructivism" appealed to the four FAA members who would join him in founding Mavo—Shūzō Ōura (1890-1928), Masamu Yanase (1900-1945), Kamenosuke Ogata (1900-1942), and Shinrō Kadowaki (ca. 1900-1924).

Although the *Mavo Manifesto,* with its muted aggression and unclear objectives, departs from the modern European manifesto tradition, both Murayama and his FAA collaborators had goals that coincided with those of their European counterparts. They advocated "art of the future" that experimented with nonobjective forms and unconventional materials while reflecting on and engaging in the conditions

⁜ Key Facts

Time Period:
Early 20th Century

Movement/Issue:
Aesthetics; Avant-gardism; Constructivism

Place of Publication:
Japan

Language of Publication:
Japanese

THE GENESIS OF THE MAVO NAME

Although Mavoists seemingly rejected dadaism, futurism, and expressionism in their formulation of a new artistic movement, the group took a cue from Dada when its members put into circulation several legends about the origins of the Mavo name. One such legend—similar to the dadaist tale that the nonsensical word *Dada* had been pinpointed by plunging a paper knife into a French-German dictionary—explains that the five founding members chose the four random letters *m, a, v,* and *o* from an alphabetic soup that had been created from the cut-up letters of the members' Romanized names (although the *v* remains unaccounted for). Another legend holds that the letters stand for *masse* (mass), *vitesse* (speed), alpha (beginning), and omega (end). Although neither of these legends has been verified, one fact is indisputable: the stories have inspired a sense of mystery that its founders knew would help attract and sustain public interest in the movement for years to come.

Programme of the eighth Dada soirée, Zurich, Switzerland, April 9, 1919. The work of the members of the Mavo movement was often compared to that of the Dadaists. © INTERFOTO /ALAMY

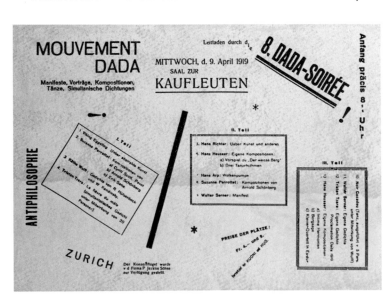

of modern life. Murayama, like many of the constructivists he had met in Germany, disdained the overly romantic subjectivity associated with abstract expressionism; experimented with collage, assemblage, performance art, theater, architecture, and design; and championed art as a means of social renewal.

Less than two months after the manifesto appeared, renewal became an overriding theme in Japan as the Great Kantō Earthquake devastated Tokyo, creating an opportunity for the Mavoists to contribute to the city's material and spiritual reconstruction. The Mavoists' decoration of temporary housing, production of plans for future permanent structures, and introduction of high art into cafes, department stores, and streets influenced commercial culture for years

to come. Nevertheless, the anarchic nature of the movement—so evident in the acute tension between affirmation and negation, commercialism and communism, egoism and collectivism, and construction and deconstruction, which the manifesto directly and indirectly expresses—ultimately led to the dissolution of the group (which included fifteen members at its peak) and left an aesthetic-political legacy that was more dialectical than programmatic.

THEMES AND STYLE

One of the central themes of the *Mavo Manifesto* is contradiction. Murayama states in the second section that Mavoists "ceaselessly affirm and negate," essentially negating the affirmative series of declarations he provides in the first section about Mavo "stand[ing] at the vanguard." He claims in the manifesto's central portion that the Mavoists "do not subscribe to the convictions ... of any existing groups" and that "[n]othing can be compared to [their] work." However, these statements contradict previous references to the influence of an already flourishing "constructivist" movement and the subsequent assertion that what "ties" the Mavoists together is "the approximation of the forms of constructivist art." These references imply that Mavo's work is meant to be compared to constructivist art, as well as to futurism, expressionism, and dadaism—movements that an advertising flier for the first Mavoist exhibition both acknowledges and negates in order to build awareness of and controversy around the organization.

Rhetorically, the manifesto reflects the contradictions that surround the group's identity. Although Murayama describes the Mavoists' organization into a commonly "inclined" group the opposes institutionalized Japanese art, he refrains from detailing Mavo's "inclinations" and naming its enemies—presumably in order to avoid institutionalizing the group. Nevertheless, he introduces the initials *MV* as the group's institutionalizing trademark—though he is quick to explain that the Mavoists are "definitely" not united by "identical principles" and do not "aggressively try to regulate [their] artistic convictions." He goes on to say that each of Mavo's members "possess[es] ... passions" that he "feels" he "must elevate to the level of objectivity" but refrains from doing so out of "respect" for his Mavoist peers who may disagree with him. He admits that Mavo is the product of expedience (a "matter of timing" and "a thing of the moment") even as he paradoxically describes the group as a "negative entity."

Stylistically, the manifesto, particularly its final section, is vague and willfully indefinite. Murayama appeals to future artist-participants in, and donor-supporters for, Mavo's newly, loosely defined movement first by announcing that Mavo will host exhibitions between one and four times a year. Then he calls upon members of the public to submit works to be considered for inclusion in future shows. But he neither suggests any theme for these exhibitions nor indicates the standards by which submissions might be judged in order to avoid exhibiting the same exclusivity of Mavo's establishment enemies. However, he continues, Mavo cannot abandon exclusivity altogether and thus "must be forgiven for accepting" only existing Mavo works "at the present time." He alludes to the necessity of judging the "scope" and "merit" of any submitted works but undercuts these requirements by adding that the "scope" he speaks of may be "extremely broad." He states that the "merit" Mavoists seek can be only determined by the Mavoists themselves because they are critically empowered not by any absolute standards but by the work they have thus far produced as artists.

CRITICAL DISCUSSION

The *Mavo Manifesto* calls on readers to look at Mavo's works in order to understand the movement's aims; the document's consciously unclear statements are intended to be more comprehensible alongside Mavoist art. Early reactions to the first Mavoist show at Denpōin came mostly from artist-critics who knew the group's members or were associated with the FAA. An acquaintance of Yanase, for instance, criticized the show and the manifesto for their comprehensive attempts to integrate art and daily life. One member of the FAA, angered by his exclusion from the first Mavo exhibition, directly lashed out at the manifesto's author for the exclusivity of Mavo's approach to art. Whereas the former review prompted Murayama to publish in a popular periodical a more specific description of constructivist art that was closer to daily life, the latter review moved him to invite the FAA critic to join Mavo. Thus, it was precisely because the manifesto raised so many questions that its author was able to sustain interest in the movement by providing answers in subsequent papers.

However, Murayama's mastery of public relations could not keep an increasingly radicalized Mavo movement together long after 1925. Nevertheless, his skill in public relations helped him find a place for the avant-garde in the world of commercial design. Although he and other former Mavoists would come to be associated with a proletarian art movement that gave them greater political satisfaction, Mavo's most pivotal role was aesthetic, helping to develop modern Japanese design, today one of the country's most celebrated artistic fields. Interest in Mavo was initially rekindled in the late 1950s by critics, art historians, and exhibition curators eager to link the movement to the post-World War II avant-garde.

Western writings on Japanese modernism that acknowledge the movement's multihemispheric influences have proliferated in the past decade. However, very few critics have examined the *Mavo Manifesto*'s relationship to the broader tradition of early twentieth-century European manifestoes in any specific detail. When scholars like Toshiko Ellis, Alexandra Munroe, and William Gardner reference the document in relation to comparable Western texts, they quote its boldest and most optimistic passage about Mavo "stand[ing] at the vanguard" in order to emphasize similarities between Western and Eastern avant-gardes. Today's preeminent Mavo expert Gennifer Weisenfeld astutely observes that the founding document of the Mavo movement was much more internally conflicted than the manifestos that European artists were producing at the time, with its refusal to provide a unified platform or to declare ideological solidarity because its signatories were understandably wary of the "coercion" and "tyranny" that establishment art communities had been exercising for centuries.

BIBLIOGRAPHY

Sources

Ellis, Toshiko. "The Japanese Avant-Garde of the 1920s: The Poetic Struggle with the Dilemma of the Modern." *Poetics Today* 20.4 (1999): 723-41. Web. 15 Oct. 2012.

Gardner, William. *Advertising Tower: Japanese Modernism and Modernity in the 1920s.* Cambridge, MA: Harvard UP, 2006. Print.

Munroe, Alexandra. *Japanese Art after 1945: Scream against the Sky.* New York: Abrams, 1994. Print.

———. Rev. of *Mavo: Japanese Artists and the Avant-Garde, 1905-1931,* by Gennifer Weisenfeld. *The Society for Japanese Studies* 30.1 (2004): 215-19. *JSTOR.* Web. 15 Oct. 2012.

Omuka, Toshiharu. *Taishōki no shinkō bijutsu undō no kenkyū* (A study of the new art movements of the Taishō period). Tokyo: Skydoor, 1995. Print.

Weisenfeld, Gennifer. *Mavo: Japanese Artists and the Avant-Garde, 1905-1931.* Berkeley: U of California P, 2002. Print.

———. "Mavo's Conscious Constructivism: Art, Individualism, and Daily Life in Interwar Japan." *Art Journal* 55.3 (1996): 64-73. *JSTOR.* Web. 15 Oct. 2012.

Wu, Chinghsin. "Transcending the Boundaries of the 'isms': Pursuing Modernity through the Machine 1920s and 1930s Japanese Avant-Garde." *Rethinking Japanese Modernism.* Ed. Roy Starrs. Boston: Global Oriental, 2012. 339-61. Print.

Further Reading

Harootunian, Harry. *Overcome by Modernity: History, Culture, and Community in Interwar Japan.* Princeton: Princeton UP, 2000. Print.

Murayama, Tomoyoshi. *Engekiteki jijoden* (Theatrical autobiography). Vol. 1. Tokyo: Tōhō Shuppansha, 1970. Print.

———. *Engekiteki jijoden 1922-1927* (Theatrical autobiography). Vol. 2. Tokyo: Tōhō Shuppansha, 1971. Print.

Omuka, Toshiharu. "David Burliuk and the Japanese Avant-Garde." *Canadian-American Slavic Studies* 20.1-2 (1986): 113-30. Print.

Silberman, Bernard, and H. D. Harootunian, eds. *Japan in Crisis: Essays on Taishō Democracy.* Princeton: Princeton UP, 1974. Print.

Silverberg, Miriam. "Constructing the Japanese Ethnography of Modernity." *Journal of Asian Studies* 51.1 (1992): 30-54. Web. 15 Oct. 2012.

Starrs, Roy. *Modernism and Japanese Culture.* New York: Palgrave Macmillan, 2011. Print.

———, ed. *Rethinking Japanese Modernism.* Boston: Global Oriental, 2012. Print.

Thornton, Richard S. *Japanese Graphic Design.* London: King, 1991. Print.

Tipton, Elise K., and John Clark, eds. *Being Modern in Japan: Culture and Society from the 1910s to the 1930s.* Honolulu: U of Hawaii P, 2000. Print.

Tyler, William J., ed. *Modanizumu: Modernist Fiction from Japan, 1913-1938.* Honolulu: U of Hawaii P, 2008. Print.

Katie Macnamara

THE NON-OBJECTIVE WORLD
The Manifesto of Suprematism
Kazimir Malevich

OVERVIEW

Written by Russian painter Kazimir Malevich, *The Non-Objective World: The Manifesto of Suprematism* (1927) describes Malevich's nonobjective, geometric style of painting, which sought to express a "supremacy of pure feeling" by rejecting the use of traditional representational forms. Although the treatise was composed around 1919, the same year that Malevich exhibited 153 suprematist works in a triumphant one-man show, it was not published until Malevich visited Berlin, Germany, for an exhibition in 1927. By then, according to Malevich, "Suprematism as a movement had come to an end," and, thus, despite its publication by the Bauhaus (an avant-garde German school of design), the manifesto did not exert as much influence in the world of avant-garde art as did his suprematist paintings. Central to the suprematist manifesto is the argument that feeling is the primary factor in determining the artistic value of a piece of art and that the artist must cast aside any representations of realistic or familiar objects in order to heed this pure feeling.

Whereas the public was hostile to the emergence of suprematism, and the art world hailed Malevich as the acknowledged leader of the avant-garde, the manifesto itself was barely noticed when published more than a decade after the first suprematist exhibition. The manifesto did, however, help articulate the theoretical underpinnings of Malevich's aesthetic. According to the manifesto, suprematism disavows the use of representational forms, as well as political and religious ideas, because they are mere "things, which conceal its [an artwork's] true value—the feeling that gave rise to it." Art critics in the twenty-first century view *The Non-Objective World* not only as an important document in the development of nonrepresentational art but also as an intellectual work that influenced contemporary American art beginning in the latter half of the twentieth century.

HISTORICAL AND LITERARY CONTEXT

The suprematist manifesto responds to the rise and development of the Russian avant-garde at the beginning of the twentieth century. A decade prior to the first suprematist exhibition, an art collector named

Sergei Shchukin catalyzed the development of the Russian avant-garde by introducing young Muscovite painters to the impressionist and postimpressionist schools, including works by Paul Cézanne, Vincent van Gogh, Henri Matisse, and Pablo Picasso. These collections gave Russian artists a crash course in forty years of revolutionary Western European painting. Much of this artwork, especially that of Picasso, rendered familiar objects abstractly in order to examine and present these forms so that the viewer might behold them with greater fullness. According to the *New York Review of Books,* "Malevich, on the other hand, saw this analysis as an attempt to shatter the subject completely." It was this creative misinterpretation that led Malevich to use the simple, abstract, geometric forms, which, as the suprematist manifesto argues, "gives the fullest possible expression to feeling as such" by ignoring "the familiar appearance of objects."

By 1927, when *The Non-Objective World* was published as part of the Bauhaus series of books, suprematism as a movement had come to an end, in part because of political pressure. In the early 1920s, Malevich had taught at the Vitebsk Art School, where he worked with students, anonymously, on suprematist-inspired flags, orator's platforms, fabric, and placards. The school was regarded as politically suspicious. In 1924 Malevich was named the leader of the Institute of Artistic Culture in Petrograd (now St. Petersburg), Russia, where he worked with his most advanced pupils on suprematist-inspired architectural models, but severe criticism of the artists' work and increasing political pressure forced the institute to close. The Soviet government denied Malevich's request to exhibit his new work in Dessau, Germany, in collaboration with the Bauhaus, but they allowed him a retrospective show in Poland and Berlin, where he exhibited his pre-suprematist and suprematist paintings. It was during this trip that *The Non-Objective World* was translated into German by A. Von Reisen and published in Munich, Germany, by Albert Langen.

The suprematist manifesto responds to a long history of avant-garde manifestos, most specifically the futurist manifesto *The Exhibitors to the Public* (1912), in which Italian painter Umberto Boccioni

✣ *Key Facts*

Time Period:
Early/Mid-20th Century

Movement/Issue:
Suprematism;
Avant-gardism

Place of Publication:
Germany

Language of Publication:
German

THE OCTOBER REVOLUTION

In the fall of 1917, the Bolsheviks, a group of people assembled from the Russian Social-Democratic Workers' Party and led by Vladimir Lenin, attacked the Winter Palace in Petrograd in order to overthrow the provisional government, which had just recently replaced the tsar's rule. The avant-garde artists of the day, with Kazimir Malevich among them, hailed the revolution as an extermination of the old order and an opportunity to build a greater industrialized society. Malevich claimed that "Cubism and Futurism were the revolutionary forms in art foreshadowing the revolution in political and economic life of 1917." These artists of the left threw their full weight behind the Bolshevik Revolution by announcing their allegiances and reordering the artistic life of the country. They encouraged artists to abandon the idle canvas and paint the squares and bridges of their cities.

By 1926, however, Malevich was feeling the repressive nature of the Soviet regime. The Petrograd State Institute of Artistic Culture, where Malevich had worked as director, was closed after a young, militant critic condemned Malevich's exhibition as openly counterrevolutionary. In that same year, Malevich petitioned for a travel permit in order to visit a fellow artist in Paris, but the government denied the request. He was granted an exit visa in order to show his works in Poland and Germany, however, and he subsequently left much of his work in Berlin. He hoped to continue exhibiting his paintings in the West, but some critics have suggested that Malevich did not bring his work back to Russia because he feared that, in such a repressive environment, his paintings might be lost to history.

advances the idea of force lines that imply the "simultaneousness of the ambient, and, therefore, the dislocation and dismemberment of objects." This lack of traditional perspective and vanishing point is taken to extremes in Malevich's suprematist paintings. Malevich also wrote other suprematist manifestos, such as *From Cubism and Futurism to Suprematism* (1915), which exemplifies, in its argument that suprematism surpasses futurism through its decision to abandon representational forms, the Hegelian idea of spiritual progression and the triumph of spirit over matter.

In the decades following its publication, *The Non-Objective World* continued to function as a theoretical touchstone for artists of geometric abstraction. Although the late date of its publication in relation to Malevich's actual work and the extremity of Malevich's aesthetics prevented the development of an enduring school, suprematism influenced a broad range of artists in the Russian avant-garde, including constructivists such as Alexander Rodchenko and El Lissitzky. Lissitzky's propagandistic lithograph *Beat the Whites with the Red Wedge* (1919), for example, incorporates suprematist geometric forms and a Bolshevik political ideology.

THEMES AND STYLE

The central theme of the suprematist manifesto is that the objective representation of the world has nothing to do with art; the essence of art is found in the feeling it expresses, and suprematism, by casting aside any representation of "ideas, concepts, and images," cleaves most closely to this pure feeling. The manifesto argues that "art no longer cares to serve the state and religion, it no longer wishes to illustrate the history of manners, it wants to have nothing further to do with the object, as such, and believes that it can exist in and for itself, without 'things.'" Suprematism goes so far as to "dispute the reality of human faces (human forms) altogether." To this end, the manifesto proposes a suprematist art that embraces nonobjectivity, the displacement or rearrangement of object and foreground, the dismissal of traditional perspective, and the exclusion of a "conglomeration of countless 'things,'" an aesthetic that, in one of Malevich's most famous paintings, *Black Square* (1915), takes the form of "a black square on a white field."

The manifesto achieves its rhetorical effect through appeals to a sense of unity among the Russian avant-garde. It envisions a group of artists, the suprematists, committed to aesthetics of nonobjectivism. This sense of unity is primarily achieved through the exclusion of other groups. Malevich frequently dismisses the "critics" or the "general public," who fail "to recognize the real, true value of things." In contrast, the reader is included in the avant-garde—as well as in this newly founded group, the suprematists—through the use of the first person plural: "We have seen how art, at the turn of the century, divested itself of the ballast of religious and political ideas … and came into its own."

Stylistically, the suprematist manifesto is distinguished by its unsystematic and, at times, chaotic prose. Malevich was largely self-taught, and, according to British modern art scholar John Golding, "even those fluent in Russian find his writings difficult." Much of the manifesto is characterized by short paragraphs and repetition, but the velocity of these sections, along with Malevich's elevated diction ("The ascent to the heights of non-objective art is arduous and painful …"), contribute to the urgency and passion of his prose. The manifesto often juxtaposes serious theoretical arguments and poetic passages. Malevich's use of aviation metaphors, from the "ballast" of religion to the "yearning for speed … for flight," echo the aesthetic demands of suprematism, which inverted the humanist and thus Earth-centric traditions of the past: "the contours of the objective world fade more and more."

CRITICAL DISCUSSION

When *The Non-Objective World* first appeared in 1927, it garnered little attention, except as a postscript to the suprematist movement, which in itself generated interest, criticism, and controversy before the first suprematist showing had even occurred at the Dobychina Gallery in Petrograd in 1915. Early negative publicity involved

Vladimir Tatlin, a founding member of constructivism (an art movement similar to suprematism in its abstract geometric nature), who argued with Malevich and threatened not to show his paintings at the gallery. The dispute became so serious that, prior to the show, a fistfight broke out between the two artists. Although the public and the critics were scornful of the exhibition, Malevich soon gathered a large following. According to art historian Camilla Gray, "By 1918 it was reported: 'Suprematism has blossomed throughout Moscow. Signs, exhibitions, cafes, everything is Suprematist. One may with assurance say that Suprematism has arrived.'"

After a series of suprematist exhibitions in Moscow, culminating in Malevich's one-man show in 1919, the suprematist manifesto remained an important articulation of Malevich's aesthetics. By 1920 the influence of suprematism was evident in the geometricization of forms in Russian painter Wassily Kandinsky's work. While at the Bauhaus, the Hungarian artist and teacher László Moholy Nagy coedited *The Non-Objective World,* along with German architect and Bauhaus director Walter Gropius. Some of Moholy-Nagy's paintings, done in the suprematist style, hang in the Museum of Modern Art in New York. In 1939 the American philanthropist and art collector Solomon R. Guggenheim championed suprematism by founding the Museum of Non-Objective Painting. In 2011 the Gagosian Gallery's New York exhibition, *Malevich and the American Legacy,* claimed that "It is not only formal analogy that connects Malevich and American artists but also deeper aesthetic, conceptual, and spiritual correspondences."

In the decades since the manifesto was written, it has attracted considerable scholarly attention for its significance as a theoretical text underpinning the suprematist movement and subsequent geometric abstract art. Some scholarship has focused on the suprematist manifesto, as well as Malevich's other writings, as a religious and spiritual text. In her book *Kazimir Malevich* (1994), Charlotte Douglas claims that Malevich "embarked upon a concentrated study of philosophy that propounded Suprematism as a further step in the evolution of religious understanding, a development that in its universality supplanted Russian Orthodoxy and even Christianity as a whole." Scholars have also emphasized the influence of science and technology on suprematism. The suprematist manifesto makes explicit reference to aviation and technology, and Robert L. Herbert argues in "The Arrival of the Machine: Modernist Art in Europe, 1919-25" that Malevich "likened modern technology's defeat of earth-born gravity to his self-invented Suprematist forms."

BIBLIOGRAPHY

Sources

Douglas, Charlotte. *Kazimir Malevich.* New York: Abrams, 1994. Print.

Gagosian Gallery. *Malevich and the American Legacy.* Gagosian Gallery, 2011. Web. 25 July 2012.

Golding, John. "Supreme Suprematist." *New York Review of Books* 38 (1991): n. pag. Web. 25 July 2012.

Gray, Camilla. *The Russian Experiment in Art: 1863-1922.* New York: Abrams, 1962. Print.

Herbert, Robert L. "The Arrival of the Machine: Modernist Art in Europe, 1910-25." *Social Research* 64.3 (1997): 1273-1305. *JSTOR.* Web. 25 July 2012.

Malevich, Kazimir. *The Non-Objective World: The Manifesto of Suprematism.* Mineola: Dover, 2003. Print.

Simmons, W. Sherwin. *Kasimir Malevich's Black Square and the Genesis of Suprematism 1907-1915.* New York: Garland, 1981. Print.

Further Reading

Douglas, Charlotte. *Malevich: Artist and Theoretician.* Paris: Flammarion, 1991. Print.

Drutt, Matthew. *Kazimir Malevich: Suprematism.* New York: Guggenheim Museum, 2003. Print.

Kovtun, Evgueny. *Russian Avant-Garde.* New York: Parkstone, 2007. Print.

Malevich, Kazimir. *From Cubism and Futurism to Suprematism: The New Realism in Painting.* Maria Elena Buszek, n.d. Web. 25 July 2012.

Néret, Gilles. *Kazimir Malevich.* Cologne: Taschen, 2003. Print.

Gregory Luther

Suprematist Composition No. 56, a 1916 painting by Kazimir Malevich. STATE RUSSIAN MUSEUM, ST. PETERSBURG, RUSSIA/GIRAUDON/THE BRIDGEMAN ART LIBRARY

PROCLAMATION FOR ART!

Lajos Kassák

✣ *Key Facts*

Time Period:
Early 20th Century

Movement/Issue:
Aesthetics; Avant-
gardism; Socialism

Place of Publication:
Hungary

**Language of
Publication:**
Hungarian

OVERVIEW

Composed by Hungarian poet and artist Lajos Kassák, "Proclamation for Art!" (1918) decries the Austro-Hungarian Empire's censorship of art during World War I and demands democratic politics that will provide freedom of expression. The essay was published in *Ma*, Kassák's arts journal, which was dedicated to the socially and politically transformative role of the Hungarian avant-garde. While the essay advocates for a socialist government, it also argues for the absolute freedom of art from any party or ideology. It calls on "Artists! Painters! Sculptors! Actors! Writers!" and the working class to become spokespeople "for a new and free human society." Central to the text is the idea that artists have an active role to play in a moral and intellectual revolution.

Ma eventually gained enough political clout to be censored by the Hungarian government, but its readership was relatively small at the time "Procla-mation for Art!" was published. Thus, the essay received little attention outside of Kassák's artistic circle, though it did help define the political and social goals of the burgeoning Hungarian avant-garde. In addition, scholars have argued that the essay succeeded in its goal of influencing Hungarian politics: its call for a ministry of arts was later met by Béla Kun's communist regime, which formed the Directorate of Arts, a body that sought to aid artists both financially and academically. Today "Proclamation for Art!" is considered to be an important document in the history of the Hungarian avant-garde.

HISTORICAL AND LITERARY CONTEXT

"Proclamation for Art!" was written in response to the political upheaval in Hungary following the nation's defeat in World War I. Three years prior to its publication, Kassák had issued his first literary magazine, *A Tett*, which sought to offer a forum for expressionist literature with an antiwar stance. The Austro-Hungarian government issued an official ban on *A Tett* after it published an international issue featuring the work of artists whose countries were at war with Hungary. Within weeks, Kassák began publishing *Ma*, but his personal, non-nationalistic brand of socialism caused artists with stronger ties to the communist and socialist parties to leave the magazine.

By 1918 World War I was ending and a new government had temporarily gained control of Hungary. Approximately nine months prior to the appearance of "Proclamation for Art!" Kassák published an issue of *Ma* that was dedicated to the Hungarian composer Bela Bartok, whom Kassák considered a fellow artist-revolutionary. In November 1918, just a few days before "Proclamation for Art!" was published, a bourgeois republic was established in Hungary, and Mihaly Karolyi became the country's leader. However, Hungary's fractured economy; the encroaching Romanian, Czech, and Serbian armies, and the rise of socialist and communist movements weakened the government. Consequently, Karolyi handed over power to a coalition led by the communist Kun by early 1919.

Although "Proclamation for Art!" exhibits the influence of other manifestos, especially F. T. Marinetti's *Futurist Manifesto* (1909), Kassák was primarily informed by the German art magazines *Die Aktion* and *Der Sturm*. *Die Aktion* was published from 1911

LAJOS KASSÁK: WORKING-CLASS POET

Born in Ersekujvar (now Slovakia) on March 21, 1887, to a Slovak father and a Hungarian mother, Lajos Kassák grew up in a large, poor family. By the age of twelve he had learned the locksmith trade. He moved to Budapest in 1904, where he lived with his mother and sisters and worked as an iron worker. His participation in the labor movement as a strike organizer made further employment difficult, but he used this time, as well as the materials provided by the Social Democratic Party, to educate himself. In 1909, at the age of twenty-two, he journeyed from Budapest to Paris on foot as the culmination of his studies.

In western Europe, Kassák was exposed to the avant-garde for the first time. Upon his return to Budapest, he began to publish short stories and poetry. Soon both of his literary magazines, *A Tett* and *Ma*, were banned by the government, and by 1920 he and his family had fled for Vienna, where *Ma* was reissued and became one of the prominent magazines of the central European avant-garde. Despite several interruptions, such as the period from 1950 to 1956 when he was living in Budapest and the Hungarian government disallowed his work, Kassák built up a significant body of poetic work. In 1965, two years before his death, he was given the Kossuth Prize, Hungary's highest cultural award.

to 1932 under the editorship of Franz Pfemfert, a longtime critic of German politics and one of the few to oppose Germany's involvement in World War I. It was primarily the political content of the magazine that appealed to Kassák, whereas *Der Sturm,* with its presentation of the international avant-garde, influenced his aesthetics. However, according to scholar Marian Mazzone in *Modernism between East and West: The Hungarian Journal* Ma *(1916-1925) and the International Avant-Garde,* both magazines were "among the earliest to address political and social issues."

In the decades following its publication, "Proclamation for Art!" served as a touchstone for Kassák's continued political and artistic activism. In 1919, after Kun criticized *Ma* at a party assembly, Kassák published his *Letter to Bela Kun, in the Name of Art,* in which he outlines the revolutionary work accomplished by the avant-garde and defends art's autonomy from the dictatorship of a single party. Forced into exile in Vienna because of his political views, Kassák continued to publish *Ma* until 1925. Today his political writing, poetry, and novels still command significant scholarly interest.

THEMES AND STYLE

The central theme of "Proclamation for Art!" is that artists must engage in peaceful, political struggle in order to establish and protect their artistic freedoms. These freedoms, the essay laments, were compromised during World War I, when "the dastardly ruling class throttled us in our holy infancy!" In order to prevent such censorship, Kassák calls on artists to advocate for their social and economic rights: "Artists! Those of you who have ever taken the measure of your strength, who are no longer content prostituting yourselves in the unconditional service of those in power, but are aware of your active role in destroying the barriers and pointing the way for the great evolution—we call upon you to adopt our demands." To this end, the essay demands that the newly founded government establish a ministry of the arts and that art be recognized as "vital and indispensable for promoting the development of human society!"

The essay achieves its rhetorical effect through appeals, often in declamatory language, to a sense of unity among young Hungarian artists. Kassák drives these appeals home with his use of the first-person-plural "we" and by playing to the aspirations of the artists. In calling art the "bread and wine" of contemporary life, he concomitantly praises and flatters artists. Addressed to these "Artists!" and "Brothers!" the "Proclamation for Art!" envisions a single body of artists committed to political struggle for freedom of expression. By aligning this group with the "subjugated working man," the text places this movement into the context of the larger political struggle of the day, when the "masses" roared "their demand for a socialist order."

Stylistically, "Proclamation for Art!" is distinguished by its declamatory prose, which serves to amplify the urgency of its argument. "If you don't speak up now," writes Kassák, "you will once again be stuck in an economic and moral morass!" He draws on the language of social agitation but also includes poetic or artistic devices such as metaphor. Thus, the essay comes to embody its primary thematic concern: that the reader recognize the social and political task of art. According to the scholar Éva Forgács in her 2006 essay in *Arcadia,* the language in the work shows the influence of the futurists. For example, the futurist preoccupation with technology in art is evident in phrases such as "Art is the bread and wine of motor-powered life!"

CRITICAL DISCUSSION

When "Proclamation for Art!" was first issued in 1918, it received limited attention within the avant-garde. Kassák's essay "Activism," published a few months later, conveyed many of the same views as "Proclamation for Art!" but garnered considerably more interest. "Activism" was first delivered as a speech in 1919, and it expressed even more adamantly Kassák's ambivalence toward political parties and his belief that art should not tie itself to any particular ideology. His idiosyncratic form of socialism demanded not only

Portrait of Lajos Kassák, by Tihonyi Lajos. Kassák was a major figure in the Hungarian avant-garde. HUNGARIAN NATIONAL GALLERY, BUDAPEST, HUNGARY/THE BRIDGEMAN ART LIBRARY

higher standards of living but also the development of collective individuals who believed in a post-state political environment. "Activism," Mazzone writes, "strongly reflects his belief in the individual's power and duty to revolutionize the spirit and ultimately create political and social change."

In the years following its publication, "Proclamation for Art!" remained an important source of political and artistic inspiration for Hungarians. Forgács addresses Kassák's dual influence, saying that the "founder and pillar of the Hungarian Avant-Garde ... united in his personality the often diverging avant-garde roles of the high priest and the politically committed artist-activist." Further, Joseph Remenyi argues in "Lajos Kassák: Hungarian 'Avant-garde" Writer and Poet" that Kassák's "prose inaugurated in Hungary a kind of polemic and imaginative writing which was considered an example for revolutionary authors." Today, "Proclamation for Art!" continues to be the subject of a small body of criticism examining its political and artistic legacy.

Although little scholarship has considered the essay itself, academics have focused on Kassák's relationship with leftist ideology. Remenyi has analyzed the socialist leanings in Kassák's literary works, writing that "there is subtlety, deftness and originality in his writings, transcending the horizons of class-consciousness. On the other hand his place in Hungarian literature is to a large extent determined by his proletarian attitude." Other commentators have focused on Kassák's contentious relationship with the Hungarian Commune of 1919. Forgács argues in "Between Cultures: Hungarian Concepts of Constructivism" that Kassák wanted "to play a leading part in the official culture of the Commune and, at the same time, to be entirely independent of its political leadership."

BIBLIOGRAPHY

Sources

Forgács, Éva. "Between Cultures: Hungarian Concepts of Constructivism." *Central European Avant-Gardes: Exchange and Transformation 1910-1930.* Ed. Timothy O. Benson. Cambridge: MIT P, 2002. Print.

———. "You Feed Us So That We Can Fight against You: Concepts of Art and State in the Hungarian Avant-Garde." *Arcadia* 41.2 (2006): 260-85. *Literature Online.* Web. 12 Oct. 2012.

Kassák, Lajos. "Proclamation for Art!" *Between Worlds: A Sourcebook of Central European Avant-Gardes, 1910-1930.* Ed. Timothy Benson. Boston: MIT P, 2002. 147-64. Print.

Mazzone, Marian. *Modernism between East and West: The Hungarian Journal Ma (1916-1925) and the International Avant-Garde.* Columbus: The Ohio State University, 1997. *ProQuest.* Web. 12 Oct. 2012.

Remenyi, Joseph. "Lajos Kassák: Hungarian 'Avant-Garde' Writer and Poet." *Modern Language Journal* 35.2 (1951): 119-23. *JSTOR.* Web. 12 Oct. 2012.

Further Reading

Ferenczi, L. "On Lajos Kassák." *Hungarian Quarterly* 37.1 (1996): 57-62. Print.

Lengyel, B. "The Other Kassák + Kassák, Lajos." *New Hungarian Quarterly* 30.1 (1989): 148-51. Print.

Miller, Tyrus. "Rethinking Central Europe: The Symbolic Geography of the Avant-Garde." *Modernism/modernity* 10.3 (2003): 559-67. University of Montana Libraries. Web. 12 Oct. 2012.

Nemeth, Lajos. *Modern Art in Hungary.* Budapest: Corvina, 1969. Print.

Szabo, Julia. "Kassák and the International Avant-Garde." *New Hungarian Quarterly* 28.1 (1987): 117-24. Print.

Gregory Luther

PROGRAM OF THE BAUHAUS IN WEIMAR

Walter Gropius

OVERVIEW

Written by Walter Gropius, "Program of the Bauhaus in Weimar" (1919) is a manifesto that outlines the mission of Germany's Bauhaus school (Staatliches Bauhaus), which was to combine the fine and applied arts and create an international community of artists. The manifesto appeared at the moment of the school's inception, during a time when Germany was instituting the liberal Weimar Republic following the nation's defeat in World War I. The demise of the German monarchy had brought an end to government-sponsored censorship, and many artists were experimenting within the new cultural atmosphere. The "Program of the Bauhaus in Weimar" addresses artists, both of the high and low arts, with the intent of leveling the distinction between artist and craftsman. As a call to action, it is marked by its desire to unify fine and practical arts and create a utopian collective of art practitioners.

The "Program of the Bauhaus in Weimar" elicited criticism from Weimar residents because of its connection to German expressionism and the Berlin gallery Der Sturm, which was perceived to be left wing and revolutionary. The Staatliches Bauhaus received some funding from the Social Democratic state Thuringia and therefore opened itself to conservative political pressure. Gropius, however, maintained that Bauhaus was apolitical, and the "Program of the Bauhaus in Weimar" describes a school in which the only criterion for entrance is a sufficient education. His manifesto helped to outline the goals of the Staatliches Bauhaus, which persisted in some form until 1933, and defined a Bauhaus style that proved to have a lasting influence on artists throughout the world.

HISTORICAL AND LITERARY CONTEXT

Appearing as a new German republic was being established, Gropius's manifesto reflects the belief among revolutionary German artists that they had a central role in the development of a transcendent German culture. The "Program of the Bauhaus in Weimar" reacts against the marginalization of artists that had occurred as a result of state-sponsored fine-arts academies in Germany. In addition, Gropius outlines an experiment in arts education that would eliminate the professional divide that such arts academies had created between fine artists and craftsmen. Countering

a post-World War I rise in German nationalism, the manifesto suggests the formation of a supranational artistic community.

Following the Russian Revolution of 1917 and the end of World War I in 1918, Germany had become a revolutionary outpost, influenced by communists and leftist ideology. It was in this political atmosphere that Gropius founded the Bauhaus school and began to recruit an international faculty that included Swiss painters Johannes Itten and Paul Klee, German sculptor Gerhard Marcks, and German designer, painter, and sculptor Oskar Schlemmer. Although these Bauhaus masters did not always agree with each other, their ideological clashes were welcomed. The central focus of the Staatliches Bauhaus was on training students in specialized workshops with the intent of bridging the gap between art and life.

The "Program of the Bauhaus in Weimar" draws on earlier works, such as the *Communist Manifesto* (1848), in its aesthetic proclamation and outline for a plan of action. Attributed to Friedrich Engels and Karl Marx, the *Communist Manifesto* was published in London by German political refugees and was highly influential in establishing the features of the manifesto as a genre. Gropius, influenced by German expressionism and later Russian constructivism, was likely familiar with other avant-garde manifestos of the time, such as the 1918 *Dada Manifesto* and the 1909 *Futurist Manifesto*. The "Program of the Bauhaus in Weimar" rests firmly in a tradition of literary and artistic manifestos that began with romanticism following the French Revolution of the late eighteenth century.

Following the publication of the "Program of the Bauhaus in Weimar" in a pamphlet for an April 1919 exhibition titled "Exhibition of Unknown Architects," the Bauhaus school established itself as a unique educational community. Art students arrived in Germany from other European countries, drawn by the international slant of the Bauhaus project and Germany's modern democratic constitution. Indeed, the inclusive language of the manifesto appealed to artists of all stations and nationalities, including many women and German-speaking Jews. The Bauhaus school would publish a number of manifestos, including Oskar Schlemmer's *Bauhaus Manifesto* (1923), as

❖ Key Facts

Time Period:
Early 20th Century

Movement/Issue:
Aesthetics; Bauhaus;
World War I

Place of Publication:
Germany

Language of Publication:
German

WALTER GROPIUS: FOUNDER OF STAATLICHES BAUHAUS

Walter Gropius (1883-1969), the author of the "Program of the Bauhaus in Weimar," was a German architect and the founder of the Staatliches Bauhaus, or the Bauhaus school. He is considered to be one of the most important pioneers of modern architecture. Gropius had a promising early career as an architect in Germany, despite the fact that he could not draw, and helped to design one of the hallmark modernist buildings of that era, the Fraguswerk, located in Alfed-an-der-Leine, Germany. In 1914 he was drafted into World War I, where he was almost killed on the western front.

Gropius's Bauhaus period stretched from 1919 to 1932. During this time, he was master of the Bauhaus school, which employed notable faculty members such as Paul Klee and Wassily Kandinsky. While involved with the Bauhaus movement, he designed his now-famous door handles, which are considered to be emblematic of the Bauhaus style. In 1934 he was able to leave Nazi Germany with the aid of English architect Maxwell Fry. He moved to the United States in 1937 and died in Boston in 1969.

it changed ideological orientation and relocated from Weimar to Dessau to Berlin. Today, artists such as the avant-garde Danish filmmakers who make up a group called Dogme 95 still use the "Program of the Bauhaus in Weimar" as a blueprint.

THEMES AND STYLE

The "Program of the Bauhaus in Weimar" presents a vision of a revolutionary style of education in which artists and craftsmen are treated on equal terms and the metaphysical quality of true art is explored. Gropius writes:

> The Bauhaus strives to bring together all creative effort into one whole, to reunify all the disciplines of practical art—sculpture, painting, handicrafts, and the crafts—as inseparable components of a new architecture. The ultimate, if distant, aim of the Bauhaus is the unified work of art—the great structure—in which there is no distinction between monumental and decorative art.

The manifesto goes on to outline specifics for the implementation of this project, detailing the structure of the school, the methods of workshop instruction, and the open and inclusive requirements for admission.

In the manifesto Gropius establishes a practical plan of action for the school and invites artists interested in a utopian educational experiment to enroll and participate. He stresses the egalitarian format of the school by declaring that the school is to be "the

servant of the workshop and will one day be absorbed into it. Therefore there will be no teachers or pupils in the Bauhaus but masters, journeymen, and apprentices." Furthermore, "any person of good repute, without regard to age or sex, whose previous education is deemed adequate by the Council of Masters will be admitted, as far as space permits." The "Program of the Bauhaus in Weimar" is both an abstract description of the Bauhaus school and a practical plan for the project's realization.

In comparison to other avant-garde manifestos of the time, the "Program of the Bauhaus in Weimar" is formal and reasoned in both tone and style. Gropius employs organizational headings such as "AIMS OF THE BAUHAUS" and "ADMISSION," as well as bullet points, to present the proposed structure of the Staatliches Bauhaus systematically. The reasoned structure of the manifesto helps lend credibility to the school's idealized aims. Gropius does not, however, stray entirely from lofty and enthusiastic language. For example, he writes:

> Let us then create a new guild of craftsmen without the class distinctions that raise an arrogant barrier between craftsman and artist! Together let us desire, conceive, and create the new structure of the future, which will embrace architecture and sculpture and painting in one unity and which will one day rise toward heaven from the hands of a million workers like the crystal symbol of a new faith.

Such visionary language resonated with artists who saw themselves as the leaders of the cultural revolution.

CRITICAL DISCUSSION

The publication of the "Program of the Bauhaus in Weimar" and the concurrent establishment of the Staatliches Bauhaus provoked criticism from members of both the avant-garde and the political right. Conservatives reacted against a perceived leftist influence. In the essay "Un-German Activities: Attacks from the Right, 1919-1933," Justus H. Ulbricht examines this response, noting that "when Emil Herfurth, a prominent local spokesman for the Bauhaus opponents, asserted that 'a city like Weimar is too small for a Schwabing' (the artists' district in Munich), his words revealed what the established citizenry feared: the disruption of their bourgeois lifestyle by bohemians, whose intent was to do exactly that." Meanwhile, members of the avant-garde were dismissive of the Bauhaus project. As Philipp Oswalt observes in his book *Bauhaus Conflicts, 1919-2009: Controversies and Counterparts*, "Dutch avant-garde artist Theo van Doesburg criticized the new educational institution as too 'mystical' and 'Romantic,' and in his Weimar studio offered an art course in opposition to the instruction at the Bauhaus."

The Bauhaus building in Dessau, Germany, designed by Walter Gropius (completed in 1926-27). VANNI/ART RESOURCE, NY

Despite this initial criticism from conservatives and liberals alike, the "Program of the Bauhaus in Weimar" helped to establish the Staatliches Bauhaus as an avant-garde stronghold throughout its existence until 1933. In the essay "The Bauhaus," Éva Forgács, points out that "the Bauhaus was a unique institution as a state-funded—and later, in Dessau, municipally-funded—art school where cutting edge ideas and technologies were advanced by faculty that drew regular salaries and a student body that was not intimidated by tradition." Its legacy as a movement is considerable. Although shifting political and ideological trends have appropriated and transformed the idea of the Bauhaus style, its influence on art, architecture, and industrial design is undeniable.

Recent scholarship on the "Program of the Bauhaus in Weimar" centers on the Bauhaus movement's significance in the study of modernism and the often misguided tendency of ideologues to ascribe political purpose to the tenets of the school in their attempts to advance their agendas. In the introduction to her book *Bauhaus Culture*, Kathleen James-Chakraborty discusses the movement's contribution to modernism, writing that "the abstraction characteristic of the objects and works of art created by those who taught and studied at the Bauhaus still appear to represent a central fact of modernity: the rationalization implicit in industrialization." As for the manner in which the school's ideals have been hijacked for political reasons at various points in history, Greg Castillo notes in the essay "The Bauhaus in Cold War Germany" that

"prior to the imposition of cold war politics on the Bauhaus legacy, it had been ideologically indeterminate. Arguments for the application of Bauhaus pedagogy to promote socialism or capitalist democracy both could be found within the school's eclectic political past."

BIBLIOGRAPHY

Sources

Castillo, Greg. "The Bauhaus in Cold War Germany." *Bauhaus Culture.* Ed. Kathleen James-Chakraborty. Minneapolis: U of Minnesota P, 2006. 171-94. Print.

Forgács, Éva. "The Bauhaus." *Between Worlds: A Sourcebook of Central European Avant-Gardes, 1910-1930.* Ed. Timothy Benson. Cambridge: MIT, 2002. 452-53. Print.

Gropius, Walter. "Program of the Bauhaus in Weimar." Trans. Wolfgang Jabs and Basil Gilbert. *Between Worlds: A Sourcebook of Central European Avant-Gardes, 1910-1930.* Ed. Timothy Benson. Cambridge: MIT, 2002. 204-06. Print.

James-Chakraborty, Kathleen. Introduction. *Bauhaus Culture: From Weimar to the Cold War.* Ed. Kathleen James-Chakraborty. Minneapolis: U of Minnesota P, 2006. xi-xix. Print.

Oswalt, Philipp. Introduction. *Bauhaus Conflicts, 1919-2009: Controversies and Counterparts.* Ed. Philipp Oswalt. New York: Museum of Modern Art, 2009. Print.

Ulbricht, Justus H. "Un-German Activities: Attacks from the Right, 1919-1933." *Bauhaus Conflicts, 1919-2009: Controversies and Counterparts.* Ed. Philipp Oswalt. New York: Museum of Modern Art, 2009. Print.

Further Reading

Bajkay, Éva. "Weimar." Trans. John Bákti. *Central European Avant-Gardes: Exchange and Transformation, 1910-1930.* Ed. Timothy Benson. Los Angeles: MIT, 2002. 205-12. Print.

Bayer, Herbert, ed. *Bauhaus, 1919-1928.* New York: Museum of Modern Art, 1986. Print.

Fox, Nicholas Weber. *The Bauhaus Group: Six Masters of Modernism.* New York: Knopf, 2009. Print.

Lidtke, Vernon. "Abstract Art and Left-Wing Politics in the Weimar Republic." *Central European History* 37.1 (2004): 49-90. JSTOR. Web. 10 August 2012.

Sauer, Wolfgang. "Weimar Culture: Experiments in Modernism." *Social Research* 39.2 (1972): 254-84. JSTOR. Web. 10 August 2012.

Weingarden, Lauren S. "Aesthetics Politicized: William Morris to the Bauhaus." *Journal of Architectural Education* 38.3 (1985): 8-13. JSTOR. Web. 10 August 2012.

Kristen Gleason

THE REALISTIC MANIFESTO
Naum Gabo

OVERVIEW

Published by brothers Naum Gabo and Antoine Pevsner, "The Realistic Manifesto" (1920) describes a responsibility in art to reflect the changing modernity that affected Russians after the October Revolution of 1917. Although the essay was written by Gabo, it was signed by both men and published as an explanation of their works as part of an avant-garde art exhibition in Moscow. As this alliance of artists suggests, "The Realistic Manifesto" was designed to speak to artists about aesthetic goals and techniques. Addressed to "artists, painters, sculptors, musicians, actors, poets," the essay calls on all artists to create works that reflect the growth of human knowledge through science, philosophical thought, and new political realities. Central to the work are five "renunciations and affirmations" aimed at producing a new art that exists in four dimensions in an age of social and scientific revolution.

Although Gabo himself was a marginal figure in the artistic avant-garde before 1920, "The Realistic Manifesto" and its bold demands generated attention for his art while he lived in Russia, and the essay achieved international recognition. Particularly in the West, the text is considered an early doctrine of the aesthetic movement known as international constructivism. Within the Soviet Union the aesthetic and philosophical musings in "The Realistic Manifesto" were superseded by the boldly utilitarian art created by Vladimir Tatlin and Aleksander Rodchenko and the collective art proposed by Alexei Gan. Still, Gabo and Pevsner's doctrine established a methodology and a metaphorical link between artistic construction and construction of a new society. "The Realistic Manifesto" is considered an important aesthetic treatise of nonobjective art, particularly outside the Soviet Union, exerting a significant influence on design, sculpture, and architectural movements in the West.

HISTORICAL AND LITERARY CONTEXT

"The Realistic Manifesto" responds to the political and aesthetic crises facing Russians around 1920, when the call for newly relevant art forms were intensified by revolution, civil war, and the rise of the Soviet Union. Three years before the essay was written, the October Revolution had inspired a new optimism and purposefulness in avant-garde artists. The revolution and subsequent Russian civil war created chaos in their aftermath; the collapse of Russian infrastructure made practical life for artists such as Gabo and Pevsner nearly impossible. Nevertheless, artists retained idealism and enthusiasm for the new state. When the Bolsheviks seized power, avant-garde artists became closely allied with the government, creating propaganda and founding institutions to establish a scientific basis for the creation of art. Such artistic organizations as the Department of Fine Arts (IZO), led initially by Wassily Kandinsky, set out a program in an attempt to create a plastic language suited to new social and political realities.

By the time "The Realistic Manifesto" was written, diverse avant-garde artists were working in forms inspired by futurist and cubist discoveries. In 1913 Tatlin created the first nonutilitarian constructions in Russia—called counter-corner reliefs—crafting experimental three-dimensional objects with metal, glass, and wood. Kazimir Malevich incorporated cubist collage into his increasingly nonobjective paintings as part of his suprematist group, taking up the work of Russia's diminished futurist avant-garde. Tatlin's follower Rodchenko made his own three-dimensional nonobjective constructions. Plans for Tatlin's architectural tower *Monument to the Third International* generated enthusiasm and inspired Gabo and Pevsner to create their own manifesto and exhibition. When "The Realistic Manifesto" appeared, it provided a lucid platform that a diverse group of constructivist artists would debate.

"The Realistic Manifesto" draws on a history of aesthetic declarations that can be traced to Italian futurism and Russian suprematism. Malevich's essay "From Cubism and Futurism to Suprematism: The New Realism in Painting" (1915) praises a realistic art that is conveyed through nonnaturalistic and abstract styles and that embraces the profound changes brought with modern life. Malevich's text contains critical observations of cubism and futurism but suggests that these early avant-garde movements offered a new picture of reality. Gabo and Pevsner also framed "The Realistic Manifesto" as a critique of other avant-garde groups but found inspiration in the discoveries of cubism and futurism. Moreover, Gabo and Pevsner drew on the bold irreverence of Italian and Russian futurist manifestos, rejecting canonical traditions and

✧ *Key Facts*

Time Period:
Early 20th Century

Movement/Issue:
Aesthetics; Rise of the Soviet Union; Realism

Place of Publication:
Russia

Language of Publication:
Russian

GROWTH OF AN ARTIST

Naum Gabo was born in 1890 in Belarus, the seventh child of a Jewish industrialist. Inspired by the failed revolution of 1905, he became committed to radical politics. His interest in art was inspired by his older brother Antoine (born Natan) Pevsner, an art student in Kiev. In 1910 Gabo moved to Munich, where he discovered avant-garde art theory, including *Abstraction and Empathy* (1908) by Wilhelm Worringer and *Concerning the Spiritual in Art* (1912) by Wassily Kandinsky. The outbreak of World War I compelled Gabo and Pevsner to leave Germany for Norway. There, Gabo began to experiment with making flat planar sculptures inspired by cubism and Russian icon paintings.

After the October Revolution, Gabo and his brother returned to Russia. In 1920 they organized a small group exhibition for which Gabo wrote "The Realistic Manifesto." Gabo made the leap into conceptual art with such sculptures as *Kinetic Construction* (1920), composed of a thin metal rod that is caused to vibrate with a motor. In 1922 he left Russia for Berlin, where he enjoyed modest acclaim. He found greater success when he moved to London in 1936, contributing to *Circle* (1937), a book-length celebration of constructivist art. He gained recognition in the United States with the rise of kinetic art in the 1950s. Throughout his life, Gabo wrote about his aesthetic ideas; he was positive about creation but increasingly combative toward the work and the legacy of his fellow artists and artistic movements.

praising new art forms that suited the kinetic energy of their time.

In the years after its publication, "The Realistic Manifesto" was followed by a resonant body of literature and artwork that crystallized the international constructivist movement, including "The Catastrophe of Architecture" (1921) by El Lissitsky, "The Line" (1921) by Rodchenko, and *Constructivism* (1922) by Alexei Gan. Rodchenko's "Program of the Productivist Group" (1920) and Osip Brik's productivist ideas moved the First Working Group of Constructivists (1921) to reject painting in favor of the mechanized processes of photography, montage, and graphic design. Tatlin's *Monument,* though constructed only as a model, signaled the role of the new Russian avant-garde: synthesizing formal innovation with revolutionary politics. Constructivist artists dedicated themselves to agitprop, industrial design, sculpture and architecture, and documentary film. The legacy of constructivist artists and architects continues to attract significant scholarly attention.

THEMES AND STYLE

The central theme of "The Realistic Manifesto" is that art should reflect Russia's social and scientific revolutions as an indispensable mirror of human experience. The essay opens with a grandiose appeal to all artists about their responsibilities: "to you people to whom

Art is no mere ground for conversation but the source of real exaltation … the impasse into which Art has come to in the last twenty years must be broken." To this end, the text evaluates the strengths and weaknesses of previous avant-garde movements and then proposes five renunciations and affirmations in order to suggest techniques that will allow artists to reproduce the inner forces of their subjects.

The essay achieves its rhetorical effect through rousing appeals to avant-garde artists working in a variety of media. A sense of artistic unity is achieved through the repeated interrogation and characterization of the nature of "Art." Addressing a broad audience of "sculptors, musicians, actors, poets," "The Realistic Manifesto" envisions an exalted group of practitioners whose passions are unified in their enthusiasm and concern for creating work that reflects the compelling changes of the era. The single ambition of art, the essay suggests, is the realization of perceptions "in the forms of space and time." Notably, Gabo does not refer to construction but instead uses derivatives of the Russian word *stroit* ("to build") throughout essay—using the act of "building" to refer to practical techniques of making art, particularly sculpture. The essay alludes to constructivist concerns by using the word *build* to refer to the broader acts of building a new society and culture after the revolution.

Stylistically "The Realistic Manifesto" is distinguished by its exalted assertions. Written as an introduction for an art exhibition in Moscow, the essay demands credibility through its sweeping judgments of preceding artistic movements. It uses the bombastic technique of earlier futurist manifestos to question the continued usefulness of futurist art: "It is obvious now to every one of us that by the simple graphic registration of a row of momentarily arrested movements, one cannot re-create movement itself. It makes one think of the pulse of a dead body." At the same time, by acknowledging the advances of earlier avant-garde groups, Gabo and Pevsner demonstrate that their aesthetic movement proceeds from earlier discoveries and problems. Although its elevated and aggressive stance renders "The Realistic Manifesto" similar to other futurist tracts, the essay achieves its rhetorical force through a careful explanation of a new plastic language and technique to match its aesthetic ambitions.

CRITICAL DISCUSSION

When "The Realistic Manifesto" was first published as introduction to an art exhibition in Moscow, it received more attention than the group exhibition. It was frequently reproduced, including publication in Hungary's *Unity* journal in 1922, and helped to solidify Gabo's career as an artist. Gabo and Pevsner's ideas lost sway in Russia when the brothers left the country in the early 1920s, but Gabo was perceived

as an emissary of constructivism in the West. In his 1967 essay in *Art Journal*, German critic Eckhard Neumann asserts that constructivism "brushed aside with a single stroke the previous work of the Expressionists and brought to light the Abstractionists." Simultaneously, a more politicized constructivism gained strength in the Soviet Union. Richard Andrews and Milena Kalinovska, in their introduction to *Art into Life* (1990), explain that the movement "was synonymous with the fledgling Soviet state; incorporat[ing] … the new leaders' aspirations for a revolutionary society built on new principles of governance and a faith in the promise of twentieth century industrial technology."

After the constructivist movement died out following the rise of Joseph Stalin's state-mandated socialist realism in the 1930s, "The Realistic Manifesto" remained a significant aesthetic treatise in the West, where constructivist émigrés, such as Lissitsky, influenced design at the Bauhaus school. In *Russian Constructivism*, Christina Lodder explains that "Gabo's cogent expositions of 'the Constructivist idea' and his use of the term 'constructive' to describe his works acted … to camouflage the differences which existed in Russia between the constructive artist and the Constructivist … two categories of activity [that] became subsumed under the one aesthetic theory enunciated by Gabo." In the years since it was written, the essay has been the subject of much disagreement and criticism regarding its role in Russian art history and Western abstract art.

Scholars have debated the role of "The Realistic Manifesto" as a source text for the constructivist movement. Andrews and Kalinovska note that "it is more accurate to regard [the essay] as transitional, forming the boundary between the destructive phase, in which the traditional stereotypic images were overthrown, and the early stages of Constructivism." Scholars also have observed the relation between Soviet public policy and the development of constructivism. In *Constructing Modernity* (2000), Martin Hammer and Lodder point out that "the birth of the Constructivist movement in 1921 coincided with the implementation of Lenin's New Economic Policy (NEP). The official emphasis on reviving industrial production may have given added impetus to their adoption of a utilitarian stance." Other commentators have drawn attention to Gabo's eventual alienation from the Russian constructivist group because of personal and ideological differences. Moreover, scholars note Gabo's somewhat misleading role as a constructivist in the West, where his artwork and ideas overlooked the more industrial and utilitarian aspects of the movement.

BIBLIOGRAPHY

Sources

Andrews, Richard, and Milena Kalinovska, eds. *Art into Life: Russian Constructivism, 1914-1932.* New York: Rizzoli, 1990. Print.

Gabo, Naum. *Gabo on Gabo: Texts and Interviews.* Ed. Martin Hammer and Christina Lodder. East Sussex, UK: Artists Bookworks, 2000. Print.

Hammer, Martin, and Christina Lodder. *Constructing Modernity: The Art and Career of Naum Gabo.* New Haven, CT: Yale UP, 2000. Print.

Lodder, Christina. *Russian Constructivism.* New Haven, CT: Yale UP, 1983. Print.

Neumann, Eckhard. "Russia's Leftist Art in Berlin, 1922." *Art Journal* 27.1 (1967): 22. Print.

Further Reading

Compton, Michael. *Naum Gabo: Sixty Years of Constructivism.* London: Tate Gallery Publications, 1987. Print.

Gabo, Naum. *Gabo: Constructions, Sculpture, Paintings, Drawings and Engravings.* London: Lund Humphries, 1957. Print.

Meecham, Pam, and Julie Sheldon. *Modern Art: A Critical Introduction.* New York: Routledge, 2000. Print.

Newman, Teresa. *Naum Gabo: The Constructive Process.* London: Tate Gallery, 1976. Print.

Karen Bender

TANK MANIFESTO
Avgust Černigoj

OVERVIEW

Authored by Slovenian painter Avgust Černigoj and originally published in *tank* magazine, the *Tank Manifesto* (1927) calls on artists to discard outmoded cultural ideas in favor of a new and politically revolutionary art that is free of ego and is focused on utility and progress. In 1918, after the defeat of Austro-Hungary in World War I, the modern-day territory of Slovenia was incorporated into the Kingdom of the Serbs, Croats, and Slovenes (renamed Yugoslavia in 1929). Slovenian intellectuals who had gone to university abroad returned with progressive ideas but were met with opposition from a population that considered artists degenerate and dangerous to national values. Addressed to artists, specifically Slovenians who were familiar with the current art scene in Ljubljana (the modern-day capital of Slovenia), the essay outlines a constructivist project and asks artists to demolish the barriers between art forms, to overcome individualism, and to enact progress by ignoring old artistic discourses.

The general population of Ljubljana ignored the *Tank Manifesto*, considering the avant-garde movement evidence of Western influence. Nevertheless, the work helped to establish and promote a uniquely Slovenian brand of constructivism, which had originated in Russia and attacked universal aesthetic values. Many Slovenians saw such an attack as threatening to nationalist and humanist values and as indicating Russian influence. Additionally, the essay's emphasis on modernization and proletarian revolution frightened the bourgeoisie and leftist reformers alike. Despite lack of widespread recognition, the *Tank Manifesto* influenced Yugoslavia's neo-avant-garde movement of the 1960s and provided an important link between historical and contemporary Slavic art.

HISTORICAL AND LITERARY CONTEXT

The *Tank Manifesto* is primarily concerned with de-stabilizing traditional artistic establishments in Ljubljana and beyond and with making use of politically revolutionary tactics to create an aesthetic aligned with life. At the time of its publication, Slovenia was neither independent nor unified—in spite of its nationalist tendencies. In 1918 the Slovenian population became partially governed by the Kingdom of Serbs, Croats, and Slovenes, and a region of Slovenia,

the modern-day state of Carinthia, became part of the newly democratic Austria in 1920. The same year, the Treaty of Rapallo also aligned a portion of the Slovene population with Italy. One effect of the fragmentation of the Slovenian population was the search for new forms of Slovenian nationalist culture.

Among Slovenian artists, traditionalism reigned. In the 1920s the avant-garde had only just appeared. Central to the international avant-garde movement was the magazine *tank*, edited by Ferdo Delak. The magazine's contributors included Černigoj; architect Dragotin Fatur; composer Marij Kogoj; and painters Ivo Spinčič, Veno Pilon, and Miha Maleš. Although *tank* and the Slovenian avant-garde failed to gain a foothold in Ljubljana (for a time Černigoj was a political refugee and the last issue of *tank* was banned), the magazine's publication established a Slovenian presence in the international art community and gave the *Tank Manifesto* an audience. Černigoj, influenced by

AVGUST ČERNIGOJ: SLOVENIAN CONSTRUCTIVIST

Avgust Černigoj (1898-1985), a Slovenian painter, became famous for his role in introducing constructivism to the Kingdom of the Serbs, Croats, and Slovenes. Born in Trieste, Italy, he continued his studies in Germany, eventually attending the Weimar Bauhaus in 1924. While there, he was influenced by Russian painter Wassily Kandinsky, a constructivist, and began a lifelong adherence to constructivist principles. Correspondence with revolutionary poet Srečko Kosovel prompted Černigoj to return to Ljubljana, where he mounted the first Slovenian constructivist exhibit in 1924.

Shortly thereafter, he was accused of possessing communist propaganda and was forced to return to Trieste in 1925. In Trieste he began a constructivist group and collaborated with Ferdo Delak on the magazine *tank*. Between 1927 and 1937 Černigoj painted ships in order to make a living. Throughout his life he participated in exhibitions at home and abroad and made contributions in the areas of theater and collage. He returned to Slovenia and lived his last five years in Lipica in Slovenia's Karst region, where a gallery now maintains 1,400 of his works.

PRIMARY SOURCE

TANK MANIFESTO

the first issue of our review is a document of the time of our activities and of the strivings of our perceptive youth. we, the artists got together to found a new world of beauty–goodness–justice. but our striving is not only theoretical or sentimentally individual: our new striving is the multiplier of all that exists: of the visible and perceptible moment of being. we're not held back by any kind of intimacy or local adversity; we are ready each and every moment for *every struggle*.

> *architecture*
>
> *painting–sculpture*
>
> *music–poetry*
>
> are the main vehicles of the new generation. europe must fall due to overbearing egoism

= = = = subconscious individualism

= = = = free terrorism.

our striving begins where european decadence stops forever.

our warrior is absolute power

= = = the collective "me" comes first

we do not fear the local metaphysics and the stupidly feeble slogans of the intimate ego.

our striving is and must be

revolutionary and *not* evolutionary.

europe saw the awakening of a kind of new–centrism (among the latiners), expressionism

(among the anglo–saxons) = a reaction of each and every new spirit? again, some kind of *classicism*.

let us beware!

Streets of Trieste, Italy, on the border of Slovenia. In 1925 Černigoj fled from Yugoslav police to Trieste, his hometown, and composed the *Tank Manifesto*. © RAFA PÉREZ/ IBERFOTO/THE IMAGE WORKS

futurism and Russian constructivism, as well as by the time he spent in Germany at the Bauhaus, advocated that Slovenian artists break with limiting traditional conceptions of art in order to bring Ljubljana into the modern artistic milieu.

The *Tank Manifesto* follows in the avant-garde tradition of presenting an artistic project in manifesto form. Borrowing a revolutionary tone from political pronouncements such as Karl Marx's *The Communist Manifesto* (1848), the *Tank Manifesto* focuses on creating a call to action and outlining an artistic project. Like other works popular among the avant-garde, such as F.T. Marinetti's *Futurist Manifesto* (1909); Guillaume Apollinaire's *L'Esprit nouveau et les poetés* (1918);

and Ljubomir Micić's, Ivan Goll's, and Boško Tokin's *Zenithist Manifesto* (1921), Černigoj's uses the manifesto form to make a revolutionary pronouncement.

Following its publication, the *Tank Manifesto* helped inspire constructivist ideas in many areas of Slovenian culture, including architecture, theater, typography, and graphic arts. The magazine *tank*, although published only twice, inspired later Slovenian art movements, especially as a result of the magazine's experimentation with photo collage and typography. The neo-avant-garde movement OHO, which began in the Slovenian town of Kranj near Ljubljana, began in the 1960s with the cross-media experimentations of Iztok Geister and Marko Pogačnik, whose work arose out of a fresh examination of the historical Slovenian avant-garde. Additionally, the new collectivism of the 1980s referred to important influences on the Slovenian avant-garde, including Russian constructivism and the Bauhaus school. Today the *Tank Manifesto* marks an important link between modern Slovenian artistic tendencies and their radical origins.

THEMES AND STYLE

The main theme of the *Tank Manifesto* is that Slovenian artists must break with traditional conceptions of art in order to build a new culture that favors collective and, above all, useful art. Černigoj begins by calling on Slovenian artists to abandon distinctions between art forms in order to begin anew:

> may all the old brain-creations perish in the galleries and palaces, where they have no other function but to gather dust and perish with time.

we must put a stop to every movement of this kind: we must nip it in the bud. the old european culture cannot make do with old poetries, so it is shaping and building a new poetic age from the old, shoddy, monumental materials of its tradition. i.e. today's *expressionism = new–centrism*. (in ljubljana we've been observing a kind of over–promotion on the architecture of plečnik's or vurnik's school, which is called national architecture, but is in fact modeled on the secession; and the same is true of painting and sculpture: the kralj brothers, the dolinars and others, may they perish in little, philistine ljubljana.)

we know that we must fight against such localisms.

the strongest must win.

may all the old brain–creations perish in the galleries and palaces, where they have no other function but to gather dust and perish with time.

long live the new art–without the gallery–museum and church

= = it must *live, be useful and serve.*

let us be proud of our new movement and let us agitate for it to prove our absolute quality or existence.

welcome delak, our friend

SOURCE: *Between Worlds: A Sourcebook of Central European Avant-Gardes, 1910–1930.* Cambridge, MA: MIT Press, 2002. Pp. 574–575.

long live the new art-without the gallery-museum and church

= = it must *live, be useful and serve.*

Černigoj describes old conceptions of art and accompanying traditional institutions as no longer useful; by contrast, utilitarian and proletariat artistic projects should be prized. Thus, he asks Slovenian artists to bring art into the arena of life and to consider art as a tool of progress so that Ljubljana might participate on the international stage.

The essay uses a form of collective address and urgent, revolutionary pronouncements in order to achieve its rhetorical effect. Addressed to artists, the *Tank Manifesto* urges political action in art: "our striving is not only theoretical or sentimentally individual; our new striving is the multiplier of all that exists; of the visible and perceptible moment of being. we're not held back by any kind of intimacy or local adversity; we are ready each and every moment for *every struggle.*" The work positions itself in opposition to an individual aesthetic, decreeing,

europe must fall due to overbearing egoism

= = = = subconscious individualism

= = = = free terrorism.

our striving begins where european decadence stops forever.

Such leftist political statements, although addressed to a domestic audience, contributed to *tank*'s reputation as dangerous to Slovenian national values.

Stylistically, the *Tank Manifesto* uses experimental capitalization, punctuation, and spacing to achieve its revolutionary effect. Černigoj's decision to forgo capitalization echoes the manifesto's message of removing individual aesthetic concerns from artistic practice. The author declares,

our warrior is absolute power

= = = the collective "me" comes first

we do not fear the local metaphysics and the stupidly feeble slogans of the intimate ego.

In addition, Černigoj's use of the hyphen to join words demonstrates the constructivist project of eliminating distinctions between the arts.

architecture

painting-sculpture

music-poetry

are the main vehicles of the new generation.

Through the layout of the words on the page, the manifesto creates a visual representation of the intertextual, multimedia orientation of the Slovenian avant-garde.

CRITICAL DISCUSSION

Members of the avant-garde and traditionalists alike criticized Černigoj's essay upon its publication. Lev Kreft, in an essay in *Central European Avant-Gardes: Exchange and Transformation, 1910-1930* (2002), notes that Slovenian constructivists "frightened artistic, political (even Communist), and bourgeois circles." Černigoj's critique of traditional Slovenian artists increased the divide between the avant-garde and traditional artistic institutions in Ljubljana. In addition, even among the Slovenian avant-garde, the *Tank Manifesto* had its critics. Esther Levinger, also in an essay in *Central European Avant-Gardes,* notes, "After close collaboration with the Slovene artists, Ferdo Delak, and his journal *tank,* Micič condemned their overt identification with Constructivism and censured Černigoj's contributions."

Despite its mixed reception, the *Tank Manifesto* continues to affect artistic developments in Slovenia and elsewhere. Černigoj's contributions to Slovenian culture are significant. As Kreft notes, "Černigoj and Delak's collaboration represents the highest point of the Slovenian avant-garde, both for their clear and manifest ideology and for the artistic value of their works." Although ignored following World War II, when avant-gardism was viewed as bourgeois, the *Tank Manifesto,* and the activities of the Yugoslavian avant-garde, became the subject of scholarship in the 1970s. As Miško Šuvaković notes in *Impossible Histories: Historical Avant-Gardes, Neo-Avant-Gardes, and Post-Avant-Gardes in Yugoslavia, 1918-1991* (2003), "Aleksandar Flaker began complex and detailed research into the theory and history of the avant-gardes in Zagreb … [triggering] study in other Yugoslav centers as well." An exhibition in Ljubljana in 1998 titled "*Tank*! The Slovenian Historical Avant-Garde" also sparked an increase in critical discussion of the essay.

Scholarship regarding the *Tank Manifesto* highlights its unique place in the Yugoslav avant-garde. Šuvaković describes the impact of *tank* magazine on the development of the avant-garde and neo-avant-garde, noting that avant-garde publications were "not only literary works or literary mediators (communicators) with a specific art typography, but intertextual and interpictorial experimental creations forming an avant-garde model of textual visual expression." Critics have also explored the particulars of the Slovenian constructivist project and its differences from other international constructivist forms. In a 1990 essay in *Journal of Decorative and Propaganda Arts,* Vida Golubič and Ann Vasič explore the intersection of poetics and theater in the Slovenian avant-garde, noting

that "the model's predominant principle is syncretist and is evident in its insistence on destabilizing the traditional connection between the arts."

BIBLIOGRAPHY

Sources

Černigoj, Avgust. "*Tank Manifesto.*" Trans. Marjan Golobic. *Between Worlds: A Sourcebook of Central European Avant-Gardes, 1910-1930.* Ed. Timothy Benson. Cambridge: MIT, 2002. 574-75. Print.

Golubič, Vida, and Ann Vasič. "Constructivism and the Slovenian Model." *Journal of Decorative and Propaganda Arts* 17 (1990): 60-69. *JSTOR.* Web. 23 Aug. 2012.

Kreft, Lev. "Ljubljana." *Central European Avant-Gardes: Exchange and Transformation, 1910-1930.* Ed. Timothy Benson. Cambridge: MIT, 2002. 283-88. Print.

Levinger, Esther. "Ljubomir Micić and the Zenitist Utopia." *Central European Avant-Gardes: Exchange and Transformation, 1910-1930.* Ed. Timothy Benson. Cambridge: MIT, 2002. 260-78. Print.

Šuvaković, Miško. "Impossible Histories." Trans. Jelena Babsek and Stephen Agnew. *Impossible Histories: Historical Avant-Gardes, Neo-Avant-Gardes, and Post-Avant-Gardes in Yugoslavia, 1918-1991.* Ed. Dubravka Djurič and Miško Šuvaković. Cambridge: MIT, 2003. 2-35. Print.

Further Reading

Bojtár, Endre. *East European Avant-Garde Literature.* Trans. Pál Várnai. Budapest: Akadémiai Kiadó, 1992. Print.

Caws, Mary Ann. *Manifesto: A Century of Isms.* Lincoln: U Nebraska P, 2001. Print.

Erjavec, Aleš. "The Three Avant-Gardes and Their Context." *Impossible Histories: Historical Avant-Gardes, Neo-Avant-Gardes, and Post-Avant-Gardes in Yugoslavia, 1918-1991.* Ed. Dubravka Djurič and Miško Šuvaković. Cambridge: MIT, 2003. 38-52. Print.

Rickey, George. *Constructivism: Origins and Evolution.* New York: G. Brazillier, 1967. Print.

Subotič, Irina. "Avant-Garde Tendencies in Yugoslavia." *Art Journal* 49.1 (1990): 21-27. *JSTOR.* Web. 23 Aug. 2012.

———. "Concerning Art and Politics in Yugoslavia during the 1930s." *Art Journal* 52.1 (1993): 69-71. *JSTOR.* Web. 23 Aug. 2012.

Kristen Gleason

TOWARD AN ARCHITECTURE

Le Corbusier

OVERVIEW

First published in 1923, *Toward an Architecture* (*Vers une architecture*) is a compilation of essays by Swiss architect Le Corbusier (1887-1965) advocating architectural functionalism: a systematic and disciplined focus on the physical requirements of a building at the expense of ornamentation. Dissatisfied with much of contemporary architectural practice—which he views as obsessed with re-creating historical styles—Le Corbusier offers the famous observation that "the house is a machine for living in" (*machine à habiter*) and asserts that both architects and clients would be better served by treating it as such. Le Corbusier finds precedents for this position in a vast historical range of built objects, from the Parthenon to the ocean liner, and argues that utilitarian buildings such as factories and grain silos are the sincerest expressions of the early twentieth-century zeitgeist. The author also voices admiration for the assembly-line production of automobiles recently implemented by Henry Ford; he devotes a chapter, "Mass-Production Housing," to discussing ways of translating this vision of standardization and interchangeability into home building practices. The book's closing chapter, "Architecture or Revolution?" turns to the political implications of architecture, arguing that thoughtfully constructed housing will be essential to preserving "social equilibrium" in the modern age.

Simultaneously hailed as a work of genius and critiqued for its polemical style, *Toward an Architecture* quickly became a classic of architectural theory. The book was in part responsible for a twentieth-century boom in publications that sought solutions to architectural problems in related disciplines—and that, conversely, sought to apply architectural insights to questions of philosophy and cultural theory. Particularly notable successors to Le Corbusier's collection include Robert Venturi's *Complexity and Contradiction in Architecture* (1966) and Rem Koolhaas's *Delirious New York* (1978). In the twenty-first century, critical studies of *Toward an Architecture* continue to elucidate Le Corbusier's impact not only on architectural writers but also on the decades-long series of movements and countermovements that constitute architectural modernism.

HISTORICAL AND LITERARY CONTEXT

The early twentieth century was an era of rapid progress for aeronautic and automotive engineering. The fixed-wing aircraft went from its first successful powered flight in 1903 through a period of prototyping and production in World War I to emerge in the postwar years as a full-fledged commercial technology; similarly, the automobile, an experimental curiosity in the 1890s, was by 1920 available in a profusion of styles and makes. Charles-Édouard Jeanneret (later and better known by his pen name, Le Corbusier) found this same spirit of experimentation and progress slow to apply to contemporary architecture, especially to the building of homes. In the essays that would appear in *Toward an Architecture,* he resolved to demonstrate the relevance to architecture of key engineering practices, such as iterative design and the development of industry-wide standards.

By the time he published *Toward an Architecture,* Le Corbusier had a modicum of experience with the style of building he championed—and with the indifference of clients. In the 1910s he had worked with the Société d'Applications de Béton Armé, promoting reinforced concrete as a suitable material not only for dams and apartment blocks but also for bespoke (custom-built) residences. By 1917 the company had folded, with Le Corbusier still better known for his commentary on contemporary art than for his architectural work. In the years prior to the publication of *Toward an Architecture,* he was a frequent contributor to *L'Esprit Nouveau,* which he cofounded with the artists Amédée Ozenfant and Paul Dermée. There, between 1920 and 1922, Le Corbusier published more than a dozen of the articles that, in 1923, he would edit and expand into his most famous written work.

Le Corbusier had several potential models for his book, which gathered observations on seemingly disparate topics under a unifying emphasis on functionality. Among the texts thought to be most influential is *The Blue Rider Almanac,* a 1912 collection of essays by a Munich-based group of expressionist artists including the painter Wassily Kandinsky and the composer Arnold Schoenberg. According to Jean-Louis Cohen in his introduction to the 2007 edition of *Toward an Architecture,* the almanac has several traits in common with Le Corbusier's book but anticipates

Key Facts

Time Period:
Early 20th Century

Movement/Issue:
Architectural theory; Modernism

Place of Publication:
France

Language of Publication:
French

THE RADIANT CITY

Although the radical ideas espoused in *Toward an Architecture* made Le Corbusier famous and had a massive influence on the course of modern architecture, one of the first structures he designed and built after the text's publication was a small house on Lake Geneva for his parents. In 1924 he established his architectural office in Paris and continued to write and design buildings, including a housing complex near the French city of Bordeaux. His interests in design, architecture, and urban planning came together in 1928, when he helped establish the Congrès Internationaux d'Architecture Moderne (CIAM), a group devoted to implementing modernist architectural theory.

In 1929 one of Le Corbusier's best-known houses was built outside Paris. Called Villa Savoye, it incorporates many of his theoretical precepts. Sitting on stilts, the structure is composed of reinforced concrete; features elegant, clean lines; and represents the architect's vision of a house as "a machine for living in." Soon after its completion, however, he increasingly turned his attention from the design of single-family homes to the project of mass urban housing. The result was Ville Radieuse, a series of plans for ideal modern cities, which he completed in 1930. Although none of Le Corbusier's model cities was ever built, his concepts contributed to the design of the Brazilian capital, Brasilia, and the planned Indian city of Chandigarh.

the work most strikingly in its wide range of illustrations, which, like Le Corbusier's hundreds of photographs and drawings, are taken from far-flung places and periods in the history of the arts it addresses.

Toward an Architecture quickly sparked the interest of a wide range of cultural commentators and became, in the author's lifetime, among the preeminent texts on architectural thinking. Le Corbusier himself further developed his views on modularity and functionalism in subsequent texts such as *Urbanism* (1925) and in such "physical manifestos" as the iconic Villa Savoye (begun in 1928). Other major twentieth-century architectural manifestos, such as the aforementioned works by Venturi and Koolhaas, drew comparison to Le Corbusier's work insofar as they sought to extend architectural thought beyond an ever-widening set of disciplinary boundaries.

THEMES AND STYLE

Le Corbusier argues that in the twentieth century, architecture had failed to keep step with engineering: the latter is "in full flower," while the former has fallen into "painful regression." The author advocates, in the manner of a cure, the close study and emulation of the methods (and, more crucially, the mental disposition) that have allowed engineers to produce such modern marvels as skyscrapers. Le Corbusier does not, however, seek to do away with the architectural imperative to create emotionally resonant work.

Acknowledging that a well-engineered house would not necessarily "touch the heart" of the occupant, he declares that "architecture is the use of raw materials to establish stirring relationships.... Passion can make drama out of inert stone." It is these seemingly contradictory impulses—to produce a rationally constructed "machine for living in" that is nonetheless edifying and evocative—which Le Corbusier seeks to reconcile in writing *Toward an Architecture*.

Key to Le Corbusier's work is the assertion that architectural excellence is a transhistorical phenomenon; by implication, those who seek it out in a particular historical period are misguided. He treats efforts to reproduce past styles with contempt: "Louis XV, XVI, XIV and Gothic are to architecture what feathers are to a woman's head; … pretty sometimes, but not always, and nothing more." By contrast, the author valorizes modern works that, though not explicitly architectural, seem to him to preserve the essence of the great buildings of the past. Among these are the signature achievements of twentieth-century mechanical engineering, such as the airplane, which "mobilized invention, intelligence, and daring: *imagination* and *cool reason*. The same spirit built the Parthenon." Le Corbusier looks as well to ocean liners and automobiles as examples of precisely posed and elegantly solved physical problems.

Toward an Architecture has been both praised and criticized for presenting the author's idiosyncratic judgments with the certitude of theoretical maxims. The eleventh chapter, "The Lesson of Rome," exemplifies this method with its claim that the Romans of antiquity "built superb chassis but designed dreadful coachwork" and its sifting of Renaissance Romans into two groups: Michelangelo, the great creator, and a superfluous "fine bunch of fellows who had talent." Le Corbusier encourages readers' assent by hailing them as privileged observers: "the lesson of Rome," he concludes the foregoing, "is for the wise, for those who know and can appreciate." Moreover, Le Corbusier takes deliberate aim at his colleagues, characterizing them as possessed of "Eyes That Do Not See" the lesson in the quasi-architectural feats of modern engineering. This dogmatism would prove quite divisive among the book's initial readers.

CRITICAL DISCUSSION

Toward an Architecture brought Le Corbusier almost instant notoriety, both positive (especially among his Parisian colleagues) and negative (for instance, his virtual shunning by the Dutch practitioners of De Stijl). The author, an expert publicist, greatly improved the book's exposure by circulating copies among not only architects and architecture critics but also historians and political personages. The reaction of the Bauhaus architect Walter Gropius typifies the work's reception among many continental European readers. According to Cohen, Gropius wrote to Le Corbusier that despite the book's critical stance on German

The Villa Savoye in Paris, designed by Le Corbusier and finished in 1931, exemplifies the five architectural points that he put forth in *Toward an Architecture.*
© BILDARCHIV MONHEIM GMBH/ALAMY

architecture, he had "never read a publication that, at its very core, comes as close to my own thoughts and writings as your book does." Interest among Anglophone critics was soon spurred by a 1927 translation by Frederick Etchells. F.X. Velarde, reviewing this English edition, praises Le Corbusier as an exemplar of the "capacity for clear, logical reasoning, and the ability to abide by its conclusion."

By midcentury *Toward an Architecture* had been indisputably canonized as a major work of architectural theory. In 1949 a committee led by Carroll L.V. Meeks declared Le Corbusier's text one of the "One Hundred Great Architectural Books Most Influential in Shaping the Architecture of the Western World." *Toward an Architecture* was one of only twelve books after 1900 to be ranked alongside works by such Renaissance masters as Vitruvius and Leonardo da Vinci. Critics also came to associate Le Corbusier's work with the flurry of avant-garde arts movements contemporary with its publication, especially Dada, and thus to uphold Le Corbusier as a commentator on arts well outside the ambit of architecture proper. In his 1967 essay in *Journal of Aesthetics and Art Criticism,* Richard Kuhns considers both Le Corbusier and the Dada artist Marcel Duchamp to offer salient answers as to what, in the "indiscriminate gathering" of the machine age, might be counted "art-worthy."

Later critics often sought out the intellectual and aesthetic influences of Le Corbusier's formative years, establishing a context for the opinions presented in *Toward an Architecture.* A comprehensive example is Adolf Max Vogt's *Le Corbusier, the Noble Savage* (2000), which presents in detail the contemporary and historical works that made an impression on the young architect. Vogt's book is of further interest in that it shows the omissions, alterations, and sometimes outright falsifications Le Corbusier practiced in shaping *Toward an Architecture* from his early travels and studies. In his 2009 survey of new literature, art historian Tim Benton provides a much broader cross-section of recent scholarship on Le Corbusier as both architect and author.

BIBLIOGRAPHY

Sources

Benton, Tim. "New Books on Le Corbusier." *Journal of Design History* 22.3 (2009): 271-84. *JSTOR.* Web. 1 Oct. 2012.

Cohen, Jean-Louis. Introduction. *Toward an Architecture.* By Le Corbusier. Trans. John Goodman. Los Angeles: Getty, 2007. Print.

Kuhns, Richard. "Art and Machine." *Journal of Aesthetics and Art Criticism* 25.3 (1967): 259-66. *JSTOR.* Web. 1 Oct. 2012.

Le Corbusier. *Toward an Architecture.* Trans. John Goodman. Los Angeles: Getty, 2007. Print.

Meeks, Carroll L.V. "Books and Buildings, 1449-1949. One Hundred Great Architectural Books Most Influential in Shaping the Architecture of the Western World." *Journal of the Society of Architectural Historians* 8.1-2 (1949): 55-67. *JSTOR.* Web. 1 Oct. 2012.

AVANT GARDES

Velarde, F.X. Rev. of *Toward an Architecture,* by Le
  Corbusier. *Town Planning Review* 13.3 (1929):
  201-02. *JSTOR.* Web. 1 Oct. 2012.

Vogt, Adolf Max. *Le Corbusier, the Noble Savage: Toward
  an Archaeology of Modernism.* Trans. Radka Donnell.
  Cambridge: MIT P, 2000. Print.

Further Reading

Brooks, H. Allen. *Le Corbusier's Formative Years: Charles-
  Édouard Jeanneret at La Chaux-de-Fonds.* Chicago:
  U of Chicago P, 1999. Print.

Nervi, Pier Luigi. *Aesthetics and Technology in Building.*
  Trans. Robert Eiaudi. London: Oxford UP, 1966.
  Print.

Vidler, Anthony. *Histories of the Immediate Present:
  Inventing Architectural Modernism.* Cambridge: MIT P,
  2008. Print.

Von Moos, Stanislaus. *Le Corbusier: Elements of a Synthesis.*
  Rotterdam: 010 Press, 2009.

Michael Hartwell

WE

Variant of a Manifesto

Dziga Vertov

OVERVIEW

Composed by Dziga Vertov, "WE: Variant of a Manifesto" (1922) describes a cinematic tradition of "leprous" Russo-German film drama and demands a change in approach and subject for filmmakers in the Soviet state. Vertov's filmmaking tract derived from journalistic work he did in conjunction with his cameraman brother Mikhail Kaufman and Vertov's wife, editor Elizaveta Svilova. The filmmakers called themselves the "Group of Three," and as their alliance suggests, the manifesto speaks to practitioners of filmmaking as well as to audiences. The manifesto is without address; instead, it is a declaration of self-definition. "WE" is described as a group of outsiders, "a herd of junkmen" who defiantly exclude themselves from the prevailing cinematic trends. Central to the manifesto are oppositions between the conventions of cinema and a scientific and kinetic approach to filmmaking, aimed at creating a dynamic cinema to reflect the feel of the world.

Initially resisted by filmmaker colleagues, "WE" is filled with bold declarations and aesthetic rules that eventually became a model for documentary filmmaking later in the twentieth century. In effect, Vertov's criticisms engage an important artistic discourse about the definition and methods of documentary filmmaking. Although Sergei Eisenstein, the *de facto* leader of Soviet filmmaking and film theory, rejected a number of Vertov's techniques as "formalist jackstraws," Vertov's philosophy and techniques—examining intervention, performance, and ethics in nonfiction filmmaking—remain notable for the work of documentarians. The manifesto inspired Jean-Luc Godard and Jean-Pierre Gorn to form the Dziga Vertov Group (1968), which was devoted to producing worker-generated political documentary films; in 1972 they adopted the first French translation of Vertov's collected writings as their "little red book." "WE: Variant of a Manifesto" is also vital to understanding the construction of Vertov's masterpiece, *Man with a Movie Camera.*

HISTORICAL AND LITERARY CONTEXT

"WE: Variant of a Manifesto" responds to a time when Russians utilized cinema in service of the Bolshevik regime. Several years before the October Revolution of 1917, Russian futurists issued a manifesto urging a rejection of canonical Russian literature. Their doctrine reassesses the role of art in response to sudden industrialization and social shifts; the movement dispersed with World War I. During the Russian Civil War, journalism and newsreels were dominant forces in communication, demanding new theories and approaches to filmmaking.

By 1922, the Soviet state had been formed as an official republic. Bolshevik leader Vladimir Lenin understood the importance of filmmaking in creating propaganda in support of the state. Soviet journalism and constructivist drama groups produced several notable practitioners and theorists, including Eisenstein, who began his career working for Prolekult, a Soviet artistic group that formed in 1917, and then for Vsevolod Meyerhold's theater. Early in his film career, Eisenstein studied with Vertov, who was an innovative director of newsreels. When "WE" appeared in 1922, it provided an aesthetic platform for discourse among filmmakers. Vertov's cinematic ideas informed some of Eisenstein's early work, but became a more notable aesthetic force later in the twentieth century.

"WE: Variant of a Manifesto" draws on a tradition of declarations about the nature and content of Russian arts that dates back to the first Russian futurist manifesto, "A Slap in the Face of Public Taste" (1912) by David Burliuk, Victor Khlebnikov, Alexander Kruchenykh, and Vladimir Mayakovsky. Written in emulation of Marinetti's *Futurist Manifesto* (1909), it advocates modernization of Russian arts and letters by embracing modern symbols—city, machine, speed. Vertov advocated a similar radical revision of aesthetic canons and artistic practices. In composing "WE," Vertov also drew upon the principles of constructivists, whose "Realistic Manifesto" (1920) advocates making art for social purposes.

"WE" has inspired a body of film and film theory that supports it aims and techniques. Vertov created effective propaganda films according his creative principles, notably *Three Songs about Lenin* (1934). Within the Soviet state, social realism became a dominant style in cinema, and Vertov's influence waned. In the decades that followed, however, innovative documentarians turned to Vertov's theories. The "Free Cinema" school of film directors in England in the 1950s, including Lindsay Anderson, Karel Reisz, Tony Richardson, and Lorenza Mazetti, emulated Vertov's irreverent attitude toward cinematic conventions.

⁘ Key Facts

Time Period:
Early 20th Century

Movement/Issue:
Aesthetics; Leninism; Constructivism

Place of Publication:
Russia

Language of Publication:
Russian

THE LIFE OF DZIGA VERTOV, *THE MAN WITH A MOVIE CAMERA*

Denis Arkadyevich Kaufman was born in 1896 to Jewish intellectuals in Bialystok. When his music studies were interrupted by the invading German army during World War I, he settled in Moscow. There, he began to write science fiction that was influenced by the artists and intellectuals of the futurist movement. He studied medicine in St. Petersburg before joining the Film Committee of the People's Commissariat of Public Education in Moscow.

At the start of his career, Kaufman took on his artistic name, Dziga Vertov ("spinning gypsy"). Vertov reported on current events and worked as cameraman for the Bolshevik newspaper *Pravda,* where he created *Kinopravda,* newsreel reportage on a wide variety of subjects. This enterprise allowed Vertov to develop his own system of editing and filmmaking. Vertov, his brother Mikhail, and his wife, editor Elizaveta Svilova, began to publish aesthetic tracts under the name "Group of Three." The majority of Vertov's subsequent cinematic works were commissions that addressed specific issues of the Soviet state. His most significant period of artistic experiment coincided with his work with VUFKU, a pan-Ukrainian production group. There, he created his masterpiece, *The Man with a Movie Camera* (1929). With the rise of the Stalinist regime, Vertov faced increasing difficulties with few assignments, and by the end of his career he had returned to creating newsreels.

North American photojournalists Robert Drew, Richard Leacock, Albert and David Maysles, D.A. Pennebaker, and Frederick Wiseman used technological advances with unobtrusive cameras to pursue Vertov's aim of catching life unaware. Other avant-garde filmmakers, such as Stan Brakhage, explored the eye as a participant-observer and alluded to the inseparability of seeing and filmmaking. In 1995 a group of Danish filmmakers issued the manifesto *Dogme 95,* echoing the manifestos of the New Wave and the Dziga Vertov Group. Although Eisenstein's theories of montage had greater influence among Soviet filmmakers, Vertov's essays and films continue to command significant artistic influence and scholarly interest.

THEMES AND STYLE
The central theme of "WE: Variant of a Manifesto" is that dominant film culture manipulates its audience by relying on the conventions of other art forms to generate reactions. With the force of the futurists' manifesto "A Slap in the Face" echoing behind it, "WE" opens with a rejection of the conventions of popular cinema: "WE affirm the future of cinema by denying its present. / Cinematography must die so that the art of cinema may live. We call for its death to be hastened." To this end, the manifesto outlines its terms for a new cinema: a rejection of the conventions of Romantic cinema and theater in favor of "radical

necessity, precision and speed"—suggesting that this formalist and constructivist dynamism is the correct approach to filming in the emergent Soviet state.

The manifesto achieves its rhetorical effect through a bold rejection of artistic conventions and a proud claim of an "outsider" status. This sense of the bold and unique importance of its message is achieved first through Vertov's use of the capitalized term "WE." By constructing his manifesto as a series of statements that alternate the opinions of WE with the weakness of other film traditions—namely, of American and Russo-German filmmaking—the essay discredits old and unexamined traditions with a new vitality: "Everyone who cares for his art seeks the essence of his own technique. / Cinema's unstrung nerves need a rigorous system of precise movement." As Vertov asserts in "Artistic Drama and Kino-Eye," cinema exists "to record and organize the individual characteristics of life's phenomena into a whole, an essence, a conclusion."

Stylistically, "WE: Variant of a Manifesto" is distinguished by its defiant and aggressive tone. Written as an aesthetic tract with some shared priorities of earlier artistic doctrines, "WE" was first published in *LEF,* a magazine edited by former futurist leader and poet Vladimir Mayakovsky. Despite a more general avant-garde concern with artistic form and purpose, "WE" announces its authority by addressing technical matters along with issues of taste. Vertov differentiates his practices by creating a new vocabulary for film. Practitioners of Kino-Eye (cinema-eye), or *kinoks,* "should be able to jot [a film idea] down with precision so as to give it life on the screen." Although its aggressive stance renders "WE" somewhat belligerent in tone, the manifesto achieves its rhetorical force through its thoughtful proposal of technical solutions to conventional shortcomings.

CRITICAL DISCUSSION
When "WE: Variant of a Manifesto" was released in 1922, it received mixed reactions both within and outside of filmmaking circles. Some film practitioners felt that its principles were focused too much on formal issues derived from newsreels, which in practice impart what Eisenstein calls an "unmotivated mischief" to sequences. Many followed Eisenstein's ideas of montage, which, as Thomas Sheehan notes in "Wittgenstein and Vertov: Aspectuality and Anarchy" (2002), had a didactic element "synthesizing juxtapositions or superimpositions, creating a graphic succession of frames that circle back around a single theme or meaning." Still, critics admired Vertov for calling attention to the framework of films, to the limits of the human eye and the camera's eye. Many who watched Vertov's film *Man with a Movie Camera* (1929) understood the power of his techniques. In *Kino: A History of the Russian and Soviet Film* (1960), Jay Leyda notes, "The camera action in Kino-Eye was alert, surprising, but never eccentric. Things … were 'caught' but less for the catching's sake than for the close observation of the things themselves."

After Vertov's film career was curtailed with the rise of social realism, his manifesto remained an important source of inspiration for documentary filmmakers. In the 1950s and 1960s, Vertov's ideas reemerged in popular culture. His self-reflective cinema can be seen in the work of Chris Marker and Jean-Luc Godard. The 1960s Canadian *cinéma direct* ("direct cinema") group—filmmakers at the National Film Board of Canada, including Michel Brault, Gilles Grouix, and Terrence Macartney-Filgate—emulated Vertov's approach to unperformed documentary. In the journal *Cahiers du cinéma,* Jean-Louis Comolli writes, "Thirty years after his time it became possible to apply Vertov's injunctions without any loss between the idea—to film everything, record everything, to be in life without disturbing or falsifying it—and its realisation."

Much scholarship has been focused on the formal and theoretical differences between Vertov's manifesto and Eisenstein's theories. While Vertov's manifesto and work fell into disfavor in his own time, commentators have drawn attention to the manifesto's ideas as forerunners to later cinematic developments. Jerry White observes that Vertov's work was the forerunner for practitioners of *cinema vérité,* including Pierre Perrault. "Vertov's belief that Radio-Eye [and Kino-Eye] was about 'eliminating distance between people' connects strongly with [Perrault's] ideas about cinema vecu and the connection between [subjects] and between the [subjects] and filmmakers themselves." Critics also note that Vertov's manifesto exerted considerable influence on New Wave directors. When Godard's work became politicized in service of the May 1968 protests, he turned to Vertov's work to debate the conventions of classical cinema, particularly, as described in *Aesthetics of Film* (1992), "its transparency and effacement of marks of enunciation."

BIBLIOGRAPHY

Sources

Aumont, Jacques et al., eds. *Aesthetics of Film.* Austin: U of Texas P, 1992.

Comolli, Jean-Louis, and J. Narboni. "Cinema/Ideologie/Critique." *Cahiers du cinéma* (Oct./Nov. 1969).

Hicks, Jeremy. *Dziga Vertov: Defining Documentary Film.* New York: I. B. Tauris, 2007.

Leyda, Jay. *Kino: A History of the Russian and Soviet Film.* Princeton: Princeton UP, 1960.

Papazian, Elizabeth Astrid. *Manufacturing Truth: The Documentary Moment in Early Soviet Culture.* DeKalb: Northern Illinois UP, 2009.

Roberts, Graham. *The Man with the Movie Camera.* New York: I. B. Tauris, 2000.

Sheehan, Thomas W. "Wittgenstein and Vertov: Aspectuality and Anarchy." *Discourse* 24.3 (2002): 95+. *Literature Resource Center.* Web. 7 Aug. 2012.

Vertov, Dziga. *Kino-Eye. The Writings of Dziga Vertov.* Ed. Annette Michelson. Trans. Kevin O'Brien. Berkeley: U of California P, 1984.

White, Jerry. *The Radio Eye: Cinema in the North Atlantic, 1958-1988.* Waterloo: Wilfred Laurier UP, 2009.

Further Reading

Delgado, Sergio. "Dziga Vertov's *Man with a Movie Camera* and the Phenomenology of Perception." *Film Criticism* 34.1 (2009): 1+. *Literature Resource Center.* Web. 7 Aug. 2012.

Feldman, Seth R. *Evolution of Style in the Early Work of Dziga Vertov.* New York: Arno, 1977.

Flaxman, Gregory, ed. *The Brain Is the Screen: Deleuze and the Philosophy of Cinema.* Minneapolis: U of Minnesota P, 2000.

Petrić, Vladimir. *Constructivism in Film:* The Man with the Movie Camera: *A Cinematic Analysis.* New York: Cambridge UP, 1987.

Tsivian, Yuri, ed. *Lines of Resistance: Dziga Vertov and the Twenties.* Trans. Julian Graffy. Gemona, Udine: Le Giornate del Cinema Muto, 2004.

Karen Bender

A poster designed by the Stenberg brothers advertising Dziga Vertov's 1929 film *Man with a Movie Camera.* ARCHIVES CHARMET/THE BRIDGEMAN ART LIBRARY

ZENITHIST MANIFESTO

Ivan Goll, Ljubomir Micić, Boško Tokin

✢ *Key Facts*

Time Period:
Early 20th Century

Movement/Issue:
Avant-gardism;
Aesthetics

Place of Publication:
Yugoslavia

**Language of
Publication:**
Serbian

OVERVIEW

Composed by Serbians Ljubomir Micić and Boško Tokin and German Ivan Goll, the *Zenithist Manifesto* (1921) describes the zenithist art movement and calls for the abandonment of Western rationalism in favor of Eastern mysticism in art and literature. Published shortly after the inception of the Kingdom of Serbs, Croats, and Slovenes in 1918 and the nearly concurrent Russian Revolution, the manifesto reflects a growing radicalism in the Croatian artistic community. The manifesto appeared in the international journal *Zenit,* which was founded by Micić, and proposed that other artistic movements, such as cubism, futurism, and expressionism, were insufficient in spirit and spirituality. The authors address Balkan intellectuals, writers, musicians, and editors, as well as an international community of artists and publishers. Chaotic and aggressive in tone, the *Zenithist Manifesto* advocates a barbarian primitivism in art and culture, as exemplified by the "Barbarogenius," the personification of the mystical Eastern man who would do battle with Western rational thought.

The *Zenithist Manifesto* was not received positively by a culture that marginalized its avant-garde, though the manifesto was read with interest in the international arena. Although zenithism was officially active from 1921 to 1926, the movement remained on the fringes of Yugoslavian culture and persisted largely as a result of the efforts of Micić and his brother, Branko Ve Poljanski. Having much in common with the Italian futurist blend of nationalist politics and internationalism in art, the *Zenithist Manifesto* reflects the embattled stance of the Croatian avant-garde in Zagreb during a time when artists were reconsidering their role in the political, social, and cultural milieu. Although zenithism was ignored as part of the intellectual and artistic heritage of Yugoslav cultures for decades, current study of its principles and manifestations situates the movement firmly in the tradition of the influential avant-garde of central Europe.

HISTORICAL AND LITERARY CONTEXT

The *Zenithist Manifesto* addresses the influence of Western rationalism on art and artistic study and capitalism's influence on artistic production. Following the assassination of Archduke Franz Ferdinand, Yugoslav nationalism took hold in the Balkans, resulting in the formation of an independent Yugoslav state. Zenithists participated in that nationalistic spirit, calling for the Balkanization (used as a pejorative term for the breakdown of society) of Europe even as they urged brotherhood among artists. The *Zenithist Manifesto* calls for the disintegration of the capitalist West and its reinvention through primitive, ancestral culture. The authors prescribe mysticism, spirituality, and aggressive simplicity as an antidote to the dominant rationalism of Western culture.

Around the time the *Zenithist Manifesto* was published, avant-garde artists, writers, and musicians in Yugoslavia were reorienting themselves within a progressively permissive political, social, and cultural atmosphere. Micić founded zenithism as a postexpressionist movement. *Zenit,* the movement's publication, featured contributions in a number of languages from representatives of international movements, including cubism, futurism, Dada, and poetism—despite the renunciation of these movements in the zenithists' first manifesto. Although pivotal in the formation of zenithism, writers Milos Crnjanski, Rastko Petrović, Tokin, and Stanislav Vinaver eventually abandoned the zenithists and formed the individualist modernist group Alfa in response to Micić's collective definition of art and culture. Zenithism and *Zenit* maintained contact with the international avant-garde movement, inspired Slovenian constructivism, and largely ignored any discussion of labor conditions until its later stages, when Micić became more explicitly leftist and published "Zenithism through the Prism of Marxism" (1926), which resulted in the censorship of the magazine.

The *Zenithist Manifesto* employs the urgent prescriptive language of political manifestos, particularly the declarations that were crucial to the French, American, and Russian revolutions. Indeed, Kaiser Franz Joseph used a manifesto to declare World War I. Micić, Goll, and Tokin were undoubtedly influenced in the writing of the *Zenithist Manifesto* by such revolutionary political manifestos, as well as by literary manifestos arising from romanticism in the 1820s and 1830s, such as Alexandre Guiraud's "Nos doctrines. Manifeste de la Muse française" (Our Doctrines. Manifesto of the French Muse, 1824). Other members of the avant-garde began to employ the manifesto as a declaration of the program of their respective artistic movements, most notably Italian futurist Filippo Marinetti, who published a manifesto on futurism in *Le Figaro* in 1909.

The *Zenithist Manifesto* advanced the avant-garde tradition of literary manifesto as a declaration of an artistic project. Micić wrote a number of manifestos on zenithism, including "Man and Art," "The Spirit of Zenithism," "Expressionism Is Dying," and the controversial "Zenithism through the Prism of Marxism." After *Zenit* was censored for fear it would foment a socialist revolution, Micić worked to advance the same project in the avant-garde magazine *tank*. The *Zenithist Manifesto* was key to the advancement of Yugoslavia's participation in the avant-garde of central Europe and to the exposure of the Yugoslav art movement to the international arena, which later allowed for the development of Slovenian constructivism.

THEMES AND STYLE

The central theme of the *Zenithist Manifesto* is that artists and makers of culture must fight against the dominant rationalism of the West, invoking a primitive Eastern mysticism in order to simplify and spiritualize art. Tokin, in his section of the manifesto, outlines the zenithist project when he writes:

New movements which are surreal in principle are not always such in practice, and we need this kind of practice: the expression of essential constructions, the emanation of a *healthy, pure, barbaric dynamism.*

- *One needs to be a barbarian.*

- This is what it means to be a barbarian: beginning, possibility, creation.

(Nietzsche, Whitman and Dostoevsky are barbarians because they are beginnings.)

We, the Yugoslavs, are barbarians.

In order to achieve such a "beginning," zenithists advocate for a radical primitivism in pursuit of sublimity; artists are urged to return to a primeval experience, equated with barbarianism, Easternism, and Balkanism, that breaks with limiting Western institutions.

To achieve its radical communication, the *Zenithist Manifesto* subverts normal modes of expression by embracing paradox and breaking with traditional literary forms of the manifesto, including text conventions. A primary contradiction contained within the manifesto is the simultaneous calls for the Balkanization of Europe and for the unity of all

LJUBOMIR MICIĆ: CHAMPION OF *ZENIT*

One of three authors of the *Zenithist Manifesto,* Ljubomir Micić (1895-1971) was a Serbo-Croatian avant-gardist and founder of the international magazine *Zenit*. Along with his brother, Branko Ve Poljanski, Micić was central to the advancement of zenithism in the newly instated Kingdom of Serbs, Croats, and Slovenes. *Zenit* was centered on zenithist aesthetics and poetics and until 1923 was based in Zagreb, Croatia. After Micić published a controversial article on Stjepan Radic and Croatian culture, he moved *Zenit* to Belgrade, Serbia. *Zenit* established contact with artists in Prague, Paris, and Vienna, where Yugoslavian artists and writers were entering universities after the end of World War I.

Zenit's publication ceased in 1926 after forty-three issues. After making trips to Munich and Berlin and contacting Russian revolutionaries, Micić published an article, "Zenitism through the Lens of Marxism," that prompted the state prosecutor to charge him with spreading communist propaganda. He was arrested, but he was later freed as a result of intervention by Italian futurist Filippo Marinetti. Micić lived in exile in Paris for nine years, from 1927 to 1936. After having faded into relative obscurity, Micić died in a nursing home in Serbia in 1971.

artists. Goll outlines the need for a specifically Balkan primitivism when he writes:

Back to the primeval source of experience— SIMPLICITY

THE WORD

back to barbarism!

We need to become the BARBARIANS of poetry once more.

The Barbarism of Mongolians Balkanites Negros

Indians

Then, just a few beats later, Goll expands his definition of zenithism to include all artists:

The New Poet is always INTERNATIONAL

He sings SIMPLY

for all Nations

for PEOPLE

Again and always the *first words of the worlds.*

The *Zenithist Manifesto* constantly disorients the reader with its numerous contradictions and breaks with convention, thereby mimicking its own prescribed departure from traditional artistic institutions.

The manifesto is chaotic in style, making use of nontraditional forms, excessive punctuation and

Writer Ivan Goll in 1948. Goll, Ljubomir Micić, and Boško Tokin produced the *Zenithist Manifesto* (1921). © HENRI MARTINIE/ ROGER-VIOLLET/THE IMAGE WORKS

italics, and aggressive, imagistic language. These elements of its style, in combination with its three different authors, communicate disintegration, urgency, and violence to the reader. Micić's section in particular is provocative in form, breaking with conventions of poetics and prose, as demonstrated here:

The sun has fallen into my soul

into the limitless spaces of All-love.

Red glass crosses have shattered

Man has died in the yellow car.

Letters are dancing, thrown above the crosses

R S U C R

E C E A

Here, the manifesto's intended break with rationalism and traditional order is played out in a literal break with normal typographic order, while its concrete and vivid images work to invite the reader to reenter the text. Each paradox is countered by a reorienting poeticism to achieve the dual objectives of Balkan nationalism and poetic brotherhood.

CRITICAL DISCUSSION

The *Zenithist Manifesto* was received with skepticism. Esther Levinger, in her 2002 essay "Ljubomir Micić and the Zenitist Utopia," notes, "To some, Zenitism looked 'chaotic, intoxicated with burning confusion that destroys … creation.'" Želimir Koščević outlines

key reasons the avant-garde was ignored in Yugoslav culture in his 2002 essay "Zagreb." Writing of the Croatian capital, he notes that "although possessing all the features of Central European urbane culture, Zagreb—with its Austro-Hungarian heritage and typical bourgeois citizenry—was neither able nor willing to accept artistic excess."

Although the *Zenithist Manifesto* was largely ignored by international and Yugoslavian scholars until the 1950s—due in part to Micić's radical and off-putting rejection of traditionalism—the work is now regarded as an important contribution to the avant-garde and to the internationalization of Croatian art and literature. Following World War II, communist efforts to inhibit expression and dissuade nationalism played a role in marginalizing the zenithist legacy. Zenithism was re-examined in the 1970s and 1980s, when divisions in the Communist Party led intellectuals to push for democratic reform, and trials of dissident scholars and writers decreased. In 1983, during a surge in intellectual experimentation in Yugoslavia, exhibitions on zenithism at the National Museum in Belgrade and in Zagreb reintroduced the movement into critical discussion. The revolutionary pronouncements in the *Zenithist Manifesto* cement its importance in Yugoslavia's social, cultural, and political evolution. As Éva Forgács notes in her 2002 essay "Form as the Agent of Social Change," "In cultures where aesthetics, ethics, and politics were often not clearly separable, the choice manifested in form or style carried more weight than in the West. It was a manifestation of freedom—of free choice—in a world where deficit in freedom was the tradition."

Scholarship on the *Zenithist Manifesto* examines its place in the avant-garde, its central concerns, and its unique form and typography. Levinger notes that zenithism resembled other art movements, but "it did not propose to advance Enlightenment rationalism but to invert it. [Micić] ignored production forces and conditions of labor." Highlighting the opposition with which zenithism was met, Želimir Koščević points out that "The Academy of Fine Arts in Zagreb, founded in 1907, supported rejections of the avant-garde, thereby bestowing legitimacy and authority to its disavowal." Irina Subotić, in "*Zenit* and Zenitism" (1990) notes the movement's revolutionary form: "In a clearly antimilitary spirit, with unconventional behavior and a decidedly critical disposition towards all existing norms and values, *Zenit* presented the ideas of free artistic forms—from free verse ('words in space') to the most radical art trends using new typographic and graphic solutions—that followed its ideological commitment."

BIBLIOGRAPHY

Sources

Forgács, Éva. "Form as the Agent of Social Change." *Between Worlds: A Sourcebook of Central European Avant-Gardes, 1910-1930.* Ed. Timothy Benson. Massachusetts: MIT P, 2002. 237-38. Print.

Goll, Ivan, Ljubomir Micić, and Boško Tokin. "The Zenithist Manifesto." Trans. Maja Starčević. *Between Worlds: A Sourcebook of Central European Avant-Gardes, 1910-1930.* Ed. Timothy Benson. Massachusetts: MIT P, 2002. 284-91. Print.

Levinger, Esther. "Ljubomir Micić and the Zenitist Utopia." *Central European Avant-Gardes: Exchange and Transformation, 1910-1930.* Ed. Timothy Benson. Los Angeles: MIT P, 2002. 260-69. Print.

Koščević, Želimir. "Zagreb." *Central European Avant-Gardes: Exchange and Transformation, 1910-1930.* Ed. Timothy Benson. Los Angeles: MIT Press, 2002. 255-59. Print.

Subotić, Irina. "*Zenit* and Zenitism." Trans. Ann Vasić. *The Journal of Decorative and Propaganda Arts* 17 (1990): 14-25. *JSTOR.* Web. 1 Aug. 2012.

Further Reading

Bojtár, Endre. *East European Avant-Garde Literature.* Trans. Pál Várnai. Budapest: Akadémiai Kiadó, 1992. Print.

Djurić, Dubravka and Miško Šuvaković. *Impossible Histories: Historical Avant-gardes, Neo-avant-gardes, and Post-avant-gardes in Yugoslavia, 1918-1991.* Massachusetts: MIT P, 2003. Print.

Milojković-Djurić, Jelena. *Tradition and Avant-Garde: Literature and Art in Serbian Cultures, 1900-1918.* New York: Columbia UP, 1988. Print.

Subotić, Irina. "Avant-Garde Tendencies in Yugoslavia." *Art Journal* 49.1 (1990): 21-27. *JSTOR.* Web. 1 Aug. 2012.

Yanoshevsky, Galia. "Three Decades of Writing on Manifesto: The Making of a Genre." *Poetics Today* 30.2 (2009): 257-86. Print.

Kristen Gleason

Harlem Renaissance

AFRICAN FUNDAMENTALISM

Marcus Garvey

OVERVIEW

Written by Marcus Garvey from an Atlanta penitentiary in 1925, "African Fundamentalism" is a semi-religious statement of black racial pride and unity that calls for the establishment of a racial empire but does not directly imply the notion of racial superiority. The essay, first published as an editorial on the front page of the *Negro World* on June 6, 1925, articulates major ideological themes that were prevalent throughout Garvey's work, including claims of black racial greatness and an understanding of history that is ideologically independent from those of white theorists. "African Fundamentalism" addresses the history of the abuses and oppression of blacks across the globe. Garvey wrote his essay at the height of the religious fundamentalist revival that dominated the United States following World War I. It plays with notions of social Darwinism by presenting northern Africans as representatives of an established form of life and culture that subtly criticized that of their white European counterparts, challenging the claims of white eugenicists to the biological inferiority of the black race. Garvey's message spoke to a wide international intellectual sphere made up predominantly by blacks in the Americas, Africa, and Europe.

"African Fundamentalism" received a mixed response from the black community in the United States. It was embraced by black nationalists and supporters of the United Negro Improvement Association (UNIA) and Pan-Africanism but scorned by more integrationist African American leaders, such as W. E. B. Du Bois and Alain Locke. Garvey's essay was one of the earlier works that contributed to the polemic on the role/responsibility of the black artist and intellectual in the United States, which was later taken up by Locke, Langston Hughes, and George Schuyler, among others. "African Fundamentalism" proclaims the necessity of a political function in black art, calling for the recognition of Africans' historical achievements and a return to the principles of self-rule and black dignity. Central to Garvey's ideology was the notion of Pan-African allegiance and solidarity and the development of racial pride. The essay is considered to be the defining statement for "Garveyism" and is widely quoted and anthologized in studies of black nationalism and Pan-Africanism.

HISTORICAL AND LITERARY CONTEXT

"African Fundamentalism" arose in response to several contemporary phenomena, including the religious fundamentalist revival in the United States following World War I, the growing influence of eugenics and social Darwinism, and the increasingly prominent role of the integrationist movement in the United States, supported by the National Association for the Advancement of Colored People (NAACP) and its African American leaders, such as Du Bois. The religious revival of the 1920s was manifested both as a theological doctrine and as a conservative neopolitical movement. While U.S. fundamentalists called for a return to a traditional belief system uninfluenced by modernity and an agricultural economy that would assuage the impact of industrialization and urbanization, social Darwinists and proponents of eugenics were simultaneously propagating a virulently racist understanding of biology that asserted the inherent inferiority of blacks and other nonwhite races. From the perspective of Garvey and many other blacks during the period, the NAACP's approach to addressing this type of blatant racism was insufficient to bring about the true change that the community needed. The organization's heavy reliance on the clearly biased justice system through lawsuits was seen as a slow and indirect path toward equality that catered too frequently to the power and influence of the white community.

At the time of the publication of "African Fundamentalism" in 1925, the widespread lynching of blacks in the American South, although occurring a little less frequently than it had in the nineteenth century, continued largely unimpeded, with the NAACP's attempts at passing legislation against lynching continually blocked by southern white Democrats in Congress. White vigilantism spurred on by the presence of the Ku Klux Klan (KKK) led to the murders of hundreds of blacks throughout the South during this period, including the slaughter of more than 200 black tenant farmers in Philips County, Arkansas, by federal troops and white civilians in October 1919, an event known as the Elaine Race Riots. Garvey founded the United Negro Improvement Association (UNIA) in 1914 based on his belief in the need for a more effective solution to the abuses endured by blacks across the globe, advocating

✜ *Key Facts*

Time Period:
Early/Mid-20th Century

Movement/Issue:
Black nationalism;
Pan-Africanism

Place of Publication:
United States

Language of Publication:
English

MARCUS GARVEY: LEADER OF THE PAN-AFRICANIST MOVEMENT

Marcus Mosiah Garvey Jr. (August 17, 1887-June 10, 1940) was a Jamaican political leader, journalist, orator, and entrepreneur and a central figure in the Pan-Africanist and black nationalist movements. Garvey is perhaps best known for his founding and leadership of the Universal Negro Improvement Association (UNIA). Born in St. Ann's Bay, Jamaica, he spent two formative years in London (1912-14), studying law and working with Dusé Mohamed Ali, publisher of the *African Times and Orient Review*. Upon returning to Jamaica, Garvey founded the UNIA (in 1914), which advanced a Pan-African philosophy partially reflected in his creation of the Black Star Line in 1919. The shipping line was a central part of the Back-to-Africa movement, which advocated for individuals of African ancestry to return to their ancestral lands on the African continent.

Upon arriving in the United States in 1916, Garvey introduced a new gospel of racial pride that drew on a unique combination of the American "dream" of success and his Jamaican ambitions for cultural and economic independence. These values developed into what became known as Garveyism and served as a source of inspiration for the global African diaspora that yearned to escape colonialism and racism. Garvey's untainted inspirational leadership faced irreparable damage, however, when he was federally indicted on mail fraud charges related to the Black Star Line in 1922. After Garvey had served two years in prison, President Calvin Coolidge commuted his sentence, and he was deported to Jamaica in November 1927. In 1928 Garvey presented the Petition of the Negro Race to the League of Nations in Geneva, which summarized the abuse endured by Africans worldwide. Following this, in 1929, he founded the People's Political Party in Jamaica, the first "modern" political party to focus on education, workers' rights, and aiding the impoverished classes. Returning to London in 1935, Garvey lived and worked there until his death in 1940. He continues to be widely lauded for his significant contributions to African American advocacy during the early twentieth century.

for African Americans to leave the United States to permanently reside in Africa rather than attempt to resolve the boiling racial tension they faced in North America. According to David Van Leeuwen in his October 2010 article for *National Humanities Center*, Garvey's radical thinking and interaction with certain whites who wanted blacks to go back to Africa, as well as his meeting with leaders of the KKK, drew sharp criticism and concern from African American leaders such as James Weldon Johnson and Chandler Owen.

"African Fundamentalism" falls within the literary tradition of credos and statements of African American artists in the nineteenth and early twentieth centuries. This tradition dates back to U.S. slave narratives, such as *Narrative of the Life of Frederick Douglass* (1845), and early reflections on black life in America, as exemplified by Booker T. Washington's 1895 "Atlanta Compromise" speech to the Atlanta Cotton States and International Exposition. The work of Harlem Renaissance intellectuals such as John Edward Bruce ("The Negro in Poetry," 1923) and the debates on African American culture and politics in emerging black cultural and political publications such as *Crisis, Opportunity*, and the *Negro World* served as inspiration for Garvey's own creed for Pan-Africanism and the African diaspora.

Despite many Harlem Renaissance writers' repudiation of Garvey and his ideology, it is clear that his work, specifically "African Fundamentalism," had a clear impact on the emerging debates on "Negro" art that so closely followed its publication. Schuyler's 1926 "The Negro-Art Hokum" and Hughes's "The Negro Artist and the Racial Mountain" published later that year both address the role that African American art and the African American artist should play in society. The work of such creative writers as Richard Wright (*Uncle Tom's Children*, 1938; *Native Son*, 1940) and Ralph Ellison (*Invisible Man*, 1952) also reflect the African American artist's attempt at composing socially and politically conscious works of fiction, as advocated by Garvey in his 1925 essay. Today "African Fundamentalism" continues to be studied as a foundational text of the black nationalist and Pan-African movements and heralded as religious gospel by Rastas and modern-day Garveyites.

THEMES AND STYLE

"African Fundamentalism" stresses the need for the Pan-African community to regain a proud sense of selfhood by reviving the fundamental beliefs in black greatness that Garvey saw embodied in ancient African civilization. Garvey begins his essay, "The time has come for the Negro to forget and cast behind him his hero worship and adoration of other races, and to start out immediately, to create and emulate heroes of his own." He stresses the need to escape from white notions of race and privilege in order to develop an original "Negro idealism" grounded in religion. Garvey incorporates Christian beliefs but encourages an African worldview that promotes the worship of the image of a black God.

Garvey's essay achieves its impact by drawing on a Christian ethos and emphasizing the unity and solidarity of all blacks. Addressing the people of the African diaspora, he proclaims, "We must inspire a literature and promulgate a doctrine of our own without any apologies to the powers that be. The right is ours and God's." Garvey's use of the first-person collective voice reaffirms the unity of the global black community through the pronoun *we* and possessive *ours*. He incorporates civil and human rights rhetoric while simultaneously emphasizing the holy nature of the literature he calls for by associating it with the right of God. "Africa has produced countless numbers of men and women," Garvey notes, "whose lustre and bravery outshine that of any other people. Then why not see good and perfection in ourselves?" He further emphasizes the collectivity of blacks by naming their shared ancestral homeland of Africa.

"African Fundamentalism" is defined by its rational yet assertive tone, which at times adopts a defiant and angry tenor. Garvey relies on comparisons, rhetorical questions, and logical examples to drive home the point that blacks deserve to celebrate and honor their own culture and history. "The world today is indebted to us for the benefits of civilization," he writes. "They stole our arts and sciences from Africa. Then why should we be ashamed of ourselves?" Garvey challenges dominant historical narratives perpetuated by the white ruling classes by appropriating their own advanced vocabulary to assert alternative truths that call into question the supposedly inferior position of blacks. His language inverts traditional racial hierarchies, asserting that whites are *indebted* to blacks and reversing stereotypical racial roles by characterizing the whites as thieves and the blacks as victims. While the defiant, clever writing style of "African Fundamentalism" may initially catch the reader off guard, it also is actively engaging and elicits an emotional reaction.

CRITICAL DISCUSSION

Upon its publication in 1925, "African Fundamentalism" received mixed reactions from its predominantly black readership, as certain sectors of the black population aligned with the Pan-African and black nationalist movements embraced the essay, but the more conservative black population that identified with the integrationist cause of the NAACP rejected and denigrated it. Many middle-class black intellectuals, including Walter White, found Garvey's pro-black message to be divisive and exclusionary. "In New York City," according to White, "this feeling between black and mulatto has been accentuated ... by the propaganda of Marcus Garvey and his Universal Negro Improvement Association.... It is true beyond doubt that such a doctrine created ... greater antagonisms among colored people." White's essay "The Paradox of Color" appeared in Alain Locke's 1925 anthology *The New Negro,* which remarkably excluded any mention of Garvey or the UNIA with the exception of White's comment. This decision to marginalize Garvey and the essay his movement lauded as its manifesto reflects the low opinion that Locke, Du Bois, and associates had of the ideology propagated by Garvey in "African Fundamentalism."

Following the heyday of the Harlem Renaissance, Garvey's 1925 essay remained a foundational work in the ongoing polemic on the black artist and also continued to be a source of inspiration for new Pan-African movements. In *Literary Garveyism* (1983), Tony Martin recognizes that "art, for [Garvey], had

Marcus Garvey in 1924.
© WORLD HISTORY ARCHIVE/ALAMY

to serve the cause of freedom, justice and equality. His view of the place of art in his people's struggle was a succinct statement of what, in the 1960s, came to be known as the 'Black aesthetic.'" Garvey's ideology influenced many of the great minds of the twentieth century, including Kwame Nkrumah and Malcolm X. He continues to be celebrated by the Rastafarian movement today, and many Rastas view Garvey as a religious prophet.

Much scholarship on "African Fundamentalism" focuses on its significance for the Pan-African movement and regards it as the defining statement of Garveyism. In the introduction to his book *The Marcus Garvey and Universal Negro Improvement Association Papers* (1983), Robert A. Hill explains how Garvey's followers saw the essay as the new creed of the UNIA, which is reflected in the decision of the *Negro World* publishers to reprint "African Fundamentalism" in the next three consecutive issues of the newspaper following its initial publication on June 6, 1925. Other scholarship focuses on the universal nature of Garvey's message and its subsequent influence on the African diaspora. Robbie Shilliam notes how "Garvey attempted to cohere a Black Jacobin 'general will,' one that spoke to the sovereign status of all Black political subjects regardless of their socioeconomic status or national affiliation," and was thus influential among the African diaspora worldwide. "African Fundamentalism" is widely quoted as a reflection of Garvey's general philosophy of black solidarity and self-determination in the face of historical injustice.

BIBLIOGRAPHY

Sources

Garvey, Marcus. "African Fundamentalism." *Marcus Garvey: Life & Lessons Sample Documents.* UCLA African Studies Center, 1995. Web. 20 July 2012.

Hill, Robert A., ed. *The Marcus Garvey and Universal Negro Improvement Association Papers.* Berkeley: U of California P, 1983. Print.

Martin, Tony, ed. *Literary Garveyism: Garvey, Black Arts, and the Harlem Renaissance.* Dover: Majority, 1983. Print.

Shilliam, Robbie. "What about Marcus Garvey? Race and the Transformation of Sovereignty Debate." *Review of International Studies* 32.3 (2006): 379-400. Print.

Van Leeuwen, David. "Marcus Garvey and the Universal Negro Improvement Association." *National Humanities Center* Oct. 2000. Web. 21 July 2012.

White, Walter. "The Paradox of Color." *The New Negro: An Interpretation.* Ed. Alain Locke. New York: Arno, 1968. Print.

Further Reading

Hill, Robert A., ed. *Marcus Garvey: Life and Lessons.* Berkeley: U of California P, 1987. Print.

Lewis, Rupert. *Marcus Garvey: Anti-Colonial Champion.* Trenton: Africa World, 1988. Print.

Martin, Tony. *African Fundamentalism: A Literary and Cultural Anthology of Garvey's Harlem Renaissance.* Dover: Majority, 1991. Print.

———. *Race First: The Ideological and Organizational Struggles of Marcus Garvey and the Universal Negro Improvement Association.* Dover: Majority, 1986. Print.

Parascandola, Louis J., ed. *"Look for Me All around You": Anglophone Caribbean Immigrants in the Harlem Renaissance.* Detroit: Wayne State UP, 2005. Print.

Solomon, Mark. *The Cry Was Unity: Communists and African Americans, 1917-36.* Jackson: UP of Mississippi, 1998. Print.

Stein, Judith. *The World of Marcus Garvey: Race and Class in Modern Society.* Baton Rouge: Louisiana State UP, 1986. Print.

Watkins-Owens, Irma. *Blood Relations: Caribbean Immigrants and the Harlem Community, 1900-1930.* Bloomington: Indiana UP, 1996. Print.

Katrina White

BLUEPRINT FOR NEGRO WRITING

Richard Wright

OVERVIEW

Richard Wright's 1937 essay "Blueprint for Negro Writing," published in the *New Challenger* journal, formalizes his philosophy regarding African American literature, arguing that creative writing should play a more central role in the black community. Appearing years after the heyday of the Harlem Renaissance and in the wake of the Great Depression, Wright's essay initiated a new era for the African American community that was represented by the Chicago Black Renaissance. Wright responded to the intellectual polemic on "negro writing" begun by George Schuyler and Langston Hughes more than a decade earlier in 1926, elaborating a more thoroughly developed understanding of African American prose. Addressing a broad audience that included, as Caroline Sanchez notes in "Richard Wright, 1908-1960," "black America and the oppressors of black America," the essay reflects on the shortcomings of the historical role played by black writers who focused solely on proving the humanity of the African American, and it calls on black writers to assume a new, more invested position in their community.

For many in black America during the mid-1900s, Wright's essay was representative of the emerging generation of African American writers. It was largely celebrated for its critical, politically minded nature, which differentiated it from earlier writing on black arts and literature. "Blueprint for Negro Writing" was one of the founding works of "protest literature," a genre of African American writing that loudly proclaims its allegiance to a progressive future. Wright's text heavily influenced his contemporaries, and his Marxist ideology set the stage for black nationalism and communism as significant political movements within the African American community. Since its publication, Wright's essay has become one of the most widely read works of African American cultural criticism.

HISTORICAL AND LITERARY CONTEXT

"Blueprint for Negro Writing" responds to the tendency of many African American writers to cater their writing to a white audience in order to disprove denigrating black stereotypes such as Uncle Tom and the mammy. Leading up to the 1930s, the perpetual economic subordination of blacks, no matter where they went in the United States, was emphasized by the migration of thousands of African Americans from the south to northern urban centers such as Chicago and New York in search of better opportunities. The Great Depression, which began in 1929, had debilitating effects on the already-impoverished African American community in the urban north, leading many blacks to seek new forms of cultural expression to reflect their harsh daily reality. While writers from the earlier New Negro movement had sought to establish their equality with whites, Wright and others of his generation began to portray a more faithful, complex representation of the countless adversities faced by blacks in mid-twentieth-century America.

By the time Wright's essay was published in 1937, a growing artistic movement of which he was a leader had emerged in Chicago. This new generation of black artists and intellectuals was much more progressive and politically committed, constantly advocating for change within the black community. One of the main shifts during the period between World War I and World War II was an emerging black labor movement and the slow incorporation of African Americans into the previously whites-only labor unions. A. Phillip Randolph became the first African American head of a union within the American Federation of Labor when he assumed leadership of the Brotherhood of Sleeping Car Porters in 1925. In addition, in the late 1920s and the 1930s the Communist Party began to gain more African American support, including that of Claude McKay and Wright, striving to establish a popular front between socialists and non-socialists in the north beginning in 1935.

Wright's essay was a reaction not only to the work of his literary antecedents, the New Negro writers, but also to the contemporary experiences of African Americans. The period between the wars, and specifically the years of the Harlem Renaissance in the 1920s and into the 1930s, had established what Robin Lucy calls in a *Journal of American Folklore* article a "self-conscious literature" that struggled with the "(re)construction of African American identity and its corollary of authenticity" in its representation of blacks, and in black writers' understanding of their role within their community. "Blueprint for Negro Writing" denounces Harlem Renaissance works such as Schuyler's "The Negro-Art Hokum" (1926) and

⁘ *Key Facts*

Time Period:
Early 20th Century

Movement/Issue:
Black nationalism;
Protest literature

Place of Publication:
United States

**Language of
Publication:**
English

THE CHICAGO BLACK RENAISSANCE

Although the Harlem Renaissance of the 1920s is a better-known African American literary movement, the Chicago Black Renaissance of the mid-twentieth century was also influential. The "Great Migration" from 1910 to 1930 brought a large influx of African Americans from the southern United States to Chicago, including Richard Wright, and they contributed to a developing urban culture in literature, visual and performing arts, and music. In addition to Wright, notable artists associated with the Chicago Black Renaissance include Langston Hughes, Arna Bontemps, Margaret Walker, and Gwendolyn Brooks.

Publications such as the *Chicago Defender* publicized the work of black artists and promoted the institutions that nurtured their creativity. Furthermore, the New Deal's Works Progress Administration, as well as the South Side Community Art Center, organized artistic events and workshops for African Americans in the city. Art served as an outlet for black migrants growing up in the impoverished south side of Chicago, specifically in the Bronzeville district. Some of the central themes addressed by members of the renaissance include questions of identity, the search for meaning and dignity for blacks, the spirit of urban Chicago, and racial conflict between blacks and whites. To provide a space of inspiration and encouragement for emerging writers, Wright founded the South Side Writers' Group in 1936.

Novelist Richard Wright in Paris. © PHOTOS 12/ ALAMY

Hughes's "The Negro Artist and the Racial Mountain" (1926) because, as Sanchez notes, they "keep writing separate from the Negro experience and [are] more entertaining than human" instead of calling out injustices and demanding concrete change.

In the years following its publication, Wright's essay had an impact on African American literature in general and on black cultural criticism in particular. African American novels such as Ralph Ellison's *Invisible Man* (1952) were directly influenced by Wright's Marxist ideology and innovative writing style, elements that Wright further developed in his 1940 novel *Native Son*. Wright's work also inspired several black publications that emerged over the following decade, including the magazine *Negro Story*, which appeared in May 1944 and presented virulently antifascist, antiracist, and unwaveringly polemical pieces reflective of Wright's style. "Blueprint for Negro Writing" is still taught in college courses on black cultural studies.

THEMES AND STYLE

The main theme of "Blueprint for Negro Writing" is that African American writers owe more to their community and need to become advocates for social and political change rather than continue to engage in racial debates generated by white intellectuals. It is in this statement that Wright so powerfully denounces the work of Harlem Renaissance writers, criticizing them for penning "humble novels, poems, and plays" and calling them "prim and decorous ambassadors who went a-begging to white America. They entered the Court of American Public Opinion dressed in the knee-pants of servility, curtsying to show that the Negro was not inferior, that he was human, and that he had a life comparable to that of other people." In his condemnation of earlier black writers, Wright calls for a more autonomous literature that is committed to the concerns and needs of blacks, not to entertaining or legitimating themselves to the white public.

"Blueprint for Negro Writing" employs both a Marxist and nationalist rhetoric to convey its message to black writers and the black public at large. In "Richard Wright's '12 Million Black Voices' and World War II-era Civic Nationalism," Dan Shiffman writes that Wright developed a type of nationalism based on "black oral traditions and familial interactions," revealing "a nation that exists largely outside of the boundaries of America's capitalist driven values." Wright's unique form of black nationalism emphasizes the similarities among African Americans and encourages black writers to draw on these common histories and traditions in their works. "In the absence of fixed and nourishing forms of culture," he writes, "the Negro has a folklore which embodies the memories and hopes of his struggle for freedom … [it] contains, in a measure that puts shame to more deliberate forms of Negro expression, the collective sense of Negro life in America." Wright stresses the collectivity of the African American population throughout his essay, reaffirming the need for black writers to advocate for their own community.

In "Blueprint for Negro Writing," Wright departs from the colloquial language that is prevalent in much of his narrative writing and opts instead for a sophisticated, precise style. Divided into sections with points that are spelled out clearly, the essay functions as a blueprint, or a set of guidelines, for black writing. Wright's formal language and elaborate sentence structure communicate to the reader that he knows how to write well and that he would rather demonstrate his prowess than brag about it. Discussing the responsibility of the black writer, he asserts, "In order to do justice to his subject matter, in order to depict Negro life in all of its manifold and intricate relationships, a deep, informed, and complex consciousness is necessary; a consciousness which draws for its strength upon the fluid lore of a great people." The sophistication of Wright's language reflects the complex level of consciousness he demands from his colleagues and the larger black public, which, at its base, is the working class.

CRITICAL DISCUSSION

Overall, "Blueprint for Negro Writing" received a positive response from its audience of leftist readers when it emerged in the radical *New Challenger* journal in 1937. As Robert Bone notes in "Richard Wright and the Chicago Renaissance," the essay embodies the artistic consensus of the South Side Writers' Group on "the national question" that the "Negro" writer must relate to his folk tradition. Therefore, the black intellectuals of the popular front movement identified with Wright's statement and were quick to embrace it, as did many progressive whites. Writers of the day such as Cedric Dover saw Wright's essay as an essential resource for black artists. Dover writes in "Notes on Coloured Writing" that "Blueprint" was "so basic for all coloured writing that it is his [Wright's] duty to make it widely available as an enlarged pamphlet." Most of all, Dover lauds the text's "artist-audience interaction." However, because of its publication in such a radical, alternative publication, Wright's essay did not make it into the homes of mainstream America and was known mostly in black intellectual circles.

There is no doubt that the progressive ideology presented in "Blueprint" had a direct impact on the black nationalist and civil rights movements that emerged in the two decades following its publication. Although Wright would eventually distance himself from the radical socialist values communicated in this early essay, it continues to be viewed as a central text in the history of mid-twentieth-century black America. Scholar Seymour Gross situates Wright's work in a specific moment in the evolution of black art, when "the party line on Negro art ... was patently propagandistic." Indeed, Wright's text is both an important literary contribution and a central political work that is representative of the black labor movement and popular front politics of the 1930s and 1940s. It is for this reason that the essay continues to be studied not only in literature courses but also in the fields of cultural studies, ethnic studies, black studies, and history.

A large body of current scholarship on "Blueprint for Negro Writing" focuses on the role of the black writer in a socially engaged literary practice. Scholars such as Houston A. Baker, Jr. have drawn on Wright's ideology to introduce cultural theories such as the black public sphere and critical memory, which necessitates that black writers be invested in recording the history of their community. Wright's issue with black writers pandering to white America has resurfaced as a topic of debate in recent years. In *Critical Memory: Public Spheres, African American Writing, and Black Fathers and Sons in America*, Baker writes that "perhaps black public figures are to white 'liking' as black public figures' discourses are to what Wright called America's 'self-draped cloak of righteousness.' To leave undisturbed America's fear of 'fact ... history ... necessity' ... is to gain a dubious American spotlight of likeableness."

BIBLIOGRAPHY

Sources

Baker, Houston A., Jr. *Critical Memory: Public Spheres, African American Writing, and Black Fathers and Sons in America*. Atlanta: U of Georgia P, 2001. Print.

Bone, Robert. "Richard Wright and the Chicago Renaissance." *Callaloo* 28 (Summer 1986): 446-68. Print.

Dover, Cedric. "Notes on Coloured Writing." *Phylon (1940-1956)* 8.3 (1947): 213-24. Web. 2 July 2012.

Gross, Seymour L. "The Negro in American Literary Criticism." *The Review of Politics* 28.3 (July 1966): 273-92. Web. 2 July 2012.

Lucy, Robin. "'Flying Home': Ralph Ellison, Richard Wright, and the Black Folk during World War II." *Journal of American Folklore* 120.477 (Summer 2007): 257-83. Print.

Sanchez, Caroline. "Richard Wright, 1908-1960." *Modern America, 1914-Present*. U of North Carolina at Pembroke. Web. 2 July 2012.

Shiffman, Dan. "Richard Wright's '12 Million Black Voices' and World War II-era Civic Nationalism." *African American Review* 41.3 (Fall 2007): 443-58. Print.

Further Reading

Bigsby, C.W.E. "Richard Wright and His Blueprint for Negro Writing." *PN Review* 19 (1980): 53-55. Print.

Fabre, Michel. *The Unfinished Quest of Richard Wright*. Isabel Barzun, trans. New York: Morrow, 1973. Print.

Gates, Henry Louis, and Gene Andrew Jarrett, eds. *The New Negro: Readings on Race, Representation, and African American Culture, 1892-1938*. Princeton: Princeton UP, 2007. Print.

Mullen, Bill. "Popular Fronts: 'Negro Story' Magazine and the African American Literary Response to World War II." *African American Review* 30.1 (Spring 1996): 5-15. Print.

Napier, Winston, ed. *African American Literary Theory: A Reader.* New York: New York UP, 2000. Print.

Skerrett, Joseph T., Jr. "Richard Wright, Writing and Identity." *Callaloo* 7 (Oct. 1979): 84-94. Print.

Tracy, Steven C., ed. *Writers of the Black Chicago Renaissance.* Urbana: U of Illinois P, 2011. Print.

Wright, Richard. *Richard Wright Reader.* Eds. Ellen Wright and Michel Fabre. New York: Harper & Row, 1978. Print.

Katrina White

DECLARATION TO THE WORLD

W. E. B. Du Bois

OVERVIEW

Drafted primarily by William Edward Burghardt (W.E.B.) Du Bois, the "Declaration to the World" (1921), also known as the "London Manifesto," is a series of statements criticizing colonial powers' administration of colonies—particularly in Africa, the West Indies, and India—and industrialized nations' treatment of people of color in both domestic and foreign affairs. Its preamble addresses racial problems in France, Great Britain, the United States, Belgium, Spain, and Portugal and in these countries' empires. In addition, the document lists six demands of the "Suppressed Races." The manifesto arose from the first session of the Second Pan-African Congress held from August 27 to 29, 1921, in London. The meeting was organized by Du Bois and had about 120 people in attendance.

Primarily because of its call for land redistribution to native peoples in Africa, the "London Manifesto" was initially considered to be too extreme by some delegates at the subsequent Brussels and Paris sessions of the Second Pan-African Congress. French-speaking leaders—such as Blaise Diagne, a Senegalese member of the French chamber of deputies—were especially critical, as they were reluctant to call out the French government in front of English-speaking outsiders. American journalist and entrepreneur Marcus Garvey and his followers, who also promoted Pan-Africanism, were among those who saw the manifesto as too radical. Nevertheless, except for the land redistribution resolution, the manifesto was approved by a majority of the 113 delegates at the Paris session of the congress. As a result, Du Bois was encouraged to compose the "Manifesto to the League of Nations" only weeks later. "The London Manifesto" served as a basis for statements later issued at Pan-African congresses held in 1923, 1927, and 1945.

HISTORICAL AND LITERARY CONTEXT

The "London Manifesto" was issued in the face of a lack of self-government in Europe's colonies, Jim Crow segregation in the United States, and the ongoing exploitation of labor in King Leopold II's Belgian Congo, among other colonies. Du Bois had played a major role in organizing the National Association for the Advancement of Colored People (NAACP) in the United States in 1910, and he had attended an International Races Congress in London in 1911 and organized the

First Pan-African Congress in 1919. Post-World War I treaties in 1919 had, to an extent, carved new nation-states from the defeated Central Powers according to the principle of "self-determination" that U.S. President Woodrow Wilson had articulated in his Fourteen Points. However, self-determination did not apply to Europe's colonies, and Du Bois wished to make this clear to the League of Nations, the international body envisioned by Wilson that became a postwar reality. Furthermore, postwar violence between whites and African Americans had occurred in over thirty U.S. cities and towns in 1919, which added urgency to Du Bois's desire for blacks to organize.

When the "London Manifesto" was drafted in 1921, Du Bois's vision of Pan-Africanism and the empowerment of nonwhites saw several challenges. In the United States, the Jamaican-born Garvey proclaimed himself a king of Africa with his organization the Universal Negro Improvement Association, which had many followers. Among his other issues, Du Bois shared leadership in the NAACP with many whites, such as Oswald Garrison Villard and Joel Spingarn, whose beliefs about social equality were not as far reaching as his own. Nevertheless, a few Americans, such as African American Walter White and white activist Florence Kelly, gave Du Bois much-needed support, and the Second Pan-African Congress also inspired several nationalist leaders, including Vietnamese revolutionary Ho Chi Minh, Indian revolutionary Shapuiji Saklaatvala, and Ghanaian journalist W. F. Hutchinson.

With its six demands to remedy the evils of the "Suppressed Races," the "London Manifesto" harks back to the People's Charter in England in 1838. The call for "absolute legal and social equality" with whites also echoes the egalitarian theme from the American Declaration of Independence. Du Bois's authorship is evident when, before its six central demands, the manifesto refers to the "evils of the colour line." Du Bois's first issue of *Crisis,* the NAACP magazine that he founded in 1910, included a section called "Along the Color Line," which addressed violence against African Americans. Although Du Bois denounced Garvey as a "demagogue," the manifesto contains some of the same sentiments as Garvey's "Declaration of Rights of the Negro People" (1920), a document stating that "we, the duly elected representatives of the

Key Facts

Time Period:
Early 20th Century

Movement/Issue:
Pan-Africanism;
Colonialism; Racism

Place of Publication:
England

**Language of
Publication:**
English

W. E. B. DU BOIS: CIVIL RIGHTS TRAILBLAZER

William Edward Burghardt (W.E.B.) Du Bois was born in Great Barrington, Massachusetts, in 1868 and went on to become the first African American to earn a doctorate from Harvard (1895). From there, he made a significant impact on civil rights, starting with his pioneering sociological study *The Philadelphia Negro* (1899), which concluded that a permanent underclass, a "submerged tenth," existed. In 1903, he began to advance a converse view that an intellectual elite—"The Talented Tenth"—was needed to lead African Americans to an improved status.

Studying as an undergraduate at Fisk University in the 1880s and teaching at Clark Atlanta University from 1897 to 1910 and in the 1930s, Du Bois was exposed to the plight of African Americans in the South. This helped to spur his push for immediate civil rights and his advocacy for a well-rounded education for African Americans. His ideas stood in contrast to those of Booker T. Washington, a southern African American educator who believed that blacks should pursue economic advancement through vocational and industrial education.

Du Bois was a key organizer of the National Association for the Advancement of Colored People (NAACP). He also wrote prose and poetry, including *The Souls of Black Folk* (1903), *The Quest of the Silver Fleece* (1911), and *Darkwater* (1920). After visiting the Soviet Union in the late 1920s, he openly became a socialist. Du Bois died in Ghana in 1963.

Negro peoples of the world, invoking the aid of the just and Almighty God, do declare all men, women and children of our blood throughout the world free denizens, and do claim them as free citizens of Africa."

In addition to the "Manifesto to the League of Nations," the "London Manifesto" inspired further dramatic demands for rights of people of color, especially as Du Bois continued to organize Pan-African congresses. The Third Pan-African Congress in Lisbon (1923) and the Fourth Congress in New York (1927) adopted similar resolutions. The Fifth Pan-African Congress (1945), which Du Bois attended at age seventy-seven, used even stronger language, stating, "We are unwilling to starve any longer while doing the world's drudgery, in order to support, by our poverty and ignorance, a false aristocracy and a discredited imperialism."

THEMES AND STYLE

The primary theme of the "London Manifesto" is that the world's colonial and industrial powers have, following World War I, reached a point where they must give all their peoples full political rights and economic opportunities. Some nations, the document states, have done better than others in this regard. France "has sought to place her cultured black citizens on a plane of absolute legal and social equality with her white, and given them representation in her highest legislature." Belgium, despite its history of slavery emanating from the Congo, "has but recently assumed responsibility for her colonies and has taken steps to lift them from the worst abuses of the autocratic regime; but … she has not confirmed to the people the possession of their land and labour." Spain and Portugal, the manifesto adds, "have never drawn a caste line against persons of culture who happen to be of Negro descent." On the other hand, the United States threw "the freed man on the world penniless and landless, educating them without thoroughness and system and subjecting them the while to lynching, lawlessness, discrimination, insult and slander, such as human beings have seldom endured and survived." The manifesto's harshest criticism is aimed at Britain, which has "systematically fostered ignorance among the Natives, has enslaved them, and is still enslaving them." Central to the manifesto are its six demands of the "Suppressed Races": (1) "the recognition of civilised men as civilised despite their race and colour"; (2) "local self-government"; (3) "education in self-knowledge, in scientific truth and in industrial technique undivorced from the art of beauty"; (4) "freedom in their own religion and customs"; (5) "co-operation with the rest of the world in government, industry and art on the basis of Justice, Freedom and Peace"; and (6) "the ancient common ownership of the Land and its natural fruits and defence against the unrestrained greed of invested capital."

Among its rhetorical strategies, the document draws from the American Declaration of Independence in its listing of grievances against governments that abuse their power. To build a consensus, Du Bois appeals to peoples of different faiths, including Muslims, Buddhists, and Christians. Unlike Garvey, Du Bois stresses that in order to make progress, races need to be unified, not separated. Du Bois writes, "This is a world of men,—of men whose likenesses far outweigh their differences; who mutually need each other in labour and thought and dream, but who can successfully have each other only on terms of equality, justice and mutual respect."

Despite his conciliatory tone toward some nations, Du Bois employs powerful, Marxist language to convey the need for social and economic justice, emphasizing the struggle between classes, between the haves and have-nots. For example, the manifesto calls for the correction of the "outrageously unjust distribution of the world income between the dominant and suppressed peoples." This language was, however, too radical for some of the attendees at the Congress, as well as for some of the European governments being addressed.

CRITICAL DISCUSSION

The "London Manifesto" was received well among those predisposed to follow Du Bois's views, and it also garnered positive reviews in some newspapers, such as the *London Times* and the *London Challenge*, which saw Du Bois as the embodiment of the "New Negro." However, others with their own ambitions or more moderate approaches did not view it favorably. Diagne and his fellow French West African leaders were unwilling to appear so critical of their government, although, as David Levering Lewis points out in *W.E.B. Du Bois: The Fight for Equality and the American Century, 1919-1963,* when one Francophone delegate spoke out, opposition to the manifesto in Paris wavered sufficiently for its passage. Du Bois himself theorized that animosities from World War I had not yet subsided; thus, the world was not ready for such calls for equality among races.

The "London Manifesto" not only inspired subsequent Pan-African congresses but also gave Du Bois more confidence to lead the movement from the United States, especially as Garvey fell from grace because of legal troubles and was deported from the United States. With Garvey's decline, Du Bois appealed to West Indians in particular for greater participation in his Pan-African movement. The "Manifesto to the League of Nations," which the "London Manifesto" immediately inspired, was ultimately accepted by the league with a pledge to establish a native affairs research section within the International Labor Organization (ILO) and to appoint someone of African descent to the league's mandates committee. As Lewis states, the ILO native affairs research section "eventually disappeared due to inattention," while "the Mandates Commission continued to be staffed exclusively by Europeans." Lewis concludes that "the London Resolutions ... comprised one of the earliest displays by educated men and women of African descent of the dramatic art of racial protest and liberation ... but [it was] a drama still much too far ahead of its time really to educate or alarm the critics."

More recently, Laura Winkiel, in *Modernism, Race, and Manifestos* (2008), places the manifesto in a tradition of documents intended to undermine the control of a master class. Examining the "London Manifesto" along with the English suffragettes' manifestos in the 1910s, Winkiel asserts that manifestos of this period became harbingers of modernism. They provided "the methodological focal point for demonstrating that modernist texts: (1) open the present moment to temporal reconceptualizations of history and historical agency" and "(2) stage alternative cosmopolitan and transnational communities through the structure of feeling of racial belonging."

BIBLIOGRAPHY

Sources

"'Declaration of the Rights of the Negro Peoples of the World': The Principles of the Universal Negro

Portrait of W.E.B. Du Bois by Laura Wheeler Waring. Du Bois wrote "Declaration to the World" as a result of the Second Pan-African Congress. NATIONAL PORTRAIT GALLERY, SMITHSONIAN INSTITUTION/ART RESOURCE, NY

Improvement Association." *History Matters: The U.S. Survey Course on the Web.* American Social History Productions. Web. 30 July 2012.

Du Bois, W.E.B. "My Evolving Plan for Negro Freedom." *What the Negro Wants.* Ed. Rayford W. Logan. Chapel Hill: U of North Carolina P, 1944. Print.

———. *Dusk of Dawn: An Essay toward an Autobiography of a Race Concept.* New York: Schocken, 1968. Print.

Lewis, David Levering. *W.E.B. Du Bois: The Fight for Equality and the American Century, 1919-1963.* New York: Holt, 2000. Print.

Pan-African Congress 1921. "London Manifesto." *Cengage College History Primary Sources.* Cengage Learning Web Site. Web. 20 July 2012.

Winkiel, Laura. *Modernism, Race and Manifestos.* New York: Cambridge UP, 2008. Print.

Further Reading

Edwards, Brent Hayes. "The Uses of Diaspora." *Social Text* 19. 1 (2001): 50. Print.

Guterl, Matthew Pratt. "The New Race Consciousness: Race, Nation, and Empire in American Culture, 1910-1925." *Journal of World History* 10.2 (1999): 345-47. Print.

Ogot, Bethwell A. "Rereading the History and Historiography of Epistemic Domination and Resistance in Africa." *African Studies Review* 52.1 (2009): 13. Print.

Wesley Borucki

THE LEGACY OF THE ANCESTRAL ARTS

Alain Locke

✥ *Key Facts*

Time Period:
Early 20th Century

Movement/Issue:
Harlem Renaissance;
African American rights;
Aesthetics

Place of Publication:
United States

**Language of
Publication:**
English

OVERVIEW

Alain Locke's "The Legacy of the Ancestral Arts," published in 1925, signaled a paradigm shift in thinking about African American culture and artistic production. It originally appeared in *The New Negro,* a groundbreaking compilation of essays, fiction, poetry, art, and music that included contributions from nearly every prominent member of the Harlem, or "New Negro," Renaissance. As the editor of *The New Negro,* Locke provided the volume's overarching vision and goals, and "The Legacy of the Ancestral Arts" served as an important philosophical foundation for the whole project. This piece engaged both the racial struggles of the time and the various movements associated with modernism.

In "The Legacy of the Ancestral Arts," one of four essays he contributed to *The New Negro,* Locke redefined the relationship between African art and the art and culture of African Americans, and, while not everyone agreed with Locke, there was no debating that his interpretation was unique. First, Locke used his essay to reject racist beliefs about African Americans as inherently "primitive" or "savage" based on their ancestral origins in Africa. Second, he stirred debate among some in the African American community who claimed an intellectual lineage from Western Europe by asserting the value and distinction of their African heritage. Third, he signaled his and, by association, the New Negro's allegiance to the modernist movements sweeping Europe, an aesthetic argument that went against the political goals of many in the African American elite. Locke's bold reinterpretation worked within *The New Negro* to announce the arrival of a new way of thinking about African American culture that resonated throughout the twentieth century and endures today.

HISTORICAL AND LITERARY CONTEXT

With "The Legacy of the Ancestral Arts," Locke sought to reconcile two issues: the belief in African Americans' primitiveness and the potency of the period's Pan-African political movements. These issues had garnered heightened attention as European nations engaged in "the scramble for Africa," the effort in the late nineteenth and early twentieth centuries to expand imperial power through the exploitative colonization of Africa. Locke aimed to reject racist suppositions that arose during the period while developing a reinterpretation of African heritage. In 1925, the Harlem Renaissance was in full swing, and *The New Negro* suggested a cohesiveness that was in reality, complicated by debates within the black community about its political goals and the purpose of African American art. As a volume, *The New Negro* emphasized the Harlem Renaissance as a vibrant artistic movement, and essays such as "The Legacy of the Ancestral Arts" noted that the movement included a theoretical base. Thus, Locke's essay functioned as more than an intellectual exercise because it used sophisticated arguments to advance an understanding of African American art that undermined racist assumptions.

Urban migration, an economic boom, and the First World War's legacy of disillusionment contributed to a period marked by racial violence in the United States—lynching and riots abounded—and, paradoxically, a flourishing of art, philosophy, and activism in the African American community. This outpouring of African American cultural production invigorated the black elite and inspired an enthusiastic audience among whites who were either seeking art or exciting provocations of their racist conceptions of black life. Locke, the country's first African-American Rhodes scholar, who held a doctorate in philosophy from Harvard University, found a deep purpose in the Harlem Renaissance. He proclaimed himself a mentor, a parental figure, and the intellectual heart of the movement—a contentious position he shared with James Weldon Johnson, Jessie Redmon Fauset, and W.E.B. Du Bois. Debate among this elite included arguments about the appropriate way to depict African Americans in art and literature. These arguments have made defining the Renaissance challenging, but they also contributed to its fascinating legacy.

"The Legacy of the Ancestral Arts" works like other essays that assert the value of black culture and reject racist beliefs. It aligns even more strongly, however, with the various manifestos of modernism, such as F.T. Marinetti's "Futurist Manifesto" or Mina Loy's (then unpublished) "Feminist Manifesto." Modernist manifestos were usually brash, iconoclastic declarations of the principles of the new art and its ideals. Like all manifestos, Locke's has a political component, but, like other modernist manifestos, it primarily focuses on invigorating art. The essay also establishes the boundaries of the movement it champions—much like the manifestos of Marinetti, Wyndham Lewis, and others—and asserts the importance of the movement's perspective. Just as the Vorticists aimed to blast that which restrains the artist, so Locke argues that the New Negroes must throw off the shackles of oppression that limit their artistic development.

"The Legacy of the Ancestral Arts," along with *The New Negro*, provided a source for understanding the importance and value of the Harlem Renaissance. African-American artists and thinkers found themselves represented as a legitimate movement rather than a cluster of individual strivers. Despite continued debates, the impact of this group identity and sense of shared endeavor cannot be overstated. Today, *The New Negro* continues to receive much scholarly attention. "The Legacy of the Ancestral Arts" has also proven a focus of rich critical discussion because of its intellectual connection to other modernist movements and its importance to subsequent debates about the interconnections between Africa and African Americans.

THEMES AND STYLE

The primary theme of "The Legacy of the Ancestral Arts" distinguishes the art of Africa from the art of African Americans, rejecting any essential similarity between them. According to Locke, "the characteristic African art expressions are rigid, controlled, disciplined, abstract, heavily conventionalized." He includes several Images of African sculptures and masks to illustrate the formality and rigidity of African art. African American art, in contrast, is "free, exuberant, emotional, sentimental, and human." Locke contends that African Americans inherited a "deep-seated aesthetic endowment" from their African heritage but that African Americans' artistic expression is otherwise completely different due to their "peculiar experience in America and the emotional upheaval of [their] trials and ordeals." With this rhetorical position, Locke stages a sophisticated argument that works on many levels to reject prevailing beliefs and establish an opposing position.

By differentiating between African and African-American art, "The Legacy of the Ancestral Arts" achieves two effects. First, it belies racist arguments that African Americans are "primitives" or "savages," as their African ancestors were widely believed to be, Africa serving at the time as a metaphor in American culture for exoticism and sensuality as well as savagery and primitivism. This argument insists on the sophistication and uniqueness of African-American culture. Second, it establishes African art as a feature of classical cultures on a par with ancient Greece and Rome. Locke thus argues that the African American should no longer be burdened by a "sense of cultural indebtedness" to European cultures and should realize that he is not a "cultural foundling without his own inheritance." Locke, referring to many great European

EXPANDING INFLUENCE: LOCKE ON ART AND POLITICS

Alain Locke's "The Legacy of the Ancestral Arts" (1925) helped to establish him as the ideological leader of the New Negro Movement and provided the foundation for a number of influential ideas regarding art and identity. In "Art or Propaganda?" (1928), he expands on the notion that African American art should focus on the authenticity of its aesthetic appeal rather than on making overtly political statements. Published as an introductory essay for the new journal *Harlem: A Forum of Negro Life*, "Art or Propaganda?" rejects the thinking of W.E.B. Du Bois and other black leaders who argued for a politicized African American art. Locke asserts that a beautiful and imaginative work, even one devoid of political content, has a far greater appeal to the general public and is ultimately a more effective tool in the fight for acceptance and equality. Although this proposition put him at odds with Du Bois and his followers, Locke's ideas proved enormously influential, inspiring African American artists and writers, including Zora Neale Hurston and Langston Hughes, to create some of the most powerful and enduring works of the twentieth century.

and American artists who value African art, emphasizes how modernist artists in Europe and the United States, perceiving that the Western world is decadent or decaying, have drawn inspiration from African art. He calls on African Americans to find an even deeper engagement with African art: "(I)f African art is capable of producing the ferment in modern art that it has, surely this is not too much to expect of its influence upon the culturally awakened Negro artist of the present generation." Locke reframes the discussion so that African art is seen as an ancient triumph, a shift in perception that he hopes will inspire young African Americans to create a true artistic movement for themselves and the world.

Even though "The Legacy of the Ancestral Arts" serves as an artistic manifesto, it avoids the fiery rhetoric of other modernist manifestos such as those of the Futurist and the Vorticist movements. Typically, modernist manifestos emphasize the newness, youth, and vigor of their aesthetic projects, and they do so by trumpeting their virtues and aggressively tearing down their predecessors. Locke presents his manifesto, in contrast, as the thoughtful, methodical argument of the philosopher and aesthetic theorist. This style and tone clearly fit his background as an academic; it also hints at the pressure Locke and other African American intellectuals felt to present themselves as reasoning humans capable of logic and the cultivation of aesthetic ideals, pressures exerted by the deep institutional racism in the United States during that time. Locke's manifesto does double duty, not only in terms of its theme but also in its rhetorical style.

A Nagaady-A-Mwaash mask from Zaire. Philosopher Alain Locke urged African American artists to make art expressive of their own experience. DETROIT INSTITUTE OF ARTS/THE BRIDGEMAN ART LIBRARY

CRITICAL DISCUSSION

Critics did not review "The Legacy of the Ancestral Arts" at the time of its publication, instead focusing on *The New Negro*. With his piece, Locke indicated his affiliation with the Pan-African movements that sought to rally peoples of African descent in a global cause. Locke's emphasis on aesthetics, however, remained a source of debate between Locke and Du Bois, the Harlem Renaissance's most influential thinker. Du Bois favored politics within art, and he clashed with Locke on this essential issue. Nevertheless, *The New Negro* featured an array of styles and opinions, providing space for Locke's opinion as well as the viewpoints of Du Bois and others.

Since its publication, "The Legacy of the Ancestral Arts" has been viewed as a significant defense of African American art and its connections to an African lineage. As Michael Harris observes, Locke's "call for African-American artists to look to African art for inspiration, although much debated, laid a foundation for a more significant subjectification of blacks: a visualization of self as part of a cultural, historical continuum." In sum, Locke's essay informed others interested in the cultural heritage of Africa, including participants in the Black Arts Movement and the "Back to Africa" activists of the 1960s and '70s as well as the creators of later postmodern, hybrid works of visual art, sculpture, and literature (see Harris). This interest in Africa's cultural legacy can be seen in literary works by Audre Lorde, Amiri Baraka, Toni Morrison, Alice Walker, and others.

Locke's important argument has not saved his essay from continued debate, especially philosophical debates that arose during the 1920s and afterward on aesthetics, pluralism, and cultural relativism. Wahneema Lubiano reads Locke as favoring African art over African American art. She calls his argument "a cute move for the time," even as she emphasizes her and others' essential disagreement with his view. More recently, scholars have sought to rescue Locke's work from relative obscurity. Mary Ann Calo argues that Locke was an under-recognized critic of visual art, who "sought to historicize, analyze, and classify African American art and to position it in relation to both black experience and mainstream American culture." Eric King Watts emphasizes the political relevance of Locke's work on *The New Negro* based on its vision of creating an African-American *ethos* in which pragmatism grounds ideals: "Locke's point is that a New Negro *ethos* should inhabit a place of antiquity, making black cultural expression both Old and New." Such scholars, even those who disagree with Locke's argument, acknowledge his importance in drawing attention to the nature of Africa's legacy for African Americans.

BIBLIOGRAPHY

Sources

Calo, Mary Ann. "Alain Locke and American Art Criticism." *American Art* 18.1 (2004): 88-97. Print.

Harris, Michael D. "From Double Consciousness to Double Vision: the Africentric Artist." *African Arts* 27.2 (1994): 44-53. Print.

Locke, Alain. "The Legacy of the Ancestral Arts." *The New Negro: Voices of the Harlem Renaissance*. Ed. Alain Locke. New York: Atheneum, 1992. 254-67. Print.

Lubiano, Wahneema H. "Mapping the Interstices between Afro-American Cultural Discourse and Cultural Studies: A Prolegomenon." *Callaloo* 19.1 (1996): 68-77. *JSTOR*. Web. 7 Aug. 2012.

Watts, Eric King. "African American Ethos and Hermeneutical Rhetoric: An Exploration of Alain Locke's *The New Negro*." *Quarterly Journal of Speech* 88.1 (2002): 19-32. Print.

Further Reading

Caws, Mary Ann. *Manifesto: A Century of Isms*. Lincoln: U of Nebraska P, 2001. Print.

Charles, John C. "What Was Africa to Him? Alain Locke, Cultural Nationalism, and the Rhetoric of Empire during the New Negro Renaissance." Ed. Australia Tarver and Paula C. Barnes. *New Voices on the Harlem Renaissance: Essays on Race, Gender, and Literary Discourse.* Madison: Fairleigh Dickinson UP, 2006. 33-58. Print.

Gikandi, Simon. "Africa and the Idea of the Aesthetic: From Eurocentrism to Pan-Africanism." *English Studies in Africa* 43.2 (2000): 19-46. Print.

Harris, Leonard, and Charles Molesworth. *Alain L. Locke: Biography of a Philosopher.* Chicago: U of Chicago P, 2008. Print.

Locke, Alain. "Art or Propaganda?" *The Making of African American Identity: Vol. III, 1917-1968.* National Humanities Center, 2007. Web. 29 July 2012.

————. *The Philosophy of Alain Locke: Harlem Renaissance and Beyond.* Ed. Leonard Harris. Philadelphia: Temple UP, 1989. Print.

————. *The Works of Alain Locke.* Ed. Charles Molesworth. Oxford: Oxford UP, 2012. Print.

Lyon, Janet. *Manifestoes: Provocations of the Modern.* Ithaca: Cornell UP, 1999. Print.

Rampersad, Arnold. Introduction. *The New Negro: Voices of the Harlem Renaissance.* Ed. Alain Locke. New York: Atheneum, 1992. ix–xxiii. Print.

Wright, Louis E. "Alain Locke on Race Relations: Some Political Implications of His Thought." *Journal of Black Studies* 42.4 (2011): 665-89. Print.

Sarah Stoeckl

THE NEGRO ARTIST AND THE RACIAL MOUNTAIN

Langston Hughes

❖ *Key Facts*

Time Period:
Early/Mid-20th Century

Movement/Issue:
Aesthetics; Black
nationalism; Harlem
Renaissance

Place of Publication:
United States

**Language of
Publication:**
English

OVERVIEW

"The Negro Artist and the Racial Mountain," an essay written by Langston Hughes for the American journal the *Nation* in 1926, served as a catalyst for African American artists and writers of the Harlem Renaissance (1918-37) to explore their own cultural roots as inspiration for their craft. In his essay, Hughes criticizes black artists who strive to emulate white standards in order to be accepted by popular culture. He champions black cultural forms such as blues, jazz, and spirituals as being equally as worthy in terms of artistic inspiration as white or Nordic poetic forms. "The Negro Artist and the Racial Mountain" became a manifesto for black authors of the Harlem Renaissance, encouraging them to write from their own experience and history rather than try to assimilate and write for mainstream white audiences.

Hughes had already received mixed reviews for his collection of poetry *The Weary Blues* (1926), but "The Negro Artist and the Racial Mountain" polarized the African American community. On the one hand, there were those who felt that art should not be defined in terms of race and, on the other, those who felt that the African American collective cultural experience and struggle for equality did define their art. As a representative of the first group, African American poet Countee Cullen chose to write in the established, traditional forms. Cullen is generally considered the young Negro poet that Hughes, representing the second group, speaks of in the first sentence of his essay: the one who wants to be a "poet—not a Negro poet" and who wants to "write like a white poet." Cullen wrote sonnets, translated Greek poetry, and followed the established rules of poetic craft that Hughes considered a betrayal of the African American racial identity. Hughes's essay paved the way for the black arts movement of the 1960s and early 1970s and black pride politics by embracing rather than refuting the collective heritage of African Americans. Hughes sought the development of a black aesthetic by using racial art to promote social change.

HISTORICAL AND LITERARY CONTEXT

"The Negro Artist and the Racial Mountain" directly addresses the faction of African Americans who attempted to hide their blackness and assimilate into white, Nordic culture. Hughes believed that many middle-class African Americans were embarrassed by their blackness and ashamed of being related to the people of their own race, whom he calls "low-down folks" in his essay. Additionally, he felt that African American writers and the black middle class as a whole should embrace their cultural background, accept their African heritage, and express these experiences in their own way, including musical forms such as the blues, jazz, and spirituals, as well as the black vernacular.

Hughes's "The Negro Artist and the Racial Mountain" was published in the middle of the Harlem Renaissance, which was an artistic awakening that began in the black middle-class neighborhood of Harlem, New York. Originally named the New Negro movement after an African American literary anthology of the same name, the Harlem Renaissance centered upon several African American publications such as *Crisis* and *Opportunity*, which employed and published black writers. The writing in these publications appealed to both black and white audiences, and many Harlem Renaissance writers wishing to have their work picked up by mainstream publishing houses adjusted their standards in an attempt to meet white audiences' expectations. Hughes saw this tendency of some black writers to follow traditional white models as an affront to black culture and responded with "The Negro Artist and the Racial Mountain."

Hughes's work was a direct response to George Schuyler's "The Negro-Art Hokum," which appeared in the *Nation* a week earlier and claimed that there was no such thing as true African American art, merely black artists mimicking white culture. Schuyler, a conservative African American author, claims, "As for the literature, painting, and sculpture of Aframericans … it is identical in kind with the literature, painting, and sculpture of white Americans: that is, it shows more or less evidence of European influence. In the field of drama little of any merit has been written by and about Negroes that could not have been written by whites." In contrast, Hughes believes that "An artist must be free to choose what he does, certainly, but he must also never be afraid to do what he might choose.... We younger Negro artists who create now intend to express our individual dark-skinned selves without fear or shame."

Other writers who expressed similar sentiments to Hughes include Zora Neale Hurston, Claude McKay, and Jean Toomer. Toomer's experimental novel *Cane* (1923) explores the oftentimes gritty world of the "low-down folks" and is mentioned in Hughes's essay as "the finest prose written by a Negro in America ... it is truly racial." In Hurston's novel *Their Eyes Were Watching God*, heroine Janie Mae finds solace and freedom through embracing her heritage, flaws and all, among the "low-down folks."

THEMES AND STYLE

The central theme of "The Negro Artist and the Racial Mountain" is that African American artists and writers should embrace their cultural heritage and write from their own experience rather than tailor their works to fit white standards or please white audiences. Hughes further explains that the approval of white audiences is not needed to validate African American art: "If the white people are pleased, we are glad. If they are not, it doesn't matter. We know we are beautiful." Hughes encourages African Americans to write about their own experiences from a personal perspective that includes the history, language, and traditions of their own culture rather than an idealized version of what other people perceive black culture to be.

Hughes presents his essay from a first-person point of view with a friendly tone, as if he is sharing information with the reader in confidence. He uses multiple allusions to his contemporaries—by name when he is praising them and anonymously when he is not. Though the young negro poet wishing to be white is never mentioned by name, he is commonly accepted to be Cullen, one of Hughes's contemporaries. By not criticizing his subjects by name, Hughes sought to bring the African American writing community together to pursue the common goal of a black aesthetic. He offers words of encouragement: "Certainly there is for the American Negro artist ... a great field of unused material ready for his art. Without going outside his race ... there is sufficient material to furnish a black artist with a lifetime of creative work."

As in his earlier work *The Weary Blues*, Hughes uses the rhythmic nature of blues, jazz, and spirituals to enhance his writing. Walter C. Farrell, Jr. and Patricia A. Johnson, in their article "How Langston Hughes Used the Blues," state:

> Hughes became one of the most innovative voices in American poetry, and the first poet in the world to transform the idioms of blues and jazz into poetic verse. He himself was demonstrating what he had called for in 'The Negro Artist and The Racial Mountain'....

HUGHES'S BIOGRAPHY

James Mercer Langston Hughes was born in Joplin, Missouri, on February 1, 1902, to Carrie Mercer Langston and James Nathaniel Hughes. Both sides of his family were of mixed race and included African American, Native American, and European American ancestry. Hughes's parents divorced when he was young, and he lived with his maternal grandmother in Lawrence, Kansas. From a young age, he was raised to be proud of his African American heritage, and he expressed this sentiment throughout his writing career. In the early 1920s Hughes attended Columbia University in New York City, which placed him near Harlem, New York, an area that he would champion throughout his works. He later graduated from Lincoln University in Pennsylvania but lived in Harlem for most of his adult life.

Hughes served as a major voice throughout the Harlem Renaissance. His poems and short stories provide a vivid depiction of the black experience in the United States. He incorporated his beliefs in the validity of African American culture into his own works throughout his life. He published more than fifty books, including poetry collections, short stories, plays, novels, and children's books. Hughes died on May 22, 1967, following surgery for prostate cancer.

Hughes suggested that creative individualism should be the guiding aesthetic value for the black artist.

In "The Negro Artist and the Racial Mountain," Hughes mentions the blues and jazz greats by name: Paul Robeson, Bessie Smith, and Clara Smith. He also employs the beat of the tom-tom as a rallying cry for artists to embrace their cultural heritage: "But Jazz to me is one of the inherent expressions of Negro life in America: the eternal tom-tom beating in the Negro soul—the tom-tom of revolt against weariness in a white world. ...the tom-tom of joy and laughter, and pain swallowed in a smile."

CRITICAL DISCUSSION

As mentioned above, Hughes's "The Negro Artist and the Racial Mountain" polarized the African American art community into two camps: those who felt art should be devoid of race and those who felt that all art should have a racial element. In the introduction to an anthology of Hughes's work, Christopher C. De Santis comments:

> At stake in the essay was no less than the very existence of a distinct African American aesthetic, an art originating in the confluence of African folk culture and the black experience of the Middle Passage, slavery, Reconstruction, and the long era of segregation.... Hughes challenged black artists and writers to embrace

Two prominent African American writers: Alice Walker with a replica of a Langston Hughes commemorative stamp following a 2002 news conference in Lawrence, Kansas. AP PHOTO/ORLIN WAGNER

a racial aesthetic and a source of creativity generated from within the black communities of the United States rather than from without.

Taking an opposite viewpoint, Schuyler felt that a writer's work should stand alone as the sole element for critique. In his essay "Harlem Renaissance," William R. Nash states that "Schuyler argues that aside 'from his color, which ranges from very dark brown to pink, your American Negro is just plain American.' For artists this assertion assumes a uniformity of work based on commonality of influence; in Schuyler's view, black artists cannot vary substantially from their white peers." In contrast, Hughes believed that the unique nature of the African American experience called for racial pride, which should be reflected in the writer's work. Nash describes Hughes's work thusly:

> In addition to producing one of the seminal aesthetic position papers of the period, Hughes also wrote poetry that embodied the values he articulated in 'The Negro Artist and the Racial Mountain.' Working with the idioms of jazz and blues and taking the mundane actions of the folk as subject matter, Hughes bridged the gap between vernacular culture and the realm of high art.

Following the Harlem Renaissance, artists within the black arts movement built upon Hughes's concept of racial pride and the creation of art and writing from the African American experience. The black arts movement, founded by writer Amiri Baraka in the wake of African American leader Malcolm X's assassination, urged African American writers to start their own publishing houses and write about the urban black experience from their own perspectives. Writers involved in the movement included Maya Angelou, Nikki Giovanni, and Sonia Sanchez. In *A Langston Hughes Encyclopedia,* Hans Ostrom explains Hughes's influence: "Although the Black Aesthetic movement did not explicitly embrace Hughes' writing as a source of inspiration, the movement's ideas echo many of Hughes' and specifically fulfill aspirations for African American literature that he expressed in 'The Negro Artist and the Racial Mountain.'"

BIBLIOGRAPHY

Sources

Farrell, Walter C., Jr. and Johnson, Patricia A. "How Langston Hughes Used the Blues." *MELUS* Spring 1979: 55-63. Web. 8 July 2012.

Hughes, Langston. "The Negro Artist and the Racial Mountain." *Nation* 23 June 1926: 692-94. Print.

———. *Essays on Art, Race, Politics, and World Affairs.* Ed. Christopher C. De Santis. Columbia: U of Missouri P, 2002. 3-4. Print.

Nash, William R. "Harlem Renaissance." *The Oxford Encyclopedia of American Literature.* Ed. Jay Parini. New York: Oxford UP, 2004. 153-59. Print.

Ostrom, Hans. *A Langston Hughes Encyclopedia.* Westport: Greenwood, 2002. Print.

Schuyler, George. "The Negro-Art Hokum." *Nation* 16 June 1926: 662-63. Print.

Further Reading

Hughes, Langston. *Good Morning Revolution: Uncollected Writings of Social Protest.* New York: Citadel, 1992. Print.

Langston Hughes: The Contemporary Reviews. Ed. Tish Dace and M. Thomas Inge. Cambridge: Cambridge UP, 2009. Print.

Montage of a Dream: The Art and Life of Langston Hughes. Ed. Cheryl R. Ragar and John Edgar Tidwell. Columbia: U of Missouri P, 2007. Print.

Rampersad, Arnold. *The Life of Langston Hughes, Vol. I 1902-1941: I, Too, Sing America.* New York: Oxford UP, 2002. Print.

West, Sandra L. *Encyclopedia of the Harlem Renaissance.* New York: Facts On File, 2003. Print.

Ron Horton

THE SOULS OF BLACK FOLK

W. E. B. Du Bois

OVERVIEW

Composed by sociologist W.E.B. Du Bois, *The Souls of Black Folk* (1903) is widely viewed as one of the most vital and enduring works on the African American experience. Du Bois wrote at a time of deep racial divide and tension in the United States, particularly in the South, where institutionalized segregation and racism still plagued African Americans despite their legal emancipation. Through the works' various essays, autobiographical writings, and even short fiction, Du Bois makes a personal and sociological argument for race as the preeminent American problem at the dawn of the twentieth century. Central to this argument is the concept of the "veil," which Du Bois introduces in the book's opening essay, "Of Our Spiritual Strivings." This "veil" creates for African Americans the "sense of always looking at one's self through the eyes of others, of measuring one's soul by the tape of a world that looks on in amused contempt and pity."

Widely hailed as a classic even by Du Bois's contemporaries, *The Souls of Black Folk* provided a powerful and enduring account of the separation between blacks and whites in the United States. The argument set forth in "Of Our Spiritual Strivings" and extended through the rest of the book gave voice to the conflicted and difficult experience of black Americans. The legacy of Du Bois's text can be seen in a broad range of later literary and sociological writings on race. *The Souls of Black Folk* also helped to catalyze the long, ongoing struggle for African American civil rights and equality. In the century since its publication, *The Souls of Black Folk* has since been enshrined as a seminal work of African American literature. "Of Our Spiritual Strivings" is considered a powerful précis of the text's larger argument.

HISTORICAL AND LITERARY CONTEXT

Like the other essays in *The Souls of Black Folk,* "Of Our Spiritual Strivings" responds to the long-standing racist oppression and dehumanization of blacks in the United States. Although the Emancipation Proclamation (1863), the Union's victory in the Civil War (1865), and the Thirteenth Amendment (1865) had brought an official end to slavery in the United States, African Americans remained in a state of persecution, subjugation, and exploitation at the beginning of the twentieth century. In the South, their position

was particularly grim. Jim Crow law institutionalized segregation, discrimination, and disenfranchisement. Lynchings and other forms of violence were not suppressed and were used to intimidate blacks. Though conditions were better in the North, blacks there were ghettoized and discriminated against. The cruel treatment of blacks in the United States that had been in existence for centuries was justified by pseudoscience that deemed blacks biologically inferior and therefore subhuman.

When "Of Our Spiritual Strivings" was first published, in *Atlantic Monthly* as "Strivings of the Negro People" (1897), the leading African American response to racial oppression was that of influential educator Booker T. Washington, who made limited demands for access to technical education and economic opportunity. Du Bois considered Washington an accommodationist to white rule. Du Bois advocated for an uncompromising campaign that would achieve not only equal opportunity and full civil rights in all political, social, educational, and economic aspects but also the recognition of the humanity of blacks. When he began to assemble, edit, and compose the essays that would make up the *The Souls of Black Folk* in 1902, Du Bois was largely motivated to offer a vision of African American liberation that would counteract Washington's philosophy of accommodation.

"Of Our Spiritual Strivings" draws on a rich history of African American writing on the divide between blacks and whites in the United States that can be traced back to civil rights leader Frederick Douglass's "The Color Line." Published in 1881, Douglass's essay employs the metaphor of "the color line" to describe the ongoing racial divide in the United States after the end of slavery. "Slavery, stupidity, servility, poverty, dependence, are undesirable conditions," Douglass writes. "When these shall cease to be coupled with color, there will be no color line drawn." Throughout *The Souls of Black Folk,* Du Bois declares, "The problem of the twentieth century is the problem of the color line." In "Of Our Spiritual Strivings," the metaphor of the "veil," describing the black experience of American culture, extends and alters Douglass's idea of a "color line."

In the century following its publication, "Of Our Spiritual Strivings," along with the other essays in *The*

÷ *Key Facts*

Time Period:
Early 20th Century

Movement/Issue:
Civil Rights Movement;
Anti-accommodationism

Place of Publication:
United States

Language of Publication:
English

PRIMARY SOURCE

THE SOULS OF BLACK FOLK

BETWEEN ME and the other world there is ever an unasked question: unasked by some through feelings of delicacy; by others through the difficulty of rightly framing it. All, nevertheless, flutter round it. They approach me in a half-hesitant sort of way, eye me curiously or compassionately, and then, instead of saying directly, How does it feel to be a problem? they say, I know an excellent colored man in my town; or, I fought at Mechanicsville; or, Do not these Southern outrages make your blood boil? At these I smile, or am interested, or reduce the boiling to a simmer, as the occasion may require. To the real question, How does it feel to be a problem? I answer seldom a word.

And yet, being a problem is a strange experience,—peculiar even for one who has never been anything else, save perhaps in babyhood and in Europe. It is in the early days of rollicking boyhood that the revelation first bursts upon one, all in a day, as it were. I remember well when the shadow swept across me. I was a little thing, away up in the hills of New England, where the dark Housatonic winds between Hoosac and Taghkanic to the sea. In a wee wooden schoolhouse, something put it into the boys' and girls' heads to buy gorgeous visiting-cards—ten cents a package—and exchange. The exchange was merry, till one girl, a tall newcomer, refused my card, —refused it peremptorily, with a glance. Then it dawned upon me with a certain suddenness that I was different from the others; or like, mayhap, in heart and life and longing, but shut out from their world by a vast veil. I had thereafter no desire to tear down that veil, to creep through; I held all beyond it in common contempt, and lived above it in a region of blue sky and great wandering shadows. That sky was bluest when I could beat my mates at examination-time, or beat them at a foot-race, or even beat their stringy heads. Alas, with the years all this fine contempt began to fade; for the words I longed for, and all their dazzling opportunities, were theirs, not mine. But they should not keep these prizes, I said; some, all, I would wrest from them. Just how I would do it I could never decide: by reading law, by healing the sick, by telling the wonderful tales that swam in my head, —some way. With other black boys the strife was not so fiercely sunny: their youth shrunk into tasteless sycophancy, or into silent hatred of the pale world about them and mocking distrust of everything white; or wasted itself in a bitter cry, Why did God make me an outcast and a stranger in mine own house? The shades of the prison-house closed round about us all: walls strait and stubborn to the whitest, but relentlessly narrow, tall, and unscalable to sons of night who must plod darkly on in resignation, or beat unavailing palms against the stone, or steadily, half hopelessly, watch the streak of blue above.

SOURCE: A.C. McClurg & Sons/Cambridge University Press, 1903.

Souls of Black Folk, helped launch Du Bois's prolific and wide-ranging writing career and inspired many other African American writers. Over the next sixty years of his life, Du Bois wrote some twenty books of fiction and nonfiction that explored the black experience not only in North America but also in Africa. The influence of "Of Our Spiritual Strivings" and the metaphor of the veil can be felt far beyond the bounds of Du Bois's oeuvre. Ralph Ellison's novel *Invisible Man* (1952), for example, furthered Du Bois's interrogation of African American alienation and identity. In the twenty-first century, "Of Our Spiritual Strivings" commands significant scholarly interest for its profound influence not only on twentieth-century African American literature but also on history itself.

THEMES AND STYLE

The central theme of "Of Our Spiritual Strivings" is that racial discrimination against blacks is the "vastest social problem" in the United States, for it has not only tormented African Americans but also sown discord throughout the nation. Like each chapter of *The Souls of Black Folk,* "Of Our Spiritual Strivings" is preceded by a passage from a "Sorrow Song," a hymn that expresses the unrest and longing of enslaved black Americans. The hymn quoted before "Of Our Spiritual Strivings" is "Nobody Knows the Trouble I've Seen." Du Bois then begins the chapter itself by introducing a question: "How does it feel to be a problem?" This is the question, he argues, that implicitly confronts African Americans throughout their lives and makes them social outcasts in their own country. He answers this question through the rest of the chapter, describing the pervasive alienation of blacks, tracing this feeling's origin, and outlining its effect on American culture at large.

"Of Our Spiritual Strivings" achieves its rhetorical effect through its appeals to all people in the United States to acknowledge the humanity of blacks. This appeal is made in the first person, a point of view that imbues Du Bois's argument with authority while evoking sympathy. He introduces his conception of racial alienation with an anecdote from his own life that begins, "I was a little thing …" In this way, he grounds his argument in the specifics of experience. He quickly moves, however, to a more general, historical argument about the difficulty of black experience. "The history of the American Negro is the history of this strife," he writes, then offers a succinct version of this history. From this history, Du Bois offers an idealized vision of the future, a vision not only of liberty and equality but also of civic responsibility and engagement.

Stylistically, "Of Our Spiritual Strivings" is distinguished by its lyricism. Rather than the staid objectivity of academic or polemical prose, Du Bois's language is rich in imagery and metaphor. The essay revolves around the metaphor of the "veil," which Du Bois employs to suggest blacks' double consciousness and their estrangement from a white United States, which both alienates blacks and provides them with a unique perspective. The use of metaphor allows Du Bois to evoke not only the fact but also the feeling of the African American experience. The evocation of emotion is furthered by the use of lyrical language throughout the essay. Du Bois's personal experience is described with vivid imagery in phrases such as "the hills of New England, where the dark Housatonic winds between Hoosac and Taghkanic to the sea." Later, contemporary black strife is described in lyric metaphor: "storm and stress to-day rocks our little boat on the mad waters of the world sea." The result is a text that imbues its sociological argument with a powerful emotional tenor.

CRITICAL DISCUSSION

When "Of Our Spiritual Strivings" appeared in *Atlantic Monthly,* its brilliance was immediately recognized, and its importance was widely acknowledged. The scholar Edward J. Blum writes in *W.E.B. Du Bois: American Prophet* (2007) that "America's cultural landscape was rocked by *The Souls of Black Folk*" and cites a range of the contemporary response that illustrates the book's impact. For example, a *Nation* review called *The Souls of Black Folk* "a profoundly interesting and affecting book, remarkable as a piece of literature." In the *South Atlantic Quarterly,* historian John Spencer Bassett, who founded the journal, used the book's erudition and ornate style to illustrate the absurdity of arguments that blacks were subhuman and soulless "beasts." Prominent contemporary intellectuals such as the novelist Henry James and the sociologist Max Weber also expressed their admiration of Du Bois's argument.

In the century since its publication, the argument made in "Of Our Spiritual Strivings" has remained relevant and influential. As Henry Louis Gates Jr. notes in "The Black Letters on the Sign," an essay included in the Oxford University Press edition of *The Souls of Black Folk,* "Du Bois's metaphor of double consciousness came to have a life of its own." The notion of fragmented identity was explored so thoroughly in the ensuing decades, Gates stresses, that it eventually was "no longer seen as a problem, but as a solution—a solution to the confines of identity itself." This solution to Du Bois's problem can be evidenced in everything from jazz to hip-hop.

Much scholarship has focused on the role of "Of Our Spiritual Strivings" in shaping African American identity in the twentieth century. In his 2009 biography of Du Bois, the scholar David Levering Lewis argues that the idea of double consciousness responded to the contemporary dialectic between separatism and assimilation "by affirming it in a permanent tension. Henceforth, the destiny of the race could be conceived as leading neither to assimilation nor separatism but to proud, enduring hyphenation. It was a revolutionary conception." Commentators have also drawn attention to the theological aspects of Du Bois's argument. Blum comments, "Read in dialogue with the religious battle over the sacred status of blacks and whites, *Souls* stood as a spectacular

intervention, an act of religious defiance and theological creation at the very same moment."

BIBLIOGRAPHY

Sources

Blum, Edward J., and Jason R. Young, eds. *The Souls of W.E.B. Du Bois: New Essays and Reflections.* Macon, GA: Mercer UP, 2009. Print.

Blum, Edward J. *W.E.B. Du Bois: American Prophet.* Philadelphia: U of Pennsylvania P, 2007. Print.

Du Bois, W.E.B. *The Souls of Black Folk.* New York: Oxford UP, 2007. Print.

Lewis, David Levering. *W.E.B. Du Bois: A Biography.* New York: Holt, 2009. Print.

Rabaka, Reiland. *W.E.B. Du Bois and the Problems of the Twenty-First Century: An Essay on African Critical Theory.* New York: Lexington, 2007. Print.

Further Reading

Aptheker, Herbert. *The Literary Legacy of W.E.B. Du Bois.* White Plains, NY: Kraus, 1989. Print.

Baker, Houston A., Jr. "The Black Man of Culture: W.E.B. Du Bois and *The Souls of Black Folk.*" *Long Black Song: Essays in Black American Literature and Culture.* Charlottesville: U of Virginia P, 1972. Print.

Hubbard, Dolan, ed. *The Souls of Black Folk One Hundred Years Later.* Columbia: U of Missouri P, 2003. Print.

Juguo, Zhang. *W.E.B. Du Bois and the Quest for the Abolition of the Color Line.* New York: Routledge, 2001. Print.

Smith, Shawn Michelle. *Photography on the Color Line: W.E.B. Du Bois, Race, and Visual Culture.* Durham, NC: Duke UP, 2004. Print.

Wolters, Raymond. *W.E.B. Du Bois and His Rivals.* Columbia: U of Missouri P, 2002. Print.

Zamir, Shamoon. *Dark Voices: W.E.B. Du Bois and American Thought, 1888-1903.* Chicago: U of Chicago P, 1995. Print.

Theodore McDermott

A schoolgirl in class. In *The Souls of Black Folk,* W.E.B. Du Bois advocates for education for African Americans to help establish leaders and educators in the black community. © IMAGE SOURCE/CORBIS

SOCIAL AND POLITICAL UPHEAVALS

ANARCHISM

What It Really Stands For

Emma Goldman

OVERVIEW

Emma Goldman's essay "Anarchism: What It Really Stands For," first published in its current form in the volume *Anarchism and Other Essays* (1910), explains Goldman's conception of anarchism and defends the political philosophy against popular notions that equate it with chaos. The lecture evolved from several previous versions delivered during Goldman's many lecture tours throughout the United States and Canada during the years 1907-1909. It sets out to dispel misconceptions of anarchism, particularly those claiming that it is impractical or essentially violent. Intended for her audience, which included intellectuals and laborers alike, the essay is equally accessible to anarchists and to the uninitiated. Unlike many other anarchist manifestos, this work refrains from using sweeping agitational language, preferring instead to mitigate the sensationalist view of anarchism propagated by the American news media.

Like many anarchist lectures, "Anarchism: What It Really Stands For" was highly controversial and drew mixed reactions. During her lecture tour, police occasionally prevented her from speaking on the subject and even forcibly removed her from meeting halls. In 1908, after she had been prevented from speaking in Chicago, the *Chicago Daily Journal* published the text of her speech. This text, an early version of her later "Anarchism" essay, was titled "Anarchy and What It Really Stands For" and was published later that year by J. C. Hart & Company under the title *A Beautiful Ideal*. Despite the strong reactions to Goldman's views, her "Anarchism" essay was reasoned and collected. It is a sharp critique of authoritarian power structures, especially those of religion and government. Today, it remains one of the best expressions of Goldman's political thought and a compelling argument for libertarianism.

HISTORICAL AND LITERARY CONTEXT

Goldman's essay responds to a history of violence associated with anarchists and delineates a notion of anarchism that distances itself from such violence. In 1892 Goldman's comrade and lover Alexander Berkman attempted to assassinate Henry Clay Frick, the factory boss responsible for the Homestead Strike conflict, a labor battle that ended with many workers' deaths. In 1901 the anarchist Leon Czolgosz, who had attended Goldman's lectures, assassinated President William McKinley. After these events, Goldman strongly opposed violent tactics and stood apart from those branches of anarchism that advocated "propaganda by the deed." Although there were few bomb-making anarchists, American newspapers associated anarchists with violence, especially after the 1886 Haymarket Affair, in which anarchists were blamed for a bomb blast.

When the essay was published in 1910, the American labor movement was still in its infancy. There had been several minor successes for American workers, such as the Coal Strike of 1902, but labor unions were still not given legal recognition, and working conditions remained abysmal. Just a few months later, the Triangle Shirtwaist Factory fire would claim the lives of 146 workers owing to poor workplace safety standards. Socialism, and in particular the anarchist communism that Goldman promoted, acknowledged the plight of the working class and provided hope for a fairer standard of living. The authorities, however, viewed anarchists as threats to order. In 1908, for instance, Theodore Roosevelt famously declared to the U.S. Congress: "The Anarchist is the enemy of humanity, the enemy of all mankind, and his is a deeper degree of criminality than any other."

Ideologically, Goldman owes much to the work of her friend, the mutualist anarchist Peter Kropotkin, who wrote a critique of the prison system from which Goldman quotes at length in her essay. American transcendentalists also play a major role in her argument: she quotes Ralph Waldo Emerson's maxim that "all government in essence is tyranny" and Henry David Thoreau's statement that "all voting is a sort of gaming." Thoreau, she declares, is "the greatest American anarchist."

In the following decades, Goldman's brand of anarchism proved to be among the most sustained, and her works were influential in the development of American radical politics. Labor unions, such as

Key Facts

Time Period:
Early 20th Century

Movement/Issue:
Anarchism

Place of Publication:
United States

Language of Publication:
English

EMMA GOLDMAN

Emma Goldman is remembered as one of the twentieth century's most vocal anarchists, antiwar activists, and workers' rights advocates. As a political speaker, she lectured throughout the United States, Canada, and Australia to lively receptions by hundreds of people. Her controversial views landed her in prison on several occasions, and her deportation was called for in internal U.S. government documents from at least as early as 1908. During the Red Scare of 1919, she was deported to Russia, where she lived for two years. She lived the rest of her life in exile in Europe, where she became involved with the anarchist factions CNT (Confederación Nacional del Trabajo) and FAI (Federación Anarquista Ibérica) during the Spanish Civil War.

A major figure in the history of women's rights, Goldman argued in favor of birth control, preached free love, and criticized the institution of marriage. The prominent feminist Gloria Steinem said of Goldman that she "understood the importance of seemingly small things, the right to music and dancing, the need for loving kindness, the importance of beauty in a revolutionary's life, the power of listening." Her major publications include *Mother Earth,* a monthly anarchist magazine she published with Alexander Berkman; *Anarchism and Other Essays*; and *Living My Life,* her autobiography.

the largely anarcho-syndicalist Industrial Workers of the World, with which Goldman was closely associated, experienced greatly increased membership in the early 1910s. In contrast, more violent forms of anarchism, such as that of Luigi Galleani and his followers, declined in popularity, especially after the highly controversial trial of Galleanists Nicola Sacco and Bartolomeo Vanzetti in the early 1920s. Goldman's manifesto stands as a pivotal work of this transformation in anarchist politics and remains relevant today among anarchists and labor activists.

THEMES AND STYLE

The major themes of "Anarchism: What It Really Stands For" are those of liberty, social justice, and direct action. Goldman defines anarchism as the "philosophy of a new social order based on liberty unrestricted by man-made law; the theory that all forms of government rest on violence, and are therefore wrong and harmful, as well as unnecessary." Free association and consensus, she argues, are the only ways to ensure justice and equality; a government based on the threat of force could never truly represent its people. Methodologically, Goldman advocates the use of direct action, such as general strikes, in lieu of indirect forms of political action, such as voting or petitioning. Direct rebellion, she claims, is responsible for many social victories, such as the abolition of slavery. Finally, Goldman asserts the necessity of a revolution, arguing that "no real social change has ever come about without a revolution."

The rhetoric of the essay is that of a practiced, persuasive orator. After dispelling popular misconceptions of anarchism, Goldman explains how many common ideas about the state and society are themselves misconceptions. In particular, she attacks religion as an ideological manifestation of statist politics, a leitmotif that repeats "man is nothing, the powers are everything." Whereas religion is "the dominion of the human mind," government is "the dominion of human conduct." Anarchism, therefore, as it stands for total liberation, means "liberation of the human mind from the dominion of religion; the liberation of the human body from the dominion of property; liberation from the shackles and restraint of government."

Through the use of nature imagery, such as references to "the earth" and "the Dawn" (Goldman's monthly magazine was titled *Mother Earth*), Goldman implicitly invokes a harmonious primeval past, a time before governments. Human nature, she argues, is not that which it may appear to be under a capitalist system. In the sense that an "experimental study of animals in captivity is absolutely useless," human nature may not be accurately studied under the captivity of the state. Crime, therefore, is not a natural function of some dark human nature, but a function of inequality, and thus "naught but misdirected energy." She defends herself against possible accusations of idealism, however, by stressing the practicality of anarchism, especially in the form of direct action.

CRITICAL DISCUSSION

Emma Goldman made newspaper headlines in nearly every city she visited during her lecture tours of 1908-1909. Whereas many of the news articles relied on the sensationalism of a "red priestess" arriving in town and the anticipated police response, many were sympathetic. A *New York Times* article from 1909 admits that "to the average newspaper reader" she is imagined as a "red spectre, a wild-eyed inciter of violence, shrieking madly against government, and getting weak-minded folks to kill Kings," but that, in reality, she is a "well-read, intellectual woman with a theory of society not very different from that entertained by a lot of college professors." Hutchins Hapgood, in a beaming 1911 review of *Anarchism and Other Essays,* confirms this apparent dichotomy by arguing of Goldman that "there is probably no living man or woman who has been so thoroughly misrepresented." While one *London Free Press* account of Goldman as a lecturer calls her "most emphatic in speech, clever and having the ability to move an audience to the wildest pitch of excitement," a review of her book in the *Independent* laments that she "cannot … write with the ability of Kropatkin [*sic*] or Tucker."

Although public interest in anarchism waned, or was repressed, after the First Red Scare, Goldman's writings were rediscovered in the 1960s, and "Anarchism: What It Really Stands For" was memorialized as one of the most definitive essays of the most prominent twentieth-century American anarchist. In the past thirty years, several books have been published about Goldman. In a 1984 review of four of these books, Karen Rosenberg declares, "One would be hard-pressed to find another woman of the past who enjoys her privileged status in contemporary America, who is emblazoned on as many tee-shirts and postcards." Her ideas continue to be controversial as well—in 2003, the University of California at Berkeley censored two antiwar quotations by Goldman from a fund-raising mailing of the Emma Goldman Papers Project, for fear that they might be construed as university-sanctioned statements about the Iraq war. After the *New York Times* ran a front-page article about the censorship, however, the university reversed its decision.

Contemporary scholarship recognizes the significance of this and other essays by Goldman, although many scholars, as Goldman perhaps would have anticipated, still view her anarchism as naive or idealistic. Don Herzog argues that Goldman "reproduced in her relationship to anarchism that side of romantic love she so despised." Meanwhile, Allan Antliff, in citing "Anarchism: What It Really Stands For," emphasizes Goldman's individualist tendencies, claiming that she "posits a situated politics in which individuality differentiates endlessly, according to each subject's desires, tastes, and inclinations."

BIBLIOGRAPHY

Sources

"Anarchist Looks on Darker Side." *London Free Press* 21 Feb. 1908: 10. Print.

Antliff, Allan. "Anarchy, Power, and Poststructuralism." *SubStance* 36.2 (2007): 56-66. *JSTOR*. Web. 4 July 2012.

Goldman, Emma. *Anarchism: What it Really Stands For.* New York: Mother Earth Publishing, 1911. *Google Book Search*. Web. 24 July 2012.

Hapgood, Hutchins. "Emma Goldman's 'Anarchism.'" Rev. of *Anarchism and Other Essays,* by Emma Goldman. *The Bookman: a Review of Books and Life* 32.6 (1911): 639-40. *ProQuest*. Web. 4 July 2012.

Herzog, Don. "Emma Goldman, Romantic Anarchism, and Pedestrian Liberalism."_*Political Theory* 35.3 (Jun 2007): 313-33. *SAGE Journals*. Web. 4 July 2012.

"Literary Notes." *The Independent* 26 Jan. 1911: 204. *ProQuest*. Web. 4 July 2012.

"Roosevelt Demands Action on Anarchy." *New York Times* 10 Apr. 1908: 5. Print.

Rosenberg, Karen. "Emma's Ambiguous Legacy." Rev. of *Red Emma Speaks: An Emma Goldman Reader,* by Alix Kates Schulman; *Love, Anarchy and Emma Goldman,* by Candace Falk; *Emma Goldman: An Intimate Life,* by Alice Wexler; and *Vision on Fire: Emma Goldman on the Spanish Revolution,* by David Porter. *Women's Review of Books* Nov. 1984: 8. *JSTOR*. Web. 4 July 2012.

Thompson, Charles Willis. "An Interview with Emma Goldman." *New York Times* 30 May 1909: 37. Print.

Further Reading

Avrich, Paul. *Anarchist Voices: An Oral History of Anarchism in America.* Princeton: Princeton UP, 1995. Print.

Falk, Candace, Barry Pateman, Jessica M. Moran, and Robert Cohen, eds. *Emma Goldman: A Documentary History of the American Years, Volume Two: Making Speech Free, 1902-1909.* Berkeley: U of California P, 2005. Print.

Ferguson, Kathy E. *Emma Goldman: Political Thinking in the Streets.* Lanham: Rowman & Littlefield, 2011. Print.

Goldman, Emma. *A Beautiful Ideal.* Chicago: J. C. Hart & Co., 1908. Print.

———. *Anarchism and Other Essays.* New York: Dover, 1969. Print.

———. *Living My Life.* New York: Penguin, 2006. Print.

Murphy, Dean. "Old Words on War Stirring a New Dispute at Berkeley." *New York Times* 14 Jan. 2003: A1. *ProQuest*. Web. 4 July 2012

Wexler, Alice. *Emma Goldman: An Intimate Life.* New York: Pantheon, 1984. Print.

An illustration from the Parisian newspaper *Le Petit Journal,* 1901. Following the assassination of President William McKinley, an angry mob moves to lynch Emma Goldman, whose anarchist philosophy had inspired McKinley's assassin, Leon Czolgosz. © INTERFOTO / ALAMY

Jonathan Reeve

ANNIHILATION OF CASTE

B. R. Ambedkar

✤ *Key Facts*

Time Period:
Mid-20th Century

Movement/Issue:
Caste discrimination;
Democratic reform

Place of Publication:
India

**Language of
Publication:**
English

OVERVIEW

Composed by B.R. Ambedkar, *Annihilation of Caste* (1936) condemns the injustice of Hinduism's caste system of hierarchical social organization and calls for legal and religious reforms that will abolish that system. The manifesto was prepared as a speech for a conference organized by the Jat-Pat-Todak Mandal of Lahore, a liberal group that shared Ambedkar's aim to eradicate the caste system. However, upon receipt of the speech, the organizers of the conference rescinded Ambedkar's invitation because of his critique of Hinduism as a fundamentally divisive and unjust religion. Undeterred, Ambedkar published the text himself. Addressed to the attendees of the conference, Ambedkar's manifesto argues that the destruction of caste is a prerequisite for all other political, economic, and social reforms. Central to *Annihilation of Caste* is its call for an end to the caste system and its comprehensive critique of Hindu society and religion at large.

Despite its rejection by conference organizers, *Annihilation of Caste* quickly became popular within and outside of India when it appeared in book form. The manifesto's argument appealed particularly strongly to members of India's lowest caste groups, collectively known as "untouchables" (and, later, "dalits"), of which Ambedkar himself was a member. As a result it helped catalyze Ambedkar's career as a politician and reformer. In 1936, the year *Annihilation of Caste* was issued, he formed a political party devoted to representing India's lowliest citizens. He went on to form two other parties, served in the cabinets of British and independent India, and authored numerous books and tracts, as well as the constitution of India. Ambedkar's critical views of Hinduism eventually led him to convert to Buddhism, which inspired a massive conversion of Indians—untouchables, in particular—to his new faith. Today, the *Annihilation of Caste* is considered a vital document in the expansion of rights for India's oppressed lower classes during the twentieth century.

HISTORICAL AND LITERARY CONTEXT

Annihilation of Caste responds to the social, economic, and political plight of the untouchable caste in the mid-1930s, when the process of modernization in India threatened the stability of the nation's existing cultural order. Untouchables were subject to discrimination in every aspect of life. They were required by Hindu law to perform certain kinds of demeaning menial labor and were forbidden to interact with higher castes. They could not enter Hindu temples, draw water, attend school, or move freely. The movement to combat the comprehensive oppression of these people began to take shape in 1923, when Ambedkar helped form the Depressed Classes Welfare Association to promote the educational, economic, and legal rights of India's lowest social group. From 1927 to 1932, he led several nonviolent protests to challenge discrimination against untouchables at temples and wells.

By the time the manifesto was written, the movement to end caste discrimination was growing. Because of vehement opposition from upper-caste Hindus, Ambedkar began to advocate for increasing the economic and political power of untouchables. To that end, he established the Independent Labour Party in 1936 to represent his constituents. In *Annihilation of Caste,* Ambedkar makes a case for the interrelatedness of politics, economics, and religion. "If the source of power and dominion is at any given time or in any given society social and religious," he writes, "then social reform and religious reform must be accepted as the necessary sort of reform." When the manifesto appeared, its appeal for fundamental change resonated with untouchables and engendered a movement against caste oppression and discrimination that continues today.

Annihilation of Caste draws on a diverse history of human rights declarations and on the French *Declaration of the Rights of Man and of the Citizen* in particular. Adopted in 1789 during the French Revolution, the *Declaration* announced in its first article, "Men are born and remain free and equal in rights. Social distinctions may be founded only upon the general good." The second article listed these rights as "liberty, property, security, and resistance to oppression." In *Annihilation of Caste,* Ambedkar calls for reforms that would bring about an open and free society based on equality and liberty, principles that would allow people to work together for the "general good" of all. In explicit reference to the French national motto, which derives from the *Declaration,* he writes that his "ideal would be a society based on *Liberty, Equality* and *Fraternity.*"

Annihilation of Caste proved to be a foundational text for a lifetime of important polemical writings by Ambedkar. In texts such as *What Congress and Gandhi Have Done to the Untouchables* (1945), he continued his argument about the incompatibility of freedom and the caste system. In 1947 and 1948, after India achieved independence, Ambedkar helped design and draft a constitution for the new nation that ended the legal practice of untouchability. The argument he made in *Annihilation of Caste* regarding the injustice of Hinduism culminated in 1956 with his conversion to Buddhism and the publication of his book *The Buddha and His Dhamma,* which explained Buddhism to the common man and convinced masses of people to convert with him. Today, Ambedkar's writings on caste and religion command significant scholarly attention around the world as well as popular interest in India.

THEMES AND STYLE

The central theme of *Annihilation of Caste* is that the caste system derives from a moral flaw in Hinduism and that, as a result, the system should be abolished and the religion should be reformed. The manifesto opens with the author's acknowledgement of the unpopularity of his ideas. He then proceeds to harshly critique Hinduism, the caste system it engenders, and the defenders of the religion and the system. "Caste does not result in economic efficiency," he writes. "Caste cannot and has not improved the race.

AMBEDKAR'S CONTRIBUTIONS TO INDIA

While *Annihilation of Caste* is still viewed as a vital document in twentieth-century Indian history, it is but one of B.R. Ambedkar's many contributions to his nation's process of independence and reform. Born an untouchable in 1891, Bhimrao Ramji Ambedkar was protected from some of the discrimination a person of his caste would normally experience, and he received a better education, because his father and grandfather had served in the military. Still, he could not escape prejudice, and he left India for schooling at Columbia University, where he earned a master's degree and a PhD, and the London School of Economics, where he received a second master's degree. When he returned to India in 1923, he began his life's work of advocating for the people of his caste and reforming his nation socially and politically.

Ambedkar successfully secured rights for untouchables and then, upon India's independence from Britain in 1947, served as the chairman of the drafting committee of the constitution. In addition to his political work Ambedkar advocated for increased literacy and education for India's untouchables. He founded several newspapers aimed at informing the poor and helped start schools and universities that were open to all. Believing that Hinduism would never reform to his satisfaction, Ambedkar converted to Buddhism two months before his death in 1956.

Caste has however done one thing. It has completely disorganized and demoralized the Hindus." To reform the system, he argues, one must reform the religion.

A Dalit woman in front of a portrait of B.R. Ambedkar during a 2004 rally to increase awareness of the continued plight of the Dalit, or "untouchable," caste. © ANTOINE SERRA/IN VISU/CORBIS

"Caste has a divine basis," he argues. "You must therefore destroy the sacredness and divinity with which Caste has become invested." To this end, he argues that Hindus themselves must question their faith in tradition.

Ambedkar achieves his rhetorical effect by appealing to a desire for practical improvement that transcends fidelity to religious custom. In a series of enumerated sections, Ambedkar gradually builds his case, systematically countering the opposition and presenting his argument in an evenhanded and logical progression. He repeatedly quotes experts from a variety of fields, cites historical precedent, and refers to the larger international context. In addition he examines the structure and characteristics of the caste system with dispassion and objectivity. He even confronts the question of whether his kind of argument can be effective: "Can you appeal to reason and ask the Hindus to discard Caste as being contrary to reason?" His answer is that you cannot, that "a Hindu cannot resort to rational thinking." Ambedkar presents his reasoned argument as an antidote to the irrationality of the Hindu belief system.

Stylistically, the *Annihilation of Caste* is distinguished by its casual discursiveness. Throughout the manifesto, Ambedkar assumes a posture of self-deprecation that only enhances his sense of assurance about his argument. "I would not be surprised if some of you have grown weary listening to this tiresome tale of the sad effects which caste has produced," he writes. In this way, he humbles himself before his audience while implicitly chastising his readers for their presumably blasé treatment of this vital issue. The manifesto also repeatedly asks rhetorical questions as a means of including the reader in the progress of the text's argument. "Why not allow liberty to benefit by an effective and competent use of a person's powers?" By asking questions of this kind, Ambedkar leads his audience from controversial opinions to seemingly incontrovertible conclusions.

CRITICAL DISCUSSION

When *Annihilation of Caste* was completed, it received a mixed response within the anti-caste movement. Upon receipt of a draft of the speech, Har Bhagwan, a member of Jat-Pat-Todak Mandal, argued in a letter that Ambedkar had "unnecessarily attacked the morality and reasonableness of the *Vedas* and other religious books of the Hindus" and requested that he excise the speech's religious critique. Ambedkar refused to make the requested changes, withdrew his speech, and published his text in book form. According to the preface to the second edition, it was met with "an astonishingly warm reception from the Hindu public for whom it was primarily intended." It was also met with criticism. In a pair of reviews for the newspaper *Harijan*, Mohandas Gandhi expressed qualified admiration for the manifesto's critique of caste while refuting Ambedkar's claim that caste is connected to Hinduism.

For decades after its publication, *Annihilation of Caste* remained an important source of pride and defiance for India's untouchables and other impoverished groups. The manifesto's calls for equality and justice without regard for caste were carried forward as the nation moved toward, and eventually achieved, independence. When the Ambedkar-designed constitution was ratified in 1949, the manifesto's call for an end to institutionalized discrimination became law. This was more than a symbolic change: according to the scholar Eleanor Zelliot, it engendered a political and literary movement that represented "a new level of pride, militancy, and sophisticated creativity" for those the manifesto had sought to uplift. In the more than seventy years since it first appeared, *Annihilation of Caste* has been the subject of an extensive body of criticism that has considered its legacy in historical, religious, and political terms.

Much scholarship focused on *Annihilation of Caste* as a critique of religion within a larger socio-political context. The scholar Christopher S. Queen, for example, compares the manifesto's critique of Hinduism to Christian theologizing about injustice. Queen writes, "Ambedkar's preoccupation with religious meaning of social oppression suggests parallels to the rise of twentieth-century liberation theology in the West." Commentators have also considered the manifesto in relationship to the way historians approach temporality. The scholar Debjani Ganguly sees Ambedkar within the context of the work of German theorist Walter Benjamin, calling Ambedkar a "Benjaminian historical materialist who has been singled out by history at a moment of immense peril and who must perforce, in an act of urgent constellating, cobble together scraps and fragments from the ruins of the past and invest them with a power that would shatter the lethal continuum of Hindi Brahminical history in the subcontinent."

BIBLIOGRAPHY

Sources

Ambedkar, B.R. *Dr. Babasaheb Ambedkar: Writings and Speeches, Vol. 1.* Bombay: Education Dept. of Maharashtra, 1989. Print.

Ganguly, Debjani. "History's Implosions: A Benjaminian Reading of Ambedkar." *Journal of Narrative Theory* 32.3 (2002): 326-47. Web. 19 July 2012.

Pritchett, Frances W. *Annihilation of Caste* Multimedia Study Environment. New York: Columbia Center for New Media Teaching and Learning, 2004. Web. 18 July 2012.

Queen, Christopher S. "Dr. Ambedkar and the Hermeneutics of Buddhist Liberation." *Engaged Buddhism: Buddhist Liberation Movements in Asia.* Ed. Christopher S. Queen and Sallie B. King. Albany: State U of New York P, 1996. Print.

Sangharakshita. *Ambedkar and Buddhism.* Glasgow: Windhorse, 1986. Print.

Zelliot. Eleanor. *From Untouchable to Dalit: Essays on the Ambedkar Movement.* New Delhi: Manohar, 1992. Print.

Further Reading

Ambedkar, B.R. *The Buddha and His Dhamma.* Bombay: People's Education Soc., 1984. Print.

Jondhale, Surendra, and Johannes Beltz, eds. *Reconstructing the World: B.R. Ambedkar and Buddhism in India.* New Delhi: Oxford UP, 2004. Print.

Keer, Dhananjay. *Dr. Ambedkar: Life and Mission.* 3rd ed. Bombay: Popular Prakashan, 1971. Print.

Narain, A. K., ed. *Studies in the History of Buddhism.* Delhi: B.R., 1980. Print.

Pilchick, Terry. *Jai Bhim!: Dispatches from a Peaceful Revolution.* Glasgow: Windhorse, 1988. Print.

Webster, John B.C. *Religion and Dalit Liberation.* New Delhi: Manohar, 1999. Print.

Wilkinson, T. S., and M. M. Thomas. *Ambedkar and the Neo-Buddhist Movement.* Madras: Christian Literature Soc., 1972. Print.

Theodore McDermott

THE BATTLE CRY

Women's Social and Political Union

✣ *Key Facts*

Time Period:
Early 20th Century

Movement/Issue:
Women's suffrage
movement in Britain

Place of Publication:
England

**Language of
Publication:**
English

OVERVIEW

"The Battle Cry" was a statement published in the inaugural issue of the journal *Votes for Women* in October of 1907. It was a call to action for British women to commit themselves to the cause of women's suffrage. Published by the Women's Social and Political Union (WSPU), "The Battle Cry" signaled a turn toward militancy in Britain's female suffrage movement, with the new motto "deeds not words" calling for women to assert themselves in the male-dominated public sphere through actions rather than merely vociferating about their cause. As a manifesto for the WSPU, "The Battle Cry" urged women throughout Britain to join the struggle for equality and reflected the WSPU's use of publicity and advertising to disseminate their message to a wide audience. The text presents the fight for women's suffrage as a universal battle, emphasizing the common experience of womanhood as a bond of solidarity across diverse backgrounds and classes.

"The Battle Cry," along with *Votes for Women,* was received with anger and indignation by a large sector of the male population who felt threatened by the increasing influence of the women's movement during the early twentieth century. Many women who supported a less militant approach to obtaining suffrage also criticized the WSPU's publication for inciting women to act illegally and for challenging the traditional role of women as wives and mothers. Nevertheless, the WSPU gained influence over the next few years, partially as a result of the wide distribution of WSPU publications such as "The Battle Cry." The WSPU continued to function actively until the outbreak of World War I in 1914, when union leader Christabel Pankhurst called for a suspension of militant acts during wartime. Today, "The Battle Cry" and *Votes for Women* are regarded as the seminal publications of the WSPU, an organization whose role in the women's suffrage movement continues to be studied today.

HISTORICAL AND LITERARY CONTEXT

"The Battle Cry" was written following a split within the WSPU that led to the formation of the Women's Freedom League (WFL), which advocated for less militant suffrage tactics and opposed the WSPU's autocratic leadership and strategy of attacking public and private property. Convinced that the union needed to escalate its blatant acts of vandalism, destruction of property, advertising, and propaganda, the authors of the WSPU's impassioned manifesto called on British women to join the battle by replacing passive speech with assertive action. WSPU leaders were frustrated with their failed attempts to communicate productively with government officials and politicians who repeatedly informed them that the public sphere and politics were not places for women.

The WSPU was originally founded in October 1903 by, among others, Emmeline and Christabel Pankhurst, who soon emerged as the group's leaders. Realizing that the vote could only be won by a change in strategies that differed from the constitutional and legal lobbying of more established women's organizations such as the National Union of Women's Suffrage Societies (NUWSS), the WSPU adopted an increasingly radical policy of militancy that sparked frequent violent encounters over the next ten years. In October 1907, a month after the WSPU-WFL split, the union founded its journal, *Votes for Women,* edited by WSPU leader Emmeline Pethick-Lawrence and her husband, Frederick. It began as a monthly but quickly became a penny weekly, with a circulation of more than 40,000. The publication was renamed the *Suffragette* in 1912, when it split from the Pethick-Lawrences, until it ceased publication in 1920. Other prominent leaders of the union included a small group of relatively wealthy women, among them the Pankhursts, Clare Mordan, and Mary Blathwayt. Notably, the split earlier in 1907 was also related to social class. Many of the former WSPU members who defected to the WFL were from the working class and felt that the more affluent union leaders did not take their interests seriously.

"The Battle Cry" draws on a history of earlier publications advocating for women's suffrage, both in England and the United States. While many earlier publications were less militant, the publicity they brought to the cause and the rhetoric they employed are reflected in the WSPU's 1907 statement. Early journals and newspapers included the weekly American women's rights journal the *Revolution,* published by Susan B. Anthony beginning in 1868, as well as the British feminist publication *English Woman's Journal,* published by Emily Davies from 1858 to 1864. Davies and fellow feminist Barbara Bodichon both published early books on women's rights and suffrage, including Davies's *Higher Education for Women* (1866) and Bodichon's *Women and Work* (1857) and *Enfranchisement of Women* (1866). These authors paved the way for later publications such as the WSPU's *Votes for Women*.

Many of the WSPU members who responded to "The Battle Cry" of 1907 published their own memoirs and autobiographies later on. A number of these books highlighted the mistreatment and violence the female militants had endured as a result of their association with the WSPU, both in prison and during public protests and other WSPU activities. These include Christabel Pankhurst's *Unshackled: The Story of How We Won the Vote* (1959), Annie Kenney's *Memories of a Militant* (1924), and Emmeline Pethick-Lawrence's *My Part in a Changing World* (1938). In their memoirs, these women employed military and revolutionary rhetoric similar to that used in "The Battle Cry." While feminist literature has evolved dramatically since the early twentieth century, "The Battle Cry" and *Votes for Women* are regarded as important precedents to contemporary feminist literature.

THEMES AND STYLE

The central theme of "The Battle Cry" is that the struggle for women's suffrage requires the participation, resolve, and commitment of all women; it cannot be won by a select few. It begins, "To women far and wide the trumpet call goes forth, Come fight with us in our battle for freedom.... Come and join us, whatever your age, whatever your class, whatever your political inclination." The article emphasizes the need for solidarity among a diverse collective of women, highlighting the shared bond of womanhood that crosses all economic, religious, and social boundaries. "The Battle Cry" functions as a tool to recruit additional members and sympathizers in order to strengthen the WSPU's cause.

The article's force is achieved through inclusive rhetoric that emphasizes the shared nature of the struggle, which includes all members of society, not just women. The call to action states that "this is a battle in which we all must take part; they must come ready for active endeavor and for strenuous service; they must be prepared not to flinch in the hour of difficulty." Employing gender-neutral terms such as "we all" and "they," the authors suggest they need the support and participation of men as well as women, painting the struggle as one in which society as a whole has a stake. The brief and vague nature of the text is its strength; it is short and to the point, a direct call to action addressed to all members of British society. Notably, the article does not detail the WSPU's tactics but rather seeks to generate passion from its readers, thus inspiring them to join the union.

"The Battle Cry" is written in an emotional, impassioned tone that relies on military and revolu-

ACHIEVING THE VOTE FOR WOMEN: BRITAIN'S LONG STRUGGLE

The fight for women's suffrage began in Britain in the mid-nineteenth century with pioneering women's rights leaders such as Emily Davies and Barbara Bodichon. Interestingly, women were allowed to vote in Britain until the Reform Act, also called the Representation of the People Act, was passed in 1832, enfranchising only "male persons." Women's suffrage became a national movement only in 1872, five years after Lydia Becker founded the National Society for Women's Suffrage (NSWS). The National Union of Women's Suffrage Societies (NUWSS) did not emerge until the turn of the twentieth century, but then it quickly gained more widespread influence than the NSWS ever had.

The NUWSS sought to legalize women's suffrage by encouraging politicians and members of parliament to enact constitutional changes. However, the ineffectiveness of this approach became apparent after several years. The WSPU was formed as an alternative to the NUWSS's constitutional campaign, but its radicalism made it unpopular with the majority of British citizens. As a result, most women's rights activists continued to support the NUWSS. At the outbreak of World War I in 1914, the suffrage cause took a backseat to wartime concerns. A partial victory came for suffragists and suffragettes alike with the passage of the People Act in 1918 that enfranchised female property owners over thirty years of age. It was not until 1928, however, when another Representation of the People Act extended the vote to all women over the age of twenty-one. The law took effect only weeks after the death of revered WSPU leader Emmeline Pankhurst.

tionary language to convey its message. The authors caution that "the battle is not to the weak or to the downhearted, or to the indifferent, but to those who resolutely set before themselves the determination of victory." They are clearly seeking militantly minded members who will exhibit a soldier-like resolve and dedication to the cause of women's suffrage and to the union itself. The struggle for the woman's vote is presented as a war, as evidenced by such terms as "battle" and "victory." Interestingly, the statement eschews directness in favor of vague phrases such as "battle for freedom," revealing the WSPU's attempt to appeal to a broad cross-section of British society, which may have been skittish about the term "women's suffrage."

CRITICAL DISCUSSION

"The Battle Cry" received a generally negative response from its British audience due to its militaristic tone. Condemning the radical nature of the WSPU's campaign, the *Times* published an article a few years later, under the title "Insurgent Hysteria," which stated that "the suffragettes are a regrettable by-product of our civilization, out with their hammers

The subject of this illustration, Emmeline Pankhurst, was the founder of the United Kingdom-based Women's Social and Political Union. This militant organization sought women's suffrage, the focus of "The Battle Cry." PRIVATE COLLECTION/© LOOK AND LEARN/THE BRIDGEMAN ART LIBRARY

did much to promote women's suffrage in Britain. Whether the attention it garnered was negative or positive, the controversy surrounding the WSPU's militancy and radical tactics kept the issue in the spotlight. According to author Barbara Green in *Spectacular Confessions* (1997), one of the keys to the WSPU's widespread influence was its strategic reliance on publicity and advertising through journal publications, pamphlets, and other written material. Green notes the organization's long-term influence on "the feminist publication industry [that] created a space for feminist speech in the public arena, hence the increased participation of working-class women in the genre of autobiography." Today, "The Battle Cry" is one of the most frequently quoted works associated with the WSPU and is regarded as representative of their militant ideology.

Much scholarship on "The Battle Cry" has addressed the emphasis on female solidarity in the WSPU's statement. As June Purvis writes in a 1995 article in *Women's Studies International Forum,* "That such solidarity should be expressed should come as no surprise since the cornerstone of WSPU rhetoric and politics was the common bond of womanhood." Other scholars have focused on the warlike rhetoric and ideology of the WSPU in "The Battle Cry" and its alienating effect on British society. In *Suffrage Discourse in Britain During the First World War* (2005), Angela Smith writes that "the WSPU had always taken the view that theirs was a moral 'war', and many of Emmeline and Christabel's speeches, articles and pamphlets had been filled with belligerent language, typically … the suffragettes, at the Pankhursts' instigation, saw themselves as soldiers, fighting for a righteous cause."

and their bags full of stones because of dreary, empty lives and high-strung, over-excitable natures," as Brian Howard Harrison quotes in his essay in *Peaceable Kingdom* (1982). WSPU members were the first to be called "suffragettes" disparagingly by a reporter, in contrast to the accepted term "suffragist" that was used to refer to members of the NUWSS. A few select newspapers did react more favorably to the WSPU's cause. A reporter for the *Daily Chronicle* praised the work of the WSPU on May 5, 1911, stating that "with sure and certain steps the cause of women's suffrage is marching to victory." However, the consensus in Britain was that WSPU members were unladylike radicals who violated women's natural role in society, a view that "The Battle Cry" reinforced somewhat with its rhetoric.

"The Battle Cry," along with other WSPU propaganda during the early twentieth century,

BIBLIOGRAPHY

Sources

Green, Barbara. *Spectacular Confessions: Autobiography, Performative Activism, and the Sites of Suffrage, 1905-1938.* New York: St. Martin's, 1997. Print.

Harrison, Brian Howard. "The Act of Militancy: Violence and the Suffragette, 1904-1914." *Peaceable Kingdom: Stability and Change in Modern Britain.* Oxford: Oxford UP, 1982. 80-122. Print.

Pugh, Martin. *The March of the Women: A Revisionist Analysis of the Campaign for Women's Suffrage, 1866-1914.* Oxford: Oxford UP, 2000. Print.

Purvis, June. "'Deeds not Words': The Daily Lives of Militant Suffragettes in Edwardian Britain." *Women's Studies International Forum* 18 (1995): 91-101. Print.

Smith, Angela. *Suffrage Discourse in Britain during the First World War.* Burlington: Ashgate, 2005. Print.

Stowell, Sheila. *A Stage of Their Own: Feminist Playwrights of the Suffrage Era*. Ann Arbor: U of Michigan P, 1994. Print.

Further Reading

Cowman, Krista. *Women of the Right Spirit: Paid Organisers of the Women's Social and Political Union (WSPU) 1904-18*. New York: Manchester UP, 2007. Print.

DiCenzo, Maria. *Feminist Media History: Suffrage, Periodicals and the Public Sphere*. New York: Palgrave Macmillan, 2010. Print.

Holton, Sandra, and June Purvis, eds. *Votes for Women*. New York: Routledge, 2000. Print.

Mayhall, Laura E. Nym. *The Militant Suffrage Movement: Citizenship and Resistance in Britain, 1860-1930*. New York: Oxford UP, 2003. Print.

Rosen, Andrew. *Rise Up, Women! The Militant Campaign of the Women's Social and Political Union 1903-1914*. London: Routledge, 1974. Print.

Vellacott, Jo. "Feminist Consciousness and the First World War." *History Workshop* 23.1 (1987), 81-101. Print.

Winkiel, Laura. *Modernism, Race and Manifestos*. New York: Cambridge UP, 2008. Print.

Katrina White

DECLARATION OF INDEPENDENCE FOR THE DEMOCRATIC REPUBLIC OF VIETNAM

Ho Chi Minh

✧ *Key Facts*

Time Period:
Mid-20th Century

Movement/Issue:
Vietnamese
independence;
Communism;
Anticolonialism

Place of Publication:
Vietnam

**Language of
Publication:**
Vietnamese

OVERVIEW

Written by Ho Chi Minh, the president of Vietnam, and first presented as a speech given by Ho on September 2, 1945, the Declaration of Independence for the Democratic Republic of Vietnam is a revolutionary writing intended to unite all of Vietnam, both the privileged south and the impoverished north, into one nation independent from colonial influence or invading forces. Ho was an early proponent of socialism and communism and had traveled and studied political theory extensively in the United States, China, and France prior to becoming the leader of Vietnam. Using lessons learned abroad from other political struggles, he sought to remedy what he considered great injustices at the hands of foreign oppressors, specifically the long-established French colonial government and the Japanese army that invaded during World War II.

The Declaration of Independence for the Democratic Republic of Vietnam was met with great fervor in the north by the Viet Minh, an organization founded by Ho in 1941 to oppose the French rule of Vietnam. In reaction to Ho's speech, leaders of the south abdicated to his new authority but still felt a certain allegiance to the French colonial leaders they had served for more than a century. The French, already weak from the devastation at home and abroad because of World War II, were faced with the reality that they very well might lose their colonial hold over Vietnam. Ho's declaration of Vietnam's independence and his presentation of the Declaration of Independence for the Democratic Republic of Vietnam as a speech in 1945 was a watershed moment as it forced the hand of French colonial rulers to either retreat and accept Vietnamese independence or to stay and fight to retain their stronghold over the country.

HISTORICAL AND LITERARY CONTEXT

The Declaration of Independence for the Democratic Republic of Vietnam announces the liberation of the Vietnamese people from colonial governments and invading forces. It urges all Vietnamese people nationwide to stand up against oppression and establish a Republican government to gain control of their land rights, natural resources, and political voice. The document also cites specific problems, including the division of the country, the robbing of natural resources, the control of trade, and the unlawful imprisonment and execution of patriots. Ho had strong ties with the peasant population, and he sought to unite the country under his leadership.

The Japanese invaded Vietnam in 1940 during World War II and surrendered in late August 1945. Shortly thereafter, Viet Minh forces deposed the colonial puppet emperor, Bao Dai, who, sensing the futility of resistance, asked the Viet Minh to form a government and contacted French leader Charles de Gaulle, urging him not to intervene. Ho became president of Vietnam, and along with General Vo Nguyen Giap and other Viet Minh officers, he set about meeting with members of the former government. According to author David Halberstam in his book *Ho* (1971), one official present during the August Revolution recalled Ho's preparation for his speech, saying, "On September 1, the eve of the declaration of independence, he arrived with a scrap of paper on which he had drafted his proclamation to the people. He submitted it to us, passing it around, accepting amendments."

Ironically, Ho modeled his groundbreaking declaration after France's *Declaration of the Rights of Man* and the U.S. *Declaration of Independence*. Given that the Vietnamese spent most of the years between 1945 and 1975 at war with either France or the United States, it might be considered ironic that Ho begins his declaration by quoting these two works. However, he was making a direct appeal to the universal values represented in them, in part hoping to find allies for his cause in the West. The Declaration of Independence for the Democratic Republic of Vietnam states,

> "All men are created equal." This immortal statement appeared in the Declaration of Independence of the United States of America in 1776 ... The Declaration of the Rights of man and the Citizen, made at the time of the French Revolution, in 1791, also states: "All men are born free and with equal rights, and must always remain free and have equal rights." Nevertheless, for more than eighty years, the French imperialists, abusing the standard of Liberty, Equality, and Fraternity, have violated

our fatherland and oppressed our fellow citizens. They have acted contrary to the ideals of humanity and justice.

Ho's declaration not only had a political effect on his country, but it also had a literary impact. Written in the style of previous declarations of independence, the document sets the tone for Ho's subsequent writings on the topic of his nation's liberation. In October 1945 he wrote "To the People's Committees in the Whole Country (North, South, Centre) and at All Levels (Province, District, and Village)," citing specific injustices placed on the Vietnamese by their French oppressors, including abuse of power, corruption, and sowing of discord, among other grievances. His declaration and subsequent writings forever cast him as an enemy of colonialism and Western influence where his country's independence was concerned.

THEMES AND STYLE

The main goal of the Declaration of Independence for the Democratic Republic of Vietnam is the establishment of a democratic republic with an independent government free from any invading force or colonial influence. The declaration states, "We, members of the Provisional Government, representing the whole Vietnamese people, declare that from now on we break off all relations of a colonial character with France; we repeal all the international obligation that France has so far subscribed to on behalf of Vietnam and we abolish all the special rights the French have unlawfully acquired in our Fatherland." This statement directly challenges the French colonial government to either relinquish colonial control of

HO CHI MINH'S POLITICAL WORLDVIEW

Ho Chi Minh was born May 19, 1890, in a small village in the Nghe An province of north-central Vietnam. Early in life he witnessed the oppressive poverty that surrounded him, a situation caused by the French colonial government that ruled Vietnam at the time. As a young man, he traveled extensively, spending time in France, China, and the United States as an activist and disciple of both socialism and communism. His travels helped him to develop a well-rounded political worldview, giving him the tools to work toward independence for the Vietnamese people upon his return to his country in 1941.

Ho was a revolutionary, a prophet, and a dictator over the North Vietnamese forces in both the French Indochina War of 1946-54 and in the Vietnam War (1956-75). He was a slight, soft-spoken, humble man of the people by all accounts, but his political voice motivated the People's Army of North Vietnam to continue struggling for independence even after his death at the age of seventy-nine on September 2, 1969.

the country or face an armed revolt on the part of the ruling Viet Minh.

By modeling the declaration after those of France and the United States, Ho sets a familiar emphatic tone for his wide audience: France, Japan, Vietnam, and other Western nations. In the body of the document, he lists his grievances against the current colonial government in order to challenge his

Relief depicting French commanders surrendering to Viet Minh soldiers at the Battle of Điên Biên Phu in 1954. © BJORN SVENSSON/ ALAMY

countrymen to rise up against their oppressors in order to rule their own country. He writes, "In the field of politics, they have deprived our people of every democratic liberty. They have enforced inhuman laws … They have built more prisons than schools. They have mercilessly slain our patriots … They have invented numerous unjustifiable taxes and reduced our people, especially our peasantry, to a state of extreme poverty." By referring to the Vietnamese people as "We" and the colonial forces as "They," Ho establishes himself as a member of the people, fighting on the frontlines for freedom.

After establishing himself as leader and citing specific instances of colonial injustice, Ho explains the steps his Viet Minh compatriots have taken to cooperate with the French government prior to this plea for independence. He writes,

> On several occasions … the Vietminh League urged the French to ally themselves with it against the Japanese. Instead of agreeing to this proposal, the French colonialists so intensified their terrorist activities against the Vietminh members that before fleeing they massacred a great number of our political prisoners. Notwithstanding all this, our fellow-citizens have always manifested toward the French a tolerant and humane attitude.

By explaining the French government's systematic oppression and lack of support during the Japanese occupation, Ho incites his audience to direct action in liberating the Vietnamese people from the burden of colonial rule.

CRITICAL DISCUSSION

The Declaration of Independence for the Democratic Republic of Vietnam was met with a variety of different reactions, depending on the audience. South Vietnamese leader Bao Dai abdicated his throne, acknowledging Ho as the new leader. Many Vietnamese, from both the north and the south, became interested in the Viet Minh cause after Ho's rousing nationalist speech and joined the fight for an independent Vietnam. In his book, *Vietnam 1945* (1995), David G. Marr describes the significance of Ho's speech:

> The organizers of the celebrations … on 2 September 1945 made a point of displaying the flags of the Allied powers, minus the French tricolor, alongside the banners of the Viet Minh—Democratic Republic of Vietnam … The story of Vietnam during the next fifteen months is symbolized by the removal of one after another of these flags, until only the banners of the French and the [Democratic

Republic of Vietnam] remained, held by citizens about to lock together in mortal combat.

The declaration catalyzed a moment that led to two wars that spanned thirty years and resulted in the loss of millions of American, French, and Vietnamese lives. Since it bears such striking resemblance to the declarations of independence of both France and the United States, it has been studied more as a political document than as a work of literature. Halberstam explains the political legacy of the work: "Ho had achieved the legitimacy of power. When the French dealt with the Vietnamese from now on, they would have to deal with him. When they challenged him now they would only increase his authority; when they fought him in battle they would strengthen him more … He had … become the arbiter of Vietnamese nationalism."

Although Ho set out to gain independence for Vietnam in 1945 with his declaration, it would take thirty years for the last remnants of Western imperialism to leave Vietnam, an event he did not live to see. Ho passed away on September 2, 1969, in the middle of the Vietnam War (1956-75). The words of his declaration, however, continued to motivate his forces even after his death. The Declaration of Independence for the Democratic Republic of Vietnam, along with Ho's other writings that span a political career of nearly sixty years, are viewed by many scholars as lasting examples of socialist-communist literature aspiring to free Vietnam of political oppression at the hands of outside colonial governments and invading forces.

BIBLIOGRAPHY

Sources

Halberstam, David. *Ho*. New York: Random, 1971. Print.

Marr, David G. *Vietnam 1945: The Quest for Power*. Berkeley: U of California P, 1995. Print.

Minh, Ho Chi. *Down with Colonialism!* London: Verso, 2007. Print.

Further Reading

Brocheux, Pierre. *Ho Chi Minh: A Biography*. Cambridge: Cambridge UP, 2007. Print.

Chi, Hoang Van. *From Colonialism to Communism: A Case History of North Vietnam*. New York: Praeger, 1964. Print.

Duiker, William J. *Ho Chi Minh*. New York: Hyperion, 2000. Print.

Fenn, Charles. *Ho Chi Minh: A Biographical Introduction*. New York: Scribner's, 1973. Print.

Pike, Douglas. *PAVN: People's Army of Vietnam*. New York: Di Capo, 1986. Print.

Ron Horton

DECLARATION OF THE WORKERS' AND FARMERS' RIGHTS AND PURPOSES

Louis Budenz, A. J. Muste

OVERVIEW

The "Declaration of the Workers' and Farmers' Rights and Purposes" (1933), by noted socialist advocates Louis Budenz and A.J. Muste, urges the unemployed and poor during the Great Depression to mobilize and protest the injustice of their economic conditions. One-third of the U.S. civilian population was jobless in March 1933—the highest unemployment rate in the country's history. The social and emotional impacts were tremendous; millions of people left their homes and families to find work, suffered in poverty, and lost faith in their government. The "Declaration" attempted to restore a collective viewpoint, a vision of the individual as a member of a nation, with shared political rights and responsibilities. Based on the tenets of the Declaration of Independence, Muste and Budenz's document is a prime example of civic nationalist rhetoric. It emphasizes an explicitly "American approach" to social reform by asserting the legitimacy of the American Dream of social mobility through hard work as it was established by the Founding Fathers.

Delivered at a convention held at the Ohio State Fairgrounds in Columbus on July 3 and 4, 1933, the "Declaration" was immediately and unanimously accepted by eight hundred delegates from across the nation. The gathering was organized by the Conference on Progressive Labor Action (CPLA), a group formed by Muste in 1929. The document was a more radical version of one Muste and Budenz had presented two months earlier at a meeting in Washington DC, "A New Declaration of Independence by the Continental Congress of Workers and Farmers." The July treatise explicitly articulates a desire for a change in the distribution of resources in the United States. At the convention Muste also founded the National Unemployed League, which directed the CPLA and the Socialist Party in joint efforts to engage workers in united actions such as demonstrations and strikes. One goal of the league was to obtain federal unemployment insurance for workers, a program that came into being with the Social Security Act of 1935.

HISTORICAL AND LITERARY CONTEXT

The "Declaration" was primarily designed to highlight the discrepancy between the perceived wealth of the United States and the notably unequal distribution of that wealth. In language that shows the influence of the Socialist Party, it describes "a nation possessing unlimited resources, along with the greatest industrial and transportation equipment the world has ever known"; at the same time, however, "millions of citizens are forced into dire destitution and starvation through being denied access to the tools of production." The inequality between an upper class of business leaders and a lower class of workers and farmers gave the latter the "duty to organize to change these conditions." Delineating the deplorable conditions they faced, the "Declaration" pronounces the "home, the corner-stone of the American nation [...] destroyed." It describes the "heartless" and "ruthless" mechanisms that led to this destruction as well as their negative effects on the people, who are left "struggling hopelessly under [the] overwhelming burden of debt" and "helpless against the aggression of concentrated wealth." To this end they seek to undermine the dominion of the "profit system" by establishing the sovereignty of a "workers' and farmers' republic."

The authors had long wanted to establish an American radical movement that demanded government policies supporting the rights of workers. They envisioned themselves as part of the tradition of civic nationalism that had formed the basis of the labor movement since the nineteenth century. The Panic of 1893, the worst financial disaster in the United States up until that point, gave way in 1897 to a period of relative prosperity, paving the way for the Progressive Era (1890-1920s). The achievements of this wave of social activism and political reform included standardized working hours. Unions, including the American Federation of Labor (AFL), established progressive agendas. In 1929 Muste organized the CPLA to assist U.S. workers in organizing as a revolutionary movement. As chairman of the faculty of Brookwood Labor College from 1921 to 1933, he also encouraged student participation. Unemployed leagues were created in numerous states: their greatest following was in Ohio, the site of the 1933 convention. Working-class participation declined significantly in the 1920s but grew again after the inauguration of Franklin Delano Roosevelt as president in 1933. His New Deal Coalition united the unions, and his National Industrial Recovery Act

✣ **Key Facts**

Time Period:
Mid-20th Century

Movement/Issue:
Civic nationalism; Great Depression-era workers' rights movement

Place of Publication:
United States

Language of Publication:
English

A. J. MUSTE: UNEMPLOYED ORGANIZER

Abraham Johannes Muste was born in 1885 in the Netherlands. His parents immigrated with their families to the United States in 1891, when Muste was around six years old. In 1896 he became a naturalized U.S. citizen. He attended Hope College in Michigan, where he excelled in sports and, in 1905, earned a BA as a valedictorian of his class. Muste was one of the major figures in a 1919 textile strike in Lawrence, Massachusetts, an almost four-month ordeal. This experience inspired him to become a labor organizer, and he served as a leader in the newly created Amalgamated Textile Workers of America from 1919 to 1921.

In 1925, influenced by John L. Lewis, president of the United Mine Workers, Muste joined Louis Budenz to engender a radical American movement that could foment interest in labor rights. To realize this goal, the two men organized the Conference on Progressive Labor Action in 1929, a body that was designed to assist workers in their attempts to unionize. They continued their efforts by coordinating the National Unemployed League in 1932 and the American Workers Party in 1933. Muste used his role in these organizations to mobilize 10,000 workers in Toledo, Ohio, in 1934 in a well-known American Federation of Labor strike against an auto company. He continued to be influential in the labor movement until his decision to end his connections with socialism in 1936; at this point in his career, he opted instead to dedicate his efforts toward Christian pacifism.

of 1933 provided support for them. The workers felt their protests were vindicated.

The "Declaration" uses rhetoric first employed by John L. Lewis, president of the United Mine

The *Declaration of the Workers' and Farmers' Rights and Purposes* was written in reaction to the Great Depression. This illustration shows a group of men marching during the Depression to protest the lack of work, a consequence of the actions taken by the "industrial system" called out in the manifesto. PRIVATE COLLECTION/© LOOK AND LEARN/THE BRIDGEMAN ART LIBRARY

Workers from 1920 to 1960. Lewis strove to infuse politics and actual workplaces with a much more potent enactment of democratic principles. Muste and Budenz's May 1933 "New Declaration of Independence by the Continental Congress of Workers and Farmers" more openly asserted its connection to the Declaration of Independence and more specifically indicted the federal government for its transgressions against the unemployed workers and struggling farmers and its failure to take action to ameliorate the desperate economic conditions.

In aligning more radical rhetoric with patriotic language, the July "Declaration" expanded the understanding of the rights that workers should possess in a democratic society. Subsequent governmental legislation included the 1935 National Labor Relations Act (NLRA; also called the Wagner Act), which strengthened collective bargaining rights, established workers' right to strike, and inhibited harmful private sector labor practices. The bill's passage was a strong victory for advocates of workers' rights in the United States and has remained crucial in engendering successful labor relations. Muste continued his heavy involvement in labor activism, although he formally dissociated himself from the Socialist Party in 1936. Budenz remained a Socialist Party member and worked as a journalist and an editor at the *Daily Worker*, a publication sponsored by the U.S. Communist Party.

THEMES AND STYLE

The "Declaration of the Workers' and Farmers' Rights and Purposes" calls for the individual's right to work rather than having to receive "sustenance" from the government. It echoes the Declaration of Independence not only in its language but also in recalling the conditions faced by the American colonists, correlating them with workers' circumstances in the early 1930s. Urging working men to challenge the federal government as the colonists had confronted the British, the "Declaration" alludes to the positive outcome of earlier American men taking action in the face of oppression: in fighting the "tyranny of kings, America was born." The document also uses the Civil War as an example: "When the men of 1860 destroyed chattel slavery, America's development as a great industrial state was made possible." Muste and Budenz conclude by emphasizing that "when the men and women of today shall finally crush the tyranny of bankers and bosses, America shall at last be free." This final sentence forecasts a victory similar to those of the past and elevates the level of suffering in the 1930s to match that of historical conditions that required warfare to ameliorate them.

Through its similarities with and references to the Declaration of Independence, the "Declaration" establishes its status. The phrase "We hold that" prefaces a list of specific demands, mimicking the similar (albeit longer) 1776 list, which begins: "We hold these truths to be self-evident." The parallelism draws an implicit comparison between the oppressive conditions of the two eras.

Boldly describing grievances in systematic, unemotional language, the "Declaration" insists on the authority and legitimacy of a rational approach. The introductory passages utilize legal-sounding, objectively constructed phrases that echo the authority and command of the Declaration of Independence. For example, Muste and Budenz open with "When, in a nation possessing unlimited resources," recalling the original's "When in the Course of human events, it becomes necessary …" By delineating the transgressions enacted by "banks and bosses" against U.S. farmers and workers, the "Declaration" provides its own evidence for indicting "tyranny." The formal tone connects the grandeur of the American Revolution with the "fight" for rights of the 1930s.

CRITICAL DISCUSSION

The eight hundred delegates at the 1933 convention in Columbus responded to the "Declaration" with a rousing rendition of "America the Beautiful." The unemployed leagues were carrying patriotic signs featuring the slogan "Don't Tread on Me" and the rattlesnake flag of the Revolutionary period. Near the beginning of the convention, a delegation known as the "Stars and Stripes" group, comprised of Ku Klux Klan members and other racist extremists, objected to the omission of the "Star Spangled Banner" in the opening ceremonies. Temporarily seizing control during the proceedings, they led the song. By the convention's second day, however, when the "Declaration" was introduced, the original leaders had regained their authority. Twenty-five leaders of various smaller unemployed leagues joined Muste in signing the document.

The "Declaration of the Workers' and Farmers' Rights and Purposes" helped inspire a massive 1934 demonstration composed of 10,000 workers in Toledo, Ohio. The rally featured a banner with the dates "1776-1865-1934," linking the Declaration of Independence, Abraham Lincoln (who delivered his Second Inaugural Address, one of history's greatest speeches, in 1865 and was murdered the same year), and the contemporary protests. Over the course of the 1930s, a period of labor activism supported by Roosevelt's New Deal policies, successive pieces of legislation gradually enlarged the unions' capacity to protect U.S. workers. In the years following the "Declaration," the federal government established the National Labor Relations Board (NLRB) to investigate and resolve charges of unfair labor practices and organize elections for union representation.

The "Declaration" has received very little critical attention. It has earned mention in some studies within the social sciences, particularly in sociology and economics. In "The Unemployed Workers Movement of the 1930s" (1990), scholar Steve Valocchi discusses the document within the broader context of Muste's legacy and his involvement in the organized protests of the unemployed leagues and other organizations.

BIBLIOGRAPHY

Sources

"The Charters of Freedom: The Declaration of Independence." *National Archives.* National Archives and Records Administration, n.d. Web. 4 Oct. 2012.

Folsom, Franklin. *America before Welfare.* New York: New York UP, 1991. Print.

Fox-Piven, Frances, and Cloward, Richard. *Poor People's Movements: Why They Succeed and How They Fail.* New York: Pantheon, 1977. Print.

Gerstle, Gary. *American Crucible: Race and Nation in the Twentieth Century.* Princeton: Princeton UP, 2001. Print.

Lucia, Danny. "Bringing Misery out of Hiding: The Unemployed Movement of the 1930s." *International Socialist Review* 71 (2010). Center for Economic Research and Social Change. Web. 2 Oct. 2012

National Unemployed Leagues. "Declaration of Workers' and Farmers' Rights and Purposes." *We the Other People: Alternative Declarations of Independence by Labor Groups, Farmers, Woman's Rights Advocates, Socialists, and Blacks, 1829-1975.* Ed. Philip Sheldon Foner. Urbana: U of Illinois P, 1976: 159-62. Print.

Further Reading

Gaul, Teresa. *Letters and Cultural Transformations in the United States, 1760-1860.* Burlington: Ashgate, 2009. Print.

Lyon, Janet. *Manifestoes: Provocations of the Modern.* Ithaca: Cornell UP, 1999. Print.

Rosenzweig, Roy. "Radicals and the Jobless: The Musteites and the Unemployed Leagues, 1932-1936." *Labor History* 16.1. (1975): 52-77. Print.

Valocchi, Steve. "The Unemployed Workers Movement of the 1930s: A Reexamination of the Piven and Cloward Thesis." *Society for the Study of Social Problems* 37.2. (1990): 191-205. Print.

———. "External Resources and the Unemployed Councils of the 1930s: Evaluating Six Propositions from Social Movement Theory." *Sociological Forum* 8.3 (1993): 451-70. Print.

Grace Waitman

AN EXHORTATION TO PROGRESS

B. Mustafa Kemal

✣ *Key Facts*

Time Period:
Early 20th Century

Movement/Issue:
Turkish nationalism;
Secularism; Democratic
reform

Place of Publication:
Turkey

**Language of
Publication:**
Turkish

OVERVIEW

"An Exhortation to Progress" (1925) is a speech by B. Mustafa Kemal (he acquired the surname Atatürk in 1934) outlining his plan to redefine the Turkish national identity. The speech was delivered on August 30 in the northern Black Sea province of Kastomonu, a stop on one of Mustafa Kemal's many tours of the countryside to personally introduce the Turkish people to a sweeping program of political and cultural reform. Mustafa Kemal had been elected president of the newly created Republic of Turkey in 1923 following his victorious military campaign in the Turkish War of Independence (1919-22). Riding the tide of nationalistic fervor, he sought through his speeches to build support for his massive social revolution, which would transform Turkey from a deeply Islamic state into a secular democracy based on the Western model. An English version of the speech appeared in the American magazine *Living Age* on October 31, 1925, translated from the September 1, 1925, Constantinople daily *Akşam.*

"An Exhortation to Progress," more commonly known as the Kastomonu speech, is considered especially significant as marking the first time Mustafa Kemal publicly announced a new dress code that would outlaw the wearing of the traditional Islamic turban and fez in favor of the Western-style hat. The so-called "hat law," passed two months later, was widely publicized in the Western press as evidence of Turkey's emerging modern consciousness. However, among all of Mustafa Kemal's progressive measures, it was the one most seriously opposed in the country itself as too radical a challenge to the Muslim identity. Riots broke out over the ban, and hundreds of demonstrators were arrested and sentenced to be executed. The controversy surrounding the hat law highlights the biases of the Mustafa Kemal government and the often brutal manner of their enforcement, issues that are central to a consideration of his legacy. The "Exhortation" became newly relevant in 1982 when the Turkish government unleashed a firestorm of controversy with its ban on women wearing the traditional headscarf in the public sector.

HISTORICAL AND LITERARY CONTEXT

Kemalism, the ideology producing the progressive reforms, was launched to reverse several centuries of political and economic decline that had culminated in the Ottoman Empire's defeat by the Allies in World War I. Following the war, British, French, Greek, and Italian forces occupied western and southern parts of Anatolia and the Ottoman capital of Constantinople. This foreign presence, combined with a proposed peace treaty that would partition the empire into several independent territories, mobilized the nationalist forces under the leadership of Mustafa Kemal. The Turkish War of Independence ensued, the outcome of which was the proclamation of the Republic of Turkey on October 29, 1923.

At the start of the war for independence, Mustafa Kemal resigned from the Ottoman army and convened a national assembly in the stark provincial city of Ankara, far from the tradition-rich capital of the Ottoman Empire, Constantinople. The consolidation of power in the new national assembly forced the abdication of the sultan. In his most decisive break with the past, Mustafa Kemal rejected the political authority of the caliph, the spiritual head of the Islamic state, as a symbol of a medieval way of life destructive to progress and the new spirit of science and reason. This reform marked the first time in Turkish history Islamic law was subordinated to the state and confined solely to matters of religion.

The idea of reform was not new to Turkey. Mustafa Kemal had participated in the Young Turk Revolution of 1908, a movement largely composed of military officers that succeeded in overthrowing the absolutist rule of the Ottoman sultan Abdülhamid II (1876-1909). The Young Turks liberalized education and promoted industrialization, but they remained attached to the ideas of empire and religious law. By 1919, when Mustafa Kemal spearheaded the national resistance, he had already distanced himself from the Committee of Union and Progress, which ruled the empire between 1908 and 1918, orchestrating the Ottoman Empire's entry into World War I and perpetrating the Armenian genocide. According to Robert I. Rotberg in his essay in *Transformative Political Leadership* (2012), "Many, if not all, of Kemal's envisaged reforms had been suggested in print and in conversation years before by prominent novelists and coffee-house intellectuals." Mustafa Kemal famously summarized the history of the national resistance movement and the founding principles of the new republic in his *Nutuk* (the Speech), which he delivered over the course of six days in October 1927 to the congress of the Republican People's Party.

"An Exhortation to Progress" set the stage for a string of radical reforms implemented in the next decade. These include a ban on Dervish brotherhoods and religious schools (madrasahs) and courts, the replacement of the Arabo-Persian script with the modified Latin alphabet, the adoption of the Christian calendar, the extension of the vote to women, and the removal of all Ottoman words from the vocabulary. To this day, Turkey remains the only secular Muslim country, but Kemalist nationalism, still the official state ideology, has come under increasing fire by Islamic conservatism. The conflict in Turkey between secularism and Islam informs contemporary issues as diverse as the proposed entry of the nation into the European Union and the 2010 repeal of the 1982 headscarf law.

THEMES AND STYLE

Civilized modernity, as mandated by an expansive vision of reform that celebrates rational inquiry over the "absurd superstitions and prejudices" of the Islamic religion, is the main idea put forth in "An Exhortation to Progress." Mustafa Kemal announces a variety of restrictions on religious practice as remedies for a pervasive ignorance that cripples Turkey's advancement: "I can never tolerate the existence, in the bosom of a civilized Turkish society, of those primitive-minded men who seek material or moral well-being under the guidance of a sheik, possibly blind and hostile to the clear light of modern science and art." He calls for the closing of Muslim shrines, Dervish lodges, and sacred tombs; the routing of sham holy men; and the elimination of the fez and the turban as elements of the national costume for men. Mustafa Kemal very deliberately makes clothing the site of identity construction. Wearing a Western-style Panama hat himself during the speech, he pointed to a man in the audience outfitted in a fez and turban and vest with billowing sleeves and charged that such "outlandish garb" made Turkey appear "ridiculous" in the eyes of the West. On November 25, 1925, the headwear decree was converted into law.

Mustafa Kemal is careful to address his audience in terms that presuppose allegiance. He speaks of "we," "us," and "our" when referring to the revolution and the civilizing project. At one point, in a strategy designed to assure the people he acts solely in their best interests, he refers to himself as "your twin brother, your friend and father." In her 2011 essay in *Journal of Social History*, Camilla T. Nereid describes the speech as carefully organized to establish the logical necessity of the reforms:

> Reading the speech in a historical context, it is obvious how [Mustafa Kemal] tries to persuade his listeners and to confront anticipated

AN EYEWITNESS ACCOUNT OF THE HAT LAW

British historian Arnold J. Toynbee made some interesting firsthand observations of the Turkish hat law in his travel diary of the country, which was published in *A Journey to China, or Things Which Are Seen* (1931). Writing four years after the passage of the law, Toynbee notes that the only men wearing the fez in Turkey were foreigners. Remarking on the omnipresence of the fez in the neighboring countries of Bulgaria and Syria, he writes, "The impression is like that made by a Russian newspaper in which the censor has covered the paragraph with a pall of ink.... The print has merely been draped; it has not been erased. And so I believe it is with hats in Turkey. Many a self-consciously beheaded man is still wearing an invisible fez."

Although no such prescription as the hat law presides over Turkish women's dress, Toynbee comments on the emancipation of Turkish women under the reforms of Mustafa Kemal. Riding the streetcar, he is surprised to discover that a sliding curtain is no longer used to separate the male and female passengers. He also notes that most Turkish women have abandoned the face veil, yet many favor the wimple, a piece of cloth covering the hair and neck.

disagreement. A closer look at the sequence in which the various topics are presented makes it possible to discover a hierarchy of values, a ranking where the revolution figures as number

In his *Design for a Modern Secular Turkish State*, Mustafa Kemal Atatürk called for Turkey to adopt western dress like the suit he wears here. Although he is also sporting a fez in this portrait, he states that the fez and other types of clothing traditionally associated with Turkey should be reformed. © WORLD HISTORY ARCHIVE/ ALAMY

one, followed by the nation (millet), the Turkish republic, the civilized Turkish people who wear civilized attire, and, lastly those Turks who claim to be civilized, and yet who do not don civilized attire. And it is precisely this hierarchy of values that served to legitimize the measures employed to secularize Turkish society, including the enactment of the Hat Law.

The tone of Kemal's speech is uncompromising: "Friends, gentlemen, fellow countrymen! You well know that the Republic of Turkey can never be a country of dervishes and sheiks and their disciples. The only true congregation is that of the great international confraternity of civilization." Far from superficial, the sartorial regulations go to the heart of Muslim religious practice. Headgear had been a mark of religious authority throughout the history of the Ottoman Empire. Further, the rimmed European hat, formerly the mark of the infidel, is particularly unsuited to Muslim worship: the fez, because it has no rim, allows Muslims to touch their foreheads to the ground when they prostrate themselves in canonical prayer.

CRITICAL DISCUSSION

In line with the populist platform of his Republican People's Party, Mustafa Kemal had claimed that the hat law would help to eliminate social stratification, such as the status grades implied by Ottoman head coverings, which had reserved the turban for the clergy and the fez for civil and military officials. In reality, however, the Turkish population remained firmly divided between highly educated urbanites and the majority rural population, despite government literacy campaigns. The government's quick suppression of the Kurdish Revolt of 1925 and a plot on Mustafa Kemal's life the following year effectively discouraged any further organized opposition to his one-party rule. Still, a vocal resistance developed among left-wing intellectuals to the speed, scope, and rigor of the reforms.

Among the earliest dissenters to Kemalism was the pioneering female novelist and politician Halide Edib Adivar. A former patriot and friend of Mustafa Kemal, she and her husband escaped to France in 1926 when the government accused them of the public denigration of Turkishness. Three years later, she published an indictment of Mustafa Kemal's dictatorial regime in the *Yale Review* in which she directly addresses the subject of the hat law:

> In a week it made the Turks don European hats ... and made them look like Westerners, although the manner in which it was accomplished was utterly un-Western.... The Westernization of Turkey is not and should not be a question of mere external imitation and

gesture.... To tell the Turk to put on a certain headdress and "get civilized" or be hanged, or imprisoned, is absurd, to say the least.

Turkey's most well-known contemporary writer, Orhan Pamuk, was charged with treason in 2005 for daring to publicly discuss the state-sponsored massacres of the Armenians and the Kurds. The charges were dropped, but Pamuk's selection as the first Turkish recipient of the Nobel Prize in Literature in 2006 is widely reported to have been politically motivated by his defense of ethnic minorities. Although he is well known for resuscitating the Ottoman past in his fiction, Pamuk has published only one overtly political novel, *Kar* (2002), which dramatizes the controversy over the government's 1982 headscarf ban and describes a rash of suicides among teenage girls persecuted for refusing to remove their headscarves in the classroom. Pamuk is internationally known as the most articulate spokesperson for the East/West cultural divide that increasingly fractures the Turkish national identity, throwing a spotlight on Mustafa Kemal's two-edged legacy as savior and tyrant and fueling the debate about the relevance of his precepts for twenty-first-century society.

BIBLIOGRAPHY

Sources

"Halide Edib [Adivar], Dictatorship and Reform in Turkey (1929)." *Middle East and Islamic World Reader.* Ed. Marvin Gettleman and Stuart Schaar. New York: Grove, 2003. 127-32. Print.

Kemal, Mustafa. "An Exhortation to Progress." *Living Age* 31 (1925): 232-33. *UNZ.org.* Web. 25 Sept. 2012.

Nereid, Camilla T. "Kemalism on the Catwalk: The Turkish Hat Law of 1925." *Journal of Social History* 44.3 (2011). *BioMedSearch.com.* Web. 26 Sept. 2012.

Rotberg, Robert I. "Kemal Ataturk: Uncompromising Modernizer." *Transformative Political Leadership: Making a Difference in the Developing World.* Chicago: U of Chicago P, 2012. 119-44. Print.

Further Reading

Kinross, Patrick Balfour. *Atatürk.* New York: William Morrow, 1965. Print.

Mango, Andrew. *Atatürk: The Biography of the Founder of Modern Turkey.* New York: Overlook, 2002. Print.

"Mustafa Kemal, Design for a Modern Secular Turkish State (1925)." *The Middle East and Islamic World Reader.* Ed. Marvin Gettleman and Stuart Schaar. New York: Grove, 2003. 125-27. Print.

Scott, Georgia. *Headwraps: A Global Journey.* New York: Public Affairs, 2003. Print.

Zürcher, Erik J. *The Young Turk Legacy and Nation Building: From the Ottoman Empire to Atatürk's Turkey.* London: I. B. Tauris, 2012. Print.

Janet Mullane

FEMINIST MANIFESTO

Mina Loy

OVERVIEW

Composed in 1914 but not published until 1982, the "Feminist Manifesto" by Mina Loy is a critique of contemporary feminism and a strident call for a radical form of women's liberation. The manifesto was, in part, an outcome of Loy's affiliation with futurism, a modernist Italian artistic movement that advocated the destruction of tradition and embraced modernity's speed and chaos. Through her personal and artistic involvement with the futurists, Loy was compelled by the movement's liberating artistic vision but repelled by the group's misogynistic tenets and practices. Her manifesto reflects her ambivalence about not only futurism but also the feminist movement, whose tactics she rejected. Addressed to all women, the "Feminist Manifesto" rejects mainstream feminist efforts for reform and equality as "inadequate" and outlines Loy's often violent vision for liberating women from oppression.

Loy shared the "Feminist Manifesto" only with her patron Mabel Dodge Luhan, and it was never published during her lifetime; nevertheless, the work quickly became a popular and influential feminist document when it appeared in the late twentieth century in such anthologies as *The Gender of Modernism* (1990). Loy's manifesto was important for establishing an early alternative to reform-minded mainstream feminism and for asserting a vision of female autonomy that rejects modernism's support of impersonality. The manifesto is also important for its radical claims regarding the political nature of the body. The "Feminist Manifesto" is one of Loy's most widely read works and is recognized as a foundational document of feminism.

HISTORICAL AND LITERARY CONTEXT

The "Feminist Manifesto" responds to the oppression of women in the early twentieth century, when patriarchal authority over the lives and bodies of women was being challenged and resisted. Opposition to the Comstock Law of 1873, which criminalized birth control and abortion in the United States, provided an important rallying point for feminism. According to Linda A. Kinnahan in *Poetics of the Feminine* (1994), "An insistent and vocal resistance to this law helped publicly heighten the issue of a woman's right to control her body." At the turn of the century, activists known as suffragettes began to advocate for women's right to vote. In England, where Loy was born, the Women's Social and Political Union formed in 1903 and initiated various violent actions to protest women's oppression. In the 1910s feminists protested the institution of marriage and the state's regulation of women's bodies. Protests, tracts, and speeches proliferated as the fight for political freedom intensified.

When Loy penned her manifesto in 1914 in Florence, Italy, she was romantically and artistically involved with Filippo Tommaso Marinetti, the leader of the futurist movement. Although he claimed to support the women's suffrage movement, he was dismissive of femininity. As quoted by Carolyn Burke in *Becoming Modern* (1996), Marinetti maintained that, however their political status and roles might change, women would remain within the "closed circle" of femininity, "as a mother, as a wife, and as a lover." This scornful and condescending attitude spurred Loy's interest in the ongoing movement to empower women and expand their rights. Loy was particularly interested in the work of the activist Margaret Sanger, who argued that a woman's right to control her own body was the first necessary step in her liberation and who rejected the idea that love and reproduction were the purposes of sex. In the letter to Mabel Dodge Luhan that included her "Feminist Manifesto," Loy inquired about Sanger's controversial new magazine, the *Woman Rebel*.

The "Feminist Manifesto" was written in response to the *Manifesto of Futurism* by Marinetti. Published in 1909, the *Manifesto of Futurism* outlines the aims of a new style of art that embraced aggression, energy, and freedom; that sought to "glorify war—the world's only hygiene—militarism, patriotism"; and that vowed to "fight moralism, feminism, every opportunistic or utilitarian cowardice." With the "Feminist Manifesto," Loy appropriates the literary technique and tone of the *Manifesto of Futurism* in order to critique both the futurist movement's misogyny and the feminist movement's inadequacy. Like Marinetti's manifesto, Loy's work rejects "the rubbish heap of tradition" and declares that violence and destruction are the only true methods of progress. The manifesto's critique of patriarchy, feminism, and

✣ Key Facts

Time Period:
Early 20th Century

Movement/Issue:
Feminism

Place of Publication:
United States

Language of Publication:
English

MINA LOY: UNMOORED ARTIST

Raised in a strict Victorian household in nineteenth-century London, Mina Loy escaped to art school as soon as she could. She traveled to Munich and Paris, the heart of the burgeoning avant-garde. She studied to be a painter, married a fellow British artist, had several children, and moved to Florence, where she befriended such luminaries as the writer Gertrude Stein. Although Loy exhibited her paintings in Paris and London, she soon turned to experiments in poetry and prose as her main creative output. Her "lewd and lascivious writing," as the critic Alfred Kreymborg described it in a quote cited by Linda Kinnahan, was published in small but prestigious journals.

Venturing to New York City in 1916, Loy moved even closer to the center of the modernist revolution in art and became involved with the ready-made artist Marcel Duchamp, the surrealist photographer Man Ray, the experimental writer Djuna Barnes, and the imagist poet William Carlos Williams. After moves to Mexico, South America, and Berlin, Loy spent nearly fifteen years in Paris as the owner of a shop that sold lamps and other objects of her design. When she returned to New York, she created art from the city's garbage and wrote poetry about the street people with whom she, as a social outsider, identified. In 1953 she moved for the last time, to Aspen, Colorado, where she continued to make art but ceased writing poetry. Loy died in Colorado in 1966.

tradition are themes that Loy also confronted in the poetry she was writing at the time.

Although the "Feminist Manifesto" was never published during Loy's lifetime, its influence can be felt strongly in Loy's subsequent and highly influential literary output. In the two years following the composition of the "Feminist Manifesto," Loy published a number of poems that explore similar ground. "Parturition," also from 1914, describes in explicit detail the experience of childbirth and contrasts what Kinnahan calls the "creative capacity arising from such specifically woman's pain" with the "shallow and calculated lust of male sexuality." In the poetry that followed over the next several decades, Loy wrestled with her female experience and with the feminist aim of reimagining society. When the "Feminist Manifesto" finally appeared in the 1982 edition of Loy's poetry collection *The Lost Lunar Baedeker*, and as Loy's reputation as a poet was revived, Loy became a major influence on contemporary poets, who were inspired by her inventive explorations of the female experience.

THEMES AND STYLE

The central theme of the "Feminist Manifesto" is that women must repudiate the prospect of reform, dismantle their preconceptions about femininity, and rebuild themselves free of patriarchal illusions. With the verve of futurism propelling it forward,

the "Feminist Manifesto" opens emphatically: "The feminist movement as at present instituted is Inadequate[.]" It then addresses its audience directly: "Women if you want to realise yourselves—you are on the eve of a devastating psychological upheaval—all your pet illusions must be unmasked—the lies of centuries have got to go—are you prepared for the Wrench—?" The manifesto goes on to list the illusions women must "demolish" and the sacrifices they must make. They must rid themselves of "virtue," undergo "the unconditional surgical destruction of virginity" at puberty, embrace maternity outside marriage, destroy "the desire to be loved," retain their "deceptive fragility of appearance," and acknowledge that "there is nothing impure in sex."

The manifesto achieves its rhetorical aims through direct appeals to the power and potential of women. Loy addresses readers in the second person, as a collective, united, and empowered "you." The "Feminist Manifesto" dispenses with the idea of victimhood and appeals instead to the ambition of her female readers. "Professional & commercial careers are opening up for you—Is that all you want?" The manifesto also explicitly rejects the "clap-trap war cry" of equality for women. Loy instructs readers to "leave off looking to men to find out what you are not," urging women instead to "seek within yourselves to find out what you are." In Loy's view, "Men and women are enemies," but conflict between them can generate freedom for women, if they are willing to renounce their illusions and embrace the destruction of comfort and virtue. Rather than promising her reader any defined victories, Loy offers "an incalculable & wider social regeneration than it is possible for our generation to imagine."

Stylistically, the "Feminist Manifesto" is distinguished by its grammatical and typographical inventiveness. With its unconventional punctuation and capitalization, its boldface and underlined words, and its variations in font size, the manifesto takes a poetic and spontaneous form. These stylistic decisions set the document in immediate opposition to convention and tradition. Unlike an enumerated list of aims (the form in which the *Manifesto of Futurism* is arranged), Loy's manifesto appears chaotic and open on the page. This presentation reflects the tone and tenor of her argument. She is not making a closed and limited case for certain political or social aims; instead, Loy is offering a fluid critique of feminism and an unconstrained investigation of female liberation.

CRITICAL DISCUSSION

When the "Feminist Manifesto" was finally published nearly seventy years after its composition, it received immediate attention from scholars of feminism and modernism. Numerous critics saw the manifesto as a kind of key to Loy's entire artistic career. Loy's poetry was characteristically open, indirect, and obscure, and the "Feminist Manifesto" offered an unusually direct statement of her aims as a woman and as an artist. Scholars who had viewed her work through the lens of modernism and futurism had to reevaluate their interpretations in light of the passionate and complex stance of the "Feminist Manifesto." When the manifesto appeared in the anthology *The Gender of Modernism,* Loy was placed alongside such writers as Djuna Barnes, Willa Cather, Marianne Moore, Ezra Pound, and Sylvia Townsend Warner. Situating the manifesto in this context helped define Loy's place as a rebellious female voice in the canon of modernist literature.

Since its appearance, the "Feminist Manifesto" has remained an important source for discussion of Loy's place in modernist poetics and feminist politics. According to Kinnahan, "The revolt against tradition informing the modernist project, for this modern woman, depended upon a feminist commitment to radical change of sexual conventions." In the decades since its publication, Loy's manifesto has been the subject of a growing body of criticism that has explored its legacy in terms of class, identity, and gender.

Several scholars have begun to consider the ways in which the "Feminist Manifesto" critiques the relationship between economics and gender. In *Cultures of Modernism: Gender and Literary Community in New York and Berlin* (2005), Cristanne Miller observes that "women are never independent of a heterosexual and sexist economy in Loy's 'Feminist Manifesto.'" In "The Manifest Professional: Manifestos and Modern Legitimation" (2000), Johanna E. Vondeling places Loy's manifesto in the context of the Vorticist manifestos of Ezra Pound and Wyndham Lewis, as well as the futurist manifestos of Marinetti and others, arguing that "the proliferation of manifestos in the early years of [the twentieth] century suggests the modernist artist's efforts to forestall marginalization by the corporate economy that has predominated in England and America since roughly the 1890s." Scholars have also begun to examine the manifesto as a response to Loy's identity, not only as woman but also as a Jew. Aimee L. Pozorski, in her article "Eugenicist Mistress and Ethnic Mother: Mina Loy and Futurism, 1913-1917" (2005), determines that the "Feminist Manifesto" "demonstrates an intense ambivalence about [Loy's] Jewish heritage."

BIBLIOGRAPHY

Sources

Burke, Carolyn. *Becoming Modern: The Life of Mina Loy.* New York: Farrar, 1996. Print.

Kinnahan, Linda A. *Poetics of the Feminine: Authority and Literary Tradition in William Carlos Williams, Mina Loy, Denise Levertov, and Kathleen Fraser.* New York: Cambridge UP, 1994. Print.

Loy, Mina. "Feminist Manifesto." *The Lost Luna Baedeker.* Ed. Roger Conover. New York: Farrar, 1996. 153-56. Print.

Marinetti, F.T. *Manifesto of Futurism.* 1909. New Haven: Yale Library Associates, 1983. Print.

Miller, Cristanne. *Cultures of Modernism: Gender and Literary Community in New York and Berlin.* Ann Arbor: U of Michigan P, 2005. Print.

Pozorski, Aimee L. "Eugenicist Mistress and Ethnic Mother: Mina Loy and Futurism, 1913-1917." *MELUS* 30.3 (2005): 41-69. Web. 8 June 2012.

Vondeling, Johanna E. "The Manifest Professional: Manifestos and Modernist Legitimation." *College Literature* 27. 2 (2000): 127-45. Web. 9 June 2012.

Further Reading

Fields, Kenneth. "The Poetry of Mina Loy." *Southern Review* 3.2 (1967): 597-607. Print.

Jaskoski, Helen. "Mina Loy Outsider Artist." *Journal of Modern Literature* 28.4 (1993): 349-68. Print.

Kouidis, Virginia M. *Mina Loy: Modern American Poet.* Baton Rouge: Louisiana State UP, 1980. Print.

Poster for the *Suffragette* newspaper, circa 1910-1915. The women's suffrage movement was gaining support when Mina Loy wrote her "Feminist Manifesto" in 1914. © HERITAGE IMAGES/CORBIS

Loy, Mina. *Stories and Essays of Mina Loy.* Ed. Sara Crangle. Urbana: Dalkey Archive, 2011. Print.

Lusty, Natalya. "Sexing the Manifesto: Mina Loy, Feminism, and Futurism." *Women: A Cultural Review* 19.3 (2008): 245-60. Web. 8 June 2012.

Schaum, Melita. "'Moon-flowers out of Muck': Mina Loy and the Autobiographical Epic." *Massachusetts Studies in English* 10.4 (1986): 254-76. Print.

Scott, Bonnie Kime, ed. *The Gender of Modernism: A Critical Anthology.* Bloomington: Indiana UP, 1990. Print.

Shreiber, Maerra, and Keith Tuma, eds. *Mina Loy: Woman and Poet.* Orono: National Poetry Foundation, 1998. Print.

Stauder, Ellen Keck. "On Mina Loy." *Modernism/ Modernity* 4.3 (1997): 141-46. Print.

Theodore McDermott

FOURTEEN POINTS

Woodrow Wilson

OVERVIEW

On January 8, 1918, less than a year after the United States entered World War I by declaring war on Germany, U.S. president Woodrow Wilson presented his Fourteen Points, outlining the American terms of peace, at a joint session of Congress. The statement came only months after the October Revolution in Russia, when the Bolsheviks seized power and withdrew from the Allies, accusing Allied nations of imperialistic motives. In presenting the Fourteen Points, Wilson sought to clarify American objectives and to enumerate the conditions for lasting peace. Compiled by a group of U.S. foreign policy experts, Wilson's plan contains fourteen objectives: the first five are broad in scope, the next eight address specific territorial matters, and the final point proposes an association of nations to mediate future conflicts and to advocate for world peace.

Allied leaders, including British foreign secretary Arthur Balfour, initially resisted the proposal, expressing concerns about its applicability and the efficacy of Wilson's idealism. However, the American and European public embraced the plan, and pressure from German citizens eventually led Prince Maximilian of Baden, who briefly took power as German chancellor in 1918, to cease fighting and begin peace talks on the basis of the Fourteen Points. Although Wilson's policy program was substantially modified during the Paris Peace Conference in 1919, his idealistic vision helped to shape the terms of the German surrender. Today the Fourteen Points are considered an important turning point in global diplomacy and a crucial step in outlining the rationale for the League of Nations and its successor organization, the United Nations.

HISTORICAL AND LITERARY CONTEXT

The Fourteen Points were formulated in response to the increasingly complex state of global affairs that helped initiate World War I. In December 1916, although the United States had not officially entered the conflict, President Wilson attempted to facilitate the peace process by convening negotiations between the Allies and Germany. Neither side found the other's terms acceptable, however, and talks broke down. Until that point, the United States

had practiced a strict noninterventionist policy, but German submarine attacks on U.S. naval fleets prompted Congress to declare war on Germany on April 6, 1917. The declaration changed the role of the United States in the peace process, making Wilson an official partner in subsequent negotiations.

Wilson delivered his speech only weeks after the Bolsheviks declared their own six-point program for peace, entering into independent talks with Germany. Months earlier, the Bolsheviks had instituted a socialist regime in Russia, ending Russia's partnership with the Allies under allegations of imperialist designs. Although Wilson had previously requested the Allies to publicly declare their war aims, none had heeded his call. Enlisting the help of a team of some 150 academics led by foreign policy advisor Edward M. House and known as the Inquiry, Wilson devised a proposal that applied the same progressive principles used to create domestic reform in the United States—free trade, open agreements, democracy, and self-determination—to resolving the global political crisis.

The Bolsheviks' six points and Wilson's Fourteen Points share similarities; however Wilson dismissed the Russian plan out of distrust of the new Soviet government and its socialist ideologies. The Bolshevik plan demanded an end to militaristic annexation, independence for formerly sovereign nations, self-determination for oppressed regions, protection of the rights of minorities, an international fund to compensate citizens for loss of property, and a review of colonial disputes according to the first four points. Although Wilson agreed in principle with the proposal's ideals of liberalization and self-determination, he wished to draft a statement that reflected an American, and more generally an Allied, point of view.

The Fourteen Points have been adopted as a model for numerous independence movements around the globe. Only months after Wilson delivered the points to Congress, a group of leading Korean citizens, inspired by his insistence on self-determination, organized the March First Movement, demanding Korean independence from the Japanese empire. In 1941 the Atlantic Charter, which defined the goals of Allied forces during World War II, took the Fourteen Points as their foundation. Similarly,

❖ *Key Facts*

Time Period:
Early 20th Century

Movement/Issue:
World War I

Place of Publication:
United States

Language of Publication:
English

THE LEAGUE OF NATIONS: A DREAM NOT QUITE REALIZED

At the center of Wilson's Fourteen Points is his vision of a League of Nations, which was formed after the Paris Peace Conference in 1919. The goals outlined in the League's covenant took inspiration from Wilson's points and included imposing sanctions for violation of international agreements, monitoring threats to peace, and arbitrating disputes. Although the forty-two member states all approved of these general principles and an overall structure of governance, they had difficulty agreeing on the specific functions and constitution of the League. Members also disagreed on whether or not to restrict permanent membership to major world powers only. They finally settled on an assembly in which representatives would meet annually to set global policy. The League also had a smaller council that met more frequently. All decisions of the assembly and of the council had to be unanimous in order to be binding.

By 1926 the League had fifty-five member states. The United States refused to join, however, largely owing to dissent among American political leaders. Although Germany and the Soviet Union eventually joined, they withdrew in the 1930s, as did Japan and Italy, crippling the ability of the League to address diplomatic issues among the major world powers. By 1940 the League had crumbled, though it would be resurrected five years later as the United Nations.

the Prague Manifesto (1944), a fourteen-point statement produced by an anticommunist coalition to overthrow Joseph Stalin's regime in Russia, reflected Wilson's Fourteen Points. Today, Wilson's vision of peace and world diplomacy is remembered as laying the groundwork for twentieth-century U.S. foreign policy and international diplomacy.

THEMES AND STYLE

The central concerns of the Fourteen Points are to restore peace and institute principles of freedom and self-determination to stave off future conflict. The manifesto's preamble emphasizes the ideological reasons for U.S. involvement: "We entered this war because violations of right had occurred which touched us to the quick and made the life of our own people impossible unless they were corrected and the world secure once and for all against their recurrence." In enumerating his points, Wilson describes general principles of global democracy, such as "open covenants of peace, openly arrived at" and "absolute freedom of navigation upon the seas." He then applies these principles to the resolution of specific disputes, emphasizing sovereignty, restoration of territory, and "free and secure" access for all. In closing, he asserts that "the new world in which we live" necessitates an end to imperialism and the creation of new "covenants of justice law and fair dealing."

The declaration acquires its rhetorical strength through appeals to unity and to the fair application of democratic principles to all nations, aggressors and the oppressed alike. Aware that the Allies might resist compromise out of self-interest, Wilson emphasizes that the best interest of all nations is the same: "What we demand in this war, therefore, is nothing peculiar to ourselves. It is that the world be made fit and safe to live in; and particularly that it be made safe for every peace-loving nation which, like our own, wishes to live its own life [and] determine its own institutions." Although the Allies wished to impose harsh sanctions on the Germans, Wilson disavows any ill will against Germany: "We grudge her no achievement or distinction of learning or of pacific enterprise such as have made her record very bright and very

An illustration depicting Woodrow Wilson pressing for a League of Nations at the 1919 Paris Peace Conference. The Fourteen Points would provide the theoretical basis for the League of Nations and, later, the United Nations. © BLUE LANTERN STUDIO/LAUGHING E/BLUE LANTERN STUDIO/CORBIS

enviable." Instead, he extends to Germany the same invitation "to associate herself with us and the other peace-loving nations of the world."

The tone of the Fourteen Points is frank, optimistic, and conciliatory. Although written as a formal declaration, the document uses plain language that mirrors Wilson's call to openness and free access. He declares, "The day of conquest and aggrandizement is gone by," calling the end of the age of imperialism a "happy fact." In order to be transparent about U.S. objectives in the peace process, he assures listeners, "We have no jealousy of German greatness, and there is nothing in this programme that impairs it." Unwavering in his idealism, he avers that all nations are united under the new world order and "cannot be separated in interest or divided in purpose. We stand together until the end." By frankly confronting fears of imperialism and reasserting the goal of "a place of equality" for all nations, he encourages governments to be transparent and optimistic as they enter the peace negotiation process.

CRITICAL DISCUSSION

The Allied nations generally considered Wilson's Fourteen Points either too idealistic or too ambitious. French prime minister Georges Clemenceau famously stated, "Even the good Lord contented Himself with only ten commandments, and we should not try to improve upon them." Many Allied leaders vehemently disagreed with particular terms of the document. The British, for instance, felt the second point—"freedom of navigation upon the sea"—threatened their national defense and longstanding naval superiority. However, the American and European public generally embraced Wilson's declaration, which helped to urge world leaders to incorporate several of the points into the 1919 Treaty of Versailles and declare an official end to World War I.

Despite the fact that only four of the original Fourteen Points survived the drafting of the treaty, Wilson's declaration continued to guide foreign conflict resolution for decades. Although the League of Nations, which grew out of the "general association of nations" proposed in the Fourteen Points, ultimately failed, the United Nations, formed following the 1941 ratification of the Atlantic Charter, succeeded in gaining widespread support and staving off yet another world war. In the midst of World War II, British historian and author Bernard Newman, in his book *The New Europe* (1943), asserts that in the effort against Nazi Germany the Allies "must accept … as a guide to equity not only the Atlantic Charter, but the Fourteen Points. In some respects the latter are more important than the former. Germany has not accepted the Atlantic Charter … [but] she *did* accept the Fourteen Points." Thus, Wilson's idea of an international organization dedicated to avoiding war ultimately persisted, and it continues to undergird international diplomacy.

Most contemporary criticism of the Fourteen Points focuses on a revisionist understanding of self-determination, often held as the central tenet of the declaration for its role in inspiring numerous twentieth-century independence movements. Many critics, however, point to the fact that the term was not used in the document itself. Trygve Throntveit, in a 2011 article in *Diplomatic History*, states, "These distortions have obscured the true character of Wilson's internationalism, which was not disintegrative, but integrative, and in the context of his times, radically so." Pointing out that Wilson's model for the League of Nations demanded "significant concessions of sovereignty from its members"—thereby contradicting the principle of self-determination—Throntveit states that Wilson relied on the misconception of his aims as a means to an end.

BIBLIOGRAPHY

Sources

Glusker, Irwin, and Richard M. Ketchum. *American Testament: Fifty Great Documents of American History.* New York: American Heritage Pub. Co, 1971. Print.

Newman, Bernard. *The New Europe.* New York: Macmillan Co., 1943. Print.

Smith, Leonard V. "The Wilsonian Challenge to International Law." *Journal of the History of International Law* 13.1 (2011): 179-208. *Academic Search Complete.* Web. 22 June 2012.

Smith, Page. *America Enters the World: A People's History of the Progressive Era and World War I.* New York: McGraw-Hill, 1985. Print.

Throntveit, Trygve. "The Fable of the Fourteen Points: Woodrow Wilson and National Self-Determination." *Diplomatic History* 35.3 (2011): 445-481. *Academic Search Complete.* Web. 21 June 2012.

Further Reading

Bullington, J.R. "Woodrow Wilson's Fourteen Points and the Long Debate in U.S. Foreign Policy." *American Diplomacy* Jan. 2008. *Academic OneFile.* Web. 22 June 2012.

"The Eight and Fourteen." *Saturday Evening Post* 214.16 (1941): 26. *Academic Search Complete.* Web. 22 June 2012.

MacMillan, Margaret. *Paris 1919: Six Months That Changed the World.* New York: Random House, 2002. Print.

Reisser, Wesley J. "Self-Determination and the Difficulty of Creating Nation-States: The Transylvania Case." *Geographical Review* 99.2 (2009): 231-247. *Academic OneFile.* Web. 22 June 2012.

Sharp, Alan. "Dreamland of the Armistice." *History Today* 58.11 (2008): 28-34. *Academic Search Complete.* Web. 22 June 2012.

Stolberg, Benjamin. "Third Party Chances." *Nation* 118.3065 (1924): 364-367. *Academic Search Complete.* Web. 22 June 2012.

Clint Garner

THE GREAT SCOURGE AND HOW TO END IT

Christabel Pankhurst

✣ *Key Facts*

Time Period:
Early 20th Century

Movement/Issue:
First-wave feminism;
Women's suffrage

Place of Publication:
England

**Language of
Publication:**
English

OVERVIEW

Christabel Pankhurst's 1913 book, *The Great Scourge and How to End It,* demands voting rights for women as a remedy for the turn-of-the-century syphilis and gonorrhea epidemics, which Pankhurst blames on male promiscuity and men's social, legal, and fiscal control of women's bodies. A decade before the manifesto was published, Pankhurst had helped her mother, Emmeline, found London's most prominent militant suffrage organization, the Women's Social and Political Union (WSPU). The organization emphasized the unity of women as an independent social force and the use of tactics such as vandalism and even arson to call attention to women's plight. Addressed to English men and women, the book argues that the primary opposition to women's suffrage comes from men who fear that enfranchisement would interfere with their access to extramarital sex; therefore women should be wary of sexual contact with men until women receive the right to vote.

Although the book proved unpopular with segments of the suffrage movement that resisted fundamentalist notions of chastity, marriage, and monogamy, the public generally embraced *The Great Scourge.* Contributions to the WSPU, which independently published the document, grew. Several suffragettes publicly stated that Pankhurst's manifesto, with its representation of sexual equality, was directly responsible for their decision to join the movement. Although the notions put forth in the document were by no means novel—they had been widely discussed by feminist activists since the 1860s—Pankhurst's outspoken activism became the focus of international media interest, and her ideas eclipsed those of other activists of the day. Today *The Great Scourge* is remembered for providing an invaluable boost to the cause of suffrage, which succeeded in gaining voting rights for women over thirty in 1918.

HISTORICAL AND LITERARY CONTEXT

In the years leading up to the manifesto's publication, suffragettes coped with increasing government attempts to violate or control women's bodies. For example, after 1909, suffragist hunger strikers were forcibly fed by nasal tubes. Moreover the state legally equated prostitution with idiocy, sending prostitutes to mental asylums. A Royal Commission on Vene-

real Disease threatened to impose draconian public policies reminiscent of the Contagious Diseases Acts of the 1860s, which authorized forced vaginal examination of women suspected of soliciting sex, and hospital incarceration for those with the slightest trace of vaginal discharge. In 1910 the U.S. Congress passed the White Slave Traffic Act, also known as the Mann Act, a long-awaited bill targeting traffickers of women and children. However, activists were angered when critical clauses were stripped from the bill and some provisions were used to punish prostituted women.

As outrage grew over government policies toward women, WSPU activities became increasingly radical. By the time *The Great Scourge* was published, more than one thousand suffragettes had been incarcerated for smashing windows, setting fires, or engaging in other acts of protest. Christabel Pankhurst, WSPU's main strategist and organizer, in 1912 exiled herself to Paris to avoid imprisonment and to continue to direct WSPU's activities. There she drafted *The Great Scourge,* articulating her idea that venereal disease outbreaks and patriarchal control of women's bodies are symptomatic of a single social pathology—the only panacea for which is "votes for women, chastity for men," a popular suffragette slogan.

Although many women had written about the link between sexually transmitted disease and the disenfranchisement of women, most employed syphilis as a literary metaphor for male corruption. In contrast, Pankhurst grounded her arguments in medicine and social psychology, building on the work of Louisa Martindale, a doctor and suffragette. In the book *Under the Surface* (1908), Martindale, a member of the nonmilitant London Women's Suffrage Society, argues that venereal disease is the result of prostitution, which in turn is the result of the patriarchal system. Pankhurst distinguished her work from that of Martindale's through her insistence that women must seize control of their bodies rather than simply petition to have it handed back to them.

Pankhurst's assertiveness caused the media to take note of her as a leader and as an author. Her notoriety garnered widespread exposure for *The Great Scourge* upon its release. Her arguments for physical independence would later be expanded upon by Virginia Woolf, who in *A Room of One's Own* (1929) argues that women require control of their bodies and intellects, as well as a dedicated space within which to practice that control. These notions continue to inform contemporary feminist writing, forming the central themes of major works such as Margaret Atwood's dystopian classic *A Handmaid's Tale* (1985).

THEMES AND STYLE

The main theme of *The Great Scourge* is that patriarchal structures are psychologically and biologically pathogenic. Pankhurst asserts, "A community which tolerates prostitution is a community which is morally diseased. The man prostitute … has his soul infected as well as his body." By giving equal weight to the twin threats of biological and moral disease, she posits enfranchisement as a kind of cure-all. In addition, she claims, enfranchisement would act as a prophylactic: "prevention … is not only better than cure, but it is the only cure, for whether these diseases are curable even in the narrowest sense of the term is very doubtful, and even when cured they can be contracted again." Therefore, she argues, to successfully address both the persistent threat of venereal disease and the patriarchal culture that allows it to proliferate, society must grant women the right to vote.

Pankhurst's arguments derive their rhetorical power from her ability to anticipate and respond to opponents' counterarguments. She predicts that her petition for the eradication of prostitution will be met with tired appeals to "'human nature' and 'injury to man's health.'" Thus, she responds, "Human nature is a very wide term, and it covers a multitude of sins and vices which are not on that account any the more to be tolerated." She states that robbing, killing, and cannibalism are naturally occurring behavioral tendencies; yet they are socially and legally forbidden. Why then, she asks, "is human nature to have full scope only in the one direction of sexual vice?" By referencing the unequal treatment of women in her arguments, she reinforces her message that a patriarchal double standard underlies the structure of public policy.

The tone of the manifesto is direct, logical, and militant. Pankhurst's methodical prose is unwavering in its denunciation of patriarchy: "The cause of sexual disease is the subjection of women. Therefore to destroy one we must destroy the other." Moreover she is conscious of her tone and anticipates that her writing, and the suffrage movement as a whole, will be criticized for its militancy: "There has been vigorous criticism of the policy of destroying property for the sake of Votes for Women. That criticism is silenced by the retort that men have destroyed, and are destroying, the health and life of women in the pursuit of vice." Such succinct, decisive language posits women's health as a basic right and enfranchisement as a way of guaranteeing that right. It also paints the argument about women's suffrage in unambiguous terms:

CHRISTABEL PANKHURST: MILITANT ACTIVIST

One of the first public acts of protest by Christabel Pankhurst occurred in 1905 when she and fellow suffragist Annie Kenney attended a Liberal Party election meeting. After candidate Winston Churchill evaded the question of whether he would support voting rights for women, they began shouting and were eventually arrested. Refusing to pay a fine, they were imprisoned for several days, a tactic that succeeded in gaining media coverage. As a result, membership in their organization, the Women's Social and Political Union (WSPU), swelled and other members began to take militant action, also electing to be imprisoned.

When WSPU headquarters moved from Manchester to London in 1906, Pankhurst relocated to act as organizing secretary. Known as "Queen of the Mob," she was voluntarily jailed for leading a protest march in 1907 and again for leading a "rush" on the House of Commons in 1908. In 1912 she expatriated to Paris to evade imprisonment, but the start of World War I compelled her to return in 1914. After she was arrested, she set out on a hunger strike, ultimately serving only thirty days of her three-year sentence. Decades later the British government recognized her efforts in the suffrage movement, and in 1936 she was appointed a Dame Commander of the Order of the British Empire.

"Those who want to have women as slaves, obviously do not want women to become voters."

CRITICAL DISCUSSION

Although many women embraced Pankhurst's manifesto and her argument for sexual equality, others criticized *The Great Scourge* as overly simple and based on inaccurate data. Dora Marsden, a suffragette and editor of *The Egoist: An Individualist Review*, argues in a 1914 issue of the magazine that Pankhurst's statistics about sexually transmitted infections—such as that 75-80 percent of men contract a venereal disease before the age of thirty—were so greatly exaggerated that they voided her argument. Prominent feminists such as Rebecca West also voiced their disapproval, echoing Marsden's conclusion that "if Miss Pankhurst desires to exploit human boredom and the ravages of dirt she will require to call in the aid of a more subtle intelligence than she herself appears to possess."

Even after women gained the right to vote in England, historians, particularly scholars of the militant suffrage movement, attacked Pankhurst's notions of sexuality. Many criticized her ideas as outdated and stifling to sexual liberation movements. Roger Fulford, in *Votes for Women* (1958), dismissed her explanation of social psychology as superfluous, concluding that her "arguments and facts need not detain the reader." Andrew Rosen in *Rise Up, Women!* (1973) echoed Fulford's disdain and pondered why

Portrait of Christabel Pankhurst, circa 1905-1914, by an unknown artist. MUSEUM OF LONDON/THE ART ARCHIVE AT ART RESOURCE, NY

women. Similarly, Margaret Jackson argues in *The Real Facts of Life: Feminism and the Politics of Sexuality c. 1850-1940* (1994) that Pankhurst combines sexual accountability and a vindication of unmarried life for women in order to make a "powerful challenge to the sexual-economic basis of male power."

BIBLIOGRAPHY

Sources

Fulford, Roger. *Votes for Women: The Story of a Struggle.* London: Faber & Faber, 1958. Print.

Jackson, Margaret. *The Real Facts of Life: Feminism and the Politics of Sexuality, c 1850-1940.* London: Taylor & Francis, 1994. Print.

Marsden, Dora. "The Chastity of Women." *The Egoist: An Individualist Review* 1.3 (1914): 44-46. *Modernist Journals Project.* Web. 17 July 2012.

Martz, Linda. "An AIDS-Era Reassessment of Christabel Pankhurst's *The Great Scourge and How To End It.*" *Women's History Review* 14.3/4 (2005): 435-46. *Academic Search Complete.* Web. 16 July 2012.

Pankhurst, Christabel. *The Great Scourge and How to End It.* London: E. Pankhurst, 1913. Print.

Purvis, June. *Emmeline Pankhurst: A Biography.* London: Routledge, 2002. Print.

Rosen, Andrew. *Rise Up, Women!: The Militant Campaign of the Women's Social and Political Union, 1903-1914.* London: Routledge & Kegan Paul, 1974. Print.

Sarah, Elizabeth. "Christabel Pankhurst: Reclaiming Her Power." *Feminist Theorists: Three Centuries of Women's Intellectual Traditions.* Ed. Dale Spender. London: Women's Press, 1983. 256-84. Print.

Further Reading

Jeffreys, Sheila. *The Spinster and Her Enemies: Feminism and Sexuality, 1880-1830.* London: Pandora, 1985. Print.

Kent, Susan Kingsley. *Sex and Suffrage in Britain, 1860-1914.* Princeton: Princeton UP, 1987. Print.

Phillips, Melanie. *The Ascent of Women: A History of the Suffragette Movement and the Ideals behind It.* London: Little, Brown, 2003. Print.

Pugh, Martin. *The March of the Women: A Revisionist Analysis of the Campaign for Women's Suffrage.* Oxford: Oxford UP, 2000. Print.

———. *The Pankhursts.* London: Penguin, 2001. Print.

Savage, Gail. "'The Wilful Communication of a Loathsome Disease': Marital Conflict and Venereal Disease in Victorian England." *Victorian Studies* 34.1 (1990): 35-54. *Academic One File.* Web. 16 July 2012.

Thomas, Sue. "Crying 'The Horror' of Prostitution: Elizabeth Robins's 'Where Are You Going To … ?' and the Moral Crusade of the Women's Social and Political Union." *Women* 16.2 (2005): 203-21. *Academic Search Complete.* Web. 16 July 2012.

Clint Garner

the text did not cause Pankhurst's fellow militant suffragettes to doubt her fitness as a leader. It was not until the 1980s, when feminist historians began examining the text in terms of its feminist contributions, that *The Great Scourge* was finally subjected to thoughtful critique.

Today, scholarship on *The Great Scourge* examines it as more than simple propagandist ranting, focusing instead on the document's importance to the women's suffrage movement. Elizabeth Sarah was one of the first to resituate key aspects of Pankhurst's feminist agenda. In a 1983 essay in *Feminist Theorists: Three Centuries of Women's Intellectual Traditions,* Sarah observes, "It is impossible to understand the campaign for the vote and the methods adopted by suffragettes to achieve it without explaining their ideas about the subordination of women." She argues that *The Great Scourge* became the most cogent expression of the consequences of the subordination of

HIND SWARAJ OR INDIAN HOME RULE

Mohandas K. Gandhi

OVERVIEW

First published in Mohandas K. Gandhi's journal *Indian Opinion* (1903-14) on December 11 and 18, 1909, *Hind Swaraj or Indian Home Rule* articulates the nationalist leader's growing concern about the militant faction of his country's movement for independence from the British Empire. The document repositions the debate about how to achieve independence by proposing that nationalism is not a political but a moral issue. Gandhi condemns both British rule and those independence fighters willing to use violence to evict the British. The treatise provides an overarching critique of materialist Western culture, urging the development of a homegrown, grassroots, spiritually based movement. *Hind Swaraj* also introduces and promotes the principles of *satyagraha,* or nonviolent resistance to illegitimate authority. Gandhi developed the concept and practice during his twenty-one years (1893-1914) as a lawyer and civil rights activist in South Africa. He first publicized it for a larger audience in his South Africa-based journal, making a clear distinction between satyagraha and other forms of protest.

After its initial publication *Hind Swaraj* was reprinted and distributed in pamphlet form in Gujarati and English. It was promptly banned by the British colonial government as a seditious tract. When Gandhi returned to India during World War I and emerged as a leader in the nationalist movement, the text was republished and recirculated. In a 1921 article in his weekly journal, *Young India* (1919-32), Gandhi explained how his ideals had changed during the past ten years, writing that although he continued to conceive of the spiritual discipline described in *Hind Swaraj* as a personal ideal, his "corporate activity is undoubtedly devoted to the attainment of Parliamentary Swaraj, in accordance with the wishes of the people of India." While Gandhi's political hopes for India changed over the years, his adherence to satyagraha was unflinching, and the principles of nonviolent protest that he championed were deeply influential throughout the world, notably in the American civil rights movement of the 1960s and 1970s.

HISTORICAL AND LITERARY CONTEXT

Hind Swaraj responds directly to a crisis within the Indian nationalist movement in the early twentieth century. Indian nationalism had developed as an intellectual and political force in the late nineteenth century in response to increasing discontent with British rule, which had begun with the East India Company holdings in 1600. Leading figures adamantly supported Indian independence, and a number of religious and advocacy groups proclaimed the benefits of indigenous religion and social structures. At the beginning of the twentieth century, the nationalist leader Til Gagadhar Tilak proposed the radical and, if necessary, violent overthrow of the British government in India, coining the phrase "*Hind Swaraj*" to describe his desire for a self-governed India. Tilak's rise led to a split in the Indian National Congress between his followers and the moderates, led by Dadabhai Naoroji, who favored the expansion of political rights for native Indians within the framework of British rule. *Hind Swaraj* intervened in this debate, presenting a third alternative—independence from Britain through nonviolent means.

Hind Swaraj's commitment to nonviolent resistance was a product of Gandhi's advocacy work on behalf of the Indian population of South Africa, which was also a British colony. In 1908, in a move to regulate and police the Indian population of the country, the British decreed that all Indians must register with the government. The practice of satyagraha was first implemented that year during a mass protest in Johannesburg against the Asiatic Registration Act. A seven-year nonviolent campaign ensued, during which many South African Indians were persecuted, jailed (including Gandhi), or killed for passive resistance. In 1919 Gandhi founded the Satyagraha League, making nonviolent resistance one of the hallmarks of his life and works.

In addition to responding to the immediate political situation in colonial India, *Hind Swaraj* draws on a history of Western and Eastern philosophy that critiques modern society for its materialist aims and urges a simpler life of the soul. Although the work's bibliography includes Dadabhai Naoroji's *Poverty and Un-British Rule in India* (1901) and Romesh Chunder

Time Period:
Early 20th Century

Movement/Issue:
Indian independence;
Nonviolent protest

Place of Publication:
India

Language of Publication:
Gujarati

THE FIRST INDIAN MEMBER OF PARLIAMENT: DADABHAI NAOROJI

One of Gandhi's early mentors, the Indian nationalist leader Dadabhai Naoroji was known in his later years as the "Grand Old Man of India." Born on September 4, 1825, in Bombay (now Mumbai), he was one of the first Indians to be educated at Bombay's Elphinstone Institute and became the first Indian to hold an academic position there. He soon left teaching and, after a period working in trade in London, where he witnessed firsthand the inequality of the colonial relationship between India and Britain, Naoroji returned to India and entered politics. From the 1860s onward he was at the center of the budding independence movement, helping establish the East India Association (1866); the Indian National Association (1876); and, finally, the Indian National Congress (INC; 1885).

Back in England, Naoroji was elected member of parliament (MP) for Central Finsbury, London, in 1892, the first Asian to hold such a position. He served as president of the INC several times, notably for the 1906 session, in which he provided a voice of moderation, strongly opposing the extremist faction's desire for violent revolution. Of Naoroji's many works of nonfiction, the best known is *Poverty and Un-British Rule in India* (1901), which focuses on the effect of the British government's taxation of Indian people, lands, and goods, showing Britain's rule to be a central cause of Indian poverty. Naoroji died in India in 1917 at the age of ninety-two.

Dutt's *Economic History of India* (1902), which specifically address the effect on India of Britain's economic policies, the majority of Gandhi's influences are spiritual and philosophical thinkers who offered alternatives to modern urban life. Alongside Russian novelist Leo Tolstoy, who became a social reformer in his later years; American transcendentalist Henry David Thoreau (whose "Resistance to Civil Government" Gandhi read during one of his several imprisonments in South Africa); and Victorian arts-and-crafts movement leader John Ruskin, Gandhi cites Henry Sumner Maine and his comparative study *Village Communities in the East and West* (1871), which lauds Eastern culture for its communal values; Robert Harb Sherard's critique of nineteenth-century British industry, *The White Slaves of London* (1897); socialist Edward Carpenter's *Civilization: Its Cause and Cure* (1889); and Thomas Taylor's tribute to a slow life, *The Fallacy of Speed* (1909). Gandhi also appends a series of "Testimonials by Eminent Men"—quotes from spiritual, political, and social leaders of the nineteenth century who reasserted the primacy of Eastern spirituality over Western civilization.

Gandhi's ideals, as laid out in *Hind Swaraj* and enacted during the struggle for Indian independence, were deeply influential on later twentieth-century philosophies of peaceful political change and nonviolent protest. American civil rights leaders of the 1960s were particularly strong supporters of the principle of satyagraha, which African American activist leader Martin Luther King, Jr. referred to in his 1958 writing "My Pilgrimage to Nonviolence" as "the only morally and practically sound method open to oppressed people in their struggle for freedom." Some politicians and activists involved in South Africa's antiapartheid movement (1959-94) espoused the use of nonviolent means of protest. The 1974 Mahlabatini Declaration of Faith, signed by South African political leaders Harry Schwarz and Mangosuthu Buthelezi, called for a peaceful transition to a multiracial government, and the Soweto uprising of 1976 was planned as a peaceful demonstration.

THEMES AND STYLE

Hind Swaraj stresses the enslavement of both India and England to commercialism and the desire for material wealth, arguing that only self-control and passive resistance can create widespread change. The tract perceives colonial culture—both British society and culture and the lifestyle of the educated Indian urban classes—as corrupt, while in the traditional Indian village system, hundreds of millions of people live simple, communal, frugal lives. Providing a vision of "civilization" as a morass of manufacturing, professionalization, and monetization (covered in chapters titled "Railways," "Lawyers," and "Doctors") under which "the nations of Europe are becoming degraded and ruined every day," he explains that true Hind swaraj begins with spiritual and physical self-discipline. Such discipline leads to true civilization, "that mode of conduct which points out to man the path of duty." In the final portion of *Hind Swaraj*, Gandhi addresses the question of violence. Responding to the stance that assassinations and guerilla warfare are the only way for India to achieve independence, Gandhi insists that such action would "make the holy land of India unholy." He advocates for the use of "soul force" rather than "the force of arms." Arguing that men are not bound to obey "laws which are repugnant to their conscience," he asserts the right of any man to refuse compliance and suffer the consequences.

Hind Swaraj is structured as a dialogue between a proindependence "editor," who articulates Gandhi's point of view, and an unconvinced "reader," who ostensibly represents the radical nationalist standpoint. This format reflects *Indian Opinion*'s larger stance toward the exchange of ideas, which Gandhi describes in his 1929 autobiography as a method of bringing the Indian community together, saying that readers knew they could depend on the journal for a "trustworthy account of the *Satyagraha* campaign as also of the real condition of Indians in South Africa.... I always aimed at establishing an intimate and clean bond between the editor and the reader." In "Gandhi, 'Truth,' and Translatability" (2006), Javed Majeed suggests that the nationalist leader's use of the dialogue format in *Hind Swaraj* is part of an overall rhetorical strategy that emphasizes the author's own uncertainties and limitations, saying that "the fore-grounding of vulnerability is an important strategy for winning the trust of his readers and interlocutors."

The tone of *Hind Swaraj* is less exhortatory than conversational, as witnessed by its mode of discourse. Gandhi uses the question-and-answer presentation to redefine terms that the "reader" and, presumably, his readership, would see as self-evident, such as "swaraj" and "civilization." The author candidly exposes the conflict within the Indian community as he perceived it, acknowledging his opponents' humanity and beliefs while taking the opportunity to present his own ideas.

CRITICAL DISCUSSION

The initial circulation and influence of *Hind Swaraj* was relatively limited, especially after it was banned by the British colonial government in 1910. It took on a second life after Gandhi returned to India to work in the nationalist movement in 1919, when it was reprinted and became widely known and read throughout the subcontinent. Although criticism of the work came from both sides of the political spectrum, with Marxists complaining that Gandhi ignored the effects of class and parliamentarians calling him an anarchist, satyagraha subsequently became one of the primary modes of political action in the Indian independence movement. In *Nationalism and Post-Colonial Identity* (2003), Anshuman Ahmed Mondal notes the discrepancy between the scornful responses of the intellectual elites in India and abroad to *Hind Swaraj* and its popularity among the masses, maintaining that the book's utopian principles and respect for village life depicted an Indian nation that the ordinary rural peasant could envision and, therefore, support and fight for.

Hind Swaraj is generally considered an important early articulation of Gandhi's ideas about the relationship between the spiritual and the political. The 2009 centenary of its initial publication in *Indian Opinion* was the occasion of several academic conferences as well as of the republication of the Cambridge University Press's authoritative edition of the book. The Cambridge volume, edited by the Indian-born historian and scholar Anthony J. Parel, includes Gandhi's preface and introduction, extensive notes and annotations that address issues of translation and of historical and political context, and a selection of related writings and correspondence.

Scholarship has followed various strains. Some critics examine the differences between the early, idealistic Gandhi of *Hind Swaraj* and the more realistic activist of later years. Dipesh Chakrabarty and Rochona Majumdar, in "Gandhi's Gita and Politics as Such" (2000), argue that, although Gandhi entered politics with the desire to enact a higher ethical standard, by the 1920s he recognized that that arena was

A statue of Mohandas Gandhi at Malpe Beach in Udupi, Karnataka, India. © CLEMENTE DO ROSARIO/ALAMY

fundamentally driven by self interest, and he sought spiritual means of protecting himself and his disciples from being corrupted by it. The authors note that Gandhi appropriated both the Hindu-language term "swaraj" and the use of the Hindu scripture the Bhagavadgita from the extremists that he contested, repositioning ideals and beliefs so that they undergirded a system of nonviolent politics. A number of postcolonial critics have focused on the relationship between the self and the state in *Hind Swaraj*, demonstrating that, in opposing modern capitalism, the text also sets itself against the bourgeois liberal state. As Shruti Kapila writes in *Modern Intellectual History* (2007), the text "subordinates history to the creation of a new self," imagining a political system fueled by the inner transformation of each participant, in which personal self-government would generate and guide communal government.

BIBLIOGRAPHY

Sources

Chakrabarty, Dipesh, and Rochona Majumdar. "Gandhi's Gita and Politics as Such." *Modern Intellectual History* 7.2 (2000): 335-53. Print.

Gandhi, Mohandas K. *An Autobiography, or The Story of My Experiments with Truth.* Boston: Beacon, 1929. Print.

———. *Indian Home Rule, or, Hind Swaraj.* Ahmedabad: Desai, 1938. Print.

Kapila, Shruti. "Self, Spenser, and *Swaraj*: Nationalist Thought and Critiques of Liberalism: 1890-1920." *Modern Intellectual History* 4.1 (2007): 109-27. Print.

King, Martin Luther, Jr. "My Pilgrimage to Nonviolence." 1958. *The Papers of Martin Luther King.* Vol. 4: *Symbol of the Movement, January 1957-December 1958.* Ed. Clayborne Carson, et al. U of California P, 2000. n. pag. Print.

Majeed, Javed. "Gandhi, 'Truth,' and Translatability." *Modern Asian Studies* 40.2 (2006): 303-32. Print.

Mondal, Anshuman A. *Nationalism and Post-Colonial Identity: Culture and Ideology in India and Egypt.* New York: Routledge, 2003. Print.

Further Reading

Birla, Ritu, and Faisal Devli, eds. *Itineraries of Self-Rule: Essays on the Centenary of Gandhi's* Hind Swaraj. Spec. issue of *Public Culture* 23.2 (2011). Print.

Brown, Rebecca M. "Spinning without Touching the Wheel: Anticolonialism, Indian Nationalism, and the Deployment of Symbol." *Comparative Studies of South Asia, Africa, and the Middle East* 29.2 (2009): 230-45. Print.

Chatterjee, Partha. *Nationalist Thought and the Colonial World: A Derivative Discourse?* Minneapolis: U of Minnesota P, 1993. Print.

Hardiman, David. *Gandhi in His Times and Ours: The Global Legacy of His Ideas.* London: Hurst, 2003. Print.

Lelyveld, David. "Words as Deeds: Gandhi and Language." *Annual of Urdu Studies* 16 (2001): 64-75. Print.

Jenny Ludwig

HUMANIST MANIFESTO I

Raymond Bragg, Roy Wood Sellars

OVERVIEW

Composed primarily by Raymond Bragg and Roy Wood Sellars, the "Humanist Manifesto I" (1933) articulates the secular principles of religious humanism and proposes that these tenets replace traditional theistic religious beliefs. Bragg and Sellars argue that religious humanism will serve mankind better than theism because it replaces the role of a deity and the expectation of an afterlife with a secular emphasis on improving human life as it is lived. Bragg, then secretary of the Western Unitarian Conference, and Sellars, a philosophy professor at the University of Michigan, composed the text with the input of numerous scholars, public intellectuals, and religious officials who had an interest in humanist ideology. Thirty-four contributors signed the "Humanist Manifesto I," which first appeared in *New Humanist* magazine, a predecessor to *The Humanist* magazine. In addition to the manifesto, Sellars published an explanatory article concerning religious humanism in the same issue of the magazine.

The manifesto received extensive but mixed media coverage upon its publication. Many traditional religious commentators reacted negatively; other critics found merit in several of the manifesto's affirmations but rejected the idea of human beings addressing these affirmations without the aid of a deity. Despite the uneven reviews, the "Humanist Manifesto I" played a large role in shaping the twentieth-century humanist movement in the United States and represents an important first attempt by religious humanists to articulate their beliefs in the form of unifying principles.

HISTORICAL AND LITERARY CONTEXT

The "Humanist Manifesto I" was published in a spirit of social reform and revolution dating back to the mid-nineteenth century. The failure of the traditional theistic religious belief structure to address new societal tensions brought on by industrialization, popular democratic uprisings, and the expanding plurality of modernity in Western culture had all contributed to broad popular and intellectual discontent with contemporary religious institutions. The emergence of political socialism as a viable alternative to autocratic and capitalist regimes added to the sense among some Western intellectuals that a cultural shift away from traditional religious belief was necessary to accommodate a more secular, cooperative cultural paradigm. The outbreak of World War I only exacerbated these long-running tensions, presenting what appeared to be a clear failure of traditional religious and political institutions to meet the challenges of twentieth-century modernity.

In the early 1930s, a global economic depression further discredited traditional cultural authorities—as did the rise of fascism in Europe, a phenomenon that foreshadowed another world war—and by association another dramatic failure of conventional religion to protect mankind from its worst impulses. The ongoing struggles of colonized peoples in Africa and southeast Asia also cast the traditional religious beliefs of the "oppressor" nations in a hypocritical light. In 1933, when the "Humanist Manifesto I" was published, Adolf Hitler was appointed chancellor of Germany, the Vatican signed an accord with the Nazi regime, and Mohandas Gandhi led a much-publicized hunger strike in British-controlled India. Thus, 1933 became the year the humanist movement came of age.

The literary roots of the "Humanist Manifesto I" can be traced to classical antiquity through the works of both Eastern and Western skeptics and materialist philosophers. These roots also include eighteenth-century Enlightenment thinkers such as David Hume and nineteenth-century Romantics such as Ralph Waldo Emerson, an early member of the Free Religious Association and proponent of Unitarian ideals. Frank Carlton Doan's *Religion of the Modern Mind* (1909), which emphasizes religion's duty to the physical as opposed to the spiritual world, was an important influence on early twentieth-century humanists, as was Sellars's *The Next Step in Religion* (1918). Curtis Reese published a pivotal collection titled *Humanist Sermons* in 1927 that explores the shrinking divide between some proto-secular Unitarian beliefs and religious humanism. Karl Marx's writings on the subject of dialectical materialism also had an impact on the humanists.

The "Humanist Manifesto I" has had a wide-ranging literary effect. Most directly—in keeping with Bragg's claim that the work was not intended to be a defining creed but merely a starting point for discourse—many commentaries, criticisms, and

Key Facts

Time Period:
Early 20th Century

Movement/Issue:
Religious humanism

Place of Publication:
United States

Language of Publication:
English

THE AUTHORSHIP QUESTION

Although Roy Wood Sellars undoubtedly wrote one of the earliest drafts of "Humanist Manifesto I," he has often been uncredited in subsequent publications of the work. According to coauthor Raymond Bragg, the document underwent numerous and extensive revisions after Sellars submitted his draft, the reason Sellars was not credited as the author. Bragg presided over the composition of the final draft and was responsible for taking into account the suggestions of the other signatories and of other intellectuals and religious officials who chose not to add their signatures to the finished product.

Until his death in 1973, Sellars maintained that he wrote the original draft of the manifesto. However, he was unable to produce the original draft after misplacing it during a move. There is also some question as to whether his draft was actually the first version of the manifesto. Another draft was uncovered containing ten affirmations that neither Sellars nor Bragg recognized. Edwin H. Wilson, coauthor of the "Humanist Manifesto II," maintains that Sellars made a significant contribution to the "Humanist Manifesto I," even if the exact nature of his authorship cannot be established.

suggested revisions for the text were published in *The Humanist* magazine in the decades following its original appearance. These derivative documents culminated in *The Humanist* hosting Symposiums I and II in its 1953 issues to reappraise the "Humanist Manifesto I" in light of world events since 1933. This reexamination ultimately resulted in the publication of the "Humanist Manifesto II" (1973), written by

Philosopher John Dewey was one of the signees of "Humanist Manifesto I." In addition to supporting humanism, Dewey was also a psychologist and educator. © BETTMANN/ CORBIS

Paul Kurtz and Edwin H. Wilson. In a broader context, the "Humanist Manifesto I" has influenced numerous, often reactionary publications by proponents of religious and political conservatism in the United States, and it also informed the work of science-fiction writer Isaac Asimov.

THEMES AND STYLE

The central theme of the work is that human beings are essentially alone in the universe and are responsible for improving their lives without the aid of a deity. This theme is addressed through fifteen humanist affirmations regarding cosmology, biological and cultural evolution, human nature, epistemology, ethics, religion, self-fulfillment, the quest for freedom, and social justice. The affirmations are intended to guide humankind toward a more joyful and life-affirming existence; they range from simple declarations ("Religious Humanists regard the universe as self-existing and not created") to more complex assertions such as the need to replace the "profit-motivated" and "acquisitive" order with a more "cooperative" economic structure. The affirmations are contextualized by a preface, which argues for the adoption of religious humanism by claiming "that any religion that can hope to be a synthesizing and dynamic force for today must be shaped for the needs of this age." The document's closing paragraph states that "the religious forms and ideas of our fathers are no longer adequate" and calls "the quest for the good life … the central task for mankind."

The manifesto achieves its rhetorical effect by articulating its concerns in a short, easily digestible list of generalized principles and by appeals to intellectual and religious authorities. Each affirmation is specific enough to speak to a variety of religious and secular positions while still general enough not to alienate most groups. Such balance is particularly noteworthy in the seventh affirmation: "Religion consists of those actions, purposes, and experiences which are humanly significant. Nothing human is alien to the religious. It includes labor, art, science, philosophy, love, friendship, recreation…. The distinction between the sacred and the secular can no longer be maintained." The signatures lend intellectual and religious authority to the manifesto, even if some of the signatories had minimal input—such as John Dewey, the most prominent signatory—or disagreed with the wording of the affirmations, as Bragg acknowledges in the preface.

The language of the document is largely secular. According to Wilson, writing in *Genesis of a Humanist Manifesto* (1995), the text was repeatedly edited to seek "verbal integrity and a semantic change from traditional religious terms in order to clarify their naturalistic approach." In this regard, the preface and affirmations avoid theistic terminology that might otherwise seem appropriate considering the subject matter. The traditional theistic religious terms that are included are ecumenical and often serve as a foil for the religious humanists' secularism.

CRITICAL DISCUSSION

The "Humanist Manifesto I" elicited varied responses both inside and outside humanist intellectual circles and was reviewed in newspapers across the country. The *Boston Evening Transcript* lauded the work, while the *Los Angeles Times* claimed the manifesto's argument was flawed. Several of the signatories expressed trepidation over its release, including E. A. Burtt, who Wilson quotes in *The Genesis of a Humanist Manifesto* as saying that it contained "positions and ideas which are irreconcilable with the essential matters on which those in profound sympathy with the humanist movement take their stand." Arthur E. Morgan ultimately chose not to sign the manifesto after offering several suggestions to the authors. Other contributors were more enthusiastic, such as Robert Morss Lovett, who expressed great pride in being part of it.

Historical events in the decades following the publication of the document—notably World War II, the Holocaust, and the rise of Soviet totalitarianism—served to intensify criticism of its affirmations. Many people within the humanist movement found fault with its scientific and technological optimism. Writing in *The Humanist*'s Symposium I issue, Wilson refers to the original manifesto as "a dated document representing a general agreement of thirty four men at a particular moment in history." The attacks continued after the much-revised and expanded "Humanist Manifesto II" was published in 1973, as both works were singled out by U.S. religious and political conservatives, including television evangelists Jerry Falwell, Pat Robertson, and Jimmy Swaggart in the 1980s.

Criticism in this vein has continued into the twenty-first century. According to *The Genesis of a Humanist Manifesto,* James T. McKenna, general counsel of the conservative Heritage Foundation, cited the two documents as "[t]he final blow to parental and public confidence in education" and as "value systems based on ethical opportunism and … shallow paganism."

The documents also have been challenged by postmodernist intellectuals such as Jacques Derrida, Jacques Lacan, and Michel Foucault, who reject the humanist ideal of human progress. Wilson responds to these charges in *The Genesis of a Humanist Manifesto,* admitting that "The Humanist Manifesto I" was a product of "the hopefulness that socialism brought to the 1930s" but claiming that "humanism should not attach itself to any particular economic system."

BIBLIOGRAPHY

Sources

Bragg, Raymond B. "Humanist Manifesto I." *American Humanist Association.* American Humanist Association, 2008. Web. 4 Oct. 2012.

Edwards, Fred. "A Humanist Manifesto Turns Seventy-Five." *Humanist* 68.3 (2008): 14-19. *Academic Search Complete.* Web. 2 Oct. 2012.

Kurtz, Paul. *The Humanist Alternative: Some Definitions of Humanism.* Buffalo: Prometheus Books, 1973. Print.

Mondale, Lester. "The Lingering 'Humanist Manifesto I' (Defining Humanism: The Battle Continues)." *Free Inquiry* 16.4 (1996): 28. *Academic One File.* Web. 2 Oct. 2012.

Wilson, Edwin H. *The Genesis of a Humanist Manifesto.* Ed. Teresa Maciocha. Washington DC: Humanist Press, 1995. Print.

Further Reading

Ericson, Edward L. *Humanist Way: An Introduction to Ethical Humanist Religion.* New York: Continuum, 1988. Print.

Lamont, Corliss. *The Philosophy of Humanism.* 5th ed. New York: Frederick Ungar Publishing, 1965. Print.

Kurtz, Paul. "Humanist Manifesto 2000." *Free Inquiry* 19.4 (1999): 5. *Academic One File.* Web. 3 Oct. 2012

Kurtz, Paul, and Edwin H. Wilson. "Humanist Manifesto II." *American Humanist Association.* American Humanist Association, 2008. Web. 4 Oct. 2012.

Wills, Gary. "Critique of the Humanist Manifesto." *Humanist* 34.1 (1974): 6. Print.

Wilson, Edwin H. "Humanist Manifesto II: Defended." *Humanist* 38.6 (1978): 57. Print.

Craig Barnes

MANIFESTO OF THE CHINESE PEOPLE'S LIBERATION ARMY

Mao Zedong

✥ *Key Facts*

Time Period:
Mid-20th Century

Movement/Issue:
Communism; Chinese
Civil War

Place of Publication:
China

**Language of
Publication:**
Chinese

OVERVIEW

Composed in 1947 by Mao Zedong and issued at a conference on land reform in North Shensi province, the *Manifesto of the Chinese People's Liberation Army* describes the long history of injustices that the Chinese people suffered—and were still enduring—during the Chinese Civil War (1927-1950), particularly under Chiang Kai-shek, chairman of the Republic of China's Nationalist Party. In addition, the document demands the immediate overthrow of Chiang Kai-shek's regime. Written for the general headquarters of the People's Liberation Army (PLA), the manifesto sought to enlist participation in the war between the communist PLA, led by Mao, and the National Revolutionary Army. It is addressed to "the people of all strata through the country" and urges citizens to "take up their own arms" against Chiang Kai-shek. Central to the treatise are eight basic policies aimed at deposing the Nationalist regime and instituting economic policies that would give relief to China's poverty-stricken peoples.

Although there is little mention of immediate reaction to the manifesto, its declaration of a counteroffensive against Chiang Kai-shek's depredations contributed to the continued growth and final military dominance of the PLA. Soon its ranks would swell as hundreds of thousands of soldiers defected from the Nationalist cause. By 1948 the communist forces had won a decisive battle in Mudken, consolidating their control of Manchuria. Within two years the PLA would drive the Nationalist ruler into exile in Taiwan and unify mainland China under communist rule as the People's Republic of China. Today the *Manifesto of the Chinese People's Liberation Army* is considered among the most important political documents of the Chinese Civil War.

HISTORICAL AND LITERARY CONTEXT

Mao's manifesto responds to the political crises that faced China in the 1930s and 1940s. Although the Chinese Communist Party (CCP) and the Nationalist government had been at war since the 1920s, the 1937 invasion of China by the Japanese during the Second Sino-Japanese War forced the two factions to fight as a united front. This tentative compact ended

with the defeat of the Japanese in 1945. The Chongqing negotiations that year resulted in a resolution to avoid civil war, but the Nationalist government refused to recognize the territory held by the CCP. Less than a year later civil war broke out, with Chiang Kai-shek's troops launching several offensives against the CCP's Liberation Army.

By the time the manifesto was issued in October 1947, full-scale civil war was underway and the Chinese economy was in a shambles. During the Sino-Japanese war the Nationalist government had printed substantial amounts of money in order to support the war effort, causing rapid inflation and the disintegration of the financial system. Average prices rose by more than two thousand percent in the decade spanning 1935 to 1945. According to the historian Suzanne Pepper, writing in *Civil War in China* (1999), the inflation "did more than any other single issue to undermine confidence" in the Nationalist government's ability to rule. In the *Manifesto of the People's Liberation Army,* Mao criticizes the governance of the country and seeks to rally peasants and soldiers alike against Chiang Kai-shek.

Mao's 1947 treatise draws on a long history of left-wing political manifestos and is analogous in many ways to Karl Marx and Friedrich Engels's *Communist Manifesto* (1848), which provides an analysis of class struggle between exploited workers and landowning bourgeoisie within a European context. The idea that only a revolution can overthrow the capitalist system, with its inherent economic disparities, is a theme echoed by Mao. He also draws on other revolutionary documents, among them his predecessor Sun Yat-sen's *Three People's Principles* (1924), which opposes imperialism and expresses support for the movements of workers and peasants.

In the decades following the publication of the manifesto, Mao consolidated his political and cultural power, becoming the leader of the most populous country on earth, the People's Republic of China, a position he would hold until his death in 1976. His *Quotations from Chairman Mao Tse-tung* (1966), known in the West as the Little Red Book, was enormously popular and was an essential accoutrement for party members; it consists of memorable excerpts from the Chinese leader's longer political works. Mao flourished as the center of a cult of personality. He is still a hero of the working classes and of communist movements around the world, and his manifesto remains an icon of revolutionary culture.

THEMES AND STYLE

The central theme of the *Manifesto of the Chinese People's Liberation Army* is that the Nationalist government, ruled by Chiang Kai-shek, had failed to provide peace and prosperity for the Chinese people and must be ousted. After a brief introduction detailing the accomplishments of the PLA, the manifesto launches into a historical criticism of Chiang Kai-shek's "dictatorship": his government was "passive against Japanese invaders" during the Second Sino-Japanese War; he failed to institute democracy after the defeat of the Japanese; he "amassed vast fortunes" while instituting policies that "plunged the overwhelming majority of the people throughout the country into an abyss of suffering"; and he sold "the country's sovereign rights" to U.S. imperialism. It is noteworthy that the manifesto emphasizes the political nature of the struggle, particularly in relation to agrarian reform. According to Mao, military victory would hinge on the party's ability to win the support of the rural masses through these reforms rather than on the army's ability to defeat Chiang Kai-shek in the cities. He calls on his countrymen to participate in both the civil and martial aspects of the struggle: "take up arms," "carry through land reform," "consolidate the foundations of democracy," and "support the fighting at the front."

The manifesto achieves its rhetorical impact by fostering a sense of unity among the suffering people of China. It lists eight communist policies, the first of which defines a broad social group of "workers, peasants, soldiers, intellectuals and businessman, all oppressed classes, all people's organizations, democratic parties, minority nationalities, overseas Chinese and other patriots." The other policies call for punishing the crimes of the Nationalists, establishing democracy, protecting minorities, instituting land reform that will "give relief" to "poverty stricken peoples, and establishing the economic and political sovereignty of China. Mao primarily cultivates unanimity through the repeated use of the first person plural, "we." For example, he declares, "We are shouldering the most important, the most glorious task in the history of our country's revolution." The manifesto takes a stance against the Nationalist army but not against its soldiers. "Our army," Mao writes, "does not reject all Chiang Kai-shek's personnel but adopts a policy of dealing with each case on its merits." This principle of tolerance, which promises that "accomplices under duress shall go unpunished and those who perform deeds of merit shall be rewarded," encouraged Nationalist soldiers to defect and join the ranks of the PLA.

MAO ZEDONG: A REBELLIOUS YOUTH

Mao Zedong, the eventual chairman of the Communist Party of China, was of humble origins. Like four-fifths of the Chinese population at the time, the members of his family were peasants. Unlike many, however, Mao's father, Mao Rhensheng, owned land—thirty acres of paddy fields that produced a comfortable income. Mao began to work in the fields at the age of seven while attending primary school. Along with mathematics and language, the school's focus was on Confucian ethics, which stressed good behavior and filial piety. Mao was a good student interested in the classics, but his deference to his father would not last long.

Rhensheng had hoped that Mao would learn more practical skills in order to manage the farm. Unimpressed by his son's scholarship, he was by many accounts abusive, beating Mao frequently. Mao ran away twice during his childhood; he refused to marry the woman that his father had selected for him; and he once criticized his father in front of his friends and then refused to apologize. Later Mao used his father to draw humorous revolutionary analogies, such as that his father represented "the Ruling power" while the rest of the family was "the Opposition united front."

Stylistically, the manifesto is distinguished by its historical purview and revolutionary spirit. Its detailed analysis of twentieth-century Chinese politics, economics, and war imbue the document with intellectual authority. By detailing his knowledge of the historical forces at play in the country's politics, Mao demonstrates both his fitness as a leader of the PLA and his sympathy for the economic privations that the Chinese people have endured. Mao's confidence that "we will win" and the manifesto's enthusiastic calls to arms—"Down with Chiang Kai-shek! Long live New China!"—embolden "the people" toward one of the manifesto's goals: active participation in the revolution.

CRITICAL DISCUSSION

When the *Manifesto of the Chinese People's Liberation Army* was first issued in late 1947, little was published in response, perhaps because its appearance coincided with that of the first edition of the Outline Agrarian Law. Formalized during the Senshi land reform conferences, the law, according to Pepper, "called for the equalization of village land and property" and was essential to the communist struggle because it "destroyed the political and economic domination of the ruling class." Mao articulates the same theme in less strident terms in his manifesto, which had a broader (though less quantifiable) purpose than the law. It strives to engender peasant support not only through land reform but also with a more comprehensive indictment of the crimes and greed of Chiang Kai-shek's regime.

The PLA's 1949 victory secured many of the manifesto's goals. Mao confiscated and redistributed all private property (including that belonging to schools and temples) equally among the people of each village, regardless of gender or age; and, as promised, he pardoned former landowners and the officials and civil servants who had been part of the Nationalist government. These policies of patience and accommodation ended, however, when China became embroiled in the Korean War in support of communist North Korea less than a year after China's revolutionary victory. According to Michael Lynch's biography *Mao* (2004), "The demands of a ferocious military struggle destroyed all thought of tolerant economic and political policies." In the decades since its publication, the *Manifesto of the Chinese People's Liberation Army* has been the subject of a small body of scholarly inquiry that has considered its legacy within the context of the Chinese Civil War.

Most scholarship on the civil war makes only passing mention, if any, of the *Manifesto of the Chinese People's Liberation Army*. Han Suyin's biography of Mao, *The Morning Deluge*, briefly analyzes the historical context surrounding its publication. Hinting at a possible reason for Mao's having issued it, Suyin writes that the leader "appears to have been worried by the slackening of discipline in the armies; this was natural, since by now they were swollen with deserters." Many studies focus on Mao's use of land reform as a tactic in the war. Anna Louise Strong quotes Mao as saying, "A people's war is not decided by taking or losing a city, but by solving the agrarian problem,"

which Mao believed would stimulate the economy, provide food for ailing soldiers, and win peasants over to the communist cause.

BIBLIOGRAPHY

Sources

Lynch, Michael. *Mao*. London: Routledge, 2004. Print

Mackerras, Colin. *China in Transormation, 1900-1949*. Harlow: Pearson, 1998. Print.

Pepper, Suzanne. *Civil War in China: The Political Struggle, 1945-1949*. Lanham: Rowman, 1999. Print

Schram, Stuart R. *The Political Thought of Mao Tse-tung*. New York: Praeger, 1963. Print.

Suyin, Han. *The Morning Deluge: Mao Tse-tung and the Chinese Revolution*. Boston: Little, 1972. Print.

Tse-Tung, Mao. "Manifesto of the Chinese People's Liberation Army." *Selected Military Writings of Mao Tse-Tung*. Peking: Foreign Language, 1967. Print.

Further Reading

Griffith, Samuel. *The Chinese People's Liberation Army*. New York: McGraw, 1967. Print.

Lynch, Michael. *The Chinese Civil War*. Oxford: Osprey, 2010. Print.

Schwartz, Benjamin I. *Chinese Communism and the Rise of Mao*. Cambridge: Harvard UP, 1952. Print.

Short, Philip. *Mao: A Life*. New York: Holt, 1999. Print

Thornton, Richard. C. *A Political History, 1917-1980*. Boulder: Westview, 1982. Print.

Tse-Tung, Mao *On Guerrilla Warfare*. Champaign: U of Illinois P, 1961. Print.

Gregory Luther

Opposite page: Chinese propaganda poster from 1949, two years after Mao Zedong issued the *Manifesto of the Chinese People's Liberation Army*. It says, "Progress under Mao Zedong" and depicts Mao being greeted by the people as he leads the army. THE ART ARCHIVE AT ART RESOURCE, NY

Manifesto of the Communist International

Leon Trotsky

✛ **Key Facts**

Time Period:
Early 20th Century

Movement/Issue:
Communism; World War
I; Imperialism

Place of Publication:
Soviet Union

**Language of
Publication:**
Russian

OVERVIEW

Leon Trotsky's 1919 *Manifesto of the Communist International* is a call to the "workers of the world" to organize for international political action. Adopted by the founding congress of the Third International (Comintern), the document begins with an affirmation of allegiance to communism's founding fathers, Karl Marx and Friedrich Engels. Trotsky then broadly indicts capitalist imperialism and its role in World War I. Offering the promise of the new Soviet democracy as a model for workers around the world, Trotsky concludes with an exhortation to his audience to seize the moment and organize for revolution.

The manifesto failed to find a wide audience initially, owing in part to the circumstances of its delivery. In *International Communism and the Communist International 1919-43*, Tim Rees and Andrew Thorpe describe the First World Congress of the Comintern as "somewhat shambolic ... with few genuine delegates from outside Russia." Invitations, issued in the name of the Central Committee of the Russian Communist Party, were kept secret, and few of the invitees were able to make the journey to Moscow. Moreover, historians report that the manifesto was composed during the congress and that Trotsky was simultaneously writing articles to be printed in newspapers once the Comintern went public. Nevertheless, the *Manifesto of the Communist International* remains interesting as a snapshot of internationalist yearnings in the Soviet Union's nascent years, as well as of Trotsky's revolutionary politics.

LEON TROTSKY: A BIOGRAPHY

Born Lev Davidovich Bronstein in 1879, Leon Trotsky spent his childhood in an area of present-day Ukraine that was then part of Russia. Raised in a comfortable Jewish family, a teenage Trotsky participated in underground political activities that resulted in his exile to Siberia, where he became involved with the Social Democratic Party. Trotsky eventually escaped from Siberia and lived abroad for years, returning to Russia after the outbreak of the 1917 Bolshevik revolution. Trotsky then committed to the Bolshevik ideals and played a key role in bringing the communist government to power. In the civil wars that followed, Trotsky was also key in raising the Red Army, which would emerge victorious against the White Armies.

Despite playing an important role in installing the Bolshevik government, Trotsky was among the losers of a struggle within the Communist Party following the 1924 death of Soviet Premier Vladimir Lenin. In 1927, Trotsky was expelled from the party. After 1929, he lived in exile, first in Turkey and later in Mexico, where he became involved with Diego Rivera and Frida Kahlo. During this period, he was also active in helping to establish the Fourth International as an alternative to the Joseph Stalin-controlled Comintern. In the Moscow Show Trials of 1936, Trotsky was tried and convicted in absentia for conspiracy crimes against the state, including plotting to murder Stalin. On August 20, 1940, Trotsky was attacked with an ice pick by Ramón Mercader, who was acting on Stalin's orders. He died the following day.

HISTORICAL AND LITERARY CONTEXT

The *Manifesto of the Communist International* responds to the fracturing of the socialist movement in the early twentieth century. Marx and Engels's *The Communist Manifesto* (1848) ends with the iconic phrase "workers of the world, unite!" and establishes a program of internationalist goals. Marx and Engels viewed international proletarian revolution as both essential and inevitable. Indeed, the first major international proletarian movement, made up of trade unionists, was founded at a workingmen's meeting in 1864 by Marx himself. The International Workingmen's Association, also known as the First International, was an attempt to unite various left-wing groups under the banner of workers' rights and revolution. The group, which was riven by disputes over economic vs. political action, disbanded in 1876. The Second International, first convened in 1889, took over that banner, although many of the original trade unionists, as well as the pro-union syndicalists, were excluded from the new organization.

The *Manifesto of the Communist International* is directed at the failures of the Second International during World War I. The group had put forth an antiwar message at the onset of the war but became segmented along national lines, with members prioritizing patriotic commitments in their own countries, such as war spending, over a proletarian unity of purpose. The Zimmerwald Conference (1915) issued documents reaffirming the socialist antiwar stance, but the rift between communist revolutionaries and social-democrat reformists deepened. Meanwhile, the Bolshevik triumph in the October Revolution in 1917 implied the possibility of a revolutionary solution to the problems of the proletariat. The manifesto was issued at the 1919 founding congress of the Third International, or Comintern, as Bolshevik and anti-Bolshevik forces warred for control of Russia.

Trotsky's manifesto draws heavily on Marx and Engels's *The Communist Manifesto,* including the original title of their work (*Manifesto of the Communist Party*) and their iconic exhortation ("workers of the world, unite!"). *The Communist Manifesto* is an analysis of history as the elaboration of class struggle and a critique of capitalism as a system that mercilessly exploits the labors of the working class. Trotsky aligns his manifesto with that of Marx and Engels, framing it as a return to the principles of communism's founding document. Influenced more broadly by a socialist rhetorical tradition encompassing works such as *The Manifesto of The Socialist League* (1885) by William Morris and E. Belfort Bax, Trotsky's manifesto treats the poverty and dispossession of slaves and the working class as a consequence of the moral impoverishment of exploitive capitalist systems.

The internationalist argument set forth in Trotsky's manifesto remained relatively uncontested in the early years of the Comintern. In fact, he revisited similar concerns in his *Manifesto of the Second World Congress* (1920.) However, a major change occurred when Joseph Stalin began to consolidate his power following the 1924 death of Soviet Premier Vladimir Lenin. Trotsky, who had previously differed with Stalin over the role of trade unions in the Soviet state, was critical of Stalin's "Socialism in One Country" sloganeering. This criticism has been cited, along with other factors, in Trotsky's marginalization in the government and his eventual expulsion from the country.

THEMES AND STYLE

The necessity of revolution on a global scale is the defining theme of Trotsky's manifesto. After the opening remarks, which portray the Comintern delegates as "heirs and consummators" of Marx and Engels, Trotsky places his arguments against a backdrop of the "smoking ruins" of post-World War I Europe. Trotsky places the blame for the war, and for the current "epoch of crisis," at the feet of capitalist societies and the "insatiable greed" of the propertied classes, particularly those in Great Britain and the United States. He argues that the capitalist-induced war, though devastating for the proletariat movement and the advances it had previously made, revealed the "moral savagery" of capitalism on a global scale. With the period of "final, decisive struggle" at hand, Trotsky urges members of the Comintern to recognize "the world character of

The cover of a 1927 issue of a German satirical magazine *Simplicissimus* depicts Leon Trotsky being attacked by red wolves, a reference to conflict within the Communist Party. Trotsky's feud with Joseph Stalin would lead to Trotsky's assassination in 1940. BIBLIOTHÈQUE NATIONALE, PARIS, FRANCE/ ARCHIVES CHARMET/THE BRIDGEMAN ART LIBRARY

their tasks" and to organize to lead an international revolution.

The manifesto seeks to establish that the members of Comintern have not only a shared theoretical paternity but also a common goal of ending oppression worldwide. Trotsky promotes this bond through inclusive language, such as the phrase "we communists" of the opening paragraph. His appeals are directed to the "small peoples" and slaves of the world's less-developed countries in addition to the proletariat. Further, Trotsky makes clear that the goals of the Comintern delegates are truly noble, focused on "the need of saving the starving masses," the desire to "heal the gaping wounds inflicted by war," and the intention to "raise mankind to new and unprecedented heights."

Trotsky employs graphic and inflammatory language to impart the "moral savagery" of capitalist regimes and the need to establish an alternative. He repeatedly portrays capitalists as criminals, calling them "pyromaniacs" and "pimps," and paints capitalist theoreticians and teachers as ineffectual "eunuchs of bourgeois professordom and mandarins of Socialist opportunism." Further, capitalist democracies are "kingdoms of destruction," their industries and political policies "blood-soaked stumps." This tone of moral outrage works in tandem with Trotsky's strategy to foster a communist solidarity among representatives from countries that had been divided by the war. Trotsky speaks to "the peasant in Bavaria and Baden who still cannot see beyond the spires of his village church, the small French wine producer who is being driven into bankruptcy by the large-scale capitalists who adulterate wine, and the small American farmer fleeced and cheated by bankers and Congressmen."

CRITICAL DISCUSSION

The inaugural meeting of the Comintern in 1919 has been described as somewhat improvised, with neither the congress nor the manifesto providing a detailed analysis of the nature or directives of the movement. However, because the Comintern was made up primarily of Soviet delegates and because of the primacy of the ruling Bolsheviks within the movement, Russian interests directed the Comintern from the start. Although the second congress would see a number of parties across Europe become affiliated with the Comintern and the internationalist goals raised in the manifesto, scholars have noted that the Comintern eventually devolved into little more than a mouthpiece for Stalin's government.

The Comintern's goal of an international socialist revolution was never realized, and it was disbanded in 1943. However, as Kevin McDermott and Jeremy Agnew point out in *The Comintern: A History of International Communism from Lenin to Stalin,* the International "nurtured an impressive array of theoretical responses to the problems of the day … and inspired various sections of the left well into the 1970s and 1980s." For example, the authors cite communist agitation on behalf of working-class people in the Little Moscow communities of Scotland and Wales. McDermott and Agnew also speculate that the "threat" of international communism as a political alternative appealing to workers might have been influential in sparking social and labor reform by capitalist governments in the twentieth century. In *Manifestoes: Provocations of the Modern,* Janet Lyon detects more generally an assumption of the manifesto's function as "a reliable discursive form" that

could be used to disseminate the communist platform and internationalize the Bolshevik success. Despite Trotsky's ability to, as Lyon writes, "narrativize the political unconscious," his internationalist vision never became manifest.

Trotsky's manifesto is now largely neglected as a subject of critical interest, either as a stand-alone document or as one of the founding texts of the Comintern. The second congress, which took place in 1920, is often considered to be the first substantive meeting of the group, and the documents produced there, including the "Statutes of the Communist International" and the "Theses on the Conditions for Admittance to the Communist International," are treated accordingly. In particular, "Theses" has generated a great amount of historical debate, with experts arguing that its promotion of a centralized policy and a rigid ideology fostered the seeds of Stalinization in the Comintern, which would play a significant part in its eventual demise.

BIBLIOGRAPHY

Sources

Lyon, Janet. *Manifestoes: Provocations of the Modern.* Ithaca: Cornell UP, 1999. Print.

McDermott, Kevin, and Jeremy Agnew. *The Comintern: A History of International Communism from Lenin to Stalin.* New York: Saint Martin's, 1997. Print.

Rees, Tim, and Andrew Thorpe, eds. *International Communism and the Communist International 1919-43.* Manchester: Manchester UP, 1998. Print.

Trotsky, Leon. *Manifesto of the Communist International to the Workers of the World. Marxists Internet Archive.* Marxist.org, March 1919. Web. 3 Aug. 2012.

Further Reading

Hallas, Duncan. *The Comintern.* Chicago: Haymarket, 2008. Print.

Read, Anthony. *The World on Fire: 1919 and the Battle with Bolshevism.* New York: W. W. Norton, 2008. Print.

Thatcher, Ian. *Trotsky.* London: Routledge, 2003. Print.

Trotsky, Leon. *The Permanent Revolution & Results and Prospects.* Seattle: Red Letter, 2010. Print.

Worley, Mathew; Norman LaPorte; and Kevin Morgan, eds. *Bolshevism, Stalinism and the Comintern: Perspectives on Stalinization, 1917-53.* Basingstoke, Hampshire: Palgrave Macmillan, 2008. Print.

Daisy Gard

THE MANIFESTO OF THE FASCIST STRUGGLE

Alceste de Ambris, Filippo Tommaso Marinetti

OVERVIEW

Written by futurist Filippo Tommaso Marinetti and syndicalist Alceste de Ambris, "Il manifesto dei fasci di combattimento" ("The Manifesto of the Fascist Struggle," often shortened in English to "The Fascist Manifesto") was published in Benito Mussolini's newspaper *Il Popolo d'Italia* ("The People of Italy") on June 6, 1919. The essay expresses Italian nationalists' dissatisfaction with the peripheral status of Italy in global politics and outlines the founding principles of the Italian Fascist Party. Intended to rally what the authors perceived as a frustrated Italian populace, "The Fascist Manifesto" comprises four sections cataloging the party's objectives for political, social, military, and financial reform. Ultimately, it calls for a nearly complete overhaul of the existing political infrastructure. Though many of the text's democratic and socialist ideals would later be abandoned in favor of the dictatorial framework with which fascism is now more commonly associated, "The Fascist Manifesto" gave voice to Italians' desire for popular sovereignty.

Upon its release, "The Fascist Manifesto" was scarcely noted outside nationalist circles, and it effected little change. What change the Fascist Party did manage to bring about had little to do with the principles outlined in the essay, as the brutality of Mussolini's regime subverted the text's promises of equity and progress. The Italian public quickly became more disenchanted with fascist rule than they had been with the monarchy, and the party's legacy became one of unflagging infamy. Among scholars today, "The Fascist Manifesto" exemplifies the disparity between thought and action in sociopolitical revolution.

HISTORICAL AND LITERARY CONTEXT

"The Fascist Manifesto"—and the growing political movement it accompanied—responded to the perceived shortcomings of the World War I peace treaties, as well as to the Italian leaders' reactions to them. A number of Italian nationalists felt slighted by the land-distribution terms of the Treaty of Saint-Germain (1919) and other provisions of the Paris Peace Conference (1919-20). They viewed the Allied Powers' treatment of Italy—ostensibly a member of the alliance—as patronizing. Moreover, the weak reactions of the Italian monarchy and socialist leaders to such condescending treatment seemed woefully inadequate. Among those disillusioned nationalists

was Mussolini, a former socialist leader who had advocated for Italy's participation in the war. Espousing a more militant doctrine, he had founded *fasci di combattimento* ("fighting leagues") to push for a stronger expression of Italian nationalism. These groups, whose members came to be known as fascists, harassed socialists as well as local government officials.

Mussolini's sentiments were shared by de Ambris, a prominent syndicalist (a type of working-class anarchist) who had founded a "league" of his own in 1914, and Marinetti, an experimental author whose *Futurist Manifesto* had attracted Mussolini's attention in 1909. The pair had worked closely with Mussolini since 1915, and "The Fascist Manifesto" they drafted in June 1919 gave voice to the burgeoning fascist movement, which arose from a collective frustration with existing nationalist ideologies. Although the essay was devised as a first step toward deposing the monarchy, it eschewed denigration of the existing government. Rather, it detailed the framework of an entirely new, more populist political system. Among its guarantees would be drastically improved labor rights, the equitable redistribution of wealth via radical tax reform, and truly universal suffrage. The promise of such progress galvanized the Italian public behind the fascist cause. In practice, however, few of the work's principles were upheld. When Mussolini took power in 1922, his government increasingly took on the oppressive, dictatorial form with which fascism is now associated.

In its calls for reform, "The Fascist Manifesto" draws on a longstanding literary tradition of enumeration—the listing of grievances or proposed solutions to provoke change. Such list making has taken many forms, from the disenchanted interrogation of Martin Luther's Ninety-five Theses (1517) to the outraged defiance of the U.S. Declaration of Independence (1776) and subsequent Constitution (1789). Marinetti even uses enumeration in his earlier *Futurist Manifesto,* which argues for forward thinking and technical innovation over nostalgia and traditional methods. Yet "The Fascist Manifesto" stands out from other enumerated declarations by foregoing the typical denunciation of existing practices. Lacking a preamble and a conclusion, the essay consists only of four groups of principles by which the authors feel a "genuinely Italian movement" ought to be undertaken. In this way, "The Fascist Manifesto" most closely resembles a

⁂ *Key Facts*

Time Period:
Early 20th Century

Movement/Issue:
Fascism; Italian nationalism

Place of Publication:
Italy

Language of Publication:
Italian

DE AMBRIS AND MARINETTI:
BEFORE AND AFTER THE MANIFESTO

Alceste de Ambris had been a prominent member of the Unione Sindacale Italiana (Italian Syndicalist Union) prior to its division into two syndicalist movements at odds with one another, which some argue he helped orchestrate. In early 1914, de Ambris penned the founding charter for the Fasci d'Azione Internazionalista (League of International Action), a document that grabbed the attention of then-unknown Benito Mussolini, who headed his own Fasci Autonomi d'Azione Rivoluzionaria (Autonomous League of Revolutionary Action). Both "leagues" were aimed at reversing socialist opposition to Italy's intervention in World War I. The two leaders got along very well and merged their groups in December 1914. They continued to collaborate until de Ambris became disgusted with the direction of the fascist movement in 1921. For de Ambris's vocal disapprobation of the Fascist Party and its activities, Mussolini revoked his citizenship in 1926.

Filippo Tommaso Marinetti, meanwhile, had gained prominence at the turn of the twentieth century as a poet and an editor. In 1909 he founded the futurist movement, penning *Futurist Manifesto* as its founding document. The body of the manifesto held that art could be "nothing but violence, cruelty, and injustice," and it asserted by extension that life could be nothing more either. As he rose to relative acclaim in his collaborations with de Ambris, Marinetti became an active and vocal supporter of Mussolini. After coauthoring "The Fascist Manifesto," Marinetti pled with Mussolini for many years to establish futurism as the official state art, to no avail.

contemporary document, Woodrow Wilson's Fourteen Points (1918). Both propose a straightforward set of principles that represent a path to progress.

"The Fascist Manifesto" was originally published in the newspaper *Il Popolo d'Italia*, owned by Benito Mussolini. Mussolini, depicted here, later became the Fascist dictator of Italy. EILEEN TWEEDY/ THE ART ARCHIVE AT ART RESOURCE, NY

When Mussolini abandoned the manifesto's principles in favor of a more self-interested, militant ideology, Marinetti and de Ambris became increasingly frustrated. Marinetti seemed content with the political path taken by Mussolini—his own *Futurist Manifesto* had promoted precisely the kind of military-industrial complex Mussolini began to build—but he was perturbed by Mussolini's refusal to establish futurism as Italy's official art form. De Ambris, meanwhile, became disenchanted with the Fascist Party altogether. He deplored the ever more militant and dictatorial character of fascism, and he was exiled for publicly defaming the party in 1926. De Ambris continued to speak and write in opposition to the Fascist Party for most of his life; he published his *Lettere dall'esilio* (*Letters from Exile*) from France. Supplanted by Mussolini's own "La Dottrina del Fascismo" ("The Doctrine of Fascism") in 1932, "The Fascist Manifesto" and its authors were relegated to relative obscurity.

THEMES AND STYLE

The sole theme of "The Fascist Manifesto" is the broadening of democratic policy in post-World War I Italy. The essay calls for several categories of reform to strengthen the country. Its proposed political reforms include a lowered voting age and the creation of a "national technical council on intellectual and manual labor, industry, commerce, and agriculture." Among its social reforms are a minimum wage, an eight-hour work day, and improved insurance for the care of disabled and elderly Italians. One of its military reforms is the creation of a national militia to "defend the nation's rights and interests." Proposed financial reforms include a redistribution of wealth among the general populace through the expansion of government-sponsored social programs, funded by taxes on affluent individuals and the seizure of religious property. The demands are unencumbered by either preamble or epilogue.

The text's utilitarian sparsity serves as its primary rhetorical strategy. Marinetti and de Ambris avoid the grand, ornate prose and rallying cries used by fascist leaders during public addresses. Instead, they focus solely on their demand for rights so basic that they need neither introduction nor elaboration. Underlying this strategy is an acknowledgement of the Italian public's intelligent participation in the discussion. The authors begin by addressing all Italians ("*Italiani!*") and thereafter employ the phrase "we demand"—thereby including in the fascist project every Italian who values fair and equal treatment under the law. "The Fascist Manifesto" thus reminds the Italian people of their right, as a nation, to determine their own governance.

The dispassionate tenor of the writing gives the essay a constitutional air. It refrains from pleading for political equity and justice per se; instead, "The Fascist Manifesto" calls for "a dynamic policy that contrasts with one inclined to reinforce the hegemony of the current plutocratic powers." Likewise, social reforms are couched in straightforward, legal terms: the authors demand "a legal workday of eight *actual* hours of work" and, simply, "a minimum wage." All reforms are aimed at forming a "state bureaucracy motivated by a sense of individual responsibility and leading to a significant reduction in bulk of the overseeing bodies" and the "decentralization and simplification" of social services. The authors thus propose a political dynamic in which the government is of less importance than the rights of the governed.

CRITICAL DISCUSSION

"The Fascist Manifesto" had little immediate impact and was accordingly afforded scarce media attention outside nationalist circles. Reactions to the essay did not appear in any substantial form, or with any regularity, until Mussolini and the Fascist Party rose to power in Italy in 1922. Indeed, the doctrine proposed in the manifesto received significant attention only after Mussolini seemed to abandon it in 1923, when he invaded the Greek island of Corfu. That action contradicted the text's call for a peaceful foreign policy and the exercise of military force only in a defensive capacity. Philip V. Cannistraro, in an article for the *Journal of Contemporary History,* contends that shortly thereafter, "it was apparent to everyone that there was little to justify the myth" of fascism as a viable path "to a young, virile, new Italy."

Few of the proposals set forth by "The Fascist Manifesto" were realized, as the brutality of Mussolini's reign effectively undermined the intentions of the essay. As a literary model, the manifesto stands as only one example in a long history of enumerative proclamations. Nevertheless, in the anthology *A Primer of Italian Fascism,* Jeffrey T. Schnapp notes that the essay is perhaps one of the earliest expressions of an amalgam of "militant but disaffected political forces within the fold of an antiparty movement." In the decades since, this almost amorphous "antiparty" ethos has influenced the shape of countless social and political revolutions.

Recontextualizing "The Fascist Manifesto" in accordance with Schnapp's view, contemporary scholarship often sees the essay as more important to the understanding of social revolution as a concept than to the understanding of the fascist movement in particular. Clarence H. Yarrow, in an article for the *Journal of the History of Ideas,* posits that the manifesto's real value is as "a revealing exercise in the history of ideas," within which "to study the parallel movements of action and thought." Another group of scholars cites the disparity between its proposals and Mussolini's actions as evidence that the Fascist Party had no discernible doctrine until nearly a decade into its reign. Walter L. Adamson, writing for the *Journal of Modern History* in 1992, goes so far as to argue that by not publishing an official doctrine until it issued "La Dottrina del Fascismo" in 1932, the fascist movement "made a fetish out of being an 'anti-ideology.'" Thus, according to many scholars, "The Fascist Manifesto" remains more useful to the study of the cultural climate out of which it arose than it is to the study of the movement it introduced.

BIBLIOGRAPHY

Sources

Adamson, Walter L. "The Language of Opposition in Early Twentieth-Century Italy: Rhetorical Continuities between Prewar Florentine Avant-gardism and Mussolini's Fascism." *Journal of Modern History* 64.1 (1992): 22-51. *JSTOR.* Web. 3 Oct. 2012.

Cannistraro, Philip V. "Mussolini's Cultural Revolution: Fascist or Nationalist?" *Journal of Contemporary History* 7.3-4 (1972): 115-39. *JSTOR.* Web. 2 Oct. 2012.

Schnapp, Jeffrey T., Olivia E. Sears, and Maria G. Stampino. *A Primer of Italian Fascism.* Lincoln: U of Nebraska P, 2000. Print.

Yarrow, Clarence H. "The Forging of Fascist Doctrine." *Journal of the History of Ideas* 3.2 (1942): 159-81. *JSTOR.* Web. 4 Oct. 2012.

Further Reading

Adamson, Walter L. "Modernism and Fascism: The Politics of Culture in Italy, 1903-1922." *American Historical Review* 95.2 (1990): 359-90. *JSTOR.* Web. 3 Oct. 2012.

Elazar, Dahlia S. *The Making of Fascism: Class, State, and Counter-Revolution, Italy 1919-1922.* Westport, CT: Praeger, 2001. Print.

Finaldi, Giuseppe. *Mussolini and Italian Fascism.* Harlow: Pearson Longman, 2008. Print.

Gentile, Giovanni, and A. J. Gregor. *Origins and Doctrine of Fascism: With Selections from Other Works.* New Brunswick: Transaction, 2002. Print.

Lazzaro, Claudia, and Roger J. Crum. *Donatello among the Blackshirts: History and Modernity in the Visual Culture of Fascist Italy.* Ithaca: Cornell UP, 2005. Print.

Roberts, David D. *The Syndicalist Tradition and Italian Fascism.* Chapel Hill: U of North Carolina P, 1979. Print.

Vivarelli, Roberto. "Interpretations of the Origins of Fascism." *Journal of Modern History* 63.1 (1991): 29-43. *JSTOR.* Web. 4 Oct. 2012.

Clint Garner

MANIFESTO OF THE SIXTEEN

Jean Grave, Peter Kropotkin

✧ *Key Facts*

Time Period:
Early 20th Century

Movement/Issue:
Anarchism; Militarism;
World War I

Place of Publication:
France

**Language of
Publication:**
French

OVERVIEW

Anarchists Peter Kropotkin and Jean Grave first published "Manifesto of the Sixteen" ("*Manifeste des seize*") in *La Bataille* on March 14, 1916, in order to declare their support for World War I, which they saw as a noble battle against authoritarianism and German imperialism. The war, which began in 1914, pitted the Allies (Great Britain, France, and Russia) against the Central Powers (principally Germany and Austria-Hungary) in a struggle for dominance of Europe. During the early years of the war, European anarchists were divided over the issue of militarism: most criticized the war for benefiting the elite at the expense of the working classes, while a minority supported the conflict as a way to resist the spread of authoritarian government. Addressed to the European public, the pro-war manifesto, which describes the need for militarism in the face of global domination, initially had only fifteen signatories, including eminent European anarchists Varlam Cherkezishvili and Christian Cornelissen.

Because the manifesto takes a position in stark contrast to that of the larger anarchist movement, many anarchists accused the authors and signatories of nationalism and betraying core anarchist principles. Despite being largely dismissed by the European anarchist community, the manifesto would later be echoed in U.S. President Woodrow Wilson's landmark "Fourteen Points" address, which ultimately shaped the conditions for lasting peace. However, Wilson and his administration denied any association with the anarchist document, and the manifesto was largely overlooked as an important statement of values during the war. Today scholars have rediscovered the manifesto and its similarity to Wilson's "Fourteen Points," examining the authors' influence on Western thought during the war.

HISTORICAL AND LITERARY CONTEXT

"Manifesto of the Sixteen" responds to the growing divisions between Marxists, socialists, and anarchists—and within the anarchist movement—over the correct way to deal with authoritarian governments and militarism. During the nineteenth century, left-wing groups were largely united through their commitment to labor rights. However, anarchists gradually differentiated themselves from Marxists in their denouncement of imperialism and their belief in the eradication of all authoritarian government. As World War I loomed, divisions appeared within the anarchist community between those who wished to avoid war at all costs and those who believed military intervention was necessary to fight off the authoritarian threat of the Central Powers.

Pro-war anarchists, isolated through their disagreement with the majority of the anarchist movement, drew closer together after the dawn of World War I. Kropotkin, influenced by fellow anarchist Mikhail Bakunin, blamed German imperialism for stifling anarchism and concluded that pacifism could no longer aid the anarchist movement in the face of militarism. Grave, a prominent French journalist and anarchist, convinced Kropotkin to write the manifesto in order to galvanize support for the war among anarchists. Although the two anarchists had previously published their arguments in the British newspaper *Freedom,* their writings had only provoked controversy and resistance from others in the anarchist movement. *La Bataille,* the controversial periodical in which "Manifesto of the Sixteen" would be published, was known for publishing pro-war writings and was labeled by Marxists as government propaganda.

Kropotkin was not the first anarchist to take a stance on World War I. An international assembly of anarchists had released an antiwar statement in February 1916, signed by such figures as Emma Goldman, Rudolf Rocker, and eventually Errico Malatesta and Alexander Schapiro. The statement claimed that all wars were the product of prevailing social and political systems; therefore, all governments were to blame. The signatories also agreed that there was little difference between military aggression and militaristic defense and that the best way to resolve conflict was to empower the working classes, not enslave them through war.

The publication of the manifesto garnered some attention from the mainstream press, which portrayed it as representing the whole of the anarchist movement. This misrepresentation angered many in the anarchist movement, some of whom simply dismissed the manifesto and alienated Kropotkin. Even those who seemed to have been directly influenced by the ideas of the document, such as Wilson in his "Fourteen Points" address, distanced themselves from

Kropotkin because of his proximity to socialism. Thus, aside from widening the divide within the anarchist movement, the manifesto exercised little clear influence on later political writings.

THEMES AND STYLE

The central theme of "Manifesto of the Sixteen" is that German aggression and authoritarianism are intolerable; therefore, even pacifist anarchists should support the Allied war effort. The document begins by confirming that, in an ideal world, anarchists could totally denounce militarism and imperialism and that peace could be brought about by an international conference of European workers. Kropotkin and Grave further state that Germany's threat extends not just to the working classes but also to the whole of humanity. Hence, pacifism is inadequate in addressing the crisis facing the world and even weakens humanity's defense against the spread of authoritarianism. The authors conclude that the only way to empower the German people in overthrowing their government is to support the war effort and thereby weaken the German military.

The manifesto relies on rhetorical appeals to logic and pragmatism, addressing the anarchist community's pro-socialist beliefs rather than its antinationalist sentiments. Kropotkin and Grave begin by offering a brief social and political history of Germany, asserting that the country's imperialist designs in the late nineteenth and early twentieth centuries made war inevitable. They argue that German workers have shown they are unprepared to independently overthrow their government—the solution most anarchists advocated. The authors conclude that peace through pacifism is unrealistic and the only intervention that can stop German aggression is defensive war. Moreover, they argue, the trend toward independent bartering with Germany, most notably on the part of Belgium and France, will result in poorer conditions for workers, who will be excluded from territorial and financial negotiations. Therefore, to resist the war effort is to abandon the people, leaving them at the mercy of authoritarian governments.

The tone of the manifesto is practical, urgent, and at times derisive. In the closing paragraphs, for instance, Kropotkin and Grave imply that peace talks with a persistently militant Germany would be naïve. They chide anarchist ideas of a pacifist solution, calling such notions "illusions" and stating that, unlike their antiwar brethren, pro-war anarchists prefer to look "danger" in the "face." The authors refer to their profound sense of conscience and even call themselves true "*antimilitaristes.*" They claim to side with La Résistance, implying that antiwar anarchists are disengaged with the actual problems facing the people of Europe. In the signatory block, the authors further deride the anarchist community for its cowardice, noting that only fifteen comrades would risk signing their names to the text.

THE MANIFESTO'S SIXTEENTH SIGNATURE

In contrast to the document's title, the original signatories of the "Manifesto of the Sixteen" numbered only fifteen. Along with Peter Kropotkin and Jean Grave, only thirteen continental European, Russian, African, and Asian comrades signed the document: Christian Cornelissen, Henri Fuss, Jacques Guérin, Charles-Ange Laisant, Francois Le Lève, Charles Malato, Jules Moineau, Antoine Orfila, Marc Pierrot, Paul Reclus, P. Richard, Sanshirō Ichikawa, and Varlam Cherkezishvili. A sixteenth signatory, Hussein Dey, was mistakenly listed but was in fact the name of the Algerian city in which signatory Antoine Orfila lived.

In spite of the error, the name "Manifesto of the Sixteen" persisted. Some have supposed that James Guillaume—a supporter of the war and a leading member of the Jura Federation, the anarchist wing of the First International—should have been an initial signatory; however, the reason his name does not appear is unknown. Although the manifesto gained more signatures when it was republished in the Swiss publication *La Libre Fédération* in April 1916, it still failed to attract widespread support. In fact, one of the later signatories, Jean Wintsch, an editor of *La Libre*, was—like Kropotkin—estranged from the anarchist community in his country for expressing support for the document.

CRITICAL DISCUSSION

Upon publication, the manifesto met with disapproval in the international anarchist movement. Later republished in *La Libre Fédération* in April 1916 with additional signatories, the document failed to gain major support from anarchists. The International Group of London Anarchists responded by publishing a 1916 declaration repudiating the manifesto and claiming that the only reason pro-war anarchists had succeeded in gaining publicity was that "their enemy of yesterday and ours for all time, the State, allowed them to express their opinions openly and freely." Italian anarcho-communist Malatesta also published a 1916 response to the manifesto in *Freedom*, recognizing the "good faith and good intentions" of the signatories but accusing them of having betrayed anarchist principles. He writes, "It will never be possible to prevent the German patriots thinking of, and preparing for, revenge…. Militarism will become a permanent and regular institution in all countries." He was later joined in his denunciation by prominent anarchists Luigi Fabbri, Sébastien Faure, and Goldman.

The lasting impact of the manifesto was to further entrench opposing anarchist camps. In *Peter Kropotkin: From Prince to Rebel* (1990), George Woodcock states that the effect of the document was to "merely [confirm] the split which existed in the anarchist movement." Camillo Berneri in *Peter Kropotkin: His*

A caricature of the German army from the June 1915 cover of the French satirical magazine *Le Rire*. In the "Manifesto of the Sixteen," issued the following year, anarchists voiced their support for the Allied powers' war against Germany. © CHRIS HELLIER/ ALAMY

Michaël Confino's investigation of previously unpublished correspondence between Kropotkin and Russian anarchist Marie Goldsmith in the months leading up to the manifesto's publication. Confino's essay, published in *Cahiers du Monde Russe et Soviétique* in 1981, reproduces several letters between Kropotkin and Goldsmith and offers an analysis of the ideological tension between the different anarchist camps.

BIBLIOGRAPHY

Sources

Berneri, Camillo. *Peter Kropotkin: His Federalist Ideas.* London: Freedom Press, 1943. Print.

Confino, Michaël. "Anarchisme et internationalisme. Autour du *Manifeste des Seize.* Correspondance inédite de Pierre Kropotkine et de Marie Goldsmith, janvier-mars 1916." *Cahiers du Monde Russe et Soviétique* 22.2-3 (1981): 231-49. *JSTOR.* Web. 12 July 2012.

Malatesta, Errico. "Pro-Government Anarchists." *Freedom* Apr. 1916: 28. Web. 14 Aug. 2012. Web. 14 Aug. 2012.

Richards, Vernon. *Errico Malatesta: His Life & Ideas.* London: Freedom Press, 1965. Print.

Vilain, Éric. *Kropotkine et la Grande Guerre.* Paris: Cercle d'études libertaires-Gaston-Leval, 2011. Web. 14 Aug. 2012.

Woodcock, George. *Peter Kropotkin: From Prince to Rebel.* Montreal: Black Rose, 1990. Print.

Woodcock, George, and Ivan Avakumovic. *The Anarchist Prince: A Biographical Study of Peter Kropotkin.* London: Boardman, 1970. Print.

Further Reading

Avrich, Paul. *The Russian Anarchists.* Edinburgh: AK Press, 2005. Print.

Ghe, Alexandre. *Lettre ouverte a P. Kropotkine.* Alexandria: Chadwyck-Healey, 1987. Print.

Goldman, Emma. *Living My Life.* New York: Dover, 1930. Print.

Guérin, Daniel. *No Gods, No Masters: An Anthology of Anarchism.* Edinburgh: AK Press, 2005. Print.

Nettlau, Max. *Errico Malatesta: The Biography of an Anarchist.* New York: Jewish Anarchist Federation, 1924. Print.

———. *A Short History of Anarchism.* London: Freedom Press, 1996. Print.

Skirda, Alexandre. *Facing the Enemy: A History of Anarchist Organization from Proudhon to May 1968.* Edinburgh: AK Press, 2002. Print.

Federalist Ideas (1922) calls the "Manifesto of the Sixteen" "the culmination of incoherence in the pro-war anarchists." As Kropotkin's popularity dwindled, owing to his staunch support of the war, many of his former friends ostracized him. (Two exceptions included Rocker and Schapiro.) In *Errico Malatesta: His Life & Ideas* (1965), anarchist scholar Vernon Richards supposes that were it not for the equitable efforts of *Freedom* editor Thomas Keell, a vocal antiwar activist, Kropotkin and his cohort might have found themselves politically quarantined even earlier than 1916.

Given its nearly immediate relegation to obscurity, "Manifesto of the Sixteen" has been afforded limited scholarly treatment. Most scholarship focuses on the anarchist dealings of those involved in the drafting of and reaction to the document and on historical treatments of the document in the context of the larger anarchist movement. One notable example is

Clint Garner

MEIN KAMPF

Adolf Hitler

OVERVIEW

A work of political philosophy containing elements of autobiography, Adolf Hitler's *Mein Kampf* (*My Struggle*), published in two volumes in 1925 and 1926, offers a blueprint for post–World War I Germany to reclaim its place as a European superpower through armed conquest and racial superiority. Hitler calls for the unification of the German people under a single *reich*, or empire, and identifies the enemies of this *reich*: Jews, communists, and pacifists, to name a few. Hitler wrote much of the book in Germany's Landsberg prison while serving one year of a five-year sentence for an attempt to seize power in Munich in 1923. This relatively light punishment reflected the court's sympathy for militaristic nationalism in the wake of Germany's catastrophic defeat in World War I, which left nearly two million Germans dead and millions more looking for a more effectual government than the democratic Weimar Republic.

Initially, the book saw some success. In its first year of publication, *Mein Kampf* sold just under 10,000 copies; however annual sales figures declined steadily until 1929. As Hitler's National Socialist (Nazi) Party rose to prominence, so did *Mein Kampf*, becoming a best seller (and the "bible" of the Nazi Party) by 1933, the year Hitler was appointed chancellor. The book came under international scrutiny in the 1930s as Hitler's policies of rearmament and territorial expansion raised the possibility of a second, deadlier world war. He would eventually carry out many of the plans he outlines in *Mein Kampf*, and the book—sales of which now number in the millions—is considered fundamental to the scholarship of National Socialism and the causes of World War II.

HISTORICAL AND LITERARY CONTEXT

Hitler's chief concern in *Mein Kampf* is creating a dominant empire in which ethnic Germans across central Europe are united within a single set of territorial borders. After the German defeat in World War I, the victorious Allied powers dictated the terms of peace to Germany in the Treaty of Versailles: financial reparations, a neutering of the armed forces, and great losses of territory. With large populations of Germans dispersed across areas of Poland, Czechoslovakia, and Austria, Hitler calls in *Mein Kampf* for a "reunion" of the German people within a new state. The implied

borders of this new Germany would violate the Treaty of Versailles as well as infringe upon the territorial sovereignty of Germany's neighbors.

In the aftermath of World War I, however, Germany underwent such a volatile transition from monarchy to democracy that national expansion would have proved impossible. The seemingly sudden surrender in November 1918 had left many soldiers—including Hitler, who served bravely at the front—convinced that civilians at home had betrayed the army, had initiated the surrender, and had forced Kaiser Wilhelm II to abdicate. After the Weimar Republic replaced the monarchy in 1919, the democratic government was crippled by ineffectiveness and hyperinflation. Deeming the republic weak and corrupt, Hitler staged an armed uprising in Munich to unseat the local government and seize power. The uprising failed, and Hitler was charged with high treason and sentenced to five years in prison (of which he served but one year). The leniency of his sentence can be attributed to the court's sympathy for the nationalist cause in the shadow of the humiliation of Versailles.

Hitler's ideas of a "Jewish danger" and an Aryan master race echo the writings of other nineteenth- and early twentieth-century writers. In *Mein Kampf*, Hitler's only book published during his lifetime, he invokes virulent anti-Semites such as Houston Stewart Chamberlain and Karl Lueger. It is probable, though difficult to prove, that he also drew on the monumental and far less discredited theories of Charles Darwin to justify his ideas of racial superiority and natural selection in which the strong eliminate the weak. Hitler, however, relied upon particular interpretations of Darwin's theories that Darwin did not endorse. The idea of Social Darwinism, in which social groups compete for superiority, offered a convenient justification for Hitler's Aryan law in which the powerful conquer and subjugate the weak.

Mein Kampf's literary legacy is largely one of political propaganda. In what would later become official ideology, Hitler presents himself as an infallible and providential leader. With proper guidance, the book claims, the German nation can reclaim its mythological, historical, and racial greatness—and defeat the existential threats to Aryan superiority posed by Judaism, Marxism, democracy, and compassion—by sacrificing individual well-being for that of society

✣ *Key Facts*

Time Period:
Early 20th Century

Movement/Issue:
German nationalism;
Nazism

Place of Publication:
Germany

Language of Publication:
German

THE LIFE OF ADOLF HITLER

Adolf Hitler was born in Austria in 1889 into unremarkable circumstances. As a child he exhibited a strong intellect but poor work habits, later failing at both painting and architecture. Moving to Vienna as a young man, he encountered poverty as well as the anti-Semitic ideas that would inform his particular brand of nationalism. In 1914, with the outbreak of World War I, he put this nationalism to use, volunteering for the German army.

Having served bravely at the front, he became involved in right-wing politics after the armistice of 1918, quickly discovering a talent for public speaking. As the head of the National Socialist German Workers' Party, he attracted enough support to stage a coup against the Bavarian government in 1923, though he was unsuccessful. Released after a single year in prison, he returned to politics, working to democratically seize power and accomplishing his goal in 1933. He and the Nazis instituted single-party rule as they rearmed the military, persecuted Jews, and expanded Germany's territory by annexing Austria and the Sudetenland (German-speaking areas in what is now the Czech Republic and Slovakia).

By the end of World War II in 1945, more than fifty million people had died, including some six million Jews who had perished in death and labor camps, in the horrid conditions of the ghettos, and at the hands of roving execution squads. After Russian forces encircled Berlin in 1945, Hitler committed suicide in his bunker with his wife, Eva Braun, at age fifty-six.

Book 2 of *Mein Kampf*, 1926. Part autobiography, part political screed, *Mein Kampf* outlines Hitler's anti-Semitism and National Socialism. BPK, BERLIN/(NAME OF MUSEUM) /(NAME OF PHOTOGRAPHER)/ART RESOURCE, NY

as a whole. Other Nazi writers such as Alfred Rosenberg and Gottfried Feder would later write tracts to be assumed by the party as doctrine, but no other text—both within Germany and without— would be regarded as so fundamental to Nazi ideology as *Mein Kampf.*

THEMES AND STYLE

For the German people to fulfill their historic destiny, Hitler writes in *Mein Kampf,* new territory must be acquired. This so-called *lebensraum,* or living space, is not only a necessity in Hitler's mind but also a right. He holds that the government must "secure for the German people the land and soil to which they are entitled." Any additional territory, however, would come at the expense of another country: "If we speak of soil in Europe today, we can primarily have in mind only Russia and her vassal border states." To conquer such territory, Hitler maintains, the German must bring to heel the "lesser" peoples of Eastern Europe. Far from considering this an unfortunate necessity, however, he views this proposition as natural and well suited to the warlike "superior" Aryan race: "Those who want to live, let them fight, and those who do not want to fight, in this world of eternal struggle, do not deserve to live."

To further his bellicose arguments, Hitler identifies various "common enemies" as a rhetorical strategy in *Mein Kampf.* This idea unites people around a common goal—to defeat the opposition—and privileges the success of the group to that of the individual. Hitler's plan to acquire *lebensraum* in the east was predicated upon first destroying France so as to take revenge for the Treaty of Versailles and avoid a two-front war. To do so, however, public opinion in Germany would have to be solidly anti-French. Hitler played on lingering animosity by calling France "the inexorable mortal enemy of the German people" in the wake of the humiliating terms of the Treaty of Versailles. He also considered Jews, eastern Europeans, and Marxists as enemies of the German people— a rhetorical strategy he would employ with success for the rest of his life.

The language and emotional tenor of *Mein Kampf* leaves little doubt that Hitler considers his own beliefs and leadership instincts to be infallible. Considering himself uniquely qualified to determine Germany's future course, his self-importance reflects his contempt for the republic he attempted to overthrow in 1923 (and would later eliminate in 1933), terming it as "democratic nonsense." Further, Hitler attacks many social and economic freedoms inherent to liberalism as "corrupt," the product of a global Jewish conspiracy, and he maintains that the state must assume a dominant role. To that end, he advocates an authoritarian society in which "there must be no majority decisions"; every "decision will be made by one man." His uncompromising nature, however, may have left him resistant to suggestions about improving the ponderous and verbose writing style of *Mein Kampf.* With its endless repetition; a complete lack of irony; and meandering, affected prose, the book led Hitler's ally Benito Mussolini, fascist dictator of Italy, to describe it as "a boring tome I have never been able to read."

CRITICAL DISCUSSION

Reaction to the book was initially mixed. Hitler acolytes such as Rudolf Hess and Alfred Rosenberg regarded the book as truth, while others rejected it as hateful warmongering. Retired German General Karl Haushofer, a man who pioneered the concept of *lebensraum* as vital to a nation's self-sufficiency (and therefore security), was so appalled by Hitler's racial diatribes that he refused to write a review for the book when asked to do so by Hess. In published reviews, many critics lambasted it as pretentious and dull. Author George Orwell was more to the point, writing in a review of the English edition republished in *George Orwell: My Country Right or Left, 1940-1943* (1968): "A thing that strikes one is the rigidity of his mind … It is the fixed vision of a monomaniac." In an essay reprinted in *The Second World War* (1976), British statesman Winston Churchill remarks on the lackluster prose but identifies the powerful and dangerous significance of the work: "the new Koran of faith and war: turgid, verbose, shapeless, but pregnant with its message."

In the years immediately following World War II, it became evident that many of the principles articulated in the book mirrored the course of German policy from 1933 to 1945. With Hitler at the helm, Nazi Germany realized many of the fantasies laid out in *Mein Kampf*: the annexation of Austria, the persecution of the Jews, the strongman head of state, the invasions of France and Russia, and the ruthless adherence to "survival of the fittest." William Shirer, a journalist who worked in Germany during Hitler's reign, writes in *The Rise and Fall of the Third Reich* (1960): "The blueprint of the Third Reich … is set down in all its appalling crudity at great length and in detail between the covers of this revealing book." John Toland writes in his 1976 biography of Hitler that the French "should have heeded the significance of … certain Francophobic passages in *Mein Kampf.*"

Over the past thirty years, the deterministic nature of *Mein Kampf* has been challenged by a new debate among Nazi scholars—that of intentionalism versus functionalism. Intentionalists, such as Daniel Goldhagen, maintain the determinacy ascribed to the book by earlier historians and contend that the actions of the Nazi state from 1933 to 1945, particularly the Holocaust, were the product of a well-developed plan Hitler conceived long before taking power, as evidenced by the anti-Semitism of *Mein Kampf.* Functionalists, however, such as Christopher Browning and Hans Mommsen, respond by noting that Hitler makes no specific reference to a plan for Jewish genocide in the book. In arguing that the Holocaust was largely a product of the ideas of his subordinates—most notably SS chief Heinrich Himmler—functionalists reject the notion that Hitler's book determined the future course of action of Nazi Germany.

BIBLIOGRAPHY

Sources

Churchill, Winston. *The Second World War.* 6 vols. Boston: Houghton Mifflin, 1976. Print.

Hitler, Adolf. *Mein Kampf.* Boston: Houghton Mifflin, 1943. Print.

Littell, Franklin H., ed. *Hyping the Holocaust: Scholars Answer Goldhagen.* Merion Station: Westfield, 1997. Print.

Orwell, George. Rev. of *Mein Kampf,* by Adolf Hitler. *George Orwell: My Country Right or Left, 1940-1943.* Vol. 2. Ed. Sonia Orwell and Ian Angus. Boston: Nonpareil, 1968. 12-15. Web. 3 Oct. 2012.

Shirer, William. *The Rise and Fall of the Third Reich.* New York: Simon and Schuster, 1960. Print.

Smith, Denis Mack. *Mussolini: A Biography.* New York: Vintage, 1983. Print.

Toland, John. *Adolf Hitler.* New York: Doubleday, 1976. Print.

Further Reading

Browning, Christopher, and Jürgen Matthäs. *The Origins of the Final Solution: The Evolution of Nazi Jewish Policy, September 1939-March 1942.* Lincoln: U of Nebraska P, 2004. Print.

Bullock, Alan. *Hitler: A Study in Tyranny.* New York: Harper & Row, 1962. Print.

Fest, Joachim. *Hitler.* New York: Vintage, 1975. Print.

Goldhagen, Daniel Jonah. *Hitler's Willing Executioners: Ordinary Germans and the Holocaust.* New York: Knopf, 1996. Print.

Kershaw, Ian. *Hitler: A Biography.* New York: Norton, 2008. Print.

Lane, Barbara Miller. "Nazi Ideology: Some Unfinished Business." *Central European History* 7.1 (1974) 3-30. *JSTOR.* Web. 7 Sept. 2012.

Rosenberg, Alfred. *Race and Race History and Other Essays.* New York: Harper & Row, 1970. Print.

David Love

OCTOBER MANIFESTO

Nicholas II, Sergey Yulyevich Witte

✣ **Key Facts**

Time Period:
Early 20th Century

Movement/Issue:
Democratic reform

Place of Publication:
Russia

Language of Publication:
Russian

OVERVIEW

Issued by Russian Emperor Nicholas II and authored primarily by his senior advisor, Sergey Yulyevich Witte (S. Iu. Witte) the *October Manifesto* (1905) initiated the Russian empire's transformation from a strict autocracy to a more participatory, constitutional monarchy. The manifesto was a direct response to the Russian Revolution of 1905, a series of protests, strikes, terrorist actions, and riots staged by a wide range of discontented social groups seeking greater democratic participation in government. Nicholas II and his advising ministers formulated the manifesto to quell national unrest and to unify the citizenry, which had splintered into various ideological factions. An appeal to "all true sons of Russia," the *October Manifesto* promises three governmental reforms in exchange for an end to the revolution: institution of civil rights, expansion of the electorate, and creation of a powerful, popularly elected legislative body.

Although the manifesto did not appeal to radical revolutionaries, it satisfied many demands of moderates and workers and effectively ended the revolution. The government enacted the manifesto's promised reforms in a very limited manner through the 1906 Fundamental Laws, which served as Russia's first constitution but did not establish the democracy that many had envisioned. Only one of the two houses of the new legislative body, called the Duma, was popularly elected and its laws were subject to the emperor's approval. Although the constitution granted Russian citizens some civil rights, including freedoms of speech, assembly, religion, and movement, it excluded Jews, women, and others. Today, some scholars credit the *October Manifesto* with undermining autocratic rule in Russia and initiating a slow but deep change in Russian governance that eventually led to the end of the monarchy and the rise of communism in 1917. Other scholars view the manifesto as having a more limited role in catalyzing later reforms in Russia.

HISTORICAL AND LITERARY CONTEXT

The *October Manifesto* responds to the political and labor unrest that had been brewing in Russia since the mid-nineteenth century. As Europe began moving toward constitutional governments, the Russian monarchy's claim to autocratic power became more entrenched. The first article of the empire's Fundamental Laws of 1832 stated, "The Emperor of all the Russias is a sovereign with autocratic and unlimited powers." In response to unrest, Tsar Alexander II initiated a series of liberal reforms in the 1860s and 1870s known as the Great Reforms. The result included the liberation of millions of serfs, the creation of local democratic institutions, the introduction of jury trials, and the creation of a modern military. Yet by the end of the nineteenth century, the emperor and his police controlled nearly every aspect of life for the empire's approximately 129 million people. Citizens had no freedom of speech, religion, assembly, or the press. Because the growing paternalism of the autocratic state coincided with rapid industrialization and modernization, the result was the growth of organized liberal and radical movements.

By the time the *October Manifesto* was written in 1905, workers had begun to organize and demonstrate for increased civil and political rights, intellectuals had begun to turn to radicalism, and professionals had begun advocating for liberal reforms. On January 9, 1905, between 50,000 and 100,000 people marched to the Winter Palace in St. Petersburg to present Emperor Nicholas II with a call for democratic rights and civil liberties. Although the demonstration was peaceful, troops killed 130 people and wounded 299. The event, known as Bloody Sunday, catalyzed the revolution. In October 1905 a general strike broke out across Russia. S. Iu. Witte urged the emperor either to crush the revolution by force or to issue a manifesto ensuring democratic reforms. The emperor chose the latter option and within days issued the *October Manifesto*.

The *October Manifesto* draws from foundational democratic documents such as England's *Magna Carta* (1215) and from the traditions of Russian imperial decrees such as the *February Manifesto* (1899). Also issued by Emperor Nicholas II, the *February Manifesto* ended Finland's long-standing autonomy and placed it under the Russian emperor's direct rule. Like the *February Manifesto,* the *October Manifesto* appeals to a spirit of cooperation but retains the right of the autocrat to rule by fiat. The *October Manifesto* balances its domineering paternalism with a commitment to empowering the citizenry, a concept that originated in the *Magna Carta.*

The first six weeks following the issuance of the *October Manifesto* saw explosive growth in political writings of all kinds as Russians embraced an unprecedented freedom of speech. An illegal ("underground") press gave way to legally published journals and newspapers founded by liberals, Marxists, conservatives, and anarchists to propagate their respective ideologies and to attack the political and social beliefs of others. The Bolshevik party printed the newspaper *Novaia zhizn,* and the moderate liberal Kadet party established *Pravo, Rech,* and other organs for its progressive, democratic ideas. Although such expansive freedom of the press was short-lived, the ideas expressed during this period continued to influence Russian society. Today scholars credit revolutionary post-*October Manifesto* publications for the rise of Russian avant-garde writing, such as that of the Futurists and their manifesto, *A Slap in the Face of Public Taste* (1912).

THEMES AND STYLE

The central theme of the *October Manifesto* is that of ending the Russian Revolution through the cooperation of the emperor and the people. To this end, the manifesto opens not with an appeal or a pledge but with an expression of sympathy: "Unrest and Disturbances in the capitals and in many parts of Our Empire fill Our heart with great and heavy grief." The emperor ingratiates himself with his subjects by appealing to their common humanity and by reinforcing the notion that they are united in their aim "to restore peace and quiet in our native land." The emperor vows to make several changes to the mechanisms of the imperial government, such as granting basic civic freedoms, democratizing elections to the Duma, and giving the Duma the power to approve all legislation.

The manifesto achieves its rhetorical aim through appeals to a cooperative spirit that transcends political differences. The document reminds the people that their fates are intertwined with those of the state and the emperor: "The welfare of the Russian Sovereign is inseparable from the welfare of the people, and the people's sorrow is His sorrow." In listing the new rights that the people will receive, the manifesto describes these freedoms as "measures designed by Us for the pacification of the State," without reference to particular political factions or ideologies. Appeals to loyalty toward the state continue throughout the manifesto as the emperor and his government "call upon all the faithful sons of Russia to remember their duty to their Fatherland … and together with Us to make every effort to restore peace and quiet in our native land."

Stylistically, the manifesto is distinguished by its domineering and paternalistic tone. Although the document promises new democratic rights, it appeals to the authority of the same imperial autocracy that the revolutionaries sought to undermine. In outlining the reasoning behind the concessions, the *October Manifesto* describes in detail the emperor's wisdom and munificence: "The great vow of Tsarist service

THE POLITICAL CAREER OF S. IU. WITTE

Long before S. Iu. Witte helped author the *October Manifesto,* he was a noted engineer of modernization and industrialization in late-nineteenth-century Russia. He was born in 1849 to a noble family and at age sixteen enrolled in university, where he studied mathematics. He entered the civil service and at age forty-three became Russia's Minister of Finance. During his eleven years in this influential position, from 1892 to 1903, he guided Russian industry to dramatic growth. He doubled the nation's length of railway track, more than tripled its coal production, increased iron and steel production nearly tenfold, and doubled cotton and thread production. However, his motive was not to increase the laboring masses' standard of the living but, as Abraham Ascher writes in *The Revolution of 1905: Russia in Disarray* (1988), "to assure the political power and greatness of the state."

On October 17, 1905, the day the *October Manifesto* was issued, Witte became prime minister and inherited a government that he described as being in "absolute chaos." Although he attempted to accommodate the various factions of liberals, radicals, and conservatives, the task was too large. Within six months of becoming the first prime minister of Imperial Russia, he was replaced.

enjoins Us to strive with all the force of Our reason and authority for the quickest cessation of unrest so perilous to the state." The document lists several of the reforms that revolutionaries desire but fails to acknowledge the protesters as the inspiration for change. Instead, the emperor takes credit for "hav[ing] recognized the necessity to coordinate the activities of the high government," granting reforms for representative institutions with the imperious rhetoric of autocracy.

CRITICAL DISCUSSION

When the *October Manifesto* was issued, the vast majority of Russians were relieved at the prospect of both ending autocratic rule and avoiding further unrest. The day after the document was printed, 50,000 people gathered in Moscow to listen to speeches hailing the manifesto's significance. The strikes that had wracked the nation ended abruptly. Newspapers hailed the document as a "great historical event" and the victory of a "peaceful national revolution." However, acceptance of the manifesto, although widespread, was not unanimous. The Russian Social Democratic Workers Party, a protocommunist group, denounced the document and called for creation of an entirely new state. Even many of those who approved of the manifesto in principle were wary. As Abraham Ascher writes in *The Revolution of 1905: Russia in Disarray* (1988), "Among those who understood the [emperor's] concession and welcomed it, there were many who harbored serious doubts about the government's determination to implement it fully."

The *October Manifesto* irrevocably altered the course of Russian politics by creating representative institutions that participated in the legislative process. It resulted in the creation of a constitution, the formation of political parties, and the extension of limited civil rights. Despite these reforms, the manifesto had the long-term consequence of delaying the revolutionary change that many common Russians sought. As Robert Service writes in *A History of Modern Russia: From Tsarism to the Twenty-First Century* (2009), "The Manifesto drew off the steam of the urban middle-class hostility and permitted Nicholas II to suppress open rebellion."

Many scholars have examined the ways in which the *October Manifesto* altered the course of Russian history despite its failure to achieve lasting and substantial democratic reform. In *First Blood: The Russian Revolution of 1905* (1964), Sidney Harcave argues that many were "dissatisfied with what had been achieved" but that this dissatisfaction propelled greater gains. "Their ambitions had changed," he writes, "having advanced with the revolution and expanded with each additional concession from the government, so that now they were likely to be aspiring to goals far ahead of those that had been reached." Commentators have noted the ways in which the manifesto and its aftermath mobilized the proletariat. Ascher writes, "The working class, though numerically small, emerged as an organized group capable of exerting decisive influence on public affairs." That decisive influence was felt during the Russian Revolution of 1917, in which the Bolsheviks seized power in the name of the working class and established the Soviet state.

BIBLIOGRAPHY

Sources

Ascher, Abraham. *The Revolution of 1905: A Short History.* Stanford: Stanford UP, 2004. Print.

———. *The Revolution of 1905: Russia in Disarray.* Stanford: Stanford UP, 1988. Print.

Harcave, Sidney. *First Blood: The Russian Revolution of 1905.* New York: Macmillan, 1964. Print.

Lieven, Dominic. *Nicholas II: Twilight of the Empire.* New York: St. Martin's, 1993. Print.

Ruthchild, Rochelle Goldberg. *Equality and Revolution: Women's Rights in the Russian Empire, 1905-1917.* Pittsburgh, PA: Pittsburgh UP, 2010. Print.

Service, Robert. *A History of Modern Russia: From Tsarism to the Twenty-First Century.* 3rd ed. Cambridge, MA: Harvard UP, 2009. Print.

Further Reading

Bonnell, V.E. *Roots of Rebellion: Workers' Politics and Organizations in St. Petersburg and Moscow: 1900-1914.* Berkeley: U California P, 1983. Print.

Emmons, Terence. *The Formation of Political Parties and the First National Elections in Russia.* Cambridge, MA: Harvard UP, 1983. Print.

Galai, Shmuel. *The Liberation Movement in Russia, 1900-1905.* New York: Cambridge UP, 1973. Print.

Leontovitsch, Victor. *The History of Liberalism is Russia.* Pittsburgh, PA: Pittsburgh UP, 2012. Print.

Rawson, Donald C. *Russian Rightists and the Revolution of 1905.* New York: Cambridge UP, 1995. Print.

Smele, Jonathan D., and Anthony Heywood, eds. *The Russian Revolution of 1905: Centenary Perspectives.* London: Routledge, 2005. Print.

Wcislo, Francis W. *Tales of Imperial Russia: The Life and Times of Sergei Witte, 1849-1915.* Oxford: Oxford UP, 2011. Print.

Weeks, Theodore R. "Defending Our Own: Government and the Russian Minority in the Kingdom of Poland, 1905-1914." *Russian Review* 54.4 (1995): 539-51. Print.

Weinberg, Robert. *The Revolution of 1905 in Odessa: Blood on the Steps.* Bloomington: Indiana UP, 1993. Print.

Theodore McDermott

OXFORD MANIFESTO

Salvador de Madariaga, et al.

✥ *Key Facts*

Time Period:
Mid-20th Century

Movement/Issue:
Liberalism; Democratic
reform; Human rights
movement

Place of Publication:
England

**Language of
Publication:**
English

OVERVIEW

The *Oxford Manifesto* (1947) was the founding document for Liberal International (World Liberal Union), initiated by Salvador de Madariaga to generate international recognition of liberal policies as an alternative to antiliberal or nonliberal political views. The members of Liberal International aimed to promote democracy and support liberal political parties at an international level, but they did not want to establish any kind of central control over those parties. The group believed that world issues such as poverty and famine were caused by ignoring liberal principles and, consequently, human rights. Written after the two world wars, which left much of Europe devastated both economically and politically, the manifesto outlines the organization's foundational principles and defines political liberalism in terms of its international benefits.

The *Oxford Manifesto* initially met with more criticism than praise from political theorists for being too vague in its definition of liberalism and in its application of that definition in an international context. The text's discussion of human rights and property ownership could be applied to other political theories, and the specific qualities that set Liberal International apart were considered unclear. Despite the critics, however, the generalities of Liberal International have allowed the organization to adapt to the changing social, economic, and political times of the twentieth and twenty-first centuries. The organization still exists and continues to be based on the ideas outlined in the *Oxford Manifesto.*

HISTORICAL AND LITERARY CONTEXT

Written shortly after World War II, when much of Europe was suffering from the devastating effects of the war, the *Oxford Manifesto* presents the union of liberalists from nineteen countries who wanted to establish international support for liberal politics based on human rights and true democracy. Before World War I, liberalism had enjoyed something of a growing monopoly, but an onslaught of challengers to the ideology followed in the ensuing decades. The document responds to this ideological debate, focusing on the individual and how that individual relates to society. The *Oxford Manifesto* is concerned with defining and upholding basic human rights, promoting free trade

and diversity of ideas, and establishing a true democracy whereby the majority decision works with a sympathetic view of minority positions. Members of the Liberal International organization believed that all of these qualities were missing from totalitarian, fascist, and communist systems of government and that only by adopting a liberal political standpoint could these components of human rights and of true democracy come to pass.

By the time the *Oxford Manifesto* was written, World War II was over, but the global economy and European nations were still suffering from financial and political turbulence. The manifesto's writers were concerned with settling the political atmosphere in the favor of liberal democracy, whereby citizens would have recognized rights and freedom of speech and trade. One of the principal organizers of Liberal International and a primary writer of the text was Madariaga, a Spanish engineer and journalist who was forced to flee his home country at the outbreak of civil war because of his pronounced liberal beliefs. Such scenarios prompted Madariaga and the other members of Liberal International to combine their international strength and organize their official political standpoint in combating systems of government that put the rights and freedoms of citizens at risk. The base of this organization was the *Oxford Manifesto.*

The manifesto was influenced by previous international liberal theories, including the political writing of Immanuel Kant. Its primary literary influences, however, were the works of Lord William Henry Beveridge, particularly the report *Social Insurance and Allied Services* (1942), which deals with the five "giant evils" of society that affect unemployment and poverty. In this report, Beveridge draws attention to the accountabilities of the individual in relation to the state and the responsibilities of both required for a productive economic future. In their *Oxford Manifesto,* the members of Liberal International draw on these ideas to express their standpoint on individual rights and responsibilities in a political setting.

The text fostered political discussion as well as criticism. The ideas outlined in manifesto and practiced by Liberal International members increasingly gained support and are reflected in the social and economic development of the United States during the Cold War. Liberal International policies began to garner international recognition after the war was over. In 1997 a supplement to the *Oxford Manifesto* was written and approved to assess new threats to liberal politics and to true democracy, such as discrimination based on race and sexuality, organized crime, and depletion of natural resources.

THEMES AND STYLE

The main theme of the *Oxford Manifesto* is that the state of Europe in the late 1940s is a direct result of the "abandonment of liberal principles" and of a subsequent lack of true democracy that led to two world wars. The manifesto declares that true democracy is "inseparable from political liberty and is based on the conscious, free and enlightened consent of the majority, expressed through a free and secret ballot, with due respect for the liberties and opinions of minorities." In order to achieve this ideal, the document outlines four major issues that are essential to establishing and maintaining the liberal principles of true democracy: understanding and protecting universal human rights, promoting economic and political freedom, exhibiting moral responsibility toward community, and creating the conditions for world peace.

The *Oxford Manifesto* achieves its rhetorical effect by creating the sense of a united liberal organization concerned with the basic human rights of each person. The text begins by calling attention to the collective members responsible for composing the document: "We, Liberals of nineteen countries assembled at Oxford at a time of disorder, poverty, famine and fear caused by two World Wars." The first article, however, deals with the individual citizen with whom these collective claims are concerned: "Man is first and foremost a being endowed with the power of independent thought and action, and with the ability to distinguish right from wrong." The effect of using the international collection of liberals to discuss the issues and independence of the individual citizen creates the notion of unity among people at the national and international level.

The *Oxford Manifesto* is a formally written document designed to outline the mandate for the Liberal International organization to a political audience. Although initially written in English, it was translated into numerous languages and distributed internationally. The formality of the language allows the expressions of freedom, peace, and true democracy to be established as achievable and practical goals rather than excessive emotional ideals. The numerous translations make the manifesto accessible to people around the world and help to establish a sense of international unity. It ends with a call to action: "We call upon all men and women who are in general agreement with these ideals and principles to join us in an endeavour to win their acceptance throughout the world." This statement urges the common people to exercise their rights and express their opinions in an effort to establish global true democracy.

SALVADOR DE MADARIAGA

One of the founding members of Liberal International and the primary composer of the *Oxford Manifesto* was Salvador de Madariaga (1886-1978), a Spanish intellectual and diplomat whose career proved highly influential in the establishment of liberalism as an international political mandate. In the 1920s Madariaga served as the leader of the disarmament section of the Secretariat of the League of Nations and would later become a permanent delegate to that organization. During the 1930s he was appointed as Spain's ambassador to the United States and France. In 1936 the outbreak of the Spanish Civil War forced Madariaga to flee to Great Britain, where he continued to write politically charged pieces that criticized Francisco Franco's regime. It was during his time in exile that Madariaga headed up the writing of the *Oxford Manifesto*.

In addition to his charged political career, Madariaga was a prolific writer, composing fiction and nonfiction works in Spanish, English, German, and French and sometimes translating works among these languages. In addition to his political writings, he composed plays, poetry, novels, biographies, and histories. Some of his most influential works include his biographies of Christopher Columbus (1939) and Hernán Cortes (1941), the novel *The Heart of Jade* (1944), the historical work *The Rise and Fall of the Spanish American Empire* (1947), and the literary essay *On Hamlet* (1948).

CRITICAL DISCUSSION

The *Oxford Manifesto* initially generated critical reactions that accused the Liberal International organization of being too general in its declarations. For example, a July 23, 1949, article in the *Economist* states that "so far the twenty nations affiliated to the organization have not yet been able to define in any but the most general terms the principles they hold in common." Despite its initial critics, however, the Liberal International order survived and played a role in the way international politics unfolded during the decades following the release of the *Oxford Manifesto*.

While the text did not produce the initial political overhaul that the members of Liberal International may have been hoping for, it did develop the mandate associated with liberal politics that would eventually become the recognized international political order at the end of the Cold War. David Williams, in *International Development and Global Politics* (2012), discusses the difficulty of dating the start of liberal internationalism but states that the "liberal international order is certainly in place all through the 1990s and into the first half of the 2000s." Nevertheless, the politics associated with international liberalism were highly influential in the U.S. and European social and economic development after World War II.

A volunteer with Habitat for Humanity, a nonprofit organization dedicated to building affordable housing. The *Oxford Manifesto* states that every citizen has a duty to perform community service to fulfill a moral responsibility toward others. BILLY HUSTANCE/STONE/GETTY IMAGES

well, and no liberal state has been able to perfect all of them. In *British Liberal Internationalism* (2009), Casper Sylvest also illustrates this trend in his introduction, noting that "liberal political thought has always been in part a vision of international relations, but this is similarly not fixed."

Current trends in scholarship tend to lose sight of the *Oxford Manifesto* within the politically turbulent milieu of postwar Europe and the overshadowing politics of the Cold War. This tendency to overlook the manifesto stems from its contemporary criticism of being too generalized and failing to define liberalism specifically in terms of international politics. In "Liberalism and World Politics" (1986), Michael Doyle explains that "there is no canonical description of liberalism. What we tend to call *liberal* resembles a family portrait of principles and institutions," such as "individual freedom, political participation, private property, and equality of opportunity." While these qualities are outlined in the *Oxford Manifesto,* they are not distinctly liberal qualities because they apply to other political theories as

BIBLIOGRAPHY

Sources

Doyle, Michael W. "Liberalism and World Politics." 1986. *Liberal Peace: Selected Essays.* London: Routledge, 2012. 61-80. Print.

"Liberals at Deauville." *Economist* [London] 23 July 1949: 182. *Economist Historical Archive.* Web. 25 Sept. 2012.

Oxford Manifesto 1947. Liberal International. Liberal International. Web. 25 Sept. 2012.

Sylvest, Casper. *British Liberal Internationalism, 1880-1930: Making Progress?* Manchester, UK: Manchester UP, 2009. Print.

Williams, David. *International Development and Global Politics: History, Theory, and Practice.* London: Routledge, 2012. Print.

Further Reading

Doyle, Michael W. "An International Liberal Community." 2009. *Liberal Peace: Selected Essays.* London: Routledge, 2012. 145-64. Print.

Green, E.H.H., and D.M. Tanner, eds. *The Strange Survival of Liberal England: Political Leaders, Moral Values and the Reception of Economic Debate.* Cambridge: Cambridge UP, 2007.

Madariaga, Salvador de. *Democracy versus Liberty? The Faith of a Liberal Heretic.* Trans. M. Marx. London: Pall Mall, 1958. Print.

Oxford Manifesto 1997. Liberal International. Liberal International, 1997. Web. 25 Sept. 2012.

Katherine Barker

PREAMBLE TO THE CONSTITUTION AND BY-LAWS OF INDUSTRIAL WORKERS OF THE WORLD

Thomas J. Hagerty

OVERVIEW

The 1905 "Preamble" to the *Constitution and By-laws of Industrial Workers of the World,* written by Catholic priest and union activist Thomas J. Hagerty, is a landmark document in U.S. labor history. Speaking out against the growing economic divide between labor and capital, this document anticipates a time when the working class will take from the employing class the means of production. In particular, it indicts the existing trade unions for fostering divisiveness among workers and failing to address their needs in an era of industrial-capitalist consolidation. Hagerty's proposal is for the working class to unite as a whole under the auspices of the newly formed Industrial Workers of the World (IWW) in order to throw off capitalism and rebuild society along the lines of more socialistic principles.

The radical politics of the "Preamble"—as put into practice by IWW founders such as William D. "Big Bill" Haywood, Eugene Debs, and Daniel De Leon—affronted the establishment. Politicians and the press alike perceived the IWW as a serious threat to the market economy and condemned the mix of socialism, anarchism, and unionism put forth in the document. In the following years, employers, often with police enforcement, took extreme and sometimes even lethal measures to curb the organization's influence and disrupt its activities. In time, these forces succeeded in crippling the IWW. Yet more than a hundred years later, the IWW continues to fight on behalf of labor, with Hagerty's preamble, revised and updated, still preceding the *Constitution.*

HISTORICAL AND LITERARY CONTEXT

Around the turn of the twentieth century, a period marked by bloody and brutal confrontations between labor and capital, Hagerty was working as a Roman Catholic priest in Texas and New Mexico. Incensed by the maltreatment of railroad workers, he became involved with the American Labor Union (ALU) and the Socialist Party of America (SPA). As an active recruiter for both organizations, he initially toured Colorado mining camps alongside Debs and eventually traveled across the United States to deliver speeches on behalf of SPA. Radicalized further by what he saw

of the appalling working-class conditions throughout the country, he lost patience with the socialists for their faith in gradual reform. In 1905, having taken on the role of editing the ALU's *Voice of Labor* magazine, Hagerty and other union activists were invited to a secret meeting in Chicago to plan a new union. The *Industrial Union Manifesto* that Hagerty helped to write on this occasion was politically and intellectually foundational for the subsequent formation and constitution of the IWW.

Hagerty wrote the "Preamble" at a moment when, as he saw it, the power of the working class had been stifled by the increasing influence of the American Federation of Labor (AFL)—a relatively conservative association of trade unions founded in 1886. Organized along craft-union lines, the AFL maintained distinctions between trades and between skilled and non-skilled workers that, in the view of the IWW, prevented any genuine worker solidarity. Furthermore, relying on arbitration, collective bargaining, and political affiliation, the AFL seemed only to displace and diffuse the power of the workers. The AFL led workers to believe that employers shared their interests and secured, at best, token gains that did nothing to alter inequitable labor-capital relations. The "Preamble" calls for a vastly different mode of organization, one seeking not to ameliorate the wage system but to abolish it entirely.

Hagerty's "Preamble" shares with the *Industrial Union Manifesto* the core concern of a working class disunited by employers and trades unions, though its matter-of-fact language sets it apart from that earlier, more flamboyant document. It similarly owes much to the labor-capital analysis of *The Communist Manifesto* (1848) by Karl Marx and Friedrich Engels, except that the "Preamble" strives to be less technical and figurative. As a priest in the southwestern United States, Hagerty had translated European socialist literature into Spanish to help awaken the Mexican railroad workers to their plight as a class, and a sense of Marx and Engels pervades the "Preamble."

The "Preamble" is perhaps best known for its closing rallying cry that "an injury to one [is] an injury to all." In his autobiography, Haywood attributes authorship of the phrase not to Hagerty but to David

❖ Key Facts

Time Period:
Early 20th Century

Movement/Issue:
Trade unionism;
Socialism; Anarchism

Place of Publication:
United States

Language of Publication:
English

PRIMARY SOURCE

PREAMBLE TO THE *CONSTITUTION AND BY-LAWS OF INDUSTRIAL WORKERS OF THE WORLD*

The working class and the employing class have nothing in common. There can be no peace so long as hunger and want are found among millions of working people and the few, who make up the employing class, have all the good things in life.

Between these two classes a struggle must go on until the workers of the world organize as a class, take possession of the earth and the machinery of production, abolish the wage system, and live in harmony with the Earth.

We find that the centering of the management of industries into fewer and fewer hands makes the trade unions unable to cope with the ever-growing power of the employing class. The trade unions foster a state of affairs which allows one set of workers to be pitted against another set of workers in the same industry, thereby helping defeat one another in wage wars. Moreover, the trade unions aid the employing class to mislead the workers into the belief that the working class have interests in common with their employers.

These conditions can be changed and the interest of the working class upheld only by an organization formed in such a way that all it's members in any one industry, or in all industries if necessary, cease work whenever a strike or lockout is on in any department thereof, thus making an injury to one an injury to all.

Instead of the conservative motto, "A fair day's wage for a fair day's work, " we must inscribe on our banner the revolutionary watchword, "Abolition of the wage system." It is the historic mission of the working class to do away with capitalism. The army of production must be organized, not only for the everyday struggle with capitalists, but also to carry on production when capitalism shall have been overthrown. By organizing industrially we are forming the structure of the new society within the shell of the old.

Coates, another radical present at the founding convention of the IWW. However, it also resembles the official motto of the Knights of Labor, a more conservative workers' organization whose popularity peaked in the 1880s: "that is the most perfect government in which an injury to one is the concern of all." Regardless, the closing slogan in the "Preamble" continues to be shouted and waved aloft on banners at union protests and rallies around the world.

THEMES AND STYLE

The primary themes of Hagerty's "Preamble" are class struggle and the irreconcilable divide between the "working class and the employing class," which "have nothing in common." On the strength of this observation, he directs the brunt of his criticism toward the trade unions that "aid the employing class to mislead the workers into the belief that the working class have interests in common with their employers."

Thus, the trade unions generate antagonisms *within* the working class in that "they foster a state of things which allows one set of workers to be pitted against another." As Marx would have it, the historic mission of the workers to overthrow capitalism is made impossible.

Consisting of only seven sentences, the document achieves its rhetorical ends concisely and swiftly. Hagerty offers the proposition that "there can be no peace so long as hunger and want are found among millions of working people and the few, who make up the employing class, have all the good things of life." Economic disparity, he says, guarantees social unrest, a claim general enough to sound like common sense. As he continues, however, the polemic comes unequivocally to the surface: "Between these two classes a struggle must go on until the workers of the world organize as a class, take possession of the earth and the machinery of production, abolish the wage system, and live in harmony with the Earth." Wasting no time, Hagerty has proposed a revolutionary solution to social inequity: the workers must unite, politically and economically, to keep the fruits of their labor for themselves and undo the capitalist mode of production.

As noted, the "Preamble" draws on the Marxist analysis of class struggle but without employing many of the usual Marxist keywords: Hagerty speaks of "labor," "toilers," the "working class," "wage wars," and the "employing class" but not of the "proletariat," the "bourgeoisie," or "capital." In fact, the language—perhaps appropriately for a working priest with a political conscious—is at times more characteristic of the social gospel, with the stakes laid in terms of "peace," "hunger," "want," and "sad conditions." But Hagerty more typically opts for plain descriptive terms: "The rapid gathering of wealth and the centering of the management of industries into fewer and fewer hands make the trade unions unable to cope with the ever-growing power of the employing class." The result is a polemic couched in what appears to be neutral language. With no recourse to similes, metaphors, or abstract constructions, Hagerty seems to want to make a simple and realistic account of how things are and how they ought to be in the working world.

CRITICAL DISCUSSION

Samuel Gompers, founder and president of the American Federation of Labor, understandably took exception to the aims and ideology represented by the IWW's *Constitution.* He objected publicly in the pages of the *American Federationist,* saying of the authors behind the IWW's manifesto and constitution that "one will look in vain to find the name of one man who has not for years been engaged in the delectable work of trying to divert, pervert, and disrupt the labor movement of the country." Similar hostility was expressed by the popular newspapers, in which IWW members were typically depicted as violent, criminal, and without scruples. One early critical work providing a useful account of the composition of (and disputes over) the *Constitution* and "Preamble" is Paul Brissenden's 1913 book *The Launching of the Industrial Workers of the World.*

The politics of the "Preamble" and *Constitution* found their way into labor songs that have become internationally famous. The IWW published the first song collection in a 1909 volume, *Songs of the Workers, on the Road, in the Jungles, and in the Shops—Songs to Fan the Flames of Discontent,* which came to be called *The Little Red Songbook.* Since the 1960s, scholars have shown serious interest in the musical legacy of the IWW and its contribution to the genres of protest and labor songs. In recent years, the *Songbook* has been a topic of folklore, music education, and American history studies by scholars such as, respectively, Thomas Walker, Terese M. Volk, and Mariana Whitmer. "Solidarity Forever," written by Ralph Chaplin in 1915, is commonly regarded as one of the best union songs of all time and is still sung at union meetings, rallies, and protests across the United States.

The *Constitution,* to say nothing of the "Preamble," is rarely discussed as a topic in its own right, though the conventions leading to their drafting are commonly referenced in histories documenting the organization. In addition to general histories, the dominant trend in the scholarship has been to look at the IWW within industrial contexts—agriculture (Greg Hall), bush working (J. Peter Campbell), logging (Richard Rajala), and oil and wheat (Nigel Sellars). Recently, scholars have looked anew at the political legacy exemplified by the "Preamble" and *Constitution,* with Patrick Renshaw and Ahmed A. White examining the IWW's syndicalism, Nicholas Thoburn class and minorities, and Francis Shor gender politics.

Recruitment poster for the IWW, circa 1910.
© EVERETT COLLECTION INC/ALAMY

BIBLIOGRAPHY

Sources

Hall, Greg. *Harvest Wobblies: The Industrial Workers of the World and Agricultural Laborers in the American West, 1905-1930.* Corvallis: Oregon State UP, 2001. Print.

Haywood, William D. *Autobiography of Big Bill Haywood.* New York: International Publishers, 1966. Print.

Rajala, Richard. "A Dandy Bunch of Wobblies: Pacific Northwest Loggers and the Industrial Workers of the World, 1900-1930." *Labor History* 37.2 (1996): 205-34. Print.

Shor, Francis. "'Virile Syndicalism' in Comparative Perspective: A Gender Analysis of the IWW in the United States and Australia." *International Labor and Working-Class History.* Cambridge: Cambridge UP, 1999. Print.

Volk, Terese M. "Little Red Songbooks: Songs for the Labor Force of America." *Journal of Research in Music Education* 49.1 (2001): 33-48. Print.

White, Ahmed A. "The Crime of Economic Radicalism: Criminal Syndicalism Law and the Industrial Workers of the World, 1917-1927." *Oregon Law Review* 8 5 (2006): 649-770. Print.

Whitmer, Mariana. "Using Music to Teach American History." *Organization of American Historians Magazine of History* 19.4 (2005): 4-5. Print.

Further Reading

Buhle, Paul, and Nicole Schulman. *Wobblies! A Graphic History of the Industrial Workers of the World.* New York: Verso, 2005. Print.

Dubofsky, Melvyn. *We Shall Be All: A History of the Industrial Workers of the World.* Champaign: U of Illinois P, 2000. Print.

Marvin, Thomas F. "Joe Hill and the Rhetoric of Radicalism." *Journal of American Culture* 34.3 (2011): 247-63. Print.

May, Matthew S. "Hobo Orator Union: Class Composition and the Spokane Free Speech Fight of the Industrial Workers of the World." *Quarterly Journal of Speech* 97.2 (2011): 155-77. Print.

Mitchell, Don. "Which Side Are You On? From Haymarket to Now." *ACME* 7.1 (2008): 59-68. Print.

David Aitchison

Sinn Féin Manifesto

Henry Boland, Robert Brennan, Tom Kelly, Michael O'Flanagan

Key Facts

Time Period:
Early 20th Century

Movement/Issue:
National independence;
Anti-imperialism

Place of Publication:
Ireland

**Language of
Publication:**
English

OVERVIEW

Composed by Roman Catholic priest Father Michael O'Flanagan, politicians Tom Kelly and Henry ("Harry") Boland, and journalist Robert Brennan, the *Sinn Féin Manifesto* (1918) describes the Sinn Féin party's plan for securing an independent Irish republic and appeals for votes from the Irish electorate to facilitate that aim. At the time of the manifesto's issuance, Ireland's centuries-long struggle to end British control and establish independence was near its tipping point. Following unsuccessful nonviolent attempts to end British rule, the manifesto and the electoral victories it engendered helped provoke a violent struggle that ended in the partitioning of Ireland into two states: Northern Ireland, which was granted complete autonomy, and the Irish Free State, which was allowed self-governance within the British Commonwealth. Addressed "to the Irish People," the *Sinn Féin Manifesto* calls for Irish voters to unyoke their homeland from imperialist oppression and to embrace the liberating potential of an independent national republic. Central to the manifesto are four points that outline the means by which Sinn Féin would "secur[e] the establishment" of an independent Irish republic.

The *Sinn Féin Manifesto* appealed strongly to Irish voters and helped contribute to the overwhelming success of the Sinn Féin party in the 1918 election. Party candidates won 73 of 105 Irish seats in the British Parliament, a result that indicated a decisive change in national mood. The manifesto asked Ireland's people to end their concessions to Britain's colonial authority, and the people heeded this message. Following its sweeping electoral gains, Sinn Féin refused to sit in the British Parliament and instead established an alternative parliament in Dublin called Dáil Éireann. Contemporary scholars consider the *Sinn Féin Manifesto* to be a vital document in the history of Ireland's pursuit of true independence in the twentieth century.

HISTORICAL AND LITERARY CONTEXT

The *Sinn Féin Manifesto* responds to Ireland's long struggle to establish political independence from Britain, which had ruled the island throughout its modern history. The mass political movement in support of Irish nationalism began in the 1790s, when the French and American revolutions inspired pride in traditional Gaelic culture and a sense of national cultural unity. During the nineteenth century, efforts to establish an

Irish parliament began to take shape. The movement for "home rule," a loosely defined term that referred to various plans for greater Irish autonomy, became increasingly organized in the 1880s under the leadership of Charles Parnell, an Irish nationalist and member of the British Parliament. In 1905 the Sinn Féin party was officially established to advocate passively for Irish cultural and economic independence. The party became more visible after the Easter Rising of 1916, a violent insurrection against British rule that was brutally extinguished. Though Sinn Féin had not in fact taken part in the violence, the British government held the party responsible, and Sinn Féin subsequently rose in prominence.

By the time the *Sinn Féin Manifesto* was issued in 1918, the Irish desire for independence was mounting, but the movement toward autonomy was not well organized. In the aftermath of the Easter Rising, many politically moderate Irish people turned against their British rulers, who had destroyed much of Dublin and declared martial law while suppressing the rebellion. The British also imprisoned many members of Sinn Féin, who spent their time in custody organizing against British repression and control. When radicals and moderates came together to oppose the British, Sinn Féin supplanted the Nationalist Party, which had been organized in 1882 by Parnell, at the forefront of the political effort to establish nationhood. Under the leadership of American-born rebel Eamon de Valera, the party increased its popular support and drafted its manifesto in time for the 1918 elections.

The 1918 *Sinn Féin Manifesto* draws on the history of Irish polemical writing and, in particular, on *The Resurrection of Hungary,* a manifesto completed in 1904. Written by Arthur Griffith, the founder of the Sinn Féin party, *The Resurrection of Hungary* was initially published in twenty-seven installments in the *United Irishman,* a newspaper published by Griffith. The manifesto provided an in-depth analysis of the Austro-Hungarian Empire in the mid-nineteenth century, during which time Austria and Hungary established a dual monarchy that the independent states shared equally. Griffith used this example to advocate for a similarly peaceful political solution to the Irish conflict with Britain. Though the authors of the *Sinn Féin Manifesto* dropped the notion of a dual monarchy, they echoed Griffith's call for Irishmen to abstain from being seated in the British Parliament as an act of passive resistance that would lead to national independence.

Since its issuance, the *Sinn Féin Manifesto* of 1918 has inspired a series of manifestos and other political writings by the Sinn Féin party. In 1921, de Valera drafted a new party manifesto in response to the threat of northern Ireland's partition. This manifesto also appealed to the national electorate and argued that Sinn Féin was "for Ireland against England, for freedom against slavery, for right and justice against force and wrong." It also called for the protection of minority parties, such as Protestants. Throughout the twentieth century, Sinn Féin continued to produce manifestos outlining its political policy; by the twenty-first century, the party was capitalizing on the ease of technology, and it began to issue the manifestos online and through video-sharing sites, such as YouTube.

THEMES AND STYLE

The central theme of the *Sinn Féin Manifesto* is that the election of Sinn Féin party members to Parliament will facilitate Ireland's long-awaited independence from Britain. Issued at a moment of gathering political unrest, the manifesto opens by offering its reader a stark choice: "The coming General Election is fraught with vital possibilities for the future of our nation." Ireland must choose, the manifesto declares, between "the full sunlight of freedom" and "the shadow of base imperialism." Sinn Féin will lead the country down "the path of national salvation" and establish the independent Irish republic. To this end, the manifesto outlines four strategies: withdrawing elected representatives from Parliament; "making use of any and every means available to render impotent the power of England to hold Ireland in subjection by military force or otherwise"; establishing an independent Irish legislative assembly; and appealing to the international community for Ireland's right of self-determination.

The manifesto achieves its rhetorical effect through appeals to a historically distinct and united Irish people. This winning discourse is achieved through repeated use of the first person plural ("we" and "our") and references to the people's shared historical struggle for freedom. Within its first paragraph, the manifesto refers to Ireland as "our nation" and to the Irish people as "our race." Later in the document, the authors describe their aims in historical rather than political terms: "Sinn Féin stands less for a political party than for the Nation; it represents the old tradition of nationhood handed on from dead generations." The manifesto's final, three-fold sentence expresses confidence that "the people of this ancient nation will be true to the old cause"; refers to numerous former advocates for independence; and declares that "the only status befitting this ancient realm is the status of a free nation."

Stylistically, the *Sinn Féin Manifesto* is distinguished by its grandiosity. The second sentence poses the question of Irish independence as a choice between "march[ing] out into the full sunlight of freedom" or "remain[ing] in the shadow of a base imperialism that has brought and

FATHER MICHAEL O'FLANAGAN: NATIONALIST PRIEST

If his role in the cause of Irish independence had been limited to being one of the four authors of the *Sinn Féin Manifesto*, Roman Catholic priest Father Michael O'Flanagan would be remembered as a minor figure in Irish history. In fact, however, O'Flanagan's role extended far beyond the composition of the manifesto. Born in 1876 and raised on a farm in rural County Roscommon, he was ordained a priest in 1900 and became a key figure in the movement to revive the Irish language. While he worked toward that goal, he became deeply involved in the independence movement.

In early 1917, O'Flanagan rose to prominence within Sinn Féin after campaigning for a successful party candidate in a local election. Later that year, O'Flanagan and party founder Arthur Griffith were elected joint vice presidents of the party. After helping to draft the party's manifesto in 1918, O'Flanagan supported the Irish War of Independence while also seeking its peaceful resolution. When a treaty to end the war and establish an Irish dominion within the British Commonwealth was announced, however, he strongly opposed it and became a radical proponent of a truly independent Ireland. Over the next decade, he embraced communism, continued agitating for Irish nationalism, and was suspended from the priesthood. In 1933 he was elected president of Sinn Féin. Near the end of his life, O'Flanagan was restored to the priesthood, and he worked as a chaplain until his death in 1942.

ever will bring in its train naught but evil for our race." This kind of elevated, metaphorical language removes the coming election from the mundane milieu of contemporary politics and couches it in the terms of a mythopoeic struggle between good and evil. In so doing, the *Sinn Féin Manifesto* places the Sinn Féin party at the vanguard of a righteous cause rather than in the midst of a battle for seats in Parliament. While the authors do outline specific strategies for success, the manifesto achieves its rhetorical force through the use of a grandiose style that elevates its argument above politics.

CRITICAL DISCUSSION

When the *Sinn Féin Manifesto* was first published, its message was greeted enthusiastically by the Irish electorate and negatively by the British authorities. After its release, the Sinn Féin party swept to power. As scholar Eoin O'Malley writes in *Contemporary Ireland* (2011), "the mood of the country had changed" in the wake of the *Sinn Féin Manifesto*—and the authorities responded forcefully. After its issuance, the British repeatedly raided Sinn Féin's headquarters and arrested three successive directors of elections for the party. According to the scholar Michael Laffan in his *Resurrection of Ireland* (1999), "The imprisonment of party activists, the dispersal of meetings, the removal of posters and the seizure of leaflets all disrupted the campaign, but at the

This illustration depicting Sinn Féin rebels appeared in the Italian newspaper *La Domenica del Corriere* in 1922. ALFREDO DAGLI ORTI/THE ART ARCHIVE AT ART RESOURCE, NY

document within the context of Ireland's early attempts to establish an independent constitutional government. According to the scholar Eoin Ó Broin in *Sinn Féin and the Politics of Left Republicanism* (2009), the manifesto was indicative of the party's focus "on the single issue of the republic, arguing that its precise form would be a matter for the Irish people once it was established. Industrial, agrarian and gender radicalism was acceptable only in the context of the broader strategic requirements of undermining British government authority in Ireland." Commentators have also situated the manifesto within the larger European historical moment. According to Laffan, "The fall of so many European monarchies towards the end of the First World War made Sinn Féin's demand for an Irish republic seem less absurd or unrealistic than might have been the case a year or two earlier."

BIBLIOGRAPHY

Sources

English, Richard. *Armed Struggle: The History of the IRA.* New York: Oxford UP, 2003. Print.

Laffan, Michael. *Resurrection of Ireland: The Sinn Féin Party, 1916-1923.* New York: Cambridge UP, 1999. Print.

Murray, Patrick. "O'Flanagan, Michael (1876-1942)." *Oxford Dictionary of National Biography.* New York: Oxford UP, 2004. Print.

Ó Broin, Eoin. *Sinn Féin and the Politics of Left Republicanism.* London: Pluto, 2009. Print.

O'Malley, Eoin. *Contemporary Ireland.* London: Palgrave MacMillan, 2011. Print.

Standing Committee of Sinn Féin. *The Manifesto of Sinn Féin as Prepared for Circulation for the General Election of December, 1918.* Corpus of Electronic Texts, 1997. Web. 20 July 2012.

Further Reading

Bew, Paul. *Ideology and the Irish Question: Ulster Unionism and Irish Nationalism, 1912-1916.* New York: Oxford UP, 1994. Print.

Buckland, Patrick. *Irish Unionism 1: The Anglo-Irish and the New Ireland, 1855-1922.* Dublin: Gill, 1973. Print.

Burleigh, Michael. *Sacred Causes: The Clash of Religion and Politics, from the Great War to the War on Terror.* New York: Harper, 2007. Print.

Connolly, S.J. *The Oxford Companion to Irish History.* New York: Oxford UP, 2002. Print.

Farrell, Brian. *The Irish Parliamentary Tradition.* Dublin: Gill, 1973. Print.

———. *The Creation of the Dáil.* Dublin: Gill, 1994. Print.

Garvin, Tom. *Nationalist Revolutionaries in Ireland, 1858-1928.* Oxford: Oxford UP, 1987. Print.

Hutchinson, John. *The Dynamics of Cultural Nationalism: The Gaelic Revival and the Creation of the Irish Nation-State.* London: Allen, 1987. Print.

Kissane, Bill. "The Constitutional Revolution That Never Was: Democratic Radicalism and the Sinn Féin Movement." *Radical History Review* 2009.104 (2009): 77-102. Print.

Russell, G.W. *The National Being: Some Thoughts on an Irish Polity.* Dublin: Irish Academic, 1982. Print.

same time these measures provided Sinn Féin with favourable publicity and gave it the halo of martyrdom."

After the manifesto appeared, it became an important catalyst for the Irish War of Independence (1919-21; also called the Anglo-Irish War). Sinn Féin did as their manifesto promised and established an Irish parliament in Dublin, the Dáil Éirann. According to the scholar Richard English in his work *Armed Struggle* (2003), "The First Dáil became, for republicans, the truly legitimate authority in Ireland." At its first meeting in January 1919, a Declaration of Independence was endorsed. Almost immediately, violence erupted between the Irish Republican Army, a paramilitary organization formed in 1919 to seek the end of British rule and the formation of an Irish republic, and the British authorities. In 1922 the Anglo-Irish Treaty created a self-governing Irish dominion within the British Commonwealth. Thus, while the manifesto's strategies had been implemented, its objective of establishing a "free nation" was only partially fulfilled.

Though few scholars have written extensively about the manifesto itself, historians have discussed the

Theodore McDermott

SPARTACUS MANIFESTO

Rosa Luxemburg

OVERVIEW

The *Spartacus Manifesto,* written by Rosa Luxemburg in December 1918 and first published as "What Does the Spartacus League Want?" in the newspaper *Die rote Fahne* (*The Red Flag*), is the defining document of the Spartacus League, the revolutionary movement that later became the Communist Party of Germany (KPD). During the founding congress of the KPD on New Year's Day 1919, a revised version of the manifesto was ratified as the party program. Intended for German workers, soldiers, and revolutionaries, it enumerates the demands of the Spartacists, criticizes the incumbent Social Democratic government, and charts a specific plan of action for a communist revolution. Among its demands are an expropriation of bourgeois wealth by the state, an abolition of ranks and titles, legal equality of the sexes, and the establishment of a six-hour work day.

Not long after the manifesto was first published, an armed communist rebellion and general strike in Berlin known as the Spartacist Uprising began in January 1919, lasting roughly two weeks. Although the uprising was quickly repressed by the *Freikorps,* a militia supported by some members of the Social Democratic government, and Luxemburg and her collaborator Karl Liebknecht were promptly assassinated, the KPD remained a major German political party until its dissolution by the Nazis in 1933. Today, the KPD manifesto is recognized as one of the strongest dissenting voices of the Weimar Republic era and an important work of internationalist communism. It functioned as a vanguard for future German labor movements and contributed greatly to the discussion of intra-party politics during the Third International.

HISTORICAL AND LITERARY CONTEXT

The *Spartacus Manifesto* responds to the rise of the Social Democratic Party of Germany (SPD) during the German Revolution of November 1918. That month, as World War I came to a close, Kaiser Wilhelm II abdicated his position as emperor, effectively dissolving the German Empire, and the SPD, led by Friedrich Ebert, rose to power. Although it was established in 1875 as a Marxist organization, the SPD had since exhibited centrist tendencies. Once in power, the party immediately allied itself with the bourgeoisie and maintained most of the imperial state apparatus.

Luxemburg and others criticized these moves as failures of socialism, and called for a full proletarian revolution as a corrective measure. The German left split over this debate between revisionism and Bolshevism, spawning the Independent Social Democratic Party (USPD) and the Communist Party of Germany (KPD).

When the manifesto was written in late 1918, Germany was in a state of political turmoil. Both the right and the left faced mass discontent over the outcome of World War I. Returning soldiers were restless and felt betrayed by both their former leadership and the new government. Many, especially Luxemburg and Liebknecht, had opposed the war from the beginning. Thus, the manifesto interprets the war as a bourgeois imperialist fight and calls for its "chief criminals" to be tried. Luxemburg proposes a communist revolution in part as a means to prevent future wars through the leveling of economic imbalances.

❖ *Key Facts*

Time Period:
Early 20th Century

Movement/Issue:
Communism; German Revolution

Place of Publication:
Germany

Language of Publication:
German

MARXIST MARTYRS: LUXEMBURG AND LIEBKNECHT

Rosa Luxemburg was one of the most influential Marxist activists of the twentieth century and the best-known female Marxist in history. She was born in 1870 in Poland, where, along with Leo Jogiches, she founded the country's Social Democratic Party. She moved to Berlin in 1898 and became an active member of the Social Democratic Party of Germany (SPD), sharply criticizing its reformist politics and advocating total revolution. She campaigned strongly against World War I and was imprisoned for more than two years as a result. From prison, she clandestinely published antiwar pamphlets with Karl Liebknecht, which were signed "Spartacus."

Along with Liebknecht and others, Luxemburg established the Spartacus League in 1915. When she was released from prison in November 1918, she and Liebknecht reestablished the organization and began publishing the newspaper *Die rote Fahne* (*The Red Flag*). On January 1, 1919, the Spartacus League became the Communist Party of Germany (KPD), and just a few days later, the Spartacus Uprising broke out. Although Luxemburg thought the uprising was a mistake, she supported it once it was under way. On January 15, 1919, after the failure of the uprising, Luxemburg was tortured and murdered by *Freikorps* soldiers, and her body was later found in the Landwehr Canal. Liebknecht was assassinated on the same day. The date of their deaths continues to be commemorated among socialists worldwide.

There were demonstrations in German cities during the Spartakus uprising, including the one depicted here. This march took place in about 1919 in Berlin. HULTON ARCHIVE/GETTY IMAGES

The *Spartacus Manifesto* explicitly builds on Karl Marx and Friedrich Engels's 1848 *Communist Manifesto*: in a speech explaining the KPD program, Luxemburg argues that "we connect ourselves to the threads which Marx and Engels spun precisely seventy years ago in the *Communist Manifesto*." In fact, she considers her manifesto more faithful to ideals of the 1848 work than later writings by Engels himself. The structured presentation of the demands—three groups of eight items each—and many of the demands themselves are very similar to those of Marx and Engels. At one point, Luxemburg cites Marx's imperative "Socialism or barbarism!" and declares that it "flares like a fiery *menetekel*"—that is, like a biblical omen—"above the crumbling bastions of capitalist society."

After their assassinations, Luxemburg and Liebknecht became revered as martyrs in Marxist circles. Labor movements throughout Europe owe much to Luxemburg's ideas, which, like those of the Marxist theorist Leon Trotsky, departed from Bolshevism and supported intra-party democracy. The Dutch communist organization Marx-Lenin-Luxemburg Front, for instance, active during the years 1940-42, published an underground journal called *Spartacus* in honor of the Spartacus League. When the Soviet government took power in East Germany after World War II, they named a Berlin square "Rosa-Luxemburg-Platz" in her honor, despite the many ideological differences between Luxemburg and the Bolsheviks.

THEMES AND STYLE

The major theme of the *Spartacus Manifesto* is that a second, proletarian revolution is necessary to finish the work begun by the German Revolution. Luxemburg calls for a "complete transformation of the state and a complete overthrow of the economic and social foundations of society." This transformation, she argues, must be carried out by the workers themselves, and not by parliamentary representatives. The economic transformation is outlined in detail, beginning with the "confiscation of all dynastic wealth" and "expropriation of the lands and fields of all large and medium agricultural enterprises." Internationalism is also a major concern; Luxemburg calls for the "immediate establishment of ties with the fraternal parties in other countries, in order to put the socialist revolution on an international footing." This aspect of the manifesto would later be criticized by Bolsheviks such as Joseph Stalin.

The rhetoric of the *Spartacus Manifesto* appeals to antiwar sentiment, builds on the left's disillusionment with the SPD's revisionism, and incites armed revolution. World War I is framed as the ultimate result of capitalism, and Luxemburg prophesies further wars if capitalism is allowed to continue. The opening passages remind the reader repeatedly of the events of November 9 that began the German Revolution and insist that socialism, beyond that which had been nominally established, "is the only salvation for humanity." By the final section, the paragraphs and sentences have become shorter, amplifying their urgency. Luxemberg argues that the capitalists and "petty-bourgeois" call for the "crucifixion" of the proletariat—Luxemburg's imagined capitalists repeatedly cry "crucify it!", a refrain which vividly colors the critique of the Ebert government.

The language of the manifesto is fiery, insistent, and at times, even violent. Luxemburg uses religious metaphors to mythologize the communist struggle. Capitalism, for instance, is described as "the insatiable god Baal, into whose bloody maw millions upon millions of steaming human sacrifices are thrown." In a similar metaphor, the proletarian revolution "seizes the entire power of the state in its calloused fist—like the god Thor his hammer—using it to smash the head of the ruling classes." The closing sentence of the manifesto proclaims in unambiguous violent fervor, "our slogan toward the enemy is: Thumbs on the eyeballs and knee in the chest!" Luxemburg uses this language—which contrasts greatly with her more collected, intellectual writings—to incite anger against the state and promote immediate action against it.

CRITICAL DISCUSSION

When the *Spartacus Manifesto* was initially published, it met with strong approval among communists and fierce rejection among social democrats. When Luxemberg reiterated key points of the manifesto in her speech "On the Spartacus Programme," there were moments of "tumultuous applause" from the audience, as recorded in a transcript of the proceedings. The SPD government, however, perhaps fearing a Bolshevik revolution like that in Russia, criticized the Spartacus League for attempting to take by force what should be won by election. One propaganda pamphlet from the SPD, quoted by Eric Waldman in his book on the Sparticist Uprising, declared that, where the KPD has power, "The people are not permitted to speak; their voices are suppressed.... Where Spartakus rules, all personal freedom and security are suspended."

After Luxemberg's assassination, her work quickly became canonized among communists, and discussions of her work became more complimentary. During the first congress of the Third International (Comintern) in 1919, Vladimir Lenin began his speech with a requiem for Luxemberg and Liebknecht, even though Luxemberg had been one of the more vocal critics of Leninist Bolshevism. In 1931, however, Stalin would deride her intra-party democracy and internationalism as "utopian and semi-Menshevik"—that is, in line with the views of the socialist minority. In response, Leon Trotsky, in a speech titled "Hands Off Rosa Luxemburg!", admits that "Stalin has sufficient cause to hate Rosa Luxemburg" for her critique of Bolshevist totalitarianism but concludes by urging the necessity to "pass on this truly beautiful, heroic, and tragic image" of Luxemburg's "to the young generations of the proletariat in all its grandeur and inspirational force." Later generations, in fact, would put Luxemburg's ideas regarding democracy to use: in January 1988, East German demonstrators used Luxemburg's slogans to criticize their Bolshevik government, as described in Jon Berndt Olsen's article "Memory in East Germany."

Modern critical commentary on the *Spartacus Manifesto* is somewhat scant. Ernst Vollrath remarks on the ways in which Luxemberg's theories depart from those of Marx and Lenin, and he observes that, in contrast to the latter, "Rosa Luxemburg's concept—which characterizes revolution as the conquest of a share in self-determining action—corresponds completely to the modern non-Marxist concept." Similarly, W. Stark, in an introduction to her work *The Accumulation of Capital,* calls Luxemburg "that rarest of all rare phenomena—a Marxist critical of Karl Marx." The anonymous commentators ("Autorenkollektiv") on a recent Marxist edition of the manifesto are more critical; they contend that there are several significant "errors" in the work. The necessity of breaking the old bourgeois state apparatus is not made clear, they argue; the ultimate goal of communism is not mentioned; and the role of the Party as vanguard is not adequately treated. Despite these problems, however, they conclude that the manifesto is a "great, revolutionary, communist program, a conscious declaration of war against revisionism and opportunism, ... the real founding document of the young Communist Party."

BIBLIOGRAPHY

Sources

Autorenkollektiv [Multiple Unnamed Authors]. *Rosa Luxemburg, Karl Liebknecht und das Revolutionäre Programm der KPD (1918).* Offenbach: Olga Benario und Herbert Baum, 2004. Print.

Luxemburg, Rosa. "On the Spartacus Programme." *Marxists Internet Archive.* Marxist Internet Archive Steering Committee, 2008. Web. 27 July 2012.

———. *The Rosa Luxemburg Reader.* New York: Monthly Review, 2004. Print.

Olsen, Jon Berndt. "Memory in East Germany." *Making the History of 1989.* Roy Rosenzweig Center for History & New Media, 2007. Web. 26 July 2012.

Stalin, J.V. "Some Questions Concerning the History of Bolshevism." *Protelarskaya Revolutsia.* Moscow: Foreign Language Publishing, 1954. *Marxists Internet Archive.* Web. 27 July 2012.

Stark, W. "A Note on Rosa Luxemburg." *The Accumulation of Capital,* by Rosa Luxemburg. London: Routledge & Kegan Paul, 1951. Print.

Trotsky, Leon. "Hands Off Rosa Luxemburg!" *The Militant* (13 Aug. 1932). *Marxists Internet Archive.* Web. 27 July 2012.

Vollrath, Ernst, and E.B. Ashton. "Rosa Luxemburg's Theory of Revolution." *Social Research* 40.1 (1973): 83-109. *JSTOR.* Web. 27 July 2012.

Waldman, Eric. *The Spartacist Uprising of 1919 and the Crisis of the German Socialist Movement: A Study of the Relation of Political Theory and Party Practice.* Milwaukee: Marquette UP, 1958. Print.

Further Reading

Bassler, Gerhard P. "The Communist Movement in the German Revolution, 1918-1919: A Problem of Historical Typology?" *Central European History* 6.3 (1973): 233-77. Print.

"Die rote Fahne." *ZEFYS Zeitungsinformationssystem.* Staatsbibliothek zu Berlin, 2011. Web. 27 July 2012.

Frölich, Paul. *Rosa Luxemburg, Ideas in Action.* London: Left Book Club, 1940. Print.

Kuhn, Gabriel. *All Power to the Councils!: A Documentary History of the German Revolution.* Oakland: PM, 2012. Print.

Luxemburg, Rosa. *The Accumulation of Capital.* Ed. W. Stark. London: Routledge & Kegan Paul, 1951. Print.

Meyer, Karl W. *Karl Liebknecht: Man Without a Country.* Washington, DC: Public Affairs, 1957. Print.

Jon Reeve

TO MY PEOPLES!

Franz Joseph I

✣ *Key Facts*

Time Period:
Early 20th Century

Movement/Issue:
World War I; Militarism

Place of Publication:
Austro-Hungary

Language of Publication:
German; Czech;
Hungarian

OVERVIEW

"To My Peoples!"—a document signed by Franz Joseph I, emperor of Austria-Hungary, on July 28, 1914—explains the declaration of war upon Serbia and marked the beginning of World War I. One month earlier, Archduke Franz Ferdinand, the nephew of Franz Joseph I, was assassinated in Sarajevo, precipitating a series of events that led to this testimony. The document is directed at the various peoples of Austria-Hungary, a massive empire made up of diverse Germanic, Hungarian, and Slavic ethnic groups, with the purpose of rallying them against Serbia. "To My Peoples!" presents Serbia as a violent, hate-filled, and plotting nation that is ungrateful for everything Austria-Hungary—in particular, Franz Joseph I—has done for it. By conflating the threat to Franz Joseph I and his family with a larger, existential threat to the Austro-Hungarian empire, "To My Peoples!" attempts to legitimize Franz Joseph's position as ruler of the sprawling multicultural state and reveals much about the politics of Europe as it verged on the Great War.

The document was greeted with a mix of trepidation and enthusiasm. Some groups within the Austro-Hungarian empire were anxious to teach the Serbs a lesson in what they assumed would be a short and decisive war. The descent toward hostilities was actually due to the careful planning and manipulation of two of Franz Joseph's top advisors. After the assassination of Franz Ferdinand, Chief of Staff General Franz Conrad von Hötzendorf and Foreign Minister Leopold von Berchtold drafted an ultimatum to Serbia that they knew would be rejected, thereby justifying a declaration of war. Many other governments that were entwined in a variety of relationships, pacts, and mutual understandings were then forced into actions they would have rather avoided. The situation that created this series of falling dominoes is known as the "Powder Keg of Europe." Franz Joseph's text is of great historical value because it formally documents the start of what would be the bloodiest conflict the world had ever known and also provides insights into the faltering politics of multinational empires and hereditary monarchies.

HISTORICAL AND LITERARY CONTEXT

"To My Peoples!" constitutes the official government explanation for why Austria-Hungary went to war with Serbia. It first refers to the thirty-year military occupation of the disputed Sandžak region on the southwestern border of Serbia, initiated by the ruling of the Congress of Berlin in 1878 as an act of support to Serbia in order to maintain peace. Rather than gratitude, the document argues, Serbia responded with hatred and acts of sabotage and violence. The text further describes Serbia's response to Austria-Hungary's "paternal affection" as ongoing criminal propaganda that misled its youth and incited its people to "mischievous deeds of madness and high treason." Though the assassination of Archduke Ferdinand is not referenced by name, the document states that the act was the latest in a long series of well-organized, bloody provocations that would no longer be tolerated. As a last attempt to preserve peace, Austria-Hungary had drafted a list of "just and moderate demands," which Serbia rejected, therefore leaving no alternative but war.

"To My Peoples!" was signed on July 28, 1914, the same day the declaration of war was delivered to Serbia. Earlier, von Hötzendorf and von Berchtold had drafted a document consisting of ten highly unreasonable demands, with the expectation that it would be rejected by Serbia and Austria-Hungary would then declare war. To ensure success, the Austrians obtained the assurance of William II of Germany, whose military might, they wrongly assumed, would prevent Russia from intervening in the matter. The ultimatum was approved on July 19, but its delivery was postponed until July 23, when French President Raymond Poincaré would be traveling and would be unable to communicate with his Russian ally. Serbia responded to the ultimatum on July 25, accepting all but two conditions and offering to submit the issue to international arbitration. Austria-Hungary immediately severed all diplomatic ties and began mobilizing its forces. On July 29, Austro-Hungarian artillery began shelling the city of Belgrade.

Unlike many other manifestos that publicly outline plans of action, "To My Peoples!" was designed to be a tool of propaganda. Reminding readers of the decision at the Congress of Berlin in 1878, which allowed for Austro-Hungarian occupation of Bosnia and Herzegovina, the manifesto portrays the Austria-Hungary empire as a victim in a struggle it did not want but was now forced to resolve. In a newspaper article published a couple months after the start of the war, the foreign minister who had coauthored the ultimatum to Serbia echoed the "victim" stance suggested in the document, stating, "Austria-Hungary looks upon this war as a purely defensive one, which has been forced on her by the agitation directed by Russia against her very existence. Austria-Hungary has given many proofs in late years of her peaceful intention."

Early in the war, coverage by newspapers throughout the Austro-Hungarian empire focused much of the blame for the conflict on Russia, portraying the nation as the leader of a Pan-Slavic conspiracy aimed at destroying the monarchy and dominating Europe. In a *New York Times* article dated November 1, 1914, Dr. Bernhard Dernburg, a German ex-colonial secretary, took a slightly different path to exonerating Austria-Hungary of wrongdoing by holding the British accountable for the start of the war. It would not be long before everyone was pointing fingers at everyone else for the misery that would kill more than nine million soldiers over a four-year period.

THEMES AND STYLE

A major theme of "To My Peoples!" is that peace-loving Austria-Hungary is declaring war upon Serbia only because of the constant and brutal attacks it has suffered at Serbian hands over the years. This theme begins with the very first sentence, as Franz Joseph pleads, "It was my fervent wish to consecrate the years which, by the grace of God, still remain to me, to the works of peace and to protect my peoples from the heavy sacrifices and burdens of war." Further into the document, he once more emphasizes this point with the suggestion that Austria-Hungary was beyond lenient in its quest to maintain peace and that it "only requested Serbia to reduce her army to a peace footing and to promise that, for the future, she would tread the path of peace and friendship." The document is sprinkled with phrases such as "the patience and love of peace of my Government," and "my paternal affection." In all, the word "peace" and variations of it are used seven times to describe the goals and stance of the Austro-Hungarian empire.

The phrase "paternal affection" and Franz Joseph's frequent use of the possessive "my" underscore another important concern of the document: the preservation of traditional hereditary monarchies as the predominant form of government in Europe. Monarchies had existed for centuries in Europe to unite disparate cultures and ethnicities under a single ruler whose authority was said to come directly from God, but the nineteenth century brought increased opposition to these types of governments and a rising demand for political autonomy spurred by ethnic nationalism and Enlightenment ideals. Franz Joseph's repeated references to "my peoples" and "my government" highlight the paternalistic view of governance espoused by monarchs, whereas the "mischievous deeds of madness and high treason" that he attributes to Serbia are depicted not only as a threat to the Austro-Hungarian empire but also to the very political

This illustration from the French publication *Le Petit Journal* depicts the assassination of Archduke Franz Ferdinand, the heir to the throne of Austria-Hungry, and his wife, Sophie. This murder led to a declaration of war against Serbia by Franz Joseph I, Franz Ferdinand's uncle. © AKG-IMAGES/ALAMY

system under which much of the continent was organized. Indeed, such concerns were well founded: World War I led to the collapse of the Austro-Hungarian, Russian, German, and Ottoman empires.

Stylistically, "To My Peoples!" is carefully crafted to build a sense of patriotic passion and outrage among its readers. The document provides a calculated contrast between the fatherly, benevolent empire and the out-of-control villain. It contains no long-term plans or philosophical ideals; instead, it is filled with rationalizations for going to war. Even so, the text does not offer a single detailed instance of provocation. The assassination of Archduke Ferdinand is implied but not specifically referenced. In fact, much of the writing immediately following the assassination indicates that the death of the archduke was more of an excuse for war than a cause. There is one phrase near the conclusion of "To My Peoples!" that most clearly and honestly explains the possible true reason for the declaration of war upon the Serbs: "The honor and dignity of my monarchy must be preserved unimpaired."

CRITICAL DISCUSSION

"To My Peoples!" was published in various newspapers using the predominant languages of the empire, and the initial response to it by people around Europe was mixed, often reflecting the uneasy relationships between different ethnic groups living together within arbitrary borders. Troy Paddock observes in *A Call to Arms: Propaganda, Public Opinion, and Newspapers in the Great War* (2004), "Austria's nationalities responded to metropolitan papers in their own local presses. Some chose overt declarations or demonstrations of loyalty; others opted for coded references to injustice and oppression, as well as a refusal to denigrate the monarchy's enemies." In *After Sarajevo: The Origins of the World War* (1966), Sidney B. Fay also examines the mixed nature of the reaction to the manifesto, writing, "Given the generally partisan nature of European newspapers, even an impressionistic glance at the Austro-Hungarian press in 1914 … means analyzing a splintered and fragmented public sphere, riven by political and national divisions."

Of those scholars who have studied "To My Peoples!" in recent years, most view the work as either an elaborate rhetorical ploy to bolster a failing sense of unity among the diverse subjects of the Austro-Hungarian empire or as a revealing glimpse into the psychology of Franz Joseph as his empire began to crumble. For example, George V. Strong, in his *Seedtime for Fascism,* views "To My Peoples!" as evidence of "the senile egoism residing at the center of the state."

However, despite the voluminous output of World War I studies, relatively little has been written about Franz Joseph's document. This paucity of analysis may be the result of the importance placed upon the assassination of Archduke Ferdinand and the details of the ensuing rush to war. A secondary reason may be that the text contains little in the way of specifics, serving more of a footnote to the declaration of war that had already been set into motion. Whatever the reasons, "To My Peoples!" is a document that, for the most part, has faded into the recesses of history.

BIBLIOGRAPHY

Sources

Bled, Jean Paul. *Franz Joseph.* Cambridge: Blackwell, 1992. Print.

Bridge, F.R. *From Sadowa to Sarajevo: The Foreign Policy of Austria-Hungary, 1866-1914.* Boston: Routledge and Paul, 1972. Print.

Coetzee, Frans, and Marilyn Shevin-Coetzee. *World War I: A History in Documents.* New York: Oxford UP, 2002. Print.

Cooper, John Milton. *Causes and Consequences of World War I.* New York: Quadrangle Books, 1972. Print.

Fay, Sidney B. *After Sarajevo: The Origins of the World War.* Vol. 2. New York: The Free Press, 1966. Print.

Paddock, Troy, R.E., ed. *A Call to Arms: Propaganda, Public Opinion, and Newspapers in the Great War.* London: Praeger, 2004. Print.

Strong, George V. *Seedtime for Fascism: The Disintegration of Austrian Political Culture, 1867-1918.* Armonk: M. E. Sharpe, 1998. Print.

Further Reading

Afflerbach, Holger, and David Stevenson, eds. *An Improbable War: The Outbreak of World War I and European Political Culture before 1914.* New York: Berghahn Books, 2007. Print.

Albertini, Luigi. *The Origins of the War of 1914.* New York: Oxford UP, 1957. Print.

Livesey, Anthony. *The Historical Atlas of World War.* New York: H. Holt, 1994. Print.

Neiberg, Michael S. *Dance of the Furies: Europe and the Outbreak of World War I.* Cambridge: Belknap Press of Harvard UP, 2011. Print.

Palmer, Alan Warwick. *Twilight of the Habsburgs: The Life and Times of Emperor Francis Joseph.* London: Weidenfeld & Nicolson, 1994. Print.

Remak, Joachim. *The Origins of World War I, 1871-1914.* New York: Holt, Rinehart and Winston, 1967. Print.

Smith, David James. *One Morning in Sarajevo: 28 June 1914.* London: Weidenfeld & Nicolson, 2008. Print.

Van der Kiste, John. *Emperor Francis Joseph: Life, Death and the Fall of the Hapsburg Empire.* Gloucestershire: Sutton, 2005. Print.

James Mladenovic

VOTES FOR WOMEN
New Movement Manifesto
Women's Social and Political Union

OVERVIEW

An official publication of the Women's Social and Political Union (WSPU), *Votes for Women: New Movement Manifesto* (1906) urges British women of all classes to unite and speak out against the patriarchal legislation that keeps them politically disenfranchised and unable to vote. Most likely written by Emmeline Pankhurst, one of the WSPU's founding members, the manifesto draws attention to the lack of political freedoms granted to women because of the supposedly inherent "disabilities" of being female. The WSPU, active from 1903-1917, was similar to unions formed by male trade workers to draw attention to their collective rights. The WSPU, the first women to be called suffragettes, succeeded in gaining publicity that attracted enough members to organize massive demonstrations, during which many women were arrested and jailed for their principles.

The manifesto was met with immediate derision from members of Parliament, who scoffed at the idea of women making any valid political statement. This reaction caused frustration and anger among women's organizations, including the WSPU, and resulted in the rise of the more militant activism that became associated with the suffrage movement. *Votes for Women* received both positive and negative criticism from women as well, with many women's organizations disagreeing over such issues as women's traditional roles and the rights of women in the workplace. Ideas about how to proceed with protests and activist campaigns also diverged. The manifesto was ultimately successful, however, helping gain women over the age of thirty the right to vote in 1918. It was also a driving force behind subsequent waves of feminism, which led to a further expansion of women's rights.

HISTORICAL AND LITERARY CONTEXT

Votes for Women protests the decree embedded in British law proclaiming women to be inferior and unable to responsibly exercise the rights of citizenship. The WSPU treatise argues that this notion denied fully half of the population representation in the British government. After the Liberal Party's 1906 landslide election victory, the WSPU worked unsuccessfully with liberal politicians to affect legislative reform. A group of 300 representatives was able to meet with the prime minister, Sir Henry Campbell-Bannerman that year. He declared his agreement with their ideas but insisted that he was helpless to affect change and that they must continue to fight patiently. His patronizing attitude toward women, especially those who had already been fighting for their rights for decades, drew a generalized anger, which expressed itself in *Votes for Women* as a call to more aggressive measures.

Votes for Women was published at a time when women's organizations had despaired of effecting

❖ *Key Facts*

Time Period:
Early 20th Century

Movement/Issue:
First-wave feminism;
Suffragism

Place of Publication:
England

Language of Publication:
English

EMMELINE GOULDEN PANKHURST: "I LOOK UPON MYSELF AS A PRISONER OF WAR."

One of the most influential women involved in the British suffrage movement was Emmeline Pankhurst (1858-1928), founding member of the WSPU and the most likely author of *Votes for Women*. Born into a life of comfort, thanks to her father's successful textile firm, Pankhurst used her social connections to reach important members of Parliament in her fight for the political enfranchisement of women. When her peaceful demonstrations and gatherings were ignored, she altered her approach to include more confrontational action and was arrested seven times in total. Imprisoned for the first time in 1908 for six weeks, she called herself a "political prisoner" and eventually a "prisoner of war." She afterwards publicized the deplorable conditions of the prison system.

One of the more violent protests Pankhurst organized was a glass-breaking campaign, which she initiated by throwing a rock through a window of the prime minister's residence. Hundreds of women smashed the windows of commercial buildings in the central boulevards of London that night, causing a crisis the next day when businesses could not open because of the shattered glass in the streets. In June 1909, while in jail for initiating this protest, Pankhurst organized a hunger strike among the women prisoners, who were brutally force-fed, an act that sparked a public outcry against the treatment of prisoners and led to a call for women's rights within the prison system. During a protest in November 1910, fight broke out with police, and many women were physically and even sexually abused; the event came to be known as "Black Friday."

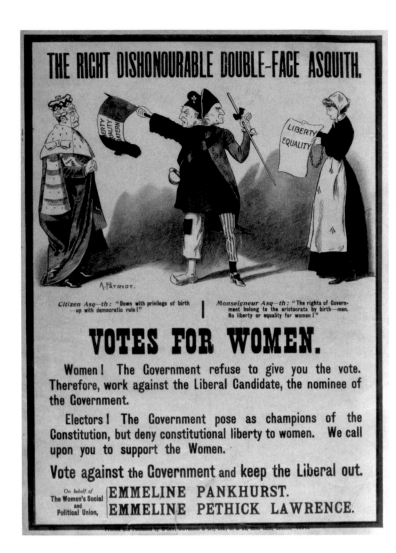

"THE RIGHT DISHONOURABLE DOUBLE-FACE ASQUITH.

Citizen Asq—th: "Down with privilege of birth
—up with democratic rule!"

Monseigneur Asq—th: "The rights of Government belong to the aristocrats by birth—men. No liberty or equality for women!"

VOTES FOR WOMEN.

Women! The Government refuse to give you the vote. Therefore, work against the Liberal Candidate, the nominee of the Government.

Electors! The Government pose as champions of the Constitution, but deny constitutional liberty to women. We call upon you to support the Women.

Vote against the Government and keep the Liberal out.

On behalf of
The Women's Social and
Political Union,
EMMELINE PANKHURST.
EMMELINE PETHICK LAWRENCE.

"The Right Dishonourable Double-Face Asquith," a poster promoting women's suffrage in England, circa 1910. The Women's Social and Political Union (WSPU) produced this poster as well as the newspaper *Votes for Women.* PRIVATE COLLECTION/THE BRIDGEMAN ART LIBRARY

change through political channels and had begun to protest more visibly. Pankhurst sought to remedy women's political silencing by creating a large enough public outcry to sway parliamentary decisions. Three thousand women marched in February 1907, and in June 1908 three to five hundred thousand are said to have gathered Hyde Park. Already well-known as an activist leader, Pankhurst was arrested numerous times beginning in 1908 and was criticized by politicians and feminists alike for her extreme tactics. She is often credited with the ultimate success of the suffrage movement. The manifesto marked the beginning of the WSPU's militant phase, earning the organization recognition as a trailblazer in political feminist activism.

Votes for Women draws on the language and style of previous human rights manifestos, including the American *Declaration of Independence* (1776), primarily composed by Thomas Jefferson, and the French National Constituent Assembly's *Declaration of the Rights of Man and of the Citizen* (1793), adopted during the French Revolution. All three share the influence of the

Age of Enlightenment, expressing the values of natural (as opposed to religious) law and of unconditional universal rights. By generating a sense of unity, *Votes for Women* applied an already successful style of manifesto writing to the cause of women's suffrage.

The WSPU platform inspired a wave of protests that ultimately became violent and even deadly, as the women's suffrage movement adopted extreme measures in order to convince the British government of the legitimacy of its demands. Political writings also followed in the manifesto's wake, including several leaflets issued by the National Women's Social and Political Union (NWSPU), a group that split from the WSPU over the issue of which women should get the vote: the WSPU focused on women heads of households, whereas the NWSPU worked for universal suffrage. NWSPU articles include *Our Demand: What It Is and What It Is Not* (1908) and *Votes for Women: The Conciliation Bill Explained* (1911). In addition, the WSPU continued to publish articles in their periodical, also called *Votes for Women,* in an effort to document the group's official and changing views. The newsletter also advocated the group's militaristic protests and included parliamentary coverage, reviews of literature, and open forums in which academics and activists discussed the problems facing working women. Because each issue cost only a penny, the newsletter became widely accessible and had a large following.

THEMES AND STYLE

The main theme of *Votes for Women* is that women deserve the right to vote and that activist methods need to change in order to achieve that goal. "The Members of the Union," the author writes, "believe that the time has come for vigorous and determined propaganda, and for the adoption of new methods of agitation in the place of old methods which have produced so little result for the past forty years." The manifesto declares that most of the British public—regardless of gender and including many politicians—feel it is time to recognize women as citizens. Advocating for men and women to unite in the fight for change, the treatise laments that "social reform can never be satisfactory as long as only one half of the nation is represented."

The manifesto develops its argument by illustrating the success of trade unions for working men and stating that adopting such a strategy for women's rights would be equally successful: "Working men have found out that political action is needed to supplement Trades Unionism and so they formed a Labour Party." When the Liberal Party's 1905 parliamentary bill mandating women's suffrage, introduced only grudgingly at the behest of women's groups, failed, the experience only catalyzed the movement. The manifesto's persuasive tactical statement that "all who work for Political or Social Reform know by experience that Members of Parliament, however sympathetic, are powerless to urge legislation, unless a strong, persistent and united pressure of public opinion is brought to bear upon the Government." The manifesto claims it is the business of the WSPU to provide a means for that public opinion to be recognized.

The manifesto combines the formal tone associated with the political atmosphere of its protest with powerful and provocative language, sometimes containing clichéd allusions to sexuality. "The New Movement for the political enfranchisement of women," the treatise begins, "initiated by the Women's Social and Political Union, is a people's movement, and is not confined to any section of the community." This opening introduces a formal tone, demonstrating the political legitimacy of a union of women. By contrast, statements such as "THE WORKING WOMEN OF LONDON ARE AROUSED" highlight existing female role expectations and call direct attention to the manifesto's central focus on women. The interplay of the two approaches emphasizes the manifesto's rhetorical strategy, calling attention to the strength of women's ability to organize for political recognition despite the stereotypes they faced in early 1900s Britain.

CRITICAL DISCUSSION

Despite the manifesto's resonance among women, which resulted in the radicalization of many, the manifesto and its stated objectives were initially derided by members of Parliament, who insisted that women were being selfish in putting their own wishes before the needs of others. Sylvia Pankhurst, Emmeline Pankhurst's daughter and a notable suffrage activist, reflects on politicians' reactions to the demands of the WSPU in her memoir *The Suffragette* (1911), reporting that members of the Liberal Party "were very deeply incensed by the thought that women should dare to put the question of their own enfranchisement before every other consideration." The Labour Party, established by the workers and their organizers, complained that the women were "subordinating its interests to the getting of votes for themselves." Sylvia Pankhurst also discusses the reaction of the press, which "merely professed amusement that we should be so foolish and conceited as to think that anything we could say or do would influence elections."

The initial disrespect for the WSPU and its manifesto only infuriated women involved with the organization. Years of militant protest followed, resulting in damage, violence, arrests, and even deaths, as the suffragettes showed they would stop at nothing to gain political enfranchisement. In *The Militant Suffrage Movement* (2003), Laura Mayhall notes that

PRIMARY SOURCE

VOTES FOR WOMEN

The New Movement for the political enfranchisement of women, initiated by the Women's Social and Political Union, is a people's movement, and is not confined to any section of the community.

The Members of the Union believe that the time has come for vigorous and determined propaganda, and for the adoption of new methods of agitation in the place of the old methods which have produced so little result for the past forty years.

All who work for Political and Social Reform know by experience that Members of Parliament however sympathetic are powerless to urge legislation, unless a strong, persistent and united pressure of public opinion is brought to bear upon the Government. It is the business of this Union to arouse and concentrate public opinion.

The Prime Minister and the majority of the Members of the House of Commons, irrespective of party, have declared themselves personally in favour of removing the disabilities of women, and throughout the country there can scarcely be found an individual who is prepared to defend seriously in public the continued exclusions of women from the ranks of voters. *Therefore, the time for argument is past!* The time for action is come.

The London W. S. & P. Unions adopt the policy, initiated in Manchester and intend to carry on in London a determined and persistent campaign. Since the adoption of this new policy great progress has already been made. THE WORKING WOMEN OF LONDON ARE AROUSED. The long struggle for political existence is in view.

All true lovers of justice must now combine in serious united effort to remove this obstacle of sex disability out of the path which leads to the wholehearted co-operation of men and women in the work of further Social Reform. Social reform can never be satisfactory as long as only one half of the nation is represented.

We confidently appeal to the women of London to join our ranks, enroll their names at once and to become active workers in a movement for getting the VOTE FOR WOMEN. Working men have found out that political action is needed to supplement Trades Unionism and so they formed a Labour Party. Women Trades Unionists and Social Reformers now realize that the possession of the Vote is the most effective way of securing better social and industrial condition, better wages, shorter hours, healthier homes, and an honourable position in the State which will enable women as well as men to render that Citizen Service so necessary to the development of a truly great nation.

HON. SECRETARY, MISS SYLVIA PANKHURST, 45 PARK WALK, CHELSEA

HON. TREASURER, MRS. F.W. PETHICK LAWRENCE, 87, CLEMENT'S INN, W.C.

SOURCE: *New Geographies, Complex Interactions.* Ed. Bonnie Kime Scott. University of Illinois, 2007.

the previous "forty years of political agitation with limited success could, and did, operate as a rallying cry." *Votes for Women* initiated the radical stance of the feminist movement's ensuing decades.

Current trends in scholarship on *Votes for Women* and the WSPU generally call attention to the multiplicity of feminist organizations that united in the cause of women's suffrage; facing a wide range of issues, these diverse contributors were not unanimous in their ideas about how to pursue the goal. In her introduction to "Manifestoes from the Sex War" (2007), Janet Lyon notes that women were divided between "a radically democratic project that included working-class representation and economic reforms" and the destruction of traditional "forms of cultural femininity—maternalism, sexual purity, political honesty—[that had created] a badly damaged and unreflective system of political practices." In *Feminist Media History* (2011), Maria DiCenzo, Lucy Delap, and Leila Ryan also study *Votes for Women* and maintain that the diversity of the feminist movement's claims and manifestos have ensured that "the meaning of the suffrage movement continues to be debated." Although the WSPU's manifesto was influential in its day, it is often lost among the numerous publications released around the same time that also deal with issues of women's political rights.

BIBLIOGRAPHY

Sources

DiCenzo, Maria, Lucy Delap, and Leila Ryan. *Feminist Media History: Suffrage, Periodicals and the Public Sphere*. New York: Palgrave, 2011. Print.

"Emmeline Pankhurst, Women's Social and Political Union: *Votes for Women: New Movement Manifesto*." 1906. Rpt. in *Gender in Modernism: New Geographies, Complex Intersections*. Ed. Bonnie Kime Scott. Chicago: U of Illinois P, 2007. 76-77. Print.

Lyon, Janet. Introduction. "Manifestoes from the Sex War." *Gender in Modernism: New Geographies, Complex Intersections*. Ed. Bonnie Kime Scott. Chicago: U of Illinois P, 2007. 67-76. Print.

Mayhall, Laura E. Nym. *The Militant Suffrage Movement: Citizenship and Resistance in Britain, 1860-1931*. Oxford: Oxford UP, 2003. Print.

Pankhurst, E. Sylvia. *The Suffragette: The History of the Women's Militant Suffrage Movement, 1905-1910*. New York: Sturgis, 1911. *Internet Archive*. Web. 15 Oct. 2012.

Further Reading

Bush, Julia. *Women against the Vote: Female Anti-Suffragism in Britain*. Oxford: Oxford UP, 2007. Print.

Cowman, Krista. *Women of the Right Spirit: Paid Organizers of the Women's Social and Political Union (WSPU), 1904-18*. Manchester: Manchester UP, 2007. Print.

"Emmeline Pankhurst." *Contemporary Heroes and Heroines*. Vol. 4. Detroit: Gale, 2000. *Gale Biography in Context*. Web. 15 Oct. 2012.

Holton, Sandra Stanley. *Suffrage Days: Stories from the Women's Suffrage Movement*. London: Routledge, 1996. Print.

Mercer, John. "Media and the Militancy: Propaganda in the Women's Social and Political Union's Campaign." *Women's History Review* 14.3 (2005): 471-86. Web. 13 Oct. 2012.

Pankhurst, Emmeline. *My Own Story*. New York: Hearst, 1914. Print.

Purvis, June. *Emmeline Pankhurst: A Biography*. London: Routledge, 2002. Print.

Katherine Barker

WOMEN'S SUFFRAGE
A Short History of a Great Movement
Millicent Garrett Fawcett

OVERVIEW

Written by the British suffragist Millicent Garrett Fawcett, *Women's Suffrage: A Short History of a Great Movement* (1912) chronicles the saga leading up to women's enfranchisement in Great Britain. Addressed to a general audience, the manifesto raises awareness for the suffrage cause overall and for Fawcett's group, the National Union of Women Suffragist Societies (NUWSS), in particular. Written as a historical account of the political and cultural events that led to the founding and continuation of the women's suffrage movement, *Women's Suffrage* records these events from a perspective that legitimizes Fawcett's approach over that of others within the suffrage movement.

Published at the same time as a spate of similar histories, *Women's Suffrage* found favor among suffrage advocates but was largely disregarded by nonsuffragist readers. After a lull in the movement, several suffragists put their struggle to paper in order to reignite the movement and galvanize supporters. Fawcett's manifesto stands apart for its core principle of intellectual and moral progress resulting in women's voting rights. As the leader of the "constitutionalist" group NUWSS, Fawcett foregrounds gradual legal changes throughout her manifesto, promoting this tactic as the best way to gain women the vote. In 1918, six years after the manifesto was published, women over thirty years of age won the vote, and by 1928 all women over the age of twenty-one had become enfranchised. Penned by one of the foremost leaders of the suffrage movement, *Women's Suffrage* offers unique insight into a critical stage of the movement and its eventual success.

HISTORICAL AND LITERARY CONTEXT

The British women's suffrage movement can be understood broadly as a response to the Reform Act of 1832, which disenfranchised poor men and all women. *Women's Suffrage* documents the political events and intellectual developments that gave rise to women's dissatisfaction, which by the end of the nineteenth century had coalesced into a national suffrage movement. While historicizing the movement, *Women's Suffrage* arguably responds more directly to flagging support for and divisive factions within

the cause. During the first decade of the twentieth century, Britain's involvement in the South African War (1899-1902) diminished interest in the issue. At the same time, radical members of the Women's Social and Political Union (WSPU) captured the public's attention—and ire—with their militancy and violent demonstrations. Fawcett's manifesto attempts to generate interest in and positive public opinion for the method of legal protest.

By the time *Women's Suffrage* was written in 1912, women had been agitating for voting rights for nearly three decades. Universal male suffrage was still six years away, and universal female suffrage was another ten years out. Among the thousands of women striving for change, Fawcett stood out as a leader of the constitutionalist faction and of the largest suffragist group, the NUWSS. Other groups favored deeds over actions, but Fawcett put her faith in legal progress toward women's suffrage. When her manifesto appeared, it provided an account of the movement from the perspective of a pragmatic leader, and the cogent text counterbalanced extremist actions recently associated with the movement.

In form, *Women's Suffrage* participates in a contemporary trend of recording history, patterned after such texts as Helen Blackburn's *Women's Suffrage: A Record of the Women's Suffrage Movement* (1902), W. Lyon Blease's *The Emancipation of English Women* (1910), and Sylvia Pankhurst's *The Suffragette* (1911). Each author documents the same political movement but inflects her account with a different guiding principle. For example, whereas the latter two works emphasize militant, terrorist actions in forwarding women's voting rights, Fawcett's pragmatism builds on previous declarations of women's rights, tracing back to Mary Wollstonecraft's *A Vindication of the Rights of Woman* (1792). Indeed, Fawcett had authored an introduction to an 1891 edition of Wollstonecraft's text. *Women's Suffrage* presumes moral equality between the sexes and declares women integral to a nation. These ideas appear in Wollstonecraft's text and in John Stuart Mill's seminal work *The Subjection of Women* (1869), which declares that women's moral and intellectual advancement would result in a happier society.

✣ *Key Facts*

Time Period:
Early 20th Century

Movement/Issue:
Women's suffrage; First-wave feminism

Place of Publication:
England

Language of Publication:
English

EMMELINE PANKHURST AND THE WOMEN'S SOCIAL AND POLITICAL UNION

Although women's suffrage supporters strove for the same goal—voting rights for women—two major factions within the movement divided participants. Millicent Fawcett and the National Union of Women Suffragist Societies (NUWSS) represented peaceful resolution and gradual change. In opposition stood the Women's Social and Political Union (WSPU), led by the self-described "hooligan" Emmeline Pankhurst and her daughters, Christabel and Sylvia. Called "militant" by its detractors, the WSPU employed aggressive and even violent tactics to attract attention to the suffrage cause.

Founded in 1903, several years after the NUWSS and with only a fraction of the membership, WSPU quickly became infamous for its extremist actions. Dedicated to "deeds not words," the WSPU supporters hurled rocks at windows, assaulted police officers, and staged protests at Parliament. While these tactics achieved notoriety, as the attacks escalated into acts of "terror" (such as arson), public favor soon turned against the group. Many members, including Pankhurst and her daughters, were imprisoned and then staged hunger strikes and endured brutal force-feeding. Pankhurst and her followers lost support in 1914, when the WSPU shifted focus to the national war effort in World War I. Named one of *Time* magazine's one hundred most influential people of the twentieth century, Emmeline Pankhurst—right or wrong—significantly altered the climate and discussion surrounding women's suffrage.

In the decades following the publication of *Women's Suffrage,* several similar histories were published, documenting new events in the suffrage movement. Nevertheless, only Fawcett and the suffragist Rachel "Ray" Strachey would do so from a constitutionalist perspective. Strachey's *The Cause* (1928) was the last of this genre to advocate for voting rights as a moral imperative. (Three years later, Strachey penned the biographical study *Millicent Garrett Fawcett.*) Fawcett wrote other works on the suffrage movement, including *The Women's Victory and After* (1920) and a biographical account in *What I Remember* (1925). Even though documentation of the suffrage movement subsided after women were granted the vote in 1928, the recording of events remains a way for other protest movements to validate their causes in the public eye. Today the many suffrage histories provide an overview of how the movement evolved and offer insight into the beginnings of modern feminism.

THEMES AND STYLE

The central theme of *Women's Suffrage* is that, because of their education, morality, and loyal support of the government, women deserve to participate in Britain's democratic government. This overriding theme is colored by Fawcett's particular brand of protest.

The manifesto describes political and cultural changes leading up to the present moment and discusses at length recent events in the movement, thus stressing its continuous evolution. Continuity distinguishes the constitutionalist suffragists from their militant counterparts, and some have read Fawcett's opening line—"We suffragists have no cause to be ashamed of the founders of our movement"—as a challenge to Pankhurst's militant history, which emphasizes breaking with tradition.

The manifesto achieves its rhetorical effect through appeals to rationality and constitutional provision, transcending any semblance of sentimentalism. Addressing an audience of nonsuffragists, Fawcett informs a broad readership, in a pragmatic and logical manner, of suffragists' qualms and their recent struggle. To this end *Women's Suffrage* details both legislative actions and responses within the movement as a way to explain both the origins of women's dissatisfaction and their dissent. Fawcett's didactic attitude toward readers indicates an assumption that her audience is not involved with the movement and may have only scant information about it. Over the course of seven chapters, Fawcett delineates history as a series of inevitable causes and effects, such that setbacks are recounted with neutrality and even optimism: "But though fatal to immediate Parliamentary success the events of 1884 strengthened our cause in the country. Everything which draws public attention to the subject of representation and to the political helplessness of the unrepresented makes people ask themselves more and more 'Why are women excluded?'" Injustices are rendered illogical rather than sensationalized—a strategy that perhaps marks the true rhetorical force of the manifesto: women's suffrage seems to be the reasonable outcome of a continuous process.

Stylistically *Women's Suffrage* follows many of the conventions in historical accounts. The manifesto progresses chronologically through major events from the movement's beginnings and recent past. In keeping with convention, the tone of the manifesto is matter-of-fact and ostensibly objective. Problematic areas of the movement, such as Fawcett's censure of militant suffragists and a discussion of antisuffragists, are dealt with in a cogent and evenhanded manner. When discussing the more militant suffragists' violent methods, Fawcett acknowledges that they "were regarded by many suffragists with strong aversion, while others watched them with sympathy and admiration for the courage and self-sacrifice which these new methods involved." This apparent balance masks the fact that *Women's Suffrage* represents only one point of view within the movement and ultimately advocates for that segment.

CRITICAL DISCUSSION

Initial responses to *Women's Suffrage* were largely confined to suffrage publications but were generally positive. A review of the book in the suffragist periodical the *Common Cause* calls attention to Fawcett's own emphasis on continuity, while a review in the suffragist journal *Votes for Women* interprets the text as generous to the militant side and highlights Fawcett's critique of their common enemies. The Church League for Women's Suffrage raved about the book, hailing it as a reliable resource and praising Fawcett's critique of militant groups. For many within the suffrage movement, Fawcett—as the leader of the NUWSS—had a commanding voice, and her account of the movement's history reflects the constitutional, legal approach she championed. The lack of coverage by more mainstream publications makes it impossible to know what kind of impact the manifesto had on broader audiences. For Fawcett's followers, however, while the manifesto contained few surprises, it validated their own actions and beliefs and asserted their place in history.

The struggle for women's suffrage continued in the years following the publication of *Women's Suffrage,* and in the process more men and women contributed their voices to documenting the cause. *Women's Suffrage* succeeded in generating support for the movement and in helping women to win the vote. Fawcett's methodology of gradual legal change and belief in the inevitability of women's enfranchisement proved successful in the suffrage campaign: in 1918 women over the age of thirty gained voting rights, and by 1928 all women over the age of twenty-one had the same voting rights as men. In the decades that followed Britain's universal suffrage, histories such as *Women's Suffrage* became a rich source for historians seeking to understand the movement, yet analysis of many of these works remains generalized.

Scholarship dealing with *Women's Suffrage* is scant and often groups Fawcett's text with other suffrage histories. Discussed in concert with other constitutionalist texts or in opposition to militant histories of the same era, *Women's Suffrage* has largely been considered by scholars in the context of the historiography of the movement and of the effect of historical accounts on shaping public perception of the suffragist cause. In "Justifying Their Modern Sisters: History Writing and the British Suffrage Movement" (2005), Maria DiCenzo asserts that the phenomenon of history writing as a whole was contested ground and that these narratives were "instrumental in constructing different feminist/activist identities" for the varying factions. Joyce Pedersen, in "The Historiography of the Women's Movement in Victorian and Edwardian England" (1996), considers liberal suffragists' historical tactics and analyzes Fawcett's manifesto to understand its ideological underpinnings. Some scholarship also evaluates the role of these histories in setting the stage for later feminist history and studies.

BIBLIOGRAPHY

Sources

DiCenzo, Maria. "Justifying Their Modern Sisters: History Writing and the British Suffrage Movement." *Victorian Review* 31.1 (2005): 40-61. Print.

Fawcett, Millicent Garrett. *Women's Suffrage: A Short History of a Great Movement.* London: T.C. & E.C. Jack, 1912. Print.

Pedersen, Joyce Senders. "The Historiography of the Women's Movement in Victorian and Edwardian England: Varieties of Contemporary Liberal Feminist Interpretation." *European Legacy: Toward New Paradigms* 1.3 (1996): 1052-57. Print.

Leaflet of the National Union of Women's Suffrage Societies (NUWSS), 1909. Millicent Garrett Fawcett served as president of the NUWSS for more than twenty years. HIP/ART RESOURCE, NY

Further Reading

Caine, Barbara. "Feminism, Suffrage, and the Nine-teenth-Century English Women's Movement." *Women's Studies International Forum* 5.6 (1982): 537-50. Print.

Fawcett, Millicent Garrett. *What I Remember.* New York: Putnam, 1925. Print.

Garner, Les. *Stepping Stones to Women's Liberty: Feminist Ideas in the Women's Suffrage Movement.* London: Heinemann Educational, 1984. Print.

Howarth, Janet. "Mrs. Henry Fawcett: The Widow as a Problem in Feminist Biography." *Votes for Women.* Ed. June Purvis and Sandra Stanley Holton. London: Routledge, 2000. 84-108. Print.

Joannou, Maroula. *The Women's Suffrage Movement: New Feminist Perspectives.* Manchester, UK: Manchester UP, 1998. Print.

Kelly, Katherine E. "Seeing through Spectacles: The Woman Suffrage Movement and London Newspapers, 1906-13." *European Journal of Women's Studies* 11.3 (2004): 327-53. Print.

Rubinstein, David. *A Different World for Women: The Life of Millicent Garrett Fawcett.* Columbus: Ohio State UP, 1991. Print.

Spender, Dale. *Feminists Theorists: Three Centuries of Women's Intellectual Traditions.* London: Women's Press, 1983. Print.

Elizabeth Boeheim

ZIMMERWALD MANIFESTO

Leon Trotsky, et al.

OVERVIEW

In September 1915 antimilitarist socialist parties convened the International Socialist Conference in Zimmerwald, Switzerland, to protest the inactivity of the Socialist, or "Second," International organization in actively protesting the outbreak of World War I. Delegates from socialist parties in eleven countries called for peace and the right of peoples to national self-determination. The "Zimmerwald Manifesto," as the document came to be known, was drafted by members of various delegations, most notable among them "Lev" (Leon) Trotsky and "V.I." (Vladimir Ilyich) Lenin. The text was subject to much revision by opposing delegates, who could not agree whether its ultimate goal was peace or revolution. Unable to reconcile their differences, the delegation appointed Trotsky to write the final draft, which was then signed by representatives from Germany, France, Italy, Russia, Poland, Romania, Bulgaria, Sweden, Norway, Switzerland, and The Netherlands.

Composed by an already divided group, the "Zimmerwald Manifesto" was presented to a world deeply affected by an all-encompassing war, and it served as an inspiration to antiwar movements, which continued to grow as Europe became mired in military conflict. Although the socialists of the warring nations generally supported the call for peace, a small faction of the International Socialist Committee, which would become known as the "revolutionary left" or the "Zimmerwald Left," called for something greater—an international workers' revolution. Led by Lenin, the members of the Zimmerwald Left at first appeared extreme in their beliefs, but as war casualties mounted—with more than one million deaths in a six-month period in 1916—the movement gained some momentum. It planted the seed for what later became the Communist International, and these plans came to fruition in 1917, when workers and soldiers turned against their governments and effectively ended World War I on the Eastern Front.

HISTORICAL AND LITERARY CONTEXT

The "Zimmerwald Manifesto" provided a pointed response to the decision of Europe's socialist leaders to support their respective countries' war aims, rather than to rally for peace, at the outset of the World War I in 1914. Socialist Party members perceived both the French and German leaders as putting the nationalistic aims of their respective countries ahead of the larger workers' struggle. Heeding the call to arms against fellow workers in neighboring countries was clearly a betrayal of the principles put forth at the foundation of the Socialist International in 1889, where delegates assembled as "brothers with a single common enemy … private capital, whether it be Prussian, French, or Chinese." Further, in 1912 Socialist Party leaders had called for improvements in social welfare in the "Manifesto of the International Socialist Congress at Basel." However, the reality only one year later was one of "want and privation, unemployment and high prices, undernourishment

❖ *Key Facts*

Time Period:
Early 20th Century

Movement/Issue:
Socialism; Proletarian revolution

Place of Publication:
Switzerland

Language of Publication:
Various

LEON TROTSKY—BEYOND ZIMMERWALD

The "Zimmerwald Manifesto," although an important document because of the impetus it gave to the revolutionary movement, remains one of Leon Trotsky's lesser known works. Following the Zimmerwald Conference, Trotsky continued to publish his newspaper, *Nashe Slovo,* from Paris, which led to his eventual expulsion from France. After a brief time in New York, he returned to Russia with a U.S. passport he had obtained with the help of President Woodrow Wilson. The Russian Revolution had erupted, and Trotsky wanted to be present for this much anticipated moment. The provisional government, however, perceived Trotsky as a threat and had him arrested. When the provisional government was overthrown in November 1917, Trotsky's years of labor on behalf of the Socialist Party came to fruition when Lenin appointed him commissar of foreign affairs and, later, leader of the Red Army, a position at which he proved to be quite successful. Trotsky continued to serve in Lenin's government after the White Army's defeat.

Lenin's death in 1924 virtually signaled the end of Trotsky's political career, as he was slowly pushed out of Joseph Stalin's government and, eventually, out of Russia. In August 1940, at the age of sixty, Trotsky died in exile in Mexico; he was stabbed with an ice pick by an undercover agent for the Soviet police. Although discredited for years, Trotsky's reputation has been restored within the past decade, and he is now respected as a great intellect, an inspiring orator, and a tireless worker for the causes in which he believed.

PRIMARY SOURCE

"ZIMMERWALD MANIFESTO"

Proletarians of Europe!

The war has lasted more than a year. Millions of corpses cover the battlefields. Millions of human beings have been crippled for the rest of their lives. *Europe is like a gigantic human slaughterhouse.* All civilization, created by the labor of many generations, is doomed to destruction. The most savage barbarism is today celebrating its triumph over all that hitherto constituted the pride of humanity.

New fetters, new chains, new burdens are arising, and it is the proletariat of all countries, of the victorious as well as of the conquered countries, that will have to bear them. Improvement in welfare was proclaimed at the outbreak of the war – want and privation, unemployment and high prices, undernourishment and epidemics are the actual results. *The burdens of war will consume the best energies of the peoples for decades,* endanger the achievements of social reform, and hinder every step forward. Cultural devastation, economic decline, political reaction these are the blessings of this horrible conflict of nations. Thus the war reveals the naked figure of modern capitalism which has become irreconcilable, not only with the interests of the laboring masses, not only with the requirements of historical development, but also with the elementary conditions of human intercourse....

Workers!

Exploited, disfranchised, scorned, they called you brothers and comrades at the outbreak of the war when you were to be led to the slaughter, to death. And now that militarism has crippled you, mutilated you, degraded and annihilated you, the rulers demand that you surrender your interests, your aims, your ideals – in a word, *servile subordination to civil peace.* They rob you of the possibility of expressing your views, your feelings, your pains; they prohibit you from raising your demands and defending them. The press gagged, political rights and liberties trod upon – this is the way the *military dictatorship* rules today with an iron hand....

In this unbearable situation, we, the representatives of the Socialist parties, trade unions and their minorities, we Germans, French, Italians, Russians, Poles, Letts, Rumanians, Bulgarians, Swedes, Norwegians, Dutch, and Swiss, we who stand, not on

and epidemics." The "Zimmerwald Manifesto" also brought attention to the plight of less powerful nations, such as Poland, Belgium, and Armenia, which faced the threat of annexation by the "Great Powers" of Europe, and called for socialists to defend the right to free speech and civil liberties, which had been largely suppressed because of war censorship imposed for the sake of national security.

By the time the "Zimmerwald Manifesto" was written, the socialist antiwar movement was already growing in strength and numbers. Although the document marked the socialist movement's first official denunciation of the war, peace movements began to gain strength throughout Europe. An anti-conscription campaign took root in Great Britain and was almost unanimously supported by the British Left. The same year in Germany, Karl Liebknecht, the only member of the German legislature to have voted against participation in World War I, penned the pamphlet "The Main Enemy Is at Home," in which he argued that Germany, with its pro-war policy, was a greater threat to its own citizens than was the enemy abroad. Liebknecht, along with Rosa Luxemburg, founded the underground *Spartacus Letters* newspaper, a vehicle by which they could share their views with the public. In 1916 Trotsky, the principal author of the "Zimmerwald Manifesto," was deported from France because of his involvement with the Zimmerwald Conference and the revolutionary nature of his articles in *Nashe Slovo,* the Russian-language newspaper he published in Paris.

The "Zimmerwald Manifesto" adheres to the socialist tradition of antiwar resolutions written in the era leading up to World War I. Similar to the Stuttgart Resolution of 1907 and the Basel Manifesto of 1912, the "Zimmerwald Manifesto," while lambasting the authors of the previous documents, calls anew for mass mobilization against the war. Contrary to previous resolutions and manifestos, however, the "Zimmerwald Manifesto" also insists upon the right of self-determination for nations and peoples: "Peace, however, is only possible if every thought of violating the rights and liberties of nations is condemned.... The right of self-determination of nations must be the indestructible principle in the system of national relationships of peoples."

The "Zimmerwald Manifesto" was the first of what would become many written denunciations of the war. Trotsky himself continued his writings, which now called for an international workers' revolution. His articles in *Nashe Slovo* and in *Novy Mir,* the paper he published while in exile in New York City at

the ground of national solidarity with the exploiting class, but on the ground of the international solidarity of the proletariat and of the class struggle, have assembled to retie the torn threads of international relations and to call upon the working class to recover itself and to fight for peace.

This struggle is the struggle for freedom, for the *reconciliation* of peoples, for Socialism. It is necessary to take up this struggle for peace, for a peace without annexations or war indemnities *Such a peace, however, is only possible if every thought of violating the rights and liberties of nations is condemned.* Neither the occupation of entire countries nor of separate parts of countries must lead to their violent annexation. No annexation, whether open or concealed, and no forcible economic attachment made still more unbearable by political disfranchisement. *The right of self-determination of nations must be the indestructible principle in the system of national relationships of peoples.*

Proletarians!

Since the outbreak of the war, you have placed your energy, your courage, your endurance at the service of the ruling classes. Now you must stand up for your own cause, for the sacred aims of Socialism, for the emancipation of the oppressed nations as well as of the enslaved classes, by means of the irreconcilable proletarian class struggle.

It is the task and the duty of the Socialists of the belligerent countries to take up this struggle with full force; it is the task and the duty of the Socialists of the neutral states to support their brothers in this struggle against bloody barbarism with every effective means. Never in world history was there a more urgent, a more sublime task, the fulfillment of which should be our common labor. No sacrifice is too great, no burden too heavy in order to achieve this goal: peace among the peoples.

Working men and working women! Mothers and fathers! Widows and orphans! Wounded and crippled! We call to all of you who are suffering from the war and because of the war: Beyond all borders, beyond the reeking battlefields, beyond the devastated cities and villages –

Proletarians of all countries, unite!

---

the outbreak of the Russian Revolution, followed in the Zimmerwald tradition. At the same time, Lenin continued to write from his own exile in neutral Switzerland; his "Letters from Afar" essentially echo Trotsky's sentiments.

The central theme of the "Zimmerwald Manifesto" is that workers and peasants of all nations, powerful or weak, have been exploited by the ruling classes and their nationalist and imperialist wars. The essay begins by recounting the destruction caused only one year into the Great War: millions of deaths, occupied countries, the loss of civil liberties, and a massive decline in welfare and living standards. Trotsky places the responsibility for this not only on the "mighty business organizations, the bourgeois parties, the capitalist press, the Church" but also on "the appointed representative bodies of the Socialists of all countries" for betraying their ideals and thus failing the people. The text concludes with a message of mobilization: "Since the outbreak of the war, you have placed your energy, your courage, your endurance at the service of the ruling classes. Now you must stand up for your own cause, for the sacred aims of Socialism, for the emancipation of the oppressed nations as well as of the enslaved classes, by means of the irreconcilable proletarian struggle.... No sacrifice is too great, no burden too heavy in order to achieve this goal: peace among the peoples."

The "Zimmerwald Manifesto" is persuasive because it draws upon common grievances in order to unite its audience. It emphasizes the shared "struggle for freedom, for the *reconciliation* of peoples, for Socialism." It addresses all workers, regardless of national origin: "Germans, French, Italians … have assembled to retie the torn threads of international relations and to call upon the working class to recover itself and to fight for peace." The rhetoric of the sorrows of war—"want and privation, unemployment and high prices, undernourishment and epidemics"—and the narrative of the betrayal of the workers by their own party, whose representatives "called upon the working class to give up the class struggle" in order to serve the interest of their own governments, work together to unite the audience.

Stylistically the essay relies heavily on an appeal to the reader's emotions. Trotsky reiterates the horror of war in its many forms: "Millions of corpses cover the battlefields…. Europe is like a gigantic human slaughterhouse. All civilization … is doomed to destruction." He speaks to the people as a single unit, rallying workers of all nations, belligerent, neutral, or occupied, behind the cause of peace. "New fetters, new chains, new burdens are arising, and it is the

M. Chermnykh's *The Proletarian's Hammer*, a 1917 cartoon depicting proletarians (workers) in Russia's October Revolution, whose leaders included Leon Trotsky and Vladimir Lenin. Two years earlier both had signed the Marxist revolutionary "Zimmerwald Manifesto."
© AKG-IMAGES/ALAMY

proletariat of all countries, of the victorious as well as of the conquered countries, that will have to bear them." By invoking the betrayal by the socialist leaders at the outset of the war, Trotsky further raises the ire of his audience: "Exploited, disfranchised, scorned, they called you brothers and comrades at the outbreak of the war when you were to be led to the slaughter, to death. And now that militarism has crippled you, mutilated you, degraded and annihilated you, the rulers demand that you surrender your interests, your aims, your ideals—in a word, *servile subordination to civil peace*." The essay concludes with an emotional call to peoples from across the spectrum of humanity to unite for peace and for a kind of internationalism.

CRITICAL DISCUSSION

Even when the "Zimmerwald Manifesto" was first published in 1915, there was dissatisfaction with the document from both the radical Zimmerwald Left, led by Lenin, and the more conservative faction of the socialist movement, led by Swiss delegate Robert Grimm. For this reason, the document was drafted as a manifesto rather than as a more formal resolu-

tion. Russian delegates felt that the "Zimmerwald Manifesto" did not go far enough because it neglected to denounce tsarism specifically, and the Italian delegate, Oddino Morgari, wanted the document to absolve France from any responsibility for the war. Despite signing the final draft of the "Zimmerwald Manifesto," Lenin went on to criticize the document soon after in his article "The First Step": "In practice, the Manifesto signifies a step towards an ideological and practical break with opportunism and social-chauvinism. At the same time, the Manifesto, as analysis will show, contains inconsistencies, and does not say everything that should be said." While a harbinger of hope to the socialist antiwar movement, the "Zimmerwald Manifesto" was an imperfect document in the eyes of many of the delegates to the conference, who, in fact, had helped to create it.

The "Zimmerwald Manifesto" laid the groundwork for future manifestos and for the emergence of the revolutionary Communist. or "Third," International in 1919. After the Zimmerwald Conference of 1915 and the subsequent publication of the essay, a second conference was held in Kiental, Switzerland, in April 1916. The manifesto that resulted from this conference was more in line with the ideas of the Zimmerwald Left and moved toward a more internationalist point of view. The third, and final, socialist antiwar conference was held in September 1917, again in Zimmerwald, Switzerland. It resulted in a document distrustful of the initiatives toward peace being made by "bourgeois governments" and stated that true peace could only be won through international socialist struggle. The piece presciently supported a revolution in Russia, which began just a few days before publication. In the century since the "Zimmerwald Manifesto" was published, there has been relatively little comment, though some critics have suggested that it sounded much more impactful than it really was.

The scant amount of recent scholarship on the "Zimmerwald Manifesto" focuses to a large degree on the figure of Lenin. In *Lenin Rediscovered* (2006), Lars T. Lih suggests that with Zimmerwald, Lenin exhibited an "aggressive unoriginality" of ideas about socialism. In contrast, R. Craig Nation contends in *War on War: Lenin, the Zimmerwald Left, and the Origins of Communist Internationalism* (1985) that Lenin's obsession with promoting the right of national self-determination ultimately set him apart from other delegates and alienated him from the Zimmerwald Left.

BIBLIOGRAPHY

Sources

Bronner, Stephen Eric. "Modernism, Surrealism, and the Political Imaginary." *Logos: A Journal of Modern Society and Culture* 11.2-3 (2012). Logos International Foundation. Web. 2 Oct. 2012.

Lih, Lars T. *Lenin Rediscovered: "What Is to Be Done" in Context.* Leiden: Brill, 2006. Print.

Manifesto of the International Socialist Congress at Basel. 1912. *University of Nevada, Las Vegas.* Web. 2 Oct. 2012.

Nation, R. Craig. *War on War: Lenin, the Zimmerwald Left, and the Origins of Communist Internationalism.* Durham: Duke UP, 1985. Print.

Shepherd, B. "After Zimmerwald—Radical Chains." Rev. of *War on War: Lenin, the Zimmerwald Left, and the Origins of Communist Internationalism,* by R. Craig Nation. *Libcom.org.* 2 Nov. 2011. Web. 2 Oct. 2012.

Trotsky, Leon, et al. "Zimmerwald Manifesto." 1915. *Memorial University Libraries.* Web. 2 Oct. 2012.

Woods, Alan. "In Memory of Leon Trotsky." *Trotsky.net.* In Defence of Marxism, 24 Jan. 2000. Web. 2 Oct. 2012.

Further Reading

Daniels, Robert V. *A Documentary History of Communism and the World: From Revolution to Collapse.* Hanover: UP of New England, 1994. Print.

Pelz, William A. *Against Capitalism: The European Left on the March.* New York: P. Lang, 2007. Print.

Trotsky, Leon. *Leon Trotsky Speaks.* New York: Pathfinder, 1972. Print.

Woods, Alan. *Zimmerwald: The Road to Revolution: A History of the Bolshevik Party from the Early Beginnings to the October Revolution.* London: Wellred, 1999. Print.

Lisa Mertel

SUBJECT INDEX

Bold *volume and page numbers (e.g.,* **3:269–272**) *refer to the main entry on the subject.*
Page numbers in italics refer to photographs and illustrations.

A

a bis z (newspaper), **2:**206, 207–208

À la recherche du temps perdu (Proust)
  literary criticism experiments, **2:**104–106
  themes and writing, **2:**104

À Rebours (Huysmans). *See Against Nature* (Huysmans)

A Tett (journal), **2:**203, 204, 220

Abaporu (do Amaral), **2:**64

Abbey, Edward, **3:**282

Abbey Theatre (Dublin, Ireland), **1:**43, 44

"The ABCs of Cinema" (Cendrars), **2:138–140**

Abd-el-Krim, **2:**82

Abdulhamid II, **2:**290

"The Abolition of Work" (Black), **1:**345

Abolitionist movement (Cuba), **1:**274

Abolitionist movement (Europe), **1:**202, 209, 211, 252, 262

Abolitionist movement (U.S.), **1:**120–121, 121–122, 169, 191, 252–254, 259, 263
  Appeal in Four Articles (Walker), **1:**234–237
  Declaration of Independence use, **1:**250, 252–253
  Declaration of Sentiments of the American Anti-Slavery Society (1833), **1:**252–255

Ethiopian Manifesto (Young), **1:**262–266
  satirical illustrations, **1:** *253*
  women's rights movement links, **1:**249, 254, 359, 361, **3:**97, 98

Abolitionist press, **1:**121–122, 234–235, 236, 252, 253, 263, 264, 359, 371

Abortion laws
  Comstock Law (1873), **2:**293
  France, **3:**108, 109, *109*
  United States, **3:**119, 126

Abortion rights
  Manifesto of the 343 (Beauvoir), **3:**108–111
  protests, **3:**119

Abraham, Arthur, **3:**346

Abram, David, **3:**23

Abrams, M. H., **1:**78

Absinthe Drinker (Manet), **1:**93

Abstract expressionism (art), **3:**55
  Gutai art critiques, **3:**49
  mid-to-late 20th century, **2:**163, **3:**42, 49, 50, 218
  poetry compared, **3:**218
  public opinion and accessibility, **3:**55

Abstraction in art
  cubism, **2:**182, 183
  expressionism, **2:**160, 189, 190, **3:**218
  suprematism, **2:**217, 218

Abstraction in literature
  creationist poetry, **2:**170
  poetry, **3:**218, 219

"The Mechanics for a Literary 'Secession'" (Munson), **2:**93

Abstractionists, **2:**166, 229

Absurdism
  Beckett writings, **2:**104–105, 106
  dada, **2:**69, 72, 73, 111, **3:**84, 85
  "The _____ Manifesto" (Betancourt), **3:**84, 85
  theater of the absurd, **2:**104–105, 106

Abu Yasir, **3:**166

Abu-Jamal, Mumia, **3:**270

Academic manifestos
  "Digital Humanities Manifesto 2.0" (Presner, et al.), **3:**352–354
  feminist criticism on language, **3:**115–117
  literary realism, **3:**192–195
  "The _____ Manifesto" (Betancourt), **3:**84–85
  Manifesto for Philosophy (Badiou), **3:**189–191
  Manifesto of a Tenured Radical (Nelson), **3:**19–21
  On the Poverty of Student Life (Khayati), **3:**315–318
  Sexual Politics (Millett), **3:**126–128

Académie des Beaux-Arts Salon, **1:**48, 49, 70–71, 86, 87, 93

Accuracy in Academe, **3:**29

Acheson, James, **2:**106

N

V

AUTHOR INDEX

The author index includes author names represented in The Manifesto in Literature. *Numbers in* **Bold** *indicate volume, with page numbers following after colons.*

TITLE INDEX

The title index includes works that are represented in The Manifesto in Literature. *Numbers in* **Bold** *indicate volume, with page numbers following after colons.*